EU EMPLOYMENT LAW

This book traces the evolution of European Union employment law and social policy from its essentially economic origins in the Treaty of Rome through to the emerging themes post-Amsterdam: co-ordination of national employment policies, modernisation of social laws and combating discrimination. Each stage of development of Community employment law and social policy is analysed in depth to give a sense of perspective to this fast changing field. As the European Union seeks to meet the challenges of globalisation the need to develop social policy as a productive factor has come to the fore. The author explains how the social, economic and employment imperatives of European integration have always been intertwined and how the emergence of Community employment law from its hitherto twilight existence is best understood through an examination of consistent strands of policy development.

EU Employment Law

*From Rome to Amsterdam
and Beyond*

JEFF KENNER

·HART·
PUBLISHING

OXFORD AND PORTLAND, OREGON
2003

Published in North America (US and Canada) by
Hart Publishing
c/o International Specialized Book Services
5804 NE Hassalo Street
Portland, Oregon
97213-3644
USA

Distributed in Netherlands, Belgium and Luxembourg by
Intersentia, Churchillaan 108
B2900 Schoten
Antwerpen
Belgium

Hart Publishing is a specialist legal publisher based in Oxford, England.
To order further copies of this book or to request a list of other publications
please write to:

Hart Publishing,
Salters Boatyard, Folly Bridge, Abingdon Rd,
Oxford, OX1 4LB
Telephone: +44 (0)1865 245533 Fax: +44 (0) 1865 794882
email: mail@hartpub.co.uk
WEBSITE: http//:www.hartpub.co.uk

British Library Cataloguing in Publication Data
Data Available

ISBN 1-901362-69-8

Typeset by SNP Best-set Typesetter Ltd., Hong Kong
Printed and bound in Great Britain by
Bell and Bain Ltd, Glasgow

In memory of my mother and father,

Lily and Len Kenner

Preface

My aim in writing this book is to offer a contextual and multi-dimensional analysis of European Union employment law. The idea for the book arose out of a desire to explain the law as seen and understood through the prism of its constant evolutionary development over a fifty-year period. By adopting this methodology I hope to offer fresh insights and to challenge commonly held assumptions about the present state of the law and its future direction. It has also enabled me to approach EU employment law and broad themes of social policy unencumbered by the conventional requirement to strictly categorise and isolate each area of development. In this way it has been possible, in a thematic fashion, to explore the interconnectedness of law and policy and identify hierarchies of norms in fields as diverse as equalities, employment protection, health and safety and employment promotion.

In particular I will seek to show how the economic and social imperatives of European integration have always been intertwined and how the emergence of Community employment law from its hitherto twilight existence is best understood through an examination of consistent strands of policy development. It is hoped that this approach will be attractive not only for legal scholars but also for students of other disciplines who wish to engage with the law in this area.

In the long process of writing this book I have been indebted to many people who kindly offered me advice and support. I would like to especially thank Tamara Hervey and Joanne Scott who generously gave their time to read draft chapters and provide helpful comments and suggestions. I am very grateful to Richard Hart for immediately grasping the idea behind this book and being prepared to run with it. All of the team at Hart Publishing have been most understanding and supportive throughout this project. I would also like to thank my colleagues at the University of Nottingham and the University of Leicester for their constant encouragement. Finally, I would like to record my gratitude, as ever, to Jacqueline Abbott for her patience, constructive criticism and unstinting support.

Jeff Kenner
Nottingham
October 2002

Table of Contents

Table of Cases

EUROPEAN COURT OF JUSTICE AND COURT OF FIRST INSTANCE OF THE EUROPEAN COMMUNITIES

International Court of Justice

UN Human Rights Committee (ICCPR)

Table of Legislation

EUROPEAN COMMUNITY LEGISLATION

Regulations

NATIONAL LEGISLATION

Germany

Irish Republic

Netherlands

Norway

South Africa

Sweden

United Kingdom

Table of Treaties and Other Instruments

1

The Emergence of the Social Dimension

I INTRODUCTION

WHEN THE FOUNDERS of what we now know as the European Union set about their grand scheme of building a 'European Federation' they resisted the opportunity to insert a guarantee of fundamental social rights into the Treaties establishing the European Communities.[1] This possibility was disregarded not because the founders were doctrinaire economic liberals driven by the mores of laissez-faire economics, but rather because they had a propensity for pragmatic incrementalism, or *engrenage*,[2] as a means of delivering their unique project, building a Union step-by-step in a technocratic fashion, first by integrating sectoral production, and then by removing trade barriers over a transitional period. This cumulative approach, beginning with the least controversial areas, created an irreversible dynamic for political as well as economic integration.[3] For six Western European states devastated by war and determined not to repeat the mistakes of the inter-war years, a federal order of European states that transcended the national framework was appealing so long as its initial tasks were determined by the need to rebuild industrial and agrarian production and to establish a common market for their goods and services, while anchored to a system that guaranteed economic inter-dependence as a conduit for lasting peace.[4]

---

[1] The European Coal and Steel Community (ECSC) 1951; the European Economic Community (EEC) 1957; and Euratom, 1957. The grand scheme was most clearly enunciated by Robert Schuman, the French Foreign Minister, in his famous declaration of 9 May 1950, when he proclaimed that the proposed ECSC was 'the first concrete foundation for a European Federation which is indispensable for lasting peace'. See 22 *Department of State Bulletin* 936 at 937.

[2] This literally means an enmeshing of gear wheels by which one cog drives another. See M Wise & R Gibb, *Single Market to Social Europe: The European Community in the 1990s* (Longman, Harlow, 1993) p 34.

[3] Hence the decision to deal with coal and steel first. The logic behind this strategy is explained by its architect in: J Monnet, 'A Ferment of Change' (1962) 1 *Journal of Common Market Studies* 203.

[4] The founder members were Belgium, France, Luxembourg, the Netherlands, Italy and the Federal Republic of Germany.

Within this context a Community social policy was recognised as being desirable as a humanitarian goal but it was not considered a necessity, except in those fields where it might operate to prevent an 'economically unsound' advantage being gained, or to provide economic assistance to those affected by any negative consequences of sectoral adjustment and the shake up caused by the establishment of the Common Market.[5] Social policy was to serve as a means of facilitating the Community's competitive goals rather than as an end in itself. At the most, the inclusion of a Title on Social Policy in the EEC Treaty,[6] with two chapters, was indicative of a longer-term objective of social policy harmonisation as a 'spillover' from economic integration.[7]

This book will seek to evaluate the ebb and flow of Community social policy over a period of 50 years of European integration. It will trace the gradual emergence of social policy from its relatively insignificant status in the Treaty of Rome to its present state of development after the Treaty of Amsterdam which, for the first time, endows the revised EC Treaty with an autonomous legislative base for furthering the Community's evolving social policy objectives in the form of a new 'Social Chapter'.[8]

II SOCIAL POLICY IN THE TREATY OF ROME

(1) The Ohlin and Spaak Reports

Social minimalism pervaded the EEC Treaty. The limited base of Community social policy did not derive solely from the cautious attitudes of the Member States. It was attributable also to the influential guidance of the International Labour Organisation (ILO), which had adopted a series of universal labour standards in the period immediately after the end of the

---

[5] See the 'Ohlin Report', International Labour Office, 'Social Aspects of European Economic Co-operation' (1956) 74 *International Labour Review* 99 at 105. On unfair advantage, see Art 119 EEC [now 141 EC] on equal pay between men and women, and Arts 123–28 EEC [now 146–48 EC] establishing the European Social Fund. For discussion, see S Deakin, 'Labour Law as Market Regulation: the Economic Foundations of European Social Policy' in P Davies, A Lyon-Caen, S Sciarra & S Simitis (eds) *European Community Labour Law: Principles and Perspectives* (Clarendon Press, Oxford, 1996) 62–93.

[6] Arts 117–28 EEC [now replaced by Arts 136–48 EC].

[7] This is based on the 'neo-functionalist' theory of European integration, propounded mainly by American political scientists, by which non-state actors, primarily the Commission, push forward the process of integration by integrating economic sectors and then moving on to integrate other sectors as a result of technical pressures. See generally, E Haas, *The Uniting of Europe: Political, Social and Economic Forces 1950–1957* (Stanford, California, 1968); L Lindberg, *The Political Dynamics of European Economic Integration* (Stanford, California, 1963).

[8] Arts 136–45 EC [replacing Arts 117–22 EEC].

Second World War.[9] There was little pressure on the fledgling Community to duplicate these existing, and therefore complementary, norms. In 1956 the ILO's Committee of Experts issued the 'Ohlin Report' on the *Social Aspects of European Integration.*[10] The Committee of Experts took the view that countries that were striving for, or already adhering to, ILO standards at the national level, with healthily diverse social systems, did not need to establish their own set of hybrid trans-European rules when their free trading goals could allow them to raise national social standards without any concurrent harmonisation of social policies. The Committee concluded that:[11]

International competition in a common market would not prevent particular countries from raising workers' living standards and there is no sound reason to think that freer international markets would hamper in any way the further improvement of workers' living standards, as productivity rises, through higher wages or improved social benefits and working conditions . . .

In reaching this conclusion the Committee of Experts were making several important assumptions. They believed that not only would the Common Market lead to rapid improvements in productivity, but also that the interests of workers would be taken into account as the Community developed its policies because trade unions in the European countries were strong, and further, there was general sympathy among European governments for social aspirations to ensure that labour conditions would improve and not deteriorate.[12] Moreover, the far reaching ILO Conventions, coupled with instruments drawn up by the Council of Europe, specifically the European Convention for the Protection of Human Rights and Fundamental Freedoms[13] and the proposed European Social Charter,[14] were considered to be the appropriate vehicles for the formulation of individual and collective social rights and ensuring observance of an optimum level of social standards at national level.

These views were not surprising because the notion of fair competition, taking into account social costs to prevent the 'dumping of human resources', was already well established as a basis for international labour

---

[9] The ILO, which was originally formed following the Treaty of Versailles, 1919, was re-established in 1946 under the aegis of the United Nations. Among its most notable Conventions are No 87, Freedom of Association, No 98, The Right to Organise, and No 100 on Equal Remuneration between Men and Women. For a comprehensive survey, see N Valticos & G von Potobsky, *International Labour Law*, 2nd revised edn (Kluwer, Deventer, 1995).

[10] (1956) 74 *International Labour Review* 99.

[11] *Ibid* at 115.

[12] *Ibid* at 112.

[13] The Convention was adopted in Rome on 4 Nov 1950. It was heavily influenced by the Universal Declaration of Human Rights proclaimed by the General Assembly of the United Nations on 10 Dec 1948.

[14] The Charter had been drafted at the time of the EEC Treaty and was eventually agreed by the Member States and opened for signature in Turin on 18 Oct 1961.

law conventions.[15] The ILO was not unduly concerned about differences in wages and social charges between different countries in the context of the proposed EEC so long as these reflected improvements in productivity, which tended to go hand in hand with higher social standards and decent wages. It followed that differences in social costs did not per se 'constitute an obstacle to the establishment of freer international markets'.[16] Only in the areas of equal pay between men and women and the provision of paid holidays was a case made for a guarantee at national level because an unfair advantage over competitors might be derived from any sharp differences between countries. As the Committee explained when considering equal pay:[17]

Countries in which there are large differentials by sex will pay relatively low wages in industries employing a large proportion of female labour and these industries will enjoy what might be considered a special advantage over their competitors abroad where differentials according to sex are smaller or non-existent.

Ohlin and his colleagues were shrewd judges of the *realpolitik* behind the European integration project. The Report's recommendations chimed well with the differing priorities of the ECSC members. Germany was eager to ensure that there was minimal interference with national policies on wages and prices, a view broadly supported by Ohlin.[18] France preferred a more *dirigiste* approach because they had higher social costs and sought to raise other countries to the same level.[19] These concerns were reflected by the Committee's recommendations on equal pay, paid holidays and working time. The Treaty of Rome endorsed this approach with specific commitments on equal pay and paid holidays,[20] and a Protocol allowing France to take protective measures if the working hours in other Member States were not reduced to the French level.[21] Italy regarded the establishment of a Common Market as an opportunity to alleviate economic problems, par-

---

[15] The first known advocate of this argument was the socialist pioneer Robert Owen in his petition to the Five Powers at Aix-la-Chapelle in 1818—see B Hepple, 'Harmonisation of Labour Law in the European Communities' in J Adams (ed) *Essays for Clive Schmitthoff* (Professional Books, Abingdon, 1983) 14–28 at 15. See also, H Feis, 'International Labour Legislation in the Light of Economic Theory' (1927) *International Labour Review* 425.

[16] The Ohlin Report, n 5 above at 99.

[17] *Ibid* p 107.

[18] See C Barnard, 'The Economic Objectives of Article 119' in T Hervey & D O'Keeffe (eds) *Sex Equality Law in the European Union* (Wiley, Chichester, 1996) 321–34 at 324–25.

[19] See L Betten, 'Prospects for a Social Policy of the European Community and its Impact on the Functioning of the European Social Charter' in L Betten (ed) *The Future of European Social Policy* (Kluwer, Deventer, 1989) 101–41 at 107.

[20] Arts 119 and 120 EEC [now 141 and 142 EC].

[21] Part II of the Protocol on Certain Provisions Affecting France. See P Davies, 'The Emergence of European Labour Law' in W McCarthy (ed) *Legal Intervention in Industrial Relations: Gains and Losses* (Blackwell, London, 1993) 313–59 at 322–23.

ticularly unemployment in the southern regions, and welcomed the Committee's findings on the need for a structural fund and loans,[22] as established through the European Social Fund and the European Investment Bank, and for co-ordination, not harmonisation, of social security systems that would encourage labour mobility, as provided for in Article 51 EEC [now 42 EC].[23] The Benelux countries were prepared to accept a compromise that reflected the views of their three larger partners.[24]

The Member States could hardly be faulted for strictly adhering to these recommendations while precluding specific Community powers to legislate for the purpose of social policy harmonisation. The logic behind the Ohlin Report was well understood by the inter-governmental committee chaired by the Belgian Foreign Minister, Paul-Henri Spaak. The Spaak Committee envisioned a 'gradual coalescence of social standards' but such equalisation 'far from being a *condition precedent* to the functioning of the common market' was, on the contrary, 'a *consequence* of its operation'.[25] Hence, the Common Market and free competition were regarded as paramount for a successful social policy. The European Commission's First Report on Competition Policy, published in 1971, at the zenith of the Community's economic achievements, stated that:[26]

Competition is the best stimulant of economic activity since it guarantees the widest possible freedom of action to all. An active competition policy pursued in accordance with the provisions in the Treaties . . . enables enterprises continuously to improve their efficiency, which is the *sine qua non* for a steady improvement in living standards and employment prospects within the countries of the Community. From this point of view, competition policy is an essential means for satisfying to a great extent the individual and collective needs of our society.

Thus competition was chosen over welfare at transnational level at a time when economic determinism could deliver the wealth to resource substantial increases in living standards and relatively generous social security protection at national level, and when there was a social consensus among

---

[22] As a result of this policy 543,000 Italian workers had been retrained and 340,000 resettled in France and Germany by 1968. See B Bercusson, *European Labour Law* (Butterworths, London, 1996) p 48.

[23] The Committee was not unanimous in this view but the Chairman and Mr Byé endorsed it in a supplementary note: Ohlin Report, n 5 above at 122. See also Betten, n 19 above at 107.

[24] Belgium, the Netherlands and Luxembourg formed a 'customs union' in 1948, went on to establish a 'common market' by 1956 and, later, in 1960, signed a Treaty on Economic Union.

[25] *Rapport des chefs de délégation aux ministres des affaires étrangères* (Brussels) 21 April 1956, pp 19–20 and 60–1. My emphasis. For a full discussion of Ohlin and Spaak, see Davies in McCarthy, n 21 above at 318–23.

[26] 'Competition Report' (European Commission, Brussels, 1971) p 11. See D Wyatt & A Dashwood, *European Community Law*, 3rd edn (Sweet & Maxwell, London, 1993) p 377.

Western European states. As Shanks explains, a Community 'which is purely an economic arrangement can work well in periods of growth and prosperity [but] it is unlikely to survive a period of social stress'.[27] Before turning to the circumstances which caused that 'social stress' in the early 1970s, and the consequences of the breaking down of the social policy consensus in the 1980s, the Treaty of Rome must be examined in more depth.

(2) The First Social Chapter

Apart from the application of the principle of equal pay between men and women contained in Article 119 EEC [now 141 EC], and the determination to endeavour, by unspecified means, to maintain the 'existing equivalence' between paid holiday schemes, under Article 120 EEC [now 142 EC], the social policy provisions of the EEC Treaty were essentially programmatic and proclamatory in nature.[28] There was no universal statement of the Community's social values and no linkage with notions of fundamental social rights founded on international law.[29] Rather, Article 117 EEC stated, in a matter of fact way, that:[30]

Member States agree upon the need to promote improved working conditions and an improved standard of living for workers, so as to make possible their harmonisation while the improvement is being maintained.

They believe that such a development *will ensue* not only from the functioning of the common market, which will favour the harmonisation of social systems, but also from the procedures provided for in this Treaty and from the approximation of provisions laid down by law, regulation or administrative action.

Harmonisation was posited not as a tool for the attainment of social justice but as a desirable outcome resulting from the operation of a common market. Approximation measures, whether legislative or purely administrative, were only necessary to rectify distortions in the market, an implicit reference to the facility of Article 100 EEC [now 94 EC] as a means of adopting directives.

[27] M Shanks, 'Introductory Article: The Social Policy of the European Communities' (1977) 14 *Common Market Law Review* 375 at 383. For a critique of the counterpoint between competition and welfare, see Lord Wedderburn, 'Workers' Rights: Fact or Fake?' (1991) 13 *Dublin University Law Journal* 1.

[28] Although the Ohlin Report had made a case for these exceptions it is worth noting that there was also pressure for their inclusion from the French who feared undercutting. Ohlin found that in France women's pay was 91% of that of men, compared with 78% in Germany and 66% in Britain. See B Hepple, 'Equality and Discrimination' in Davies *et al*, n 5 above, 237–59 at 241.

[29] See B Hepple, 'Social Values and European Law' [1995] *Current Legal Problems* 39 at 41.

[30] My emphasis.

This essentially static view of Article 117 EEC was challenged by those who believed that, on the basis of a purposive interpretation, it had the capacity to empower the Community to act where social progress was endangered by unfavourable economic developments. Schnorr contended that the text of the first paragraph of Article 117 EEC:[31]

... does not plainly affirm social progress as a consequence of economic integration, but ... contains an agreement between the Member States about the necessity to promote such progress. This means, indeed, a *contractual obligation* on all Member States to co-operate in achieving the Community purpose of social progress.

This notion of a 'contractual obligation' may have served to objectify attainable ends but it did not provide the means for the Community to act where co-operation alone was insufficient. At the most, this leads to a supposition that the Member States committed themselves to social progress by means of a Community social policy.[32] While Däubler has suggested that Article 117(1) EEC was 'not just a political declaration of intent but a legally binding commitment',[33] the European Court of Justice[34] preferred a more cautious approach, regarding Article 117 EEC as a guide for interpretation. For example in *Sloman Neptun*[35] the Court stated that:

Article 117 ... is essentially in the nature of a programme. It relates only to social objectives the attainment of which must be the result of Community action, close co-operation between the Member States and the operation of the Common Market.

The programmatic nature of these social objectives did not mean that they were deprived of legal effect, but rather they constituted an important aid to interpretation of *other provisions* in the Treaty and of secondary legislation in the social field.[36] In this sense social policy objectives were given a subordinate role and were subsumed by the conditions of competition.[37] Nonetheless, Article 117 EEC must be understood as a provision that was

---

[31] G Schnorr, 'European Communities' in R Blanpain (ed) *International Encyclopaedia for Labour Law and Industrial Relations* (Kluwer, Deventer, 1980) para 60. Emphasis added. Discussed by Hepple in Adams, n 15 above at 18–19.

[32] See E Vogel-Polsky, 'Legal Bases for European Employee's Rights', ETUC Technical Conference, Strasbourg, 12/13 Dec 1989. Cited by R Nielsen & E Szyszczak, *The Social Dimension of the European Community*, 2nd edn (Handelshøjskolens Forlag, Copenhagen, 1993) p 21.

[33] W Däubler, 'Instruments in EC Labour Law' in Davies *et al*, n 5 above, 151–67 at 154.

[34] Hereinafter 'the Court' or 'the Court of Justice'.

[35] Cases C–72–73/91, *Sloman Neptun Schiffahrts v Seebetriebsrat Bodo Ziesemer der Sloman Neptun Schiffahrts* [1993] ECR I–887, para 25.

[36] See Case 126/86, *Zaera v Instituto Nacional de la Seguridad Social* [1987] ECR 3697, para 14.

[37] Art 3(f) EEC [now 3(g) EC] provided for 'the institution of a system ensuring that competition in the common market is not distorted'. See S Simitis & A Lyon-Caen, 'Community Labour Law: A Critical Introduction to its History' in Davies *et al*, n 5 above, 1–22 at 5–7.

capable of operating to defend social standards and, in this sense, the provision that has replaced it, Article 136 EC, serves the same purpose. Hence, Article 117 EEC amounted to a commitment to improvements in living standards and working conditions 'to make possible their harmonisation while the improvement is being maintained'. In other words, there can be no turning back from social standards. Similar 'non-retrogression' clauses have consistently featured in Community social policy directives.[38]

Article 118 EEC was intended to encompass these social objectives by identifying a non-exhaustive catalogue of areas in the social field where Member States were urged or obliged to co-operate with each other 'without prejudice' to other provisions in the Treaty. The listed areas were:

—employment;
—labour law and working conditions;
—basic and advanced vocational training;
—social security;
—prevention of occupational accidents and diseases;
—occupational hygiene;
—the right of association and collective bargaining between employers and workers.

The Member States were the key players with the Commission being consigned to the role of bystander, only serving as a point of contact 'making studies, delivering opinions and arranging consultations'. Therefore the Commission's role was purely procedural. They could not impose any of the results of their studies or consultations on the Member States and they were powerless to act against national measures unless they contravened other provisions in the Treaty.[39] The remainder of the social policy provisions tended to confirm the secondary role of the Community institutions vis-à-vis the Member States. For example, Article 122 EEC [now 145 EC] placed an obligation on the Commission to include a separate chapter on social developments within the Community in its annual report to the European Parliament. In turn, the Parliament was allowed to invite the Commission to draw up reports on any particular problems concerning social conditions. Under Article 128 EEC [now 150 EC] the Council, acting on a Commission proposal, had the responsibility of laying down general principles for implementing a common vocational training policy 'capable of contributing to the harmonious development both of the national economies and of the common market'.[40]

---

[38] See the note by B Bercusson, 'European Labour Law in Context: A Review of the Literature' (1999) 5 *European Law Journal* 87 at 94–5.

[39] See Cases C–281/85, C–283/85, C–285/85 and C–287/85, *Germany and others v Commission* [1987] ECR 3203.

[40] In practice the only immediate steps taken to advance this goal were a 1963 Council Decision setting out 10 general principles and the setting up of an Advisory Committee, a 'very meagre' outcome. See P Venturini, *1992: The European Social Dimension* (European Communities, Luxembourg, 1989) p 16.

Article 119 EEC [now part of a wider Article 141 EC] stood out as the only provision in the first chapter of the Title on Social Policy that placed an express obligation on Member States to ensure by the first stage, 1962, and subsequently maintain, the principle that men and women should receive equal pay for equal work. In fact this period was extended to 1964.[41] Moreover, when the 'Sullerot Report' was issued to the Commission in 1972, it was found that progress had been extremely slow and there was still widespread sex discrimination in remuneration and general working practices in the Member States.[42] Article 119 EEC was only revivified by a fresh drive for social policy in the 1970s and, above all, by the determination of a Belgian air steward, Gabrielle Defrenne, who brought a series of legal actions designed to bind the Member States to their equal pay commitments.[43]

Even the obligation inherent within Article 119 EEC has to be read as a *non sequitur* because the most striking feature of the social policy of the Rome Treaty was not what it contained but what was absent. There was no specific action programme and no binding timetable for the adoption of certain matters.[44] There was no common social policy to accompany the common policies in the fields of, for example, commerce, agriculture or transport.[45] Social policy was not even listed as one of the activities of the Community in Article 3 EEC, which referred only obliquely to the establishment of a European Social Fund to improve employment opportunities and to encourage labour mobility. Most noticeable of all was the absence of any direct or explicit means of adopting binding labour laws in the form of directives or regulations for the specified purpose of fulfilling the objectives in Article 117 EEC. Measures that impinged on social policy as a consequence of market functioning could be adopted under Article 100 EEC [now 94 EC], or the provisions on the free movement of services, Article 54(3)g EEC [now 44(3)g EC], or through recourse to the general purpose clause in Article 235 EEC [now 308 EC]—all avenues pursued once a Social Action Programme was adopted in the 1970s—but for the Community's founders the anticipated social benefits were to derive axiomatically from market mechanisms and not through legislative means.[46]

---

[41] *Bulletin of the European Communities* 1962/1, pp 7–9.

[42] *The Employment of Women and the Problems it raises in the Member States of the European Community* (European Commission, Luxembourg, 1972). See Hepple in Adams, n 15 above, at 20. See generally, H Warner, 'EC Social Policy in Practice: Community Action on Behalf of Women and its Impact in the Member States' (1984) 23 *Journal of Common Market Studies* 141.

[43] Case 80/70, *Defrenne v Belgian State I* [1971] ECR 445; Case 43/75, *Defrenne v Sabena II* [1976] ECR 455; Case 149/77, *Defrenne v Sabena III* [1978] ECR 1365.

[44] See Betten, n 19 above at 108.

[45] Arts 3(b) (d) and (e) EEC, respectively.

[46] Spaak Report, n 25 above at 61. See Davies in McCarthy, n 21 above at 324–25.

In the period between 1958 and 1972 the economic achievements of the Community surpassed even the loftiest expectations of its founders and, as living standards improved,[47] there seemed little reason, and indeed there was little pressure, at least until the spring of 1968,[48] to replace 'benign neglect' with 'social activism'.[49]

(3) Substantive Obstacles to the Integration of Social Laws

While what has been described so far might suggest that the development of Community social law was delayed principally by the ineluctable logic of prevailing economic liberalism combined with the formal problems created by a limited Treaty base, this would only be a partial assessment because the most intractable obstacles inhibiting social policy harmonisation, not just in the early stages but throughout the Community's history, have been, and remain, substantive not formalistic.[50]

Community employment law and social policy has been described as a 'symbiosis' of Community law and national laws with Member States jealously guarding their own systems and traditions while, on occasion, being influenced when formulating policy at Community level, by national practices which seem particularly apt in a given situation.[51] For example, equal pay in the case of France, or, less successfully, the German system of workers' participation in companies, or, more recently, the Italian tradition of autonomous social partners and the Danish model of enacting labour law based, in part, on collective agreements.[52]

The substantive problem here is twofold. First, what Kahn-Freund described as the 'transplantation' of labour law is extremely difficult because:[53]

... variations in the organisation of power between one country and another can prevent or frustrate the transfer of legal institutions, and turn the use of the comparative method into an abuse.

In particular, the diverse and heterogeneous nature of both individual and

---

[47] In the first decade of the Community the GDP of the Member States increased at a rate of 5% per year, twice the level in the US and Britain. For discussion, see J Pinder, *European Community: The Building of a Union*, 2nd edn (OUP, Oxford, 1995) pp 70–4.

[48] Student unrest in Paris and the growth of protest movements in Western Europe were a reflection, in part, of a concern about growing inequalities in an era of economic growth.

[49] See H Mosley, 'The social dimension of European integration' (1990) 129 *International Labour Review* 147 at 149–50.

[50] See Hepple in Adams, n 15 above at 22–7.

[51] B Bercusson, *European Labour Law*, n 22 above at 8–10.

[52] *Ibid.* This only applies to Danish rules concerning 'blue collar' workers.

[53] O Kahn-Freund, 'On the Uses and Misuses of Comparative Law' (1974) 37 *Modern Law Review* 1 at 13. For discussion, see B Fitzpatrick, 'Community Social Law after Maastricht' (1992) 21 *Industrial Law Journal* 199 at 209–12.

collective labour law systems has mitigated against the harmonisation of substantive rules and tended to shift the focus of Community activity towards flexible procedural measures, most noticeably in the sensitive area of collective labour relations for, as Kahn-Freund added, 'individual labour law lends itself to transplantation very much more easily . . . than collective labour law'.[54] While Kahn-Freund was describing the problems in transplanting law from one national legal system to another, his central thesis is equally applicable in the supranational context of Community law. This is because the principal legal instruments used to give effect to Community social policy are directives that require separate implementation in each of the national legal orders.

Nielsen has explained how the position has been further complicated by the expansion of the Community from the founding members, who were all broadly of the Romano-Germanic legal family, where legislation is the dominant method of regulating labour law, to include also the Anglo-Saxon and Nordic legal families, which have traditionally relied on a voluntary approach with only a limited amount of legal regulation, but a quite different appreciation of the status of collective labour law agreements.[55] It follows that, while the Community has developed its own legal system, reflecting the combined legal heritage of the Member States, it has to operate in harmony with national and sub-national legal systems and respect their diverse labour law traditions. Directives have to be drafted to take account of this diversity and enforcement is dependent upon national procedural rules that are often, in cases of labour law dispute resolution, localised and sectoral. Indeed, the desire to respect diverse national approaches to collective labour law questions has led to an even more abstentionist policy today than at the time of the foundation of the Community, with the total exclusion of laws on 'pay, the right of association, the right to strike or the right to impose lock-outs' from the revised Social Chapter.[56]

Second, when considering proposals affecting both individual and collective labour law, Member States face national pressures from trade unions and employers' organisations, often linked to governing party groupings, making them sensitive to regulation at Community level which may tip the industrial relations balance.[57] It is for this reason that the Community has, from the outset, erred towards resolving social policy matters at national

---

[54] *Ibid* at 21.

[55] See R Nielsen, 'The Contract of Employment in the Member States of the European Communities and in European Community Law' (1990) 33 *German Yearbook of International Law* 258 at 259. In the Community of 15 there are, according to Nielsen, 10 countries belonging to the Romano-Germanic system (Germany, Austria, France, Belgium, Holland, Luxembourg, Spain, Portugal, Italy and Greece); 3 belong to the Nordic system (Denmark, Finland and Sweden); and 2 to the Anglo-Saxon system (UK and Ireland).

[56] Art 137(6) EC.

[57] See Hepple in Adams, n 15 above at 26.

or workplace level and has only introduced proposals for social laws as a last resort. There was no practical reason to write the 'principle of subsidiarity' into the provisions on social policy at Maastricht because it has always been the governing rule. The extent to which the gradual removal, over 40 years, of the formal barriers to social policy legislation has created a new dynamic for a drive towards a greater homogeneity of substantive social laws based on the principle of social justice will be a key question for consideration later in this book.[58]

III SOCIAL POLICY IN THE WIDER TREATY CONTEXT

As a counterpoint to the dearth of explicit social policy content in the EEC Treaty, one factor considered by both Ohlin and Spaak was how other Community policies would interact with social policy goals and contribute towards 'a harmonious development of economic activities'?[59] While free movement of labour was widely regarded as a positive step, particularly in combating unemployment, it was feared that free trade might restrict the Community's competence to legislate in the social arena and run counter to the national labour law regimes of the Member States.[60]

Free movement of labour and co-ordination of social security systems, as set out in Articles 39–42 EC [ex 48–51 EEC], was regarded by the Committee of Experts as a boon for workers' living standards arising from 'the more rapid growth of productivity to be expected as a result of a more international division of labour'.[61] The rationale behind these provisions was economic rather than social, to free up the labour market with migrant workers who were regarded as 'human capital' or factors of production within the common market. The wording of Article 39 EC [ex 48 EEC] emphasises the scope of the principle of non-discrimination[62] in this context by making it clear that free movement:

---

[58] Albert Thomas, the first Director of the ILO, considered that social justice 'meant much more than the removal of social injustice. It meant a possible policy through which the individual might attain his political, economic and moral rights'. E Phelan, *Yes and Albert Thomas* (Cresset Press, London, 1949) p 242. Social justice is an evolving notion and now encompasses a 'growing need for security and well-being . . . accompanied by a desire for more freedom, more equality and a greater measure of participation in the management of society, as well as for better "quality of life" and a substantial improvement in working conditions', Valticos & von Potobsky, n 9 above, p 26.

[59] Art 2 EEC.

[60] See P Davies, 'Market Integration and Social Policy in the Court of Justice' (1995) 24 *Industrial Law Journal* 49 at 50.

[61] The Ohlin Report, n 5 above at 112.

[62] Art 6 EEC [now 12 EC] has established the general principle that: 'Within the scope of application of this Treaty, and without prejudice to any special provisions contained therein, any discrimination on the grounds of nationality shall be prohibited'.

... shall entail the abolition of any discrimination based on nationality between workers of the Member States as regards employment, remuneration and other conditions of work and employment.

Articles 40 and 42 EC [ex 49 and 51 EEC] provide legal bases for Community legislation. Regulations have been adopted to ensure, inter alia, equality of treatment in employment between nationals and Community free movers, derivative rights for the family members of migrant workers, 'social advantages' in the host State,[63] and effective co-ordination of social security systems.[64] These policies are of direct social import and have been interpreted broadly by the Court.[65] Thus Community legislation and case law has explicitly recognised that workers have independent needs and are not mere units of production,[66] but these policies are still primarily motivated by economic considerations intended to *neutralise* living and working conditions as between Community nationals with any consequential raising of social standards being viewed as a desirable by-product. Moreover, while *directives* have been the predominant legislative form for binding social policy measures because they offer flexibility 'as to the choice of form and methods' of implementation, the neutralising non-discriminatory goals of free movement measures lend themselves to *regulations* which are 'directly applicable in all Member States',[67] precisely because they are intended to be transnational common market measures that may have beneficial social consequences but are not, strictly speaking, instruments concerned with the social policies of individual Member States.[68]

Ohlin was well aware of the potential restraints on the development of an activist Community social policy in a free trading area. The Committee's starting point had been to ask 'whether it would be more difficult to improve social standards once the more vigorous competition of freer markets had come into force?'[69] The Committee concluded that, whereas some harmonisation of social policy would be consistent with such an

---

[63] Reg 1612/68/EEC, OJ 1968, L257/2. In particular Arts 7, 10, 11, and 12.

[64] Reg 1408/71/EEC, OJ 1971, L149/2.

[65] For example, in Case 44/65, *Maison Singer* [1965] ECR 965 at 971, the Court asserted that freedom of movement of workers is a right that is not strictly limited by the requirements of the common market. In Case 53/81, *Levin* [1982] ECR 1035, at para 13, the Court applied Art 48 EEC [now 39 EC] in such a way as to encompass part-time workers on the basis that such employment constitutes, for a large number of persons, 'an effective means of improving their living conditions'.

[66] See C Barnard, *EC Employment Law*, 2nd edn (OUP, Oxford, 2000) pp 111–12.

[67] Directives and regulations are distinguished in Art 249 EC [ex 189 EEC].

[68] J Kenner, 'Citizenship and Fundamental Rights: Reshaping the European Social Model' in J Kenner (ed) *Trends in European Social Policy* (Dartmouth, Aldershot, 1995) 3–84 at 10–11. On free movement of workers and social security, see P Watson, *Social Security Law of the European Communities* (Mansell, London, 1980) and Barnard, *EC Employment Law*, n 66 above, ch 5.

[69] The Ohlin Report, n 5 above at 112.

approach, it was at national level where social standards should be raised to match growth in productivity.[70]

In practice the Court has tended to be cautious when presented with opportunities to interfere with national labour laws even in situations where a potential conflict may arise with other parts of the EC Treaty. For example, Article 28 EC [ex 30 EEC] provides that: 'Quantitative restrictions on imports and all measures having equivalent effect shall be prohibited between Member States'. In *Dassonville*[71] the Court defined 'measures having equivalent effect' as encompassing 'all trading rules enacted by Member States which are capable of hindering, directly or indirectly, actually or potentially intra-Community trade'.[72] It has been suggested that a literal interpretation of this formula would mean that these prohibited 'measures' might include labour laws and employment regulations that affect the cost of production, such as rules on working time or operating hours which have a restrictive effect on trade.[73] However, while *Dassonville* suggested unbridled economic liberalism, the Court swiftly provided a counterweight in *Cassis de Dijon*[74] where, in the case of indistinctly applicable measures, the aim of the State was not to restrict imports but to pursue public interest objectives.[75] Such a wide-ranging approach to the justification of indirectly discriminatory rules was capable of application beyond the limited exceptions in Article 30 EC [ex 36 EEC].[76]

For example, in *Oebel*[77] the Court upheld national rules restricting night working in bakeries on the grounds that such requirements constituted 'a legitimate part of economic and social policy, consistent with the objectives of public interest pursued by the Treaty'.[78] The Court noted that the prohibition was designed to improve working conditions in a 'manifestly sensitive industry' and was consistent with similar rules in several Member States and a specific ILO Convention.[79] *Oebel* was applied in *Torfaen*[80] where the Court held that the same consideration must apply as regards

---

[70] The Ohlin Report, at 112–13.
[71] Case 8/74 [1974] ECR 837.
[72] *Ibid* para 5.
[73] Deakin, n 5 above at 71.
[74] Case 120/78, *Rewe Zentrale v Bundesmonopolverwaltung für Branntwein (Cassis de Dijon)* [1979] ECR 649.
[75] M Poiares Maduro, *We, The Court: The European Court of Justice and the European Economic Constitution* (Hart, Oxford, 1998) p 61.
[76] Specifically: 'public morality, public policy or public security; the protection of health and life of humans, animals or plants; the protection of national treasures possessing artistic or archaeological value; or the protection of industrial or commercial property'. Such restrictions must not 'constitute a means of arbitrary discrimination or a disguised restriction on trade between Member States'.
[77] Case 155/80, *Oebel* [1981] ECR 1993.
[78] *Ibid* para 12.
[79] *Ibid* paras 12–13. ILO Convention No 20 of 1925 which, subject to certain exceptions, prohibits the production of bread, pastries or similar products during the night.
[80] Case 145/88, *Torfaen BC v B&Q* [1989] ECR 765, para 14.

national rules governing the opening hours of retail premises because such rules reflect certain political and economic choices in so far as their purpose is to ensure that working and non-working hours are so arranged as to accord with national or regional socio-cultural characteristics rather than to govern the patterns of trade between Member States.[81]

Subsequently, the Court has changed tack and ruled in *Keck and Mithouard*[82] that the application to products of other Member States of national rules restricting or prohibiting 'certain selling arrangements' falls outside the *Dassonville* formulation, subject to the qualification that such national rules must apply to all affected traders operating within the national territory and must affect in the same manner, in law and in fact, the marketing of domestic and imported products.[83] *Keck* has been specifically applied in the Sunday trading context.[84] Post-*Keck and Mithouard* the Court has been primarily concerned with the link between measures and intra-Community trade rather than the reasons behind the public policies of Member States. Measures that affect the marketing of products rather than their composition are deemed less likely to affect imports and to meet the requirements for factual and legal equality.[85]

One case that illustrates the delicate balance between the free movement of economic actors and national social policies is *Rush Portuguesa*.[86] The Court was asked to rule on the validity of a French law prohibiting the recruitment of foreign workers without a work permit. On the one hand, the Court was bold, holding that rules that adversely affected Portuguese sub-contractors in the construction industry based outside of France were capable of violating Article 49 EC [ex 59 EEC] on the free movement of services.[87] On the other hand, the Court held that such activities could be regulated by more protective French law rather than the more limited Portuguese regulations so long as France extended its labour law, including collective agreements, 'to any person who is employed, even temporarily, within their territory, no matter in which country the employer is established'.[88] Such a solution would prevent the disapplication of national labour laws while ensuring compliance with Community free movement obligations, an approach now embodied in the Posted Workers Directive[89]

---

[81] *Ibid* para 14.
[82] Joined Cases C–267–268/91, *Keck and Mithouard* [1993] ECR I–6097.
[83] *Ibid* para 16.
[84] Joined Cases C–69/93 and C–258/93, *Punto Casa and PPV* [1994] ECR I–2355.
[85] See S Weatherill & P Beaumont, *EU Law*, 3rd edn (Penguin, London, 1999) p 612.
[86] Case C–113/89 *Rush Portuguesa Ltda v Office Nationale d'Immigration* [1990] ECR 1417.
[87] *Ibid* para 12.
[88] *Ibid* para 18.
[89] Directive 96/71/EC concerning the posting of workers in the framework of the provision of services, OJ 1996, L18/1. For discussion, see P Davies, 'Posted Workers: Single Market or Protection of National Labour Law Systems?' (1997) 34 *Common Market Law Review* 571; E Kolehmainen, 'The Directive Concerning the Posting of Workers: Synchronization of the Functions of National Legal Systems' (1998) 20 *Comparative Labor Law & Policy Journal* 71.

and applied by the Court in respect of national rules concerning minimum wages[90] and paid leave.[91]

The Court's tentative approach when scrutinising the compatibility of national social laws with Community free movement rules is in tune with the political caution of the Commission and the Council in this respect. In particular, although Articles 96 and 97 EC [ex 101 and 102 EEC] offer a basis for action to eliminate 'distortions of competition' caused by national laws, the opportunities offered by these provisions have not been fully explored, even though the Spaak Report had envisaged the need to take steps to combat 'specific distortions' arising from such issues as differences in the financing of social security systems and working conditions.[92] In practice the Community's approach to differences between the social laws of the Member States, all of which are capable of producing distortions of competition, has been pragmatic. Differences in labour standards may affect market access but it does not necessarily follow that they will create distortions, or are discriminatory, in the sense that they would prevent access to domestic markets by design or effect.[93]

In the Ohlin Report a distinction was drawn between variations in *different countries* in terms of wages and social conditions that broadly reflect fluctuations in productivity, and variations in the *same country* that might arise by way of 'unfair competition' where foreign producers have to compete with subsidised national producers.[94] The competition rules applying to undertakings indicate a Community response that is consistent with this approach. Article 86(1) EC [ex 90(1) EEC] applies the competition rules to public undertakings and undertakings to which Member States grant special or exclusive rights. Member States shall 'neither enact nor maintain in force' any measure contrary to the principle of non-discrimination or the competition provisions in Articles 81–89 EC [ex 85–94 EEC]. Article 86(1) EC [ex 90(1) EEC] must be read in conjunction with Article 86(2) EC [ex 90(2) EEC], which determines whether Member States are permitted to confer exclusive rights on undertakings providing a 'service of general economic interest'.[95]

---

[90] Case C–164/99, *Portugaia Construções Ldª* [2002] ECR I (nyr) judgment of 24 Jan 2002.

[91] Cases C–49/98 and C–70–71/98, *Finalarte Sociedade de Construção Civil Ldª and others v Urlaubs- und Lohnausgleichskasse der Bauwirtschaft* and Cases C–50/98, C–52–54/98, C68–69/98, *Urlaubs- und Lohnausgleichskasse der Bauwirtschaft v Amilcar Oliveira Rocha and others* [2001] ECR I–7831.

[92] Spaak Report, n 25 above at 233–34. See Deakin, n 5 above at 79–80. An explicit reference from a national court based on Art 234 EC [ex 177 EEC] would, however, oblige the Court to consider the scope of these provisions.

[93] See further, P Syrpis, 'The Integrationist Rationale for European Social Policy' in J Shaw (ed) *Social Law and Policy in an Evolving European Union* (Hart, Oxford, 2000) 17–30 at 26; Deakin, n 5 above at 74–5.

[94] The Ohlin Report, n 5 above at 104–5. See Davies in McCarthy, n 21 above at 322.

[95] Such services 'shall be subject to the rules contained in this Treaty, in particular the rules on competition, insofar as the application of such rules does not obstruct the performance, in law or in fact, of the particular tasks assigned to them. The development of trade must not be affected to such an extent as would be contrary to the interests of the Community'.

Article 87(1) EC [ex 92(1) EEC] explicitly outlaws state aids that distort or threaten to distort competition as 'incompatible with the common market' because they favour certain undertakings and certain goods. However, 'aid having a social character' granted to individual consumers *shall* be compatible with the common market so long as it is non-discriminatory as to the origin of the products concerned.[96] Further, aid to promote the economic development of areas 'where the standard of living is abnormally low or where there is serious underemployment' *may* be deemed compatible with the common market.[97]

As with the provisions on free movement, the Court has tended to apply the rules on public undertakings and state aids with less than full rigour when interpreting labour law rules that may appear to create distortions or have the potential to be anti-competitive. For example, in *Kirsammer-Hack*[98] a German regulation that exempted employers with five or fewer employees from liability for unfair dismissal was held not to amount to a state aid. Such a measure did not entail any direct or indirect transfer of State resources to those businesses but derived solely from the legislature's intention to provide a specific legislative framework for working relationships in small businesses and to avoid imposing on those businesses financial constraints that might hinder their development.[99] Where there has been clear abuse, however, the Court has been prepared to act. Hence, in *Porto di Genova*[100] national rules that gave the state exclusive rights to organise dock work in a way that ensured that work was offered only to Italian nationals were found to be in violation of Article 86(1) EC [ex 90(1) EEC]. The Court was not prepared to accept the social argument that the scheme was the most effective means of preventing the casualisation of labour.[101] The Court was not, however, immune to such arguments. Rather, the Court was recognising the fact that the Treaty does not allow social arguments to prevail where there is blatant anti-competitive behaviour by a Member State.

---

[96] Art 87(2)(a) EC [ex 92(2)(a) EEC]. In all cases there is an obligation on the Member State to notify the Commission of the proposed aid. The Commission has the power to abolish or alter such aids (Art 88(2) EC—ex 93(2) EEC). Note that nationalisation per se is perfectly lawful under Art 295 EC [ex 222 EEC]. Nationalised entities are 'just as compatible with private enterprise on the large market as they are on a single nation', Monnet, n 3 above at 206. Thus the state aids rules cover both the public and private sectors.

[97] Art 87(3)(a) EC [ex 92(3)(a) EEC].

[98] Case C–189/91, *Kirsammer-Hack v Sidal* [1993] ECR I–6185.

[99] *Ibid* paras 16 and 17. See T Hervey, 'Small Business Exclusion in German Dismissal Law' (1994) 23 *Industrial Law Journal* 267. See further, Cases C–72/91 and C–73/91, *Sloman Neptun Schiffahrts v Seebetriebsrat Bodo Ziesemer der Sloman Neptun Schiffahrts* [1993] ECR I–887.

[100] Case C–179/90, *Merci Convenzionali Porto di Genova v Siderurgica Gabrielli* [1991] ECR I–5889. See also, Case 31/87, *Beentjes v Minister van Landbouw en Visserij* [1988] ECR 4635; and Case C–41/90, *Höfner and Elser v Macrotron* [1991] ECR I–1979. For discussion, see C Barnard, 'EC 'Social' Policy' in P Craig & G de Búrca (eds) *The Evolution of EU Law* (OUP, Oxford, 1999) 479–516 at 494–95.

[101] See Deakin, n 5 above at 75.

More recently the Court has had to address the more fundamental issue of the compatibility of national social protection systems and supplementary pension schemes with Community competition and free movement law. While the Court's general approach is not to interfere with the autonomy of national social systems,[102] there has been an increase in litigation designed to challenge national schemes for social insurance,[103] health care[104] and pensions.[105] In *Poucet and Pistre*[106] the Court held that the concept of an 'undertaking', which is referred to in Articles 81, 82 and 86 EC [ex Articles 85, 86 and 90 EEC][107] did not encompass organisations responsible for the management of compulsory social security schemes established in accordance with the principle of 'social solidarity' on the basis that it was necessary for such schemes to be managed by a single organisation with compulsory affiliation.[108] The Court's reasoning was based on an assumption that such systems cannot be effectively provided by private market actors and do not constitute economic activity as their aims are social not economic.[109]

By contrast in *Albany International*[110] the Court distinguished *Poucet and Pistre* when asked to determine whether a compulsory sectoral pension fund

---

[102] See, for example, Case 238/82, *Duphar* [1984] ECR 523, para 16; Cases C–159–160/91, *Poucet and Pistre v AGF and Concava* [1993] ECR I–637, para 6; Case C–70/95, *Sodemare SA and others v Regione Lombardia* [1997] ECR I–3395, para 27. Discussed by T Hervey, 'Social Solidarity: A Buttress Against Internal Market Law?' in Shaw, n 93 above 31–47.

[103] *Poucet and Pistre, ibid.*

[104] *Sodemare, ibid.* Case C–120/95, *Decker v Caisse de Maladie des Employés Privés* [1998] ECR I–1831; Case C–158/96, *Kohll v Union des Caisses de Maladie* [1998] ECR I–1931.

[105] Case C–244/94, *Fédération Française des Sociétés d'Assurances (FFSA)* [1995] ECR I–4013; Cases C–430 and C–431/93, *Van Schijndel and Van Veen v Stichting Pensioenfonds voor Fysiotherapeuten* [1995] ECR I–4705; Case C–67/96, *Albany International BV v Stichting Bedrijfspensioenfonds Textielindustrie* [1999] ECR I–5751; Cases C–115–117/97, *Brentjens' Handelsonderneming BV v Stichting Bedrijfspensioenfonds voor de Handel in Bouwmaterialen* [1999] ECR I–6025; Case C–219/97, *Drijvende Bokken v Stichting Pensioenfonds voor de Vervoer-en Havenbedrijven* [1999] ECR I–6121.

[106] Cases C–159–160/91, n 102 above.

[107] Art 81 EC [ex 85 EEC] sets out a variety of agreements, decisions and concerted practices involving 'undertakings' which may affect trade between Member States and which have 'as their object or effect the prevention, restriction or distortion of competition within the common market.' Art 82 EC [ex 86 EEC] bites when undertakings behave in such a way as to 'abuse' their 'dominant' market position. Art 82 EC can operate in conjunction with Art 86 EC [ex 90 EEC] where the abuse arises because of 'special or exclusive rights' granted to undertakings by a State.

[108] Cases C–159–160/91, n 102 above, para 17. Equally the concept of an 'undertaking' does not apply, individually or collectively, to 'workers' who, because of their subordinate position in the employment relationship, lack the necessary independence required to constitute an undertaking for the purpose of competition rules—Case C–22/98, *Becu* [1999] ECR I–5665, paras 20–37. For comment, see P Nihoul, 'Do workers constitute undertakings for the purpose of the competition rules?' (2000) 25 *European Law Review* 408.

[109] See Hervey, in Shaw, n 93 above at 44.

[110] Case C–67/96, n 105 above. See also, Cases C–115–117/97, *Brentjens'*, n 105 above and Case C–219/97, *Bokken*, n 105 above. Applied in Case C–222/98, *van der Woude v Stichting Beatrixoord* [2000] ECR I–7111; and Cases C–180–184/98, *Pavlov and others v Stichting Pensioenfonds Medische Specialisten* [2000] ECR I–6451. For discussion, see

established by a collective agreement between the employers and trade unions in the Dutch textile industry was in conformity with Community competition law. Notwithstanding the social aim of the fund and its 'manifestations of solidarity',[111] the Court held that it was not deprived of its status as an 'undertaking' for the purposes of Articles 81, 82 and 86 EC [ex Articles 85, 86 and 90 EEC] because the fund itself determined the amount of the contributions required and benefits provided while operating in accordance with the principle of capitalisation.[112] Unlike compulsory social security schemes, the amount of the benefits provided by the fund depended on the financial results of its investments.[113] However, having found that the fund constituted an economic activity,[114] and was therefore an 'undertaking', the Court once again struck a balance. While it was possible for such funds to 'abuse' their 'dominant position' contrary to Article 82 EC [ex 86 EEC][115] and to fall within the purview of competition law as undertakings granted 'special or exclusive rights' to operate the fund as a service of 'general economic interest' under Article 86 EC [ex 90 EEC],[116] the granting of those exclusive rights was justified as a measure necessary for the performance of a particular social task of general interest—the provision of social protection *for all workers*—with which that fund had been charged.[117] Moreover, it was necessary for the fund to be compulsory because otherwise the viability of the pension fund would be jeopardised if younger workers in good health were to seek more advantageous terms from private insurers.[118]

In perhaps the most remarkable passage in *Albany*, the Court rejected a separate line of argument based on the notion that collective agreements establishing the fund constituted an 'agreement' between 'undertakings' operating in the sector concerned, contrary to Article 81(1) EC [ex 85(1) EEC].[119] Albany contended that this was a form of collusion that distorted competition, implying an 'antitrust conspiracy' of the kind recognised as an exception in the US to the general principle in both legislation and case law

---

R Van den Bergh and P Camesasca, 'Irreconcilable Principles? The Court of Justice Exempts Collective Labour Agreements from the Wrath of Antitrust' (2000) 25 *European Law Review* 492; S Evju, 'Collective Agreements and Competition Law. The *Albany* Puzzle, and *van der Woude*' (2001) 17 *International Journal of Comparative Labour Law and Industrial Relations* 165.

[111] *Ibid* para 85.
[112] *Ibid* para 81. See also, Case C–244/94, *FFSA*, n 105 above.
[113] *Ibid* para 82. See also, the opinion of AG Jacobs, para 343.
[114] *Ibid* para 84. In particular, each fund engaged in an economic activity in competition with insurance companies.
[115] *Ibid* para 93.
[116] *Ibid* para 111.
[117] *Ibid* paras 88–123
[118] *Ibid* para 108.
[119] *Ibid* paras 54–63.

that collective labour agreements have immunity from competition law.[120] The Court's response was stark and direct. While acknowledging that 'certain restrictions of competition are inherent in collective agreements' they observed that 'the social policy objectives pursued by such agreements would be seriously undermined' if management and labour were subject to Article 81(1) EC when seeking jointly to adopt measures to improve conditions of work and employment.[121] The Court took account of the 'whole scheme of the Treaty', paying particular attention to social provisions added to the original Treaty by later amendments[122] including, inter alia, Article 1 of the Agreement on Social Policy[123] [now revised and incorporated in Article 136 EC] which lays down the broad social policy objectives,[124] Article 3(j) [ex 3(i)] EC which now refers to 'a policy in the social sphere' among the Community's activities, and the revised Article 2 EC which sets the Community a goal of a 'high level of employment and social protection'. The Court concluded that collective agreements reached 'in pursuit of such objectives' were outside the scope of Article 81(1) EC.[125]

Hence, notwithstanding the unequivocal language of Article 81(1) EC, collective agreements are exempt from competitive assessment under Community law so long as they pursue social objectives. In this context, labour law, which gives primacy to redistribution based on recognition of unequal power relationships, is preferred to competition law, which seeks to allocate resources efficiently based on an assumption of equality between parties.[126] Such an outcome is deemed tolerable because of the gains in terms of economic efficiency and social concord that arise from harmonious industrial relations founded on collective agreements.

---

[120] Discussed by AG Jacobs at paras 97–107 of his opinion. In the Unites States the legislative immunity of collective agreements can be traced back to the 'Sherman Act', 1870 and the 'Clayton Act', 1914. The Supreme Court has most recently upheld the 'antitrust immunity' in *Brown v Pro Football* [1996] 116 USSC 2116. The main concern of both legislators and the courts has been to preserve the autonomy of the parties but immunity is not unlimited. Where the parties conspire to eliminate competitors from the industry the Supreme Court has been prepared to intervene: *United Mine Workers of America v Pennington* [1965] 381 US 657. After completing a comparative assessment of the national laws of both the US and the Member States of the EU, the AG advised that there was limited 'antitrust immunity' for collective agreements between management and labour concluded in good faith on core subjects of collective bargaining such as wages and working conditions which do not directly affect third markets and third parties (para 194). He concluded that the agreement in question went beyond these limits and fell within Art 81(1) EC but it did not restrict competition because the decision to make the scheme compulsory was made separately by the State (paras 274–94 of the opinion).

[121] Judgment, para 59.

[122] *Ibid* paras 54–58.

[123] The Agreement, which applied to all Member States except the UK, was annexed to Protocol No 14 on Social Policy, annexed to the EC Treaty by the Treaty on European Union (TEU), 1993.

[124] Art 136 EC is the successor provision to Art 117 EEC.

[125] *Ibid* para 60.

[126] See Van den Bergh & Camesasca, n 110 above at 502.

In later chapters we will trace the amendments to the social provisions in the Treaty that influenced the Court in *Albany*, but it is important to note at this stage that, while the Court's judgment drew heavily on these Treaty changes and expressed itself in strikingly clear language, its approach was broadly consistent with its earlier case law, showing awareness not only of the national sensitivities involved, specifically the autonomy of the 'social partners' in the area of industrial relations, but also the fine balance between the Community's economic and social aims. Indeed, it was to rectify the *formal* imbalance in the methods available to fulfil its economic and social objectives arising from the strictly limited social provisions in the Treaty of Rome that more substantive social policies were proposed in the Community's first Social Action Programme of 1974.

2

The Community's 'New Deal'

I A 'HUMAN FACE' FOR THE COMMUNITY: THE FIRST SOCIAL ACTION PROGRAMME

THE PERIOD FROM the 1950s through to the early 1970s is often described as the Community's 'golden age' when a rapid rise in rates of growth and a corresponding increase in *overall* living standards appeared to vindicate the central tenets of the 'automatic convergence' theory expounded in the Spaak Report and crystallised in Article 117 EEC.[1] This metaphysical approach to the development of the Community was perhaps the most remarkable feature of the post-war years when man appeared to be achieving 'an unprecedented mastery over nature'[2] in a Kantian 'perfect civic association'.[3] To the rational mind the harnessing of European resources in a climate of peace meant *inevitable* economic and social convergence. By the late 1960s, however, there were undercurrents of dissent that began to challenge these cosy assumptions. In particular, a new generation, born after the Second World War, were expressing themselves in reaction against the Vietnam War and social inequality. The 'Paris Spring' of 1968 had a powerful impact on Europe's political leaders and drew their attention to the increasing reality that the benefits of the boom were being unevenly spread with many groups still excluded from the labour market. For the first time they began to question the *raison d'être* of the Community's social policy.

At the Hague European Council in December 1969 the West German Chancellor, Willy Brandt, submitted a memorandum calling for co-ordination of economic integration with social harmonisation in order to give

---

[1] Improved working conditions and living standards *'will ensue* from the functioning of the common market'. My emphasis. See S Deakin, 'Labour Law as Market Regulation: the Economic Foundations of European Social Policy' in P Davies, A Lyon-Caen, S Sciarra & S Simitis (eds) *European Community Labour Law: Principles and Perspectives* (Clarendon Press, Oxford, 1996) 62–93 at 69 and 84. On the 'golden age', see S Marglin & J Schorr (eds) *The Golden Age of Capitalism: Reinterpreting the Postwar Experience* (Clarendon Press, Oxford, 1992).

[2] J Monnet, 'A Ferment of Change' (1962) 1 *Journal of Common Market Studies* 203 at 203.

[3] F von Krosigk, 'A Reconsideration of Federalism in the Scope of the Present Discussion on European Integration' (1970) 9 *Journal of Common Market Studies* 197 at 198–200.

the Community a 'human face' which could be understood by its citizens.[4] This demand challenged the hitherto unassailable reliance on market mechanisms and echoed Roosevelt's 'New Deal'.[5] Community social policy was no longer seen as passive. It was to be attuned to Marshall's classic sociological view that social policies are necessary to modify the economic system in order to achieve results that the economic system would not achieve on its own and, in doing so, Community social policy was to be guided by values other than those determined by open market forces.[6] As Michael Shanks, a former Director-General for Social Affairs at the Commission, explained several years later:[7]

The Community had to be seen to be more than a device to enable capitalists to exploit the common market; otherwise it might not be possible to persuade the peoples of the Community to accept the disciplines of the market. The common market had to evolve into a genuine Community, a Community 'with a human face', which would be able to command the loyalties of its citizens, strong enough to resist the centrifugal forces of nationalism and sectional pressures.

The expansion of the Community from six to nine Member States from 1973 added a fresh dynamic to this evolutionary process.[8] In a reworking of Roosevelt's formula, the preamble to the final declaration of the Paris Summit in October 1972 proclaimed that:[9]

Economic expansion is not an end in itself. Its firm aim should be to enable disparities in living conditions to be reduced. It must take place with the participation of all Social Partners. It should result in an improvement of the quality of life as well as standards of living.

It was agreed to establish a Social Action Programme in 1974 as a means of fulfilling this bold vision but without any pretence that the Treaty powers would be strengthened. Nevertheless, this was an important turning point

---

[4] See M Wise & R Gibb, *Single Market to Social Europe: The European Community in the 1990s* (Longman, Harlow, 1993) pp 131–32.

[5] As Roosevelt famously declared to the 1941 ILO Conference: 'economic policy can no longer be an end in itself. It is merely a means for achieving social justice'. Rec Proc Conf 1941, p 158.

[6] See T Marshall, *Social Policy* (Hutchinson, London, 1975) p 15. For discussion, see T Hervey, *European Social Law and Policy* (Longman, Harlow, 1998) ch 1; G Majone, 'The European Community Between Social Policy and Social Regulation' (1993) 31 *Journal of Common Market Studies* 153.

[7] M Shanks, 'Introductory Article: The Social Policy of the European Communities' (1977) 14 *Common Market Law Review* 375 at 378. Shanks was Director-General from June 1973 to Jan 1976.

[8] The new members were Denmark, Ireland and the UK. Norway had also applied but a referendum in 1972 produced a 'No' vote. The well developed social policies in Denmark and Norway and the need to secure them after accession was another important factor. See A Sandler, 'Players and Process: The Evolution of Employment Law in the EEC' (1985) 7 *Comparative Labour Law Journal* 1 at 3–4.

[9] Summarised in *Bulletin of the European Communities Supplement* 2/74, p 14.

because for the first time the Member States declared that they attached 'as much importance to vigorous action in the social field as to the achievement of the economic and monetary union'.[10] Thus, notwithstanding the 'inadequate' powers available under the Treaty, the Commission now had a clear mandate to rely on existing Treaty provisions, both Article 100 EEC [now 94 EC], allowing for Common Market approximation measures,[11] and, where necessary, the gap-filling general purposes clause in Article 235 EEC [now 308 EC],[12] as a basis for proposing legislation to harmonise social policies.[13] Such a programme could only be carried through when there was unanimity in the Council of Ministers under these Treaty provisions.

The Social Action Programme (SAP) was eventually adopted by way of a Council Resolution in January 1974[14] based on the Commission's proposals.[15] The SAP strove to ensure that social objectives should be a 'constant concern' of all Community policies in order to overcome problems 'of inequalities and of the unacceptable by-products of growth' which might jeopardise 'the rhythm of growth itself in face of the social pressures and resistance it generates'.[16] This fresh drive for social progress was part of a determined, but pragmatic, attempt to transform the Community from an economic to a political union by the end of the decade.[17]

A set of bold objectives was presented:[18] full and better employment; improvement of living and working conditions; and greater participation of workers and employers in the economic and social decisions of the Community. In practice the legislative programme fell far short of expectations not only because of the formal limitations of the Treaty bases, but also for substantive reasons, including the underlying problems considered earlier and, more immediately, by a serious economic recession which undermined the political will that had existed in favour of an activist social programme and restricted the action taken, at least outside the equalities field. Moreover, the Council Resolution setting out the SAP was a form of influential but non-binding soft law. It was a manifesto that would be adhered to, in whole or part, only so long as there was the political will to apply it for

---

[10] *Ibid.*

[11] Art 94 EC provides for the issuing of approximation directives which 'directly affect the establishment and functioning of the common market'.

[12] Art 308 EC provides for appropriate measures 'necessary to obtain one of the objectives of the Community and this Treaty has not provided the necessary powers'.

[13] *Bulletin of the European Communities Supplement* 2/74, p 14.

[14] OJ 1974, C13/1.

[15] Submitted to the Council on 25 Oct 1973. Reproduced in *Bulletin of the European Communities Supplement* 2/74, pp 13–35.

[16] *Ibid* p 13.

[17] As agreed at the Paris Summit on 17 Oct 1972. For an interesting account by one of the leading participants, see E Heath, *The Course of My Life* (Hodder & Stoughton, London, 1998) pp 387–95.

[18] *Bulletin of the European Communities Supplement* 2/74, p 15.

the purposes of supporting binding legislative proposals that might emanate from the Commission.[19]

The legislative and programmatic action that followed fell broadly into four areas:

—employment protection and the working environment;
—equality between women and men;
—employee participation; and
—employment creation through vocational training and the European Social Fund.

In the following sections an attempt will be made to address key elements of the development of social policy under this programme in the period leading up to the Single European Act of 1987. There will be a focus on four main areas:

(1) Partial harmonisation—the legislative programme of the Commission in the area of employment protection.
(2) The principle of equality—the pivotal role of the Court of Justice in filling gaps left by the Community legislator.
(3) Harmonisation of technical standards—the first 'Framework Directive' on health and safety at work.
(4) Attempts to combine social dialogue at Community level with wider democratisation of the workplace.

Each of these areas has been selected to aid an evaluation of the broad development of social policy in this period by indicating how these first legislative steps and the early case law of the Court had an influence upon the content and reach of the revised Social Chapter adopted at Amsterdam in 1997.

II PARTIAL HARMONISATION AND FLEXIBLE IMPLEMENTATION OF THE EMPLOYMENT PROTECTION DIRECTIVES

The story of the SAP is one of scaled down ambition. Faced with a downward economic cycle and the need to react most immediately to domestic pressures, the Community's leaders responded with pragmatism and tailored the programme to suit their immediate economic and political concerns. These changing priorities were already apparent by the time the Commission submitted the SAP in 1974 after the first of a series of sharp rises in oil prices. The Commission was determined not to be knocked off course by economic turbulence and strove to secure political agreement for

[19] See B Hepple, 'The Effect of Community Law on Employment Rights' (1975) 1 *Poly Law Review* 50 at 51.

a limited programme of social legislation. The SAP sought to improve living and working conditions with a series of measures including, for example, a proposal to fix 'immediate targets' of a 40-hour working week and four weeks annual holiday.[20]

In essence, the Community's approach was to intervene in areas where national regulation either did not exist or was manifestly failing to improve the working environment. For example, in the context of employee participation in companies, the Commission was able to boldly state in its 1975 Green Paper on employee participation that:[21]

A sufficient convergence of social and economic policies and structures in [employee decision making within companies] will not happen automatically as a consequence of the integration of markets.

It followed that positive Community action was required to provide the necessary legislative push to attain 'sufficient convergence'. Positive and negative integration had become intertwined.[22] Social policy, in the first phase of the Community's development, was based on a series of negative assumptions that improvements would arise not through specific positive laws at Community level in the social field, but consequentially, as a result of the removal of barriers and improvements in productivity, allowing Member States to enhance social conditions at a national level leading to a general upward harmonisation of social standards. The introduction of the SAP was tantamount to an admission that positive harmonisation was necessary, not as an end in itself, but to complete the task where the market alone had failed to deliver. It was therefore appropriate that Article 100 EEC was to be the legal base for selected measures deemed to 'directly affect' the establishment and functioning of the common market.

In the event, the employment protection measures adopted were narrowly targeted at specific economic and industrial circumstances and were intended to offer only a limited amount of employment protection, or compensation, for a change of employer or for loss of employment. Directive 75/129 on collective redundancies offered a minimal degree of procedural rights in the face of mass dismissals.[23] Directive 77/187 was concerned with

---

[20] *Bulletin of the European Communities Supplement* 2/74, p 18.

[21] 'Employee Participation and Company Structure', Green Paper of the EC Commission, *Bulletin of the European Communities Supplement* 8/75, p 10. See S Simitis and A Lyon-Caen, 'Community Labour Law: A Critical Introduction to its History' in Davies *et al*, n 1 above, 1–22 at 7. For discussion, see P Davies, 'The Emergence of European Labour Law' in W McCarthy (ed) *Legal Intervention in Industrial Relations: Gains and Losses* (Blackwell, London, 1993) 313–59 at 325.

[22] See S Weatherill, *Law and Integration in the European Union* (Clarendon Press, Oxford, 1995) pp 282–83. Weatherill discusses the way in which Community law has become increasingly multi-functional combining regulation at Community level, often driven by pressure from interest groups, with deregulation at national level to improve the operation of the European market.

[23] Dir 75/129/EEC on collective redundancies, OJ 1975, L48/29.

protecting the acquired rights of employees in circumstances where there was change of the natural or legal person responsible for carrying on the business and/or a change of ownership of the employing undertaking.[24] Directive 80/987 was intended to guarantee state compensation to the employees of insolvent companies.[25] These were essentially crisis measures, driven as much by economic considerations as social needs. Their purpose was not to enhance basic working conditions but instead to alleviate the consequences of economic decline, particularly in the private manufacturing sector. [The Collective Redundancies and Acquired Rights Directives have now been amended and consolidated, while the Insolvency Directive is also due for revision.[26] For discussion of these developments and a full appraisal of the Court's more recent jurisprudence in this area, see chapter 7, Part VI(3)].

For example, the Collective Redundancies Directive, 75/129 [now 98/59][27] provides for the consultation of workers where the employer is contemplating collective redundancies[28] involving 'at least . . . ways and means of *avoiding* collective redundancies or *reducing* the numbers of workers affected, and *mitigating* the consequences'.[29] This was intended to allow time for the 'workers' representatives' to make 'constructive proposals' and to be given 'all relevant information' including 'the reasons for the redundancies'.[30] Consultation with workers' representatives is to take place 'with a view to reaching an agreement'.[31] The Directive was motivated in part by a desire to provide some protection in these circumstances, but it was also hoped that it

[24] Dir 77/187/EEC on the safeguarding of employees' rights in the event of transfers of undertakings, businesses or parts of businesses, OJ 1977, L61/26: the 'Acquired Rights Directive'.

[25] Dir 80/987/EEC on the protection of employees in the event of the insolvency of their employer, OJ 1980, L283/23.

[26] Dir 92/56/EEC on collective redundancies, OJ 1992, L245/3, consolidated by Dir 98/59/EC, OJ 1998, L225/16; Dir 98/50/EC on safeguarding of employees' rights in the event of transfers of undertakings, businesses or parts of undertakings or businesses, OJ 1998, L201/88, consolidated by Dir 2001/23/EC, OJ 2001, L82/16. For the Commission's Explanatory Memorandum on the revision of the Insolvency Dir, see COM(2000) 832.

[27] *Ibid.*

[28] Art 1(1)(a) of Dir 98/59, replacing the identical Art 1(1)(a) of Dir 75/129, defines 'collective redundancies' as 'dismissals effected by the employer for one or more reasons not related to the individual workers concerned where, according to the choice of the Member States, the number of redundancies is:—either, over a period of 30 days: (1) at least 10 in establishments normally employing more than 20 and less than 100 workers; (2) at least 10% . . . in establishments normally employing at least 100 but less than 300 workers, (3) at least 30 in establishments normally employing 300 workers or more;—or, over a period of 90 days, at least 20, whatever the number of workers normally employed . . .'.

[29] Art 2(2) of Dir 75/129. My emphasis. See ch 7 for comment on how the Dir has subsequently been strengthened in this respect by Art 2(2) of Dir 92/56, now consolidated within Art 2(2) of Dir 98/59.

[30] Art 2(3) of Dir 75/129 [now 98/59]. Other relevant information is to include the numbers to be made redundant, the number of workers normally employed and the period over which the redundancies are to be given effect.

[31] Art 2(1) of Dir 75/129 [now 98/59]. Dir 92/56 added the words 'in good time'.

would help to promote free movement of labour and a level playing field of competition.[32] The Community was effectively offering only a sticking plaster to provide temporary and limited protection for, as the Commission explained in its Explanatory Memorandum to the original draft:[33]

... economic changes, involving closing down of some companies are, however, an integral part of the evolution towards more promising activities. They should not therefore be prevented, but job mobility should be subject to adequate guarantees.

Furthermore, the Court, aware of the aspirational nature of the measure and its limitations as a procedural labour law device, has been unwilling to interfere with the employer's managerial prerogative and commercial power to decide how and when to formulate plans for collective dismissals subject only to national restraints where they may exist. As the Court explained in *Nielsen*, the procedural rules in the Directive apply only where the employer has contemplated redundancies or drawn up a plan for them.[34] For example, workers cannot pre-empt the process by terminating their own contracts in anticipation of impending redundancies.[35]

A similar approach can be found in the Insolvency Directive, 80/987. This too is essentially procedural but it places the main obligation on the State and is, therefore, bolder in practice. Each Member State is required to establish 'guarantee institutions'[36] where an employer is in a 'state of insolvency',[37] and thereby to protect employees from the consequences of their employer's insolvency in the form of a guarantee payment of their outstanding claims resulting from the contract of employment and employment relationship and relating to arrears of pay.[38] Additional guarantees ensure

---

[32] The original proposal for a Dir was based on a 1972 report from the Commission to the Council (1972) 5 *Bulletin of the European Communities* (No 9) para 42. The report is reproduced in *Bulletin No 4* (1973) Institute of Labour Relations, University of Leuven, pp 171–203. For discussion, see M Freedland, 'Employment Protection: Redundancy Procedures and the EEC' (1976) 5 *Industrial Law Journal* 24 at 26.

[33] See Davies in McCarthy, n 21 above at 327. This extract from the Commission's draft is taken from the reproduced version in the Bulletin of the University of Leuven, *ibid* pp 108 *et seq* at 206.

[34] Case 248/83, *Dansk Metalarbejderforbund v Nielsen & Son Maskin-fabrik A/S* [1985] ECR 553.

[35] *Ibid* para 10.

[36] Art 3(1) of Dir 80/987. Under Art 5 it is for the Member State to prescribe the detailed rules for organisation, finance and operation of the guarantee institution providing they adhere to three principles: (a) the assets of the institutions shall be independent of the employer's operating capital and be inaccessible to proceedings for insolvency; (b) employers shall contribute to financing, unless it is fully covered by the public authorities; and (c) the institution's liabilities shall not depend on whether or not obligations to contribute to financing have been fulfilled.

[37] Art 1(1). A 'state of insolvency' shall be deemed to exist, by virtue of Art 2(1) when a request has been made for the opening of proceedings involving the employer's assets to satisfy collectively the claims of creditors or where the competent national authority has decided to open proceedings or established that the employer's assets have definitely closed down and that available assets are insufficient to warrant the opening of proceedings.

[38] Art 3(1).

that non-payment of statutory social security contributions by insolvent employers do not adversely affect the benefit entitlement of employees,[39] and preserve the right of former employees to old age benefits, including survivors' benefits, under company schemes.[40] Although the requirement to establish a 'guarantee institution' has been found not to be 'directly effective', non-implementation by a Member State may form the basis for a damages claim before the national courts.[41]

What then was the scope of employment protection or support to be afforded to workers under these directives? Were they intended to fully equalise the rights of workers across the Community or merely to 'approximate' levels of protection in a way that would fall short of full harmonisation? The preamble of Directive 77/187 [now 2001/23][42] on Acquired Rights indicated that the latter approach was preferred. The sixth and seventh recitals of the original Directive proclaimed that:

Whereas it is necessary to provide for the protection of employees in the event of a change of employer, in particular to ensure that their rights are safeguarded;

Whereas differences still remain in the Member States as regards the extent of protection of employees in this respect and these differences should be reduced . . .

The commitment to protect workers was, therefore, to be achieved over time by reducing, but not eliminating, differences in national standards. As the Court explained 10 years later in the *Daddy's Dance Hall* case,[43] the Directive:

. . . is intended to achieve only *partial harmonisation*, essentially by extending the protection guaranteed to workers independently by the laws of the individual Member States to cover the case where an undertaking is transferred. *It is not intended to establish a uniform level of protection throughout the Community on the basis of common criteria.*

This explanation makes sense both as an interpretation of the Directive in question and as a general statement about Community social laws. For as Bercusson notes:[44]

---

[39]   Art 7.

[40]   Art 8.

[41]   Cases C–6/90 and C–9/90, *Francovich and Bonifaci v Italy* [1991] ECR I–5357. In a landmark ruling the Court established that an individual has the right to sue a defaulting state for failure to implement a directive where there is a direct causal link between the loss suffered by the individual and the breach of Community obligations by the State, and where the provisions in question are intended to benefit that individual. In *Francovich* the Commission had already successfully brought an action against Italy for non-compliance under Art 169 EEC [now 226 EC] but Italy had not yet acted (Case 22/87, *Commission v Italy* [1989] ECR 143).

[42]   OJ 2001, L82/16.

[43]   Case 324/86, *Foreningen af Arbejdsledere i Danmark v Daddy's Dance Hall A/S* [1988] ECR 739, para 16. My emphasis.

[44]   B Bercusson, *European Labour Law* (Butterworths, London, 1996) p 52.

The starting point of a policy of harmonisation is the identification of a problem *common* to various European countries and the attempt to harmonise law and practice relating to the problem. It emerges, however, that the identification of *common* problems, when related to *varying* labour laws of selected national systems, does not produce a harmonised view of law and practice.

Therefore, variations in industrial relations and labour law systems and corresponding differences in the form and substance of national labour laws represent insuperable obstacles to 'full' harmonisation.[45] The implications of breaking down such differences are also both politically and socially undesirable. For these reasons rigid harmonisation has been consistently rejected in favour of 'diversity built on common standards'. In this way a patchwork of employment protection can be provided at Community level, providing transnational protection where necessary, without creating a common set of rules governing the employment relationship. In a sense the very limitations inherent within these harmonising objectives have served as a basis for justifying them on the grounds that they help to eliminate unfair competition. As Wedderburn explains:[46]

The need for a 'level playing field' of competition therefore requires a broad equivalence in labour standards. For some the minimum level would move upwards, for others the obligatory requirements would be low; but none could agree to standards which allow incalculable advantage only to some.

By using directives the Community was able to lay down standards acceptable to all Member States, not necessarily the lowest common denominator, but sufficiently flexible to allow for improvements at national level while offering no scope for any individual State to undercut the agreed minima. It followed that in each of the employment protection directives 'upwards harmonisation' was provided for with provisions allowing Member States to apply or introduce laws 'which are more favourable to employees'.[47] This approach has helped to provide a more coherent rationale for introducing Community social policy in a flexible way and, as we shall see, it has been developed and adjusted through the notion of 'minimum harmonisation' in Article 118a EEC on the health and safety of workers, added by the Single European Act of 1987, and now contained

---

[45] *Ibid.*

[46] Lord Wedderburn, 'The Social Charter in Britain—Labour Law and Labour Courts?' (1991) 54 *Modern Law Review* 1 at 16. In the case of the Collective Redundancies Directive, 75/129, Wedderburn cites an article by the then AG Mancini who declared that: 'If a country can authorise redundancies on less stringent conditions than other countries, its industry will be given an incalculable advantage. And it is against the advantage that war is being declared'. See G Mancini, 'Labour Law and Community Law' (1985) 20 *Irish Jurist (ns)* 1 at 12.

[47] See Art 5 of Dir 77/187 and Art 9 of Dir 80/987. Art 5 of Dir 75/129 [now 98/59] was broader and allowed for measures 'which are more favourable to workers or to promote or to allow the application of collective agreements more favourable to workers'. This wording is now applied in Art 8 of Dir 2001/23, replacing Art 5 of Dir 77/187.

within Article 137(2) and (5) EC. This technique has continued to evolve and been adapted to fit the new legal bases in the Amsterdam Social Chapter.[48]

For example, in the case of the Collective Redundancies Directive, the precise scope of the procedural obligation is delegated to each Member State, not only in the choice of method for calculating the number and timing of redundancies, but also for the oversight of the notification procedures[49] and the definition of 'workers' representatives'.[50] The Court has confirmed, in *Commission v United Kingdom*,[51] that the Directive 'was not intended to bring about full harmonisation of national systems for the representation of employees', but the limited nature of such harmonisation does not deprive the Directive of its effectiveness and therefore the system of workers' representation cannot be determined unilaterally by the employer.[52]

The Insolvency Directive, 80/987, is even more flexible. Member States have a variety of choices for calculating compensation payments. The amounts awarded must be for a period of at least three months before the end of the employment contract but cover a period up to 18 months depending on the method for choosing the relevant date opted for by the Member State be it the onset of the employer's insolvency or the notice of dismissal on account of insolvency.[53] They are also able to set a ceiling to the liability for employees' outstanding claims 'in order to avoid the payment of sums going beyond the social objective of this Directive'. The Commission must be informed of the methods used to set this ceiling.[54]

Another flexible feature of the Insolvency Directive is its use of derogations to exclude groups of employees' altogether if they are deemed to have employment contracts of a 'special nature' that fall within a list in the Annex.[55] This list excludes, inter alia, part-time domestic servants in the Netherlands, some home workers and part-time workers in Ireland and the crews of sea-going vessels in several countries.[56] The existence of the Annex can only be rationally explained by the requirement for unanimous voting among the Member States under Article 100 EEC [now 94 EC]. The result

---

[48] As listed in Art 137(1) and (3) EC.

[49] Arts 3 and 4. This has been substantially revised by Dir 92/56 and the consolidated provisions are now contained in Arts 3 and 4 of Dir 98/59.

[50] Art 1(1)(b) unaltered in Dir 98/59, provides that 'workers representatives' means the 'workers' representatives provided for by the laws and practices of the Member States'.

[51] Case C–382/92 [1994] ECR I–2435.

[52] *Ibid* para 25.

[53] Arts 3(2), 4(1) and 4(2).

[54] Art 4(3).

[55] Art 1(2).

[56] See also, Art 1(2) and (3) of Dir 77/187, which limits the scope of application of that Directive to all employees where the business is situated 'within the territorial scope of the Treaty' with the exception of 'sea-going vessels'.

is extremely arbitrary for those workers unlucky enough to be excluded from the minimum degree of protection provided for in the Directive.[57]

At first glance the original Acquired Rights Directive had many similarities with the Directives on Collective Redundancies and Insolvency. It had a procedural dimension and was intended to operate flexibly. As noted above, it was concerned with reducing rather than eliminating differences between the Member States. In particular, the Directive was a response to:[58]

Economic trends . . . bringing in their wake, at both national and Community level, changes in the structure of undertakings, through transfers of undertakings, businesses or parts of businesses to other employers as a result of legal transfers or mergers.

The inclusion of this recital reflected a subtle but important change of emphasis from the original proposal of 1974. In the Commission's proposal it was explicitly stated that the primary aim of the draft directive was to 'ensure . . . that employees do not forfeit essential rights and advantages acquired prior to a change of employer'.[59] While the limited legal bases in the Treaty required an acknowledgement of the wider market functioning factors referred to in Article 100 EEC, it is clear from the final text that, after long and tortuous negotiations, the market imperative was deemed to be paramount.

Although the Directive is widely seen today as a 'champion of employees' rights'[60] its core employment protection provisions were quite restricted and circumscribed by derogations. For the Member States it was understood as only a *safeguard* in the specific context of the ending of an employment relationship by reason of a transfer of an undertaking or business or part thereof as defined in the Directive. Where such circumstances arise, the transferee inherits both the employment relationship and the rights acquired therein with the exception of any occupational pension arrangements.[61] The terms and conditions in any collective agreements are transferred although a Member State is able to limit their observance to only one year after the transfer.[62]

In the main text of the Directive the specific event of 'transfer' was defined narrowly as 'the transfer of an undertaking, business or part of a business

---

[57] In Case C–53/88, *Commission v Greece* [1990] ECR I–3931, the Court held that the Directive offers minimum guaranteed protection to all employees and the exclusions are only possible by way of an exception on implementation.

[58] First recital of the preamble of Dir 77/187.

[59] COM(74) 351. For discussion, see G More, 'The Concept of 'Undertaking' in the Acquired Rights Directive: The Court of Justice Under Pressure (Again)' (1995) 15 *Yearbook of European Law* 135 at 136–37; and P Davies, 'Acquired Rights, Creditors' Rights, Freedom of Contract, and Industrial Democracy' (1989) 9 *Yearbook of European Law* 21 at 27–9.

[60] More, *ibid* at 135.

[61] Art 3(1) and 3(3) of Dir 77/187 [now incorporated within the amended Art 3(1) and 3(4) of Dir 2001/23].

[62] Art 3(2) of Dir 77/187 [now Art 3(2) of Dir 2001/23].

to another employer *as a result of a legal transfer or merger*.[63] Therefore protection depended on the nature of the transfer or merger and did not arise simply by virtue of a change of employer or, as proposed in the original draft,[64] a mere change of control not involving a change of identity of the employer. Moreover, the transfer event did not occur where one company acquired a controlling shareholding in another, or indeed where the transferor had been adjudged insolvent and the undertaking deemed to be part of his assets.[65] In effect, operative business practices likely to alter the rights of the employees concerned, such as takeovers and the hiving-down of companies,[66] were excluded even where there was a change in ownership. When the Directive was adopted such activities were relatively rare in many of the Member States. By the end of the 1980s, these business practices had become commonplace throughout the Community and an expert report for the Commission recommended a revision of the Directive in 1990.[67] In the event the Directive was not amended until 1998.

An additional limitation in the Acquired Rights Directive is the distinction made between certain types of dismissal that may arise in the context of the transfer process. The employer does not have grounds for dismissal if the *reason for the dismissal is the transfer itself*, and is responsible for any related terminations of contracts of employment or employment relationships that involve a 'substantial change in working conditions to the detriment of the employee'.[68] This would include dismissals even before the transfer date where the reason for the dismissal is the transfer.[69] Conversely, where the dismissal is for other 'economic, technical or organisational reasons entailing changes in the workforce',[70] the employee has no recourse to Community law and therefore the level of protection is entirely determined by the existence and scope of national unfair dismissal legislation or collective agreements. The sheer breadth of this exemption, coupled with

---

[63] Art 1(1) [now Art 1(1) of Dir 2001/23. Emphasis added. [This definition has been substantially revised—see ch 7 for discussion].

[64] COM(74) 351, draft Art 11. For comment, see Davies (1989, *Yearbook of European Law*) n 59 above at 27.

[65] Case 135/83, *Abels v Bedrijfsvereniging voor de Metaalindustrie en de Electrotechnische Industrie* [1985] ECR 469.

[66] See R Rideout, 'The Great Transfer of Employees Rights Hoax' [1982] *Current Legal Problems* 233 at 237–39. Rideout describes 'hiving down' as a device that enables a receiver to transfer the assets of an insolvent company to an intermediate owner who is usually a wholly owned subsidiary of the insolvent. The insolvency company retains the liabilities, including the employees. The employees' rights become a mere bundle of assets. Their rights lie in claims against the insolvent company although any employees who are ultimately transferred will be protected.

[67] B Hepple, *Main Shortcomings and Proposals for Revision of Council Directive 77/187* (European Commission, Brussels, 1990).

[68] Art 4(2) of Dir 77/187 [now 2001/23].

[69] Case 101/87, *Bork v Foreiningen Arbejdsledere i Danmark* [1988] ECR 3057.

[70] Art 4(1) of Dir 77/187 [now 2001/23].

the problem of transposition based on translation of such arcane terms,[71] has created plenty of scope for employers to rebut the presumption of an unlawful dismissal in a transfer scenario.[72]

Not surprisingly, the introduction of a right of an employee to have their acquired rights transferred in a given situation led to a stream of litigation in which the labyrinthine wording of the Directive has been explored almost to the point of exhaustion. By the end of 1997 the Court had handed down 25 judgments interpreting the Directive.[73] Case law has led to a quite remarkable evolution in the character of the Directive. By the time of its amendment in 1998, the Directive was a quite different animal from the beast originally conceived by the Member States. For example, in the 1970s the Member States were, without exception, retaining a fairly stable level of public ownership or, in some cases, such as France, briefly after 1981, contemplating further nationalisation, particularly in the utility and banking sectors. Although public ownership had been permitted under Article 222 EEC [now 295 EC],[74] the central thrust of the Directive, as indicated by the preamble, was aimed at changes of ownership of private sector undertakings at a time of economic turbulence, particularly in the manufacturing sector. This did not mean that Member States were able to explicitly exclude the public sector as the UK sought to do, ultimately unsuccessfully,[75] but such an application was ancillary. Yet, within 10 years a dramatic transformation had taken place. Member States, led by the UK, were embarking on a variety of programmes of 'contracting out' or even

---

[71] As Lord Wedderburn complained, in a debate on the implementing legislation in the UK House of Lords, when referring to Art 4(1): 'Euro-jargon sometimes goes well into the law of France and of Germany. It rarely goes well into English law', HL Deb 1166 (10 Dec 1981) col 1491.

[72] For a comment on the impact of this provision on UK employment law at the time of implementation, see Rideout, n 66 above at 242–43.

[73] For comprehensive summaries of the case law, see C De Groot, 'The Council Directive on the Safeguarding of Employees' Rights in the Event of Transfers of Undertakings: An Overview of the Case Law' (1993) 30 *Common Market Law Review* 331; and C De Groot, 'The Council Directive on the Safeguarding of Employees' Rights in the Event of Transfers of Undertakings: An Overview of Recent Case Law' (1998) 35 *Common Market Law Review* 707.

[74] Art 295 EC reads as follows: 'This Treaty shall in no way prejudice the rules in Member States governing the system of property ownership'.

[75] Case C–383/92, *Commission v United Kingdom* [1994] ECR I–2345. Reg 2(1) of the UK's Transfer of Undertakings (Protection of Employment) Regulations (SI 1981, No 1794) defined an 'undertaking' as including: 'any trade or business but . . . not . . . any undertaking or part of an undertaking which is not in the nature of a commercial venture'. A 'commercial venture' was understood, in pleadings accepted by the UK, to refer to the investment of capital with a view to making profits and accepting the risks of losses, para 19 of the AG's opinion. The Court held that this interpretation was too narrow and found that 'the fact that an undertaking is engaged in non-profit-making activities is not in itself sufficient to deprive such activities of their economic character or to remove the undertaking from the scope of the directive', paras 44–5. The UK, anticipating this outcome, had amended the Regulations with effect from 30 Aug 1993 by virtue of s 26 of the Trade Union Reform and Employment Rights Act, 1993.

full-scale privatisation of public services. Was the Directive sufficiently *flexible* to evolve in such a way as to take account of these changed circumstances?

The response of the Court when faced with this question has been to seek to keep pace with changes on the ground while continuing to make reference to the wider economic basis for the Directive in such a way as to provide a broad discretion to national courts. The first question to be considered is strictly legal: has there been a 'legal transfer or merger'? The second question, however, is one of fact for the national court to determine whether there has been a transfer of an undertaking, business or part of a business to another employer?[76]

By the mid-1980s, when the trickle of cases was becoming a flood, the Court sought to give as much discretion as possible to the national courts. In essence, the national court is required to consider the nature of the economic activities and organisational arrangements of the transferor and transferee with the employees as passive recipients of Community safeguarding if the criteria are met. There is, however, scope for an employee to object if he does not wish to be transferred, as he cannot be obliged to work for an employer that he has not freely chosen.[77] In *Spijkers*[78] a non-exhaustive list of factors was drawn up by the Court to determine whether there had in fact been a transfer. These factors include: the type of business concerned; whether its tangible assets have been transferred; the value of those assets at the time of transfer; the retention of employees and customers; and continuation of similar activities.[79] Having considered these and any other factors, the 'decisive criterion' is 'whether the business in question retains its identity' as indicated, inter alia, by the actual continuation or resumption by the new employer of the same or similar activities.[80] The critical point here is that the operation of the Directive is not dependent on

---

[76] See More, n 59 above at 137–38.

[77] Cases C–132/91 and C–138–139/91, *Katsikas v Konstatinidis* [1992] ECR I–6577. The Court held, at paras 31 and 32, that an obligation on the employee to be transferred would 'jeopardise the fundamental rights of the employee, who must be free to choose his employer and cannot be obliged to work for an employer whom he has not freely chosen'. Although this is qualified by the Court's decision that national law may allow the contract with the transferor to be terminated by reason of the transfer, the Court's approach is consistent with the international labour law principle that 'labour is not a commodity' and the common law rule that upholds the freedom of contract. See P O'Higgins, ' "Labour is not a Commodity"— An Irish Contribution to International Labour Law' (1997) 26 *Industrial Law Journal* 225. As Lord Atkin famously stated in *Nokes v Doncaster Amalgamated Collieries Ltd* [1940] AC 1014 at 1026: 'I had fancied that ingrained in the personal status of a citizen under our laws was the right to choose for himself whom he would serve, and that this right of choice constituted the main difference between a servant and a serf'. For comment, see Davies (1989, *Yearbook of European Law*) n 59 above at 23; B Hepple, 'Social Values and European Law' [1995] *Current Legal Problems* 39 at 53–4.

[78] Case 24/85, *Spijkers v Gebroeders Benedik Abbatoir CV* [1986] ECR 1119.

[79] See also, Case C–209/91, *Rask and Christensen v ISS Kantinservice* [1993] ECR I–5755.

[80] Case 24/85, *Spijkers v Gebroeders Benedik Abbatoir CV* [1986] ECR 1119, paras 11–14.

a change of ownership but is instead applicable in any situation where, as the Court explained in *Daddy's Dance Hall*,[81] there is 'a change in the natural or legal person who is responsible for carrying on the business and who by virtue of that fact incurs the obligations of an employer'. In such a situation the employees' require equivalent protection that is comparable to that of employees of an undertaking that has been sold. It is at this point that labour law overrides commercial considerations.[82]

It followed that, by considering neutral economic factors as part of an overall assessment, it was perfectly possible, at least on a theoretical level, for the Directive to be applied to privatisations and contracting out. Moreover, such an approach was consistent with the economic objectives of the Treaty. For example in its judgment in a free movement case, *Donà*, the Court had stated that:[83]

The pursuit of an activity as an employed person or the provision of services for remuneration must be regarded as an economic activity within the meaning of Article 2 of the Treaty.

As AG Van Gerven explained in *Commission v United Kingdom*,[84] the nature of the 'economic activity' understood to be covered by any directive concerned with common market approximation was not to be determined according to the sector within which that activity was performed and could not be limited only to profit-making undertakings.[85] It was in this light that the term 'undertaking' was to be understood. For example, in *Sophie Redmond*,[86] a change in the ownership of a publicly funded charitable foundation was found to be capable of falling within the scope of the Directive. There had been a change in the legal or natural person responsible for carrying out the business albeit that this was the result of a decision by a public body to terminate its subsidy.[87] By contrast, in *Henke*,[88] the Court was not prepared to extend the Directive so far that it covered structural reorganisations and transfers of administrative functions that took place exclusively between public administration authorities.[89] Therefore, in the area of

---

[81] Case 324/86, *Foreningen af Arbejdsledere i Danmark v Daddy's Dance Hall A/S* [1988] ECR 739, para 9.

[82] See Davies (1989, *Yearbook of European Law*) n 59 above at 40.

[83] Case 13/76, *Donà v Mantero* [1976] ECR 1333, para 12.

[84] Case C–383/92, *Commission v United Kingdom* [1994] ECR I–2345, paras 22–5 of the AG's opinion.

[85] Case 66/85, *Lawrie-Blum* [1986] ECR 2121, para 20. Cited with approval by AG Van Gerven, *ibid* para 22.

[86] Case C–29/91, *Dr. Sophie Redmond Stichting v Bartol* [1992] ECR I–3189.

[87] *Ibid* para 21.

[88] Case C–298/94, *Henke v Gemeinde Schierke and Verwaltungsgemeinschaft 'Brocken'* [1996] ECR I–4989.

[89] *Ibid* para 14. For discussion, see C Barnard and T Hervey, 'European Union Employment and Social Policy Survey 1996 and 1997' (1997) 17 *Yearbook of European Law* 435 at 442–43.

government, as opposed to charities, the Directive would not normally apply where economic activities were ancillary but such a presumption could be rebutted on the facts.[90] While the Court in *Henke* can be criticised for a cautious approach, its interpretation reflected the limitations inherent within the Directive.

The Court has had the difficult task of interpreting the Directive in the context of ever more radical changes in company organisation and commercial activity in both the public and private sectors. For example, in a contracting out case, *Schmidt*,[91] it was held that, in considering the list of factors to be taken into account by the national court, the absence of any transfer of tangible assets will not preclude a transfer where the business has retained its identity and has maintained the same or similar activities even though the activity is merely ancillary. Although this case concerned only the transfer of a solitary canteen assistant, the Directive was applicable because the employee in question had the right to have her acquired rights safeguarded. This expansive approach was not followed in *Rygaard* where the Court held that a transfer 'must relate to a stable economic entity whose activity is not limited to performing one specific works contract'.[92] Moreover, in *Süzen*[93] it was held that the further sub-contracting of an activity, a 'second generation' contract, falls outside the provisions of the Directive unless there is a transfer of significant tangible or intangible assets or the taking over by the new employer of a major part of the workforce.

These cases will be examined in more depth in chapter 7, when consideration will be given to the codification of the Court's case law in the amended Directive and its more recent jurisprudence. For now, however, it is important to note that, in making these refinements to the tests for determining a transfer, the Court opened itself up to criticism for giving pre-eminence to commercial considerations while losing sight of the Directive's overriding objective of safeguarding the employee in the event of a change of employer arising out of circumstances beyond the employee's control and over which they have little or no influence. Equally it can be seen that the Court has had little room for manoeuvre. It has had to work with a Directive which, though rooted in the economic, political and industrial context of the 1970s, has had to be applied in the rapidly changing circumstances of the mid-1980s and beyond, where both public and private sector structures of ownership and control have become increasingly fragmented and

---

[90] See De Groot (1998, *Common Market Law Review*) n 73 above at 722.

[91] Case C–392/92, *Schmidt v Spar und Leikhasse* [1994] ECR I–1311, paras 13–17. See also, Case C–209/91, *Rask and Christensen v ISS Kantinservice* [1992] ECR I–5755; and Case C–171/94, *Merckx and Neuhuys v Ford Motors* [1996] ECR I–1253.

[92] Case C–48/94, *Rygaard v Strø Mølle Akustik* [1995] ECR I–2745, para 20.

[93] Case C–13/95, *Süzen v Zehnacker Gebäudereinigung GmbH Krankenhausservice* [1997] ECR I–1259. For a critique, see P Davies, 'Taken to the Cleaners? Contracting Out of Services Yet Again' (1997) 26 *Industrial Law Journal* 193.

globalised at a speed that could not have been anticipated by its authors. Moreover, in applying the Directive, the Court has remained aware of its origins as a market integration measure that, in the words of AG Mancini in *Berg*, was intended 'to facilitate mobility of enterprises while protecting the rights of their staff'.[94]

An additional feature of the original Collective Redundancies and Acquired Rights Directives can be found in the respective provisions concerning information and consultation with trade unions and/or workers' representatives.[95] The broader issues of worker involvement will be considered later in this chapter, and there has been some strengthening of these provisions in the amending directives,[96] but in the context of the directives, as adopted in the 1970s, the limitations of the procedures laid down are obvious. Article 2(1) of Directive 75/129, by providing for consultation by an employer with workers' representatives 'with a view to reaching an agreement' was designed to offer the individual worker an indirect right amounting to a minimum level of protection,[97] through his representatives, to information and consultation in a scenario where an employer was 'contemplating collective redundancies'. By contrast, the provisions of Article 6 of Directive 77/187 were operative only when the transfer was a *fait accompli* not directly challengeable by the employees' representatives. Their only function was to receive information in good time about the reason for the transfer; the legal, economic and social implications for the employees; and measures envisaged in relation to the employees.[98] This was a much weaker text than the original draft, which would have placed an obligation on both the transferor and the transferee to inform the representatives of the workforce of the proposed transfer and to indicate to them any measures proposed to be taken in relation to workers. Where the outcome may have been prejudicial to the workers, there would have been an obligation on both transferor and transferee to *negotiate* with a view to reaching an agreement and, if necessary, to go to binding arbitration.[99] Under the provisions of Directive 77/187 the managerial prerogative to proceed with the transfer without either negotiation or binding arbitration was beyond question. While, in the context of both directives, the Court has held that the Member States cannot unilaterally impose a system of designating employees'

---

[94] Cases 144–145/87, *Berg and Busschers v Besselsen* [1988] ECR I–2559, para 2 of the opinion.

[95] Art 2 of Dir 75/129; and Art 6 of Dir 77/187.

[96] See Art 2 of Dir 92/56, now consolidated in Art 2 of Dir 98/59; and Art 6 of Dir 98/50, now consolidated in Art 7 of Dir 2001/23.

[97] Case 215/83, *Commission v Belgium* [1985] ECR 1039, para 2.

[98] Art 6(1) of Dir 77/187. Art 6(1) of Dir 98/50 adds a requirement for information concerning the date or proposed date of the transfer [now Art 7(1) of Dir 2001/23].

[99] COM(74) 351, draft Art 8. For further comment, see Davies, (1989, *Yearbook of European Law*) n 59 above at 28.

representatives,[100] it remains the case, even after the revision of the directives, that employees' representatives have limited scope for bargaining in an unequal relationship.

As integrationist tools the three directives combined the technique of partial harmonisation with flexible 'forms and methods' of implementation implied by Article 189 EEC [now 249 EC]. Each directive contained a similar implementation clause placing an obligation on the Member States to 'bring into force the laws, regulations or administrative provisions' required for compliance.[101] This level of flexibility in the method of implementation can be compared with Article 19, paragraph 5(d) of the International Labour Organisation (ILO) Constitution, which provides that Member States of the ILO must 'take such action as may be necessary to make effective' the provisions of any convention that they ratify.[102] Some ILO conventions refer to the options of Member States to adopt or refer to 'national law or regulations or collective agreements' to make them effective.[103] Article 33(1) of the European Social Charter (ESC) allows collective agreements to be used to enforce certain labour standards provided that they are 'applied . . . to the great majority of the workers concerned'.[104]

References to collective agreements as methods of implementation were noticeably absent from early Community social policy directives of the SAP period. In many ways this was surprising given the long tradition in certain Member States, such as Denmark, for preferring legally binding contractual agreements to centralised legislation.[105] Indeed it has been argued that where collective agreements are legally binding and govern the working conditions of whole groups of workers and sectors, they may be more flexible and effective than legislation.[106] Was it possible, by implication, to extend the implementing provisions in directives to allow for compliance by way of collective agreements given that this would reflect both the

---

[100] Case C–383/92, *Commission v United Kingdom* [1994] ECR I–2345, para 19.

[101] Art 6 of Dir 75/129; Art 8 of Dir 77/187; and Art 11 of Dir 80/987.

[102] See N Valticos and G von Potobsky, *International Labour Law*, 2nd revised edn (Kluwer, Deventer, 1995) pp 274–75; and C Jenks, 'The Application of International Labour Conventions by Means of Collective Agreements' (1958) 19 *Zeitschrift für ausländisches öffentliches Recht und Völkerrecht* 197.

[103] For example, Art 6 of ILO Convention No 135 of 1971 concerning the protection and facilities to be afforded workers' representatives in the undertakings. For discussion, see A Adinolfi, 'The Implementation of Social Policy Directives Through Collective Agreements' (1988) 25 *Common Market Law Review* 291 at 297.

[104] 529 UNTS No 89. See O Kahn-Freund, 'The European Social Charter' in F Jacobs (ed) *European Law and the Individual* (North-Holland, Amsterdam, 1976) 181–211 at 190–91.

[105] In the case of Denmark this tradition can be traced back to the 'September Agreement' of 1899, the forerunner of successive basic agreements. See Lord Wedderburn, 'Inderogability, Collective Agreements and Community Law' (1992) 21 *Industrial Law Journal* 245 at 247–48.

[106] See Adinolfi, n 103 above at 295. Adinolfi contrasts the tradition of relying on contractual agreements in Italy and Denmark with the experience in the UK and Ireland where such agreements are not legally binding.

tradition in some Member States and practice in international labour law? Moreover, if compliance was possible by means of a collective agreement, who was to be covered by its terms?

These questions were foremost in the collective minds of the Court when asked to consider the issue in *Commission v Denmark*.[107] This case concerned the decision of the Danish Government to seek to implement Directive 75/117 on equal pay[108] by way of reference to a prior collective agreement. The Court had to consider whether this method of compliance provided the necessary legal certainty required by the Community system. The answer was a heavily qualified yes. In particular, the Court held, the Community method emphasised an inclusive approach that, unlike the ESC, took account of the interests of minorities. The Court stated that:[109]

Member States may leave the implementation of the principle of equal pay *in the first instance* to representatives of management and labour. That possibility does not, however, discharge them from the obligation of ensuring, by appropriate legislative and administrative provisions, that all workers in the Community are afforded the full protection provided for in the directive. That *state guarantee* must cover all cases where effective protection is not ensured by other means, for whatever reason, and in particular cases where the workers in question are not union members, where the sector in question is not covered by a collective agreement or where such an agreement does not fully guarantee the principle of equal pay.

Therefore the critical issue is not form but effect. The hierarchy of norms may vary between and within national jurisdictions but whatever system is in place, the ultimate obligation remains with the state. Each Member State must consider the following question. Is the method of implementation proposed capable of creating a 'state guarantee' of an *effective right* protecting all of the individuals intended to be covered by the directive and capable of enforcement by them before their national courts? In other words,

---

[107] Case 143/83 [1985] ECR 427. See also Case 102/79, *Commission v Belgium* [1980] ECR 1473.

[108] OJ 1975, L45/19.

[109] [1985] ECR 427 at 434–35. My emphasis. This remains, however, a contentious interpretation not always approved of by the Court's AGs. For example, in a subsequent case, AG Slynn expressed the view that directives cannot 'be implemented by collective bargaining agreements unless they are given the force of law by legislation . . . [a] collective bargaining agreement is not a "method" for implementing a directive under Article [249] of the Treaty', because it does not have the same binding force. In the view of the AG, collective agreements are not 'laws', 'regulations' or 'administrative provisions' within the meaning of Art 8 of Dir 77/187 (Case 235/84, *Commission v Italy* [1986] ECR 2291 at 2295). See also, AG Van Themaat's Opinion in Case 91/81, *Commission v Italy* [1982] ECR 2133 at 2145. The Court in Case 235/84 declined to follow its AG's advice and reiterated its statement in *Commission v Denmark*. For discussion, see B Bercusson, 'Collective Bargaining and the Protection of Social Rights' in K Ewing, C Gearty, and B Hepple (eds) *Human Rights and Labour Law: Essays for Paul O'Higgins* (Mansell, London, 1994) 106–26 at 109–12; and P Davies, 'The European Court of Justice, National Courts and the Member States' in Davies *et al*, n 1 above, 95–138 at 120–23.

will it achieve the 'result' required by Article 249 EC [ex 189 EEC]? Clearly no such guarantee is possible in Member States, such as the UK or Ireland, where collective agreements are not legally binding *inter partes*. In several other countries, including Spain and Germany, there is a concept akin to the Italian doctrine of *inderogabilità*, by which there can be no derogation from the norms in collective agreements to the detriment of the workers concerned.[110] Only in certain countries, however, are such agreements capable of extension by law to all relevant workers *erga omnes*.[111]

Wedderburn[112] has urged the Court to resist the superficial attractions of a quest for legal formalism but, even if collective agreements may offer short-term guarantees, the Community interest is not so much legal certainty as lasting effective protection for all intended beneficiaries. If a collective agreement ceases to be representative of all the workers concerned, or if it is no longer being complied with, then it follows that the state must be required to step in to fill the gap by providing the necessary guarantee through legislation or administrative action. The Commission retain the responsibility of monitoring, on a continuing basis, the implementation of directives by the Member States who, in turn, have the onus of satisfying the Commission that the forms and methods used are effective. In all cases the primary concern of the Court, as we shall see in the next section, is 'effective protection' of the intended beneficiaries of the Community measure in question and this must be reflected by methods of implementation that are transparent and certain.

III EQUAL PAY AND EQUAL TREATMENT—THE PIVOTAL ROLE OF THE COURT OF JUSTICE

Community provisions on equality between men and women, Article 119 EEC on the principle of equal pay, now replaced by the much broader Article 141 EC, and the ensuing SAP Directives on equal pay and equal treatment,[113] have played a prominent role in the case law of the Court.

---

[110] See Wedderburn (1992, *Industrial Law Journal*) n 105 above at 249–50.

[111] *Ibid* at 259. Wedderburn cites France, Belgium, Spain, Germany and the Netherlands as countries where a legal power exists to extend collective agreements. In Denmark and Sweden extension is unacceptable because it is contrary to contractual principles, while in Italy permanent agreements of this kind have been found to be unconstitutional.

[112] *Ibid* at 256.

[113] Dir 75/117/EEC on the approximation of the laws of the Member States relating to the application of the principle of equal pay for men and women, OJ 1975, L45/19; Dir 76/207/EEC on equal treatment for men and women as regards access to employment, vocational training and promotion and working conditions, OJ 1976, L39/40; Dir 79/7/EEC on the progressive implementation of the principle of equal treatment for men and women in matters of social security, OJ 1979, L6/24; Dir 86/378/EEC on occupational social security, OJ 1986, L225/40 [now amended by Dir 96/97/EC, OJ 1997, L46/20]; and Dir 86/613/EEC on self-employment, OJ 1986, L359/56.

This is no coincidence for it is precisely in those areas where the Treaty's objectives are strong, but its means of giving effect to them are limited, that the Court has been able to act dynamically.[114] The juridical tools used by the Court have been the twin notions of effectiveness of Community law and protection of the rights of the individual.

In its early years the Court was responsible for a 'quiet revolution' that greatly influenced the development of Community social law particularly in the equalities field.[115] In *Van Gend en Loos*,[116] the Court gave notice of how it perceived its duty to 'ensure that in the interpretation and application of this Treaty the law is observed'.[117] By granting individuals the right to invoke the Treaties before national courts and tribunals, by virtue of the principle of 'direct effect', the Court created a basis not only for references from national courts for preliminary rulings arising from individual actions under Article 234 EC [ex 177 EEC], but also, for the interpretation of national laws by domestic courts in conformity with Community law,[118] or 'indirect effect' as part of the general obligation on Member States to comply with their Community obligations under Article 10 EC [ex 5 EEC].[119] This principle would apply to national laws whether issued before or after the Community provision in question.[120]

These developments were possible because of the Court's parallel creation of the doctrine of supremacy of Community law over national law, a notion at first resisted, but later accepted with various degrees of enthusiasm by the national courts.[121] Moreover, by coupling direct effect with the principle of supremacy, the Court created a clear basis for the Commission to bring an action against a state deemed to be failing to meet its Treaty obligations under Article 226 EC [ex 169 EEC].

In one leap, followed by several smaller steps, the Court has developed the notion of *l'effet utile*, to give operative effect to the Treaty and to binding Community legislation, because it regards as its task, and the duty

---

[114] See generally, Davies in Davies *et al*, n 1 above, and P Watson, 'The Role of the European Court of Justice in the Development of Community Labour Law' in Ewing *et al*, n 109 above at 76–105.

[115] See J Weiler, 'Quiet Revolution: The European Court of Justice and its Interlocutors' (1994) 26 *Comparative Political Studies* 510.

[116] Case 26/62 [1963] ECR 1.

[117] Art 220 EC [ex 164 EEC].

[118] Case 14/83, *Von Colson and Kamann v Land Nordrhein Westfalen* [1984] ECR 1891.

[119] The first paragraph of Art 10 EC provides that: 'Member States shall take all appropriate measures, whether general or particular, to ensure fulfilment of the obligations arising out of this Treaty or resulting from action taken by the institutions of the Community. They shall facilitate the achievement of the Community's tasks'. The second paragraph adds: 'They shall abstain from any measure which could jeopardise the attainment of the objectives of this Treaty'.

[120] See Case C–106/89, *Marleasing SA v La Comercial Alimentacion SA* [1990] ECR I–4135.

[121] For example in the case of the *Conseil d'Etat*, see *Ministère de l'intérieur v Cohn-Bendit* [1980] *CMLR* 543; and W Cohen, 'The Conseil d'Etat: continuing convergence with the Court of Justice' (1991) 16 *European Law Review* 144.

also of the national courts, to fulfil the overall objectives of the Treaty through judicial supervision and enforcement. The logic is simple. Only through the invention of the principles of direct effect and supremacy, neither of which were explicitly stated in the Treaties, has the Court been able to prevent the attainment of these objectives from being jeopardised *contra* the second paragraph of what is now Article 10 EC [ex 5 EEC]. It follows that:[122]

... the law stemming from the Treaty, an independent source of law, could not, because of its special and original nature, be overridden by domestic legal provisions, however framed, without being deprived of its character as Community law and without the legal basis of the Community itself being called into question.

As the Court reasoned in *Van Gend en Loos*, the Member States had, of their own volition, created 'a new legal order' for the benefit not only of themselves but also of their 'subjects' and had therefore 'limited their sovereign rights, *albeit within limited fields*', and, consequentially, had conferred on individuals 'rights which become part of their legal heritage'.[123]

In the context of the SAP, this analysis would indicate two immediate questions. First, how could social policy rights be advanced through the juridical process when, with the arguable exception of Article 119 EEC, the Member States had quite deliberately chosen to retain their sovereign rights in this field? Secondly, as the directive was the chosen legislative instrument in this area, were social policy directives legally enforceable by way of an action brought by one individual against another, or by an individual against a state before national courts or tribunals? It is worth noting at this stage that, following the adoption of the revised Social Chapter at Amsterdam, the first question has subtly changed and the Court has been presented with a fresh challenge to give full effect to its provisions.[124] Conversely, the second question remains, as we shall see, distinctly problematic.

In considering the first question, we have already noted the very limited scope of Article 117 EEC in the eyes of the Court. On face value Article 119 EEC appeared to offer very little more. It contained a statement of the principle of equal pay 'for equal work' as a binding obligation *on Member States* but there was no inherent capacity to issue directives to compel Member States to pass implementing legislation.[125] Further, the scope of the

---

[122] Case 6/64, *Costa v ENEL* [1964] ECR 585.

[123] [1963] ECR 1 at 12. My emphasis. This followed the Court's approach in the early cases concerning the ECSC. In Cases 7/56 and 3–7/57, *Dinecke Algera v Common Assembly of the European Coal and Steel Community* [1957–8] ECR 39, the Court held that the ECSC Treaty 'rests on the derogation of sovereignty consented by the Member States to supranational jurisdiction for an object strictly determined. The legal principle at the basis of the Treaty is a principle of limited competence'.

[124] See ch 10, pp 458–65.

[125] The first paragraph of Art 119 EEC provided that: 'Each Member State shall during the first stage ensure and subsequently maintain the application of the principle that men and women should receive equal pay for equal work'.

principle appeared limited and indeed was formally much narrower than the universal standard set by ILO Convention No 100 of 1951.[126] Indeed the much broader principle that men and women 'should receive equal remuneration for work of *equal value*' was in the original 1919 ILO Constitution and appears also in Article 4(3) of the ESC. There is a clear distinction between *equal work*, meaning literally pay differentials in the same workplace, and *equal value*, meaning unequal pay for equivalent work based on an objective appraisal of comparability that can extend beyond the immediate workplace. The final paragraph of Article 119 EEC [now the second paragraph of Article 141(2) EC], states that equal pay without discrimination based on sex means:

(a) that pay for the same work at piece rates shall be calculated on the basis of the same unit of measurement;
(b) that pay for work at time rates shall be the same for the same job.

It was hardly surprising, therefore, that the UK believed that its existing Equal Pay Act of 1970, which limited equal pay comparisons to those carrying out identical work, was compatible with Article 119 EEC, a position not rectified until after the Commission brought infringement proceedings before the Court in 1981.[127] By this time Directive 75/117 had entered into force. Article 1(1) of the Directive defines the 'principle of equal pay' as 'outlined in Article 119' as meaning 'for the same work or work for which equal value is attributed, the elimination of all discrimination on grounds of sex with regard to all aspects and conditions of remuneration'. This brought the Community definition into line with international law while raising the further question, considered below, about the precise relationship between the Directive and the Treaty provision.

The scope of 'pay' under Article 119 EEC [now Article 141(2) EC] is as follows:

For the purpose of this Article, 'pay' means the ordinary basic or minimum wage or salary and any other consideration, whether in cash or in kind, which the worker receives, directly or indirectly, in respect of his employment from his employer.

This definition is almost identical to ILO Convention No 100 but it was far from clear that this would be interpreted widely. In the immediate aftermath of the Treaty of Rome there seemed to be little immediate prospect of the area being tested before the Court. Kahn-Freund, writing in 1960, reflected the prevailing mood when he stated that:[128]

---

[126] Art 141(1) EC now incorporates the 'equal value' concept.
[127] Case 61/81, *Commission v United Kingdom* [1982] ECR 2601. See generally, E Ellis, 'Equal Pay for Work of Equal Value: The United Kingdom's Legislation Viewed in the Light of Community Law' in T Hervey and D O'Keeffe (eds) *Sex Equality Law in the European Union* (Wiley, Chichester, 1996) 7–19.
[128] O Kahn-Freund, 'Labour Law and Social Security' in E Stein and T Nicholson (eds) *American Enterprise in the European Common Market: A Legal Profile, Vol 1* (University of Michigan Press, Ann Arbor, 1960) 297–458 at 329.

Article 119 is very cautiously formulated. The principle of equal pay for equal work does not *ipso facto* become part of the legal systems of the members, and the Council has not been given power to issue regulations enacting it into law. The Member States have gone no further than to accept an obligation to each other and to the Community to transform their systems of wage rates so as to ensure application of the principle in the course of the first stage of the transitional period. Article 119 does not, therefore, confer any rights or impose any obligations on any individual based on the principle of equality. It does no more than to create an obligation binding the Member States in international law.

Fifteen years on, however, the Court, having invented the principle of direct effect, breathed new life into this 'very cautiously formulated' obligation in *Defrenne II*[129] and made it effective not just as a right for individuals vis-à-vis Member States—vertical direct effect—but also, because Article 119 EEC, read in conjunction with the notion of 'solidarity' in Article 5 EEC [now 10 EC], required an interpretation placing obligations upon, and granting rights to, individuals, the principle of equal pay applied equally to individuals *inter se*—horizontal direct effect.[130]

Viewed with hindsight, *Defrenne II* conveys a certain logic that can be followed through by reference to subsequent decisions of the Court but, at the time, it was remarkable for its liberality. Indeed, even the Commission in its submission to the Court was of the view that Article 119 EEC did not affect relations between individuals.[131] Moreover, this interpretation of the bare Treaty provision is still criticised by those who argue that, on the basis of a narrow reading of the Treaty, the ruling in *Defrenne II* lends itself to the charge of being 'contrary to the text'.[132] Others contend that if the Court had chosen to leave the question of interpretation to the national courts the resulting inconsistencies would, in the words of Arnull, 'have fatally undermined the common market, which it was the purpose of the Treaty to establish'.[133] By extending these principles to equal pay, the Court was interpreting the Treaty teleologically at a time, 1976, when the political barometer was pointing in a favourable direction in the wake of the Sullerot Report's finding of persisting pay inequality and the passage of the Equal Pay Directive.[134] The Court's application of the notion of *l'effet utile* in the context of Article 119 EEC meant an appreciation of its twin objectives:[135]

[129] Case 43/75, *Defrenne v Sabena II* [1976] ECR 455.
[130] *Ibid* para 39.
[131] *Ibid* at 462. See J Usher, 'European Community Equality Law: Legal Instruments and Judicial Remedies' in C McCrudden (ed) *Women, Employment and European Equality Law* (Eclipse Publications, London) 161–77 at 167.
[132] See T Hartley, 'The European Court, Judicial Objectivity and the Constitution of the European Union' (1996) 112 *Law Quarterly Review* 95 at 97.
[133] A Arnull, 'The European Court and Judicial Objectivity: A Reply to Professor Hartley' (1996) 112 *Law Quarterly Review* 411 at 414.
[134] See Davies in Davies *et al*, n 1 above at 107.
[135] *Defrenne II*, paras 9–10 and 12.

First . . . to avoid a situation in which undertakings established in States which have actually implemented the principle of equal pay suffer a competitive disadvantage in intra-Community competition as compared with undertakings established in States which have not yet eliminated discrimination against women workers as regards pay.

Secondly, this provision forms part of the social objectives of the Community, which is not merely an economic union, but is at the same time intended, by common action, to ensure social progress and seek the constant improvement of the living and working conditions of their peoples, as emphasised by the Preamble to the Treaty . . .

This double aim, which is at once economic and social, shows that the principle of equal pay forms part of the foundations of the Community.

In these three short paragraphs the Court revealed an understanding of the evolutionary development of Community social policy moving on from purely negative integration and recognising that the social policy provisions were as important as the economic ones, although further Treaty amendments would be required to make them free-standing.[136] In the meantime the Court's equalities jurisprudence has been at the forefront of this evolutionary process. Not only has 'the principle of equality' been recognised as a general principle of law in the context of equal treatment under the Community's Staff Regulations,[137] but also equality is now clearly understood as a fundamental right, albeit presumptive,[138] whose observance the Court has a duty to ensure. Thus Article 119 EEC, and now Article 141 EC, 'is part of the *implementation* of the principle; it is not the *source*',[139] and therefore, the principle of equality extends beyond these provisions for, as the Court subsequently pronounced in 1978 in *Defrenne III*:[140]

---

[136] This was first achieved by the insertion of a specific legislative base in Art 118a EEC by the Single European Act, 1987 (now contained within the much expanded Art 137(1) and (2) EC)—see Case C–84/94, *United Kingdom v Council* [1996] ECR I–5755.

[137] Case 20/71, *Sabbatini v European Parliament* [1972] ECR 345. See also, Case 21/74, *Airola v Commission* [1975] ECR 221; and Cases 75/82 and 117/82, *Razzouk and Beydoun v Commission* [1984] ECR 1509. For comment, see Usher, n 131 above at 175–77.

[138] See S Fredman, 'European Community Discrimination Law: A Critique' (1992) 21 *Industrial Law Journal* 119. As Fredman notes, at 125, the principle of equality can be trumped by other considerations where discrimination can be justified by reasons which are not due to the sex of the worker—see Case 170/84, *Bilka Kaufhaus v Weber* [1986] ECR 1607.

[139] C Docksey, 'The Principle of Equality Between Women and Men as a Fundamental Right under Community Law' (1991) 20 *Industrial Law Journal* 258; cf G de Búrca, 'The Role of Equality in European Law' in A Dashwood and S O'Leary (eds) *The Principle of Equal Treatment in EC Law* (Sweet & Maxwell, London, 1997) 13–34.

[140] Case 149/77, *Defrenne v Sabena III* [1978] ECR 1365, paras 26–27. See also, Case C–13/94, *P v S and Cornwall CC* [1996] ECR I–2143, where the Court held, at para 22, in the context of Art 2(1) of Dir 76/207 on equal treatment in employment, that to tolerate discrimination against a transsexual undergoing gender reassignment 'would be tantamount, as regards such a person, to a failure to respect the dignity and freedom to which he or she is entitled, and which the Court has a duty to safeguard'.

... respect for fundamental personal human rights is one of the general principles of Community law ... [there] can be no doubt that the elimination of discrimination based on sex forms part of those fundamental rights.

Moreover, as we shall see when we revisit the Court's equalities jurisprudence,[141] the Court has chosen to update its formulation in *Defrenne II*, 25 years on, in *Deutsche Telekom AG v Schröder*,[142] when, taking account of Treaty changes and case law, it concluded that the economic aim pursued by Article 119 EEC [now 141 EC], namely the elimination of distortions of competition between undertakings established in different Member States, is secondary to the social aim pursued by the same provision, which constitutes the expression of a fundamental human right.[143]

In *Defrenne II* the Court went on to explain the scope of Article 119 EEC in the following terms:[144]

In fact since Article 119 is mandatory in nature, the prohibition on discrimination between men and women applies not only to the action of public authorities, but also extends to all agreements which are intended to regulate paid labour collectively, as well as to contracts between individuals.

Article 119 EEC had therefore passed the tests for direct effect summed up by AG Trebucchi as covering a 'Community provision' that is:[145]

... clear and sufficiently precise in its content, does not contain any reservation and is complete in itself in the sense that its application by the national courts does not require the adoption of any subsequent measure of implementation either by the States or the Community.

The most significant aspect of *Defrenne II* lay with the breadth of the Court's interpretation of Article 119 EEC extending beyond the 'narrow criterion' of equal work. Hence, even though Directive 75/117 provided for equal pay for work of equal value it was only capable of being given full effect once this notion was brought within Article 119 EEC itself, making it horizontally directly effective. The Court followed through this logic in *Worringham*,[146] holding that, as the Equal Pay Directive was essentially a definition of Article 119 EEC, it was binding on private employers as an integral part of the Treaty notwithstanding the parallel duty of the State to ensure that national law was in compliance. As we shall see, when we return to our second question below, the position would be quite different if the individual had to rely *only* on the provisions of the Directive in question. In *Defrenne II* the Court sought to explain the relationship between Article

---

[141] See ch 10.
[142] Case C–50/96 [2000] ECR I–743.
[143] *Ibid* para 57.
[144] Case 43/75 [1976] ECR 455, para 39.
[145] *Ibid* at 486.
[146] Case 69/80, *Worringham and Humphries v Lloyds Bank* [1981] ECR 767.

119 EEC and the Equal Pay Directive, which had not yet entered into legal force, in the following terms:[147]

It is impossible not to recognise that the complete implementation of the aim pursued by Article 119, by means of the elimination of all discrimination, direct or indirect, between men and women workers, not only as regards individual undertakings but also entire branches of industry and even of the economic system as a whole, may in certain cases involve the elaboration of criteria whose implementation necessitates the taking of appropriate measures at Community and national level.

There was no specific reference to indirect or disguised discrimination in Article 119 EEC but drawing on *Defrenne II*, the Court in *Jenkins* held that the principle applied equally to both direct and indirect discrimination.[148] The question for the national court would be one of causation.[149] As the Court explained in *Enderby*:[150]

. . . when a measure distinguishing between employees on the basis of their hours of work has in practice an adverse impact on substantially more members of one or other sex, that measure must be regarded as contrary to the objective pursued by Article 119 . . . unless the employer shows that it is based on objectively justified factors unrelated to any discrimination on the grounds of sex.

The Court has also liberally interpreted the meaning of 'pay' under Article 119 EEC [now 141 EC]. In *Garland v British Rail Engineering*[151] the Court stated that 'pay' was to be defined as including any consideration 'whether immediate or future, provided that the worker receives it, albeit indirectly, in respect of his employment from his employer'.[152] Special travel facilities for retired employees granted by their former employer were covered by this broad definition. In later cases the Court has applied this definition to include, inter alia, sick pay,[153] employers' contributions to pension schemes,[154] redundancy payments,[155] unfair dismissal compensation,[156] survivors' benefits,[157] special bonuses,[158] severance grants[159] and occupational

---

[147] Case 43/75 [1976] ECR 455, para 19.

[148] Case 96/80, *Jenkins v Kingsgate (Clothing Productions) Ltd* [1981] ECR 911. See also, Case 58/81, *Commission v Luxembourg* [1982] ECR 2175; Case 170/84, *Bilka Kaufhaus v Weber* [1986] ECR 1607; and Case 171/88, *Rinner Kühn v FVW* [1989] ECR 2743.

[149] See E Ellis, 'The Definition of Discrimination in European Community Sex Equality Law' (1994) 19 *European Law Review* 563 at 573.

[150] Case 127/92, *Enderby v Frenchay HA* [1993] ECR I–5535.

[151] Case 12/81 [1982] ECR 359.

[152] *Ibid* para 5. See A Arnull, 'Article 119 and Equal Pay for Work of Equal Value' (1986) 11 *European Law Review* 200 at 201.

[153] Case 171/88, *Rinner Kühn v FVW* [1989] ECR 2743.

[154] Case 170/84, *Bilka Kaufhaus v Weber* [1986] ECR 1607.

[155] Case C–262/88, *Barber v GRE* [1990] ECR I–1889.

[156] Case C–167/97, *R v Secretary of State for Employment, ex parte Seymour-Smith and Perez* [1999] ECR I–623.

[157] Case C–109/91, *Ten Oever* [1993] ECR I–4879.

[158] Case 58/81, *Commission v Luxembourg* [1982] ECR 2175.

[159] Case 33/89, *Kowalska v Frei und Hansestadt Hamburg* [1989] ECR I–2591.

pensions.[160] In many of these circumstances the individual might otherwise
have had to rely on the Equal Treatment Directives to be discussed below.[161]

Although the period from the mid 1970s to the late 1980s is often
regarded as the high water mark of the Court's 'judicial activism',[162] there
was, and indeed there remains today, a keen awareness at the Court of
national sensitivities. This has occasionally led to a softening of the blow
for the Member State concerned in more controversial judgments concerning equalities law. In *Defrenne II*, for example, the Court, following the
example of the US Supreme Court,[163] ruled that the direct effect of Article
119 EEC would only arise prospectively and therefore, the ruling did not
apply to claims prior to the date of judgment, except in the case of applicants who had already initiated legal proceedings or made an equivalent
claim.[164] The Court accepted economic arguments put forward by the UK
and Ireland, both new Member States at the time, that to apply the direct
effect of Article 119 EEC retrospectively would, they believed, cause acute
financial problems for companies and might even lead to bankruptcies.[165]
This highly questionable policy proposition was justified on the grounds of
legal certainty for 'all the interests involved'. Fifteen years on, the Court in
Barber[166] was to justify the prospective application of the principle of equal
pay to occupational pension schemes in near identical terms.

A further limiting factor concerns the relationship between the Court of
Justice and national courts. In order to ensure observance of Community
law on the ground, it is essential, as the Court explained in *Simmenthal*,[167]
for national courts and tribunals to operate as Community law courts and

---

[160] Case C–262/88, *Barber v GRE* [1990] ECR I–1889.

[161] For examples, see Case 69/80, *Worringham and Humphries v Lloyds Bank* [1981] ECR 767; Case 12/81, *Garland v British Rail Engineering* [1982] ECR 359; Case 23/83, *Liefting and others v Directie van het Akademisch Ziekenhuis bij Universitiet van Amsterdam* [1984] ECR 3225; and Case 33/89, *Kowalska v Frei und Hansestadt Hamburg* [1990] ECR I–2591.

[162] See H Rasmussen, 'Between Self-Restraint and Activism: A Judicial Policy for the European Court' (1988) 13 *European Law Review* 28 at 30; and T Koopmans, 'The Rôle of Law in the Next Stage of European Integration' (1986) 35 *International and Comparative Law Quarterly* 925; cf D Edward, 'Judicial Activism—Myth or Reality?' in A Campbell and M Voyati (eds) *Legal Reasoning and Judicial Interpretation of European Law* (Trenton Publishing, Gosport, 1996) 29–67.

[163] *Linkletter v Walter*, 381 US 618 (1965). This was the first case where the US Supreme Court applied a new constitutional rule only prospectively, not retrospectively. For discussion, see M Cappelletti and W Cohen, *Comparative Constitutional Law* (Bobbs-Merrill, Indianapolis & New York, 1979) pp 98–112.

[164] [1976] ECR 455, paras 69–75. According to Hartley there is 'no basis' for this interpretation in the Treaty itself and the Court's limitation of the temporal effect of its rulings is
different from the American practice of prospective overruling because an American court
applies the old rule to the case itself, but announces that it will apply the new rule in future
cases. See Hartley, n 132 above, at 97; cf Arnull, n 133 above at 413–14.

[165] See Docksey, n 139 above, at 274–75.

[166] Case C–262/88, *Barber v GRE* [1990] ECR I–1889, paras 44–5.

[167] Case 106/77, *Amministrazione delle Finanze dello Stato v Simmenthal spa* [1978] ECR 629.

exercise 'the power to do everything necessary . . . to set aside national legal provisions which might prevent Community rules from having full force and effect'.[168]

In effect, as the Court confirmed in *Von Colson*,[169] when considering the scope of Directive 76/207 on equal treatment in employment, the national court must accept a Community method of construction that overrides both national constitutional rules and established judicial principles such as the doctrine of precedent.[170] In return for this expectation of co-operation, the Court has recognised that national courts have the task of determining procedural issues in accordance with their national legal systems.[171] This is very significant in the case of the equalities directives, which invariably contain a clause intended to enable all persons who consider themselves wronged by discrimination to 'pursue their claims by judicial process after possible recourse to other competent authorities'.[172] The national court will have autonomy to determine these procedural matters, including time limits for bringing claims, providing that these rules are not less favourable than those governing similar domestic actions (the principle of equivalence)[173] nor must they render virtually impossible or excessively difficult the exercise of rights conferred by Community law (the principle of effectiveness).[174] Therefore, the effectiveness of the protection afforded to the individual under Community law depends to a large degree on the robustness of national legal and administrative procedures.[175]

We now turn to our second question, which can be reformulated as follows. Is an appropriately worded directive in the social policy field, or part thereof, capable of amounting to a 'Community provision' that may be directly effective and, if so, does the obligation apply only to Member States or extend also to individuals? The answer to this question is of critical importance in the case of the equalities directives because they seek to secure substantive equality rights *within* and not *across* Member States.[176]

---

[168] *Ibid* para 22.

[169] Case 14/83, *Von Colson and Kamann v Land Nordrhein-Westfalen* [1984] ECR 1891.

[170] See C Docksey and B Fitzpatrick, 'The Duty of National Courts to Interpret Provisions of National Law in Accordance with Community Law' (1991) 20 *Industrial Law Journal* 113 at 117–18; and A Arnull, 'The Incoming Tide: Responding to Marshall' [1987] *Public Law* 383.

[171] Case 33/76, *Rewe v Landwirtschaftskammer Saarland* [1976] ECR 1989, para 5; Case 45/76, *Comet v Produktschap voor Siergewassen* [1976] ECR 2043, paras 13 and 16.

[172] For example, Dir 76/207, Art 6; and Dir 79/7, Art 6.

[173] Derived from the principle of non-discrimination in Art 12 EC [ex 6 EEC]. See Case C-326/96, *Levez v TH Jennings (Harlow Pools) Ltd* [1998] ECR I-7835, paras 39–44.

[174] See Joined Cases C-430–431/93, *Van Schijndel and Van Veen v SPF* [1995] ECR I-4705, para 17; Case C-261/95, *Palmisani v INPS* [1997] ECR I-4025, para 27; Case C-246/96 *Magorrian and Cunningham* [1997] ECR I-7153, para 37; Case C-352/96, *Levez, ibid* para 18.

[175] For full discussion of the development of these principles, see ch 7, pp 363–74.

[176] See E Meehan, 'Sex Equality Policies in the European Community' (1990) 13 *Journal of European Integration* 185 at 188.

Therefore, common standards are dependent, first and foremost, on adequate enforcement at national level and the onus is on national courts to make appropriate references under Article 234 EC [ex 177 EEC].[177] As explained earlier while, under Article 249 EC [ex 189 EEC], a regulation is 'directly applicable' and 'binding in its entirety' in the national legal orders of the Member States, a directive is binding only 'as to the result to be achieved, upon each Member State to which it is addressed'.

The Court's solution has not been to apply the principle of direct effect to directives *in toto*, but instead to infer an analogous obligation on the State to ensure the effectiveness of the operative provisions in any Directive by reading Article 10 EC [ex 5 EEC] and Article 249 EC [ex 189 EEC] together. As the Court subtly explained in *Becker*:[178]

Particularly in cases in which the Community authorities have, by means of a directive, placed Member States under a duty to adopt a certain course of action, the effectiveness of such a measure would be diminished if persons were prevented from relying upon it in proceedings before a court and national courts were prevented from taking it into consideration as an element of Community law.

Consequently, a Member State which has not adopted the implementing measures required by the directive within the prescribed period may not plead, as against individuals, its own failure to perform the obligations which the directive entails.

Thus, wherever the provisions of a directive appear, as far as their subject matter is concerned, to be unconditional and sufficiently precise, those provisions may, in the absence of implementing measures adopted within the prescribed period, be relied upon as against any national provision which is incompatible with the directive or in so far as the provisions define rights which individuals are able to assert against the State.

Therefore the rights of an individual to rely on a directive, in a Community law context, arise *only* against a Member State where that State has failed to properly implement those provisions that are clearly intended for his or her benefit. It is a subsidiary remedy, unlike direct application by a regulation, that allows an individual to invoke the provisions of a directive but does not affect its legal nature, which remains that of an obligation addressed to Member States.[179] This has been likened to the common law principle of estoppel, for to deny the individual protection in these circumstances would be akin to allowing a defaulting Member State to escape

---

[177] For discussion on the importance of 'dialogue' between national courts and the ECJ in this area, see Docksey and Fitzpatrick, n 170 above.

[178] Case 8/81, *Becker v FZA Münster-Innenstadt* [1982] ECR 53 at 70–1. See also, Case 9/70, *Grad v Finanzamt Traunstein* [1970] ECR 825; and Case 148/78, *Pubblico Minstero v Ratti* [1979] ECR 1629.

[179] See Usher, n 131 above at 172.

from its Community law obligations.[180] Conversely, this estoppel rationale effectively excludes any separate action between private individuals in cases where a directive has not been enacted in national law because a directive does not *of itself* impose any obligation on such an individual.[181]

In equalities law, and in a wider social law context, this can lead to perverse results. Let us consider the impact upon the effectiveness of the protection afforded by Directive 76/207 on equal treatment in employment, including promotion, vocational training and working conditions.[182] The guiding principle is set out in Article 2(1) of the Directive:

. . . the principle of equal treatment shall mean that there will be no discrimination whatsoever on grounds of sex either directly or indirectly by reference in particular to marital or family status.

Further provisions deal specifically with measures to be taken by Member States to ensure that there shall be no discrimination in the conditions for access to jobs, vocational training and working conditions.[183] The Court has held in *Marshall*[184] that the guarantee in respect of working conditions in Article 5(1) of the Directive is directly effective. Whilst the Directive is of general application as part of the principle of equality,[185] it was not founded upon Article 119 EEC and was therefore derived from the broad social policy objectives in Article 117 EEC and adopted by virtue of Article

---

[180] See P Pescatore, 'The Doctrine of 'Direct Effect': An Infant Disease of Community Law' (1983) 8 *European Law Review* 155 at 169; C Plaza Martin, 'Furthering the Effectiveness of EC Directives and the Judicial Protection of Individual Rights Thereunder' (1994) 43 *International and Comparative Law Quarterly* 26 at 27–9; and Davies in Davies *et al*, n 1 above at 104–6.

[181] *Ibid* para 48. See Case C–91/92, *Faccini Dori v Recreb Srl* [1994] ECR I–3325.

[182] OJ 1976, L39/40. The same principles apply to the other directives on equal treatment: Dir 79/7/EEC on the progressive implementation of the principle of equal treatment for men and women in matters of social security, OJ 1979, L6/24; Dir 86/378/EEC on occupational social security, OJ 1986, L225/40 [now amended by Dir 96/97/EC, OJ 1997, L46/20]; and Dir 86/613/EEC on self-employment, OJ 1986, L359/56.

[183] Arts 3, 4 and 5 respectively. Art 2(2) allows for an exception for occupational activities where 'the sex of the worker constitutes a determining factor'. This derogation is subject to two tests laid down by the Court. First, there is a test derived from the principle of proportionality whereby the activities in question, such as restrictions on women serving in the police or armed forces, are limited to what is appropriate and necessary in order to achieve the aim in view and requires the principle of equal treatment to be reconciled as far as is possible with the requirements of public security which determine the context in which the activities in question are to be performed: see Case 222/84, *Johnston v RUC* [1986] ECR 1651, para 38; and Case C–285/98, *Kreil v Bundesrepublik Deutschland* [2000] ECR I–69, para 29. Second, Member States have a certain degree of discretion when adopting measures that they consider necessary in order to guarantee public security in a Member State: see Case C–83/94, *Leifer and others* [1995] ECR I–3231, para 35. Member States must periodically assess the activities concerned to decide whether, in the light of social developments, the derogation may still be maintained: see Case C–273/97, *Sirdar v The Army Board* [1999] ECR I–7403, para 31.

[184] Case 152/84, *Marshall v Southampton and South-West Hampshire AHA I* [1986] ECR 723, para 52. Art 5(1) implements the principle of equal treatment set out in Art 2(1) of the Directive.

[185] Case 248/83, *Commission v Germany* [1985] ECR 1459, para 16.

235 EEC [now 308 EC]. It follows that direct effect in the context of Directive 76/207, and the other equal treatment directives adopted on the same legal basis, is only vertical. In chapter 10, we will return to this question in the present day context of the wider Article 141 EC, which makes a direct reference to 'the principle of equal treatment' and therefore reopens the issue of the scope of the directives on equal treatment post-Amsterdam.[186]

In *Marshall* the Court held that where the UK had not properly implemented Directive 76/207, in the context of equal retirement ages between men and women, it was still possible for Mrs Marshall, who was employed by the State,[187] to have a remedy against her employer, while Mrs Duke, who was employed in the private sector, in otherwise near identical circumstances, was unsuccessful in a separate action decided by the national court.[188]

Therefore the rights of the individual relying solely on a directive fall short of horizontal direct effect. It has been forcibly argued that this approach is inconsistent with the rule, established in *Defrenne II*,[189] that the fundamental right involved is the basis of the requirement on national courts to apply it directly. The Court has preferred a narrower view that subjects the fundamental right of equality to an overriding principle that, notwithstanding any inequality of outcome, prevents the State from being allowed to profit from its own wrongdoing and, consequentially, prohibits any shift of responsibility from the State to a third party. The notion that there is any correlative obligation on others has been firmly rejected.[190] Rather a directive amounts to no more than a 'minimum guarantee' for the individual that is capable of application only against the State,[191] or an emanation thereof,[192] deemed responsible for bringing national law into line with its provisions.

Despite the limitations of this approach, the Court has remained keenly aware of its gap filling role and the need to give social policy an integra-

---

[186] Art 141(3) EC.

[187] The health authority employing Mrs Marshall was a public authority and was deemed to be an emanation of the State.

[188] *Duke v GEC Reliance Ltd* [1988] 1 AC 618. See also, *Finnegan v Clowney Youth Training Programme* [1990] 2 AC 407.

[189] Case 43/75 [1976] ECR 455, paras 31–40. See Docksey and Fitzpatrick, n 170 above at 116.

[190] See generally, D Wyatt, 'The Direct Effect of Community Social Law—Not Forgetting Directives' (1983) 8 *European Law Review* 241.

[191] See Case C–208/90, *Emmott v Minister for Social Welfare and another* [1991] ECR I–4269, at ground 5 of the judgment.

[192] The 'State' for these purposes can include a privately owned company controlled directly or indirectly, or awarded special powers, by the State, which is performing a public service. State responsibility is inferred by the degree of control exerted by the State over an essential public service regardless of ownership *per se*: Case C–188/89 *Foster v British Gas* [1990] ECR I–3313; and Cases C–253–258/96, *Kampelmann and Others v Landschaftsverband Westfalen-Lippe* and *Stadtwerke Witten GmbH v Schade* and *Haseley v Stadtwerke Altena GmbH* [1997] ECR I–6907.

tionist push. As Docksey and Fitzpatrick have shown,[193] the Court, by inter-preting ex-Article 119 EEC very widely, has ensured that the concept of 'equal pay' is capable of application to situations, such as equal retirement ages,[194] that might otherwise be regarded as a condition of employment under the Equal Treatment Directive and not horizontally directly effective. Moreover, by asserting the primacy of state responsibility, the Court has been able to rely upon the obligation in Article 10 EC [ex 5 EEC] to compel Member States to implement directives and national courts to co-operate in interpreting Community law purposively by overriding any competing national constitutional provisions or doctrinal rules and, where appropri-ate, providing a national remedy to the individual consistent with the pro-visions of the relevant directive. The scope of application of directives has been further enhanced by a liberal interpretation of the 'State' in the context of Article 249 EC [ex 189 EEC]. More recently, the Court has, as we shall in chapter 7, sought to bridge the gap further by establishing grounds for the individual to exercise a right of reparation against a Member State deemed to be in default of its Community obligations.[195]

As the social policy provisions of the Treaty have gradually widened post-1987, the place of the Court in the process has subtly changed, an ongoing evolution to be evaluated in later chapters. In assessing the Court's changing role, account will be taken of the way in which successive Treaty amendments have gradually widened the Community's legislative base for adopting directives and extended the overarching social policy objectives.

IV HARMONISATION OF TECHNICAL STANDARDS—THE FIRST 'FRAMEWORK DIRECTIVE' ON HEALTH AND SAFETY AT WORK

Community activity in the field of occupational health and safety can be traced back to the ECSC. From the outset the method followed was to estab-lish expert groups, to promote inspection and enforcement of health and safety standards consistent with ILO conventions[196] and to have in mind the possibility of harmonising technical standards, where necessary, by legisla-tive or other means to prevent accidents and diseases and promote hygiene at work.[197] A tripartite Mines Safety Commission had been established in 1957 to follow developments in the safety of coalmines particularly in the field of

---

[193] Docksey and Fitzpatrick, n 170 above at 116–20.
[194] Case C–262/88, *Barber v GRE* [1990] ECR I–1889.
[195] Cases C–6/90 and 9/90, *Francovich and others v Italian Republic* [1991] ECR I–5357.
[196] In particular, the 1947 ILO Convention No 81 on Labour Inspection in Industry and Commerce. This was derived from Art 427 of the Treaty of Versailles, 1919, which stated that: 'Each State should make provision for a system of inspection . . . in order to ensure the enforcement of the laws and regulations for the protection of the employed'. See Valticos & von Potobsky, n 102 above at 253–59.
[197] See the listing in Art 118 EEC [now 140 EC].

accident prevention.[198] The SAP promised steps to reduce the monotony of work by introducing 'techniques of job enrichment' and action to remove 'dangers and nuisances at work'.[199] The immediate response was bureaucratic with the establishment in 1974 of an expert Advisory Committee on Safety, Hygiene and Health Protection at Work to aid the Commission in the preparation and implementation of activities in these fields.[200] It was also hoped that the Committee would be able to work out a response to specific concerns about the use of dangerous substances and the number of avoidable occupational accidents. In 1975 the Council set up the European Foundation for the Improvement of Living and Working Conditions,[201] based in Dublin, as a research body in the area of social policy with a watching brief on matters concerning health and safety and the working environment. Both the Advisory Committee and the Dublin Foundation have given impetus to the Commission, through their expertise and research, and this, in turn, has driven forward the programmatic approach to this area.

Without this expertise it is unlikely that the highly technical and evolutionary legislation that followed would have been developed as quickly and effectively. Indeed it has to be borne in mind that the experts had to synthesise and seek to upgrade national standards, where they existed, while taking into account issues of regulatory fairness and effectiveness.[202] The first directives adopted under the SAP aimed at harmonising the rules concerning the provision of safety signs at work in order to indicate certain hazards,[203] and to protect the health and safety of workers from risks related specifically to exposure to vinyl chloride monomer, a dangerous carcinogen.[204] These were important steps but progress was not as rapid as the Commission would have liked and, in a method later to be transferred to other spheres of social policy, the Commission launched a series of specific Safety and Health Action Programmes in 1978 and 1984 designed primarily to focus action on preventing accidents, identifying the causes of diseases, protecting workers against dangerous substances, collating statistics, and providing training and information.[205] These programmes formed a

---

[198] ECSC Decision of 9 July 1957 concerning the terms of reference and rules of procedure of the Mines Safety Commission, OJ 1957, B28/487, para 1 of the terms of reference.

[199] *Bulletin of the European Communities Supplement* 2/74, p 18.

[200] Decision 74/325/EEC, OJ 1975, L185/15. The Commissioner responsible for Employment and Social Affairs chairs the Committee, which is now made up of 90 members with six appointed by each Member State on a tripartite basis.

[201] Reg 1365/75/EEC, OJ 1975, L139/1.

[202] See R Baldwin and T Daintith, 'The European Framework' in R Baldwin and T Daintith (eds) *Harmonization and Hazard: Regulating Workplace Health and Safety in the European Community* (Graham & Trotman, London, 1992) 1–17 at 1.

[203] Dir 77/576/EEC, OJ 1977, L229/12.

[204] Dir 78/610/EEC, OJ 1978, L197/12.

[205] Council Resolution of 29 June 1978 on an action programme of the European Communities on Safety and Health at Work, OJ 1978, C165/1; and Council Resolution of 27 Feb 1984 on a second programme of action of the European Communities on Safety and Health at Work, OJ 1984, C67/2.

basis for a logical progression starting with the gathering of information, followed by encouraging co-operation and co-ordination and, leading to, where required, legislation at Community level.[206]

One common thread running through the specific measures and programmes of this period was the concept of occupational *safety* based on the assessment, avoidance or minimisation of risks to workers to be achieved through a mix of short and long-term measures with managerial responsibility placed on the employer. Safety was linked to *health* by focusing on both accidents and disease aetiology. There was also some indication of a wider approach to health and safety embracing the improvement of 'human attitudes' at the work place and taking account of the impact of environmental conditions at work with specific attention being given to the effects on pregnant women and young workers.[207] In the period leading up to the Single European Act, however, such ideas remained largely at the formative stage.

Neal has identified four main strands of argument for Community activity in this field.[208] First, it is argued that common safety and health standards assist economic integration, by removing price differentials for products reflecting variable safety and health costs in different Member States. Secondly, the reduction of the human, social and economic costs of work-related accidents and ill health brings about an improvement in the quality of life for the whole Community. Thirdly, the introduction of more efficient work practices increases productivity and promotes better industrial relations. Fourthly, the regulation of certain major risks should be harmonised at supranational level because of the scale of resources involved. Therefore, activity in this area is a humanitarian necessity and makes sense economically. Viewed in this way, health and safety activity is essentially consensual and responsive to the fact that new technology combined with new substances and processes, including new dimensions of scale, requires a practical and programmatic response.[209]

This approach is exemplified by the first 'framework' Directive, 80/1107,[210] on the protection of workers from risks related to exposure to chemical, physical and biological agents at work. Occupational health and safety is therefore aimed at preventing or limiting the exposure of workers to hazards at the workplace in general and, if these hazards cannot be eliminated, then protection should be provided to all workers likely to be affected. The use of a 'framework' directive was also highly significant,

---

[206] A Neal, 'Promoting Occupational Safety and Health in the European Union' in A Neal and S Foyn (eds) *Developing the Social Dimension in an Enlarged European Union* (Scandinavian University Press, Oslo, 1995) 80–99 at 82.

[207] 1978 Action Programme, n 205 above, paras 11–14.

[208] Neal, n 206 above at 80.

[209] *Ibid* at 81.

[210] Dir 80/1107/EEC, OJ 1980, L327/8, amended by Dir 88/642/EEC, OJ 1988, L356/74; Dir 91/322/EEC, OJ 1991, L177/22; Dir 96/94/EC, OJ 1996, L338/86. Repealed and replaced by Dir 98/24/EC, OJ 1998, L131/11.

reflecting not only the pragmatic political consensus that pertained in the area of health and safety, even after the election of the Thatcher administration in the UK in 1979, but also the dynamism that was necessary to keep pace with change. This was in tune with the ideas of the Economic and Social Committee, in its *Prospects for the 80s* report,[211] on the need for guideline measures laying down general goals to be achieved that would then be implemented at national and sectoral levels. In this way the first 'framework' Directive spawned a series of 'daughter directives' concerning specified agents such as lead, asbestos and noise.[212] In each case assessments of risk of exposure must be made and the workplaces affected identified to determine the conditions under which the provisions apply. A 'trigger mechanism' is activated once exposure reaches a certain level bringing protective measures into play and, in addition, there are maximum permitted exposure levels, known as limit values, and counter measures that must be taken when these are exceeded.[213] The first framework Directive, and any measure that flows from it, was intended to be regularly revised taking into account progress made in science and technology and in the light of experience.[214]

Other proposals concerned with the broader working environment failed to emerge in a binding legislative form over this period. At the most there was soft law, for example a Council Recommendation on a 40-hour working week and four weeks annual paid holiday,[215] a forerunner of the Working Time Directive[216] adopted nearly 20 years later. Economic circumstances dictated that the Community's primary social policy concern was creating and protecting employment, with a nod to health and safety at the workplace, rather than tackling the broader working environment issues that were to be promoted later under the Social Charter once Article 118a EEC had been incorporated into the Treaty by the Single European Act.

While the legislation and the related action programmes of this first phase may be regarded as highly technical and limited in an ergonomic sense, as

---

[211] *Prospects for the 80s*, Bulletin of the Economic and Social Committee, 10/81, 5–12 at 8.

[212] Dir 82/605/EEC on the protection of workers from the risks related to exposure to metallic lead and its ionic compounds at work, OJ 1982, L247/12, repealed and replaced by Dir 98/24, n 210 above, Dir 83/477/EEC on the protection of workers from the risks related to exposure to asbestos at work, OJ 1983, L263/25, amended by Dir 91/382/EEC, OJ 1991, L206/16, and Dir 98/24, *ibid*. Dir 86/188/EEC on the protection of workers from the risks related to the exposure to noise at work, OJ 1986, L137/28, amended by Dir 98/24, *ibid*. Dir 88/364/EEC on the protection of workers by banning certain specified agents and/or certain work activities, OJ 1988, L179/44, repealed and replaced by Dir 98/24, *ibid*. Collectively these directives regulate every area of commercial activity except air and sea transportation.

[213] Neal, n 206 above at 89.

[214] *Ibid*.

[215] Council Recommendation 75/457/EEC, OJ 1975, L199/32.

[216] Dir 93/104/EC, OJ 1993, L307/18.

we shall see when considering later developments in chapter 3, it was by no means a narrow approach. Rather, the Community's activities were focused on a series of measures, intended to be dynamic and non-exhaustive, that built upon well-developed notions of health, safety and hygiene at the workplace. In many ways the pace of progress was remarkable given the absence of a specific Treaty base for this legislation prior to the Single European Act and the general trend towards deregulation clearly evident by the early 1980s. Technical health and safety standards made sense economically and were recognised as a necessity across the political spectrum. Moreover, the development of the 'framework' directive as an evolutionary, dynamic and highly flexible legislative technique, was to provide a building block for not only later measures that could fit within the rubric of Directive 80/1107, but also for further development under the much broader second 'framework' Directive, 89/391/EEC.[217]

V THE ADVENT OF SOCIAL DIALOGUE AND EMPLOYEE INVOLVEMENT IN UNDERTAKINGS—DEMOCRATISATION OR BARGAINING?

By the mid-1970s the Community had begun to search in earnest for a policy nexus upon which to construct a coherent programme to promote macroeconomic social dialogue between management and labour coupled with greater involvement of employees in decision-making within undertakings. This agenda was already well established at a national level but was it possible or indeed desirable to devise a transnational stratagem?[218]

The SAP had set out the core objectives in concise terms by calling for:[219]

The progressive involvement of workers or their representatives in the life of undertakings in the Community.

The promotion of the involvement of management and labour in the economic and social decisions of the Community.

From the outset the Commission's proposals for developing these ideas have exposed tensions of a political, philosophical and organisational

---

[217] OJ 1989, L183/1.

[218] This was reflected by developments in countries where the idea of industrial partnership was well rooted and being further developed. See, for example, the 'Biedenkopf Report' in Germany; Report of the Commission of Experts, *Mitbestimmung im Unternehmen*, Deutscher Bundestag, 6. Wahlperiode, Drucksache VI/334 (Kohlhaumer, Stuttgart, 1970). These ideas were also being promoted in other Member States where such developments were traditionally viewed with suspicion, notably the UK where a tripartite 'Social Contract' had been signed in 1975 rapidly followed by the 'Bullock Report'; published as the *Report of the Committee of Inquiry on Industrial Democracy*, Cmnd. 6706 (HM Stationary Office, London, 1977).

[219] *Bulletin of the European Communities Supplement* 2/74, p 10.

nature. These formative attempts to develop social dialogue and employee involvement were in many respects misguided and futile but the lessons learned were invaluable, serving to inculcate later legislative adaptations and the Amsterdam Social Chapter itself with an exciting new dynamic.

(1) The Advent of Social Dialogue

The formula contained within Article 118 EEC [now 140 EC] presented the Commission with an intriguing strategic dilemma. The Commission were given responsibility for 'arranging consultations' across a selected range of matters where primacy was to rest with the Member States. These included, inter alia, employment, labour law and collective bargaining between employers and workers. Self-evidently these consultations needed to involve the employers' and workers' organisations responsible for conducting collective bargaining at national level notwithstanding the diversity of national and sectoral bargaining systems prevalent in the Member States.

One route that the Commission might have chosen would have been to arrange consultations on the basis that employers' and workers' organisations are essentially adversarial players whose core business is, and should remain, collective bargaining for the purposes of industrial rule making. It follows from this premise that a primary objective of these consultations for the Community would be to achieve a greater degree of convergence of bargaining systems as a means of accelerating the process of market integration. This would, over time, bring collective labour relations within the ambit of Community law. A second route, apparently more ambitious, would be to seek to superimpose an architecture of Community-wide social dialogue or joint consultation leading to mutually agreed statements or, ultimately, to framework agreements based on consensual partnership between the social actors as an alternative to legislative harmonisation.

The second route was eventually chosen ahead of the first because it offered the prospect of an evolving influence for employers' and workers' organisations over the Community's decision-making process without challenging the fundamentals of jealously guarded national industrial relations processes. In this way the 'social partners' would gradually become institutionalised and, through accretion on the basis of shared objectives, exert genuine influence over the construction of Community law across a wide range of social policy fields. Thus, paradoxically, national collective bargaining actors would, when operating at a Community level, have to assume quite different and, in many cases, unrehearsed roles that, critics have argued, may be inimical to their best interests.[220] In later chapters we will

---

[220] For a critique, see T Treu, 'European Collective Bargaining Levels and the Competences of the Social Partners' in Davies *et al*, n 1 above, 269–87.

trace how this process has been brought to fruition through Treaty changes, but let us first consider the early tentative steps taken by the Community and seek to understand how these have foreshadowed later developments.

The idea of social participation in decision-making at Community level can be traced back to the 1951 Treaty of Paris establishing the ECSC. Indeed it can be argued that the ECSC Treaty, due to expire in July 2002,[221] remains the most far reaching Community constitutional document, containing both specific social goals, to expand production and raise living standards,[222] and clearly defined roles for 'producers' and 'workers' on a Consultative Committee,[223] later to form the basis for the Economic and Social Committee established under the EEC Treaty.[224] Moreover, the executive of the ECSC, the High Authority, institutional forerunner of the European Commission, was originally composed of nine members including a trade union representative.[225]

In practice the ECSC provided a useful vehicle for the launch of a sectoral approach to Community social dialogue, which was the basis for the incremental development of a European-wide framework of consultation. A joint committee was established for the coal and steel sector in 1955 and, with the launch of the EEC, further committees were formed covering agriculture, footwear, transport—road, rail and sea—and sea fishing.[226] Many of these committees were inactive, issuing occasional opinions or joint recommendations. Employers' organisations were underdeveloped at a European level and, in some Member States, at a national level. Employers were also unenthusiastic about the idea of formalised Community-wide agreements. One notable exception was the agricultural sector where the 'Joint Committee on the Social Problems of Agricultural Workers' reached an agreement in 1978 to restrict the working week of agricultural workers on arable land, an agreement extended to all agricultural workers in 1981.[227]

Alongside these joint committees there existed an array of other fora. The Economic and Social Committee, comprising representatives of employers, workers and other economic actors, has had a right to initiate opinions, published in the *Official Journal of the European Communities*, since the Paris Summit of 1972. A variety of inter-sectoral advisory committees were set up where experience could be shared concerning, inter alia, vocational training, free movement, social security and occupational health.

---

[221] By virtue of Art 97 ECSC.

[222] Preamble of the ECSC, fourth recital.

[223] Art 18 ECSC.

[224] Art 4(2) EEC [now 7(2) EC].

[225] See P Venturini, *1992: The European Social Dimension* (European Communities, Luxembourg, 1989) pp 21–5.

[226] *Ibid* pp 83–94.

[227] A useful summary of developments can be found in the Commission Communication concerning the development of Social Dialogue at Community level, COM(96) 448, Annex I.

Tripartitism, the method practised by the ILO, was not initially favoured as a Community mechanism, with the sole exception of the Standing Committee on Employment, established in 1970,[228] which brought together representatives of the social partners, the Commission and the Council. In practice the Standing Committee has had a limited impact and faced criticism by the Commission for its 'undisputed lack of efficiency'.[229] Interest in tripartitism at Community level was not to be rekindled until the late 1990s when the Standing Committee was substantially reformed[230] and a separate Employment Committee established as part of the Employment Title in the Amsterdam Treaty, Articles 125–130 EC.[231]

In conclusion, these embryonic forms of social dialogue achieved remarkably little and were widely regarded as peripheral to the Community's social policy project. There was little indication of the revolution to come. When Jacques Delors, as the incoming President of the European Commission, relaunched the Social Dialogue in 1985 and brought the social partners together at a meeting at Val Duchesse, his aim was to end this fragmentation and make the social partners an integral part of the process of social policy making, filling a vacuum left by the Member States, and creating the basis for the establishment of a 'European Industrial Relations Area'.[232] This metamorphosis may have initially been slow but, as we trace the ensuing developments, its profound impact will swiftly become apparent.

(2) Information, Consultation and Participation of Workers in Undertakings

The Commission, in its 1975 Green Paper on *Employee Participation and Company Structure*, frankly acknowledged that, by engaging in a debate about the role of employees in relation to decision-making within companies, they were raising an 'undeniably controversial and difficult issue'.[233] Not only was there a palpable disagreement over the rationale for the establishment of structures for employee involvement but also, even if such differences could be set aside, the form that such structures should take produced, and continues to emit, more heat than light. For, as the ILO noted in an influential report:[234]

---

[228] Decision 70/532/EEC, OJ 1970, L273/25.

[229] Commission Communication on adapting and promoting the Social Dialogue at Community level, COM(98) 322, p 10.

[230] Decision 99/207/EC, OJ 1999, L72/33, repealing Decision 70/532.

[231] Decision 2000/98/EC, OJ 2000, L29/21.

[232] See generally, P Teague and J Grahl, '1992 and the Emergence of a European Industrial Relations Area' (1990) 13 *Journal of European Integration* 167.

[233] *Bulletin of the European Communities Supplement* 8/75, p 7.

[234] *Workers' Participation in Decisions within Undertakings* (ILO, Geneva, 1981) p 21. My emphasis.

The belief that workers' participation in decisions within undertakings ought to be promoted for some reason does not in itself imply acceptance of a particular method of bringing it about. *The diversity of methods is as great as the diversity of aims.*

The ILO Report usefully identifies the complex reasons for such proposals at national and international level as involving one or a combination of ethical, socio-political and economic considerations.[235] The first consideration, the ethical or moral case, is the simplest and most broadly acceptable amounting, in essence, to recognition of 'human rights at the work place'.[236] Paternalism based on the master's/employer's 'right to command' his servant/employee is no longer acceptable in post-industrial society.[237] It follows that it is a pre-requisite of the concept of social justice that an employee should receive 'recognition, treatment and attention as a human being rather than a mere statistical unit of production',[238] a conception well founded in international law.[239] The Green Paper notes that decisions taken by or within the enterprise can have a substantial effect on the 'sense of dignity and autonomy as human beings' of employees.[240]

The second consideration, the socio-political underpinning for employee involvement in undertakings, is a far more controversial issue. Multifarious goals can be ranged together under the banner of 'industrial democracy'. Can political democracy be equated with a form of industrial or corporate suffrage and, if so, how far should the democratic process reach?[241] More pointedly, should 'industrial democracy' be understood in its Webbian construct[242] as beginning and ending with the workplace or plant-level collective bargaining 'substructure'?[243] Alternatively, is the concept capable of being extended to the 'superstructure', by establishing forms of representative employee participation in board-level corporate decision-making? The Green Paper suggested a broad approach based on recognition of the:[244]

---

[235] *Ibid* p 9.

[236] *Ibid* p 10.

[237] For a fascinating insight into the early development of workers' participation, see T Ramm, 'Workers' Participation, the Representation of Labour and Special Labour Courts' in B Hepple (ed) *The Making of Labour Law in Europe: A Comparative Study of Nine Countries up to 1945* (Mansell, London and New York, 1987) 242–76.

[238] ILO Report, n 234 above, p 10.

[239] Most importantly in the Universal Declaration of Human Rights (1948). Art 22 declares that: 'Everyone, as a member of society . . . is entitled to realisation . . . of the economic, social and cultural rights indispensable for his dignity and the free development of his personality'.

[240] Green Paper, n 233 above, p 9.

[241] See ILO Report, n 234 above, p 11. See also, E Batstone in 'Industrial Democracy: European Experience', reports prepared by E Batstone and P Davies for the Industrial Democracy Committee (HMSO, London, 1976) pp 10–11.

[242] See S Webb and B Webb, *Industrial Democracy* (Longmans, London, 1898). For a discussion, see O Kahn-Freund, 'Industrial Democracy' (1977) 6 *Industrial Law Journal* 77; cf P Davies & Lord Wedderburn, 'The Land of Industrial Democracy' (1977) 6 *Industrial Law Journal* 197.

[243] This terminology is derived from the 'Bullock Report', n 218 above.

[244] Green Paper, n 233 above, p 9. My emphasis.

... *democratic imperative* that those who will be substantially affected by decisions made by social and political institutions must be involved in the making of those decisions.

An ILO Symposium held in Oslo in August 1974 brought to the fore the political dimension by identifying two alternative varieties of participation:[245]

Workers' participation is an eminently political issue . . . This is least visible in those countries where workers' participation is looked upon merely as a *management technique* aimed at improving either work organisation at the shop-floor level or employer-employee communications. It is clearest in schemes that aim at redefining the respective roles of owners, managers and workers in the enterprise, and at *radically changing the power relationships* between them.

In the Community context, proposals put forward by the Commission have amounted to a hybrid approach to these socio-political conceptions. On the one hand, the Commission has, through DGV on Social Affairs, focused its legislative strategy primarily on information and consultation as a 'management technique', either for the purposes of transnational consultation in multinational enterprises in the form of proposals for a directive on 'European Works Councils',[246] or as a means of communication with employees in the specific event of a collective dismissal,[247] or the transfer of an undertaking,[248] and, more generally, for the purposes of consultation and 'balanced participation' on 'all questions relating to safety and health at work'.[249]

The corresponding directives have placed procedural obligations on management to inform and consult without affecting their ultimate decision-making prerogative or the pluralist structure and operation of companies throughout the Member States. They provide a filter for management and trade unions to be involved in 'joint regulation' of the workplace,[250]

[245] Summarised by the rapporteur: J Schregle, 'Workers' participation in decisions within undertakings' in *International Labour Review* (ILO, Geneva, Jan–Feb 1976) pp 2–3. My emphasis. Discussed in the ILO Report, n 234 above, pp 13–14.

[246] Originally proposed as the 'Vredeling Directive'—named after the Social Affairs Commissioner responsible—on procedures for informing and consulting the employees of undertakings with complex structures, in particular transnational undertakings, OJ 1980, C297/3. See also, the equally unsuccessful 'Richard Directive'—named after Vredeling's successor—OJ 1983, C217/3. The European Works Councils Directive, 94/45/EC, OJ 1994, L 254/64, was eventually adopted by virtue of the Agreement on Social Policy.

[247] Art 2 of Dir 75/129/EEC, OJ 1975, L48/29, as amended by Art 1(2) of Dir 92/56/EEC, now consolidated in Art 2 of Dir 98/59/EC, OJ 1998, L225/16.

[248] Art 6 of Dir 77/187/EEC, OJ 1977, L61/26, amended by Art 1(2) of Dir 98/50/EC, OJ 1998, L201/88, now consolidated within Art 7 of Dir 2001/23, OJ 2001, L82/16.

[249] Art 11 of Dir 89/391/EEC, OJ 1989, L183/1. This would appear to go further than mere consultation and, according to Weiss, provides for a 'stronger degree of influence'. See M Weiss, 'The European Community's Approach to Workers' Participation' in Neal and Foyn, n 206 above, 100–24 at 106–7.

[250] See, generally, A Flanders, *Management and Unions: the Theory and Reform of Industrial Relations* (Faber, London, 1970).

an approach that does not undermine the industrial freedom of action of the parties while allowing for a degree of consensus or 'conflictual partnership'.[251] Moreover, while placing a duty on management to inform and consult trade unions, works councils, or other representatives of employees in good faith, these directives do not impose a 'duty to bargain' akin to the American model by which unions can compel management to negotiate with them over pay and other conditions of employment.[252]

On the other hand, the former DGXV on Financial Services and Company Law, sought, over a period of 30 years, to directly address the issue of redefining 'power relationships' through workers' participation proposals tied in with harmonisation of company structures, as proposed in the original draft 'Fifth Company Law Directive',[253] and the establishment of the 'European Company' as an optional Community model.[254] This unitary approach to company structure and employee participation is based on the notion that companies can and should act in the best interests of shareholders *and* employees. In those circumstances, it is argued that there is genuine employee participation that transcends the plant level and leads to co-determination or, more accurately, a better form of control of, or influence over, enterprise policy.[255]

While measures primarily concerning the *nature* of management information and decision-making communicated to employees have, over time, won acceptance and been incorporated into Community directives, proposals concerning corporate structure and the *means* by which influence is exercised at a strategic level have been far less successful. Slow progress in the field of company structure can partly be blamed on the rigidity and prescriptiveness of the Commission's proposals, and in part, also, on the absence of a consensus around the link between socio-political considerations and the third element, the economic rationale.

Broadly speaking the economic case for employee involvement in decision-making within undertakings can be summarised as: increasing the efficiency of the undertaking through industrial co-operation; improving the quantity and quality of output by creating a sense of identity within the undertaking; adapting useful ideas made by workers; and reducing the capacity for industrial conflict. This is because, inter alia, workers may work more productively because they are sharing in decisions that affect

---

[251] See Davies & Wedderburn, n 242 above at 198.

[252] National Labor Relations Act, 1964, ss 7, 8 (a) (5) and (9) (a). See *Fibreboard Products Corporation v NLRB* [1964] 379 US 203. Discussed by R Rabin, 'Fibreboard and the Termination of Bargaining Unit Work: The Search for Standards in Defining the Scope of the Duty to Bargain' (1971) 71 *Columbia Law Review* 803.

[253] *Bulletin of the European Communities Supplement* 6/83.

[254] *Bulletin of the European Communities Supplement* 4/75, COM(88) 320.

[255] See S Simitis, 'Workers' Participation in the Enterprise—Transcending Company Law' (1975) 38 *Modern Law Review* 1 at 7–8.

them while the process itself may act as a spur to managerial efficiency.[256] These ideas are attractive to management so long as the structures adopted neither profoundly challenge the existing distribution of economic power nor seriously threaten the exercise of the managerial prerogative. From a trade union perspective such notions are double-edged, simultaneously offering the potential of greater influence while creating the danger of assumed responsibility without sufficient power over the ultimate decision. This may lead to a perception of elitism, arguments about accountability and a build up of pressures and conflicts within the operational structures of employee representation.

The difficulties arising from these perceptions might have been overcome in this period if the Commission had taken account of national diversity in company structures and industrial relations traditions when drawing up and augmenting its proposals. Unfortunately the company law initiatives of the 1970s and early 1980s served only to compound the problem by exacerbating the differences between the social partners, the Member States and within the Commission itself. At the root of the problem lay an attempt to impose a heavily regulated and unitary form of company structure and workers' participation throughout the Community.

In our earlier discussion we considered the variety of 'legal families' operative in the labour law of the Member States.[257] In the specific context of workers' participation within undertakings, the legal and practical elements are even more diverse and heterogeneous. Docksey helpfully divides the national employee representation mechanisms into 'dual' and 'single-channel' approaches.[258] The 'dual-channel' approach, developed most markedly in Germany and the Netherlands, divides employee representation into two distinct spheres of operation. At one level there will be the *collective bargaining* function involving trade unions both at the work place and 'externally' or industry-wide. At another level there is the *information and consultation* function performed by works councils or equivalent bodies democratically elected by the entire work force.[259] The 'dual channel' approach may also combine information and consultation mechanisms with active employee *participation* in the strategic decision-making of companies through a 'two-tier' system of directorships whereby each company will normally have a supervisory board, including representatives of employees and shareholders, responsible for overall control of a management board that is

---

[256] See K Walker, 'Workers' Participation in Management: Problems, Practice and Prospects' in 1974 *IILS Bulletin* (International Institute of Labour Studies, Geneva) No 12, 3–35.

[257] See R Nielsen, 'The Contract of Employment in the Member States of the European Communities and in European Community Law' (1990) 33 *German Yearbook of International Law* 258.

[258] C Docksey, 'Employee Information and Consultation Rights in the Member States of the European Communities' (1987) 7 *Comparative Labor Law Journal* 32 at 35.

[259] *Ibid.* This approach is broadly followed in Denmark, France, Belgium and Luxembourg.

in charge of day-to-day activities.[260] By contrast, the 'single-channel' or monist approach has traditionally involved employee representation by trade unions alone, although employers must now have mechanisms to consult all workers irrespective of trade union recognition or membership in circumstances where the directives on Collective Redundancies and Acquired Rights are operative.[261] In the UK and Ireland the 'single-channel' operates alongside a single board of directors with no employee representation.

When the Commission was considering the best way forward during the first SAP they had the option of allowing for diversity, by permitting Member States to continue with either a dualist or a monist system of company organisation alongside a compulsory element of employee involvement. This optional model was operative in France and, even within a 'single-channel', it would be possible to adjust the structure to allow for non-executive directors to represent the interests of workers, or to establish a special consultative committee akin to a works council.[262] Indeed, the Economic and Social Committee, in an Opinion of April 1974, promoted diversity.[263] The Committee found that it was 'premature' to impose a uniform company structure when the interests of shareholders and employees could be protected under either system providing that there was an element of employee involvement.

The Commission's decision to proceed with the blunt instrument of a mandatory 'dual-channel' system relying closely on the German/Dutch model of two-tier management and supervisory boards for all public companies, as set out in the early drafts of the 'Fifth Company Law Directive',[264] was based on a desire to align their proposals with a wave of company law harmonisation measures intended to remove barriers to cross-border competition relying on the somewhat ambiguous wording of Article 44(2)(g) EC [ex 54(3)(g) EEC], that provides a legal base for directives to co-ordinate:[265]

... to the necessary extent the *safeguards* which, *for the protection of the interests of members and others*, are required by member states of companies and firms . . . with a view to making such safeguards equivalent throughout the Community;

---

[260] See T Conlon, 'Industrial Democracy and EEC Company Law: A Review of the Draft Fifth Directive' (1975) 24 *International and Comparative Law Quarterly* 348 at 348–9.

[261] Following the judgment of the Court in Cases C–382–383/92, *Commission v United Kingdom* [1994] ECR I–2435. The 'single-channel' is found not only in the UK and Ireland, but also, in a differing form, in Italy and Greece.

[262] See Conlon, n 260 above at 358–9.

[263] Doc CES 861/73, 22 April 1974.

[264] OJ 1972, C131/44. For discussion, see Conlon, n 260 above; W Kolvenbach, 'EEC Company Law Harmonization and Worker Participation' (1990) *University of Pennsylvania Journal of International Business Law* 709; J Temple Lang, 'The Fifth EEC Directive on the Harmonization of Company Law' (1975) 12 *Common Market Law Review* 155; W Däubler, 'The Employee Participation Directive—A Realistic Utopia?' (1977) 14 *Common Market Law Review* 17; and J Welch, 'The Fifth Draft Directive—A False Dawn' (1983) 8 *European Law Review* 83.

[265] My emphasis.

This provision must be understood in the context of the freedom of companies to establish their operations throughout the Member States, as provided for in Article 48 EC [ex 58 EEC], and therefore any arrangements for the representation of employees on corporate boards as 'others' are essentially an adjunct to this general objective. Formulated prior to the enlargement of the Community from six to nine members, these proposals, along with similar measures for the establishment of optional European Companies,[266] were destined to fail in the face of implacable opposition from companies based in the UK and Ireland.[267] The relaunched draft Fifth Directive of 1983[268] was a pale shadow of its former self and, while it allowed for both dualist and monist boards, with separate managerial and supervisory functions, the element of employee participation was diluted to the extent that a separate and essentially toothless 'consultative council' could be substituted for employee representation on the corporate board. The result was a messy compromise that provoked opposition from all sides.[269] Ultimately company law which, in many other aspects, has converged at Community level, has proved to be an inappropriate vehicle for harmonising systems of collective labour relations and labour law that are deeply rooted in national regional, social and economic structures.[270]

While the Community's pursuit of employee participation through the reform of company structure was premature, it was also a distraction from any attempt to proffer more coherent alternative models of employee involvement in the transnational context.[271] The most important of these alternatives, emanating from the former DGV of the Commission, was first mooted in the so-called 'Vredeling' proposal on transnational procedures for information and consultation in large multinationals.[272] DGV's pragmatic proposal sought to place an obligation on large transnational enterprises, with more than 1,000 employees, to provide regular communication and consultation with employees' representatives. The Commission sought to advance this policy on the basis of shared values and good corporate practice whilst insisting that there would be no change in the structures of

[266] *Bulletin of the European Communities Supplement* 8/70. Eventually a revised proposal for establishing the 'European Company', as a voluntary option for transnational companies, allowing for either a 'single tier' or 'dual tier' board, was successful 30 years on: Reg 2157/2001/EC on the Statute for a European Company (SE) OJ 2001, L294/1; and Dir 2001/86/EC supplementing the Statute for a European company with regard to the involvement of employees, OJ 2001, L294/22.

[267] For example, see the 'Watkinson Report': *The Responsibility of the British Company*, Final Report of the Company Affairs Committee (Confederation of British Industry, London, 1973).

[268] OJ 1983, C240/2.

[269] See Weiss in Davies *et al*, n 1 above at 220–3.

[270] Lord Wedderburn, 'Industrial Relations and the Courts' (1980) 9 *Industrial Law Journal* 65 at 71. See Welch, n 264 above at 84.

[271] See Weiss in Davies *et al*, n 1 above at 223–4.

[272] OJ 1980, C297/3.

companies and the formal arrangements for worker representation afforded by the laws and practices of the Member States.[273]

The 'Vredeling' proposal represented a considered and more realistic approach to the thorny subject of employee involvement in undertakings. DGV were seeking consensus while closely attuning their ideas with principles founded in international law, specifically the ILO's Tripartite Declaration of 1977 that called for information to be conveyed in a way that enabled employees' representatives to obtain a true and fair view of the performance of the enterprise and consultation concerning matters with major employment effects.[274] 'Vredeling' provided a testing ground for ideas that, despite their pragmatism, were still launched ahead of their time. Indeed 'Vredeling' offered a blueprint for what was to emerge a decade later as the European Works Council Directive.[275] In the short to medium-term, however, these proposals had to be put into cold storage, partly because the social partners, particularly the employers' organisations, lacked enthusiasm for yet another new drive for 'Euro-corporatism', but more importantly, because there had been a sea-change in the political climate.

By 1980, when the 'Vredeling' proposal was published, the first Social Action Programme was nearly exhausted with only what one former Social Affairs Commissioner derisively described as 'fag-end measures' remaining.[276] In 1979 a new Conservative Government led by Margaret Thatcher had been elected in the UK. Thatcher, who had campaigned for British membership of the EEC, presented herself as a positive European who favoured market integration but fiercely opposed what she regarded as unnecessary regulation. The weaknesses of the social provisions of the EEC Treaty, dependent on unanimity and liberal interpretation, were swiftly exposed once a solitary and geopolitically powerful Member State sought to challenge the economic and social assumptions that had underpinned the first Social Action Programme. Along with 'Vredeling', other proposals on working time,[277] part-time work[278] and temporary work[279] fell by the wayside. Other new players were, however, about to take their place on the Community's stage: Francois Mitterand, Helmut Kohl and, most importantly in this context, Jacques Delors, the candidate supported by Mrs Thatcher to head up the European Commission in 1985.

---

[273] See Docksey (1987, *Comparative Labor Law Journal*) n 258 above at 34.

[274] ILO Tripartite Declaration of Principles concerning Multinational Enterprises and Social Policy of 16 Nov 1977. 'Vredeling' also reflected the OECD Guidelines for Multinational Enterprises of 21 June 1976. For a discussion, see C Docksey, 'Information and Consultation of Employees: The United Kingdom and the Vredeling Directive' (1986) 49 *Modern Law Review* 282 at 283–8.

[275] Dir 94/45/EC, OJ 1994, L254/64.

[276] Shanks, n 7 above at 382.

[277] Council Resolution of 18 Dec 1979 on the adaptation of working time, OJ 1980, C2/1.

[278] OJ 1982, C62/7.

[279] OJ 1982, C128/2.

3

The Single European Act—Catalyst for Action I

I INTRODUCTION

A S THE COMMUNITY entered the 1980s the prevailing mood was one of pessimism. A bleak report of the Economic and Social Committee starkly set out the challenges for the decade ahead in two concise paragraphs:[1]

On the economic and social front, unemployment is rising, economic and social inequalities are growing, ground is being lost to other large industrialised countries and the Community's economic structures are ill-equipped to cope with the rise in energy prices and technological change.

On the political and institutional front, there is a lack of solidarity between the Member States, who are incapable of transforming either the guidelines set by the European Council or the initiatives taken by the Commission or the European Parliament into Council of Ministers decisions. This shows that the political will to attain the underlying objectives of the Community is lacking.

A decade earlier, most notably at the Paris Summit of 1972, the Community had exhibited an aura of invincibility based on apparently inexorable economic growth and social progress. By 1980, this mood of optimism, or rather complacency, had been replaced by a general malaise. The US and Japan had rapidly overtaken the Community both in economic output and competitiveness and, where there was once a comfortable certainty of success based on a mix of regulated free trade, strong state sectors, social protection and industrial partnership, there was now incoherence and a policy vacuum. A new phrase entered the Community's lexicon: 'Eurosclerosis'. As Grahl and Teague explain:[2]

The notion is that slower growth, rising unemployment and stagnant productivity in advanced capitalist economies result from the impairment of market forces. The

---

[1] *Prospects for the 80s*, Bulletin of the Economic and Social Committee, 10/81, pp 5–12 at 5.
[2] J Grahl and P Teague, *1992—The Big Market: The Future of the European Community* (Lawrence & Wishart, London, 1990) p 20.

necessary adaptations and adjustments to changing tastes and technologies are seen as obstructed by rigidities in the price system or in the reallocation of productive resources, for which the main responsibility lies with government: intervention, regulation, taxation are seen as obscuring market signals or blunting the incentives to respond to them. Organised labour is also seen as contributing to economic rigidities, by imposing collective agreements which fix rigid wage rates and circumscribe the tasks which may be ascribed to workers.

Those who advanced the notion of 'Eurosclerosis' were in fact the advocates of a new certainty known as neo-liberalism.[3] For the neo-liberals the path to economic recovery depended on the swift removal of market restrictions and a minimal level of institutional or state involvement. Impetus for the rapid advancement of the neo-liberal agenda was provided by the emergence of Margaret Thatcher and Ronald Reagan on the global stage. Advocates of 'Eurocorporatism', who argued that a more interventionist approach to the labour market, promoting education and vocational training, would reduce unemployment and lead to greater productivity, earnestly countered this fresh push for 'Euroliberalism'.[4] Nonetheless, neo-liberals were in the ascendancy over Keynesians throughout the 1980s.[5]

For the Community, the challenge was to find a response that combined the advantages of the neo-liberal approach—flexibility, innovation and greater autonomy—with policies to combat its disadvantages—social division, cyclical boom and bust and unemployment. What followed was a powerful market-oriented drive for an 'area without frontiers' with a strong deregulatory emphasis, coupled with a much weaker steer towards a 'social dimension' of the market. The focus switched from legislative harmonisation to social consensus and, where necessary, both binding and non-binding measures—or a mix of 'hard' and 'soft' law—intended to establish minimum standards at Community level while leaving a wide range of discretion to the Member States.

In the next two chapters we will seek to explore the effectiveness of the two main strands of Community social policy in operation from the mid-1980s through to the entry into force of the Agreement on Social Policy in 1993. The first strand, discussed in this chapter, was the development of a 'social dimension' revolving around the Commission's Internal Market programme and buttressed by specific Treaty changes brought about by the Single European Act. As a development of the original 'market integration'

---

[3] See, for example, R Lawrence and C Schultz (eds) *Barriers to European Growth: A Transatlantic View* (Brookings, Washington DC, 1987).

[4] See W Streeck, 'Skills and the Limits of Neo-Liberalism: The Enterprise of the Future as a Place of Learning' (1989) 3 *Work, Employment and Society* 1; and D Soskice, 'Industrial Relations and Unemployment: The Case for Flexible Corporatism' in J Kriegel, E Matzner and A Roncaglia (eds) *Barriers to Full Employment* (Macmillan, London, 1988).

[5] For a balanced critique of this debate, see M Rhodes, 'The Future of the 'Social Dimension': Labour Market Regulation in Post-1992 Europe' (1992) 30 *Journal of Common Market Studies* 23.

model of the Community,[6] this policy commanded the broad support of all the Member States. Under this first strand, the Community was able to take steps to improve the working environment, by way of health and safety measures, and, on a broader front, to promote social dialogue. The second strand, considered in the next chapter, was more experimental and lacked universal support. This was based on a much wider fundamental rights orientation to social policy linked to, but not dependent upon, economic objectives. This emerging 'social citizenship' model[7] relied on two non-binding policy instruments: the Social Charter, a 'solemn declaration' made by 11 Member States at Strasbourg in 1989; and the Commission's accompanying Action Programme. While tentative steps were taken to further the second strand from the mid-1980s, it was the internal market, and the balance between its economic and social spheres, that first provided the momentum for a new, more purposive and dynamic, phase of European integration.

II THE SOCIAL DIMENSION OF THE INTERNAL MARKET

At the Fontainebleau European Council of June 1984, the Community's leaders sought to settle their outstanding differences. After much haggling, agreement was reached on a 66 per cent budget rebate for the UK in return for minor adjustments to the Common Agricultural Policy and the establishment of a framework for resolving wider budgetary issues required for the accession of Spain and Portugal in 1986.[8] The time was ripe for a new initiative that could combine the free market instincts of the British Conservatives under Margaret Thatcher with the technocratic vision of the French Socialists led by François Mitterand. Thatcher, already the Community's longest serving leader, issued an influential paper at Fontainebleau entitled *Europe—The Future*[9] which, while paying homage to inter-governmental technology programmes supported by Mitterand, marked a new drive for a market-oriented approach to job creation and competitiveness. Thatcher warned that:[10]

Only by a sustained effort to remove remaining obstacles to intra-Community trade can we enable the citizens of Europe to benefit from the dynamic effects of a fully

---

[6] See B Fitzpatrick, 'Straining the Definition of Health and Safety' (1997) 26 *Industrial Law Journal* 115 at 117–19.

[7] *Ibid.* See also, J Kenner, 'Citizenship and Fundamental Rights: Reshaping the European Social Model' in J Kenner (ed) *Trends in European Social Policy* (Dartmouth, Aldershot, 1995) 3–84.

[8] The UK's rebate was worth £1,000 million at 1984 prices and was set without the imposition of a time limit. The overall budgetary settlement was finally reached at a meeting of Finance Ministers in Dublin on 15/16 Sept 1984.

[9] The text of the paper is reproduced at (1984) 23 *Journal of Common Market Studies* 73.

[10] *Ibid* at 74.

integrated common market with immense purchasing power . . . This means action to harmonize standards and prevent their deliberate use as barriers to intra-Community trade; more rapid and better co-ordinated customs procedures; a major effort to improve mutual recognition of professional qualifications; and liberalising trade in services.

Thatcher believed that, if there was the necessary political will, these objectives could be fully achieved under the provisions of the Treaty of Rome, but others were not convinced and, as a compromise, the leaders at Fontainebleau agreed to the establishment of an *ad hoc* Committee for Institutional Affairs to look into the matter.[11] Parallel developments were taking place in the European Parliament where, shortly before the second direct election in June 1984, a radical 'Draft Treaty establishing the European Union' was adopted with the federalist pioneer, Alterio Spinelli, as *rapporteur*.[12]

The stage was now set for the appearance of Jacques Delors as President of the Commission in January 1985. Delors, who had served as Mitterand's Finance Minister, was credited with steering the French economy to success by implementing a tough austerity package and a small measure of market deregulation. He was greatly admired by Thatcher who supported him over France's preferred candidate, Claude Cheysson. Moreover, Delors was a strong supporter of the drive for the single market who recognised that market integration had to be given priority while right of centre governments were in the ascendancy in many Member States.[13] Delors was, however, approaching the task from a fundamentally different perspective. For Thatcher, the single market was an end in itself, but for Delors it was a means to an end.[14] Delors' 'Big Idea' was to vigorously pursue market integration but only because it was a necessary first step to his ultimate objective of political integration. For this reason Delors set a target date of 31 December 1992 for the completion of the single market to give his programme the necessary momentum. Delors was fortunate in his allies, receiving the support not just of the majority of the Member States, but also from Thatcher's own Commissioner, Lord Cockfield who, in his White Paper on *Completing the Internal Market*, concluded that:[15]

---

[11] The 'Dooge Committee' reported to the European Council in March 1985. A full copy of the text is reproduced in Annex II of R Bieber, J-P Jacqué and J Weiler, *An Ever Closer Union: A Critical Analysis of the Draft Treaty Establishing the European Union* (European Communities, Luxembourg, 1985) pp 330–42.

[12] Adopted by the European Parliament on 14 Feb 1984, OJ 1984, C77/33. Also reproduced as Annex I of Bieber *et al*, *ibid* pp 306–29.

[13] H Young, *This Blessed Plot: Britain and Europe from Churchill to Blair* (Macmillan, London, 1998) pp 326–7.

[14] C Grant, *Delors: Inside the House that Jacques Built* (Nicholas Brealey, London, 1994) p 70.

[15] COM(85) 310.

Just as the Customs Union had to precede Economic Integration, so Economic Integration has to precede European Unity.

For Delors, however, an 'area without frontiers' necessarily required *l'espace sociale Européenne*. As he explained in his first address to the European Parliament:[16]

The creation of a vast economic area, based on market and business co-operation, is inconceivable—I would say unattainable—without some harmonisation of social legislation. Our ultimate aim must be the creation of a European social area . . .

What would become of us if we didn't have a minimum harmonisation of social rules? What do we already see? Some member states, some companies who try to steal an advantage over their competitors, at the cost of what we have to call a social retreat.

At the European Parliament, Delors found an audience that was highly receptive to this kind of rhetoric. He was to perform a similar feat at the annual conference of the British Trades Union Congress (TUC) in September 1988, a feat that led to an almost instantaneous *volte face* in the European stance of both the TUC and the Labour Party.[17] In practice Delors moved more cautiously on social policy.

The agenda set by the Internal Market White Paper had a distinctly deregulatory bias, drawing heavily on the principle of mutual recognition derived from the Court's judgment in *'Cassis de Dijon'*,[18] a case concerned with the scope of Articles 28–30 EC [ex 30–36 EEC] on the free movement of goods. In order to secure the removal of physical, technical and fiscal barriers to the free movement of goods and services, the principle of mutual recognition in *Cassis* required that 'if a product is lawfully manufactured and marketed in one Member State, there is no reason why it should not be sold freely throughout the Community'.[19] In the social policy context, the Commission suggested that the principle of mutual recognition could be applied to the area of health and safety where the Member States had essentially equivalent legislative objectives. Moreover, 'public health' was one of the areas recognised as a mandatory requirement of Community policy in *Cassis*,[20] to be taken into account when applying the rules on free movement of goods and services. In addition, 'the protection of health and life of humans' was also recognised as an exception where justified by national

---

[16] *Bulletin of the European Communities Supplement* 1/86, p 9.

[17] See, for example, *1992: Maximising the Benefits: Minimising the Costs* (Trades Union Congress, London, 1988).

[18] Case 120/78, *Rewe Zentrale v Bundesmonopolverwaltung für Branntwein* [1979] ECR 649.

[19] COM(85) 310, para 58. A similar approach was recommended by the ad hoc Committee for a People's Europe, the 'Adonnino Report', which drew up proposals to implement the right of establishment by means of the mutual recognition of academic and professional qualifications. See COM(84) 446.

[20] [1979] ECR 649, para 8.

governments under Article 30 EC [ex 36 EEC].[21] The burden of proof would, however, be on the government of the importing country, rather than on the private exporter or its customers.[22] It followed that there might need to be legislative harmonisation to lay down essential health and safety requirements, where this could not otherwise be achieved by mutual recognition, leading to a Community standard that would entitle a product to free movement in the internal market. The Commission concluded that, in the short term, the horizon of Community social policy was to be limited to health and safety linked to free movement objectives and, pending reform of the EEC Treaty, it would be inappropriate to use Article 94 EC [ex 100 EEC] more widely.[23]

While this strategy had the advantage of promoting a broad equivalence of objectives between market integration and standardisation in the area of health and safety, the Commission was conscious of the need to identify any potentially negative implications of the single market on social conditions in the Member States, not least because of renewed fears of 'social dumping', as clearly expressed by Delors in his inaugural address to the European Parliament. As part of its strategic response, the Commission issued a report of an inter-departmental Working Party entitled, *The Social Dimension of the Internal Market*.[24]

The report identified two specific concerns about 'social dumping' expressed by countries with 'advanced social conditions'.[25] First, once differentials were transparent and obstacles were removed, market share would shift within the single market to countries with lower production costs. Secondly, there would be downward pressure on social conditions because of the demands of competition as jobs are sucked out of the economy. In such circumstances, it was suggested that a 'race to the bottom' would be inevitable.[26] The Working Party, while acknowledging that there would be an acceleration or intensification of this process in some areas, such as public works contracts and transport, concluded that these problems would be offset by other comparative advantages in terms of productivity, technical innovation, reliability and geographical location.[27] The

---

[21] COM(85) 310, para 65.
[22] Grahl and Teague, n 2 above at 32.
[23] COM(85) 310, para 65.
[24] *Social Europe*, Special Edn (European Communities, Luxembourg, 1988).
[25] *Ibid* pp 65–6.
[26] The 'race to the bottom' or 'meltdown' theory arises in a deregulatory federal system where states are allowed to unilaterally lower their social standards in order to undercut other states. Businesses relocate in response and the other states respond by lowering their standards in order to compete. In the US this is known as the 'Delaware effect', after the deregulatory policies of the State of Delaware following the Delaware Corporation Act of 1899. See C Barnard, 'Social dumping and the race to the bottom: some lessons for the European Union from Delaware?' (2000) 25 *European Law Review* 57 at 57–63.
[27] *Social Europe* (1988) n 24 above, pp 65–6.

report also gave short shrift to related concerns that flexible labour markets and decentralisation would lead to a growth in illicit work and a widening of wage differentials.[28]

In determining the way forward, the report addressed the respective merits of two contrasting and 'less than ideal' approaches to Community social policy.[29] The first option, the *normative* approach, was designed to achieve 'a single harmonizing framework to all matters at Community level . . . mainly by means of binding instruments'.[30] While the Working Party was able to refer to some notable successes for this approach in the areas of employment protection and sex equality, they recognised that the normative or regulatory method left little room for innovation and denied the social partners autonomy. It was also unrealistic given the outright opposition of some Member States and the limitations of the social provisions in the Treaties. Moreover, the authors of the report concluded that the employment crisis that had engulfed the Community, and changes both in technology and behaviour, and also the demands of international competition, called for a 'more flexible and pragmatic policy with different ambitions'.[31]

The second option, the *decentralised* approach, acknowledged the need for basic rules in the area of health and safety but its advocates wished 'to see competition between social rules and a minimisation of social legislation'.[32] While this second option had the advantage of more flexibility, promoting innovation and greater autonomy for the social partners, the Working Party concluded that reliance upon decentralisation was too localised and short-termist. It would not lead to social progress in areas where a Community yardstick was required beyond the fields of health and safety, for example, to prevent abuses of labour standards, promote equality and protect the weakest members of society.[33]

Having analysed the two approaches, the Working Party recommended a 'middle way', or perhaps what would be regarded in the language of the late 1990s/early 2000s as a 'third way'. This would draw upon the strengths of both the normative and decentralised approaches and thereby combine economic and social policy effectively. The best means of delivering this, the Commission suggested, was to promote a 'European industrial area' where the two sides of industry could meet in a Community forum to determine the mix between the two approaches.[34] At this stage, however, the Commission, while promoting the idea of a 'genuine European system of

[28] *Ibid* pp 66–8.
[29] *Ibid* pp 62–3.
[30] *Ibid.*
[31] *Ibid.*
[32] *Ibid* pp 63–4.
[33] *Ibid.*
[34] *Ibid* pp 68–70.

social relations' did not envisage formalised European collective agree-ments.[35] Although the Working Party highlighted the potential of what might be described as a deepening of the process of 'social dialogue', they were eager to indicate the potential limitations of this method of decision-making in practice when they warned that:[36]

This should not, however, be taken to mean that the Commission might in some way abdicate its role. Should the social dialogue fail, the Commission would not use it as an excuse to shirk its responsibilities.

Hence, while the Commission's 'middle way' would focus on the develop-ment of the 'social dialogue' as the favoured route for furthering the social dimension, there would also be other means available to promote specific measures at both Community and national levels. A range of methods would be considered including harmonisation, where necessary, convergence of social standards in areas such as social protection, vocational training and public health, and, as a means of giving additional momentum to the process, 'the establishment at Community level of a body of minimum social provi-sions', albeit in a far more limited form than the Social Charter that was to be launched the following year. The emergence of the Social Charter will be discussed in the next chapter, but to assess how the substantive goals of the social dimension were to be brought into legal effect we shall first turn to the Community's chosen instrument, the Single European Act.

III THE SINGLE EUROPEAN ACT—ESTABLISHING THE INTERNAL MARKET

(1) Introduction

At the Milan European Council in June 1985, the Community's leaders decided to override the opposition of Denmark, Greece and the UK, and proceed with institutional reform as the most effective means of achieving the Commission's target date of 1992 for completing the internal market.[37] One course open to the European Council would have been to adopt, in whole or in part, the 'Draft Treaty' drawn up by the European Parliament in 1984.[38] Indeed the French and German governments put forward a joint proposal for a 'European Union Treaty' as a basis for debate. In fact this fell far short of the Parliament's proposals and, in any event, the reference

---

[35] *Social Europe* (1988) n 24 above, pp 70–3.
[36] *Ibid* p 70.
[37] See E Noel, 'Reflections on the Community in the Aftermath of the Meeting of the Euro-pean Council in Milan' (1985) 20 *Government and Opposition* 444; and S George, *An Awkward Partner: Britain in the European Community*, 2nd edn (OUP, Oxford, 1994) pp 180–3.
[38] See Bieber *et al*, n 11 above.

to the establishment of a 'European Union' was anathema to the British and highly unattractive for the Danes. As a consequence, the Parliament's forward looking prognosis for a Treaty founded upon principles of fundamental rights and Union citizenship, with fully fledged social provisions, subsidiarity and legislative co-decision, was never tabled.[39] The Single European Act (SEA) that emerged from the negotiating process was a pale shadow of the Parliament's document. For the most part it adapted the suggestion of the Council's own *ad hoc* group, the 'Dooge Committee', for limited reforms designed to smooth the way for the single market and achieve closer political co-operation over foreign policy.[40] For Margaret Thatcher, the SEA was a 'modest decision', for Jacques Delors, it was a 'monstrosity'.[41] Nonetheless, once in force from 1 July 1987, the SEA represented the first substantive reform of the EEC Treaty and it is doubtful whether either the protagonists or antagonists of the final text fully appreciated the long-term impact of the institutional reforms and policy refinements that they had set in train.

The SEA combined short-term objectives with longer lasting changes to the competences of what was still formally the EEC Treaty. The core internal market provisions were contained in Articles 8a, 8b and 8c EEC[42] [now 14 and 15 EC], setting out the general principles for establishing the internal market to be implemented by Article 100a EEC [now 95 EC] and Article 100b EEC [now repealed], containing the legal bases for internal market measures.[43] The social policy context of these internal market provisions will be discussed in the next section before considering the specific amendments to the EEC Social Chapter contained in Article 118a EEC [now part of Articles 137 and 138 EC] on health and safety in the context of the working environment, and Article 118b EEC [now replaced by Articles 138 and 139 EC] on the establishment of social dialogue. As the Amsterdam Treaty has substantially altered each of these provisions, we will, to avoid confusion, refer to them in their historical context as Articles 118a and 118b EEC.

(2) The Internal Market and Social Policy

Article 14(1) EC [ex 7a(1) EC, ex 8a(1) EEC] *obliges* the Community to 'adopt measures with the aim of progressively establishing the internal

---

[39] The provisions on social and health policy can be found in Art 56 of the 'Draft Treaty'. For the text, see Bieber *et al, ibid* at 321.

[40] See Young, n 13 above, p 331.

[41] Cited by Grant, n 14 above, p 74.

[42] Renumbered as Arts 7a, 7b and 7c EC by the Treaty on European Union (TEU).

[43] For a full assessment of the impact of these provisions and related parts of the SEA, see D Wyatt and A Dashwood, *European Community Law*, 2nd edn (Sweet & Maxwell, London, 1993) pp 353–74.

market' by 31 December 1992. Responsibility is shared by the Community institutions, which must adopt the necessary measures, and the Member States, who are bound by the duty of co-operation in Article 10 EC [ex 5 EEC] to ensure their fulfilment. A wide range of Treaty provisions are identified for this purpose, including 'market approximation' under Articles 94 and 95 EC [ex 100 and 100a EEC], but there is no direct reference to the Chapter on social policy, Articles 136–145 EC [ex 117–122 EEC]. Article 14(1) EC does not, however, preclude activity in those areas not expressly mentioned because any measures are 'without prejudice to the other provisions of this Treaty'. Moreover, the SEA imposed an additional duty on the Council, set out in Article 8b EEC [now repealed], to 'ensure balanced progress in all the sectors concerned' when exercising a qualified majority vote on a proposal from the Commission. This implies that, while the 'internal market' is primarily concerned with creating the conditions for transborder free movement, account should be taken of the wider sectoral impact of removing barriers and regulating the market in areas such as the environment and social policy. Article 14(2) EC [ex 7a(2) EC, ex 8a(2) EEC] *defines* the internal market as:

... an area without internal frontiers in which the free movement of goods, persons, services and capital is ensured in accordance with the provisions of this Treaty.

Thus, while the notion of a 'common market' encompasses a broad range of Community policies not confined by specific economic objectives, the 'internal market' is a narrower conception, designed to rapidly achieve economic liberalisation through both negative and positive means by a combination of deregulation, mutual recognition and, where necessary, standardisation at Community level. While this narrow focus indicates an exercise of political restraint by the Member States reflecting a lowering of the Community's aspirations,[44] at least in the short-term, it also presented an opportunity, swiftly seized upon by the Delors Commission, to make decisions quickly, taking advantage of very specific provisions requiring qualified majority voting (QMV), to generate an institutional dynamic that would prepare the way for the next stage of political integration.[45] Moreover, even though it can be argued that Article 14(2) EC is not directly effective, because it requires implementation through Community measures, as indicated by an accompanying Declaration by the Member States,[46] its importance lies with the

[44] For a critique, see P Pescatore, 'Some Critical Remarks on the Single European Act' (1987) 24 *Common Market Law Review* 9.

[45] For support for this proposition, see J Weiler, 'The Transformation of Europe' (1991) 100 *Yale Law Journal* 2403 at 2454; and W Sandholtz and J Zysman, '1992: Recasting the European Bargain' (1989) 42 *World Politics* 95; cf A Moravcsik, 'Negotiating the Single European Act: National Interests and Conventional Statecraft in the European Community' (1991) 45 *International Organization* 19.

[46] The Member States declared that the 31 Dec 1992 deadline 'does not create an automatic legal effect'. This is no more than an interpretative non-binding statement but its

obligation on both the Member States and the Community to act within the timetable set in order to achieve a clearly *defined* objective. Article 15 EC [ex 8c EEC] provides some limited scope for the Commission to specify derogations when drawing up internal market proposals to take account of the need for economic adjustments to help less well developed economies having to cope with the opening up of markets. Any derogation must, however, be temporary in nature and cause the least possible disturbance to the functioning of the common market.[47]

In practice, Article 95(1) EC [ex 100a(1) EEC] has provided the main lever for the *implementation* of the internal market programme by way of QMV 'for the achievement of the objectives set out in Article 14'. The introduction of QMV on internal market matters had an immediate dynamic effect on the approach of the Member States to Community decision-making. The Member States, having grown accustomed to placing reliance on the threat of the national veto, have progressively lost this shibboleth as the range of areas covered by QMV has been extended by successive Treaty amendments. By contrast, under the QMV formula,[48] the Member States must negotiate with an awareness of the possibility of being outvoted and, faced with this danger, they must seek to secure the best possible terms within the framework of the Commission's proposal unless they can construct a blocking minority.[49] The results were immediate and dramatic. Within a short period, the inertia of the early 1980s rapidly gave way to an active legislative dynamic with 265 of the measures proposed in the Commission's White Paper being adopted by the end of 1993.[50]

While the sheer volume of internal market measures is impressive, their ambit has been severely circumscribed by a derogation contained in Article

unambiguous nature carries considerable force. The retention of the deadline in the Amsterdam Treaty of 1997 indicates a continuing obligation. See Wyatt and Dashwood, n 43 above, pp 358–63; cf A Toth, 'The Legal Status of the Declarations Annexed to the Single European Act' (1986) 23 *Common Market Law Review* 803. For a summary of the debate on this point, see D Chalmers and E Szyszczak, *European Union Law, Volume II: Towards a European Polity?* (Dartmouth, Aldershot, 1998) pp 5–6.

[47] For further discussion on this point, see C-D Ehlermann, 'The Internal Market Following the Single European Act' (1987) 24 *Common Market Law Review* 361 at 374.

[48] At the time of the SEA the QMV formula provided a threshold of 54 votes out of 76 to secure a majority in the Council of Ministers. Following enlargement from 12 to 15 Member States, the threshold was adjusted to 62 votes out of 87, Art 205(2) EC [ex 148(2) EEC]. The votes of each Member State are weighted taking into account population with a bias towards smaller countries. Germany, France, Italy and the UK each have 10 votes, Spain has 8, Belgium, Greece, The Netherlands and Portugal have 5, Austria and Sweden have 4, Denmark, Ireland and Finland have 3, and Luxembourg has 2. Both the QMV formula and the weighting of votes will again be substantially altered if or when the draft Treaty of Nice of 26 Feb 2001 enters into force and the next planned enlargement takes place after 2004. See the table annexed to the Final Act of the Conference, OJ 2001, C80/1 at 82–3.

[49] See R Dehousse, *Integration v Regulation? Social Regulation in the European Community* (EUI, Florence, 1992) p 17.

[50] *Community Internal Market—1993*, COM(94) 55. See Chalmers & Szyszczak, n 46 above, p 2.

95(2) EC [ex 100a(2) EEC] which states that the first paragraph of Article 95 EC 'shall not apply to fiscal provisions, to those relating to the free movement of persons nor to those relating to the rights and interests of employed persons'. This was clearly intended by its proponents, the UK and Germany, to severely limit, at least in the short-term, the notion of a 'social dimension' of the internal market. When considered at face value, Article 95(2) EC—pre-Maastricht—appeared to rule out 'Europeanisation'[51] of the social policy field except where unanimity could be reached under the original Treaty provisions in Article 94 EC [ex 100 EEC] or Article 308 EC [ex 235 EEC], or where, in the specific area of health and safety and the 'working environment', added by the SEA, a proposal could be founded upon Article 118a EEC which provided for QMV—all of which provided opportunities for the players in the 'Treaty base game'.[52]

Two main lines of argument have been put forward concerning the scope of Article 95(2) EC. First, several commentators have argued that it might be possible to limit the application of Article 95(2) EC.[53] It has been suggested that, notwithstanding the derogation, Article 95(1) EC might still be capable of covering a broader range of proposals that could be presented as not being exclusively or predominantly concerned with the rights and interests of employed persons. The Commission attempted, unsuccessfully, to test this approach when seeking to introduce legislation concerning 'atypical' or non-standard workers: specifically, part-time, fixed-term and temporary workers.[54] Rather than risk all on one piece of legislation that would almost certainly have foundered on the rocks of the unanimity rule, the Commission simultaneously launched three proposals using different legal bases. The proposals were as follows:

1) Proposal for a Council Directive on certain employment relationships with regard to working conditions (Article 94 EC [ex 100 EEC]);[55]

2) Proposal for a Council Directive on certain employment relationships with regard to distortions of competition (Article 95 EC [ex 100a EEC]);[56]

3) Proposal for a Council Directive supplementing the measures to encourage improvements in the safety and health at work of workers with a fixed-duration

---

[51] In the sense that European integration would otherwise directly infiltrate national social laws—see generally, F Snyder (ed) *The Europeanisation of Law: The Legal Effects of European Integration* (Hart, Oxford, 2000).

[52] See Fitzpatrick, n 6 above at 116–19.

[53] See, for example, E Vogel-Polsky, 'What Future is There for a Social Europe?' (1990) 19 *Industrial Law Journal* 65 at 70–2; and B Bercusson, *Fundamental Social and Economic Rights* (EUI, Florence, 1989) pp 12–14.

[54] For further discussion, see R Nielsen, *European Labour Law* (DJØF Publishing, Copenhagen, 2000) pp 148–49; E Whiteford, 'W(h)ither Social Policy?' in J Shaw & G More (eds) *New Legal Dynamics of European Union* (Clarendon Press, Oxford, 1995) 111–28 at 116–17.

[55] COM(90) 228, OJ 1990, C224/4.

[56] OJ 1990, C224/6. Amended proposal COM(90) 533, OJ 1990, C305/6.

employment relationship or a temporary employment relationship (Article 118a EEC).[57]

The first proposal—the most far-reaching—sought to apply the principle of non-discrimination to atypical workers including part-time, fixed-term, temporary and seasonal workers. The Commission's decision to rely on Article 94 EC reflected the generally cautious approach of the Delors period. The proposal may have been a harbinger of changes to come but, for the time being, it was sacrificed on the altar of the unanimity rule and the UK's inevitable veto.

The second proposed measure was subtler and potentially even more significant. The Commission sought to harmonise indirect costs for employing atypical workers as a means to combat distortions of competition. Member States would be obliged to include them in social protection schemes and employers would have had to provide, inter alia, protection against unfair dismissal, maternity protection, occupational pensions and redundancy payments. Moreover, part-time workers would have been entitled pro-rata to equal treatment with full-time employees in respect of such matters as holidays and seniority allowances. This measure was more widely opposed among the Member States who were concerned about the economic costs. It was also a victim of tactical disagreements between the Commission and the European Parliament. The latter supported the notion of one combined proposal under Article 95 EC. The result was the shelving of both proposals.

The third proposal was, however, successful. This was the most limited measure. It was more narrowly focused on health and safety matters, rather than broader employment protection, and, as such, it fell clearly within the scope of Article 118a EEC. As this was also subject to QMV, and there was wider support among the Member States for health and safety proposals, the measure was formally adopted as Directive 91/383.[58] This was no more than a pyrrhic victory for the Commission. One measure may have been adopted but this was, in itself, rather superficial given the all-embracing nature of the 1989 'framework' Directive on the Safety and Health of Workers at Work,[59] which covers all 'workers'. Moreover, the precise scope of Article 95(2) EC remained untested.

A second line of argument concerns the relationship between paragraphs 2 and 3 of Article 95 EC. It has been suggested that the derogation in Article 95(2) EC must be read together with Article 95(3) EC [ex 100a(3) EEC] which provides that, where an internal market proposal concerns health, safety, or the protection of the environment or consumers, the Commission must take 'as a base a high level of protection'. Article 95(3) EC was

---

[57] OJ 1990, C224/4.
[58] OJ 1991, L206/19. Effective from 31 Dec 1992.
[59] Dir 89/391/EEC, OJ 1989, L183/1.

intended to placate those countries that have established stringent standards and who were concerned that harmonisation would be at the level of the 'lowest common denominator'.[60]

Both of these arguments are unconvincing. Article 95(3) EC refers only to 'proposals envisaged in paragraph 1' and therefore paragraphs 2 and 3 must be understood as being mutually exclusive. More importantly, Article 95 EC was inserted into the Treaty only as a means of implementing specific internal market proposals by QMV. While it has undoubtedly acted as a restraint on social policy proposals, so long as at least one Member State has objected to them, it does not prevent the advancement of such measures where a *more specific* legal base is available, for example Article 118a EEC or now, post-Amsterdam, any one of the areas covered by Article 137 EC, which is much wider than its precursor. In order to explain this point it is first necessary to consider the place of Article 95 EC in the revised scheme of the Treaty post-SEA.

Paradoxically, despite its widespread use, Article 95 EC is, as a matter of Treaty interpretation, a *residual legal base* in two senses. Firstly, Article 95 EC operates by way of 'derogation from Article 94', hitherto the principal legal base for approximation measures in a wide range of policy fields, including social policy, where Community legislation has been deemed necessary for the 'establishment and functioning of the common market'. Article 95 EC is only concerned with approximation provisions *'which have as their object* the establishment and functioning of the *internal market'*.[61] Article 94 EC is broader, not only because of the functional distinction between the 'common market' and the 'internal market', but also, because Articles 94 and 95 EC are mutually exclusive, it is operative in those areas excluded from the main thrust of the 'internal market' programme by virtue of Article 95(2) EC. Hence, while the practical utility of Article 94 EC is necessarily limited by the requirement of unanimity, it has continued to provide the most appropriate legal base for a limited number of whole Community labour law proposals, outside the ambit of what was Article 118a EEC, in the period between the SEA and the ratification of the Treaty of Amsterdam.

Secondly, Article 95 EC must be interpreted, even within the context of the 'internal market', as residual in the sense that it only applies 'save where otherwise provided in this Treaty'.[62] Article 95 EC is therefore intended as a legal base only for those measures that have the establishment and functioning of the internal market as their *primary objective*. In all other cases a more specific provision will take precedence—*generalia specialibus non*

---

[60] See P Craig & G de Búrca, *EC Law: Text, Cases and Materials*, 2nd edn (OUP, Oxford, 1998) p 1121.

[61] My emphasis.

[62] For further elucidation on this point, see Wyatt & Dashwood, n 43 above, p 364.

derogant.[63] Where, however, the internal market objective of any measure is paramount, Article 95(3) EC must be taken into account and, as a consequence, specific 'health' and 'safety' aspects of any proposal must provide for 'a high level of protection', a point firmly reinforced in the public health context by the Court in its landmark *Tobacco Advertising*[64] judgment of 5 October 2000.

In the *Tobacco Advertising* case the Court powerfully underlined the narrow conception of the internal market bequeathed by the SEA and the specific nature of Article 95(1) EC.[65] When considering the legality of a Directive on the approximation of national laws on the advertising and sponsorship of tobacco products,[66] the Court rejected the notion that Article 95(1) EC vests in the Community legislature 'a general power to regulate the internal market'.[67] While the Court's judgment is consistent with the current trend of judicial recognition of limits on the scope of Community competence,[68] it is based on the conferred or limited powers principle that although now expressly incorporated into the EC Treaty by the TEU,[69] derives from the earlier constitutional jurisprudence of the Court.[70] It follows that a measure based on Article 95(1) EC 'must genuinely have as its object the improvement of the conditions for the establishment and functioning of the internal market'.[71]

Significantly, the Directive in question was annulled not because its 'centre of gravity' lay in the area of public health,[72] but because of the general nature of the prohibition on the marketing of tobacco products.[73] Hence, a more specific measure aimed at preventing the emergence of future

---

[63] See A Dashwood, 'The Working Time Judgment in a Wider Perspective' in C Barnard, A Dashwood & B Hepple, *The ECJ's Working Time Judgment: The Social Market Vindicated* (CELS Occasional Paper No 2, Cambridge, 1997) 23–31 at 26.

[64] Case C–376/98, *Germany v European Parliament and Council (Tobacco Advertising)* [2000] ECR I–8419, para 88.

[65] For discussion, see the annotation by J Usher (2001) 38 *Common Market Law Review* 1519.

[66] Dir 98/43/EC, OJ 1998, L213/9.

[67] Para 83.

[68] See Usher, n 65 above at 1519.

[69] The first para of Art 5 [ex 3b] EC reads: 'The Community shall act within the limits of the powers conferred upon it by this Treaty and of the objectives assigned to it therein'.

[70] See especially, Case 26/62, *Van Gend en Loos v Nederlande Administratie der Belastingen* [1963] ECR 1 at 12, where the Court held that the Member States had, by signing the EEC Treaty, 'limited their sovereign rights, albeit within limited fields'.

[71] *Tobacco Advertising*, n 64 above, para 84.

[72] Art 152 [ex 129] EC on public health does not allow for harmonisation measures. Therefore the two legal bases were not 'competing' and, as AG Fennelly graphically observed at para 58 of his opinion, 'the question of whether the Community has acted within its powers cannot be determined by a measure's putative 'centre of gravity' as between these two incommensurable objectives [health protection and the internal market]'. For further discussion of the public health issues raised by the case, see T Hervey, 'Up in Smoke? Community (anti) tobacco law and policy' (2001) 26 *European Law Review* 101.

[73] Para 117.

obstacles to trade resulting from multifarious development of national laws may be validly adopted under Article 95(1) EC so long as the emergence of such obstacles is likely and the measure in question is designed to prevent them.[74] Moreover, the Court will verify whether the distortion of competition that the measure purports to eliminate is appreciable.[75] Therefore, a general measure such as the Commission's second proposal on 'atypical work',[76] which was based on the distortion of competition argument, would almost certainly have fallen foul of this test on the basis that, even if it had promoted competition, such advantages might be regarded as 'remote and indirect' and not comparable to appreciable distortions caused by differences in production costs.[77] Further, as the Court warned in its judgment,[78] other articles in the Treaty may not be used as a legal basis in order to circumvent the exclusion of harmonisation elsewhere[79] and, by implication, the absence of a power to harmonise in certain areas.

Syrpis[80] has suggested that one consequence of the *Tobacco Advertising* case will be to restrict the capacity of the Community's legislature to utilise Article 94 EC [ex 100 EEC] for social policy measures to prevent or rectify market distortions in areas where there is no specific legal base in the Social Chapter. Notwithstanding the introduction of Article 95 EC by the SEA, the Member States chose to retain Article 94 EC as a general legal base for measures designed to achieve this broad objective where there is an 'absence of any express reference' in the Treaty.[81] For example, even after the revision of EC Treaty at Amsterdam, there is no Treaty competence for a directive concerning matters such as pay or the right to strike. Rather, there is an express prohibition against using Article 137 EC for such measures.[82] However, unlike Article 95 EC, the legal base in Article 94 EC can be utilised for measures that '*directly affect* the establishment or functioning of the *common market*'.[83] Such measures do not have to be narrowly conceived, or 'have as their object' the precise *internal market* goals in Articles 3(1)(c) EC [ex 3(c) EEC] and Article 14 EC [ex 7a EC, ex 8a EEC],[84] but can be more broadly justified on the grounds of the

---

[74] Para 86. See also, Case C–350/92, *Spain v Council* [1995] ECR I–1985, para 35.
[75] Para 106. See also, Case C–300/89, *Commission v Council (Titanium Dioxide)* [1991] ECR I–2867, para 23.
[76] OJ 1990, C224/6.
[77] Para 109.
[78] Para 79.
[79] Specifically in relation to public health in Art 152(4) [ex 129(4)] EC.
[80] See P Syrpis, 'Smoke Without Fire: The Social Policy Agenda and the Internal Market' (2001) 30 *Industrial Law Journal* 271 at 277.
[81] Case 43/75, *Defrenne v Sabena II* [1976] ECR 455, para 63. Cited by AG Léger in Case C–84/94, *United Kingdom v Council (Working Time Directive)* [1996] ECR I–5755, at para 70 of his opinion.
[82] Art 137(6) EC.
[83] My emphasis.
[84] See the express reference to these provisions in para 82 of the judgment.

Community's tasks in Article 2 EC which, even in its original form, required a balance within the common market between the pursuit of the Community's broad economic and social objectives. Therefore, the adoption of revised directives on collective redundancies[85] and acquired rights[86] on the basis of Article 94 EC, prior to the ratification of the Amsterdam Treaty,[87] was fully justified.

While the *Tobacco Advertising* case limits the scope for Community legislation in the specific area of the internal market, it does not exclude targeted measures under Article 95 EC that, for example, have the free movement of goods as their object, but have ancillary social policy benefits. Moreover, directives intended to guarantee the free movement of goods in the internal market must, by virtue of Article 95(3) EC, ensure that a high standard of health protection is incorporated into *product design and manufacture*. Conversely, the social policy objective only becomes paramount when legislation is primarily concerned with the *conditions of use* of those same products.[88] Hence, as AG Léger advised in the *Working Time* case,[89] Article 95 EC was the appropriate legal base for Directive 89/686, on the approximation of laws concerning personal protective equipment,[90] which sought, as its fundamental objective, to remove barriers to trade in the production and manufacture of such equipment while, simultaneously, ensuring that the workers using this equipment were protected by a high level of safety standards in its specifications. Similarly, Directive 89/392 on the approximation of laws relating to machinery,[91] was intended to ensure that safety was incorporated from the design stage onwards by placing an obligation on the manufacturer of machinery to eliminate or reduce risks as far as possible, to take any necessary protective measures against risks that cannot be eliminated and to provide information and training for users of the machinery.[92] Moreover, other general measures, such as Directive 88/379 on the classification, packaging and labelling of dangerous preparations,[93] are intended to have a protective effect both within and beyond

[85] Dir 92/56/EEC on the approximation of the laws of the Member States relating to collective redundancies, OJ 1992, L245/3, consolidated by Dir 98/59/EC, OJ 1998, L225/16.

[86] Dir 98/50/EC on the approximation of the laws of the Member States relating to the safeguarding of employees' rights in the event of transfers of undertakings, businesses or parts of undertakings or businesses, OJ 1998, L201/88, consolidated by Dir 2001/23/EC, OJ L82/16.

[87] Post-Amsterdam such measures can be justified based on Art 137(1) EC which allows for QMV.

[88] See *Social Europe 2/90, Health and Safety at Work in the European Community* (European Commission, Brussels, 1990) p 47.

[89] Case C–84/94, *United Kingdom v Council (Working Time Directive)* [1996] ECR I–5755, para 73 of the opinion. The AG explicitly approved of the use of Art 95 EC for the directives referred to above.

[90] OJ 1989, L399/18.

[91] OJ 1989, L183/9.

[92] See *Social Europe 2/90*, n 88 above, p 48.

[93] OJ 1988, L187/14, as amended by Dir 89/178/EEC, OJ 1989, L64/18, and Dir 91/155/EEC, OJ 1991, L76/35.

the working environment. Therefore, the specific use of Article 95 EC for internal market proposals requires a complementary approach to free movement of goods and health and safety objectives.

Where, however, the measure in question is founded primarily upon a policy objective provided for elsewhere in the Treaty, it follows that Article 95 EC should not be used because it is a residual provision and, in the context of measures principally concerned with social policy, the derogations contained in Article 95(2) EC will not come into play. In those circumstances the 'centre of gravity' argument between the relevant Treaty provisions will be of crucial importance and, as the Community's legislative powers in the field of social policy have gradually widened, it has become possible to justify Community legislation based on the autonomous legal bases in the Social Chapter. This was the interpretation applied by the Court in the *Working Time*[94] case, when considering the UK's challenge to the validity of the Working Time Directive[95] adopted under Article 118a EEC as a measure to protect the health and safety of workers 'especially in the working environment'.

In the *Working Time* case the UK argued, inter alia, that Article 118a EEC should be strictly interpreted as an exception to the general rule in Article 95(2) EC which excludes a measure that, in their view, was concerned with working conditions generally and not specifically health and safety in the context of the immediate working environment. The Court reached precisely the opposite conclusion, ruling that 'the existence of other provisions in the Treaty does not have the effect of restricting the scope of Article 118a', a point addressed in Article 95(1) EC which states that its provisions apply 'save where otherwise provided in this Treaty'.[96] Where the choice of legal base is the subject of judicial review proceedings under Article 230 EC [ex 173 EEC], it is well established that the Court will decide the case by making an objective assessment of the aim and content of the measure in question.[97] It follows that the spheres of application of Article 95 EC and now Article 137 EC [ex 118a EEC] are delimited not on the basis of a choice between general and particular measures 'but upon the *principal aim* of the measure envisaged'.[98] Where the principal aim of

---

[94] Case C–84/94, *United Kingdom v Council (Working Time Directive)* [1996] ECR I–5755. For discussion, see J Kenner, 'A Distinctive Legal Base for Social Policy?—The Court of Justice Answers a "Delicate Question"' (1997) 22 *European Law Review* 579; and Barnard *et al*, n 63 above.

[95] Dir 93/104/EC concerning certain aspects of the organisation of working time, OJ 1993, L307/18.

[96] Paras 12–13.

[97] Case 45/86, *Commission v Council* [1987] ECR 1493, para 11; and Case C–300/89, *Commission v Council* [1991] ECR 2867, para 10. For a critique, see S Crosby, 'The Single Market and the Rule of Law' (1991) 16 *European Law Review* 451.

[98] Case C–84/94, *United Kingdom v Council (Working Time Directive)* [1996] ECR I–5755, para 21 (my emphasis).

the measure is the protection of the health and safety of workers in general, Article 137 EC [ex 118a EEC] *must* be used[99] and this objective should not be subordinated to 'purely economic considerations'.[100]

We shall consider the scope of Article 118a EEC, and the Court's interpretation thereof, more fully in the next section, but for the purposes of interpreting Article 95 EC, it is now clear that even though a specific health and safety measure may have an ancillary effect on the establishment and functioning of the internal market, this will not suffice to bring it within the scope of that provision.[101] Conversely, as the *Tobacco Advertising* case subsequently demonstrated, the targeted nature of the internal market provisions effectively foreclosed any attempts to utilise QMV under Article 95 EC to circumvent the absence of a specific Treaty base for employment and social policy measures outside the area of health and safety of workers during the period of the SEA.

The operation of Article 95 EC is subject to a further specific derogation by virtue of Article 95(4) EC [ex 100a(4) EEC] where, after the adoption of a harmonisation measure, a Member State 'deems it necessary to apply national provisions on grounds of major needs referred to in [Article 30 EC—ex 36 EEC], or relating to protection of the environment or the working environment'.[102] When negotiating the SEA the Member States were not willing to give an unqualified right of pre-emption to the Community via the operation of QMV.[103] Article 95(4) EC retains a limited amount of manoeuvrability at national level. Member States seeking to have recourse to Article 95(4) EC must first notify the Commission who must be satisfied that there will be not be 'arbitrary discrimination or a disguised restriction' on intra-Community trade before they can activate the provision and, in addition, an action may be brought by a Member State or the Commission against any Member State considered to be making 'improper use' of these powers. Therefore, in the field of social policy, a Member State may seek to disapply or delimit the effects of a measure on the grounds of the 'protection of health', as one of the areas specified in Article 30 EC [ex 36 EEC], or the 'working environment'. In the *Working Time* case both of

---

[99] *Ibid* paras 20 and 22.

[100] *Ibid* para 28.

[101] Case C–426/93, *Germany v Council* [1995] ECR I–3723, para 33. See Dashwood, n 63 above, p 27.

[102] See also the interpretative and procedural provisions added by the Treaty of Amsterdam: Art 95(5)–(9) EC. In addition, Art 95(10) [ex 100a(5) EEC] provides for the inclusion of a 'safeguard clause' in harmonisation measures, in appropriate cases, authorising Member States to take provisional measures 'for one or more of the non-economic reasons referred to in [Art 30 EC—ex 36 EEC]', subject to a Community control procedure. The full list of 'grounds' in Art 30 EC is 'public morality, public policy or public security, the protection of health and life of humans, animals or plants; the protection of national treasures possessing artistic, historical or archaeological value; or the protection of industrial and commercial property'.

[103] On the theory of pre-emption, see S Weatherill, *Law and Integration in the European Union* (Clarendon Press, Oxford, 1995) pp 135–83.

these expressions were given a broad meaning,[104] albeit within the specific context of the former Article 118a EEC, and, at the time of the SEA, the inclusion of this clause aroused considerable fear that it would be frequently relied upon by Member States, particularly those outvoted in the Council, and this would undermine the whole internal market process.[105]

In practice, Article 95(4) EC has rarely been used with notification being given to the Commission in just two cases in the first five years of the operation of the SEA, the critical period for the '1992 process'.[106] Wyatt and Dashwood suggest that one of the main reasons for this inactivity has been the interplay between Article 95(3) and (4) EC that has led to higher common standards being proposed in harmonisation measures in order to deter Member States from having recourse to national provisions on the specified grounds.[107] This is a good example of how, in practice, the SEA has confounded the dire warnings of some of its sternest critics by both accelerating the process and deepening the substance of the internal market. This point was well made by AG Léger in the *Working Time* case where he noted that:[108]

[Article 95] constitutes the appropriate legal base whenever a harmonization measure has as its *fundamental object* the establishment of the *internal market* even though, in order to achieve that goal, the measure must, in accordance with [Article 95(3)], ensure a high level of protection as regards the safety and health of workers, and thereby reduce the risk of a Member State resorting to the exception in [Article 95(4)].

The completion of the internal market was not to be achieved by Community legislation alone, as indicated in the White Paper. Article 95 EC [ex 100a EEC] was supplemented by ex-Article 100b EEC,[109] an innovative mutual recognition clause, which obliged the Commission to draw up an inventory of national laws and regulations which had not been harmonised under Article 95 EC and for the Council to decide whether to recognise

---

[104] Case C–84/94, *United Kingdom v Council (Working Time Directive)* [1996] ECR I–5755, para 15.
[105] See Pescatore, n 44 above, and J Flynn, 'How Well Will Article 100a(4) Work? A Comparison with Article 93' (1987) 24 *Common Market Law Review* 689.
[106] Art 95(4) EC has been tested before the Court on just two occasions. In Case C–41/93, *France v Commission* [1994] ECR I–1829, the Court annulled a Commission decision to allow a German rule imposing stricter controls on a chemical, PCP, but only on procedural grounds. In Case C–127/97, *Burstein v Freistaat Bayern* [1998] ECR I–6005, a related challenge was also unsuccessful on procedural grounds. See E Szyszczak, 'The Working Environment v. Internal Market' (1999) 24 *European Law Review* 196 at 197.
[107] Wyatt and Dashwood, n 43 above, p 367.
[108] Case C–84/94, *United Kingdom v Council (Working Time Directive)* [1996] ECR I–5755, para 73 of the opinion.
[109] Now repealed. The obligation under this provision was intended to be operative until 31 Dec 1992.

them as equivalent.[110] Thus, mutual recognition, while central to the 'big idea' behind the White Paper, appeared to be confined to a sweeping up clause. This underestimates its importance. As subsidiarity has come to the fore, particularly in areas where Community competence is less well developed, so mutual recognition has increasingly been regarded as the preferred option with harmonisation only being introduced as a last resort where the Community objective cannot be more effectively achieved at national level. This is an approach that has, as we shall see, had important consequences for social policy, notwithstanding the gradual extension of the legal base in the social policy field in the SEA and subsequent Treaties. Taken together, Articles 95 EC [ex 100a EEC] and 100b EEC, reflect the complementary characteristics of mutual recognition, as an instrument of integration, and harmonisation, as a regulatory technique, where there is a convergence of objectives.[111] While Article 95(2) EC has provided a high hurdle for the Commission to clear when seeking an appropriate legal base for proposals aimed at furthering the 'social dimension', it has not been insurmountable, not least because of the expansive interpretation given to Article 118a EEC and the policy drive initiated by the launch of the Community's Social Charter.

IV HEALTH, SAFETY AND THE WORKING ENVIRONMENT

(1) The 'Excessively Subtle Wording' of Article 118a EEC

In the preamble to the SEA the Member States professed themselves 'determined to improve the economic and social situation by extending common policies and pursuing new objectives'.[112] To an extent, this commitment reflected a new wave of optimism flowing from the Internal Market White Paper. Advocates of the internal market programme were confidently predicting that market liberalisation would lead to a combination of cost reductions, rationalisation of industrial structures and innovative new processes and products. They predicted a doubling of GDP, a six per cent drop in consumer prices and a fall in unemployment rates throughout the Community as a consequence of the creation of 1.8 million new jobs.[113] At the same time, experts reviewing the wider social impact of the internal market were more cautiously pointing to changes in the labour force based

---

[110] Despite the obligation contained therein the Commission did not table any proposals under Art 100b EEC before the deadline. See Wyatt and Dashwood, n 43 above, p 368.

[111] See Dehousse, n 49 above, p 13.

[112] Sixth recital of the preamble of the SEA.

[113] See P Cecchini, *The European Challenge 1992: The Benefits of a Single Market* (Wildwood House, Aldershot, 1988); M Emerson, M Aujean *et al*, *The EC Commission's*

on the notion of a 'J-curve'.[114] The theory was that the immediate effect of market integration would be a short to medium-term rise in unemployment, as a consequence of structural adjustments and economies of scale, to be followed by a longer lasting fall, with better resource allocation leading to steady growth. A decade later, Tsoulakis[115] was in a position to conclude, on the basis of several studies of the economics of the internal market, that there had been only small net gains with many of the bigger expectations being dependent on the 'dynamic effects' of the whole process. As Chalmers and Szyszczak have observed, much of the success of the 1992 project depended on hype and more recent assessments have shown an overestimation of both its positive and negative effects.[116] Therefore, for those seeking to transcend the hype and identify tangible benefits in the 'social situation' arising from the 1992 project, much depended on the Commission's ability to utilise the 'new objectives' added by the only amendment to the EEC Social Chapter in the SEA, Article 118a EEC on the health and safety of workers in the context of the working environment. This has, as we shall see later, been revised and incorporated into the far wider provisions now contained in Article 137 EC.

From the time of its enactment, Article 118a EEC maintained a certain enigmatic quality attributed by AG Léger to its 'excessively subtle wording ... bearing witness to the difficulties involved in its adoption'.[117] In the following sections an attempt will be made to understand these subtleties by close scrutiny both of the provisions themselves and their practical application.

Article 118a(1) EEC [now amended by Article 137(1) EC] set out the general objective as follows:

Member States shall pay particular attention to encouraging improvements, especially in the working environment, as regards the health and safety of workers, and shall set as their objective the harmonisation of conditions in this area, while maintaining the improvements made.

Harmonisation was established as the *objective* and not the means. Article 118a(2) EEC [now 137(2) EC] provided for the adoption of directives to 'help achieve the objective'. The 'middle way' between normative regulation and decentralisation, discussed later by the *Social Dimension Working*

Assessment of the Economic Effects of Completing the Internal Market (OUP, Oxford, 1988). For discussion, see Chalmers and Szyszczak, n 46 above, pp 6–13.

[114] See *Social Europe*, Supp 7/89, *The Social Aspects of the Internal Market, vol. 2* (European Commission, Brussels, 1989) pp 15–16.

[115] L Tsoulakis, *The New European Economy Revisited*, 3rd edn (OUP, Oxford, 1997) pp 71–3.

[116] See Chalmers and Szyszczak, n 46 above, p 11.

[117] Case C–84/94, *United Kingdom v Council (Working Time Directive)* [1996] ECR I–5755, para 35 of the opinion.

Party, was an integral part of the new Treaty scheme and formed the foundation for the approach to be developed subsequently in the Agreement on Social Policy. Subsidiarity, averred to overtly in the Environment Chapter,[118] was implicit here, but was nonetheless central to an approach that retained the notion of shared competence featured in Articles 117 and 118 EEC. Article 118a(2) EEC added the missing ingredient of a specific legal base providing for directives to be adopted under QMV clearly focused on health and safety within the sphere of the working environment.

The first paragraph of Article 118a(2) EEC, while specifying the use of directives, and therefore recognising the necessity for Community legislative standardisation, required that any directives must contain 'minimum requirements for gradual implementation, having regard to the conditions and technical rules obtaining in each of the Member States'. This provision reflected the concerns of those Member States, including the UK, which had developed their own regime for health and safety and expected to make a minimal number of technical changes by way of directives.[119] For other Member States, notably Denmark, the principal concern was the reverse. They feared that 'minimum standards' might lead to a levelling down of health and safety conditions and they were determined to maintain their freedom of manoeuvre. Hence, Article 118a(3) EEC [now 137(5) EC] made plain that the provisions in any directive 'shall not prevent any Member State from maintaining or introducing more stringent measures for the protection of working conditions compatible with this Treaty'. This appears, at face value, to be the reverse of the presumption in Article 95(3) EC [ex 100a(3) EEC]. Whereas Article 95(3) EC presumes that Commission proposals 'will take as a base . . . a high level of protection', Article 137(5) EC [ex 118a(3) EEC] allows for Member States to apply higher, or 'more stringent', levels of protection set above the 'minimum requirements' contained in any directives.

A further qualification is contained in the second paragraph of Article 118a(2) EEC [now 137(2) EC] where it is stated that:

Such directives shall avoid imposing administrative, financial and legal constraints in a way which shall hold back the creation and development of small and medium-sized undertakings.

This small and medium-sized enterprises (SMEs) clause reflects both the patchwork of compromise necessary to reach agreement during the

---

[118] Art 130r(4) EEC [repealed by the TEU] provided that: 'The Community shall take action relating to the environment to the extent to which the objectives [of Community environment policy] can be attained better at Community level than at the level of the individual Member States'.

[119] In the case of the UK, the main statutory provisions had been laid down in the Health and Safety at Work Act, 1974.

negotiations, as an area of concern for several Member States, and a recognition of the central role to be played by innovative SMEs in delivering the employment creation and technological innovation that is central to the objectives of the internal market programme across a diverse range of sectors.[120]

The immediate significance of Article 118a EEC can be measured by reference to its place within the SEA Treaty scheme as an autonomous social policy base. One consequence of the introduction of Article 118a EEC was to render obsolete, for the purpose of advancing health and safety policy, the use of Article 94 EC [ex 100 EEC]. It has already been shown that Article 95 EC [ex 100a EEC] was introduced as a residual legal base and derogation from Article 94 EC. In turn, Article 94 EC was retained as a *general* provision concerning the establishment or functioning of the common market and applied, and continues to apply,[121] only in those areas of Community activity where there is an 'absence of any express reference' in the Treaty.[122] Article 118a(2) EEC provided that reference point and, therefore, as a *more specific rule*, it superseded Article 94 EC as a legal base in respect of all measures where the primary purpose was the protection of the health and safety of workers.[123] Only where the protection of health and safety, or the working environment, were ancillary objectives of the measure did Article 100a EEC [now 95 EC], and not Article 100 EEC [now 94 EC], provide the appropriate legal base so long as the primary objective had, as its object, the improvement of the conditions for the establishment and functioning of the internal market.[124] Indeed, in order to swiftly demonstrate the status of Article 118a EEC as an autonomous legal base for social policy measures, an alteration was made to two legislative proposals on health and safety, originally conceived under Article 100 EEC [now 94 EC], to enable their adoption under the new provisions.[125]

Having established the status of Article 118a in the EEC/EC Treaty prior to the Amsterdam Treaty amendments, let us now turn to the *obligation* on

---

[120] See, for example, Cecchini, n 113 above, p 8; and A Neal, 'The Industrial Relations in SMEs in the United Kingdom' (1993) 26 *Bulletin of Comparative Labour Relations* 75 at 76–7.

[121] For an analysis of the status of Art 94 EC in the light of the *Tobacco Advertising* case, see the discussion on pp 86–7 above.

[122] Case 43/75, *Defrenne v Sabena II* [1976] ECR 455, para 63. Cited by AG Léger in Case C–84/94, *United Kingdom v Council (Working Time Directive)* [1996] ECR I–5755, at para 70 of his opinion.

[123] Case C–84/94, *ibid* para 12 of the judgment.

[124] See Case C–376/98, *Germany v European Parliament and Council (Tobacco Advertising)* [2000] ECR I–8419, para 84.

[125] Dir 88/364/EEC on the protection of workers by the banning of certain specified agents and/or certain work activities (fourth individual directive within the meaning of Art 8 of Dir 80/1107/EEC) OJ 1988, L179/44; and Dir 88/642/EEC amending Dir 80/1107/EEC on the protection of workers from the risks related to exposure to chemical, physical and biological agents at work, OJ 1988, L356/74.

Member States to 'pay particular attention to encouraging improvements, especially in the working environment, as regards the health and safety of workers' and the *objective* of 'harmonisation of conditions in this area, while maintaining the improvements made'. Two questions immediately arise. What is the scope of the obligation? What is the level of protection to be afforded to most effectively achieve the objective of harmonisation?

(2) The Scope of the Obligation—A Question of Ergonomics?

An examination of the scope of the obligation in Article 118a EEC requires an assessment of the meaning of the terms 'working environment', 'health' and 'safety'. Account must also be taken of the general obligations on Member States contained in Article 117 EEC [now 136 EC] to 'promote improved working conditions', and Article 118 EEC [now 140 EC], which provides for co-operation in the fields of the 'prevention of occupational accidents and diseases' and 'occupational hygiene'. The subtleties of this terminology and the relationship between the related provisions have perplexed institutional actors and academic commentators alike. In the absence of other legal bases within the revised first Social Chapter, a great deal depended on the delineation of 'this area' to be covered by any harmonising measures. The Community was faced with a choice of interpretative options. One interpretation would focus on health and safety measures in the form of risk assessment, preventing accidents at work, maintaining a hygienic working environment and combating industrial diseases. An alternative approach would seek to encompass all working conditions that have, or potentially could have, an effect on the health and safety of each individual worker, within and beyond the work place, that is detrimental to their mental or physical well-being, including such matters as the organisation of work, maternity provision and action to combat bullying or sexual harassment.

As we have seen in chapter 2, concepts of occupational health, safety and hygiene were already well developed in Community law long before the SEA was adopted. The significance of Article 118a EEC lays with the specific placement of health and safety activity within the context of encouraging improvements 'especially in the working environment'. Article 118a EEC did not merely provide a legal base with QMV for pursuing the Community's existing health and safety programmes, it instead added a new substantive Treaty dimension of the 'working environment' that created the potential for a much wider contextual interpretation of well established concepts.[126] For those advocating a broader approach a great prize was at stake. It was suggested that several long-standing Commission proposals

---

[126] See B Bercusson, *European Labour Law* (Butterworths, London, 1996) p 70.

opposed or obstructed by the UK could potentially be channelled via the 'back door' of Article 118a EEC.[127] What was required was a logical and legally robust argument that would galvanise the institutions to act. The institution most likely to gain was the European Parliament because Article 118a EEC provided not only for QMV but also for co-operation between the Parliament and the Council in the adoption of legislation.[128] The Social Affairs and Employment Committee of the Parliament, chaired by Mrs Heinke Salisch, took up this challenge.[129]

The 'Salisch Report' of 1988 sought to bring a wide range of social policy proposals within Article 118a EEC on the basis that the 'harmonization of working conditions is essential for the completion of the internal market'.[130] While this argument fitted neatly with the Delors' notion of a 'European Social Area', it must be regarded as legally specious when account is taken of the internal market derogation in Article 95(2) EC [ex 100a(2) EEC]. Salisch's interpretation of Article 118a EEC itself, however, was more credible and very innovative. In essence, the main thrust of the Report was founded upon what Salisch described as an 'ergonomic analysis' of the concept of the 'working environment' based on:[131]

The scientific study of the relationship between man and his working environment. It is concerned with the whole person and not only with the physical environment in which people work . . . It is therefore only logical for legislation on health and safety to be based on ergonomic principles.

An ergonomic approach to the working environment takes account of the impact of economic, social, cultural and political factors affecting the worker and heightens the importance of safety at work. At the core of the analysis is an emphasis on the 'physiological and psychological capabilities of the individual, in other words, his working environment'.[132]

Ergonomics is not a newfangled philosophy. As early as 1978, the Commission had sought to apply the principles of ergonomics in the 'design, construction and utilization' of plant and machinery as part of the First

---

[127] See A Neal, 'The European Framework Directive on the Health and Safety of Workers: Challenges for the United Kingdom' (1990) 6 *International Journal of Comparative Labour Law and Industrial Relations* 80 at 81.

[128] Under Art 252 EC [ex 189c EC, ex 149(2) EEC]. This procedure allowed Parliament to make legislative amendments. The Council was able to reject the amendments but this required a majority vote. In practice the co-operation procedure gave the Parliament a greater say over the *content* of Community legislation in those areas where it applied. The Amsterdam Treaty has replaced co-operation in the social policy field with co-decision under Art 251 [ex 189b] EC, granting the Parliament an even greater influence over the legislative process.

[129] *The Concept of the Working Environment and the Scope of Article 118a of the EEC Treaty*, 'Salisch Report', PE DOC A 2–226/88, 21 Oct 1988.

[130] *Ibid* p 9.

[131] *Ibid* p 10.

[132] *Ibid*.

Action Programme on Safety and Health at Work.[133] Moreover, Salisch's ergonomic analysis of the 'working environment' was heavily influenced by the Danish concept of *arbejdsmiljø*.[134] Denmark had been the driving force behind the inclusion of the term 'working environment' in Article 118a EEC. *Arbejdsmiljø* was the philosophical underpinning for the Danish Working Environment Act of 1975.[135] In his Opinion in the *Working Time* case, AG Léger outlined the broad sweep of the Danish statute thus:[136]

> The . . . legislation is not limited to classic measures relating to safety and health at work in the strict sense, but also includes measures concerning working hours, psychological factors, the way in which work is performed, training in hygiene and safety, and the protection of young workers and worker representation with regard to security against dismissal or any other attempt to undermine their working conditions. The concept of the 'working environment' is not immutable, but reflects the social and technical evolution of society.

This dynamic conception of the working environment recognises that long working hours, regular night working and carrying out repetitive tasks may contribute to fatigue and stress, affecting the worker's concentration and endangering their health and safety. In addition, lack of job security may make the worker more susceptible and put them at greater risk.[137] Salisch concluded that the term 'this area', referred to in Article 118a(1) EEC must include all 'working conditions', and therefore all of the fields referred to in Article 118 EEC [now 140 EC], in order to achieve its objectives. It followed that Article 118a EEC should be 'used for everything directly or indirectly related to the physical or psychological make up of the worker'.[138]

The approach of the Salisch Report was so broad that it would, when taken to its logical conclusion, have been capable of extending the application of the legal base in Article 118a EEC to cover all provisions concerning workers.[139] This was clearly not the intention of the Member States. The Danish may have been the initiators of Article 118a EEC but the interpretation of Community law should not be based solely on national

---

[133] Council Resolution of 29 June 1978 on an action programme of the European Communities on Safety and Health at Work, OJ 1978, C165/1, para 9.

[134] 'Salisch Report', n 129 above, pp 11–12.

[135] Law No 681 of 23 Dec 1975, which entered into force on 1 July 1977. Nielsen and Szyszczak suggest the approach is similar in other Nordic countries, pointing to, in addition, the Norwegian Working Environment Act of 1977 which covers some aspects of the employment relationship including unfair dismissal. See R Nielsen and E Szyszczak, *The Social Dimension of the European Community*, 2nd edn (Handelshøjskolens Forlag, Copenhagen, 1993) p 233.

[136] Case C–84/94, *United Kingdom v Council (Working Time Directive)* [1996] ECR I–5755, para 42 of the opinion.

[137] 'Salisch Report', n 129 above, p 11.

[138] *Ibid* p 13.

[139] This is explicitly stated as the objective, *ibid*.

concepts, not least in areas where there is a diversity of approaches and a range of national legislation. It is significant that while AG Léger relied heavily on the Danish input into the drafting of Article 118a EEC in his opinion in the *Working Time* case,[140] the judgment of the Court makes no direct reference to either the Danish influence in general or to ergonomics in particular. It can also be argued that the inclusion of the terms 'health' and 'safety' is a reflection of the approach of the majority of Member States that have a distinct health and safety regime dealing strictly with the workplace as the designated 'working environment'.

These reservations notwithstanding, the Salisch Report was, and remains, important because it constitutes a powerful case for a more dynamic and purposive approach to the concept of the 'working environment' that embraces a wide range of factors affecting the health and safety of the individual worker. This approach has been influential not only on the strategy adopted by the European Parliament, but also on the legislative programme of the Commission, which had already resolved, by the end of 1987, in a Communication issued a year before the completion of the second Safety and Health Action Programme,[141] to embark immediately on a new work programme and to take 'full advantage of the opportunities afforded by the provisions of . . . Article 118a' which would include the promotion of 'safety and ergonomics at work'.[142] It was this legislative strategy that would ultimately give rise to the adoption under Article 118a EEC of contentious directives concerning Pregnant Workers,[143] Working Time[144] and Young Workers,[145] under the aegis of the broader Action Programme designed to give effect to the aims of the Community's 1989 Social Charter.

---

[140] Case C–84/94, *United Kingdom v Council (Working Time Directive)* [1996] ECR I–5755, paras 42–3 of the opinion.

[141] Commission Communication of 21 Dec 1987, OJ 1988, C28/2, summary to the Communication. The second action programme on safety and health at work was initiated by a Council Resolution of 27 Feb 1984, OJ 1984, C67/2. The programme prescribed a specific set of priority actions to be taken from that date until the end of 1988. The Commission's 1987 Communication was issued on the same date that the Council had adopted a Resolution on Safety, Hygiene and Health at Work, OJ 1988, C28/1. The Council Resolution was more guarded. It did, however, call for action under Art 118a EEC to be 'intensified and expanded' but recognised the need to 'place equal emphasis on achieving the economic and social objectives of the completion of the internal market'. For discussion, see A Neal, 'Regulating Health and Safety at Work: Developing European Union Policy for the Millennium' (1998) 14 *International Journal of Comparative Labour Law and Industrial Relations* 217 at 230–31.

[142] *Ibid*. Summary and Part II.A.

[143] Dir 92/85/EEC on the introduction of measures to encourage improvements in the safety and health of pregnant workers and workers who have recently given birth or are breast feeding (tenth individual directive within the meaning of Art 16(1) of Dir 89/391/EEC) OJ 1992, L348/1.

[144] Dir 93/104/EC concerning certain aspects of the organisation of working time, OJ 1993, L307/18.

[145] Dir 94/33/EC on the protection of young workers, OJ 1994, L216/12.

Hence, an expansive interpretation of the 'working environment' ineluctably leads to a much broader view of the interlinked concepts of 'health' and 'safety'. In a key passage in its judgment in the *Working Time* case the Court explained that:[146]

There is nothing in the wording of Article 118a to indicate that the concepts of 'working environment', 'safety' and 'health' as used in that provision should, in the absence of other indications, be interpreted restrictively, and not as *embracing all factors, physical or otherwise, capable of affecting the health and safety of the worker in his working environment*, including in particular certain aspects of the organisation of working time. On the contrary, the words 'especially in the working environment' militate in favour of a broad interpretation of the powers which Article 118a confers upon the Council for the protection of the health and safety of workers. Moreover, such an interpretation of the words 'safety' and 'health' derives support in particular from the preamble to the Constitution of the World Health Organisation to which all the Member States belong. *Health is there defined as a state of complete physical, mental and social well-being that does not consist only in the absence of illness or infirmity.*

In opting for a broad conceptual interpretation of Article 118a EEC that emphasises the health and safety of the individual worker *within his own working environment*, and therefore implicitly endorses ergonomic principles, the Court has not only upheld the most essential provisions of the Working Time Directive,[147] fiercely challenged by the UK in its annulment proceedings, but has also provided a justification for a wide range of other measures, allowing for full utilisation of Article 118a EEC and now Article 137 EC.

(3) A New Approach to Minimum Standards Harmonisation?

From the above discussion it has been shown that the concepts of the 'working environment', 'health', and 'safety', are capable of supporting an expansive interpretation of the obligation in Article 118a EEC. The second question must now be addressed. In essence, what is the level of protection to be afforded to workers to make effective the *objective of harmonisation* in Article 118a(1) EEC [now part of Article 136 EC]? From the perspective of the Commission, the new legal base provided an immediate

---

[146] Case C–84/94, *United Kingdom v Council (Working Time Directive)* [1996] ECR I–5755, para 15, emphasis added. The definition is contained in the preamble to the WHO constitution of July 1946.

[147] Dir 93/104/EC, OJ 1993, L307/18. The Directive regulates such matters as, inter alia, the length of the working week, night work, rest breaks and the right to paid annual leave. The Court only annulled one minor provision, contained in the second paragraph of Art 5 of the Dir, that allowed Member States to designate Sunday as a rest day when formulating their implementing legislation. The Council had failed to explain why Sunday was more closely connected to health and safety than any other day. Reference in the preamble to cultural, ethnic and religious factors was deemed insufficient, para 37 *ibid*.

opportunity for a focused approach building upon the health and safety action programmes already adopted and using the model of the first 'framework' Directive, 80/1107,[148] to favour a new, more wide ranging and inclusive, 'framework directive' as the most dynamic means of promoting health and safety in the workplace. Such an approach could, over time, be developed alongside a more expansive interpretation of Article 118a EEC portended by the ergonomics debate and clearly envisaged in the Commission's 1987 Communication establishing a Third Action Programme on Safety and Health.[149] Thus, while the Commission was well aware of the potential of Article 118a EEC as a means of relaunching several long-standing proposals opposed or obstructed by some of the Member States, their immediate priority was to accelerate the process of regulation at Community, national and sectoral levels in the health and safety field in order to promote higher standards of protection at the workplace. The springboard for achieving these objectives was the second 'framework' Directive, 89/391, on the Safety and Health of Workers at Work,[150] adopted with a view to the introduction of measures to encourage improvements in the safety and health of workers at work based on 'general principles concerning the prevention of occupational risks, the protection of safety and health, the elimination of risk and accident factors, the informing, consultation, balanced participation . . . and training of workers'.[151]

An examination of Directive 89/391 reveals two distinct features. First, as a 'framework' Directive it represents a flexible guideline method of Community legislation, laying down general objectives and obligations on employers and workers, while leaving as much scope as possible for the application of detailed rules at the appropriate level. It was made clear from the outset that there would be further directives laying down more specific rules where necessary, but there would also be scope for improvements to be achieved more directly at a national, sectoral or workplace level. Hence, the idea of a 'framework' directive is to both direct and facilitate concerted action at all levels. In this way Directive 89/391 serves as an umbrella under which Member States can exercise a degree of freedom of action, but the direction of any activity must lead to an upward harmonisation of the health and safety protection of workers at work. The Member States made this explicit in a declaration at the Hanover European Council in June 1989, when they stated that existing levels of social protection, particularly occupational health and safety, would not be reduced.[152] Further guidance can be found in the preamble of the Directive where it is proclaimed that the

---

[148] OJ 1980, L327/8.
[149] OJ 1988, C28/2.
[150] OJ 1989, L183/1.
[151] *Ibid.* Art 1(1). For a critical analysis, see Neal (1990, *International Journal of Comparative Labour Law and Industrial Relations*) n 127 above.
[152] *Social Europe* 2/90, n 88 above, p 9.

overall goal is to 'guarantee a better level of protection of the health and safety of workers'[153] and, therefore it follows that:[154]

This Directive does not justify any reduction in levels of protection already achieved in individual Member States, the Member States being committed, under the Treaty, to encouraging improvements in conditions in this area and to harmonizing conditions while maintaining the improvements made.

This statement directly assuaged concerns about a minimalist approach leading to 'lowest common denominator' standards. Moreover, the Directive was not intended to be the last word on the subject. Article 1(3) states that:

This Directive shall be without prejudice to existing or future national and Community provisions which are more favourable to protection of the safety and health of workers at work.

The framers of the Directive were seeking to provide a broad basis for action, allowing for 'daughter directives' as in the case of Directive 80/1107,[155] while, at the same time, ensuring that the full operation of Article 118a EEC was in no way delimited by the scope of the Directive. Any future measures had to be founded upon Article 118a EEC, whether or not they took the form of 'daughter' directives. Hence, it is palpably clear that activity in this field is intended to be dynamic, allowing for an ergonomic approach to develop over time. The hierarchical relationship between Directive 89/391 and Article 118a EEC was reaffirmed in the *Working Time* case where the Court rejected the UK's contention that following the adoption of Directive 89/391, health and safety measures should be applied only to particular groups of workers exposed to specific risks within the context of that Directive. The Court held that previous Council practice in this field could not justify a derogation from the Treaty's rules, nor could it create a binding precedent.[156]

The second important feature of the Directive is one of *responsibility*. The Directive is intended to be inclusive, simultaneously extending the scope of activities covered to protect workers in 'all sectors of activity, both public and private',[157] with the exception of the self-employed and domestic servants.[158] Responsibility for making the provisions effective in

---

[153] Fourth recital of the preamble.
[154] Fifth recital.
[155] OJ 1980, L327/8. Art 16 of Dir 89/391 provides that: 'The Council acting on a proposal from the Commission based on Article 118a ... shall adopt individual directives *inter alia* in the areas listed in the Annex'.
[156] Case C–84/94, *United Kingdom v Council (Working Time Directive)* [1996] ECR I–5755, para 19. See also, Case C–271/94, *Parliament v Council* [1996] ECR I–1705, para 24.
[157] Art 2(1).
[158] Art 3(a) defines a 'worker' as 'any person employed by an employer, including trainees and apprentices but excluding domestic servants'. While all workers, thus defined, are brought

the working environment is placed on both employers and workers. Responsibility rests primarily with employers[159] who have, by virtue of Article 5(1) a 'duty to ensure the safety and health of workers in *every aspect* related to the work'.[160] Moreover, Member States can choose, under Article 5(4) to either place strict responsibility on the employer, or to allow a limited defence where 'occurrences are due to unusual or unforeseeable circumstances, beyond the employers' control' or to 'exceptional events, the consequences of which could not have been avoided despite the exercise of all due care'.

The employer has a general obligation that is both broad and evolutionary as stated in Article 6(1):

Within the context of his responsibilities, the employer shall take the measures necessary for the safety and health protection of workers, including prevention of occupational risks and provision of information and training, as well as provision of the necessary organisation and means.

The employer shall be alert to the need to adjust these measures to take account of changing circumstances and aim to improve existing situations.

From this general obligation and related provisions in the Directive a wide range of duties are placed on the employer.[161] These include a:

—duty of awareness and evaluation of risk;[162]
—duty to eliminate avoidable risks;[163]

within the scope of the Directive, Art 2(2) contains an additional limitation whereby the Directive is not applicable 'where characteristics peculiar to certain specific public service activities, such as the armed forces or the police, or to certain specific activities in the civil protection services inevitably conflict with it'. Nevertheless, where this derogation applies, the health and safety of workers must be 'ensured as far as possible in the light of the objectives of the Directive'.

[159] Art 3(b) broadly defines employers to include 'any natural or legal person who has an employment relationship with the worker and has responsibility for the undertaking and/or establishment'. Employers cannot deflect their responsibilities by enlisting external services or persons, Art 5(2).

[160] Emphasis added.

[161] See Neal (1990, *International Journal of Comparative Labour Law and Industrial Relations*) n 141 above at 84–5; and C Barnard, *EC Employment Law*, 2nd edn (OUP, Oxford, 2000) pp 384–91.

[162] The employer must not only keep himself informed of technological advances and scientific findings concerning work place design, Art 6(2)(e) but also must also be aware of the capabilities of individual workers, Art 6(3)(b) and must identify and evaluate risks to their safety and health at work. By virtue of Art 6(3)(a) the employer has a duty to evaluate risks, inter alia, in the choice of work equipment, the chemical substances or preparations used, and the fitting-out of work places. Under Art 9(1)(a) the employer must assess the risks 'facing groups of workers exposed to particular risks'. As the Directive is first and foremost about establishing general principles, there is no specific guidance about formal procedures or the rigour of the risk assessment process. Art 6(5) does, however, make it clear that measures related to safety, hygiene and health of workers 'may in no circumstances involve the workers in financial cost'.

[163] Art 6(2). For example, Art 6(2)(c) obliges the employer to implement measures to, inter alia, combat risks at source. Under Art 6(2)(d) he must adapt work to the individual 'espe-

—duty to reduce the dangers posed by unavoidable risks by implementing general principles of prevention;[164]

—duty to train and direct the workforce;[165]

—duty to inform, consult and provide for balanced participation of workers and/or their representatives;[166]

—duty to record and be in possession of risk assessments and to list and report occupational accidents to the national authorities.[167]

Whilst the employer's responsibilities cover every aspect related to the safety and health of workers at work, the Directive is careful to avoid rigid

cially as regards the design of work places, the choice of work equipment and the choice of working and production methods, with a view, in particular, to alleviating monotonous work and work at a predetermined work-rate and to reducing their effect on health'. As part of the general duty the employer must also make adaptations to take account of technical progress, Art 6(2)(e) and replace the dangerous by the non-dangerous or less dangerous, Art 6(2)(f).

[164] The employer must develop a coherent overall prevention policy that must cover 'technology, organisation of work, working conditions, social relationships and the influence of factors related to the working environment', Art 6(2)(g). In effect, this amounts to a general duty to take account of ergonomic principles and to practically apply them. Additional responsibilities include regular health surveillance, Art 14; first-aid, fire fighting and evacuation of workers, Art 8(1); and to ensure that all workers are able, in the event of serious and imminent danger to their own safety and/or that of other persons, to take the appropriate steps in the light of their knowledge and the technical means at their disposal, to avoid the consequences of such danger, Art 8(5). In order to carry out his activities of protection and prevention the employer shall designate workers for these tasks or, where this cannot be organised, enlist competent external services or persons, Arts 7(1) 7(3) and 8(2). The detailed implementation of these provisions can be found in a series of 'daughter directives' on such matters as, inter alia, reducing the risks relating to exposure to carcinogens, Dir 90/394/EEC, OJ 1990, L196/1, on the use of personal protective equipment, Dir 89/656/EEC, OJ 1989, L393/181, and the manual handling of loads, Dir 90/269/EEC, OJ 1990, L156/9.

[165] Art 12 sets out an obligation on the employer to 'ensure that every worker receives adequate safety and health training, in particular in the form of information and instructions specific to his workstation or job'. Art 12(1) specifies that the worker should receive this training on recruitment; in the event of a transfer or a change of job; the introduction of new work equipment or a change in equipment; and the introduction of any new technology. The training, which should take place during working hours, must be adapted to take account of new or changed risks and repeated periodically if necessary. In addition, under Art 12(3) workers' representatives with a specific role in protecting the safety and health of workers shall be entitled to appropriate training at the employer's expense. Training must be accompanied by appropriate instructions issued to workers, Art 6(2)(i) and only workers who have received adequate instructions are to have access to areas where there is 'serious and specific danger' (Art 6(3)(d)).

[166] Art 10(1) obliges the employer to provide 'all the necessary information' to workers and/or their representatives concerning the safety and health risks and protective and preventative measures and activities in relation to the undertaking in general and each type of workstation and/or job. Art 11 provides for consultation of workers and/or their representatives including discussions 'on all questions relating to safety and health at work'. Additional consultation and balanced participation must take place with workers or workers' representatives with specific responsibility for the safety and health of workers.

[167] Art 9(1)(a)–(d). Under Art 9(1)(b) the employer must also decide on the protective measures to be taken and, if necessary, the protective equipment to be used. Art 9(2) provides that the specific obligations on employers in relation to these matters are to be defined by the Member States in the light of the nature of the activities and the size of undertakings.

obligations so long as the general duties are adhered to and practised throughout the Community. Hence, as the Directive is first and foremost about establishing general principles, there is no specific guidance about formal procedures or the rigour of the risk assessment process. These are matters that are left with the Member States who have overall responsibility to provide adequate controls and supervision.[168] Moreover, while SMEs have the same broad duties as large employers, there is discretion for Member States to address resource issues and to limit the recording and information responsibilities in line with the specific SME clause in Article 118a EEC.[169] The systems for the involvement of workers are left to the Member States' national laws and/or practices, but it is part of the scheme of the Directive that Article 11(1) presupposes the consultation of workers and the right of workers, and/or their representatives,[170] to make proposals and have balanced participation in accordance with national laws and/or practices.[171]

Responsibility is not, however, a one-way process. Inherent within the scheme of the Directive are notions of partnership, shared responsibility and even-handedness,[172] albeit that the ultimate objective is to protect the safety and health of workers. For workers to secure this basic right they must accept individual responsibility. Article 13(1) declares that:

It shall be the responsibility of each worker to take care as far as possible of his own safety and health and that of other persons affected by his acts or omissions at work in accordance with his training and the instructions given by his employer.

---

[168] Art 4(2).

[169] For example, Art 7(5) provides that the size of the undertaking is a relevant matter for determining the number of designated workers and external services or persons to be consulted in relation to the protection and prevention of occupational risks. It must also be taken into account when setting the precise numbers to be involved in first-aid, fire fighting and the evacuation of workers, Arts 8(1) and 8(2). Further, the size of undertakings may be considered when Member States define the precise record keeping obligations under Art 9 and the appropriate worker information measures under Art 10.

[170] For comment, see Bercusson, *European Labour Law*, n 126 above, pp 359–60. Bercusson argues that the notion of individual consultation may be inconsistent with Community law because the objective, structure and wording of the Directive imply involvement of both employees and their representatives. The emphasis of the Court, in Cases C–382–383/92, *Commission v United Kingdom* [1994] ECR I–2479, indicates a more nuanced approach. Whilst it is now clear that an employer cannot unilaterally choose to consult individual employees rather than their representatives, it will still be appropriate to inform and consult individuals where an employee has no representatives, or wishes to be individually involved. Moreover, the Directive presupposes a partnership approach that, as far as is possible, involves employees and their representatives *simultaneously* in information, consultation and balanced participation in health and safety matters.

[171] For a study of the effectiveness of participation, see H Krieger, 'Participation of Employees' Representatives in the Protection of the Health and Safety of Workers in Europe' (1990/91) 6 *International Journal of Comparative Labour Law and Industrial Relations* 217.

[172] See R Baldwin and T Daintith, 'The European Framework' in R Balwin and T Daintith (eds) *Harmonisation and Hazard: Regulating Workplace Health and Safety in the Community* (Graham & Trotman, London, 1992) 1–17 at 3.

Article 13 contains specific examples of these responsibilities including: inter alia, correct use of machinery, tools, dangerous substances and personal protective equipment; informing the employer or safety representatives of serious or imminent danger and other shortcomings in the protection arrangements; and co-operation with the employer's safety arrangements. In return for accepting these responsibilities the worker is granted an individual right to make health and safety proposals,[173] to stop work if in serious danger[174] and to appeal to a competent authority.[175]

The framework Directive remains dynamic today precisely because of its flexibility and evolutionary nature. It has provided a basis for 14 'daughter' Directives and a succession of action programmes.[176] Measures can be constantly updated or, if appropriate, deleted, in response to technological advances, breakthroughs in disease aetiology and cure, and even the emergence of new industries carrying fresh dangers. Although there is undoubtedly a tension between shared responsibility and effective regulation of workplace health and safety, this is not necessarily problematic and may be seen as beneficial. Each worker has an individual stake in the process but, ultimately, any obligation that he accepts does not diminish the principle of responsibility that rests with the employer.[177]

V ARTICLE 118b EEC—SOCIAL DIALOGUE: A MEANS TO AN END?

In chapter 2 we explored the concept of social dialogue and its development, both formal and informal, prior to the SEA. As early as 1980, the Economic and Social Committee, in its *Prospects for the 80s* report, had proposed 'concerted action' at European level between the two sides of industry that could, through their own initiative, and backed up by the Commission, lead to the conclusion of negotiated 'framework agreements'.[178] Jacques Delors took up this theme after his assumption of the Commission Presidency in 1985. Delors believed that the search for consensus and negotiation between the two sides of industry was a vital component of the completion of the internal market and would help European economies cope with major industrial, technological and social changes.[179] Delors convened a series of 'summit meetings' in the run up to the SEA as a means of injecting life into his conception of a 'European Industrial

---

[173] Art 11(1).
[174] Art 8(4).
[175] Art 11(6).
[176] Art 16 provides for a series of individual directives to be adopted to cover specific risks.
[177] Art 5(3).
[178] *Bulletin of the Economic and Social Committee*, 10/81, pp 5–12 at 8.
[179] See P Venturini, *1992: The European Social Dimension* (European Communities, Luxembourg, 1989) p 62.

Relations Area'. At a meeting at Val Duchesse in November 1985 the employers' organisations, UNICE and CEEP,[180] met with the European Trade Union Confederation (ETUC) and established two working parties on macroeconomic questions and new technologies.[181] These working parties and high-level meetings were intended to provide a springboard for Article 118b EEC, which declared that:

The Commission shall endeavour to develop the dialogue between management and labour at European level which could, if the two sides consider it desirable, lead to relations based on agreement.

In practice, the social partners, whilst they agreed on the desirability of social dialogue as a process, disagreed both on the need for, and status of, such 'agreements'. Nine joint opinions were issued by the social partners between 1986 and 1992 on subjects mainly relating to vocational training, new technology and the adaptability of the labour market.[182] Whilst these opinions represented important and worthwhile statements of best practice they were merely declaratory. They created no binding obligations, but instead indicated areas where there was substantive common ground but no consensus about the need for formalised agreements. On the one hand, the ETUC regarded social dialogue as *a means to an end*, developing and strengthening, rather than replacing, existing Community legislation through formalised agreements. On the other hand, UNICE regarded dialogue as *an end in itself*, seeking an understanding with the ETUC in relatively uncontroversial areas but declining, at this stage of the process, to negotiate agreements which might have had the potential for conversion into binding Community laws.

   For critics of social dialogue under the SEA its limitations were obvious. Any agreements would reflect the weakened state of trade unions at national level. They would carry no sanctions and were likely to be little used.[183] The joint opinions did, however, provide a basis for further evolutionary steps to be taken on the road from consensual dialogue to binding agreement. For example, the second Joint Opinion on new technologies,[184] while it was mainly concerned with economic issues, provided, in the view of the ETUC, a guarantee that the organisation of work and the adaptability of labour should be negotiated and subject to agreements and/or new statu-

---

[180] The Union of Industrial and Employers' Confederations of Europe (UNICE); and the European Centre of Enterprises and Public Participation (CEEP).

[181] Venturini, n 179 above, pp 61–5.

[182] These opinions are listed in the Commission's Green Paper, *European Social Policy: Options for the Union*, COM(93) 551, Annex IV, p 100.

[183] See B Hepple, 'The Crisis in EEC Labour Law' (1987) 16 *Industrial Law Journal* 77 at 85; Vogel-Polsky, n 53 above at 75.

[184] Joint Opinion of 9 Dec 1988 on 'New Technologies, Organisation of Work and Adaptability of the Labour Market'.

tory rules.[185] In its 1988 report on the *Social Dimension of the Internal Market* the Commission concluded that the Val Duchesse process needed to go further with a view to establishing a genuine system of European social relations but, at least in the short-term, it was unrealistic, because of the past heterogeneity of the systems in force in the Member States, to consider the notion of a European collective agreement.[186]

Social dialogue under the SEA left a number of questions unanswered. How representative were the parties to such 'agreements'? What was the status of any decisions arising from them? Were the social partners conducting a form of Community-wide collective bargaining or merely a structured dialogue? As we shall see in chapter 6, some of these questions have been answered by the adoption of the Social Policy Agreement and the provisions now contained in Articles 138 and 139 EC, but the fundamental issues of representativeness and dialogue or bargaining have not been fully resolved.

In the context of the SEA, legislative harmonisation under Article 118a EEC and social dialogue under Article 118b EEC provided a variety of means to further Community social policy within the confines of the general schema of the internal market. By 1987, when the ink of the signatories of the SEA was barely dry, the Belgian Presidency,[187] the Economic and Social Committee[188] and the Commission[189] were seeking to open a second social policy front. This required agreement on a minimum set of basic social rules and broad principles designed to ensure balanced progress in both the economic and social aspects of the internal market. Such rules were necessary both to avoid market distortions and to provide a stable basis for the furtherance of social dialogue.[190] In a highly influential Opinion of the Economic and Social Committee of November 1987, the notion of social rights and the single market were intertwined and explained thus:[191]

Adoption of Community legislation guaranteeing basic social rights immune to competitive pressures is therefore a key stage in the creation of the single market.

This rights-oriented conception of the internal market was a direct challenge to the deregulatory agenda being vigorously pursued domestically, and increasingly internationally, by the UK. In September 1988, Margaret

---

[185] See T Jaspers, 'Desirability of European Legislation in Particular Areas of Social Policy' in L Betten (ed) *The Future of European Social Policy* (Kluwer, Deventer, 1989) 53–81 at 74–5.
[186] 'The Social Dimension of the Internal Market', *Social Europe*, Special edn (European Communities, Luxembourg, 1988) p 73.
[187] Report to the Labour and Social Affairs Council, May 1987.
[188] *Opinion of the Economic and Social Committee on the Social Aspects of the Internal Market (European Social Area)* 19 Nov 1987, CES (87) 1069.
[189] 'The Social Dimension of the Internal Market', n 186 above, p 74.
[190] CES (87) 1069, n 188 above, para 1.5.
[191] *Ibid* para 1.6.

Thatcher set out her stall in her notable, perhaps notorious, address in Bruges when she warned that:[192]

We have not successfully rolled back the frontiers of the state in Britain only to see them re-imposed at European level; with a European super-state exercising a new dominance in Brussels.

A new and decisive phase of the period of 'Thatcherism Versus the Social Dimension'[193] had begun.

[192] Reported in *The Guardian*, 21 Sept 1988.
[193] B Hepple, 'Social Rights in the European Economic Community: A British Perspective' (1990) 11 *Comparative Labor Law Journal* 425 at 425.

4

The Community 'Social Charter'—
Catalyst for Action II

I INTRODUCTION: ONE OR TWO CHARTERS?

WHEN THE SINGLE European Act was signed, in the aftermath of the Commission's White Paper on the Internal Market, it appeared to be little more than a vehicle for implementing the 1992 programme through a limited application of qualified majority voting in the Council. In the preceding analysis, the social policy repercussions of the revised EEC Treaty, and its dynamic effects on the institutional and social policy actors, have been highlighted alongside its limitations. The substantive provisions of the SEA represented a further stepping-stone in the incremental process of social policy integration without challenging the orthodoxy of the social market/social rights dichotomy. Beneath the surface, however, there was room for development of a parallel strand of social policy rooted in an emerging conception of social citizenship. A vital clue can be found in the third recital of the preamble of the SEA, which declared that the Community was:

Determined to work together to promote democracy on the basis of fundamental rights recognised in the constitutions and laws of the Member States, in the Convention for the Protection of Human Rights and Fundamental Freedoms and the European Social Charter, notably freedom, equality and social justice.

Whilst this declaration may be regarded as essentially rhetorical,[1] weak enough to escape the attention of Mrs Thatcher's blue pencil, it helped to perpetuate a vision of Europe that transcended economic integration and recognised that without political integration there would always be a social rights deficit. As Poiares Maduro explains:[2]

---

[1] For comment, see L Betten, 'Prospects for a Social Policy of the European Community and its Impact on the Functioning of the European Social Charter' in L Betten (ed) *The Future of European Social Policy* (Kluwer, Deventer, 1989) 101–41 at 111. Betten argues that even though this is 'preamble language' the wording is considerably more precise than the original Treaty preamble and the specific reference to the ESC is important.

[2] See M Poiares Maduro, 'Striking the Elusive Balance Between Economic Freedom and Social Rights in the EU' in P Alston (ed) *The EU and Human Rights* (OUP, Oxford, 1999)

For those who argue in favour of a model of European integration restricted to economic integration, the goal is to maximise wealth (efficiency) through free trade and market integration. Social rights may be required, but only as a form of securing a level playing field and fair competition. For those who argue in favour of a model of political integration, wealth maximisation has to be complemented by some criterion of solidarity and distributive justice in the new political community. Social rights will be a requirement independent of fair competition and arising from membership of that political community.

Hitherto our analysis has been mainly confined to the development of social rights that are directly or indirectly linked to economic objectives. As we have seen in chapter 3, an increase in the pace of economic integration is not necessarily inimical to social objectives and can even be a catalyst for the establishment and further development of social rights.[3] Economic integration alone will not, however, secure social rights that are interdependent with but not dependent upon the market. This broader political vision, linked to an embryonic conception of a Community or Union citizenship, was first mooted in the European Parliament[4] and explained in the Tindemans Report of 1975 which concluded that:[5]

The gradual increase in the powers of the European institutions which will make itself felt while the Union is being built up, will make it imperative to ensure that rights and fundamental freedoms, including economic and social rights, are thus recognized and protected. In this the Union will find confirmation of its political objectives.

While an abortive attempt had been made to incorporate the European Convention on the Protection of Human Rights and Fundamental Freedoms (ECHR) into Community law in 1979,[6] it fell to the Belgian Presidency, in the first half of 1987,[7] to introduce the concept of a core of fundamental workers' rights that could provide the two sides of industry with a stable

---

449–72 at 466. See also, Lord Wedderburn, 'European Community Law and Workers' Rights: Fact or Fake in 1992?' (1991) 13 *Dublin University Law Journal* 1.

[3] Reich has described this process as 'social statisation' or *Versozialstaatlichung*, whereby the Community has approached policies at the fringes of traditional social policy, such as equal opportunities and health protection, in an interventionist fashion. See N Reich, *Schutzpolitik in der Europäischen Gemeinschaft in Spannungsfeld von Rechtsschutznormen und institutioneller Integration* (Hennies und Zinkeisen, Hanover, 1988) at 7. Cited by S Leibfried and P Pierson, 'Prospects for Social Europe' (1992) 20 *Politics & Society* 333 at 335.

[4] European Parliament Resolution of 10 July 1975 on a 'Charter of the Rights of the Peoples of the European Community', OJ 1975, C179/28.

[5] COM(75) 481, *Bulletin of the European Communities Supplement* 1/76, p 26.

[6] Commission Memorandum of 4 April 1979, *Bulletin of the European Communities Supplement* 2/79, p 5. See K Economides and J Weiler, 'Accession of the Communities to the European Convention on Human Rights: Commission Memorandum' (1979) 42 *Modern Law Review* 683.

[7] Report of the Social Affairs Council, May 1987.

and common foundation for bargaining. This offered a limited notion of what might be achieved, but what was now required, in the context of the SEA preamble, was a much more rounded and intellectually sustainable case for incorporating a social citizenship agenda into the internal market process itself. A decisive step in this direction came from the Economic and Social Committee, in its 'Beretta Report' of September 1987.[8] The Committee, having analysed the need for progress in areas such as the length of working time, work organisation and the need to restructure the labour market in response to technological changes, concluded that there was a pressing need for basic social rules to avoid market distortions and provide a stable basis for social dialogue.[9]

The Committee recommended the adoption of a framework directive setting out 'inalienable basic social rights' inspired not only by existing Commission proposals but also sourced from International Labour Organisation (ILO) declarations, the ECHR and the European Social Charter (ESC).[10] In a subsequent Opinion, in February 1989, the Committee referred to a whole raft of international obligations endorsed by the Member States to draw attention to the need for such a guarantee to be aimed not at establishing new rules, but as a way of taking account of existing rules already agreed at other levels. They specifically rejected the idea of a separate Community Social Charter.[11] It was left to the Commission to decide whether to pursue the idea of a Social Charter further.

One of the options open to the Commission at this stage would have been to propose the direct incorporation of the ESC into Community law either as a Treaty amendment or in the form of a directive.[12] This option carried a number of attractions in the late 1980s and, indeed, remains valid today because, although there is now an explicit reference to the ESC and 'fundamental social rights' in the revised EC Treaty,[13] it is purely rhetorical. Moreover, as we shall see in chapter 12, the Charter of Fundamental Rights of the European Union, proclaimed in December 2000, which also draws heavily on the ESC, is non-binding.[14]

First, all Member States of the Community have also been members of the Council of Europe from its formation in 1949 and are contracting parties to the ESC, which is long established as an international instrument of fundamental social rights, having been signed in Turin in 1961, effective

---

[8] Doc CES 225/87. Beretta was the *rapporteur* for the Committee which adopted an Opinion endorsing the report at its meeting of 19 Nov 1987, Doc CES 1069/87.

[9] Doc CES 1069/87, *ibid* para 1.5.

[10] *Ibid* para 2.1.

[11] Doc CES 270/89, 22 Feb 1989.

[12] See Betten in Betten, n 1 above at 122.

[13] Art 136 EC urges the Community and the Member States to have fundamental social rights, such as those in the ESC and the Community Social Charter, in mind when seeking to fulfil their social policy objectives.

[14] OJ 2000, C364/1.

in international law from 1965 and subsequently revised in 1996.[15] As contracting parties of the ESC the Member States have committed themselves to 'pursue by all appropriate means' the effective realisation of the 19 rights contained in the original ESC.[16] The ESC is concerned with economic and social rights as distinct from the ECHR, which guarantees civil and political rights. Although this is not always an easy distinction, it mirrors the separation at the level of universal rights maintained through the adoption of two United Nations International Covenants on, respectively, Economic, Social and Cultural Rights,[17] and Civil and Political Rights.[18] There would therefore be logic to incorporating the ESC into Community law as an accepted foundation of *European* fundamental social rights. This would also help to address the notion of a separate European approach to human rights generally and social rights in particular.[19]

Second, by incorporating the ESC, the Community would be accepting a broad conception of social rights that extends beyond rights linked directly to an employment relationship. This can be demonstrated by distinguishing between specific workers' rights contained in the ESC and other provisions that reflect social citizenship values and apply to all citizens irrespective of their employment status. For example the core workers' rights in the ESC include, inter alia:

—the right to work (Article 1);
—the right to just conditions of work (Article 2);
—the right to safe and healthy working conditions (Article 3);
—the right of workers to a fair remuneration (Article 4);
—the right to organise (Article 5);

---

[15] 529 UNTS No 89. The original ESC has been extended by Protocols issued in 1988, 1991 and 1995; now consolidated in the revised ESC adopted on 1–4 April 1996 (Council of Europe, Strasbourg, 2000). The Revised ESC entered into force in July 1999. As of 1 June 2001, three EU Member States had ratified the revised Charter: France, Ireland and Sweden. Seven others had indicated an intention to ratify: Belgium, Denmark, Finland, Greece, Italy, Portugal and the UK: <http://www.humanrights.coe.int/cseweb/GB/index.htm>. For further discussion, see D Harris, *The European Social Charter*, 8th edn (University of Virginia Press, Charlottesville, 1984); O Kahn-Freund, 'The European Social Charter' in F Jacobs (ed) *European Law and the Individual* (North-Holland, Amsterdam, 1976) 181–211; L Betten and N Grief, *EU Law and Human Rights* (Longman, Harlow, 1998) pp 42–52; N Casey, 'The European Social Charter and Revised European Social Charter' in C Costello (ed) *Fundamental Social Rights: Current Legal Protection and the Challenge of the EU Charter of Fundamental Rights* (Irish Centre for European Law, Dublin, 2001) 55–75; and V Shrubsall, 'The Additional Protocol to the European Social Charter—Employment Rights' (1989) 18 *Industrial Law Journal* 39.

[16] Art 20 ESC.

[17] 999 UNTS No 3. For analysis, see M Craven, *The International Covenant on Economic, Social and Cultural Rights* (Clarendon Press, Oxford, 1995).

[18] 999 UNTS No 171. Both Covenants were adopted in 1966.

[19] See C Leben, 'Is there a European Approach to Human Rights?' in Alston ed, n 2 above, 69–97. Leben argues that the notion of a European approach to human rights can be traced back to the age of enlightenment, notably the Glorious Revolution in England in 1689 and, most emphatically, the French Revolution of 1789.

—the right to bargain collectively (Article 6);
—the right of employed women to protection (Article 8);
—the right of migrant workers and their families to protection and assistance (Article 19).

Social citizenship rights include, inter alia:

—the right of children and young persons to protection (Article 7);
—the right to protection of health (Article 11);
—the right to social security (Article 12);
—the right to social and medical assistance (Article 13);
—the right to benefit from social welfare services (Article 14);
—the right of the family to social, legal and economic protection (Article 16).

Whilst the original version of the ESC contained some notable gaps: for example, rights to housing, rights to protection against poverty and social exclusion, the right of the elderly to social protection and other employment rights added later by three protocols adopted between 1988 and 1995;[20] it came close to fulfilling Marshall's classic definition of social citizenship encompassing:[21]

... the whole range from the right to a modicum of economic welfare and security to the right to share to the full in the social heritage and to live the life of a civilised being according to the standards prevailing in society.

Third, incorporation of the ESC into Community law would simultaneously avoid the problem of overlapping and even contradictory rights and the potential for conflict between Council of Europe and Community Charters.[22] It would also have the advantage of elevating the status of the ESC, described by Kahn-Freund as a 'big footnote' to the ECHR.[23] While the ESC creates positive legal obligations on the contracting parties in international law, its provisions are not self-executing or directly effective in the Member States of the Council of Europe. Without incorporation into domestic law it has, at most, a 'reflex effect'[24] as a source of law in the Member States and also, perhaps more importantly, for the Community. As Kahn-Freund explains, the ESC provides a general principle of Community

---

[20] Additional employment rights include, inter alia: the right to protection in cases of termination of employment; the right to information and consultation; the right to equal opportunities and equal treatment in employment. The additional rights are contained in Arts 20–31 of the Revised ESC.

[21] T Marshall, *Social Policy* (Hutchinson, London, 1975) p 7. See further, T Hervey, *European Social Law and Policy* (Longman, Harlow, 1998).

[22] See Betten in Betten, n 1 above at 126–28.

[23] Kahn-Freund, n 15 above at 182.

[24] *Ibid* at 184. See, generally, R Rogowski and T Wilthagen (eds) *Reflexive Labour Law* (Kluwer, Deventer, 1994).

law for interpretation by the Court of Justice that 'crystallises'[25] into a legal rule at Community level, but only where there is a link with Community competence. The European Court of Human Rights has no jurisdiction over the ESC and there is no executive, akin to the European Commission of Human Rights. Instead, an expert body, the European Committee of Social Rights, undertakes supervision of the ESC, and now the Revised ESC.[26] Incorporation of the ESC into Community law would make it supranational, overcoming its operative limitations within the Council of Europe structure, whilst leaving the supervisory mechanisms intact.[27]

There are a number of reasons why incorporation of the ESC was not pursued at this time and remains an open question today. First, many important social citizenship and employment rights, such as rights to education and housing and the general non-discrimination clause, were not part of the 1961 Charter, leaving important gaps in coverage. Second, there was the problem of Treaty competence. Incorporation was only possible by way of a Treaty amendment or Community legislation derived from the general powers provisions in Article 308 EC [ex 235 EEC]. As both routes required unanimity among the Member States, incorporation was, in practice, a nonstarter because of the implacable opposition of the UK to the expansion of Community social policy during this period. Moreover, the use of Article 308 EC, in the context of the social provisions applicable at the time of the SEA, would have required a request to the Court for an opinion on the compatibility of any envisaged agreement with the Treaty under the procedure in Article 300(6) EC [ex 228(6) EEC]. Although the issue had not been tested at the time, such a request would almost certainly have stopped the process in its tracks. Indeed, when the Council raised a similar question, concerning accession of the Community to the ECHR, the Court's answer was resoundingly negative.[28] Third, the Community has its own legal per-

---

[25] Kahn-Freund, *ibid* at 197–98.
[26] Following the amending Protocol of 1991 this body replaced the original Committee of Independent Experts, a move intended to increase the experts' status and power. See further, Casey, n 15 above.
[27] See Betten in Betten, n 1 above, p 134.
[28] *Opinion 2/94* [1996] ECR I–1759. The Court's judgment was based on the notion of conferred powers and the duty of the Community to act within those powers under Art 3b [now 5] EC. Although the Treaty on European Union, 1993, added Art 5 EC, the notion of conferred powers can be derived directly from Art 308 EC [ex 235 EEC], which only permits action to further 'one of the objectives of the Community'. The Court concluded: 'no Treaty provision confers on the Community institutions any general powers to enact rules on human rights or to conclude international conventions in this field' (para 27). Art 308 EC could not be used as the basis for the adoption of provisions whose effect would, in substance, be to amend the Treaty without following the procedure that it provides for that purpose (para 30). Such a modification would be of constitutional significance and beyond the scope of Art 308 EC (para 35). For discussion, see *The Human Rights Opinion of the ECJ and its Constitutional Implications* (CELS Occasional Paper No 1, Cambridge, 1996); G Gaja, 'Opinion 2/94, Accession by the Communities to the European Convention for the Protection of Human Rights and Fundamental Freedoms' (1996) 33 *Common Market Law Review* 973; and Betten and Grief, n 15 above, pp 111–23.

sonality[29] and is conscious of the separate legal personality and territorial coverage of other international institutions. This has led to sensitivity and caution whenever proposals have been put forward to adopt or incorporate rights or obligations derived from other international sources of law.[30]

In the event, the Commission decided to press ahead, in May 1989,[31] with its own proposal for a Community Social Charter and, following the publication of a further draft,[32] a final amended text was issued by 11 of the then 12 Member States as a non-binding 'solemn declaration' at the Strasbourg European Council on 9 December 1989.[33] The Community Charter of Fundamental Social Rights of Workers was born.[34] In anticipation of the Council's decision, the Commission had, two weeks earlier, published an Action Programme[35] containing 47 initiatives[36] designed to ensure the early implementation of the 'most urgent aspects'[37] of the principles set out in the Charter.

The remainder of the chapter will be broken down into two sections. First, there will be an overview of the evolution of the Social Charter and an assessment, in the light of the Charter's non-binding status, of its ambitions and legal scope. Secondly, there will be an analysis of the specific fundamental social rights contained within the Charter and the proposals in the Commission's accompanying Action Programme.

II THE EVOLUTION AND LEGAL SCOPE OF THE COMMUNITY SOCIAL CHARTER

(1) Citizens' Rights or Workers' Rights?

The Commission's draft proposals of May and September 1989 called for the adoption of a 'Community Charter of Fundamental Social Rights'. The

---

[29] Art 281 EC [ex 210 EEC].

[30] See, for example, the 'Simitis Report' on *Affirming Fundamental Rights in the European Union Time to Act* (European Commission, Brussels, 1999). A group of legal experts, appointed by the Commission, called for recognition of both economic and social rights contained in the ECHR, the ESC and ILO conventions and concluded, at p 17, that all rights should be set out in a single text to be inserted into the Treaties. For further discussion, see ch 12.

[31] COM(89) 248, reproduced in *Social Europe* 1/90, pp 92–6.

[32] COM(89) 471, reproduced in *Social Europe* 1/90, pp 97–101.

[33] The UK refused to sign the Charter. For Mrs Thatcher, commenting on the first draft, it was 'more like a socialist Charter'. House of Commons, *Official Report*, vol 153, col 474, 18 May 1989. See B Hepple, 'Social Rights in the European Community: A British Perspective' (1990) 11 *Comparative Labor Law Journal* 425 at 425.

[34] Luxembourg: European Communities, 1990. The text of the Charter is reproduced in *Social Europe* 1/90, pp 46–50. For contemporary assessments, see B Bercusson, 'The European Community's Charter of the Fundamental Social Rights of Workers' (1990) 53 *Modern Law Review* 624; B Hepple, 'The Implementation of the Community Charter of Fundamental Social Rights' (1990) 53 *Modern Law Review* 643; and P Watson, 'The Community Social Charter' (1991) 28 *Common Market Law Review* 37.

[35] COM(89) 568, 29 Nov 1989, reproduced in *Social Europe* 1/90, pp 52–76.

[36] *Ibid Social Europe* 1/90, pp 52–3.

[37] *Ibid* at 54.

title of the proposed Charter echoed the language of the second Opinion of the Economic and Social Committee on 'Basic Community Social Rights',[38] but whereas the Committee had sought a guarantee of fundamental social rights that were part of the common heritage and values of the Member States, a 'European social model',[39] they had rejected the notion of a Charter, reflecting a widely shared concern about potential conflict and confusion with the ESC.[40] The Commission's draft Charter, while also drawing inspiration from ILO Conventions and the ESC, offered its own enumeration of fundamental social rights for *citizens*.[41] By offering social rights to all 'citizens' the Commission were seeking a wide definition of social rights that transcended nationality and extended beyond the employment relationship. Hence, under the Commission's proposals, all 'citizens' were to have rights to adequate social protection, an income in retirement, education and training.[42] The draft also took account of the 'socially excluded'; noting that one of the priority objectives in the economic and social field is to combat unemployment.[43] This approach, if fully implemented, would have guaranteed a wider range of rights than those contained within the ESC and provided a foundation for a European 'social state' (*Sozialstaat*)[44] because constitutionalising social citizenship rights would create a 'European sphere of entitlements to a decent livelihood'.[45]

The Community's heightened emphasis on social citizenship and social inclusion was not to last, at least in the short term. Although the second Commission draft had reinforced references to the social rights of citizens,[46] the French Presidency of the Council presented a drastically revised draft at Strasbourg that formed the basis for the final text. Most specifically, the title of the document had been changed to the 'Community Charter of the Fundamental Social Rights *of Workers*'.[47] Every reference in the draft to 'citizens' had been deleted and replaced with 'workers' or 'persons'. Even though the UK had dissented from the final text, the other 11 Member States were only prepared to define a social dimension that granted rights

---

[38] Doc CES 270/89, 22 Feb 1989.

[39] *Ibid* para 12.

[40] See, especially, Betten in Betten, n 1 above at 126.

[41] COM(89) 248, 31 May 1989, para 5 of the draft preamble.

[42] *Ibid* Title I, draft points 9,13 and 22.

[43] *Ibid* para 3 of the draft preamble.

[44] See Leibfried and Pierson, n 3 above at 336; and Hepple (1990, *Modern Law Review*) n 34 above, who explains, at 653, that the notion of a *Sozialstaat* is derived from the German public law principle of 'social government based on the rule of law', Art 28(1) of the Basic Law, and also Art 20 thereof, which defines Germany as a 'social Federal State'. In essence, the *Sozialstaat* requires the state to create a just social order.

[45] Leibfried and Pierson, *ibid*.

[46] COM(89) 471, reproduced in *Social Europe* 1/90, pp 97–101.

[47] For a very useful comparison between the draft and the final text, see Annex 1 of the Fourth Report of the Employment Committee of the House of Commons Session 1990–91, *The European Community Social Charter* (HMSO, London, 1991).

to workers.[48] References to combating unemployment and social exclusion were struck out or watered down.[49] Hence the Charter protects workers who are not citizens but not citizens who are not workers.[50] Such an idiosyncratic outcome can be put down, in part, to the inevitable machinations and compromises that take place at the level of the European Council. This would be a comfortable conclusion to draw but a partial one. A more convincing explanation is that this push for social citizenship was premature for three main reasons.

First, the distinction between workers and citizens was reconcilable with the goals of the French Presidency that sought, as a priority, to achieve a Community policy for workers, represented by their trade unions. A bridge could be built between the French approach and that of the Federal Republic of Germany for a Community 'social market' based on policies that support allocative efficiency and optimum levels of production at national level.[51] Secondly, there was no Treaty foundation for moving further because, at this stage, there was no reference to citizenship of any kind in either the original EEC Treaty or the SEA. Third, it followed that the conditions had not yet been created for a European *Sozialstaat* where the tenets that drive national social policy—public health, education, housing and social protection—could be at the forefront of a *Community* social policy.[52] For instance, the Charter promotes health protection and safety at the workplace,[53] but not public health[54] and a minimum age of employment for children,[55] but not education.[56] Workers had a clearly established status in Community law as

[48] See Bercusson (1990, *Modern Law Review*) n 34 above at 626–27; and E Whiteford, 'W(h)ither Social Policy?' in J Shaw and G More (eds) *New Legal Dynamics of European Union* (Clarendon Press, Oxford, 1995) 111–28 at 117. As Whiteford notes: 'while the UK objections to Community actions in the social field appear to have been consistent and predictable, the positions taken by other member states diverge significantly from their public affirmation of support for the social dimension'.

[49] The reference to unemployment in para 3 of the draft preamble was excised altogether. Moreover, para 7 of the draft preamble referred to the need to combat 'every form of social exclusion'. The final text merely stated that 'it is important to combat social exclusion', para 8.

[50] House of Commons Report, n 33 above, paras 52–4. There are several references in the Charter to rights extending to 'every worker of the European Community' (points 1, 8, 9, 10, 11, 15 and 24). There is no apparent restriction concerning nationality or citizenship. Indeed, the preamble explicitly provides for equal treatment of workers who are legally resident nationals of non-member countries and members of their families (para 9).

[51] See J Story, 'Social Europe: Ariadne's Thread' (1990) 13 *Journal of European Integration* 151 at 155–60.

[52] See M Kleinman and D Piachaud, 'European Social Policy: Conceptions and Choices' (1993) 3 *Journal of European Social Policy* 1.

[53] Point 19.

[54] Kleinman and Piachaud, n 52 above at 3–4. The authors define 'allocative efficiency' as a socially efficient level of public services, such as health care and education. It follows that socially efficient state provision creates the ingredients for high levels of productivity and output from a well educated, highly trained and healthy workforce.

[55] Point 20.

[56] Kleinman and Piachaud, n 52 above at 3. The European Parliament had earlier proposed that these areas should be included in the Charter: EP Doc A2-399/88.

'market citizens' but the 'European citizen' had not yet been conceived.[57] This distinction, as it existed pre-Maastricht, was neatly summarised by Judge Mancini in his 1989 address at Harvard University where he observed that:[58]

The Treaty does not safeguard the fundamental rights of individuals affected by its application, nor does it recognise, even in an embryonic form, a constitutional right to European citizenship. Europe cannot confer citizenship: this remains the prerogative of the Member States. By the same token, individual citizens of a Member State are entitled to move from their State to another Member State exclusively by virtue of their being workers, self-employed persons or providers of services, that is *qua* units of a production factor.

Therefore, by deleting all references to citizens from the Charter, and by implication any connotations of a nascent European citizenship, the Member States were reaffirming the boundaries of Community law as they stood at the time. Citizenship had to be understood as purely a national construct and the very possibility of ambiguity predicated that the rights in the Charter had to be confined to workers. The Member States would have been wary that the very notion of 'social citizenship' carries with it ideas of entitlements and guarantees. As Everson explains, when discussing Marshall's classic citizenship thesis[59] and Dahrendorf's reformulation thereof,[60] citizenship is best understood as a 'status' because:[61]

Within this reformulation it is the notion of 'entitlement by right' which consequently creates the 'status' of citizenship; a status which is constitutive of the person, attaching to each and every individual regardless of his or her personal attributes or the prevailing labour or market conditions.

For those advocating a European *Sozialstaat* the development of social citizenship based on a foundation of social entitlements is a *sine qua non*. Indeed a powerful analogy can be drawn with the role of social policy in integrating the Nineteenth Century European nation-state.[62] Paradoxically,

---

[57] See M Everson, 'The Legacy of the Market Citizen' in Shaw and More, n 48 above, 73–90. For comment, see Poiares Maduro, n 2 above at 462.

[58] G Mancini, 'The Making of a Constitution for Europe' (1989) 26 *Common Market Law Review* 595 at 596.

[59] T Marshall, *Citizenship and Social Class and Other Essays* (CUP, Cambridge, 1950). Marshall regards the citizen as sovereign. The sovereign citizen is entitled to respect as an autonomous being and inclusion in the disposal of state power. See Everson, n 57 above, at 82–3.

[60] R Dahrendorf, *Der Moderne Soziale Konflikt* (DVA, Stuttgart, 1992).

[61] Everson, n 57 above at 83.

[62] G Majone, 'The European Community Between Social Policy and Social Regulation' (1993) 31 *Journal of Common Market Studies* 153 at 159. In Majone's view this analogy is dubious not least because, at the time, entrepreneurs were only persuaded to support the establishment of the social state in return for a promise of greater protectionism against foreign imports. Such a bargain, Majone notes at 159, 'would hardly be possible under present circumstances'.

it is precisely for this reason that the Member States have consistently rejected such an approach. From the perspective of the Member States, they have already established successful welfare states at national level and, as Majone[63] notes, it is this very success that sets limits to an expanded social policy competence of the Community. The same argument applies even in the light of welfare reform and modernisation of the social state. Indeed with greater involvement of civil society in the co-ordination or provision of welfare, or to use Streeck's terminology, 'neo-voluntarism',[64] the prospect for harmonisation either as a method or as a goal becomes weaker. Moreover, even the Commission, while asserting the rhetoric of social citizenship in the drafts of the Charter, was able to recognise the inherent limitations of this concept in the context of the Treaties and political realities. The Commission's 1989 Action Programme baldly states:[65]

The social security schemes vary greatly in nature from one Member State of the Community to another. They reflect the history, traditions and social and cultural practices proper to each Member State, which cannot be called into question. There can therefore be no question of harmonizing the systems existing in these fields.

Hence, by restricting the reach of the Charter to workers, the Member States were reinforcing the existing balance between national and Community competence while, at the same time, seeking to create a Community vehicle for establishing targeted minimum levels of employment, or employment-related, rights at national level, primarily to protect health and safety and combat social dumping, without opening up the possibility of apparently limitless *personal social rights* falling within the purview of the Community. This approach ensured that there could be no immediate possibility of a 'spill-over' from social-market rights for workers to social rights for citizens.[66] The Charter is therefore firmly placed within the social dimension of the Internal Market for, as Hervey explains, 'Community provisions are constructed according to their universalist "social" function only where to do so actually serves a latent "market" ideology'.[67] The Member States

---

[63] *Ibid* at 159–63.
[64] W Streeck, 'Neo-Voluntarism: A New European Social Policy Regime?' (1995) 1 *European Law Journal* 31 at 52. According to Streeck: 'Neo-voluntarism in social policy represents a break with the practice of the European welfare state to create 'hard', legally enforceable status rights and obligations for individual citizens and organized collectives acting in, taking advantage of, and being disadvantaged by market relations. Compared to welfare state interventionism, neo-voluntarism is *much less statist*, reflecting the European Union's lack of State capacity'.
[65] *Social Europe* 1/90, p 64. See Majone, n 62 above at 161.
[66] See Streeck, n 64 above at 45.
[67] T Hervey, 'Migrant workers and their families in the European Union: the pervasive market ideology of Community law' in Shaw and More, n 48 above, 91–110 at 110. See also, Majone, n 62 above, who argues, at 156, that 'measures proposed by the Commission in the social field must be compatible with the "economic constitution" of the Community, that is, with the principles of a liberal economic order'.

augmented this position, as we shall see, by ensuring that the Charter has a non-binding status and operates only in strict accordance with the principle of subsidiarity.

The final text is a messy compromise. The Commission's draft, although severely bullet-ridden, remained partially intact. Clauses drafted in the context of social citizenship had to be reconciled with revisions that reasserted the social dimension as an aspect of the 'internal market'. The thirteenth recital of the preamble is a case in point. The final text reads as follows:[68]

Whereas its aim is ... to declare solemnly that the implementation of the Single European Act must *take full account of the social dimension of the Community and that it is necessary in this context to ensure at the appropriate levels* the development of the social rights of *workers* of the European Community, especially *employed* workers and self-employed persons.

The Commission's September draft had read:[69]

Whereas its aim is ... to declare solemnly that the implementation of the Single European Act *must be accompanied, either at Community level or at the level of the Member State or of their constituent parts, by* the development of the social rights of *citizens* of the European Community, especially workers and self-employed persons.

The outcome is deeply ambiguous. Bercusson argues that to 'take full account of the social dimension' necessarily implies that implementation should be '*not* of the internal market only'.[70] He concludes that this is a 'fundamental guideline for both the Commission and the Court in interpreting the Charter'.[71] Therefore, providing the Commission's proposals are within the Community's area of competence,[72] a dynamic implementation of the Charter is possible notwithstanding the apparent limitation of the social dimension to 'employed workers and self-employed persons'. In order to explore this further let us first consider the preliminary question of who is a 'worker' under Community law before proceeding to examine the social rights that the Charter seeks to guarantee for these workers.

For the purposes of Community law there are two discrete conceptions of a worker. First, in the context of free movement of workers *between* Member States, a worker must be a 'Community worker' pursuing an eco-

---

[68] Words added to the final text are in italics.
[69] COM(89) 471. Words deleted are in italics.
[70] Bercusson (1990) *Modern Law Review*, n 34 above at 625.
[71] *Ibid.*
[72] A requirement stipulated in point 28 of the Charter.

nomic activity.[73] As the Court explained in *Hoekstra*[74] the definition of a 'worker', for the purposes of Articles 39–42 EC [ex 48–51 EEC], is a matter for the Community and not the Member States to determine, for otherwise the Community rules on free movement of workers would be undermined because Member States would be able to unilaterally answer the question 'who is a worker?' National laws could then be used to exclude certain categories or groups of persons from Community protection. In seeking to explain the Community concept of a 'worker' the Court, in *Lawrie-Blum*,[75] held that the definition of 'worker' must be based on objective criteria that distinguish the employment relationship by reference to the rights and duties of the persons concerned. The essential feature of an employment relationship is that for a certain period of time a person performs services for and under the direction of another person in return for remuneration.[76] The Court had earlier decided, in *Levin*,[77] that part-time work is capable of being a 'genuine and effective' economic activity of an employed person, as distinct from activities that are merely marginal and ancillary.[78] For a large number of persons such employment constitutes 'an effective means of improving their living conditions'.[79] Therefore, so long as there is a clear and dominant economic purpose to the activity, and an employment relationship based on subordination while those activities are being carried out, the individual is a worker for the purposes of Community law and entitled to equal treatment with nationals of the State in question and all the consequential rights arising from Articles 39–42 EC.[80] Moreover, these rights must be applied not only to a Community worker, but extended also, by

---

[73] Case 13/76, *Donà v Mantero* [1976] ECR 1333. For the purposes of the interpretative Regulation 1612/68/EEC, OJ 1968, L257/2, any Community national has, under Art 39 EC [ex 48 EEC], the right to take up and pursue 'an activity as an employed person', Art 1(1). Note, however, the broader reach of Reg 1408/71/EEC, OJ 1971, L149/2 [now amended and consolidated as Reg 118/97/EC, OJ 1997, L28/1] which applies national social security schemes to 'employed' and 'self-employed' *persons* and to members of their families moving within the Community.

[74] Case 75/63, *Hoekstra (née Unger) v Bestuur der Bedrijfsvereniging voor Detailhandel en Ambachten* [1964] ECR 177 at 184.

[75] Case 66/85, *Lawrie-Blum v Land Baden-Württemberg* [1986] ECR 2121.

[76] *Ibid* para 16.

[77] Case 53/81, *Levin v Staatssecretaris van Justitie* [1982] ECR 1035.

[78] *Ibid* para 17. For example if the main purpose of the activity is rehabilitation or reintegration into society, Case 344/87, *Bettray v Staatssecretaris van Justitie* [1989] ECR 1637; or education, Case 197/86, *Brown v Secretary of State for Scotland* [1988] ECR 3205. For a broader approach, see Case 196/87, *Steymann v Staatssecretaris van Justitie* [1988] ECR 6159; and Case 39/86, *Lair v Universität Hannover* [1988] ECR 3161.

[79] *Levin, ibid* para 15. For an example of the application of this test, see Case 139/85, *Kempf v Staatssecretaris van Justitie* [1986] ECR 1741, where the Court held that a part-time worker, who was earning less than the minimum level of subsistence as defined by national law, was included within the Community's meaning of a worker even though they needed to have recourse to state social protection.

[80] See C Barnard, *EC Employment Law*, 2nd edn (OUP, Oxford, 2000) ch 3.

virtue of Regulation 1612/68,[81] to the worker's spouse[82] and children under the age of 21, or dependant children, even if they are not nationals of a Member State.[83]

The second conception of a 'worker' in the Community is a wholly national one arising on implementation of Community law into national law and the interpretation thereof by national courts. On the one hand, certain specific measures guaranteeing *transnational* rights for workers will be allied to the Community notion of a worker, as in the case of the Posted Workers Directive, 96/71,[84] based on the Treaty provisions concerning the free movement of services.[85] On the other hand, the vast majority of social policy measures are primarily concerned with the rights of workers *within* Member States and are based on the specific social policy provisions in the EC Treaty.[86] In respect of these measures the question of who is a 'worker' or an 'employed person' is normally a matter of national law. In addition, while any social rights for workers contained in these directives must be extended to the nationals of other Member States, it is for each Member State, when implementing the directive in question within its own territory, to determine who are its own nationals[87] and whether any non-Community nationals are legally resident, subject to any directly effective provisions of Community association agreements with 'third countries'.[88]

As we have seen in chapter 2, Member States are granted considerable flexibility when implementing Community directives in the social policy field. For example, the framework Health and Safety Directive[89] and the

---

[81] OJ 1968, L257/2.

[82] The term 'spouse' has been narrowly defined to include married couples but not co-habitees, Case 59/85, *Netherlands v Reed* [1986] ECR 1283; nor, in the context of the Community's Staff Regulations, same-sex couples, Case T–264/97, *D and Sweden v Council* [1999] ECR–SC I–A 1 and II–1, para 26, and on appeal, Cases C–122/99P and 125/99P [2001] ECR I–4139. For discussion, see C McGlynn, 'A Family Law for the European Union?' in J Shaw (ed) *Social Law and Policy in an Evolving European Union* (Hart, Oxford, 2000) 223–41.

[83] Art 11 of Reg 1612/68, OJ 1968, L257/2.

[84] OJ 1996, L18/1.

[85] Arts 47(2) and 55 EC [ex 57(2) and 66 EEC]. The idea behind the Directive is to facilitate the provision of workers employed in one Member State, the home state, to employers based in another Member State, the host state, typically through sub-contracting of public or private sector work programmes.

[86] Originally Arts 117–122 EEC [now Arts 136–145 EC].

[87] See Case C–369/90, *Micheletti v Delegación del Gobierno en Cantabria* [1992] ECR I–4239.

[88] Workers' rights to free movement and consequential benefits under these agreements are usually quite limited. See Case C–192/89, *Sevince v Staatssecretaris van Justitie* [1990] ECR I–3461; Case 12/86, *Demirel v Stadt Schwäbisch Gmünd* [1987] ECR 3719. Workers have been successful in several cases; see Case C–18/90, *Onem v Kziber* [1991] ECR I–199; Case C–58/93, *Yousfi v Belgium* [1994] ECR I–1353; and Case C–126/95, *Hallouzi-Choho* [1996] ECR I–4807, all on the EEC-Morocco Co-operation Agreement. For further discussion on the direct effect of provisions contained in these agreements, see P Craig and G de Búrca, *EU Law: Text, Cases and Materials*, 2nd edn (OUP, Oxford, 1998) pp 179–85.

[89] Dir 89/391/EEC, OJ 1989, L183/1.

Working Time Directive[90] include all 'workers' within their ambit. In the case of the framework Directive, a 'worker' is defined in Article 3 as 'any person employed by an employer, including trainees and apprentices' but bizarrely, 'excluding domestic servants'. No express room for manoeuvre is left to the implementing Member State but, in the absence of a Community definition of a 'person employed by an employer', it must be implicit that this is a matter for national law. There is no separate definition of a 'worker' in the Working Time Directive, although it is derived from the framework Directive and Article 118a EEC [now 137 EC], which refers to the 'health and safety of workers'.[91] Outside the field of health and safety, Community social policy directives have tended to limit their scope to 'employees' with a 'contract of employment or employment relationship', or, in the case of the equalities directives, refer only to 'employment'. A standard clause usually specifies that the precise nature of the contract of employment or employment relationship is a matter for national law. For example, the scope of Directive 91/533[92] on the right of employees to be informed about 'the essential aspects' of their 'contract or employment relationship'[93] is circumscribed by Article 1(1), which sets out the following definition:

This Directive shall apply to every paid employee having a contract or employment relationship defined by the law in force in a Member State and/or governed by the law in a Member State.

Bercusson[94] suggests that inclusion of the term 'employment relationship' implies that the Directive's coverage may extend to independent contractors and self-employed workers paid by the 'employer'. In his view:[95]

The use of the term 'relationship' requires EU law to take cognisance of a multitude of forms of work which never acquire contractual status, but are nonetheless carried out in the expectation of some form of reciprocal benefit, which may fall short of the common law concept of contractual 'consideration'.

This interpretation suggests that the Community will ultimately determine the scope of the 'employment relationship'. Article 6 of the Directive, however, militates against such a broad interpretation. This sweeping-up clause states that the Directive shall be 'without prejudice' to national law

[90] Dir 93/104/EC concerning certain aspects of the organisation of working time, OJ 1993, L307/18.

[91] Art 137(1) EC now refers to 'workers' health and safety'. See also, Dir 92/85/EEC on the introduction of measures to encourage improvements in the safety and health at work of pregnant workers and workers who have recently given birth or breastfeeding, OJ 1992, L348/1; and Dir 94/33/EC on the protection of young people at work, OJ 1993, L216/12.

[92] Dir 91/533/EEC on an employer's obligation to inform employees of conditions applicable to the contract or employment relationship, OJ 1991, L288/32.

[93] *Ibid* Art 2(1).

[94] See B Bercusson, *European Labour Law* (Butterworths, London, 1996) p 431.

[95] *Ibid*.

and practice concerning 'the form of the contract or employment relation-ship'. Thus, Article 6 creates a hierarchy of norms at the head of which rests a national conception of the term 'contract or employment relationship'.[96]

What then is the significance of national law prevailing over Community law in respect of the interpretation of terms such as 'worker', 'employee', 'contract of employment' or 'employment relationship' in Community directives? Kleinman and Piachaud assume that employed nationals of Member States 'obviously qualify'.[97] In practice the position is not quite so straightforward. For example, in certain Member States, such as Italy, civil servants have 'public-law status' which takes them outside the scope of 'employment law', a view recently accepted by the Court when determin-ing the scope of the Acquired Rights Directive.[98]

Zeijen, in a 1992 study for the Commission,[99] considered the definition of the term 'contract of employment'[100] in the Member States and concluded that:[101]

The conventional elements in the definition of contract of employment common to all Member States are: agreement, work performance, length of time, remuneration and, most importantly, dependency, subordination and control. The latter issues are the subject of increasingly flexible interpretation by the courts.

In general it appears that the legal concept of contract of employment in continen-tal Member States is broader and more comprehensive than that in Ireland and the United Kingdom ...

In the United Kingdom, for instance, one third of those in employment—such as 'casual' workers and temporary workers supplied through an intermediary—is excluded from statutory employment rights.

This statement is borne out by more recent evidence from the House of Lords in the UK where, in *Carmichael and another v National Power*,[102] it

---

[96] See further, J Kenner, 'Statement or Contract?—Some Reflections on the EC Employee Information (Contract or Employment Relationship) Directive after *Kampelmann*' (1999) 28 *Industrial Law Journal* 205 at 217–18.

[97] Kleinman and Piachaud, n 52 above at 15.

[98] Dir 77/187/EC, OJ 1977, L61/26. See Case C–343/98, *Collino and Chiappero v Telecom Italia SpA* [2000] ECR I–6659, paras 36–41.

[99] H Zeijen, 'Part I. The Regulation of Individual Employment Relationships'. Reproduced in *Social Europe* 4/92 (European Commission, Brussels, 1992). See R Nielsen, *European Labour Law* (DJØF Publishing, Copenhagen, 2000) p 144.

[100] For a fascinating history, see B Veneziani, 'The Evolution of the Contract of Employment' in B Hepple (ed) *The Making of Labour Law in Europe: A Comparative Study of Nine Countries up to 1945* (Mansell, London & New York, 1987) 31–72.

[101] Zeijen, n 99 above at 4.

[102] [2000] IRLR 43. This narrow interpretation can be contrasted with the definition of a 'worker' in s 2(1) of the UK Working Time Regulations which define a 'worker' as an indi-vidual with a contract of employment *or* 'any other contract . . . to do or perform personally any work or services for another party to the contract whose status is not by virtue of the contract that of a client or customer of any profession or business undertaking carried on by the individual'—SI 1998, No 1833, now revised by SI 1999, No 3372. Available at: <http://www.legislation.hmso.gov.uk/>.

was held that tour guides who had been appointed with a letter offering them employment on a 'casual as required basis' did not in fact have a contract of employment because, when oral evidence about their relationship with the undertaking was taken into account, their case foundered on the rock of the absence of mutuality, for a contract of employment in British law requires an 'irreducible minimum of mutual obligation' between employer and employee.[103]

These examples illustrate how the Community's ideal of a Charter of Fundamental Social Rights of *Workers* must be measured against the reality of national and not Community interpretations of key concepts that, in practice, may exclude the growing numbers of workers with irregular or atypical contracts. Moreover, even if one accepts Zeijen's assessment that there are certain 'conventional elements' to the employment relationship across the Member States, specifically a relationship of 'dependency, subordination and control', these terms, which seem rather old-fashioned today, do not easily accommodate the unemployed or retired persons, or temporary agency workers, or semi-autonomous workers such as homeworkers and unpaid carers.[104] It is in this context that we should now examine the Social Charter in more detail after having first considered its legal status and *modus operandi*.

(2) The Social Charter, Soft Law and Subsidiarity

The Social Charter will illustrate this leap forward in the social dimension. It will show our political will to build a social Europe, in accordance with the essential subsidiarity and also variety.

(Jacques Delors, 8 December 1989)[105]

With this ringing declaration, echoing Mao,[106] Delors signified his approval for the outcome of the Strasbourg European Council. Delors' words signified the two-dimensional nature of the Social Charter. On the one hand, an almost metaphysical 'leap forward' could be achieved through the projection of the political aspirations contained within and contingent upon the concept of a Social Charter. The adoption of a *Charter* and an

---

[103] *Ibid* per Lord Irvine of Lairg LC at paras 18–20. See also, *Nethermere (St Neots) Ltd v Gardiner* [1984] IRLR 240, Court of Appeal, per Stephenson LJ.

[104] See Kleinman and Piachaud, n 52 above at 15. For a critique of the limitations of the concept of 'work' in the Community, see I Moebius and E Szyszczak, 'Of Raising Pigs and Children' (1998) 18 *Yearbook of European Law* 125.

[105] This quotation is placed at the front of the text of the Social Charter reproduced by the Commission in *Social Europe* 1/90, p 45.

[106] The disastrous Great Leap Forward of 1958, a policy of forced industrialisation that led to economic ruin, followed Mao's Leap Forward of 1956. See A Bullock and O Stallybrass (eds) *The Fontana Dictionary of Modern Thought* (Fontana, London, 1977) p 270.

accompanying *Action Programme* was intended to create a dynamism that would engender hope and optimism for the 1990s,[107] to contrast with the disappointment and pessimism of the 1980s. Social policy would be propelled forward notwithstanding the inherent limitations of the Social Charter in both legal form and substantive content. On the other hand, there was the hard reality of a diluted text that, stripped naked of any pretensions of social citizenship, was perceived by many as, at best, a reference point for a step-by-step programme of limited workers' rights tied to internal market goals, drawing upon, wherever possible, an elastic interpretation of Article 118a EEC as a basis for legislation oriented towards workers' health and safety and the working environment.

For those seeking to utilise the Charter to 'build a Social Europe' its formal limitations as a non-binding 'solemn declaration' were compounded by the fact that, at the time of its adoption, it was subject to the vigorous opposition of the UK whose consent was needed in most areas of social policy legislation. For Vogel-Polsky, the Strasbourg European Council was a 'bitter failure'[108] and served to 'put non-decision in concrete form'.[109] Indeed, the Charter might be regarded as too weak even to be counted as an example of indicative 'soft law'. Hence, the Commission has recognised the limitations of the Charter, at least when it is considered in isolation:[110]

The Charter, as a European act, merely states and notes the rights which were the subject of deliberations in the European Council in Strasbourg in December 1989. *In itself, it has no effect on the existing legal situation.*

This statement is transparent but it leaves an important question open. Does the Charter, although it is not legally binding *in itself*, still have *legal consequences*? In order to answer this question we need to explore the concept of 'soft law'.

Community lawyers have drawn from the conceptualisation of soft law in the sphere of public international law. A first point of reference is the Vienna Convention on the Law of the Treaties of 23 May 1969.[111] The Convention refers, in Article 2, to an 'international agreement concluded between States in written form and governed by international law' that is, under Article 26, 'binding upon the parties' and 'must be performed by

---

[107] See E Szyszczak, 'L'Espace Sociale Européenne: Reality, Dreams, or Nightmares?' (1990) 33 *German Yearbook of International Law* 284 at 284. For a pessimistic view, see E Vogel-Polsky, 'What Future Is There For A Social Europe After The Strasbourg Summit?' (1990) 19 *Industrial Law Journal* 65.

[108] Vogel-Polsky, *ibid* at 65.

[109] *Ibid* at 67.

[110] These comments are contained in the introduction to the Commission's second annual report on the application of the Social Charter, COM(92) 562. Emphasis added.

[111] This was the date when the Convention was opened for signature: UN Doc A/CONF 39/27 (1969) reproduced at (1969) 63 *American Journal of International Law* 875. For discussion, see R Baxter, 'International Law in "Her Infinite Variety"' (1980) 29 *International and Comparative Law Quarterly* 549.

them in good faith'.[112] This is a very helpful definition of 'hard law' in a public international law sense, but it leaves open the question of the status of other informal agreements and what Baxter describes as the 'infinite variety' of hortatory statements and public declarations issued collectively by states and emanating from the international bodies that they have established.[113] Therefore it is much easier to determine what soft law is not, by reference to accepted precepts of hard law, than define what it is. The most that can be said, when considering the concept in public international law, is that soft laws are norms issued by states, or persons acting on their behalf, that are of a legal character but are not intended to be legally binding in themselves. Nonetheless, soft laws have a real existence and a capacity to create obligations for states and individuals, even though they may not be enforced by sanctions.[114]

How then can this concept of soft law be applied in a Community system that 'constitutes a new legal order of international law'[115] and has 'its own institutions, its own personality, its own legal capacity and capacity of representation on the international plane'?[116] The *sui generis* nature of Community law, encapsulated in these early pronouncements from the Court, brings a new dimension to soft law as a tool for furthering and deepening European integration by building upon and around the legal *acquis* without directly creating strict legal obligations.[117] Thus, while hard laws in the form of Treaty provisions or binding regulations and directives create rules that Member States are bound to comply with, soft laws, whilst being normative in character, are essentially methods of Community guidance or rules which create an expectation that the conduct of Member States will be in conformity with them, but without an accompanying legal obligation.[118] However, the hard law/soft law dichotomy is blurred by the fact that although soft laws, in themselves, have no legally binding force, they may act as 'impulses for integration', or provide a basis for judicial interpretation

---

[112] Baxter, *ibid* at 550.

[113] *Ibid* at 566.

[114] *Ibid* at 549. See also, O Schachter, 'The Twilight Existence of Nonbinding International Agreements' (1977) 71 *American Journal of International Law* 296; and A Aust, 'The Theory and Practice of Informal International Instruments' (1986) 35 *International and Comparative Law Quarterly* 787.

[115] Case 26/62, *Van Gend en Loos v Nederlande Administratie der Belastingen* [1963] ECR 1 at 12.

[116] Case 6/64, *Costa v ENEL* [1964] ECR 585 at 593.

[117] See especially, J Kenner, 'EC Labour Law: the Softly, Softly Approach' (1995) 11 *International Journal of Comparative Labour Law and International Relations* 307; K Wellens and G Borchardt, 'Soft Law in European Community Law' (1989) 14 *European Law Review* 267; F Snyder, *Soft Law and Institutional Practice in the European Community*, EUI Working Paper LAW No 93/5 (EUI, Florence 1993); and J Klabbers, 'Informal Instruments before the European Court of Justice' (1994) 31 *Common Market Law Review* 997.

[118] On the hard law/soft law distinction, see Baxter, n 111 above at 565; and Klabbers, *ibid* at 999.

of hard laws, or serve to strengthen national legislation and thereby produce the desired legal effects.[119]

By its very nature soft law is multifaceted and serves diverse purposes. The Community has used informal instruments for a variety of reasons for, as Snyder explains, soft law is:[120]

... in part a predictable feature of administrative development, in part a comprehensible response to institutional inertia, and in part a questionable attempt to circumvent or avoid the implications of failures to reach political agreement.

This statement helps us to understand the reasons why the Social Charter was adopted as a 'solemn declaration' by 11 out of the then 12 Member States, but where does it fit in the hierarchy of soft laws? To help answer this question I have identified four distinct groups of soft laws in the field of social policy:[121]

(1) Bold statements, usually European Council or joint institutional resolutions or declarations, serving to usher in new periods of social activism.
(2) Commission and Council recommendations serving either as prompters to maintain the momentum of existing programmes or, alternatively, as reminders of the Community's unfulfilled ambition.
(3) Recommendations, resolutions and memoranda, designed to supplement existing hard law in order to give it maximum effect at national level, and to serve as a means of focusing the attention of Community institutions on priority policy areas.
(4) Broad statements of political principle reflecting areas on the fringes or even outside of existing Community competence where there is no realistic prospect, nor any clear intention, of bringing forward binding legislative proposals in the foreseeable future.

As a declaratory statement of principle and aspirational intent issued at the highest level, the Social Charter falls within my first category of soft laws. Moreover, the Social Charter and, indeed, the Action Programme, which also has soft law status, have spawned numerous soft laws that fit within the other categories outlined above. We will return to some examples of these soft laws when considering the effectiveness of the Action Programme in the next chapter. For now it is important to understand the dynamic nature of the Social Charter as a totemic tool of soft law. There are three main reasons why the Charter has had this dynamic or reflexive effect.

---

[119] Wellens and Borchardt, n 117 above at 298, and F Snyder, 'The Effectiveness of European Community Law: Institutions, Processes, Tools and Techniques' (1993) 56 *Modern Law Review* 19 at 32.

[120] Snyder, *Soft Law and Institutional Practice in the European Community*, n 117 above at 3.

[121] Kenner (1995, *International Journal of Comparative Labour Law and Industrial Relations*) n 117 above at 311–13.

First, it is possible to distinguish between the status of formal declarations adopted by an overwhelming majority of the Council, such as the Social Charter, and weaker minority statements usually intended for the minutes. Klabbers argues that the Court can rely on such declarations for interpretation and their influence may be reinforced where the Commission also expresses the majority sentiments.[122] For example, in *ex parte Antonissen*[123] the Court expressed the view that declarations may be used for interpretative purposes where 'reference is made to the content of the declaration in the wording of the provision in question'.[124] The drafters of legislation arising from the Social Charter have been astute enough to draw upon it whenever seeking to reinforce an otherwise shaky legal foundation. For example, the Article 118a EEC directives on Pregnancy and Maternity, Working Time and Young Workers each refer to the Charter as a source in the recitals contained in their respective preambles.[125]

Secondly, while the Charter itself is purely declaratory and places the obligation for its implementation firmly on the Member States,[126] it must be read together with the Commission's Action Programme which had been prepared pursuant to its right of initiative on the basis that the Charter should be followed up with urgent binding Community legislation, wherever necessary to achieve its objectives.[127] Thus, although the *obligation* to implement would remain with the Member States, the parameters of Community social policy and labour law would be greatly extended through the adoption of a 'sound base of minimum provisions'.[128] Once the European Council adopted only a 'solemn declaration' among the majority, the Commission saw no reason to hold back on proposals which were designed for immediate action and based on existing Treaty commitments. In this way the Commission, with the support of the European Parliament and the majority of Member States, was able to draw strength and inspiration from two separate but related instruments of soft law that together created an irresistible momentum. In practice, the main role of the Charter has been its capacity to act as a stimulant for action founded on the basis that the Member States intended to carry forward their purely political commitments to the extent that they would ultimately have legal consequences. Such was the dynamism of the Social Charter and the Action Programme

---

[122] Klabbers, n 117 above at 1009.
[123] Case C–292/89, *R v The Immigration Appeal Tribunal, ex parte Antonissen* [1991] ECR I–745.
[124] *Ibid* at 778.
[125] Respectively, Dir 92/85/EEC, OJ 1992, L348/1, fifth recital (point 19 of the Charter); Dir 93/104/EC, OJ 1993, L307/18, fourth recital (points 7, 8 and 19); and Dir 94/33/EC, OJ 1993, L216/12, third recital (points 20 and 22).
[126] Point 27. Discussed below.
[127] Point 28.
[128] *Third Report from the Commission on the Application of the Community Charter of the Fundamental Social Rights of Workers*, COM(93) 668 at p 3.

that, by the end of 1993, each of the legislative initiatives identified in the Programme had been presented by the Commission and the majority of those requiring legislation had been adopted.[129] In fact much of this legislation was far weaker than originally intended in the Action Programme, whether adopted as hard or soft law, as will be shown in the next chapter, and the apparent success of these instruments was to lead the Commission to take a rather rose-tinted view of the need for further binding Community legislation.[130]

Thirdly, the Social Charter provided a platform for the later proposal to amend the EEC Treaty at Maastricht by revising the social policy provisions and thereby extending the legal base. The adoption of first, the Agreement on Social Policy with the specific objective of implementing the Social Charter, and then, Article 136 EC [replacing Article 117 EEC], with its direct reference to the Charter as a source of fundamental social rights, has served to constitutionalise the principles behind the Charter within the bounds of the Treaty.

The status of the Charter is further reinforced by its preamble. There are 16 declaratory recitals in the preamble. Each recital acts as a guide to the sources of the Charter and the ambitions of its signatories. The importance of the preamble should not be understated. Fitzpatrick has noted, when discussing the EC Treaty, that the preamble is at the apex of the Community's pyramid-like structure.[131] It sets out laudable aspirations and hovers above the norms within it while providing overarching guidance for the Court to use for the purposes of interpretation of the rights contained therein.[132] The central aspirations of the EC Treaty are economic ones and this drives the whole integration process.[133] Fitzpatrick's paradigm also applies, by analogy, to the preamble of the Charter, a point reinforced later by direct references to the Charter in the Maastricht Protocol and Agreement on Social Policy[134] and the revised Social Chapter negotiated at Amsterdam.[135] Thus, while the principal thrust of the Charter is to promote workers' rights in the internal market,[136] the preamble also helps to provide an indication

---

[129] See COM(93) 551, Commission 'Green Paper' on European Social Policy, *Options for the Union*, p 6.

[130] See J Kenner, 'Citizenship and Fundamental Rights: Reshaping the European Social Model' in J Kenner (ed) *Trends in European Social Policy* (Dartmouth, Aldershot, 1995) 3–84 at 3–8.

[131] B Fitzpatrick, 'Converse Pyramids and the EU Social Constitution' in Shaw, n 82 above, 303–24 at 304–6.

[132] *Ibid* at 305.

[133] *Ibid* at 306.

[134] The preamble of the Protocol lists the Member States that wished to 'continue along the path laid down by the Charter'. The Agreement seeks to 'implement' the Charter in accordance with the Community *acquis*, also in the preamble.

[135] Art 136 EC obliges the Community to have in mind 'fundamental social rights' such as those contained in the ESC and the Social Charter when pursuing their social policy objectives.

[136] See Poiares Maduro, n 2 above at 462.

of a wider and longer-term ambition to secure 'fundamental social rights at Community level'.[137] In this way the ideal of social citizenship was kept alive even at a time when the Community was at an impasse on social policy. In due course this will help us to identify a common thread running from the Social Charter, continuing through to the Amsterdam Treaty, with its reference to 'fundamental social rights' in Article 136 EC [ex 117 EEC], and leading to an overarching soft law declaration in the form of the Charter of Fundamental Rights of the European Union signed at the Nice Inter-Governmental Conference on 7 December 2000.[138]

The preamble of the Charter is indicative of its wider, longer-term ambitions. Particular significance can be derived from the eighth, ninth, fifteenth and sixteenth recitals. The eighth recital contains a declaration that:[139]

Whereas, in order to ensure equal treatment, it is important to combat *every form of discrimination* including discrimination on the grounds of sex, colour, race, opinions and beliefs and, whereas, in a spirit of solidarity, it is important to combat social exclusion.

No specific rights listed in the Charter flow from this statement and yet its significance is twofold. First, the locus of the declaration is society at large. Neither work nor workers are mentioned. Combating discrimination and social exclusion is posited as a societal duty and it is implicit that this duty is to be shared by citizens and states. Second, the statement extended well beyond the competences of the Community at the time. The principle of equality has been discussed in chapter 2, with respect, in particular to sex discrimination under Article 119 EEC [now 141 EC]. Although the principle is recognised as all embracing, its application is selective[140] and remains so. In particular, prior to the introduction of Article 13 EC by the Amsterdam Treaty, there was no reference in the Treaties to discrimination on the grounds of racial or ethnic origin, religion or belief, disability, age or sexual orientation. Although the text of the eighth recital does not exactly match the listing that emerged later in Article 13 EC, its portent lies with the fact that it is non-exhaustive in character. Indeed a general clause concerning 'disabled persons' is included in point 26 of the Charter notwithstanding the lack of a direct reference in the preamble. As such, even as a soft law source derived from the preamble, this statement has served as an impulse for further and deeper integration of Community social laws. The extent to which this outcome may have been intended at the time is a moot

---

[137] 16th recital.
[138] OJ 2000, C364/1. The Charter of Fundamental Rights Charter is a non-binding 'solemn proclamation' although, unlike the Social Charter, it has received unanimous support and is inter-institutional. For full discussion, see ch 12.
[139] Emphasis added.
[140] See G de Búrca, 'The Role of Equality in European Law' in A Dashwood and S O'Leary (eds) *The Principle of Equal Treatment in EC Law* (Sweet & Maxwell, London, 1997) 13–34.

point, but the Community's leaders were, at the very least, prepared to leave the door open for a wider application of the equality principle in the future. In the meantime, however, the Commission were not prepared to put forward a legislative proposal in the Action Programme.[141]

The ninth recital proclaims:

Whereas inspiration should be drawn from the Conventions of the International Labour Organisation and from the European Social Charter of the Council of Europe.

The perfunctory nature of this statement belies its import. While other declarations in the preamble have the EC Treaty as their point of reference, this recital provides a universal source for both the interpretation of Community law and the initiation of new binding or non-binding legislative proposals. Moreover, it is a source founded on a broad conception of freestanding social rights. 'Labour is not a commodity' is the first principle of the ILO.[142] It is therefore a prerequisite of international labour standards that the 'law of the market' must not be the sole regulator of the employment relationship.[143] Therefore, this direct reference to the conventions of the ILO and the ESC adds a gloss to the social dimension that takes it, at least potentially, beyond the realm of market integration. In this sense the preamble acts as 'pre-law'[144] or even 'pre-pre-law' if one sees law as a continuum from an aspiration followed by a tentative proposal, further repeated declarations and, ultimately, an evolution into a firm proposition once there is sufficient political momentum for binding law in a widening horizon of social rights. For example, following the collapse of the Commission's earlier attempts to introduce legislation to protect 'atypical workers',[145] a new proposal was put forward to act in relation to part-time work as a 'first step'.[146] The Commission's decision was undoubtedly influenced by the adoption of ILO Convention No 175 on Part-time Work in

---

[141] Para 5 of the introduction states: 'While the Commission is not making a proposal in respect of discrimination on the grounds of race, colour or religion, it none the less stresses the need for such practices to be eradicated, particularly in the workplace and in access to employment, through appropriate action by Member States and by the two sides of industry'. *Social Europe* 1/90, p 54.

[142] The Declaration of Philadelphia, 1944. See *Constitution of the International Labour Organisation* (ILO, Geneva, 1992) p 22.

[143] See P O'Higgins, 'Labour is not a Commodity'—an Irish Contribution to International Labour Law' (1997) 26 *Industrial Law Journal* 225 at 226. O'Higgins traces the origins of this declaration back to an address on 'Work and the Workman' by the Irish economist, Dr John Kells Ingram, to the British Trades Union Congress in 1880.

[144] See M Rodríguez-Piñero and E Casas, 'In Support of a European Social Constitution' in P Davies, A Lyon-Caen, S Sciarra and S Simitis (eds) *European Community Labour Law: Principles and Perspectives* (Clarendon Press, Oxford, 1996) 23–48 at 36.

[145] This proposal was based on a specific legislative commitment in the Action Programme to introduce a directive on 'contracts and employment relationships other than full-time open-ended contracts'. *Social Europe* 1/90, p 52.

[146] COM(94) 33 at 31.

1994.[147] The Convention seeks, inter alia, to guarantee equivalent rights between part-time workers and comparable full-time workers. This broad guarantee was to form the basis for the negotiation and drafting of a Framework Agreement between the social partners on 6 June 1997 leading to the adoption of Directive 97/81 on part-time work.[148]

The fifteenth recital is the most important indicator of the legal scope of the Charter and, in a wider sense, of the shape of things to come. In this recital it is declared that:[149]

Whereas, *by virtue of the principle of subsidiarity*, responsibility for the initiatives to be taken with regard to the implementation of these social rights lies with the Member States or their constituent parts and, within the limits of its powers, within the European Community; whereas such implementation may take the form of laws, collective agreements or existing practices at the various appropriate levels and whereas it requires in many spheres the active involvement of the two sides of industry.

This early reference to subsidiarity,[150] in advance of the formal introduction of Article 3b [now 5] EC, is reinforced in Title II of the Charter, the 'horizontal' provisions, where it is stated that:[151]

It is more particularly the responsibility of the Member States, in accordance with national practices, notably through legislative measures or collective agreements, to guarantee the fundamental social rights in this Charter and to implement the social measures indispensable to the smooth operation of the internal market as part of a strategy of economic and social cohesion.

These references to subsidiarity and the attribution of powers and responsibilities between the Community and the Member States differ significantly in emphasis from the first draft where the Commission sought to commit the Member States to:[152]

... take such steps as are appropriate and to mobilize all the resources that may be necessary in order to guarantee the fundamental social rights in this Charter and full implementation of the social measures indispensable to the efficient operation of the internal market ... This shall be done through legislative measures, or by encouraging both sides of industry to conclude collective agreements at national, regional or company level.

---

[147] The text of the Convention and the accompanying Recommendation are reproduced in (1994) 10 *International Journal of Comparative Labour Law and Industrial Relations* 249 and 254.

[148] Dir 97/81/EC concerning the Framework Agreement on part-time work agreed by UNICE, CEEP and the ETUC, OJ 1998, L14/9.

[149] Emphasis added.

[150] For an analysis of the origins and application of subsidiarity, see N Emiliou, 'Subsidiarity: an effective barrier against "the enterprises of ambition"?' (1992) 17 *European Law Review* 383.

[151] Point 27.

[152] COM(89) 471, draft point 27.

As Shaw explains, the emphasis had switched from centralised to decentralised implementation:[153]

For it is not that the Member States are being required to implement a catalogue of binding social rights which would act as legal guarantees in the case of non-implementation. Rather it is the Member States themselves who are being asked to give these so-called rights the form of law.

On the basis of this formulation of subsidiarity, *legal competence* ultimately rests with the Member States.[154] By contrast the Commission's accompanying Action Programme defines subsidiarity as meaning that 'the Community acts when the set of objectives can be reached more effectively at this level than at that of the Member States'.[155] Therefore, in the Commission's view, the Community reserves a residual power to act to secure the *effectiveness* of the objectives in the Charter although it proceeds to limit its proposals to those areas where Community legislation 'seems necessary to achieve the social dimension of the internal market'.[156] This emphasis on effectiveness also chimes with the definition of subsidiarity in the European Parliament's draft European Union Treaty of 1984.[157] Significantly, the Commission's view also equates more closely with the definition that was to eventually emerge in the second paragraph of Article 3b [now 5] EC where it is stated that:

In areas which do not fall within its exclusive competence, the Community shall take action, in accordance with the principle of subsidiarity, only if and so far as the objectives of the proposed action cannot be sufficiently achieved by the Member States and can therefore, by reason of the scale or effects of the proposed action, be better achieved by the Community.

We will return to this definition of subsidiarity in chapter 6, when the 'principle' will be assessed in the context of the Treaty on European Union and the Protocol and Agreement on Social Policy. For now it is important to note that, when the Social Charter was launched, subsidiarity was being applied in the area of Community social policy in advance of its formal incorporation into the EC Treaty. This only serves to exemplify the extent to which the allocation of competences between the Community and Member States has, in the sphere of social policy, erred on the side of the

---

[153] J Shaw, 'The Scope and Content of European Community Social Law: A Review of Progress and a Bibliographical Note' (1992) 14 *Journal of Social Welfare and Family Law* 71 at 74–5.

[154] See Hepple (1990) *Modern Law Review* n 34 above at 646.

[155] Introduction, para 3. *Social Europe* 1/90, p 54.

[156] *Ibid* para 5. On the distinction between legal competence and effectiveness, see Hepple (1990, *Modern Law Review*) n 34 above at 646–47.

[157] OJ 1984, C77/53. Art 12(2) states that: 'The Union shall only act to carry out those tasks which may be more effectively undertaken in common than by Member States acting separately, in particular those whose dimensions and effect extend beyond national frontiers'.

Member States. As Hepple explains, the emphasis in the Action Programme on both legal competence and effectiveness has meant that subsidiarity 'adds nothing of substance to the well-established legal bases of Community competence in the social field'.[158] Rather, its substance, in the context of the Charter, is political not legal.[159]

Finally, we can complete our analysis of the preamble by considering the sixteenth recital, which decrees that:

Whereas the solemn proclamation of fundamental social rights at European Community level may not, when implemented, provide grounds for any retrogression compared with the situation currently existing in each Member State.

This notion of 'non-retrogression' was, on the face of it, a mere reinforcement of the existing approach to Community social legislation at the time. A standard clause can be found in the legislation of the 1970s and 80s allowing Member States to introduce provisions that are 'more favourable' to employees.[160] There is, however, no *explicit* requirement in this legislation to maintain existing employment standards or to prohibit retrogression. After the adoption of the Social Charter there has been a change of emphasis in the language used in directives. Upward harmonisation is encouraged but retrogression is explicitly forbidden. For example, the Pregnancy and Maternity Directive[161] contains a minimum requirement to provide a guarantee of at least 14 weeks leave before or after confinement.[162] This standard was set below the level pertaining in the majority of the Member States at the time. There was therefore little incentive for the states in question to introduce more favourable provisions. Indeed there was an underlying concern that setting such a low threshold for social policy rights might encourage a reduction in standards leading to a lowest common denominator approach to the implementation of Community labour laws. In order to avoid that scenario, Article 1(3) was inserted into the Directive to provide that:

This Directive may not have the effect of reducing the level of protection afforded to pregnant workers, workers who have recently given birth or who are breastfeeding as compared with the situation which exists in each Member State on the date on which this Directive is adopted.

Hence the importance of non-retrogression is that it acts as a bulwark against the deregulation of labour law. The reference to non-retrogression

---

[158] Hepple (1990, *Modern Law Review*) n 34 above at 647.
[159] *Ibid.*
[160] For example, Art 5 of Dir 75/129/EEC on collective redundancies, OJ 1975, L48/29; Art 7(1) of Dir 77/187/EEC on transfers of undertakings, OJ 1977, L61/26; and Art 9 of Dir 80/987/EEC on insolvency protection, OJ 1980, L283/23.
[161] Dir 92/85/EEC, OJ 1992, L348/1.
[162] *Ibid.* Art 8(1).

in the preamble of the Charter also reinforces the clause in Article 118a(3) EEC [now 137(5) EC] that allows Member States to maintain or introduce 'more stringent measures for the protection of working conditions' compatible with the Treaty. Non-retrogression can be implied from Article 118a(3) EEC but the preamble has ensured that it has been made explicit in later directives stemming from the Action Programme. Moreover, at the time of the Social Charter, the introduction of non-retrogression served as a warning shot to states, such as the UK, that were pursuing or contemplating the path of deregulation. The concept of non-retrogression is just as relevant today as the Community prepares for the next enlargement eastwards for, as new Member States with lower labour costs and, in some cases, lower labour standards, join the European Union, the pressure to deregulate at national level and even to dilute Community legislation will surely grow.

III THE CHARTER'S FUNDAMENTAL SOCIAL RIGHTS

Having considered the legal status of the Charter and the framework provided by the preamble, let us now turn to the substance of the 26 'vertical' rights listed in Title I of the Charter and the related proposals in the Commission's accompanying Action Programme. Although the Action Programme was launched immediately before the formal adoption of the Charter, it was justified by virtue of the 'horizontal' implementing provisions in Title II, points 27–30. While point 27 places responsibility on the Member States to implement the Charter and guarantee the listed social rights, as discussed above, point 28 simultaneously invites the Commission to submit 'initiatives' that fall within its powers 'as soon as possible'. These initiatives are to be submitted with a view to the adoption of legal instruments for the effective implementation of those rights coming within the Community's areas of competence. In addition, by virtue of points 29 and 30, the Commission is obliged to issue an annual report on the application of the Charter to be forwarded to the European Council, the European Parliament and the Economic and Social Committee. Hence, these horizontal points, while they preserve a degree of autonomy for the Member States, have created a momentum for implementation and monitoring of the Charter and a foundation for successive action programmes.

Title I of the Charter contains thirteen general headings as follows:

—freedom of movement (points 1–3);
—employment and remuneration (points 4–6);
—improvement of living and working conditions (points 7–9);
—social protection (point 10);
—freedom of association and collective bargaining (points 11–14);

—vocational training (point 15);
—equal treatment for men and women (point 16);
—information, consultation and participation of workers (points 17–18);
—health protection and safety at the workplace (point 19);
—protection of children and adolescents (points 20–23);
—elderly persons (points 24–25);
—disabled persons (point 26).

This enumeration is drawn from both Community and international law sources of *workers'* rights, discussed below (sections 1–2) and a small residue of the Commission's original 'social citizenship' agenda in the form of fundamental social rights of *persons* in points 10 and 24–26 (section 3).

(1) Fundamental Social Rights of Workers—Community Sources

From the outset priority is given to the 'Community worker' as a 'market citizen'.[163] Points 1 and 2, drawn from Articles 39–48 EC [ex 48–58 EEC], set out the basic rights of workers to free movement and equal treatment in occupation and profession. Point 3 declares that freedom of movement shall also imply harmonisation of conditions of residence, particularly those concerning family reunification; elimination of obstacles arising from the non-recognition of diplomas or equivalent occupational qualifications; and improvement of the living and working conditions of frontier workers. An additional clause in the Commission's draft, referring to equal treatment in all fields, including social and tax advantages, was deleted from the final text.[164] By way of new initiatives, the Commission, in the Action Programme, proposed the establishment of an employment 'observatory' to integrate employment information systems in the Community and other action targeted at employment creation.[165] It is therefore apparent that, while the principal free movement rights were targeted at the completion of the internal market, there were the also the first tentative signs of what

---

[163] See M Everson, 'The Legacy of the Market Citizen' in Shaw and More, n 48 above, 73–90.
[164] COM(89) 248, point 2 of the first draft.
[165] *Social Europe* 1/90, p 57. The first meeting of the network of employment co-ordinators (NEC) was held on 6 April 1990. The European system of documentation on employment (Sysdem) was launched in October 1989. The Mutual Information System on Employment Policies (MISEP) was swiftly established and reports periodically. NEC, Sysdem and MISEP, together, form the 'observatory' and documentation system on employment. Action Programmes on employment creation were established for specific target groups: ERGO (long-term unemployed); LEDA (local employment); and SPEC (support programme for employment creation). The European Social Fund (ESF) Regulation was amended to bring the ESF into line with the employment creation agenda, Reg 2084/93/EEC, OJ 1993, L193/39. Finally, the European system for the clearance of vacancies and applications for employment (SEDOC) was updated through the adoption of Reg 2434/92/EEC, OJ 1992, L245/1.

would later emerge as a fully-fledged Employment Title.[166] The significance here is that this new activity was derived directly from the preamble of the Charter which states that employment development and creation 'must be given first priority'[167] in the completion of the internal market.

In a separate section of the Action Programme on free movement there were several innovative proposals.[168] For example, the Commission proposed to extend Regulation 1408/71[169] concerning the co-ordination of social security to 'other categories of persons' such as public sector workers, who do not have 'worker' status in certain Member States,[170] students, and persons who are not economically active. The Commission also proposed a measure to protect the rights of workers who are sent to another Member State to perform a contract for services on behalf of their employer. It is worth noting that this proposal was proceeded with even though a reference to such protection in the draft was excised from the final text of the Charter.[171] This idea was to provide the foundation for the Directive on Posted Workers.[172] Other innovations included a Community instrument to introduce a labour clause into public contracts[173] and a Communication concerning access to services for frontier workers.[174]

Point 7 on the improvement of living and working conditions begins with the following declaration:[175]

The completion of the internal market *must* lead to an improvement in the living and working conditions of workers in the Community.

Following on from this imperative, the Charter makes specific reference in points 7–9 to the need for 'approximation' of these conditions while the improvement is being maintained. Both elements are derived from Article 117 and 118 EEC [now 136 and 140 EC].

First, points 7 and 8 refer to the need to act in respect of the duration and organisation of working time including rights to a weekly rest period and annual paid leave. The Commission included a proposal for a directive on the adaptation of working time in the Action Programme.[176]

---

[166] Now Arts 125–130 EC, added by the Treaty of Amsterdam. See further, ch 11.

[167] Fourth recital.

[168] *Social Europe* 1/90, pp 61–3.

[169] OJ 1971, L149/2. The Commission proposal was published in OJ 1992, C325/1, and led to the eventual revision of Reg 1408/71 by Reg 118/97/EC, OJ 1997, L28/1.

[170] See Case C–343/98, *Collino and Chiappero v Telecom Italia SpA* [2000] ECR I–6659, paras 36–41.

[171] COM(89) 248, point 3 of the draft Charter. For discussion, see Bercusson (1990, *Modern Law Review*) n 34 above, at 629–31. The proposal was published in COM(91) 230, OJ 1991, C225/6.

[172] Dir 96/71/EC, OJ 1996, L18/1.

[173] Subsumed within Dir 96/71, *ibid*.

[174] COM(90) 561.

[175] Emphasis added.

[176] *Social Europe* 1/90, pp 60–1. This was swiftly published in COM(90) 317; followed by an amended proposal, COM(91) 130; OJ 1991, C124/8; leading to the eventual adoption of Dir 93/104/EC, OJ 1993, L307/18.

The health protection of workers was given as a secondary reason for this proposal.

Secondly, point 7 also makes reference to forms of employment other than open-ended contracts, such as fixed-term contracts, part-time working, temporary work and seasonal work. The Action Programme contained a proposal to legislate in this area with a single measure linked to the need to prevent the distortion of competition arising from the growth in 'atypical' forms of employment.[177] In practice, the Commission was prompted to launch three separate proposals on 'atypical work'[178] by concerns expressed in the European Parliament about discrimination against predominantly female part-time, temporary and fixed-term workers.[179] While initially unsuccessful, this commitment was carried over to later action programmes and ultimately led to the adoption of Directives on Part-time and Fixed-Term Work.[180]

Thirdly, the second paragraph of point 7 identifies the need to further develop procedures for collective redundancies, in particular those regarding bankruptcies. This was followed-up with a firm proposal in the Action Programme for the revision of the Collective Redundancies Directive[181] leading, in turn, to the adoption of an amended Directive.[182] Fourthly, point 9 declares that the conditions of employment of every worker shall be stipulated in law, a collective agreement or a contract of employment, according to the arrangements applying in each country. This was backed up by a stronger proposal in the Action Programme for a directive that would place a duty on employers to provide employees with a means of proving the existence of a contract of employment or employment relationship.[183] Ultimately, this would lead to the adoption of Directive 91/533 on Employee Information (Contract or Employment Relationship),[184] which more closely resembled the original concept.

In addition to these legislative proposals, the Commission, drawing from language in the preamble, recommended that a non-binding memorandum should be issued on the social integration of migrants from non-member countries.[185] The memorandum would lay stress on the quality of

---

[177] *Social Europe* 1/90, p 59. Oddly, this appears under the separate heading of 'Employment and Remuneration'.

[178] COM(90) 228, OJ 1990, C 224/4. Discussed on pp 82–3 above.

[179] See, for example, the European Parliament's Resolution on an initiative aimed at a proposal for a directive on atypical employment contracts and terms of employment, OJ 1990, C231/32.

[180] Respectively, Dir 97/81/EC, OJ 1998, L14/9, amended by Dir 98/23/EC, OJ L131/10; and Dir 99/70/EC, OJ 1999, L175/43.

[181] *Social Europe* 1/90, p 60. Dir 75/129/EEC, OJ 1975, L48/29. For the proposals, see COM(91) 292, OJ 1991, C310/5; and COM(92) 127, OJ 1992, C117/10.

[182] Dir 92/56/EEC, OJ 1992, L245/3; now consolidated in Dir 98/59/EC, OJ 1998, L225/16.

[183] COM(90) 563; OJ 1991, C24/3.

[184] OJ 1991, L288/32.

[185] *Social Europe* 1/90, p 61. The Memorandum was adopted by the Commission in 1991, SEC(91) 1855.

administrative and social services afforded to migrants, especially in fields such as education and housing. Hence, this was only a minimalist response to the call in the preamble for equal treatment of nationals of non-member countries and no attempt was made to test the scope of, for example, the general purposes legal base in Article 308 EC [ex 235 EEC]. This Memorandum can, however, be seen as a foundation for the eventual inclusion of a legislative base in Article 137(3) EC for measures concerning the 'conditions of employment for third country nationals legally residing in Community territory'. This legal base is subject to unanimity in the Council. No such legislative proposals have been forthcoming.

The Charter's provisions concerning equal treatment for men and women appear unremarkable at first sight. Point 16 states that equal treatment 'must be assured'. There is no clear statement as to the means to be developed to achieve this objective beyond 'implementation' of the principle of equality. This is, perhaps, a somewhat obtuse reference to the lack of progress towards achieving substantive equality notwithstanding the application of equal pay under Article 119 EEC [now 141 EC] and the adoption of the sex equality directives. The first proposal under this heading in the Action Programme was for a Third Community Action Programme on equal opportunities for women and men (1991–1995).[186] The Programme was intended to be part of an 'overall integrated approach allowing the policies on equality to be given full effect'[187] and took, as its starting point, the assumption that implementation of the law 'cannot alone secure the *de facto* equality of opportunity'.[188] What was required was specific action aimed at improving the situation of women in practice.[189] This marked the beginning of an important policy shift towards a 'mainstreaming' of gender equality policies throughout the Community's activities and, at the national level, renewed encouragement for equal opportunities policies and positive action.

Separate from this programmatic activity, further legislative possibilities can be drawn from an oblique reference in point 16 of the Charter to the need to develop measures 'enabling men and women to reconcile their occupational and family obligations'. In the Action Programme the Commission used this statement as a springboard for its 'family-friendly' agenda by proposing a recommendation on childcare, eventually adopted by the Council.[190] This, in turn, can be linked directly to revived proposals on

---

[186] Proposed in COM(90) 449 and adopted as a Council Resolution on 21 May 1991, OJ 1991, C142/1.

[187] *Third Commission Report on the Application of the Community Charter of the Fundamental Social Rights of Workers*, COM(93) 668, p 14.

[188] COM(90) 449. Introduction, para 2.

[189] *Ibid.*

[190] Recommendation 92/241/EEC, OJ 1992, L123/16. For the Commission proposal, see COM(91) 233, OJ 1991, C242/3.

maternity and paternity leave, leading most immediately to the Pregnancy and Maternity Directive[191] and, in later action programmes,[192] a framework proposal on the reconciliation of family and professional life leading, ultimately, to the adoption of the Parental Leave Directive.[193]

Points 17 and 18 of the Charter, on information, consultation and participation for workers, seek to develop worker involvement along appropriate lines 'taking account of the practices in force' in the various Member States. This concerned especially companies or groups of companies based in two or more Member States. In the Action Programme, the Commission applied this commitment by seeking to revamp its ill-fated 'Vredeling' proposal of the 1980s concerning worker involvement in transnational undertakings.[194] Following publication of the Commission's proposal in 1990,[195] an updated measure was eventually adopted as the European Works Council Directive,[196] the first binding piece of legislation issued under the Maastricht Agreement on Social Policy. There was also a separate proposal in the Action Programme, not directly referred to in the Charter, for a Community instrument on equity-sharing and financial participation by workers.[197] Sounding the mantra for what we would, several years later, comprehend as the language of the 'third way', the Commission ambitiously suggested that employee participation in productive capital formation could be a device for a 'fairer distribution of wealth' and act as a means for 'attaining an adequate level of non-inflationary growth'.[198] This proposal eventually emerged in the form of a non-binding Recommendation concerning the promotion of participation by employed persons in profits and enterprise results (including equity participation).[199]

Point 19 provides that every worker must enjoy satisfactory health and safety conditions in his working environment. It was envisaged that 'appropriate measures' would be taken to harmonise conditions in this area while maintaining the improvements made. In practice, the introduction of this

[191] Dir 92/85/EEC, OJ 1992, L348/1. The original proposals can be found in COM(90) 406, OJ 1990, C281/3; and COM(90) 692, OJ 1991, C25/9. A separate proposal for a recommendation on a code of good conduct on pregnancy and maternity was not progressed.

[192] Medium Term Social Action Programme, 1995–1997, COM(95) 134, p 19.

[193] Adopted, following the agreement of the social partners of 14 Dec 1995, as Dir 96/34/EC, OJ 1996, L145/4, and later amended by Dir 97/75/EC, OJ 1998, L10/24. The Commission had originally attempted to launch a directive in the 1980s, see COM(83) 636, OJ 1983, C333/6; and COM(84) 631, OJ 1984, C316/7.

[194] *Social Europe* 1/90, p 66. The 'Vredeling proposal' on procedures for informing and consulting the employees of undertakings with complex structures, in particular transnational undertakings, OJ 1980, C297/3. See also, the 'Richard proposal', OJ 1983, C217/3.

[195] COM(90) 581, OJ 1991, C39/10; COM(91) 345, OJ 1991, C336/11.

[196] Dir 94/45/EC, OJ L254/64, as amended by Dir 97/74/EC, OJ 1998, L10/20. For the proposal, see COM(94) 134, OJ 1994, C135/8, as revised by COM(94) 228, OJ 1994, C199/10.

[197] *Social Europe* 1/90, pp 66–7.

[198] *Ibid* p 66.

[199] Recommendation 92/443/EEC, OJ 1992, L245/53. For the Commission proposal, see COM(91) 259, OJ 1991, C245/12.

rights' guarantee served to reinforce the second health and safety action programme that was already underway.[200] No fewer than 12 of the legislative proposals, some 25 per cent of the total measures proposed, were put forward under this heading in the Action Programme.[201] This bias undoubtedly reflected both the potential of Article 118a EEC [now 137 EC] and the dextrous nature of the framework Directive. Seven of the proposals were strictly sectoral, while the remainder concerned such matters as, inter alia: safety and health signs; a system of specific information for workers exposed to certain dangerous chemical agents; protection for workers exposed to risks caused by physical agents; and the establishment of a safety, hygiene and health agency.[202] While this package represented a significant gearing up of an existing legislative programme, it also highlighted the paramount importance of the health and safety objective in this period and beyond.

(2) Fundamental Social Rights of Workers—International Law Sources

Several of the rights in the Charter can be traced directly to ILO conventions and the ESC. In this grouping we find rights at the very fringes of Treaty competence both at the time of the SEA and also today. In particular, these rights can be found under the headings on employment and remuneration;[203] freedom of association and collective bargaining;[204] social protection;[205] and the protection of children and adolescents.[206] Not surprisingly, as the rights under these headings fall mainly within the bounds of national competence, the Action Programme was less ambitious in these areas.

For example, in the first of these areas, the section on employment and remuneration, the principal source is Article 4(1) ESC, which recognises 'the right of workers to a remuneration such as will give them and their families a decent standard of living'. In the Action Programme, however, the Commission emphasised that subsidiarity would be at the fore when considering action to guarantee these rights and therefore both responsibility and initiative would lie mainly with the Member States.[207] Looking in a little more detail at the substantive 'rights' to 'employment and remuneration' we find that point 4 is relatively straightforward, providing for a

---

[200] Council Resolution on safety, hygiene and health at work of 21 Dec 1987, OJ 1988, C28/1. See also, the Commission Communication on its action programme, OJ 1988, C28/2.
[201] *Social Europe* 1/90, pp 70–3.
[202] *Ibid.*
[203] Points 4–6.
[204] Points 11–14.
[205] Point 10.
[206] Points 20–23.
[207] *Social Europe* 1/90, p 58.

right for every individual to be free to choose and engage in an occupation according to the regulations governing each occupation. This is an uncontroversial statement and should be read as a stand-alone provision demanding no specific proposals for action at national level although further implementation as part of the right of establishment under Article 43 EC [ex 52 EEC] is required. Point 6, enabling every individual to have access to public placement services free of charge, is also self-executing. Point 5, however, stands out by forthrightly proclaiming that *all employment* shall be fairly remunerated. In order to determine the scope of this apparently far-reaching right, the Charter identifies three steps to be taken to this end 'in accordance with the arrangements applying in each country':[208]

—workers shall be assured of an equitable wage, i.e. a wage sufficient to enable them to have a decent standard of living;
—workers subject to terms of employment other than an open-ended full-time contract shall benefit from an equitable reference wage;
—wages may be withheld, seized or transferred only in accordance with national law; such provisions should entail measures enabling the worker concerned to continue to enjoy the necessary means of subsistence for him or herself and his or her family.

The Commission's response in the Action Programme was extremely cautious. No attempt was made to propose legislation, perhaps based on Article 94 EC [ex 100 EEC], to establish a reference or minimum wage, or a system for evaluating and setting of wages at Community level, on the grounds that such a step would promote fair competition, combat social dumping and contribute to the functioning of the common market. Instead the Commission unequivocally stated that wage setting was a matter for the Member States and the two sides of industry alone.[209] Moreover, it was not the task of the Community to fix a decent reference wage because such a concept corresponded to different criteria from one country of the Community to another.[210] This was somewhat of a climb-down by the Commission because the original draft of the Charter had referred specifically to the right to a 'decent' wage consistent with the right in Article 5 ESC.[211] Meekly, the Commission proposed to 'assert its views' by issuing a non-binding opinion on the possible means by which an 'equitable wage' would be 'guaranteed to one and all'.[212] The Commission's caution was understandable given the emphasis in the Charter on subsidiarity and the accompanying obligation in point 28 to ensure that proposals for initiatives came within the Community's competence. In the event, the

---

[208] Point 5, para 2.
[209] *Social Europe* 1/90, p 59.
[210] *Ibid.*
[211] On this point, see Bercusson (1990, *Modern Law Review*) n 34 above at 631.
[212] *Social Europe* 1/90, pp 58–9.

Commission issued its Opinion on 1 September 1993.[213] No further concrete measures have been taken to activate the right to an 'equitable wage' at Community-level. Indeed the extension of the social policy provisions at Maastricht and Amsterdam has only served, paradoxically, to constrain the Community's competence in this area by excluding 'pay' from the scope of legislative provisions under Article 137 EC [ex 2 of the Agreement on Social Policy][214] along with 'the right of association, the right to strike' and 'the right to impose lock-outs', broadly corresponding with the second heading in this grouping, freedom of association and collective bargaining in points 11–14.

Point 11 of the Charter recognises both the positive and negative right of association for *employers and workers* consistent with Article 11 ECHR[215] and the case law of the Strasbourg Court.[216] Under the ECHR, the right of association is exercisable as a means of defending the economic and social interests of both groups. In a similar vein to Article 11 ECHR, however, point 14 of the Charter leaves it to the internal order of the Member States to determine under which conditions and to what extent the rights on freedom of association and collective bargaining in points 11–13 apply to the armed forces, the police and the civil service.[217]

Further, by virtue of the first paragraph of point 12, both employers' and workers' organisations shall have the right to negotiate and conclude collective agreements 'under the conditions laid down by national legislation and practice'. This is consistent with the right to organise and bargain collectively in Articles 5 and 6 ESC. Does Article 6 ESC, read in conjunction with the Charter, Article 11 ECHR, and the related international instruments, provide a sufficient basis to recognise the right to collective bargaining on pay and other conditions of employment as a fundamental right that should be guaranteed by the Court? This was the question posed by the Commission in its submission in *Albany International*.[218] AG Jacobs, in

---

[213] COM(93) 388.

[214] This exclusion is contained within Art 137(6) EC [ex 2(6) of the Agreement].

[215] Art 11(1) ECHR declares that: 'Everyone has the right to freedom of peaceful assembly and to freedom of association with others, including the right to form and join trade unions for the protection of his interests'. The right to form and join trade unions is also recognised by Art 5 ESC; ILO Convention Nos 87 and 98; Art 22 of the UN International Covenant on Civil and Political Rights; and Art 8 of the UN International Covenant on Economic, Social and Cultural Rights.

[216] In other words, the right to join *or* not to join a trade union. See *Sigurjonnson v Iceland*, judgment of 30 June 1993, Series A No 264; *Young, James and Webster*, judgment of 13 August 1981, Series A No 44.

[217] Art 11(2) ECHR provides that: 'No restrictions shall be placed on the exercise of these rights other than such as are prescribed by law and are necessary in a democratic society in the interests of national security or public safety, for the prevention of disorder or crime, for the protection of health or morals or for the protection of the rights and freedoms of others. This article shall not prevent the imposition of lawful restrictions on the exercise of these rights by members of the armed forces, of the police or of the administration of the State'.

[218] Case C–67/96, *Albany International BV v Stichting Bedrijfspensioenfonds Textielindustrie* [1999] ECR I–5751.

a comprehensive opinion, was not prepared to reach that conclusion. Rather, he observed that the case law of the European Court of Human Rights did not establish a general right to bargain collectively. Although Article 11 ECHR has been held to safeguard 'the freedom to protect the occupational interests of trade union members by trade union action, the conduct and development of which the Contracting States must both permit and make possible',[219] this broad statement covers only a core of specific activities.[220] It does not include any right for a trade union to be consulted by the State,[221] nor an obligation on the State to conclude collective agreements.[222] There is no direct reference in this case law to a right to bargain collectively.[223] In the view of the AG, Article 6 ESC and the related clauses in international law, were not sufficiently strong to create a fundamental right to collective bargaining.[224] In the absence of such a clear-cut right in international law it was, by implication, inappropriate for the Court of Justice to move at a faster pace than the Strasbourg Court when interpreting the scope of corresponding rights under Community law and the ECHR, an approach now reinforced by the 'horizontal' provisions of the EU Charter of Fundamental Rights.[225]

The Social Charter's declarations on collective bargaining must be read together with point 13 where it is pronounced that:

The right to resort to collective action in the event of a conflict of interests shall include the right to strike subject to the obligations arising under national regulations and collective agreements.

The right to strike contained in point 13 is similar to Article 6(4) ESC,[226] although the ESC makes no reference to 'obligations arising under national regulations'. Once again the Commission's reaction was cautious. No

---

[219] *National Union of Belgian Police v Belgium*, 27 Oct 1975, Series A No 19, para 40.

[220] See paras 143–45 of the opinion. In fact the only right expressly recognised by the Court has been to be heard by the State, *ibid* para 39; and *Swedish Engine Drivers' Union v Sweden*, 6 February 1976, Series A No 20, para 40.

[221] *Belgian Police, ibid* para 38.

[222] *Swedish Engine Drivers*, n 220 above, para 39.

[223] In para 148 the AG cites the *Swedish Engine Drivers* case, *ibid* where the majority of the Commission of Human Rights had argued in favour of interpreting Art 11 ECHR to include a right of trade unions to engage in collective bargaining. The Court, however, held that it did not have to give a ruling on that question since, it said, such a right was not at issue and was granted to the applicant union under national law. See also, *Gustafsson v Sweden*, 25 April 1996, RJD. 1996–II, No 9, discussed in paras 151–56 of the opinion.

[224] Paras 146–47. In para 149 the AG points to the restrictive interpretation of Art 6 ESC in the cases concerning the *Belgian Police*, n 219 above, para 38; and *Swedish Engine Drivers, ibid* para 39. In both cases the Court of Human Rights commented upon the meaning of Art 6(1) ESC in the course of interpreting Art 11 ECHR.

[225] OJ 2000, C364/1. See Art 52(3), which does, however, allow for the provision of more extensive protection in the form of 'Union law'. See further, ch 12.

[226] Art 6(4) ESC declares that workers and employers have the right to take: 'collective action in cases of conflicts of interest, including the right to strike, subject to obligations that might arise out of collective agreements previously entered into'.

attempt was made to frame a proposal based on Article 94 EC [ex 100 EEC].[227] Another option, suggested by Bercusson, would have been a Community instrument recognising the right to strike over violations or impasses in negotiating agreements on fundamental rights with protection according to the law in each Member State.[228] Such an approach would put fundamental rights disputes on a par with industrial conflicts. It is difficult to envisage how the Community would have justified legislation on these grounds, presumably based on Article 308 EC [ex 235 EEC], even before such an option was apparently foreclosed by the exclusion of the 'right to strike' from the reach of legislation promulgated under the Amsterdam Social Chapter.[229] Moreover, the phrase 'conflicts of interests' in point 13 indicates that the right to strike is limited to protecting workers' *interests* rather than the broader notion of fundamental social *rights*.

Community legislation recognising the right to strike as a *fundamental social right* would present acute practical and philosophical difficulties as, in most Member States,[230] a fundamental distinction is drawn between conflicts of interest and conflicts of right.[231] Recognition of the right to strike places *collective interests* on a pedestal above the *rights of individuals* under the contract of employment or employment relationship. As Barnard explains:[232]

While disputes over conflicts of rights concern the interpretation and application of existing contractual clauses, disputes over conflicts of interests relate to changes in the establishment of collective rules and require the conflicting economic interest to be reconciled with a view to reaching a solution on the basis of legal or collective procedures.

It is for this reason that the Charter indicates a preference for mediation, conciliation and, if necessary, arbitration at the appropriate level.[233] Indeed, in a parallel study the Commission note that the concept of a Community 'right to strike' poses immense problems as a result of the very different and complex laws governing strike action in the Member States.[234] A Community right to strike would be incapable of definition in individual Member States where there are a multitude of forms of industrial action

---

[227] For discussion of the legality of using Article 94 EC for such a proposal in the light of the Court's judgment in Case C–376/98, *Germany v European Parliament and Council* (*Tobacco Advertising*) [2000] ECR I–8419, see ch 3, pp 86–7.

[228] B Bercusson, 'Fundamental Social and Economic Rights in the European Community' in A Cassese, A Clapham and J Weiler (eds) *Human Rights and the European Community: Methods of Protection* (Nomos, Baden-Baden, 1991) 195–291 at 230.

[229] Art 137(6) EC [ex 2(6) of the Agreement on Social Policy].

[230] With the exception of the UK and Ireland. See Barnard, n 80 above at 578.

[231] Nielsen, n 99 above, p 105.

[232] Barnard, n 80 above, p 578.

[233] Point 13(2).

[234] *Comparative Study on Rules Governing Working Conditions in the Member States: A Synopsis*, SEC(89) 1137, pp 64–5. See Bercusson in Cassese *et al*, n 228 above at 229–30.

and a variety of legal effects.[235] Instead the Commission, in its proposed 'new initiatives' in the Action Programme, steered clear of any reference to the right to strike and focused on developing social dialogue at all levels. There was to be only one specific initiative, which would involve the preparation of a communication on the development of collective bargaining, including collective agreements at European level, with specific reference to the settlement of disputes.[236] This communication was not progressed by the Commission during the course of the Action Programme. In subsequent reports the Commission made no attempt to justify why it was abdicating its responsibility to further this part of the Charter.[237]

The Court has reflected the Commission's caution in this respect. In his opinion in *Albany International*,[238] AG Jacobs observed that Article 11 ECHR does not necessarily imply a right to strike, since the interests of union members can be furthered by other means.[239] Nevertheless, he concluded that the Community legal order protects the right to form and join trade unions and employers' associations that is at the heart of freedom of association.[240] It follows that the right to take collective action in order to protect occupational interests in so far as it is indispensable for the enjoyment of freedom of association is also protected by Community law.[241] However, there is insufficient convergence of national legal orders and international legal instruments on the recognition of a specific fundamental right to bargain collectively.[242] The Court did not address the international instruments in its judgment in *Albany* although, as has already been noted,[243] it too ultimately concluded that collective agreements per se fell outside the competition rules in Article 81 EC [ex 85 EEC].

While the Commission's caution and the Court's agnosticism suggest that collective labour rights have entered a cul-de-sac notwithstanding the bold statements in the Charter, more concrete possibilities have been offered by the second paragraph of point 12 where it is stated that:

The dialogue between the two sides of industry at European level which must be developed, may, if the parties deem it desirable, result in contractual relations in particular at inter-occupational and sectoral level.

[235] Bercusson, *ibid* at 230.

[236] *Social Europe* 1/90, p 65.

[237] Despite a brief mention of the proposed communication in the first monitoring report, COM(91) 511, Annex II, the three reports that followed were silent: COM(92) 562, COM(93) 668 and COM(95) 184. See further, B Ryan, 'Pay, Trade Union Rights and European Community Law' (1997) 13 *International Journal of Comparative Labour Law and Industrial Relations* 305 at 308–9.

[238] Case C–67/96 [1999] ECR I–5751.

[239] *Schmidt and Dahlström v Sweden*, judgment of 6 Feb 1976, Series A No 21, para 36.

[240] *Albany International*, para 158.

[241] *Ibid* para 159.

[242] *Ibid* para 160. The AG concludes, at para 161, that the right to collective bargaining is sufficiently protected by the general principle of freedom of contract.

[243] Discussed in ch 1.

This statement sits rather uneasily in a document seeking to establish 'rights'. It is, however, indicative of the potential for the development of European social dialogue and by referring to 'contractual relations' rather than merely 'relations', as in Article 118b EEC, it presages the formalised establishment of European 'framework agreements' under the procedure introduced at Maastricht and now contained in Articles 138–139 EC [ex Articles 3 and 4 of the Agreement on Social Policy].

A third example of social rights in the Charter derived from international law can be found in the first paragraph of point 10. Under this provision workers have a right to 'adequate social protection' according to the arrangements applying in each country. Workers also have a right to enjoy an adequate level of social security benefits irrespective of their status and the size of the undertaking where they are employed. These commitments broadly correspond with the right to social security in Article 12 ESC and ILO Convention No 102. As an alternative to harmonisation, the Commission consulted on a strategy designed to achieve the convergence of objectives of national security systems that can act as a brake on free movement.[244] This was eventually adopted in the form of a Council Recommendation on Social Protection: Convergence of Objectives.[245]

Finally, we complete this grouping with Articles 20–23 containing a series of employment-related rights for the protection of children and adolescents derived from Articles 7, 9 and 10 ESC and ILO Convention No 138. These rights can be summarised as follows:

—a minimum employment age not lower than the minimum school leaving age and, in any case, not lower than fifteen years;[246]
—equitable remuneration for young people in gainful employment in accordance with national practice;[247]
—limitation of the duration of work;[248]
—prohibition of night work in the case of workers under eighteen years;[249]
—vocational training for the purposes of access to employment and, following the end of compulsory education, such training should take place during working hours.[250]

In this area, unlike in the other fields in this grouping, the Commission proposed a binding legislative measure in the form of a directive on the approximation of the laws of the Member States on the protection of young

---

[244] *Social Europe* 1/90, p 64.
[245] Council Recommendation 92/442/EEC, OJ 1992, L245/49. For the Commission proposal, see COM(91) 228, OJ 1991, C194/13.
[246] Point 20.
[247] Point 21.
[248] Point 22.
[249] *Ibid.*
[250] Points 22 and 23.

people.[251] In the Action Programme the Commission left the issue of the appropriate legal base open. There was a strong hint, however, that recourse would be made to Article 118a EEC. For example, the Action Programme declared that children should in no event 'take up an occupation which endangers their health'.[252] The Commission concluded that the working hours of young people less than 18 years would have to be limited 'to protect their health and safety'.[253] Further reference was made to the need for regular medical checks to ensure that the health of young workers would not be threatened by the job in question.[254] The Commission had prepared their ground well and, once proposals had been issued under Article 118a EEC,[255] the measure was eventually adopted as Directive 94/33.[256] This Directive will be considered in more detail in the next chapter. Suffice to say that the Directive does not address the issue of the 'equitable remuneration' of young workers. Nonetheless, the Commission's success under this heading demonstrates that, in the period of the SEA, it was possible to secure binding social policy legislation where there was a link made with the health, safety and working environment of workers. In the other headings falling within this grouping, where pay and collective rights are to the fore, there was no realistic possibility of progress and the Commission wisely chose to target their resources on the areas where there was the greatest possibility of success.

(3) Fundamental Social Rights of Persons

Points 24–26 on the fundamental social rights of elderly and disabled persons, and the second paragraph of point 10 on social protection, form a third grouping of fundamental social rights in the Charter applicable to both workers and persons. In one sense these rights are a hangover from the Commission's drafts of the Charter. Citizenship is not referred to in the final text but, to all intents and purposes, these are citizens' rights. In another, more practical, sense, however, these are 'safe' rights. In the light of subsidiarity and the delineation of competences in the Charter, it is clear that these are areas where the Community was in a position to have influence without, ultimately, being able to dictate policy to the Member States. The significance of this category of rights lies with the recognition that disabled and elderly persons have specific rights that extend beyond

---

[251] *Social Europe* 1/90, pp 73–4.
[252] *Ibid.*
[253] *Ibid.*
[254] *Ibid.*
[255] COM(91) 543, OJ 1992, C84/7; and the amended proposal, COM(93) 35, OJ 1993, C77/1.
[256] Dir 94/33/EC on the protection of young people at work, OJ 1993, L216/12.

the ambit of the social policy provisions. This 'mainstreaming' approach to group rights, linked with the general principles of equality and non-discrimination, was to eventually manifest itself in Article 13 EC, introduced by the Treaty of Amsterdam, and the Framework Employment Directive of 2000.[257] In the short-term, however, the Commission exhibited only limited ambitions in these areas.

Points 24 and 25 of the Charter are concerned with the rights of elderly persons. As in the case of social protection rights in point 10, it is a precondition for the exercise of these rights that they will operate according to the arrangements applying in each country. Point 24 proclaims that every worker must, at the time of retirement 'be able to enjoy resources affording him or her a decent standard of living'. Point 25 offers a more limited right to any other person who has reached retirement age but is not entitled to a pension and does not have other means of subsistence. Persons falling into this category 'must be entitled to sufficient resources and to medical and social assistance specifically suited to his needs'. The rights contained in points 24 and 25 can be directly traced to Article 23 ESC concerning the right of elderly persons to social protection.

In the Action Programme the Commission highlighted the budgetary implications of demographic change both in connection with retirement pensions and also the increasing pressures on social and medical services.[258] The Commission noted that 20 per cent of the population were over 60, a figure which they expected to increase to 25 per cent by 2000. In particular, concern was expressed about a potential fall in the numbers active in the labour market. Hence, the ground was being prepared for the development of an important strand of the Community's labour market strategy, subsequently launched at Essen, in December 1994, where a series of priorities for job creation were identified based on active labour market measures.[259] These priorities formed the nucleus of what was later to emerge in concrete form in the 'Employment Guidelines', first published in 1997[260] in the immediate aftermath of the Amsterdam Treaty. In the 1989 Action Programme, however, the Commission proposed to 'limit its activities in this area' to the establishment of a separate action programme that would provide for 'pilot projects, exchanges of experience, improved information and channels of communication between groups representing the elderly'.[261] A Council Decision was rapidly adopted[262] along with a proposal for a European Year of the Elderly and Solidarity between Generations in 1993.[263]

---

[257] Dir 2000/78/EC establishing a general framework for equal treatment in employment and occupation, OJ 2000, L303/16. For full discussion, see ch 9.
[258] *Social Europe* 1/90, p 74.
[259] Presidency Conclusions, Essen European Council, 9/10 Dec 1994.
[260] COM(97) 497.
[261] *Social Europe* 1/90, p 75.
[262] Decision 91/49/EEC, OJ 1991, L28/29. For the Commission proposal, see COM(90) 80.
[263] Decision 92/440/EEC, OJ 1992, L245/43. The Commission proposal can be found in COM(91) 508, OJ 1992, C25/5.

Point 26 of the Charter addresses the fundamental social rights of disabled persons in more forthright terms thus:

All disabled persons, whatever the origin and nature of their disablement, must be entitled to additional concrete measures aimed at improving their social and professional integration.

These measures must concern, in particular, according to the capacities of the beneficiaries, vocational training, ergonomics, accessibility, mobility, means of transport and housing.

Significantly, point 26 evokes a broad conception of disability and forms part of the drive for greater economic and social cohesion.[264] As the Commission noted in the Third Report on the Application of the Social Charter, the Community's task was to integrate an estimated 30 million disabled people economically and socially within the general context of improving the quality of life of all Community citizens.[265] Moreover, the Community had adopted a programme on the vocational rehabilitation of people with disabilities in 1974[266] and a Recommendation on the Employment of Disabled People in the Community in 1986.[267] The Recommendation espouses equal opportunities for disabled persons in training and employment and the development of comprehensive policies including positive action. Building on this approach, and following the launch of the Helios programme in 1988,[268] the Commission proposed to continue this effort with Helios II for the period 1993–96.[269] The Helios programmes were designed to promote a coherent overall policy on integration and an independent way of life for disabled persons. An additional proposal, for a directive, was to be aimed at promoting the improvement of travel conditions of workers with motor disabilities as an essential prerequisite for vocational training and employment.[270] The resulting Community instrument was in the form of a non-binding Council Resolution establishing a separate action programme.[271]

We complete this section with the general right to social protection contained in the second paragraph of point 10 of the Charter, which declares that:

---

[264] See L Waddington, *Disability, Employment and the European Community* (Maklu, Antwerp, 1995); and Hervey, *European Social Law and Policy*, n 21 above, pp 169–72.

[265] COM(93) 668, p 18.

[266] Council Resolution of 27 June 1974, OJ 1974, C80/30.

[267] Council Recommendation 86/379/EEC, OJ 1986, L225/43.

[268] *Handicapped People in the European Community Living Independently in an Open Society*, OJ 1988, L104/38. An earlier Action Programme on the Integration of Handicapped People covered the period from 1983 to 1988, OJ 1981, C347/14.

[269] Decision 93/136/EEC, OJ 1993, L56/30. For the Commission proposals, see COM(91) 350, OJ 1991, C293/2; as amended by COM(92) 482, OJ 1993, C25/1.

[270] *Social Europe* 1/90, p 76.

[271] OJ 1992, C18/1. The Commission proposals were published in COM(90) 588, OJ 1991, C68/7; and COM(91) 539, OJ 1992, C15/18.

Persons who have been unable either to enter or re-enter the labour market and have no means of subsistence must be able to receive sufficient resources and social assistance in keeping with their particular situation.

Although there is no direct reference in point 10 to combating social exclusion, it is clear that this clause is intended to apply to those who are no longer in employment or who may never have entered the labour market and, therefore, it is indicative of a general right to social protection for Community citizens, albeit subject to the arrangements established in each country. This caveat prohibits harmonisation measures but it allows for the development of a convergence of social protection objectives and, specifically, the establishment of common criteria concerning sufficient resources and social assistance in national social protection systems. The latter was adopted in the form of a Council Recommendation in 1992.[272] It seeks to establish a subjective right to a guarantee of sufficient resources and benefits, and guidance for Member States on the ways and means of implementing that right. While this measure provides no more than soft legal guidance, it serves to encourage Member States to ensure that basic social assistance should cover essential needs 'taking account of living standards and price levels'.[273] This is a clear indication that the right to social protection creates a general duty on Member States to define and combat poverty concomitant with other commitments set out in the parallel 'Poverty' programmes.[274]

From the above analysis it is clear that, even in areas on the fringes of Community competence, or falling entirely within the national sphere of social policy, the Social Charter has, directly or indirectly, acted as a catalyst for wider and deeper integration primarily through the vehicle of the Action Programme. In turn, the Action Programme, sanctioned through the horizontal clause in point 28, helped to broaden the Community's social objectives beyond the narrow confines of Articles 117–122 EEC. The Charter has, in practice, embraced all Community citizens, albeit that much of this activity has been generated through soft law programmes. In order to assess the effectiveness of Community social legislation during the Action Programme (1989–1994) let us now turn, in the next chapter, to an analysis of selected directives and non-binding instruments introduced in this period.

---

[272] Recommendation 92/441/EEC, OJ 1992, L245/46. For the Commission proposals, see COM(91) 161, OJ 1991, C163/3; and COM(92) 240.

[273] *Ibid.* Section IC.

[274] See Hervey, *European Social Law and Policy*, n 21 above, pp 163–65. At the time of the Social Charter the Community had launched the 'Poverty 3' programme linked to the goals of the Internal Market and economic and social cohesion, Council Decision 89/457/EEC, OJ 1989, L224/10.

5

Community Social Legislation in the Era of the Social Charter

I A SOLID BASE OF LEGISLATIVE ACHIEVEMENTS?

IN THE PERIOD between the launch of the Social Charter Action Programme in November 1989[1] and the publication of the Commission's Green Paper on Social Policy in November 1993,[2] the Commission, in a sustained burst of activity, presented all 47 of the specific proposals in the Action Programme. In fact many of these proposals did not require legislative action, but of the 29 prospective measures referred to the Council, 16 had been adopted at this stage.[3] Indeed, several months later, in the ensuing White Paper on European Social Policy of July 1994,[4] the Commission followed through their own logic and concluded that:[5]

Given the *solid base of European social legislation that has already been achieved*, the Commission considers that there is not a need for a wide-ranging programme of new legislative proposals in the coming period.

In order to assess the veracity of the Commission's seemingly confident claim it is necessary to evaluate the Community's legislative output over the period of the Action Programme.[6] In particular, our interest lies in questioning the assumptions that lay behind the Commission's statement. How far was it possible for Community legislation, justified primarily on internal market or health and safety grounds, to fulfil the broad *social* aims that

---

[1] COM(89) 568. Reproduced in *Social Europe*, 1/90, pp 52–76.

[2] COM(93) 551, *Options for the Union*. The purpose of the Green Paper was to set out the achievements of the Community's social dimension and to map a way forward that took account of the entry into force of the Treaty on European Union (TEU) and the changing socio-economic situation reflected most noticeably by a serious rise in the level of unemployment (Introduction, p 6). These themes will be carried forward in chs 6 and 7.

[3] *Ibid* p 10.

[4] COM(94) 333, *A Way Forward for the Union*.

[5] *Ibid*. Introduction, para 22. Emphasis added.

[6] The Action Programme covered the period from 1989 to 1994. Although the TEU entered into legal force on 2 Nov 1993, none of the proposals under discussion in this chapter were proposed or enacted under the provisions of the Agreement on Social Policy, which was annexed to the amended EC Treaty by the TEU.

underpinned the Charter, even in the denuded form in which it was ultimately issued? How valid was the Commission's claim in the light of the
apparently unflinching opposition of the UK to *European social legislation*
throughout this period?[7] To what extent did this *solid base* of legislation
amount to a minimum set of uniform exercisable social rights for Community 'workers' and 'persons' broadly consistent with the aims of the
Charter? How far was this process of 'Europeanisation' of the social laws
of the Member States dependant upon quasi-legislative or soft law measures designed to encourage rather than impose adherence by national
legislatures and courts?

For the purposes of conducting our evaluation, while taking account of
these questions, examples have been selected from three distinct streams of
'social legislation' introduced under the Action Programme. The first stream
consists of three directives adopted as health, safety and working environment measures on the basis of an expansive interpretation of Article 118a
EEC [now part of 137 EC]. The second stream contains the only measure
introduced during this period with the purpose of improving living and
working conditions in so far as they 'directly effect the establishment or
functioning of the common market' under Article 100 EEC [now 94 EC].
Finally, the third stream features two contrasting examples of Community
soft laws to provide an assessment of the legal scope and effectiveness of
Community social policy measures that are formally non-binding.

II TAKING FULL ADVANTAGE OF ARTICLE 118a EEC?

Momentum for legislative action based on Article 118a EEC grew rapidly
after the adoption of the SEA. Indeed, by the end of 1987, the Commission
had formulated a strategy to take 'full advantage of the opportunities
afforded by the provisions of . . . Article 118a'.[8] The European Parliament's
'Salisch Report' of October 1988[9] added fuel to the fire by urging an
ergonomic approach to the concepts of 'health', 'safety' and the 'working
environment', which took account not only of specific health and safety
risks at the workplace, but also the needs of the whole person and his or
her environment at work and in society.[10] In the Action Programme,

---

[7] Indeed it was precisely because of this opposition that the eleven signatories of the Social
Charter decided, with the UK's approval, to adopt a separately annexed Agreement on Social
Policy, specifically because they wished to 'implement' the Social Charter—see the first recital
of the preamble of the Agreement on Social Policy annexed to Protocol 14 of the EC Treaty
as revised by the TEU.

[8] Commission Communication of 21 December 1987 on its programme concerning safety,
hygiene and health at work, OJ 1988, C28/2; Summary and Part II.A.

[9] *The Concept of the Working Environment and the Scope of Article 118a of the EEC
Treaty*, 'Salisch Report', PE DOC A 2-226/88, 21.10.88.

[10] *Ibid* p 10. Discussed in ch 3, pp 96–8.

however, the Commission limited its ambitions, under a heading concerning health protection and safety in the workplace, to technical regulations regarding products and equipment used by workers and provisions regarding worker protection and the working environment. The main vehicle for achieving these objectives was to be the 'framework' Directive on the Safety and Health of Workers at Work.[11] In the event, however, three directives: on Pregnancy and Maternity;[12] the Organisation of Working Time;[13] and Young Workers;[14] each put forward elsewhere in the Action Programme,[15] were introduced, controversially, under Article 118a EEC, and therefore became effective in all Member States, circumventing the UK's veto.[16] While much of the debate concerning these directives has been concerned with the strategies of the players in the 'Treaty base game',[17] and the Court's justifications for broadly interpreting the concepts in Article 118a EEC,[18] our primary interest here lies with the quality of the legislation that emerged and the extent to which it has contributed to a 'solid base' of social legislation in this field.

(1) Pregnancy and Maternity

The first measure to test the scope of Article 118a EEC was the Pregnancy and Maternity Directive[19] introduced in 1992 for implementation by

---

[11] Dir 89/391/EEC, OJ 1989, L183/1.

[12] Dir 92/85/EEC on the introduction of measures to encourage improvements in the safety and health of pregnant workers and workers who have recently given birth or are breast feeding (tenth individual Directive within the meaning of Art 16(1) of Dir 89/391/EEC) OJ 1992, L348/1.

[13] Dir 93/104/EC concerning certain aspects of the organisation of working time, OJ 1993, L307/18.

[14] Dir 94/33/EC on the protection of young people at work, OJ 1994, L216/12.

[15] The proposal on pregnancy and maternity is featured in the initiatives concerning 'equal treatment for men and women' (point 16); references to limiting working time are found under the heading 'improving living and working conditions' (points 7–9); and proposals concerning young workers fall within the 'protection of children and adolescents' (points 20–23). See *Social Europe* 1/90, p 52.

[16] See ch 3 for discussion of the scope of Art 118a EEC.

[17] See B Fitzpatrick, 'Straining the Definition of Health and Safety' (1997) 26 *Industrial Law Journal* 115.

[18] See generally, C Barnard, A Dashwood and B Hepple, *The ECJ's Working Time Judgment: The Social Market Vindicated* (CELS Occasional Paper No 2, Cambridge, 1997).

[19] Dir 92/85/EEC, OJ 1992, L348/1. For academic literature on the Directive, see N Burrows, 'Maternity Rights in Europe—An Embryonic Legal Regime' (1991) 11 *Yearbook of European Law* 273; V Cromack, 'The EC Pregnancy Directive—Principle or Pragmatism?' (1993) 15 *Journal of Social Welfare and Family Law* 261; E Ellis, 'Protection of Pregnancy and Maternity' (1993) 22 *Industrial Law Journal* 63; H Fenwick, 'Special Protections for Women in European Union Law' in T Hervey and D O'Keeffe (eds) *Sex Equality Law in the European Union* (Wiley, Chichester, 1996) 63–80; C Kilpatrick, 'How long is a piece of string? European regulation of the post-birth period' in Hervey and O'Keeffe, *ibid* 81–96; and E Szyszczak, 'Community Law on Pregnancy and Maternity' in Hervey and O'Keeffe, *ibid* 52–62.

19 October 1994.[20] Whereas the Action Programme had indicated that an initiative to protect pregnant women at work would be based on equal treatment between women and men,[21] the Commission's proposals[22] and the ensuing Directive refer only to point 19 of the Charter concerning health and safety conditions in the working environment.[23] In particular, the Directive is justified on the basis that pregnant workers, and workers who have recently given birth or are breastfeeding, must be a 'specific risk group' with respect to their safety and health in line with Article 15 of the framework Directive on the Safety and Health of Workers at Work.[24] The proposals focused on specific measures concerning, inter alia, the dangers for pregnant women associated with visual display units and risks arising from exposure to carcinogens. In the view of the Economic and Social Committee the proposal offered a 'coherent health and safety package'.[25] By placing their proposals in this context, the Commission provided a basis for the Directive to be adopted as the tenth individual 'daughter directive' within the meaning of Article 16(1) of the framework Directive. In order to fit the Directive within the overall structure of Article 118a EEC and the framework Directive, its protective health and safety goals were accentuated, as an alternative to legislating specifically for the purpose of establishing maternity rights per se. In fact, when push came to shove, the UK, having secured several key amendments, was prepared to abstain rather than oppose the measure.[26] The Directive does, however, retain elements that can be traced back to its source as an equal treatment measure derived from point 16 of the Charter.

A brief examination of the resulting Directive reveals this dual health and safety/equal treatment purpose. Articles 1–7 reflect the primary objective of health and safety protection. The starting point of the Directive is for the Commission to draw up guidelines concerning health and safety hazards for pregnant workers and for workers who have recently given birth, or who are breast feeding, with a view to risk assessment for these groups of workers.[27] Member States are obliged to bring these guidelines to the attention of all employers and all female employees and/or their representatives.[28] Annex I contains a non-exhaustive list of activities liable to involve a specific risk of exposure to physical, biological and chemical agents, industrial processes and working conditions in underground mining. There is an obligation on the employer to assess these risks and take necessary measures to

---

[20] Art 14(1).
[21] *Social Europe* 1/90, p 68.
[22] OJ 1990, C281/3 and OJ 1991, C25/9.
[23] Fifth recital of the preamble.
[24] Sixth and seventh recital of the preamble.
[25] OJ 1991, C41/30.
[26] See Ellis, n 19 above at 65. Italy also abstained.
[27] Art 3(1).
[28] Art 3(2).

avoid the exposure of the worker concerned to such risks.[29] Employers must adjust the working conditions or, if this is not technically or objectively feasible and cannot be required on duly substantiated grounds, workers may have to be moved to another job,[30] or be granted leave in accordance with national legislation and practice.[31] There are also prohibitions in certain cases where there is a risk of exposure to agents and working conditions listed in Annex II,[32] with additional safeguards for women who are breastfeeding.[33] Workers are not obliged to perform night work during pregnancy and for a period after childbirth.[34] The implementing measures must, however, entail the possibility, in accordance with national legislation/or practice, for the worker in question to transfer to day work,[35] or be granted leave if this is not feasible or cannot reasonably be required on duly substantiated grounds.[36]

Articles 8–12, by contrast, contain a limited range of specific maternity rights for women. Article 8 provides a right to a continuous period of 'at least' 14 weeks maternity leave, in accordance with national legislation and practice, including at least two weeks leave before and/or after confinement. This was a reduction from the 16 weeks leave originally proposed by the Commission's equalities unit.[37] Moreover, at least two weeks of this period is determined according to coercive protective reasons rather than the personal choice of the woman concerned.[38] Under Article 11 an 'adequate' maternity allowance must be paid during the period of maternity leave guaranteeing income at least equivalent to that which the worker concerned would receive in the event of a break of her activities on grounds connected with her state of health. This will be subject to any national ceiling and also the worker may have to fulfil national conditions of eligibility for such benefits. By virtue of Article 9, women also have a right to time-off without loss of pay in order to attend antenatal examinations, if such examinations have to take place during working hours.

Article 10(1) of the Directive obliges Member States to take the necessary measures to prohibit 'dismissal' from the beginning of the pregnancy to the end of the period of maternity leave, save in 'exceptional cases' not

---

[29] Arts 4 and 5.
[30] Art 5(2).
[31] Art 5(3).
[32] Art 6(1). This list follows the same headings as Annex I but is more limited.
[33] Art 6(2).
[34] Art 7(1).
[35] Art 7(2)(a).
[36] Art 7(2)(b).
[37] See Ellis, n 19 above at 63. The European Parliament attempted to reinstate the 16-week leave period unsuccessfully. The equalities unit also proposed that the directive should cover replacement services for self-employed pregnant women, paternity leave and reversal of the burden of proof.
[38] See Fenwick, n 19 above at 76.

connected with the woman's condition which are 'permitted under national legislation and practice' and 'where applicable, provided that the competent authority has given its consent'. However, under Article 10(2) any employer seeking to justify dismissal on this basis 'must cite duly substantiated grounds' in writing. Article 10(3) places an additional obligation on Member States to take the necessary measures to protect women unlawfully dismissed under this provision from the 'consequences of dismissal'.

Article 10, which the Court has found to be directly effective,[39] appears to strongly reinforce the 'special protection' for women against pregnancy related dismissals under Articles 2(1) and 3 of Directive 76/207 as interpreted by the Court,[40] a point acknowledged in *Brown*.[41] In practice, however, the utility of this provision depends not only on the scope of Directive 92/85, but also on the interpretation and application of the concept of 'dismissal' and the grounds under which national rules may allow for dismissals in exceptional cases, including the arrangements, if any, for consent to be given by a competent authority. The Court has recently considered these issues in *Tele Danmark*[42] and *Jiménez Melgar*.[43] Before turning to the

[39] Case C–438/99, *Jiménez Melgar v Ayuntamiento de Los Barrios* [2001] ECR I–6915, paras 31–4.

[40] Dir 76/207/EEC on equal treatment for men and women as regards access to employment, vocational training and promotion and working conditions, OJ 1976, L39/40. See Case C–177/88, *Dekker v Stichting Vormingscentrum voor Jong Volwassenen* [1990] ECR I–3941; Case C–421/92, *Habermann-Beltermann v Arbeiterwohlfahrt, Bezirksverband Ndb/Opf EV* [1994] ECR I–1657; Case C–32/93, *Webb v EMO Air Cargo* [1994] ECR I–3567; Case C–394/96, *Brown v Rentokil Ltd* [1998] ECR I–4185; Case C–218/98, *Abdoulaye v Renault* [1999] ECR I–5723; Case C–207/98, *Mahlburg v Land Mecklenburg-Vorpommern* [2000] ECR I–549; *Jiménez Melgar, ibid*; Case C–109/00, *Tele Danmark A/S v Handels-og Kontorfunktionærernes Forbund i Danmark* [2001] ECR I–6993; cf Case C–400/95, *Larsson v Føtex Supermarked* [1997] ECR I–2757. For critique, see H Fenwick and T Hervey, 'Sex Equality in the Single Market: New Directions for the European Court of Justice' (1995) 32 *Common Market Law Review* 443 at 450–57; L Flynn, 'Equality between Men and Women in the Court of Justice (1998) 18 *Yearbook of European Law* 259 at 265–78; E Ellis, 'The Recent Jurisprudence of the Court of Justice in the Field of Sex Equality' (2000) 37 *Common Market Law Review* 1403 at 1416–22; and E Caracciolo di Torella and A Masselot, 'Pregnancy, Maternity and the Organisation of Family Life: An Attempt to Classify the Case Law of the Court of Justice' (2001) 26 *European Law Review* 239.

[41] *Brown, ibid*. See Flynn, *ibid* at 268. The Court held, at para 18, that it was 'precisely in view of the harmful effects which the risk of dismissal may have on the physical and mental state of women who are pregnant, women who have recently given birth or women who are breastfeeding, including the particularly serious risk that pregnant women may be prompted voluntarily to terminate their pregnancy, that the Community legislature, pursuant to Article 10 [of the Directive] . . . provided for special protection to be given to women, by prohibiting dismissal during the period from the beginning of their pregnancy to the end of their maternity leave. Article 10 . . . provides that there is to be no exception to, or derogation from, the prohibition of dismissal of pregnant women during that period, save in exceptional cases not connected with their condition'. See C Boch, 'Official: During Pregnancy, Females are Pregnant' (1998) 23 *European Law Review* 488.

[42] Case C–109/00, *Tele Danmark A/S v Handels-og Kontorfunktionærernes Forbund i Danmark* [2001] ECR I–6993.

[43] Case C–438/99, *Jiménez Melgar v Ayuntamiento de Los Barrios* [2001] ECR I–6915.

Court's case law on the Directive, however, let us first consider the Commission's periodic report on its implementation, published in 1999.[44]

In the implementation report the Commission note that Member States have, in the main, applied the Directive to all pregnant workers in both public and private sectors and to women on both indefinite and fixed-term contracts.[45] The Commission have identified a number of examples of apparent non-compliance arising either from misimplementation by Member States, or misapplication of national rules and/or practices. For example, contrary to Article 5, national law in France and Spain does not adequately provide for pregnant workers to take leave for health and safety reasons.[46] The provisions on night work in Article 7 do not amount to an outright ban, but rather a prohibition against forced night work for women covered by the Directive. According to the Commission, this means that the Directive is consistent with the equal treatment principle guaranteed by Article 5 of Directive 76/207. The Court has held in *Stoeckel*[47] and, subsequently, in infringement proceedings against France[48] and Italy[49] that a general ban against women performing night work is contrary to the principle of equal treatment. The Court did not directly address the ILO Night Work Convention No 89 which prohibited night work for women, and to which both Member States were bound at the time, although its finding is compatible with the Protocol to that Convention and a revised Night Work Convention introduced in 1990.[50] The Commission identify several Member States who ban pregnant women, or women who have recently given birth, from night work. Such a ban goes further than is necessary to achieve the protective objective of Article 7 and therefore, according to the Commission, contravenes Directive 76/207. Infringement proceedings will be brought against these Member States.[51] This litigation will address the tension inherent within the Directive between its essentially protective provisions, that can

---

[44] COM(99) 100.

[45] *Ibid* p 7. The Commission reported, however, that there were exceptions in the legislation in Austria, Greece and Gibraltar and, as no exceptions are allowed, they proposed to bring infringement proceedings in this regard.

[46] *Ibid* p 8.

[47] Case C–345/89, *Ministère Public v Stoeckel* [1991] ECR I–4047. See S Sciarra, 'Dynamic integration of national and Community sources: the case of night-work for women', in Hervey and O'Keeffe, n 19 above, 97–108; and C Kilpatrick, 'Production and Circulation of EC Night Work Jurisprudence' (1996) 25 *Industrial Law Journal* 169.

[48] Case C–197/96, *Commission v French Republic* [1997] ECR I–1489.

[49] Case C–207/96, *Commission v Italy* [1997] ECR I–6869.

[50] ILO Convention No 171, Recommendation No 178 and a Protocol to the Night Work (Women) Convention No 89. This allows the prohibition to be lifted at the express request of a woman worker on condition that neither her health nor that of her child will be endangered. This decision represents a complete volte-face in international labour law. Back in 1919, when the ILO was founded, the issue of night work for women was at the top of the agenda and led to the adoption of a Convention on the subject at the ILO's inaugural session: ILO Night Work (Women) Convention (No 4). See N Valticos and G von Potobsky, *International Labour Law*, 2nd revised edn (Kluwer, Deventer, 1995) p 208.

[51] Austria, Italy, Luxembourg and the UK (in respect of the law in Gibraltar). Proceedings against Germany are also being contemplated.

create a negative impact on women's employment by removing women from the workplace,[52] and its broader equal treatment objectives that place emphasis on the maternity entitlements of women workers.[53]

In relation to the maternity rights in Articles 8–12, the Commission found a high level of compliance. This is not surprising considering the minimalist nature of these provisions. At the time of the report maternity leave ranged from 14 weeks in the UK[54] to 28 weeks in Denmark.[55] The Commission report contains an extensive survey of maternity allowances paid by Member States and the form of payment.[56] This survey reveals wide variations both in the amounts that Member States consider to be 'adequate' and the linkage made between maternity payments and other allowances for sickness and/or incapacity. For example, payments range from 80–100 per cent of full pay in Belgium, France and the Netherlands, 65–70 per cent in Portugal and Ireland and fixed sums in Sweden and the UK. There is also evidence of blurring between maternity pay and sick pay. For example, in Austria the maternity allowance is based on the average remuneration over the previous 13 weeks and the worker is entitled to special payments such as bonuses. However, if the reason for the leave is based on a medical certificate stating health reasons the worker is entitled to a social security benefit.[57]

Although the preamble indicates that the reference to sick pay in Article 11 should not be interpreted as an analogy between pregnancy and sickness, the wording of the Directive itself does little to prevent such ambiguity in practice.[58] The problem of eligibility rules is also highlighted by the case of Gibraltar where entitlement to an allowance during maternity leave

[52] See Fenwick and Hervey, n 40 above, who observe, at 457, that the 'special protection of excluding pregnant women from night work masks a desire on the part of the State and employers to remove pregnant employees from the public and dangerous workplaces wherever possible. Where, as in this instance, the special protection model perpetuates liberal notions of equality in the public sphere, and implies that women's place lies in the private sphere, the [special protection] model is revealed as antithetical to substantive equality'.

[53] For a discussion on the equalities issues raised by the inclusion of 'protective' clauses in directives, see Fenwick, n 19 above.

[54] This was subsequently increased to 18 weeks by the Maternity and Parental Leave etc. Regs, 1999, effective from 15 Dec 1999. SI 1999 No 3312. Provisions contained within the UK's Employment Bill, 2001, on formal enactment, will increase the period of leave to 26 weeks and raise the maternity allowance from 2003 [Bill 44–7 Nov 2001].

[55] COM(99) 100, pp 10–12.

[56] *Ibid* pp 15–19.

[57] *Ibid* p 15.

[58] The Court has established through its case law that pregnancy is not in any way comparable to a pathological condition—Case C–32/93, *Webb v EMO Air Cargo* [1994] ECR I–3567, para 25. However, in Case C–394/96, *Brown v Rentokil Ltd* [1998] ECR I–4185, the Court held, at para 22, that it is a period during which disorders and complications may arise compelling a woman to undergo strict medical supervision and, in some cases, to take absolute rest for all or part of her pregnancy. Those disorders and complications, which may cause incapacity for work, form part of the risks inherent in the condition of pregnancy and are thus considered to be a specific feature of that condition.

is dependent upon the woman satisfying the conditions of entitlement for injury benefit.[59] The Commission humbly note that such a blatant linkage between maternity and sickness/injury is permissible because the Directive, in Article 11(4) allows Member States to make entitlement to an adequate allowance subject to their own national conditions of eligibility.[60]

Further guidance on the effectiveness of the Directive can be gleaned from a limited number of cases referred by the national courts to the Court of Justice. In *Boyle*[61] five specific issues were referred concerning the rights of women under their contract of employment during pregnancy and maternity leave. First, the Court was asked to determine the meaning of the terms 'payment' and an 'adequate allowance' in Article 11. The Court endorsed its earlier case law when finding that the concept of 'pay' encompasses the consideration paid directly or indirectly during the worker's maternity leave in respect of her employment.[62] By contrast the concept of an 'allowance' includes all income received by the worker during her maternity leave which is not paid to her by her employer pursuant to an employment relationship.[63] The allowance must provide a guaranteed income *at least equivalent* to a sickness allowance under national legislation whether it is paid in the form of an allowance, pay or a combination of the two.[64] It does not, however, guarantee any higher contractual sick pay normally paid by the employer.[65] Therefore, a worker who does not return to work after childbirth does have to repay the difference between the pay she received during her maternity leave and the statutory payments to which she was entitled so long as the equivalence test is satisfied.[66] Moreover, the requirement to repay does not amount to sex discrimination as a pregnant woman cannot be compared with a sick man as the maternity leave granted to a woman under Directive 92/85 is intended, *first*, to protect a woman's biological condition and, *second*, to protect the 'special relationship' between a woman and her child over the period which follows pregnancy and childbirth.[67]

[59] COM(99) 100, p 18.

[60] *Ibid* pp 18–19.

[61] Case C–411/96, *Boyle and Others v Equal Opportunities Commission* [1998] ECR I–6041. See E Caracciolo di Torella, 'Recent Developments in Pregnancy and Maternity Rights' (1999) 28 *Industrial Law Journal* 276.

[62] This is consistent with the definition of 'pay' in Art 119 EEC [now 141 EC] in Case C–342/93, *Gillespie and others v Northern Health and Social Services Board and others* [1996] ECR I–475, para 12.

[63] *Boyle*, n 61 above, para 31.

[64] Para 33.

[65] Para 35. This would not be a 'like for like' comparison: see Case C–342/93, *Gillespie and others v Northern Health and Social Services Board and Others* [1996] ECR I–475, para 16; and Case C–279/93, *Schumacker v Finanzamt Köln-Altstadt* [1995] ECR I–225, para 30.

[66] Para 36.

[67] Paras 40–41. See Case 184/83, *Hofmann v Barmer Ersatzkasse* [1984] ECR 3047, para 25; and Case C–136/95, *CNAVTS v Thibault* [1998] ECR I–2011, para 25. For a critique, see C McGlynn, 'Ideologies of Motherhood in European Community Sex Equality Law' [2000] 6 *European Law Journal* 29.

Secondly, the Court was asked to consider whether a clause in an employment contract, requiring a female worker who is on pregnancy-related sick leave immediately before a period of maternity leave to bring forward her maternity leave period, is discriminatory and contravenes either Article 119 EEC [now 141 EC], Directive 76/207 or Directive 92/85. The Court found that such a clause was lawful on the basis that Article 8 of Directive 92/85 provides for a minimum period of 14 weeks continuous maternity leave but leaves it open to the Member States to determine when the maternity leave commences.[68] The clause in the contract merely reflected the choice made in the national legislation.[69] However, the Court found, thirdly, that the right to 14 weeks continuous leave is an absolute right and a clause prohibiting a woman from taking sick leave during that period unless she terminates her maternity leave and resumes it later was unlawful.[70]

Fourthly, the Court held that the legal scope of Article 8 of Directive 92/85 did not extend beyond the continuous 14-week period. Therefore, a clause in an employment contract covering a supplementary period of maternity leave, during which time the employee ceased to accrue her entitlement to annual leave, was not prohibited even though it could be viewed as indirectly discriminatory because it worked to the disadvantage of far more women than men.[71] However, this disadvantage was cancelled out by supplementary unpaid maternity leave which constituted a 'special advantage', over and above the protection provided for by Directive 92/85 and available only to women, so the fact that annual leave ceased to accrue during that period of leave could not amount to less favourable treatment of women.[72] Finally, the Court held that a clause limiting the accrual of pension rights during the maternity leave period was unlawful.[73]

In *Høy Pedersen*[74] the Court was asked to consider Danish legislation concerning pay during incapacity for work due to pregnancy. The Court found that the fact that women, absent from work due to pregnancy-related incapacity, were paid less than workers absent due to other forms of incapacity was discriminatory.[75] Discrimination in this case could not be justified by the aim of sharing the risks and economic costs connected with pregnancy between the pregnant worker, the employer and society as a whole. That goal could not be regarded as an objective factor unrelated to any discrimination based on sex within the meaning of the case law of the

---

[68] Para 49.
[69] Para 52.
[70] Para 66.
[71] Para 76. See Case C–1/95, *Gerster v Freiestaat Bremen* [1997] ECR I–5253, para 30, and Case C–100/95, *Kording v Senator für Finanz* [1997] ECR I–5289, para 16.
[72] Para 79.
[73] Para 87.
[74] Case C–66/96, *Høy Pedersen v Kvickly Skive* [1998] ECR I–7327. See Caracciolo di Torella (1999, *Industrial Law Journal*) n 61 above.
[75] *Ibid* para 35.

Court.[76] While ruling out justification in this case, the Court made no attempt to exclude the possibility that it might be possible to justify direct discrimination in the context of the Directive.[77]

The Court was also asked to consider whether Articles 4 and 5 had been breached in a situation where an employer had sent a woman home on the grounds that she was unfit to work due to pregnancy-related incapacity without paying her salary because he considered that he could not provide work for her. The Court noted that it is true that, by reserving to Member States the right to retain or introduce provisions which are intended to protect women in connection with 'pregnancy and maternity', Article 2(3) of Directive 76/207 recognises the legitimacy, in terms of the principle of equal treatment, of protecting a woman's biological condition during and after pregnancy.[78] This argument could not be sustained in this case, however, because the employer's decision had reflected his interests rather than the aim of protecting the biological condition of the pregnant woman and therefore he had acted in contravention of Articles 4 and 5 of the Directive.[79]

The meaning of 'pay' and 'allowance' for the purposes of Article 11(2) was considered further in *Lewen v Denda*.[80] In this case an employee on parenting leave had been denied a Christmas bonus. The Court held that for the purposes of Article 119 EEC [now 141 EC] this was 'pay', even if paid on a voluntary basis and even if paid mainly or exclusively as an incentive for future work or loyalty to the undertaking or both.[81] The Court went on to reiterate, however, that the concept of payment within the meaning of Article 11(2)(b) of Directive 92/85 was different.[82] That provision is intended to ensure that, during maternity leave, female workers receive an income at least equal to that prescribed by Article 11(3) of that Directive, irrespective of whether it is paid in the form of an allowance, pay or a combination of the two. As the Christmas bonus was not intended to ensure such a level of income during a worker's maternity leave, the bonus at issue could not be regarded as falling within the concept of payment within the meaning of the Directive.[83] Article 11(2) of Directive 92/85 was not

---

[76] Case C–457/93, *Kuratorium für Dialyse und Nierentransplantation v Lewark* [1996] ECR I–243, para 31.

[77] Flynn, n 40 above, 270–71.

[78] Para 54. See Case C–32/93, *Webb v EMO Air Cargo* [1994] ECR I–3567, para 20.

[79] Para 58. See also, Case C–207/98, *Mahlburg v Land Mecklenburg-Vorpommern* [2000] ECR I–159, where the Court held, at para 26, that the exercise of the rights conferred on women under Art 2(3) of Dir 76/207 cannot be the subject of unfavourable treatment regarding their access to employment or working conditions and that, in that light, the result pursued by the Directive is substantive, not formal, equality.

[80] Case C–333/97 [1999] ECR I–7243. See E Caracciolo di Torella, 'Childcare, employment and equality in the European Community: first (false) steps of the Court' (2000) 25 *European Law Review* 310.

[81] Para 31.

[82] See *Boyle*, n 61 above, paras 31–3.

[83] *Lewen*, n 80 above, para 23.

applicable in so far as subparagraph (a) concerns rights linked to the contract of employment of a female worker which must be assured in the event of maternity leave. The Court ultimately found that as the bonus in question was paid during parenting leave rather than maternity leave, Directive 92/85 was inapplicable.[84]

Finally, two recent judgments regarding the application of the Directive to workers on fixed-term contracts have revealed both its strengths and weaknesses. In *Tele Danmark*[85] a mobile telephone company dismissed an employee after one month of a six-month fixed-term contract on the grounds that she had not informed them that she was pregnant when she was recruited and would not be able to perform a substantial part of her contract. The Court referred to the uncertainty of fixed-term contracts and held that Directive 92/85 makes no distinction as to the duration of the employment contract.[86] The Court observed that had the Community legislature wished to exclude fixed-term contracts, which 'represent a substantial proportion of employment relationships', from the scope of these directives 'it would have done so expressly'.[87]

In relation to the issue of dismissal, the Court referred to its established case law on the Equal Treatment Directive, 76/207,[88] whereby the dismissal of a woman worker on account of pregnancy amounts to direct discrimination 'on grounds of sex',[89] which is prohibited and cannot be justified on grounds relating to, either the financial loss which an employer who appointed a pregnant woman would suffer for the duration of her maternity leave[90] and pregnancy,[91] or because her presence is essential to the proper functioning of the undertaking.[92] Directive 92/85 adds a fresh dimension because, if women were obliged to inform their employer of their condition at the time of their recruitment, it could render ineffective the protection of pregnant workers established by Article 10 'even though the Community legislature intended such protection to be especially high'.[93]

---

[84] Para 31.
[85] Case C–109/00, *Tele Danmark A/S v Handels-og Kontorfunktionærernes Forbund i Danmark* [2001] ECR I–6993.
[86] Paras 32–3.
[87] Para 33.
[88] OJ 1976, L39/40.
[89] Para 25. Contrary to Art 5(1) of Dir 76/207. See Case C–179/88, *Handels-og Kontorfunktionærernes Forbund i Danmark (Hertz) v Dansk Arbejdsgiverforening* [1990] ECR I–3979, para 13; Case C–421/92, *Habermann-Beltermann v Arbeiterwohlfahrt, Bezirksverband Ndb/Opf EV* [1994] ECR I–1657, para 15; and Case C–32/93, *Webb v EMO Air Cargo* [1994] ECR I–3567, para 19.
[90] Para 28. See Case C–177/88, *Dekker v Stichting Vormingscentrum voor Jong Volwassenen* [1990] ECR I–3941, para 12.
[91] *Ibid.* See Case C–207/98, *Mahlburg v Land Mecklenburg-Vorpommern* [2000] ECR I–549, para 29.
[92] Para 29. See Case C–32/93, *Webb v EMO Air Cargo* [1994] ECR I–3567, para 26.
[93] Para 24.

The Court also referred to the fact that the protection laid down in Article 10 was motivated by concern regarding the risk that a dismissal may pose for the physical and mental state of pregnant workers 'including the particularly serious risk that they may be encouraged to have abortions'.[94] Consequently, the two directives precluded a worker from being dismissed on grounds of pregnancy where she was recruited for a fixed-term period and had failed to inform her employer of her pregnancy, even though she was aware of it at the time of her recruitment, and even in circumstances where she was unable to work during a substantial part of the term of that contract.[95]

In *Jiménez Melgar*,[96] a judgment delivered on the same date by the same Chamber,[97] the Court held that Article 10 of Directive 92/85 protects women who have a contract for an indefinite term as well as women on fixed-term contracts.[98] In a reference from a Spanish judge, the Court was asked to consider the position of a pregnant woman who argued that the non-renewal of her fixed-term contract by her employer, which had previously been renewed several times, was due to her pregnancy. The employer denied that this was the case. Referring to the same case law on Directive 76/207, the Court found that, if the reason for non-renewal was connected with her pregnancy this would be direct discrimination 'on grounds of sex', regardless as to whether or not the contract had expired at the stipulated time or the employer had acted unilaterally.[99] However, in relation to Article 10 of Directive 92/85, the Court held that non-renewal of a fixed-term contract when it comes to the end of its stipulated term cannot be regarded as a 'dismissal'.[100] Therefore, Mrs Jiménez Melgar was no longer a worker and she would have to rely on Directive 76/207 to show that the refusal of the employer to employ her, or renew her contract, was in fact motivated by her 'state of pregnancy'.[101]

The referring judge also asked the Court to determine the obligations on the State, if any, in relation to the derogations in Article 10(1) allowing for the dismissal of protected workers in 'exceptional cases not connected with their condition'. In its response, the Court found that this provision does not impose any obligation on the Member States, in their national laws and/or practices, to draw up a specific list of the reasons for dismissal in those circumstances.[102] Moreover, in reply to a separate question regarding

---

[94] Para 26.
[95] Para 34.
[96] Case C–438/99, *Jiménez Melgar v Ayuntamiento de Los Barrios* [2001] ECR I–6915.
[97] Delivered on 4 Oct 2001 by the Fifth Chamber.
[98] Para 40.
[99] Paras 41–4.
[100] Para 45.
[101] Para 46.
[102] Paras 37–8.

the procedures for 'consent' to be given by a 'competent authority' for such dismissals, the Court found that, where no such procedures exist, as is the case in Spain, Article 10(1) imposes no obligation on the Member State to introduce them because the consent requirement 'is preceded by the adverbial phrase "where applicable" '.[103]

The Commission report and the case law arising from the Directive reveal serious limitations in its scope and an element of confusion about its purpose. *Boyle* and *Lewen* confirm that the minimum 14-week protected period for paid maternity leave is guaranteed but there is no scope for coverage beyond this period unless a Member State has introduced more favourable provisions. Moreover, by referring to the 'special advantages' of women and the 'special relationship' between mother and child, the Court perpetuates an outdated stereotype of motherhood and consolidates the idea of the 'traditional family' where childcare is not shared equally between the parents.[104] As a result it is predominantly women who have to bear the dual burden of 'work' and 'care'.[105] The Court has failed to distinguish between maternity leave, linked to pregnancy, and therefore unique to women, and parent/child responsibilities that should be shared between parents.[106] This is a debate to which we shall return when we consider the scope of the Parental Leave Directive adopted in 1996.[107] In the meantime it should also be noted that the link between payment and sickness has the effect of limiting the meaning of 'pay' and 'payment' as shown in *Lewen*. The Court's judgment in *Pedersen* does, however, indicate that the more specific health and safety provisions offer greater scope for strict enforcement. It is noticeable that the Commission, while reporting wide discrepancies in respect of Articles 8–12, the maternity rights clauses, recommends concerted action mainly in respect of the 'protective' clauses in Articles 1–7.

By applying the Directive to fixed-term workers and other workers with contracts of uncertain duration, the Court, in *Tele Danmark* and *Jiménez Melgar*, has ensured that it will be broadly applied on the basis that 'the duration of the employment relationship has no bearing on the extent of the protection guaranteed to pregnant workers by Community law'.[108] Nevertheless, in the case of a dismissal during the course of a fixed-term contract, or the non-renewal of a contract on grounds connected with pregnancy, the main function of Article 10 is to complement the protection afforded by the Equal Treatment Directive. Furthermore, Member States

---

[103] Paras 50–52.

[104] See generally, McGlynn, n 67 above; Caracciolo di Torella (1999, *Industrial Law Journal*) n 61 above at 281; and E Ellis, *European Community Sex Equality Law*, 2nd edn (Clarendon Press, Oxford, 1998) p 242.

[105] See T Hervey and J Shaw, 'Women, Work and Care: Women's Dual Role and Double Burden in EC Sex Equality Law' (1998) 8 *Journal of European Social Policy* 43.

[106] See further, McGlynn, n 67 above at 40.

[107] Dir 96/34/EC, OJ 1996, L145/4.

[108] *Tele Danmark*, para 38.

are under no obligation either to stipulate the grounds permitted under national law for exceptional dismissals or to provide a procedure for consent to be granted for such dismissals. This suggests that the Court places little value on national supervision of the derogations permitted under the Directive and offers no real incentive for action in those Member States where legal protection in this area is relatively weak. Moreover, the Court's narrow approach to the concept of 'dismissal', for which there is no reasoned support, reflects a desire not to interfere with national rules concerning the creation and termination of the contract of employment or employment relationship.[109] Lastly, and perhaps most importantly, it opens the door to abuse by certain employers who choose to employ workers, who are often predominantly female, on a succession of fixed-term contracts, a practice that runs counter to the aims of the Directive on Fixed-term Work introduced in 1999.[110]

To conclude on Directive 92/85, it is clear that some advances have been made, particularly with regard to tighter rules on health protection during the period of a woman's pregnancy and maternity. In this sense the Commission is justified in concluding that women covered by the Directive have been provided with health and safety protection.[111] When it comes to the employment rights of women during pregnancy and maternity, however, the Directive has been less successful and, as Fenwick explains, it fails to maintain a principle of protection from employment disadvantage.[112] A price has been paid for the compromises that were involved in securing the adoption of the Directive under Article 118a EEC. By placing health protection first and equality second, the outcome is wrongheaded. As a result the equality objective has been subsumed by the health and safety rationale of Article 118a EEC. It is submitted that the Directive would have been much more effective if it had been founded on the equality objective and based on the substantive equality model.[113] In this way a broad approach might have been given to specific entitlements during the maternity period whereas 'special protection' would have been defined as narrowly as possible and

---

[109] For further development of this point, see the next part of this chapter.

[110] Dir 99/70, OJ 1999, L175/43. Clause 1(b) of the annexed Framework Agreement seeks to 'establish a framework to prevent abuse arising from the use of successive fixed-term employment contracts or relationships'. For discussion, see ch 6.

[111] COM(99) 100, p 22.

[112] Fenwick, n 19 above at 75. See Fenwick and Hervey, n 40 above at 455.

[113] Fenwick, n 19 above at 65–7. Fenwick defines a substantive equality approach, at 66–7, as 'one which first redefines "special" treatment, and second seeks to extend both family-related entitlements and undeniably beneficial provisions to men, while confining the latter to as narrow a scope as possible in so far as it is necessary for them to remain gender-specific. Under this approach protective measures genuinely needed to protect the foetus would be acceptable so long as they were framed in such a way as to be costless in terms of women's employment opportunities: the principle should be that the risk, rather than the woman, should be removed from the workplace'.

limited to genuine biological factors.[114] Other issues such as parental leave, not progressed in this period, and childcare, addressed only through a non-binding recommendation,[115] needed to be taken on board as part of a wider 'family friendly' agenda based on a sharing of responsibilities between working parents.[116] Recently the ILO has adopted a revised Maternity Convention, which seeks to achieve precisely this objective by attempting to unify the separate spheres of work and family.[117] Such a bold step could not, of course, be realistically contemplated during the period of the SEA, where it was necessary to heavily emphasise the Directive's protective features to bring it within the ambit of Article 118a EEC and secure QMV, but perhaps the Commission was too eager to achieve its Action Programme targets regardless of the quality of the ensuing legislation and, in the process, lost sight of the equality objective?

(2) Working Time

In chapter 3 we considered how the European Parliament, the Commission and certain Member States, most notably Denmark, have developed an ergonomic approach to the concepts of 'health', 'safety' and the 'working environment' in Article 118a EEC. Ergonomics provides a foundation for legislation that extends beyond the immediate physical environment of the worker and, as the Court found in the *Working Time* case,[118] embraces all factors capable of affecting the health and safety of the worker in his/her working environment. Such an approach is consistent with the all-encompassing definition of 'health' laid down in the Constitution of the World Health Organisation.[119]

---

[114] Fenwick, *ibid* p 79.

[115] Recommendation 92/241/EEC, OJ 1992, L123/16.

[116] In the absence of such regulation there will be, as Kilpatrick notes, a 'twilight zone between pregnancy provision, maternity provision and young child-care provision'. See Kilpatrick in Hervey and O'Keeffe, n 19 above at 81. As Kilpatrick notes, also at 81, the Pregnancy and Maternity Directive is incapable of remedying this inadequacy in post-birth regulation because it is based on a health and safety rationale. For further discussion on the 'family friendly' agenda, see E Caracciolo di Torella, 'The 'Family Friendly Workplace': the EC Position' (2001) 17 *International Journal of Comparative Labour Law and Industrial Relations* 325.

[117] ILO Convention No 183 of 2000; available at <http:/www.ilo.org>. For analysis, see J Murray, 'The International Regulation of Maternity: Still Waiting for the Reconciliation of Work and Family Life' (2001) 17 *International Journal of Comparative Labour Law and Industrial Relations* 25.

[118] Case C–84/94, *United Kingdom v Council* [1996] ECR I–5755.

[119] Health is defined in the preamble of the WHO Constitution, 1946, as 'a state of complete physical, mental and social well being that does not consist only in the absence of illness or infirmity'. Applied by the Court, *ibid* para 15.

[120] Dir 93/104/EC concerning certain aspects of the organisation of working time, OJ 1993, L307/18.

The Working Time Directive, 93/104[120] [now revised by Directive 2000/34[121]] was the centrepiece of this approach. The Council, by using Article 118a EEC as the vehicle to adopt the Directive, in line with the proposal by the Commission,[122] signalled a broad evolutionary approach to health, safety and the working environment, as dynamic concepts, which are not to be subordinated to purely economic considerations.[123] By adopting this strategy, the Community was able to shift the emphasis of the Directive from the 'improvement of living and working conditions',[124] to the right of every worker to 'enjoy satisfactory health and safety conditions in his working environment'.[125] The aim of the Directive, as simply stated in Article 1(1), is to establish 'minimum safety and health requirements for the organisation of working time'. The Directive contains two elements outlined in Article 1(2):

(a) minimum periods of daily rest, weekly rest and annual leave, to breaks and maximum weekly working time; and
(b) certain aspects of night work, shift work and patterns of work.

While the Directive bestows extensive rights on workers in relation to each of these elements, it also allows for wide exclusions and derogations from those rights. The core rights can be set out briefly as follows:

—minimum daily rest of eleven consecutive hours per 24-hour period;[126]
—a rest break where the working day is more than six hours. The duration will be determined by a collective agreement or national legislation;[127]
—weekly rest amounting to a minimum uninterrupted period of 24 hours (in addition to daily rest).[128] This will normally be calculated over a 14-day reference period;[129]

---

[121] Dir 2000/34/EC of the European Parliament and the Council amending Council Dir 93/104/EC concerning certain aspects of the organisation of working time to cover sectors and activities excluded from the Directive, OJ 2000, L195/41. Discussed below.

[122] COM(90) 317; followed by an amended proposal, COM(91) 130, OJ 1991, C124/8.

[123] Fifth recital of the preamble. As Chalmers and Szyszczak have pointed out, this declaration highlights the *lex specialis* nature of Art 118a EEC as an independent source for the development of social policy measures. See D Chalmers and E Szyszczak, *European Union Law Volume Two: Towards a European Polity?* (Ashgate, Aldershot, 1998) p 495.

[124] *Community Charter of the Fundamental Social Rights of Workers* (European Communities, Luxembourg, 1990) point 7.

[125] *Ibid* point 19. All three points are referred to in the fourth recital of the preamble of the Directive.

[126] Art 3.

[127] Art 4.

[128] Art 5. The second paragraph of Art 5, allowing for the minimum rest period to include Sunday, was annulled by the Court in Case C–84/94, *United Kingdom v Council* [1996] ECR I–5755, para 37, on the grounds that there was no direct connection between this right and the health and safety objectives of Art 118a EEC. Art 1(3) of the amending Dir 2000/34/EC, OJ 2000, L 195/41, has now formally deleted this paragraph.

[129] Art 16(1).

—maximum average weekly 'working time',[130] including overtime, not exceeding 48 hours.[131] This will normally be calculated over a four-month reference period;[132]

—paid annual leave of at least four weeks in accordance with the conditions for entitlement to, and granting of, such leave laid down by national legislation and/or practice;[133]

—night work[134] not exceeding an average of eight hours in any 24-hour period.[135] National law or collective or other industry agreements will determine the reference period.[136]

Other provisions grant night workers a right to a free health assessment and transfer to day work if they suffer from health problems;[137] and, more generally, allow for an adaptation of work patterns with a view to alleviating monotonous work and work at a pre-determined work rate, especially by allowing for breaks during work time.[138] The idea behind these provisions is that work should be adapted to the worker, leading to a more 'humanised' workplace.[139]

From a cursory review of these provisions, particularly Articles 3–13, it would appear that the Directive, by securing a maximum 48-hour working week and a minimum four-weeks paid annual leave, largely fulfilled two of the Community's most treasured outstanding social policy goals.[140] Such a conclusion would be premature. In particular, Article 1(3) in its original form is double-edged. On the one hand, the Directive applies 'to all sectors

---

[130] Art 2(1) defines working time as: 'any period during which the worker is working, at the employer's disposal and carrying out his activities or duties, in accordance with national laws and/or practice'. Working time and rest periods are mutually exclusive for a 'rest period' is 'any period which is not working time'.

[131] Art 6.

[132] Art 16(2).

[133] Art 7(1). Further, Art 7(2) provides that the period of paid annual leave may not be replaced by an allowance in lieu, except where the employment relationship is terminated.

[134] Art 2(3) defines 'night time' as 'any period of not less than seven hours, as defined by national law, and which must include in any case the period between midnight and 5 a. m.' Art 2(4) defines a 'night worker' as: '(a) on the one hand, any worker, who, during night time, works at least three hours of his daily working time as a normal course; and (b) on the other hand, any worker who is likely during night time to work a certain proportion of his annual working time, as defined at the choice of the Member State concerned: (i) by national legislation, following consultation with the two sides of industry; or (ii) by collective agreements or agreements concluded between the two sides of industry at national or regional level'.

[135] Art 8.

[136] Art 16(3).

[137] Art 9. Arts 10–12 provide additional protection for night workers and shift workers.

[138] Art 13.

[139] On this point, see B Bercusson, *Working Time in Britain, Towards a European Model*, Part I (Institute of Employment Rights, London, 1993); A Supiot, *Beyond Employment: Changes in Work and the Future of Labour Law in Europe* (OUP, Oxford, 2001) ch 3.

[140] For example, a Council Recommendation of 1975 had endorsed the principle of a maximum 40-hour working week and a minimum four week annual paid holiday: Recommendation 75/457/EEC, OJ 1975, L199/32.

of activity, both public and private'. As with the framework Directive, 89/391, the Working Time Directive refers to rights for 'workers' in general, although in practice the operative definition, derived from the framework Directive, is rather narrow.[141] On the other hand, specified sectors, 'air, rail, road, sea, inland waterway and lake transport, sea fishing and other work at sea', were excluded altogether along with 'the activities of doctors in training'. As we shall see below, it was precisely because of these exclusions that it became necessary for the Commission to launch a package of proposals in 1998 to cover the sectors and activities excluded by Article 1(3) in order to extend the coverage of the Directive.[142]

Moreover, Article 17 allows Member States derogations from certain provisions arising from the activities of particular workers and the conditions under which they work. First, a derogation may be applied for workers whose working time is not measured and/or predetermined or can be determined by the workers themselves, from all of the main provisions except paid annual leave.[143] Article 17(1) specifically refers to managing executives or other persons 'with autonomous decision-taking powers', family workers and workers officiating at religious ceremonies.[144] Although this list is not exhaustive, it is, in the view of the Commission, to be interpreted restrictively.[145] Secondly, Article 17(2) provides for further derogations concerning the provisions on rest periods, night work and the reference period for the calculation of weekly rest and maximum working time,[146] applicable to a wide range of other sectors and activities covered by the Directive.[147] Where

---

[141] Art 3 of Dir 89/391 defines a worker as 'any person employed by an employer, including trainees and apprentices but excluding domestic servants'. According to the Commission the great majority of Member States have applied their legislation to 'traditional' employees working under a contract of employment as defined by national legislation and practice. In the UK, by contrast, the Commission note that the regulations have been extended to workers performing contracts for services. See COM(2000) 787, p 5.

[142] COM(1998) 662. Three Directives have now been adopted. First, Dir 99/63/EC concerning the Agreement on the organisation of working time of seafarers concluded by the European Community Shipowners' Association (ECSA) and the Federation of Transport Workers' Unions in the European Union (FST), OJ 1999, L167/33. Secondly, the amending Dir, 2000/34/EC, OJ 2000, L195/41. Thirdly, Dir 2000/79/EC concerning the European Agreement on the Organisation of Working Time of Mobile Workers in Civil Aviation concluded by the Association of European Airlines (AEA) the European Transport Workers' Federation (ETF) the European Cockpit Association (ECA) the European Regions Airline Association (ERA) and the International Air Carrier Association (IACA), OJ 2000, L302/57.

[143] The exclusion may cover Arts 3, 4, 5, 6, 8 or 16.

[144] Art 17(1) of Dir 93/104.

[145] See the Commission's implementation report: COM(2000) 787, p 3.

[146] Arts 3, 4, 5, 8 and 16.

[147] By virtue of Art 17(2.1) these activities include, inter alia: '(a) . . . where the worker's place of work and his place of residence are distant from one another or where the worker's different places of work are distant from one another; (b) . . . security and surveillance activities requiring a permanent presence in order to protect property and persons, particularly security guards and caretakers or security firms; (c) in the case of activities involving the need for continuity of service or production, particularly: (i) services relating to the reception, treatment and/or care provided by hospitals or similar establishments, residential institutions and

these derogations are applied, the workers concerned must be afforded 'equivalent periods of compensatory rest' or where, in 'exceptional cases', it is not possible, for objective reasons, to grant such equivalent periods of compensatory rest, the workers concerned must be afforded 'appropriate protection'.[148] Thirdly, by virtue of Article 17(3), variations from the provisions referred to in Article 17(2)[149] can also be applied to other groups of workers within the scope of the Directive by means of collective agreements or other agreements concluded by the two sides of industry, subject to the same requirements for 'compensatory rest' and 'appropriate protection' where that is not possible.[150]

The Directive carries a sting in its tail. Not only do the final provisions allow for a generous three-year period for implementation,[151] and phasing-in of the paid annual leave provisions over a further three years,[152] but also, most controversially, Article 18(1)(b)(i) grants Member States the option of introducing a voluntary opt-out for individual workers from the maximum weekly working time provisions in Article 6. The workers concerned must formally agree to work longer hours following a request by the employer. Any worker unwilling to work longer hours must not be subjected to any detriment by the employer. The employer must also maintain records of the working hours of these workers and the 'competent authorities' may, for health and safety reasons, prohibit or restrict the possibility of exceeding the maximum weekly working hours. In practice these safeguards may only provide very limited protection against coercive practices in sectors where low pay and long, often unsociable, hours are the norm.

---

prisons; (ii) dock or airport workers; (iii) press, radio, television, cinematographic production, postal and telecommunications services, ambulance, fire and civil protection services; (iv) gas, water and electricity production, transmission and distribution, household refuse collection and incineration plants; (v) industries in which work cannot be interrupted on technical grounds; (vi) research and development activities; (vii) agriculture; (d) where there is a foreseeable surge of activity, particularly in: (i) agriculture; (ii) tourism; (iii) postal services'. Under Art 17(2.2) these derogations can also be applied in the event of unusual or unforeseeable circumstances beyond the employers' control, or due to exceptional events, as defined by Art 5(4) of the framework Dir 89/391, or in the case of accident or imminent risk of accident. Art 17(2.3) provides for further derogations from the daily or weekly rest periods in Arts 3 and 5 in the case of shift workers who are unable to take breaks between shifts and in respect of work, such as cleaning, where activities are split up over the day.

[148] Art 17(2).
[149] Arts 3, 4, 5, 8 and 16.
[150] Art 17(3). Also subject to the requirement for equivalent compensating rest periods.
[151] Art 18(1)(a). Until 23 Nov 1996. See the Commission's report of 1 Dec 2000 on the state of implementation of the Directive, where the Commission noted that only Germany, Sweden, Finland, Spain and the Netherlands notified them of their national measures by the date of implementation: COM(2000) 787, p 2. Successful legal action has been brought against France and Italy for failing to implement the Directive on time. See Case C–46/99, *Commission v France* [2000] ECR I–4379; and Case C–386/98, *Commission v Italy* [2000] ECR I–1277.
[152] Art 18(1)(b)(ii). The paid annual leave entitlement in this period was a minimum of three weeks.

The Commission's implementation report reveals that only the UK, the instigator of the clause, has chosen to take advantage of Article 18(1)(b)(i).[153] Under the final paragraph of that provision, a review must be conducted before seven years have expired, by 23 November 2003 at the latest. At that time the Council will decide what action, if any, to take on the basis of a Commission proposal accompanied by an appraisal report. Perhaps surprisingly, the Commission has not included any statistics in its implementation report on the number of workers in the UK who have agreed to work beyond the maximum weekly hours deemed appropriate for the protection of their safety and health at work. This might suggest that the individual opt-out mechanism will continue for an indefinite period. More recently, however, the Commission has issued the UK with an initial warning letter regarding, inter alia, the way in which 'voluntary' working time is measured.[154]

With the exception of the provisions on paid annual leave, Directive 93/104, is a decidedly weak and rather complex piece of legislation severely circumscribed by limitations and derogations which, at the time of its adoption, satisfied neither the main supporters of Community regulation in this field, notably the European Parliament, nor its principal detractor, the UK, which, having secured substantial amendments from the Commission's original proposal, abstained in the Council vote and then proceeded to lodge annulment proceedings. These proceedings were ultimately unsuccessful, not only because Article 118a EEC was deemed to be the correct legal base,[155] but also the Directive was held to have satisfied the procedural requirements for its adoption and was found to be consistent with the principles of subsidiarity and proportionality.[156]

Pressure to extend the Directive and override its limitations was immediate. Indeed, within a year of its implementation, the Commission responded to demands to widen the Directive's scope by publishing a White Paper concerning the excluded sectors and activities.[157] The Commission reported that an estimated 5.6 million workers were potentially excluded from the coverage of the Directive,[158] although in practice only the UK and

---

[153] COM(2000) 787, p 17.

[154] On 21 March 2002. This letter marks the first stage in possible infringement proceedings under Art 226 EC [ex 169 EEC]. The Commission's action is a direct response to a complaint from Amicus, a British trade union. For further details, see: <www.incomesdata.co.uk>.

[155] Case C–84/94, *United Kingdom v Council* [1996] ECR I–5755. For full discussion, see ch 3.

[156] See further, Barnard *et al*, n 18 above; and J Kenner, 'A Distinctive Legal Base for Social Policy?—The Court of Justice Answers a "Delicate Question"' (1997) 22 *European Law Review* 579.

[157] *White Paper on Sectors and Activities Excluded from the Working Time Directive,* COM(97) 334.

[158] *Ibid* para 18.

Greece have excluded all of the named sectors and activities from the scope of their national implementing measures.[159] Many other workers have restricted rights to the provisions on rest periods, weekly working time and night work.[160] Moreover, the excluded and restricted sectors and activities include areas, such as transport and health care, where there is an above average likelihood of danger and accidents resulting from, or connected with, insufficient rest and excessive working hours. Indeed, as the Commission has pointedly noted:[161]

Thus the exclusions were considered by the Council to be directly related to the type of work involved, and *not because of any suggestion that health and safety as regards working time was sufficiently protected in these sectors and activities.* A common feature of all these sectors, apart from doctors in training, is that key workers typically are required to spend time away from home as an integral part of their duties.

In other words, while the rhetoric of the preamble indicated that health and safety requirements would not be subordinated to economic considerations, the reality was deeply ambiguous. The Directive needed to be flexible to take account of specific groups of workers spending time away from home, but it was not necessary to exclude whole sectors *en bloc.* The test should relate to the nature of the activity and not to the sector in which the employee works.[162]

In the White Paper the Commission considered the options of either a vertical approach, proposing a specific directive for each of the excluded sectors, or a horizontal approach, extending the existing Directive to all sectors. The Commission concluded that there should be a combination of these methods allowing for Community-wide sectoral agreements to be negotiated by the social partners on a case-by-case basis. After lengthy negotiations between the Council and the European Parliament, a highly complex amendment to the Directive was adopted on 22 June 2000[163] with an implementation date of 1 August 2003.[164]

The amending Directive, 2000/34, adopted under the successor provision, Article 137(2) EC, is concerned specifically with health and safety protection for workers in sectors or activities excluded from Directive 93/104. Therefore, the health and safety rationale remains paramount notwithstanding the

---

[159] See the Commission's implementation report: COM(2000) 787, p 5. In the Commission's view (p 26) this is inappropriate because some of these categories fall within the partial exclusions permitted by Article 17(1).

[160] In the implementation report the Commission note that in some cases the scope of national measures in respect of the derogation in Art 17(1) may have extended beyond the scope of the derogation. *Ibid* p 26.

[161] COM(97) 334, para 13. Emphasis added.

[162] *Ibid* para 14.

[163] Dir 2000/34/EC, OJ 2000, L195/41. For the Commission proposal, see OJ 1999, C43/1.

[164] Art 2(1).

broadening of the legal bases by Article 137 EC. Seafarers are excluded from the amended Directive because they are covered by separate measures.[165] Road transport is also subject to other arrangements.[166] In relation to the other excluded sectors, the Directive seeks to distinguish between 'mobile' and 'non-mobile' workers. Any worker in these sectors who is deemed to be 'non-mobile' is entitled to the full set of rights under Directive 93/104: rest periods, breaks, maximum working time, limits on night work and annual leave. By contrast 'mobile workers', defined as 'travelling or flying person-nel'[167] employed by an undertaking which operates transport services for passengers or goods by road, air[168] and inland waterways, are only entitled to the average 48-hour maximum working week and four weeks paid annual leave.[169] There are additional limitations on the entitlements of workers in the railway sector,[170] offshore installations[171] and sea-fishing.[172]

The second part of the amended Directive addresses the activities of trainee doctors. Although trainee doctors will eventually be put in the same

---

[165] The first measure is: Dir 99/63/EC concerning the Agreement on the organisation of working time of seafarers concluded by the European Community Shipowners' Association (ECSA) and the Federation of Transport Workers' Unions in the European Union (FST), OJ 1999, L167/33. This Directive gives legislative effect, for the first time, to a sectoral agreement between management and labour. It is based on ILO Convention No 180 on seafarers' hours of work. See also, Commission Recommendation 99/130/EC on ratification of ILO Convention 180 concerning seafarers' hours of work and the manning of ships, and the ratification of the 1996 Protocol to the 1976 Merchant Shipping (minimum standards) Convention, OJ 1999, L43/9. Dir 99/63/EC was swiftly followed by: Dir 99/95/EC, OJ 2000, L14/29, which applies to seafarers' hours of work on board ships using Community ports.

[166] There are separate regulations limiting the working hours of lorry drivers predating Dir 93/104. These include: Reg 3820/85/EEC, OJ 1985, L370/1, on the harmonisation of certain social legislation relating to road transport; Reg 3821/85/EEC, OJ 1985, L371/8, on recording equipment in road transport; and Dir 88/599/EEC, OJ 1988, L325/55, on standard checking procedures on recording equipment in road transport. See further, C Barnard, *EC Employment Law*, 2nd edn (OUP, Oxford, 2000) pp 417–18.

[167] Art 1(2) of Dir 2000/34 inserting a new Art 2(7) of Dir 93/104.

[168] There is now a separate Directive covering 'mobile workers' on airlines which is intended to take precedence over the amended provisions concerning that sector: Dir 2000/79/EC concerning the European Agreement on the Organisation of Working Time of Mobile Workers in Civil Aviation concluded by the Association of European Airlines (AEA) the European Transport Workers' Federation (ETF) the European Cockpit Association (ECA) the European Regions Airline Association (ERA) and the International Air Carrier Association (IACA), OJ 2000, L302/57.

[169] Incorporated by Art 1(7) into the new Art 17a of Dir 93/104. Workers concerned with the carriage of passengers on regular urban transport services are also specifically included within this category—Art 17(2.1)(c)(viii) as amended by Art 1(5).

[170] Art 1(5) adds a new paragraph (e) to Art 17(2.1) which allows for the derogations therein to be applied to workers in railway transport: whose activities are intermittent; who spend their working time on board trains; or whose activities are linked to transport timetables and to ensuring the continuity and regularity of traffic. Mobile workers in the rail sector are also covered by a separate agreement between management and labour. See *European Industrial Relations Review*, June 2000, pp 14–17.

[171] Art 1(5) amending Art 17a and 17(2.1)(a). The definition of 'offshore work' is contained in the new Art 2(8) of Dir 93/104.

[172] Art 17b inserted by Art 1(7).

position as 'mobile workers',[173] they will not receive the benefit of the maximum working week until after the expiry of a transitional period during which the reductions in working hours will be phased in.[174] Over a five-year period expiring on 1 August 2009, their average maximum working week will be reduced from 58 to 52 hours. Extensions of the transitional period for up to three further years may also be permitted where justified on the grounds of the organisation and delivery of health care and special difficulties in meeting these responsibilities. Therefore the average 48-hour working week is unlikely to be a reality for trainee doctors until August 2012.

The Court has issued three judgments on the scope of Directive 93/104. In the first case, *SIMAP*,[175] the central issue was the meaning of the term 'working time' in Article 2(1). Under that provision, 'working time' is defined as 'any period during which the worker is working, at the employer's disposal and carrying out his activity or duties, in accordance with national laws and/or practice'. SIMAP represented Spanish doctors who were required to work lengthy hours 'on call' either when at a primary care centre or when elsewhere. In its judgment, the Court adopted an expansive interpretation of the concept of 'working time'. First of all, the Court confirmed that the concepts of 'working time' and 'rest periods' were mutually exclusive in the scheme of the Directive.[176] It was held that the characteristic features of working time were present in the case of time spent on call by doctors in primary care teams where their presence at the health centre was required. Moreover, even if the activity actually performed varied according to the circumstances, the fact that the doctors in question were obliged to be present and available at the workplace with a view to providing their professional services meant that they were carrying out their duties in that instance.[177] Such an interpretation is in conformity with the objective of the Directive, which is to ensure the safety and health of workers by granting them minimum periods of rest and adequate breaks. To exclude duty on call from working time if physical presence is required would seriously undermine that objective.[178] However, the situation was different in situations where the doctors were on call by being contactable at all times without having to be at the health centre. In those circumstances, even if they were at the disposal of their employer, in the sense that it would

---

[173] Art 17(2.1)(c)(i) as amended by Art 1(5).

[174] Art 1(6) adds a new Art 17(2.4) containing these provisions.

[175] Case C–303/98, *Sindicato de Médicos de Asistencia Pública (SIMAP) v Conselleria de Sanidad y Consumo de la Generalidad Valenciana* [2000] ECR I–7963. For discussion, see J Fairhurst, 'SIMAP—Interpreting the Working Time Directive' (2001) 30 *Industrial Law Journal* 236.

[176] Para 47.

[177] Para 48.

[178] Para 49.

be possible to contact them, the doctors concerned were managing their time with fewer constraints and pursuing their own interests. In these cases only time linked to the actual provision of primary care services was to be regarded as working time within the meaning of the Directive.[179] In addition, it does not matter whether the time worked 'on call' is classified as 'overtime' because overtime falls within the concept of working time for the purposes of the Directive which draws no distinction according to whether or not such time is spent within normal hours of work.[180]

In the second case, *BECTU*,[181] the Court was asked to consider the scope of Article 7 entitling workers to a minimum period of at least four weeks paid annual leave. Unlike other rights in the Directive, the right to paid leave, for those workers within the scope of the Directive,[182] is not subject to any specified derogations. Rather it must be granted, under Article 7(1) 'in accordance with the conditions for entitlement to, and granting of, such leave laid down by national legislation and/or practice'. BECTU, an entertainment workers' union, challenged the UK's implementing regulations which restricted the right to paid leave by applying a qualifying period of 13 weeks with the same employer before entitlement arose. Because of the short-term working arrangements commonly found in the entertainment industry many BECTU members were caught by this condition and lost their right to paid annual leave for these periods of employment. AG Tizzano advised that the right to paid annual leave is a fundamental right[183] not subject to any exceptions. In its judgment, the Court ruled in favour of BECTU, emphasising that the Directive, although based only on Article 118a EEC, maintained its originally conceived purpose, sourced from the Social Charter,[184] of laying down minimum requirements to improve the living and working conditions of workers.[185] Furthermore, the Directive does not distinguish between workers employed under a contract of indefinite duration and those employed under a fixed-term contract.[186] Therefore it follows that:[187]

---

[179] Para 50.

[180] Para 51.

[181] Case C–173/99, *R v Secretary of State for Trade and Industry, ex parte Broadcasting, Entertainment, Cinematographic and Theatre Union (BECTU)* [2001] ECR I–4881.

[182] Subject to the exclusions in Art 1(3) of the Directive prior to its amendment. See Case C–133/00, *Bowden and others v Tuffnells Parcels Express Ltd* [2001] ECR I–7031, discussed below.

[183] At paras 27–28 of his Opinion in *BECTU*, the AG referred specifically to Art 31(2) of the EU Charter of Fundamental Rights, OJ 2000, C 364/1, which guarantees every worker a right to paid annual leave, concluding that the Charter is 'the most reliable and definitive confirmation of the fact that the right to paid annual leave constitutes a fundamental right'. For further discussion, see ch 12.

[184] Para 39. The Court referred specifically to points 8 and 19 of the Social Charter.

[185] Para 37.

[186] Para 46.

[187] Para 47.

... paid annual leave of ... four weeks [after the expiry of the transitional period] constitutes a social right directly conferred by that directive on every worker as the minimum requirement necessary to ensure protection of his health and safety.

By imposing a precondition for entitlement to paid annual leave, which had the effect of preventing certain workers from any such entitlement, the UK's legislation not only negated an individual right expressly granted by the Directive, but also was contrary to its objective.[188] The scheme of the Directive, including the variations to the working time arrangements permitted under Article 17, allowed for no derogations from the right to paid leave.[189] Moreover, such legislation was likely to give rise to abuse because employers might be tempted to evade the obligation to grant the paid annual leave to which every worker is entitled by more frequent resort to short-term employment relationships.[190] Hence, although Member States are free to lay down conditions for the *exercise and implementation of the right* to paid annual leave, by prescribing the specific circumstances in which workers may exercise that right, they are not entitled to make the *existence of that right*, which derives directly from the Directive, subject to any preconditions whatsoever.

Equally significant was the Court's rationale for rejecting the UK's two main arguments in defence of its legislation. First, the UK contended that other Member States also made the exercise of the right to paid leave conditional in their legislation. The Court swiftly dispensed with this argument on the basis that it was not a defence to rely on the fact that other Member States were in breach of their obligations.[191] Secondly, the UK considered that the qualifying period was consistent with the need to avoid imposing excessive constraints on small and medium-sized enterprises (SMEs), in accordance with Article 118a(2) EEC [now 137(2) EC], on the basis that SMEs would find the administrative costs of organising annual leave for staff engaged for short periods particularly difficult to bear.[192] The Court's response was to rule that these conditions were of general application and therefore not explicitly targeted at SMEs.[193] Moreover, while the Directive took account of the needs of SMEs,[194] in accordance with the preamble, the 'improvement of workers' safety, hygiene and health at work is an objective which should not be subordinated to purely economic considerations'.[195]

---

[188] Para 48.

[189] Para 50.

[190] Para 51.

[191] Paras 54–56. See Case C–146/89, *Commission v United Kingdom* [1991] ECR I–3533, para 47.

[192] Para 57.

[193] Para 58.

[194] Para 60. See also, Case C–84/94, *United Kingdom v Council* [1996] ECR I–5755, para 44.

[195] Para 59. Fifth recital of the preamble.

The Court concluded that the UK's argument was 'incontestably based on such a consideration'.[196]

In *Bowden*,[197] the third case arising from the Directive, the Court has added a rider to the *BECTU* ruling. While *BECTU* points to the universality of the right to paid leave for 'every worker', the Court in *Bowden* reminds us that Article 1(3) of the Directive excludes many sectors and activities, a position that will only be partially rectified by Directive 2000/34. *Bowden*, also a reference from the UK, concerned the position of part-time clerical workers at a road transport depot with no contractual entitlement to holidays with pay. In fact the firm's van drivers were not allowed into their offices and had no contact with them. Further, under their contracts, the clerical workers could not be asked to work in actual transport operations. The national court was concerned that a literal interpretation of Article 1(3)—excluding *all workers* in the transport sector—would run counter to the objectives of the Directive and the Social Charter, which were based on protection of the worker rather than the activities of the employer.[198] However, the Court was satisfied that the effect of Article 1(3) and the Council's clear intention, was to exclude all workers in the road transport sector including office staff irrespective of their activities.[199] Indeed it was precisely for this reason that the Commission had published its White Paper and the Council had agreed to new legislation.[200] The Court, conscious of the separate role of the Community legislator, was not prepared to override its remit by subverting Article 1(3) even though the workers in question, whose work was indistinguishable from many others covered by the Directive, were denied their 'social right' to paid leave, at least for the time being.[201]

To conclude, Directive 93/104 represents, at best, a hesitant first step towards establishing minimum requirements concerning working time arrangements. Such is the flexibility in the system, however, that observance of the maximum working week requirements is difficult to monitor. As the Commission note in the implementation report, the structure of national legislation in several Member States differentiates between regular working time and overtime without setting an absolute limit over a given reference period.[202] The Commission also found considerable variations in the

---

[196] *Ibid.* The UK has responded swiftly to the judgment by introducing the Working Time (Amendment) Reg 2001 (SI 2001/3256) effective from 29 Oct 2001, which gives workers a right to paid annual leave from their first day of employment, and a corresponding right to compensation for any untaken leave on termination of employment. Available at: <www.legislation.hmso.gov.UK>.

[197] Case C–133/00, *Bowden and others v Tuffnells Parcels Express Ltd* [2001] ECR I–7031.

[198] Paras 23–5.

[199] Paras 39 and 44.

[200] Para 43.

[201] Until August 2003, the implementation date of Dir 2000/34.

[202] COM(2000) 787, p 26.

regulation of night work and related overtime rules.[203] In addition, the Court's ruling in *SIMAP* highlights a need to tighten up methods of calculating 'working time', particularly where workers are 'on call' or working overtime.

Further difficulties arise when a worker has two or more concurrent employment relationships, a situation not expressly provided for in the Directive. The Commission have called on Member States to introduce appropriate measures to ensure that the provisions on working time and rest periods are observed where there are concurrent employment relationships as such working arrangements are becoming increasingly common.[204]

Moreover, the provisions on working time, which were modified in order to try to garner the support of the UK, ultimately unsuccessfully, are so severely compromised by exclusions, derogations, and delaying provisions, that any positive effect has been rendered almost nugatory. As Supiot[205] has observed, the Directive is positively schizophrenic, 'its first part . . . establishes rules which the second part . . . immediately sets out to drain of any binding effect'. On a qualitative assessment, the working time provisions in the Directive provide limited benefits and, partly due to their opacity, fail to provide uniform exercisable rights for workers.

By contrast, the Directive's guarantee of a minimum four weeks paid annual leave, strongly reinforced as a 'social right' for 'every worker' in *BECTU*, is an important and, in many Member States, a novel right. Further, by stressing that the health and safety objective is not to be subordinated by economic considerations, the Court has transmitted a powerful message about the autonomy of Article 118a EEC [and now 137 EC] and its distinctive contribution as part of the Community's explicit social objectives which operates in harness with, but not dependent upon, the economic imperatives of the internal market programme. Moreover, the right to paid annual leave is transparent, easily understood and offers tangible benefits for workers within the scope of the Directive with no room for derogations or, following *BECTU*, preconditions. Even in this case, however, as *Bowden* has graphically revealed, flaws in the drafting of Article 1(3) have caused blatant unfairness. The amended Directive, and the whole patchwork quilt of protection offered by the accompanying sectoral measures, adds up to a far from seamless transition with much inconsistency remaining.

The wider significance of the Directive lies with its evolutionary approach. Over time there is further potential for gradual improvements in the legal regulation of working time at national and Community levels. The

---

[203] COM(2000) 787, p 27.

[204] *Ibid* p 26.

[205] A Supiot, 'On the Job: Time for Agreement' (1996) 12 *International Journal of Comparative Labour Law and Industrial Relations* 195 at 195.

Directive may also be regarded as ahead of its time. Operating in an inherently pliable fashion, by allowing for variation of several of the minimum standards through collective agreements, it demonstrates an essential feature of flexibility and adaptability in the workplace that takes account of the fact that there is no longer a straightforward distinction between time spent at work and leisure time.[206] In turn, the adoption of the Directive has helped to foster discussion on the potential contribution that any reduction and reorganisation of working time can make to job creation and redistribution of jobs as part of the Community's strategy to reduce unemployment.[207]

(3) Young Workers

A third Directive introduced under Article 118a EEC, on the protection of Young Workers, 94/33,[208] was founded on a range of commitments contained in points 20 and 22 of the Social Charter concerning the working age of children and the protection of young people at work. Additional sources were a European Parliament Resolution on child labour[209] and, although not directly cited, Article 7 ESC on the right of children and young persons to protection, Article 32 of the UN Convention on the Rights of the Child, and ILO Convention No 138.[210] As with the Working Time Directive, the broad objectives of the Charter were made to fit the health and safety rationale of Article 118a EEC and the overall scheme of the framework Health and Safety Directive.

The preamble of the Young Workers Directive identifies 'children and adolescents' as 'specific risk groups'[211] and proclaims that measures must be taken with regard to their health and safety. Maximum working time of young people should be 'strictly limited' and night work should be prohibited, subject to the exemption of certain jobs specified by national

---

[206] See generally, Supiot, *ibid*.

[207] See in particular, the Opinion of the Economic and Social Committee on *Working Time*, Brussels, 24–25 Oct 1995, CES 1166/95. See also, the Opinion of AG Léger in Case C–84/94, *United Kingdom v Council* [1996] ECR I–5755, who, at para 92, concludes that examination of the Directive shows that it does not, in itself, constitute a measure to combat unemployment. However, the debate that it has engendered has helped to revive the ideas behind a Council Resolution of 18 Dec 1979 on the adaptation of working time (OJ 1980, C2/1). In its Resolution the Council stressed that 'any measures to adapt working time should be assessed [with a view to improving the employment situation]'.

[208] Dir 94/33/EC, OJ 1994, L216/12.

[209] OJ 1987, C190/44.

[210] The Directive sets the same age limits of 15 and 18 as the ILO Convention. See also Convention No 90 on the night work of young persons. Both measures were adopted in a more simplified form at the first session of the ILO in 1919. See Valticos and von Potobsky, n 50 above, pp 216–26.

[211] Seventh recital of the preamble.

legislation or rules.[212] More generally, the Directive places a duty on Member States to ensure that employers 'guarantee that young people have working conditions which suit their age'[213] so as to facilitate the 'transition from childhood to adult life'.[214] It is therefore regarded as essential that young people are protected against 'economic exploitation and . . . any work likely to harm their safety, health or physical, mental, moral or social development or to jeopardise their education'.[215] The scheme of the Directive is to secure these objectives by providing stronger protection for young people under 18[216] in respect of working time,[217] night work,[218] rest periods[219] and rest breaks,[220] while banning child labour for under 15s.[221] There is also a range of obligations on employers to carry out risk assessments when young people begin work and when there is any change in their working conditions.[222] Finally, Member States must ensure that young people are protected from any 'specific risks' to their development that are a consequence of their lack of experience, of absence of awareness of existing or potential risks, or of the fact that young people have not fully matured.[223] This will

[212] Fifteenth recital.

[213] Art 1(3).

[214] Ninth recital.

[215] Art 1(3).

[216] In Art 3 the Directive defines (a) a 'young person' as any person under 18 years of age; (b) a 'child' as a young person under 15 years of age; and (c) an 'adolescent' as a young person over 15 and under 18.

[217] Art 8(2) limits the working time of adolescents to eight hours a day and 40 hours a week subject to derogations—see below. Time spent on training is counted as working time (Art 8(3)). In addition, when more than one employer employs a young person working time and working days shall be cumulative (Art 8(4)).

[218] Art 9(1)(b) prohibits adolescents from working between 10 p.m. and 6 a.m. or 11 p.m. and 7 a.m., again subject to derogations—see below.

[219] The minimum rest periods for adolescents are 12 consecutive hours for each 24-hour period, Art 10(1)(b) and two days for each seven-day period, Art 10(2)—subject to derogations, see below.

[220] Art 12 provides for a minimum rest break for young people of 30 minutes every four and a half hours. The rest break shall be consecutive if possible. This clause is not subject to any derogation except, in the case of adolescents, in the event of *force majeure*—see below.

[221] Art 1(1) and 4.

[222] Art 6(2). The following points must be given particular attention: (a) the fitting-out and layout of the workplace and the workstation; (b) the nature, degree and duration of exposure to physical, biological and chemical agents; (c) the form, range and use of work equipment, in particular agents, machines, apparatus and devices, and the way in which they are handled; (d) the arrangement of work processes and operations and the way in which these are combined (organisation of work); (e) the level of training and instruction given to young people.

[223] Art 7(1). Art 7(2)—see below—prohibits work which is likely to entail 'specific risks' for young people within the meaning of Art 7(1) including: work involving harmful exposure to the physical, biological and chemical agents listed in point I of the Annex to the Directive (the Annex contains a non-exhaustive list of agents, processes and work); and/or processes and work referred to in point II of the Annex.

mean in practice that certain forms of employment for young people will be prohibited in accordance with criteria laid down in Article 7(2).[224]

As with the Working Time Directive, the derogations are of as much interest and, inevitably, subject to more controversy than the intrinsic rights granted by the Directive. Any Member State can utilise a wide range of derogations. First, there is an option for Member States to have a general exclusion from the Directive for occasional work or short-term work involving domestic service in a private household or work regarded as not being harmful, damaging or dangerous to young people in a family undertaking.[225] This exemption, although justified in a Commission Memorandum,[226] with visions of grape picking and crop harvesting,[227] also evokes less comfortable Dickensian imagery of domestic exploitation of children. Secondly, there are limited exemptions allowing children to carry out vocational training,[228] 'light work'[229]—such as delivering newspapers and babysitting—and, more generally, cultural, artistic, sports or advertising activities.[230] Thirdly, the maximum working time for adolescents of eight hours a day and 40 hours a week is subject to derogations 'where there are objective grounds for so doing' in accordance with national rules.[231]

---

[224] Prohibited work includes: (a) work which is objectively beyond young people's physical or psychological capacity; (b) work involving harmful exposure to agents which are toxic, carcinogenic, cause heritable genetic damage, or harm to the unborn child or which in any other way chronically affect human health; (c) work involving harmful exposure to radiation; (d) work involving the risk of accidents which it may be assumed cannot be recognised or avoided by young persons owing to their insufficient attention to safety or lack of experience or training; or (e) work in which there is a risk to health from extreme cold or heat, or from noise or vibration. Derogations from the above may be authorised in the case of adolescents where the work in question is 'indispensable' for their vocational training subject to health and safety protection.

[225] Art 2(2).

[226] COM(91) 543.

[227] See Barnard, n 166 above, p 421.

[228] Under Art 4(b) children of at least 14 years of age may be allowed to work under a combined work/training scheme or an in-plant work-experience scheme, provided that such work is done in accordance with the conditions laid down by the competent authority. This derogation, along with Article 4(c) below, operates in accordance with strict limits on working time and arrangements for attendance at school laid down in Art 8(1); night work, specified in Art 9(1); rest periods, in Art 10(1)(a) and 10(2); and annual rest, Art 11.

[229] Art 4(c). This applies to 14 year olds and also, more restrictively, to 13 year olds for a limited number of hours per week in the case of categories of work determined by national legislation. Member States making use of this option shall determine, subject to the provisions of the Directive, the working conditions relating to the light work in question. Art 3(d) defines 'light work' as 'all work which, on account of the inherent nature of the tasks which it involves and the particular conditions under which they are performed: (i) is not likely to be harmful to the safety, health or development of children, and (ii) is not such as to be harmful to their attendance at school, their participation in vocational guidance or training programmes approved by the competent authority or their capacity to benefit from the instruction received'.

[230] Art 4(2)(a) and 5.

[231] Art 8(5).

Fourthly, the provisions on night work for adolescents[232] are subject to a wide range of derogations linked to areas of activity and sectors.[233] Similar derogations operate in respect of rest periods.[234] Fifth, Member States may authorise derogations from the provisions on working time, night work, daily rest and rest breaks in the event of *force majeure*[235] provided that such work is of a temporary nature and must be performed immediately, that adult workers are not available and that the adolescents are allowed equivalent compensatory rest time within the following three weeks.

The Young Workers Directive was due for implementation by 22 June 1996.[236] Notwithstanding the wide range of general derogations negotiated to ensure its adoption, its most remarkable feature is to be found in a rare and, in the social policy context, unique national concession for the UK in the final provisions contained in Article 17(1)(b).[237] In a departure from all previous precedent concerning social legislation in the whole Community

---

[232] Art 9(3) provides that prior to any assignment to night work and at regular intervals thereafter, adolescents shall be entitled to a free assessment of their health and capacities, unless the work they do during the period during which work is prohibited is of an exceptional nature.

[233] Art 9(2)(a) allows Member States to reduce the prohibited hours for night work 'in specific areas of activity' for adolescents to between midnight and 4 a.m. subject, where necessary, to supervision by an adult. However, under Art 9(2)(b) the prohibition on night work for adolescents may be removed altogether, where there are objective grounds for so doing and provided that adolescents are allowed suitable compensatory rest time and that the objectives set out in Article 1 are not called into question in respect of: work performed in the shipping or fisheries sectors; work performed in the context of the armed forces or the police; work performed in hospitals or similar establishments; cultural, artistic, sports or advertising activities.

[234] Art 10(2) allows Member States to reduce the minimum weekly rest period to 36 hours where justified by technical or organisational reasons. This shall in principle include Sunday, although the legality of this derogation must be called into question in the light of the Court's ruling, in the context of the Working Time Directive, annulling the reference to Sunday as a day of rest in the second paragraph of Art 5 of that Directive because it was not specifically linked to its health and safety objective—Case C–84/94, *United Kingdom v Council* [1996] ECR I–5755, para 37. Art 10(3) permits Member States to make provisions whereby minimum rest periods for adolescents may be interrupted in the case of activities involving periods of work that are split up over the day or are of short duration. By virtue of Art 10(4) Member States may allow for further derogations in respect of adolescents in the following cases, where there are objective grounds for so doing and provided that they are granted appropriate compensatory rest time and that the objectives set out in Art 1 are not called into question: (a) work performed in the shipping or fisheries sectors; (b) work performed in the context of the armed forces or the police; (c) work performed in hospitals or similar establishments; (d) work performed in agriculture; (e) work performed in the tourism industry or in the hotel, restaurant and café sector; (f) activities involving periods of work split up over the day.

[235] This is defined in Art 5(4) of the framework Dir 89/391, as occurrences 'due to unusual and unforeseeable circumstances, beyond the employer's control, or to exceptional events, the consequences of which could not have been avoided despite the exercise of all due care'.

[236] Art 17(1)(a). The Commission has successfully brought infringement proceedings against Luxembourg and France for non-implementation. See Case C–47/99, *Commission v Luxembourg* [1999] ECR I–8999; and Case C–45/99, *Commission v France* [2000] ECR I–3615.

[237] The transitional period did not materialise in the text of the draft directive until the Council had reached a common position on 24 November 1993, C3–0504/93–94/O383 (SYN).

sphere,[238] this provision granted the UK a further four year period after the implementation date, during which time the UK did not have to comply with the provisions concerning working time for schoolchildren and adolescents, and night work for adolescents.[239] As we have already noted, the UK negotiated an opt-out clause for individual workers, in relation to the maximum working week, as part of the Working Time Directive,[240] and has been the only Member State to take advantage of it, but that provision was not, in its legal effect, specific to the UK. In both cases these concessions were introduced notwithstanding the fact that a qualified majority vote in the Council would have secured uniform application of the requirements in question.

In support of the derogation, the UK argued that the transitional period was necessary to protect the employment and training opportunities for young people which pose no health and safety risk,[241] a view supported by British employers' representatives.[242] Once the concession had been made, however, it was the subject of scathing criticism.[243] The European Parliament's Committee on Social Affairs, Employment and the Working Environment believed that the derogations already in place allowed the UK sufficient flexibility and therefore the transitional period was 'incomprehensible'.[244] In 1996 the British Trades Union Congress (TUC) commissioned a survey indicating that many British children worked illegally and for long hours, 'adversely affecting their health and education'.[245] The transitional period increased the risk to young persons' health, education and welfare.[246] The TUC view was also supported by a survey of schoolchildren.[247]

On 20 July 2000 the Commission submitted a report on the effects of Article 17(1)(b)—one month after the formal expiry of the opt-out.[248] After

---

[238] In the sense that Art 118a EEC applied to the whole Community when, under the Agreement on Social Policy, operative by 1994, there was the option of introducing a Directive that would not be applicable in the UK, but only where an attempt to use the whole Community provisions had failed—see further, ch 6.

[239] Arts 8(1)(b), 8(2), 9(1)(b) and 9(2) respectively.

[240] Art 18(i)(b)(i) of Dir 93/104, OJ 1993, L307/18.

[241] Summarised in para 5.3 of COM(2000) 457, the Commission's report on the effects of Art 17(1)(b).

[242] *Ibid* paras 6.3–6.7. Particular concern was expressed about sectors heavily dependent on young workers; such as broadcasting, retailing, hotels and catering.

[243] In the Council vote the UK, which was formally against regulation of this area, voted in favour while Spain and Italy, nominally supportive, abstained because of the concession. See the note by A Bond (1995) 24 *Industrial Law Journal* 377 at 377.

[244] PE Doc. A3–108/94. The Parliament as a whole recommended its deletion—OJ 1994, C91/89. See COM(2000) 457, para 3.3.

[245] COM(2000) 457, paras 6.8–6.12.

[246] *Ibid* para 6.11.

[247] Conducted by Market and Opinion Research International (MORI). See COM(2000) 457, para 7.2.

[248] *Ibid.*

consultation, an independent expert engaged by the Commission had found no evidence that employment opportunities for young people would have been adversely affected if there had been no transitional period.[249] On the basis of this report the Commission recommended to the Council that the transitional period should not be extended.[250] In the meantime the UK, which had originally regarded transitional arrangements as a 'renewable opt-out',[251] has accepted the Commission's advice and has amended its national Working Time Regulations on the basis that the transitional period expired on 22 June 2000.[252]

Much of the criticism of the Young Workers Directive has been focused on the transitional period granted to the UK. On the one hand, such criticism is legitimate because, while there may be different cultural traditions in certain Member States, not least the British tradition of employing schoolchildren to deliver newspapers, there can be no justification for singling out a Member State for special treatment and thereby denying the children and adolescents affected the health and safety protection that the Directive is designed to afford. On the other hand, the importance of this issue should not be exaggerated. Article 118a EEC was designed to be flexible, allowing for 'minimum requirements for gradual implementation'. As with the Pregnancy Directive, the identification of young people as a group having 'specific risks' has tilted the balance of the legislation towards health and safety protection. Consequently, the objectives of the Social Charter, promoting employment opportunities and equitable remuneration, and limiting or prohibiting the work and exploitation of young people, without any reference to derogations, have been downgraded or lost altogether. The result is a distinctly anaemic piece of legislation considered by the ILO to fall short of the standards required by international conventions.[253]

III IMPROVING LIVING AND WORKING CONDITIONS

(1) Market Functioning under Article 100 EEC

Whereas Article 118a EEC was applied liberally for legislative purposes in the period of the Social Charter Action Programme, Article 100 EEC [now 94 EC], hitherto the main repository for Community social legislation, was utilised sparingly. In part, this caution can be explained by the place of social policy in the EEC Treaty. As explained in chapter 1, in the context

---

[249] Conducted by Market and Opinion Research International (MORI). See COM(2000) 457, para 7.3.
[250] *Ibid* para 7.4. The European Parliament passed a resolution concurring with the Commission's conclusion: A5–0021/2001 of 13 Feb 2001, OJ 2001, C276/36.
[251] *Ibid* para 5.2. See URN 97/508 (HMSO, London, 1997).
[252] URN 00/1461 (HMSO, London, 2000).
[253] WE/2/94, 20 Jan 1994. See Barnard, n 166 above, p 425.

of Article 117 EEC, approximation measures under Article 100 EEC, whether legislative or purely administrative, were only necessary to rectify distortions in the market. Moreover, as early as 1985, the Commission had concluded that, in the short term, the horizon of Community social policy was to be limited to the promotion of health and safety linked to free movement objectives and, pending reform of the Treaty, it would be inappropriate to use Article 100 EEC more widely.[254] Having failed to secure a major reform of the Treaty and, moreover, with the internal market legislative route blocked off by the exclusion of employment legislation in Article 100a(2) EEC [now 95(2) EC], a fresh look at the potential of Article 100 EEC was now needed. In particular, the Commission sought to reconcile the bold ambitions that underlay the fundamental social rights in the Charter with the mundane practicality of crafting legislative measures deemed to 'directly affect' the establishment and functioning of the common market, while also taking account of the unanimity requirement.[255] In order to facilitate this adjustment, the European Council provided a steer towards a market-oriented approach in its Presidency Conclusions at Strasbourg in December 1989, when it called on the Council 'to deliberate upon the Commission's proposals in the light of the social dimension of the internal market'.[256] The Commission, for its part, adopted three 'cardinal' principles for the enactment of legislation aimed at improving workers' living and working conditions:[257]

—the principle of subsidiarity, having regard to the specific nature of the social sphere, whereby the type of action has to be matched to the subject matter (e.g. harmonisation, coordination, convergence, cooperation, etc.) and giving due consideration to known needs and to the potential added value of Community action;
—the principle of the diversity of national systems, cultures and practices, where this is a positive element in terms of the completion of the internal market;
—the preservation of the competitiveness of undertakings reconciling the economic and social dimensions. In each initiative a balance must be sought and reached.

Therefore action to establish a 'sound basis of minimum provisions' was permissible outside the field of health and safety, to complete the internal market, but only in so far as it 'added value', taking into account the principle of subsidiarity, the diversity of national systems and the overriding consideration of competitiveness. The strengthening of economic and social cohesion, including combating unemployment, was now regarded as central

[254] European Commission White Paper, *Completing the Internal Market*, COM(85) 310, para 65.
[255] For discussion of the legal justification for utilising Art 100 EEC [and now 94 EC] in this way, see the earlier discussion in ch 3 of Case C–376/98, *Germany v European Parliament and Council (Tobacco Advertising)* [2000] ECR I–8419.
[256] Issued on 8/9 Dec 1989. See COM(92) 562, p 3.
[257] First Report on the Application of the Community Charter of the Fundamental Social Rights of Workers, COM(91) 511.

to achieving competitiveness and this helps to explain why Article 100 EEC was applied as the legal base for strengthening the Collective Redundancies Directive in 1992.[258] By contrast, Directive 91/533 on Employee Information (Contract or Employment Relationship)[259] fitted less obviously within the compass of Article 100 EEC, and yet, this was the only other item of social legislation to be successfully chartered through the Community's legislative waters as a market functioning measure during the Action Programme prior to the entry into force of the Agreement on Social Policy in November 1993. In order to find out why this happened we should now consider this relatively obscure and unheralded Directive and, in the light of two judgments of the Court, re-evaluate its importance.

(2) Employee Information (Contract or Employment Relationship)

One of the reasons why Article 100 EEC was lightly used in this period, notwithstanding the market imperative of the social dimension, was the perceived threat of the UK veto, although it was rarely applied in practice. How did the Commission's proposal for an Employee Information (Contract or Employment Relationship) Directive survive the apparently inevitable legislative axe when it reached the Council? The answer to this question is both complex and surprising. The UK abstained in the Council vote, signifying its tacit opposition to any proposal deemed to regulate the individual employment relationship. On the face of it, this decision was not unusual and yet, lying behind the habitual facade of obstinacy, there was a supreme irony. Here was a piece of Community law, adopted under the auspices of the Social Charter Action Programme, but drawing its source and inspiration from the legal regulation of this area by the UK originating from the legislative programme of a previous Conservative Government enacting its own *Industrial Charter*.[260] Indeed, at the time of the Commission's proposal for a 'proof of employment' directive in January 1991,[261] only the UK

---

[258] Dir 92/56/EEC, OJ 1992, L245/3, now consolidated within Dir 98/59/EC, OJ 1998, L225/16.

[259] Dir 91/533/EEC on an employer's obligation to inform employees of the conditions applicable to the contract or employment relationship, OJ 1991, L288/32. By virtue of Art 9 of the Directive the implementation date was 30 June 1993. For critical analysis, see J Clark and M Hall, 'The Cinderella Directive? Employee Rights to Information about Conditions Applicable to their Contract or Employment Relationship' (1992) 21 *Industrial Law Journal* 106; and J Kenner, 'Statement or Contract?—Some Reflections on the EC Employee Information (Contract or Employment Relationship) Directive after *Kampelmann*' (1999) 28 *Industrial Law Journal* 205.

[260] As acknowledged by the European Commission in its Explanatory Memorandum attached to the draft directive, COM(90) 563, para 8, OJ 1991, C24/3. UK legislation in this area can be traced back to the Contracts of Employment Act, 1963. On the source of the Directive, see R Nielsen, 'The Contract of Employment in the Member States of the European Communities and in Community Law' (1990) 33 *German Yearbook of International Law* 258.

[261] OJ 1991, C24/3.

and Ireland,[262] among the Member States, had introduced legislation placing an obligation on employers to issue their employees with a written statement of employment particulars both at the commencement of employment and, where appropriate, when seeking to make amendments to those particulars.

The Commission's proposal, however, was aimed at achieving a deeper regulatory incursion into the employment relationship. The Commission sought to require an employer to issue every employee working an average week of more than eight hours with a 'document constituting a form of proof of the main terms of his employment relationship with his employer' within one month of the commencement of their employment contract.[263] This was of particular significance in the UK and Ireland where the introduction of national statutory provisions had been accompanied by a blurring of the distinction between the employer's *declaratory statement* as an item of documentary evidence and the *contract of employment* mutually agreed between the parties.[264]

The following statement in the Commission's accompanying Explanatory Memorandum encapsulates the underlying philosophy behind the proposal:[265]

The proposal for a Directive has as its objective the creation of an instrument to make employer's responsible for providing precise information on the nature and content of working relationships in the company.

To this end, it makes provision for an obligation to provide all workers covered by this Directive with a document setting out the details of the conditions and elements of their employment relationships with their employer. As such it does not relate to the rules of national law concerning the conclusion of employment contracts. *The document in question is designed to be a declaratory element and written proof of the employment contract or employment relationship established in accordance with the national law of a Member State.*

This approach was endorsed by the European Parliament, which sought to strengthen the Commission's proposal by suggesting several amendments backed up by a Resolution.[266] Parliament proposed that the proof of employment document should 'relate both to the parties to the contract and the work to be undertaken' and that employees 'shall confirm receipt

---

[262] In the case of Ireland, the relevant legislation is contained in the Minimum Notice and Terms of Employment Act, 1977, which is broadly similar in content to the earlier UK legislation except that it provides for the statement to be issued within one month of the commencement of the employee's employment, a period identical to the one originally proposed by the Commission. See Nielsen, n 260 above at 272.

[263] OJ 1991, C24/3, sixth recital of the draft preamble.

[264] On the operation of common law and statute in the UK, see Kenner, n 259 above and P Leighton and S Dumville, 'From Statement to Contract—Some Effects of the Contracts of Employment Act 1972' (1977) 6 *Industrial Law Journal* 133.

[265] COM(90) 563, paras 11–12. Emphasis added.

[266] OJ 1991, C240/21.

thereof in a special document'. They rejected the notion of an exemption for part-time workers and sought rather unconvincingly to justify the measure on the grounds of Article 118a EEC. Therefore the Commission's proposal, as amended by Parliament, would have had the potential to transform the employer's statements into 'proof of employment' documents but only in those cases where there was an absence of written contractual documentation. In all other cases, the Commission noted that the written declarations would be 'superfluous' to any existing written contract or other documentation 'making reference to current provisions or collective agreements'.[267] The Commission's main concern was to 'clarify the legal position of employees' who were not covered by a written contract of employment or a letter of appointment, rather than to alter 'the rules of national law concerning the conclusion of employment contracts'.[268]

However, the Council not only rejected the amended text but also diluted the Commission's draft taking into account concerns expressed by the Economic and Social Committee[269] and several Member States. Significant revisions were made to accommodate these objections. These included, inter alia, extending the deadline for the statement to be provided to two months after the commencement of employment[270] and deleting a proposal for the enumerated information to include a job description and category of employment.[271] Most importantly, Article 6 of the Directive provides that:

This Directive shall be without prejudice to national law and practice concerning:
—the form of the contract or employment relationship,
—proof as regards the existence and content of a contract or employment relationship,
—the relevant procedural rules.

It followed, axiomatically, that the final agreed text represented a shift away from the original proposal. The measure was no longer primarily concerned with proof of employment and was, instead, downgraded to an apparently innocuous piece of Community legislation obliging the employer to issue documentation to qualifying employees containing a panoply of worthwhile information concerning the 'essential aspects of the contract or employment relationship'.[272] In particular, there was greater emphasis on the internal market objectives and an overall goal, summarised in the preamble, 'to provide employees with improved protection against possible infringements

---

[267] OJ 1991, C24/3, tenth recital of the preamble.
[268] COM(90) 563, paras 7 and 12–13.
[269] OJ 1991, C159/32.
[270] Art 3(2).
[271] See also, the Opinion of the Economic and Social Committee, OJ 1991, C159/32, which found that this requirement would place an 'excessive' administrative obligation on the employer.
[272] Art 2.

of their rights and to create greater transparency in the labour market'.[273] Not surprisingly, considering the Directive's legal heritage, the UK's opposition was fairly muted and aroused little media comment at the time.[274] Rather, by registering its objection, the UK was indicating opposition, not to the measure in principle, but to the necessity for harmonising legislation concerning an administrative obligation that appeared to have little direct bearing on the operation of the common market and which might be better left for more flexible regulation, where necessary, at Member State level.[275]

What then is the scope of the Directive? In chapter 4 we discussed how Article 1(1) of the Directive, limiting its application to 'every paid employee', has a significant narrowing effect when account is taken of Article 6, whereby the Directive operates 'without prejudice' to national law and practice concerning the form of the contract or employment relationship. Elsewhere there are specific derogations that, if applied by Member States, narrow its scope even further. For example, Article 1(2)(a) allows for national derogations including a one-month service qualification and the option of excluding employees who work fewer than eight hours. This derogation, while it remains on the EC 'statute book', cannot now be reconciled with the provisions of Directive 97/81 prohibiting discrimination against part-time workers.[276] Article 1(2)(b) allows Member States to exclude any 'contract or employment relationship' of a 'casual and/or specific nature provided, in these cases, that its non-application is justified by objective considerations'. Bercusson has persuasively argued that the wording of Article 1(2)(b) 'creates a *presumption* that casual and specific employment relationships *are* within the scope of the Directive'.[277] The position, however, is not so clear-cut. In particular, Article 6 creates a hierarchy of norms founded on national law, whereas Article 1(2)(b) derogates from the core definition in Article 1(1). Hence, Article 1(2)(b) is founded upon the interpretation of a 'contract or employment relationship defined by the law in force in a Member State'.

The main substantive provisions can be found in Articles 2–5. Article 2(1) obliges employers to notify their employees of the 'essential aspects of the contract of employment' covering 'at least' the following information enumerated in Articles 2(2)(a)–(j):

(a) the identities of the parties;
(b) the place of work; where there is no fixed or main place of work, the principle

---

[273] Second recital of the preamble.
[274] See Clark and Hall, n 259 above at 106.
[275] Department of Employment, *Consultation Document on EC Proposal for a Directive on Form of Proof of an Employment Relationship* (HMSO, London, 1991).
[276] Dir 97/81/EC, OJ 1998, L14/9, as amended by Dir 98/23/EC, OJ 1998, L131/10.
[277] B Bercusson, *European Labour Law* (Butterworths, London, 1996) p 432. Emphasis in the original.

that the employee is employed at various places and the registered place of business or, where appropriate, the domicile of the employer;

(c) (i) the title, grade, nature or category of the work for which the employee is employed; or

    (ii) a brief specification or description of the work;

(d) the date of commencement of the contract or employment relationship;

(e) in the case of a temporary contract or employment relationship, the expected duration thereof;

(f) the amount of paid leave to which the employee is entitled or, where this cannot be indicated when the information is given, the procedures for allocating and determining such leave;

(g) the length of the periods of notice to be observed by the employer and the employee should their contract or employment relationship be terminated or, where this cannot be indicated when the information is given, the method for determining such periods of notice;

(h) the initial basic amount, the other component elements and the frequency of payment of the remuneration to which the employee is entitled;

(i) the length of the employee's normal working day or week;

(j) where appropriate;

    (i) the collective agreements governing the employee's conditions of work; or

    (ii) in the case of collective agreements concluded outside the business by special joint bodies or institutions, the name of the competent body or joint institution within which the agreements were concluded.

Article 2(3) allows some flexibility by permitting the information referred to in paragraphs (f) (g) (h) and (i) to be transmitted in the form of a reference to the laws, regulations and administrative or statutory provisions or collective agreements governing those particular points.

Article 2(2) is not intended to be exhaustive but it does contain one glaring omission concerning disciplinary procedures. There is no obligation on the employer to provide information about the existence and form of such procedures. Member States are able to apply or introduce more favourable provisions[278] and the UK, acting in conformity with the principle of non-retrogression, has chosen to retain its existing rules obliging employers with 20 employees or more to provide this information.[279] One less obvious omission, concerning overtime, as distinct from normal working hours, was discussed by the Court in *Lange*,[280] where the relationship between Article 2(1) and 2(2) was also addressed. We will return to this question when discussing *Lange* later in this section.

Methods of conveying the essential information listed in Article 2(2) are set out in Article 3. Employers are obliged to issue a specific document or

---

[278] Art 7.

[279] The relevant provisions are contained in s 3(3) Employment Rights Act, 1996.

[280] Case C–350/99, *Lange v Georg Schünemann GmbH* [2001] ECR I–1061.

a succession of documents,[281] and/or written declarations,[282] conveying all the required information to their employees within two months of the commencement of their employment. An employer cannot simply refer to other documentation that the employee can inspect. Where the contract or employment relationship comes to an end within two months, the information must be made available to the employee at the end of this period at the latest.[283] A separate clause, in Article 9(2) obliged employers to issue the itemised documentation to employees in employment at the time when the Directive's provisions entered into force where an employee had requested this information. The employer had two months to comply with this request.

Article 4 provides additional protection where an employee is required to work outside the country whose law and/or practice governs their contract or employment relationship[284] for a period of more than one month.[285] These 'expatriate' employees are entitled to the documentation referred to in Article 3 prior to their departure together with specified information concerning the length of time to be worked abroad, the currency to be used for wages, and related matters concerning the benefits and cash in kind attendant on the employment abroad and the conditions governing their repatriation.[286] This provision, which might appear to be separated from the main thrust of the Directive, can now be regarded as fully complementary with the later Directive on Posted Workers,[287] which provides for a minimum range of protection for workers who, for a limited period, work in the territory of a Member State other than the State in which they normally work.

Article 5 is concerned with modifications of aspects of the contract or employment relationship. Any change in the details specified in Articles 2

[281] Art 3(1) provides that this information can be issued in the form of: (a) a written contract of employment; and/or (b) a letter of engagement; and/or (c) one or more other written documents, where one of these documents contains at least all the information referred to in Art 2(2) (a) (b) (c) (d) (h) and (i).

[282] This option is set out in Art 3(2). It applies where none of the documents referred to in Art 3(1) is handed over to the employee within the prescribed period. In these circumstances 'the employer shall be obliged to give the employee, not later than two months after the commencement of employment, a written declaration signed by the employer and containing at least the information referred to in Article 2(2)'. Where the documents referred to in Art 3(1) contain only part of the information required, the written declaration 'shall cover the remaining information'.

[283] Art 3(3).

[284] Art 4(1).

[285] Art 4(3).

[286] Art 4(1)(a)–(d). Art 4(2) provides that the information concerning the currency of any remuneration and cash and benefits in kind may be given in the form of a reference to the laws, regulations and administrative or statutory provisions or collective agreements governing those particular points.

[287] Dir 96/71/EC concerning the posting of workers in the framework of the provision of services, OJ 1997, L18/1.

and 4 will normally be set out in a 'written document' to be issued by the employer to the employee 'at the earliest opportunity and not later than one month after the date of entry into effect of the change in question'.[288] This written document shall not, however, be compulsory in the event of a change in the laws, regulations and administrative or statutory provisions or collective agreements. This offers Member States considerable flexibility. Moreover, with regard to clauses in collective agreements, the effectiveness of this provision depends on the legal status of such agreements in the Member State concerned. For example, in the UK, where collective agreements are not legally binding per se, an Employment Tribunal must be satisfied that the parties are bound by the collective agreement through the incorporation of its terms into the contract. Reference to a collective agreement in the employer's statement will not automatically lead to incorporation, but it can be argued that it provides strong prima facie evidence in favour of that interpretation.[289]

Finally, Article 8 provides for access to redress for the employee within 15 days of notifying the employer of his failure to comply with the obligations in the Directive by 'judicial process after possible recourse to other competent authorities'.[290] This offers Member States considerable leeway. For example, in the UK an employee has a right of recourse to an Employment Tribunal to obtain a declaration rectifying the statutory particulars. This would appear to meet this minimum requirement and yet research suggests that this provision has been infrequently used because the Tribunal cannot award compensation or impose a fine for non-compliance.[291]

Taken together, the employee information requirements specified in the Directive largely reflect the fast changing nature of labour markets and the prevalence of informal employment relationships. For these reasons the requirement to include a non-exhaustive list of detailed information in the written statement was not intended to lead to any systematic changes to the diverse formalities of the individual employment relationship in the Member States, but rather to operate as a practical means of making information issued by the employer more relevant to the employee. It does not, however, resolve the statement or contract conundrum. Nevertheless, some insight into the Directive's application can be gleaned from two cases referred from courts in Germany.

In *Kampelmann*[292] a group of employers sought to challenge the accuracy of their own statements in order to deny promotion to several of their

---

[288] Art 5(1).
[289] *System Floors Ltd v Daniel* [1981] IRLR 475 (Employment Appeal Tribunal).
[290] Art 8(1).
[291] See Clark and Hall, n 259 above at 116.
[292] Joined Cases C–253–258/96, *Kampelmann and others v Landschaftsverband Westfalen-Lippe*, and *Stadtwerke Witten GmbH v Schade*, and *Haseley v Stadtwerke Altena GmbH* [1998] ECR I–6907.

employees on the grounds that documents previously issued to them, in some cases before the Directive entered into force, had incorrectly categorised or assessed their performance. The main provisions under consideration were Article 2(2)(c)(ii) concerning information containing 'a brief specification or description of the work' and Article 9(2) obliging employers to give existing employees the documentation required by Article 3 on request. While the primary issue at stake was whether the employers' statements were binding on them, the questions raised by the referring court have much wider ramifications.[293]

The first question referred to the stated objective in the preamble of the Directive 'to provide employees with improved protection and to create greater transparency in the labour market' and asked if it was the purpose of Article 2(2) to modify the burden of proof in the employee's favour by providing a list of minimum requirements 'intended to ensure that the employee does not encounter difficulties of proof regarding the listed points when enforcing his contractual rights in employment law disputes?'[294] On a related point arising from Article 9(2) concerning documents issued before the Directive came into force, the Court was also asked, in the fourth question, whether an employer who issues a more recent notification which conflicts with the earlier ones, must prove that the latter notification is correct?

When considering the first question, AG Tesauro placed great emphasis on Article 6, which preserves national law and practice concerning proof as regards the existence and content of a contract or employment relationship. He concluded, however, that it must be recognised that 'the details given by the employer himself in the notification cannot be wholly devoid of relevance, in terms of probative value', but the Directive cannot be taken to reverse the burden of proof. This will be a matter for national procedural rules.[295] The Court concurred with this view but noted that Article 2(1) of the Directive requires the employer, for the purposes set out in the second recital in the preamble, to notify an employee of the essential aspects of the contract or employment relationship, as set out in Article 2(2).[296] It followed that:[297]

That objective would not be achieved if the employee were unable in any way to use the information contained in the notification . . . as evidence before the national

---

[293] The third and fifth questions are not considered in detail here. The third question concerned the scope of Art 2(2)(c)(i) of the Directive but this was deemed not to be relevant because Germany had legitimately chosen an alternative provision contained in Art 2(2)(c)(ii) paras 48–9. In answering the fifth question, the Court, at paras 50–3, upheld Germany's means of implementing Art 9(2) notwithstanding the fact that they had exempted employers from issuing statements to employees who already possessed written contractual documentation before the Directive entered into force.
[294] Para 24.
[295] Paras 11–12 of the opinion.
[296] Para 31.
[297] Paras 32–3.

courts, particularly in disputes concerning essential aspects of the contract or employment relationship.

The national courts must . . . apply and interpret their national rules on the burden of proof in the light of the purpose of the Directive, giving the notification . . . *such evidential weight as to allow it to serve as factual proof of the essential aspects of the contract of employment* . . . enjoying such presumption as to its correctness as would attach, in domestic law, to any similar document drawn up by the employer and communicated to the employee.

The real significance of this part of the judgment lies with the Court's application of the doctrine of effectiveness in its interpretation of any notification issued in accordance with the Directive as presumptive 'proof of employment' notwithstanding the dilution of the original proposal. It follows that where the employer's notification is accurate both at the time of issue and in operative fact, it will serve as the contract in so far as it conveys those essential aspects contained within Article 2(2) and added to by 'more favourable provisions' in domestic law. The employer will only be able to rebut the presumption by bringing evidence to show that the information in the notification 'is either inherently incorrect or has shown to be so in fact'.[298] Therefore, in circumstances where the notification, or series of notifications, issued in accordance with Article 2, amount to the only accurate and available documentary evidence of the relevant contractual terms the statement and contract may be treated as one and the same.

To what extent then does his own statement bind the employer? AG Tesauro advised that the employer is bound by his subsequent notification unless its details are shown to be inaccurate, while the employee should only have to rely upon the notification where he wishes to establish that it reflects the substance of the agreement.[299] Implicitly therefore, in all other circumstances, the employee ought to be able to rely on the written contract preceding the notification. Hence, the purpose of the notification is to help the *employee* as a matter of proof although this may not be incontrovertible or even sufficient in itself because:[300]

. . . the employer's obligations derive exclusively from the contract and not from notification given pursuant to the Directive, which merely serves as subsequent evidence of the details of the contract which it must faithfully reflect.

Although the Court did not directly address this point, it ruled that the notification amounts to a presumptive contract capable of rebuttal by the employer.[301] Hence, any inconsistency between the statement and its contractual precursor ought to be reconciled by reference to the original con-

---

[298] Para 34.
[299] Para 13 of the opinion.
[300] *Ibid.*
[301] Para 35.

tractual document. Any other interpretation would be contrary to the Directive's aim to give improved protection to employees without written proof of employment and not to undermine the rights of those who have.[302]

The second question concerned the direct effect of Article 2(2)(c). This provision allows Member States to choose between two categories of information to be issued by employers containing, *either*, 'the title, grade, nature or category of the work for which the employee is employed', *or*, 'a brief specification or description of the work'. The Court held that this provision meets the requirements for direct effect, in the sense that it is unconditional and sufficiently precise, notwithstanding the fact that Member States were given a choice of options.[303] It is still possible to determine the content of the rights conferred on individuals, the scope of which is not in the discretion of the Member State whatever choice it makes.[304] Having found that Article 2(2)(c) is directly effective, the Court noted that Germany had chosen the second option by requiring the employer to give written notification of 'the designation or general description of the work to be done by the employee'.[305] The Court concluded that 'the mere designation of an activity cannot in every case amount to a brief specification or description of the work done by an employee' as required by Article 2(2)(c)(ii).[306] Therefore, while not explicitly striking down the German legislation, the Court found that it was not open to Member States to transpose the Directive in such a way as to allow the employer, in every case, to confine the information to be notified to the employee to a mere job designation, and national courts should interpret such legislation accordingly.[307]

Kampelmann confirms that national rules concerning the formation of the contract between the parties at the commencement of employment, and when seeking to make changes, will persist. No other interpretation would have been conceivable when determining the impact of the clear provisions contained within Article 6 of the Directive. The Court has, however, given clear guidance that, in circumstances where the employer's notification accurately reflects the contract and the employee seeks to rely on it, the Directive's objective of improved protection for employees will be converted into an effective guarantee that will apply to, at least, the directly effective normative terms enumerated in Article 2(2). Simultaneously, the Court has placed a heavy burden of rebuttal on the employer seeking to disprove his own statement.

---

[302] Paras 31–2.
[303] Para 39.
[304] *Ibid.* See also, Cases C–6/90 and 9/90, *Francovich and others v Italy* [1991] ECR I–5357, para 17.
[305] Para 43.
[306] Para 44.
[307] Para 47.

The Court's interpretation of the Directive in *Kampelmann* has been further amplified in *Lange*.[308] This case concerned a dispute about overtime. Mr Lange's contract of employment specified that his working week was 40 hours with no reference to overtime. Subsequently, he refused his employer's request to work overtime and his contract was terminated. The employer claimed that it was understood that overtime would be worked in the event of sudden increases in workload while Mr Lange contended that he agreed to work overtime only in emergencies. In order to settle this dispute the *Arbeitsgericht* Bremen sought guidance from the Court on the interpretation of Article 2, concerning its application to any agreements to work overtime, and Article 6 on the exercise of national rules of evidence where an employer has failed to provide information pursuant to the Directive.

First, the Court considered the scope of Article 2(2)(i) which specifies the conveyance of information concerning the 'length of the employee's normal working day or week'. Interpreting this provision in isolation led ineluctably to the conclusion that *normal working hours* and *overtime* were mutually exclusive as overtime is performed outside, and is additional to, normal working hours.[309] The Commission had argued that the position is different where overtime is habitually worked in the undertaking and can be viewed as a feature of the employee's ordinary working day.[310] The Court rejected this argument on the basis that it was contrary to the wording of Article 2(2)(i) and, also, the purpose of the obligation to provide information is to apprise employees of their rights and obligations vis-à-vis their employers, not to give an indication of the practices observed as a general rule in the undertaking preceding their recruitment.[311]

Therefore, in isolation, Article 2(2)(i) is to be interpreted narrowly as not relating to overtime. This is not, however, the end of the matter because Article 2(1) and 2(2) must be construed together. The Court confirmed that Article 2(2) is not intended to be an exhaustive enumeration of the essential elements of the contract or employment relationship referred to in Article 2(1).[312] The Court continued:[313]

Accordingly, apart from the elements mentioned in Article 2(2) of the Directive, any element which, in view of its importance, must be considered an essential element of the contract or employment relationship of which it forms part must be notified to the employee. That applies in particular to a term under which an employee is obliged to work overtime whenever requested to do so by his employer.

Consequently, an employer is required to give written notice to an employee of such a term under which the latter is obliged to work overtime when-

---

[308] Case C–350/99, *Lange v Georg Schünemann GmbH* [2001] ECR I–1061.
[309] Para 16.
[310] Para 17.
[311] Para 18.
[312] Para 22.
[313] Para 23.

ever requested to do so by an employer under the same conditions as apply under Article 2(2) and, by analogy, Article 2(3) which allows rules concerning normal working hours to be transmitted in the form of a reference to the relevant laws, regulations and administrative or statutory provisions or collective agreements.[314]

Secondly, does it necessarily follow that, in the absence of this written notification, such a request to work overtime is inapplicable? The Court found that such an interpretation would frustrate the purpose of the Directive, which was to establish the contents of the essential elements of the contract or employment relationship.[315] Article 6 gives precedence to national rules of evidence and such proof may be produced in any form allowed by national law, and thus, even in the absence of any written notification from the employer.[316] Moreover, Article 8(1) leaves the issue of remedies to the Member States and therefore it does not necessarily follow that the element in question will be inapplicable.[317] The Court applied *Kampelmann* in holding that national rules on the burden of proof are not affected and the Directive itself does not lay down any rules of evidence.[318]

Both *Kampelmann* and *Lange* point to a broad interpretation of Article 2. The employer is bound not only to provide the information required under Article 2(2), where it forms part of the contract or employment relationship, but also any additional information which is an essential element of that contract or employment relationship. Therefore the Community obligation, founded on transparency, is a broad one, but in practice it operates, under the principles of subsidiarity and legal diversity, in strict accordance with national rules on the formation of the contract, proof of its existence and content, and procedural rules, including the means of redress.

While the central thrust of *Kampelmann* and *Lange* has fortified Directive 91/533 as a means of transmitting contractual information in a transparent form, apparently offering a 'solid base' of protection for employees, these cases have also, paradoxically, helped to reveal its most serious limitation. In particular, it neither alters the power relationship between employer and employee, nor impinges upon the framework of employment protection provided by national labour laws. Hence, Article 6 ensures that the employer retains a large measure of control over the contractual bargain subject to the interpretation of the contractual documentation, including the employer's notifications, by the national court. It follows that, although Article 2(1) contains an *assumption* that the 'essential elements of the contract' are 'at least' those items contained in Article 2(2), the precise *content*

---

[314] Para 24.
[315] Paras 27 and 29.
[316] Para 27.
[317] Para 28.
[318] Paras 30–5.

of the contract remains a matter for the parties while the Directive is concerned with how it is *conveyed*. Therefore, if the framework of regulation at national level is stripped away and no longer offers a minimum level of protection in the enumerated areas there is no compulsion on the employer to include these details in the contractual terms. Where this occurs the Directive offers no corresponding protection.[319] This was aptly demonstrated by the fact that just when the UK was taking positive steps to implement the Directive, they were simultaneously dismantling the bulk of the Wages Council machinery that had regulated employment contracts for millions of workers throughout the post-war period.[320]

IV SOFT LAW—FILLING THE GAPS?

(1) Introduction

Our discussion of the first two legislative streams has featured a range of measures that, while they reflect a health and safety or common market orientation, have fulfilled, at least in part, the objective of establishing a minimum, if not uniform, set of exercisable social rights for those Community workers within their protective scope, broadly consistent with the aims of the Social Charter. To complete the picture we need to examine a third stream of quasi-legislative[321] or soft law activity that featured prominently during the period of the Action Programme. In seeking to work through its 47 wide-ranging initiatives, the Commission had to rely heavily on soft law, not only to compensate for the limitations of the legal bases in the Treaty and the difficulty in overcoming opposition in the Council, but also because non-binding measures can help to render existing hard law more effective on the ground and act as a test-bed or filter for new initiatives in areas in which there may be no short or medium-term possibility of Community legislation. Hence soft law helps to fill legislative gaps while maintaining the momentum created by declaratory instruments such as the Charter and the Action Programme. In this section we will examine two Community instruments from this period representing the diversity and inherent flexibility of the Community soft law method.

---

[319] See S Deakin and G Morris, *Labour Law* 2nd edn (Butterworths, London, 1998) pp 252–55.

[320] Wage setting has now been restored by the National Minimum Wage Act, 1998.

[321] This term predates 'soft law' and is still used in British administrative law. See R Megarry, 'Administrative Quasi-Legislation' (1944) 60 *Law Quarterly Review* 125; and G Ganz, *Quasi-Legislation: Recent Developments in Secondary Legislation* (Sweet & Maxwell, London, 1987).

(2) Commission Recommendation and Code of Practice on Sexual Harassment

In 1984 the Council adopted a non-binding Recommendation on the pro-motion of positive action for women,[322] which sought to give practical effect to the commitment in Article 2(4) of the Equal Treatment Directive, 76/207,[323] to take measures to promote equal opportunities for men and women, 'in particular *by removing existing inequalities* which affect women's opportunities in employment and the labour market'.[324] The 1984 Recommendation sought to implement positive actions designed to elimi-nate existing inequalities affecting women in working life and to promote a better balance between the sexes in employment.[325] One of the objectives of positive action would be to eliminate or counteract the prejudicial effects on women in employment or seeking employment which arise from exist-ing attitudes, behaviour and structures based on the idea of a traditional division of roles in society between men and women.[326] High on the list of priorities was action aimed at ensuring respect for the dignity of women at the workplace.[327] Following on from this Recommendation, the Commis-sion embarked on a range of programmatic activity leading to a seminal opinion of the Advisory Committee on Equal Opportunities for Men and Women which, in June 1988, unanimously proposed a recommendation and code of conduct on sexual harassment in the workplace covering harassment of both sexes.[328] This report followed hard on the heels of a Commission study on the dignity of women at work[329] and a European Parliament Resolution on violence against women.[330] The Council

---

[322] Council Recommendation 84/635/EEC on the promotion of positive action for women, OJ 1984, L331/34. This Recommendation was, in turn, a development arising from a Council Resolution on the promotion of equal opportunities for women, OJ 1982, C186/3. The 1982 Resolution gave Council approval to the general objectives of a Community action programme on the promotion of equal opportunities for women (1982–1985) namely the stepping up of action to ensure observance of the principle of equal treatment and the promotion of equal opportunities in practice by positive action (Part B of the programme) and expressed the will to implement appropriate measures to achieve these objectives.

[323] OJ 1976, L39/40.

[324] Emphasis added.

[325] Council Recommendation 84/635/EEC on the promotion of positive action for women, OJ 1984, L331/3, point 1.

[326] *Ibid* point 1(a).

[327] *Ibid* point 4.

[328] Commission Report of 20 June 1988 (European Commission, Brussels, 1988).

[329] M Rubenstein, *The Dignity of Women at Work: A Report on the Problem of Sexual Harassment in the Member States of the European Communities* (European Communities, Luxembourg, 1987). See also, C McCrudden, 'The Effectiveness of European Equality Law: National Mechanisms for Enforcing Gender Equality Law in the Light of European Require-ments' (1993) 13 *Oxford Journal of Legal Studies* 320 at 362–65.

[330] OJ 1986, C176/73. This resolution called upon national governments, equal opportu-nities committees and trade unions to carry out concerted information campaigns to create a proper awareness of the individual rights of all members of the labour force.

responded with a Resolution on the protection of the dignity of women and men at work.[331] Finally, following the absorption of this objective into the Third Community Action Programme on equal opportunities for women and men,[332] on 27 November 1991, the Commission formally adopted Recommendation 92/131 on the protection of the dignity of men and women at work, together with an annexed code of practice on measures to combat sexual harassment.[333]

The Commission Recommendation should therefore be regarded as the culmination of an intense period of inter-institutional soft law activity that created an irresistible dynamic for a definitive Community instrument on combating sexual harassment that was designed to spur activity at both national and Community levels and which, in due course, has proved to be capable of conversion into hard law. Hence the Recommendation falls into a grouping of soft laws[334] that are designed to supplement existing hard laws in order to give them maximum effect at national level and to serve as a means of focusing the attention of the Community institutions on priority policy areas. McCrudden has neatly described this type of instrument as a 'hybrid' between legislation and litigation 'devised as much to influence national court and [Court of Justice] interpretations of existing legal provisions as to influence Member States to adopt new legal provisions or new practices'.[335]

In order to consider the *effectiveness* of the Recommendation let us first establish its legal status.[336] Under Article 220 EC [ex 164 EEC] the Court has a duty to 'ensure that in the interpretation and application of this Treaty the law is observed'. In each case the primary consideration of the Court is not the formal or informal means used to adopt the instrument but its inherent capacity to create legal effects by reference to both its content and objectives.[337] In particular, the Court will take note of the general obligation on Member States in Article 10 EC [ex 5 EEC] to facilitate the Community's tasks and abstain from all measures that could jeopardise the attainment of the Community's objectives. Hence, Community soft laws have the potential to influence and extend the scope of national laws to fully comply with Community objectives, whilst ensuring that derogations

[331] OJ 1990, C157/3.
[332] COM(90) 449. Point D (a). The Social Charter Action Programme did not directly include the proposed recommendation among its initiatives but referred instead to the need for an action programme. *Social Europe* 1/90, p 68.
[333] Recommendation 92/131/EEC, OJ 1992, L49/1. For further discussion, see F Beveridge and S Nott, 'A Hard Look at Soft Law' in P Craig and C Harlow (eds) *Lawmaking in the European Union* (Kluwer, London, 1998) 285–309 at 297–305.
[334] For my categorisation, see p 128 above.
[335] McCrudden, n 329 above at 362. Another example is the Council Recommendation on Childcare, 92/241/EEC, OJ 1992, L123/16.
[336] See further, J Kenner, 'EC Labour Law: the Softly, Softly Approach' (1995) 11 *International Journal of Comparative Labour Law and Industrial Relatiour* 307.
[337] See Case 22/70, *Commission v Council (ERTA case)* [1971] ECR 263 at 277.

from the objectives of the Treaty, in whatever form, are interpreted restrictively.[338]

The Court has recognised that recommendations 'have no binding force'[339] but this does not mean that they have no legal significance. In *Frecassetti*,[340] AG Warner advised that where a national statute had been passed for the express purpose of giving effect to a recommendation 'the correct interpretation of that statute may well depend on that of the recommendation. Whether it does so depend or not is a matter for the national court concerned'.[341] This was taken further by the Court itself in *Grimaldi*,[342] where it was held, firstly, that the legal effects, if any, of a recommendation could be the subject of an Article 234 EEC [ex 177 EC] reference from a national court seeking guidance from the Court[343] and, secondly, while recommendations are non-binding and cannot create rights upon which individuals may rely before a national court, they may, nevertheless, have certain legal consequences for Member States.[344] In its judgment the Court concluded that:[345]

. . . it must be stressed that [recommendations] cannot therefore be regarded as having no legal effect. The national courts are bound to take recommendations into consideration in order to decide disputes submitted to them, in particular where they cast light on the interpretation of national measures adopted in order to implement them or where they are designed to supplement binding Community provisions.

Therefore, recommendations are capable of 'indirect effect'[346] in the sense that they can act as an aid to interpretation where national provisions are

---

[338] For example in Case 43/75, *Defrenne v Sabena II* [1976] ECR 455 at para 56, the Court rejected a Council Resolution of 30 Dec 1961 which sought to achieve a three year delay of the effective date for the implementation of the principle of equal pay for men and women in Art 119 EEC on the grounds that such a resolution could not modify a clear Treaty provision. However, the Court acknowledged that a resolution on this subject matter could have legal effects if it operated to encourage and accelerate the full implementation of equal pay. See J Klabbers, 'Informal Instruments before the European Court of Justice' (1994) 31 *Comman Market Law Review* 997 at 1007–8. In Cases 90 and 91/63, *Commission v Luxembourg and Belgium* [1964] ECR 625 at 638, AG Roemer noted that where a Council resolution was not acted upon in due time 'this might well imply that an obligation based on the Treaty was not observed'.

[339] Art 249 EC [ex 189 EEC].

[340] Case 113/75, *Frecassetti v Amministrazione delle Finanze dello Stato* [1976] ECR 983.

[341] *Ibid* at 996–97.

[342] Case C–322/88, *Grimaldi v Fonds des Maladies Professionelles* [1989] ECR 4407. For comment, see A Arnull, 'The legal status of recommendations' (1990) 15 *European Law Review* 318. See also Case C–188/91, *Deutsche Shell AG v Hauptzollamt Hamburg-Hamburg* [1993] ECR I–363.

[343] *Ibid* paras 8–9.

[344] *Paras* 16–19.

[345] *Para* 18.

[346] For discussion, see C Docksey and B Fitzpatrick, 'The duty of national courts to interpret provisions of national law in accordance with Community law' (1991) 20 *Industrial Law Journal* 113.

vague or inconsistent in order to ensure conformity with other binding Community laws and Treaty provisions. By focusing on content rather than form the national court can reverse the presumption that soft laws do not have legal effects.[347] Thus, both formal and informal non-binding instruments are given 'legal scope' based on a legitimate expectation that the conduct of Member States will be in conformity with rules and declarations designed to fulfil the Community's aspirations.[348] In this way there is the potential for soft law to be transformed into hard law at national level where the courts are prepared to accept this form of Community guidance.

The Commission Recommendation and Code of Practice[349] seek to address the issue of unwanted conduct, sexual or otherwise, based on sex affecting the dignity of women and men at work. The first recital declares that such conduct is:[350]

... unacceptable and *may, in certain circumstances*, be contrary to the principle of equal treatment within the meaning ... of Directive 76/207 ... on the implementation of the principle of equal treatment for men and women as regards access to employment, vocational training and promotion, and working conditions, a view supported by case-law in certain Member States.

Thus the Recommendation provides further elaboration of an existing binding Community provision as a means of encouragement and guidance for national courts seeking to interpret national rules in line with Community laws in order to give them maximum 'useful effect'.[351] Without such encouragement there is a danger that 'weak enforcement or failure to sanction infringements' will inhibit women from exercising their rights, will diminish their status, and reduce their likelihood of obtaining equality of treatment in the workplace.[352]

The Recommendation is directed at the Member States exhorting them to take action to promote awareness of sexual harassment. Article 1 recommends that Member States take action to promote awareness that conduct of a sexual nature, or other conduct based on sex affecting the dignity of women and men at work, including conduct of superiors and colleagues, is unacceptable if:

(a) such conduct is unwanted, unreasonable and offensive to the recipient;
(b) a person's rejection of, or submission to, such conduct on the part of employers or workers (including superiors or colleagues) is used explicitly or implicitly as a basis for a decision which affects that person's access to

---

[347] See Klabbers, n 338 above at 1016–17.
[348] See K Wellens and G Borchardt, 'Soft Law in European Community Law' (1989) 14 *European Law Review* 267 at 281–82.
[349] Recommendation 92/131/EEC, OJ 1992, L49/1.
[350] Emphasis added.
[351] See Case 41/74, *Van Duyn v Home Office* [1974] ECR 1337.
[352] See the Commission's draft equal opportunities action programme for 1996–2000, COM(95) 381 at 26–7.

vocational training, access to employment, continued employment, promotion, salary or any other employment decisions; and/or

(c) such conduct creates an intimidating, hostile or humiliating work environment for the recipient; and that such conduct may, in certain circumstances, be contrary to the principle of equal treatment within the meaning of Articles 3, 4 and 5 of Directive 76/207/EEC.

This is a general definition of such conduct and should not be confused with a more detailed definition of sexual harassment in the Code. Part 2 of the Code gives examples of sexual harassment including unwelcome physical, verbal or non-verbal conduct. Thus, a range of behaviour may be considered to constitute sexual harassment as the Commission explain:[353]

The essential characteristic of sexual harassment is that it is unwanted by the recipient, that it is for each individual to determine what behaviour is acceptable to them and what they regard as offensive. Sexual attention becomes sexual harassment if it is persisted in once it has been made clear that it is regarded by the recipient as offensive, although one incident of harassment may constitute sexual harassment if sufficiently serious. It is the unwanted nature of the conduct which distinguishes sexual harassment from friendly behaviour, which is welcome and mutual.

Article 2 urges the Member States to implement the Code in the public sector and, through their action in 'initiating and pursuing positive measures designed to create a climate at work in which women and men respect one another's human integrity, should serve as an example to the private sector'. Article 3 recommends that Member States encourage employers' and employees' representatives to develop measures to implement the Code. Article 4 instructs Member States to inform the Commission within three years of the date of the recommendation of the measures taken to give effect to it, in order to allow it to draw up a report on these measures.

Having set out a general series of recommendations to the Member States, the Commission reinforce the Recommendation by attaching guidelines in the Code of Practice. Through the mechanism of the Code, the Commission seeks to directly address employers, trade unions and equal opportunity agencies concerned with the implementation of equal treatment on the ground in both public and private sectors and in small and medium-sized enterprises.[354] The overriding aim of the Code is to ensure that sexual harassment does not occur and, if it does occur, to guarantee that adequate procedures are readily available to deal with the problem and prevent its recurrence. The Code thus seeks to encourage the development and implementation of policies and practices that establish working environments free of sexual harassment and in which women and men respect one another's human integrity.[355] Significantly, the Commission follow through this

---

[353] Annex, Part 2, para 3.
[354] Annex, Part 1, para 2.
[355] Annex, Part 1, para 3.

logic and note that some groups are particularly vulnerable to sexual harassment:[356]

... including divorced and separated women, young women and new entrants to the labour market and those with irregular or precarious employment contracts, women in non-traditional jobs, women with disabilities, lesbians and women from racial minorities are disproportionately at risk. The Commission also note that gay men and young men are also vulnerable to harassment. It is undeniable that harassment on grounds of sexual orientation undermines the dignity at work of those affected and it is impossible to regard such harassment as appropriate workplace behaviour.

This statement was to provide a direct point of reference for the Commission when drafting its proposals on Community measures to combat discrimination under Article 13 EC,[357] added by the Treaty of Amsterdam.[358] This, in turn, led to the inclusion of specific anti-harassment clauses in both the Race Equality Directive[359] and the Framework Employment Directive.[360] In each case the definition of harassment has been closely modelled on the Recommendation, indicating direct lineage from soft law to binding Community action.

As a Community instrument the Code is a means by which formal equality guaranteed by the Directive can be translated into real equality on the ground based on best employment practice. The social policy actors are provided with a detailed definition of sexual harassment, guidance on the law, including the possibility of making sexual harassment a criminal offence. Employers are offered specific advice about investigative and disciplinary procedures. The aim, therefore, is to facilitate changes in attitudes and behaviour through both practical and legal steps.

Evidence from several Member States suggests that the Recommendation and Code have had a galvanising effect.[361] Within a year of its adoption, a Belgian decree was issued which forces employers to ensure that employees are aware that sexual harassment of a verbal, non-verbal and physical

---

[356] Annex, Part 1, para 3.

[357] Art 13 EC provides that: 'Without prejudice to other provisions of this Treaty and within the limits of the powers conferred upon the Community, the Council, acting unanimously on a proposal from the Commission and after consulting the European Parliament, may take appropriate action to combat discrimination based on sex, racial or ethnic origin, religion or belief, disability, age or sexual orientation'. For full discussion, see ch 9.

[358] COM(99) 564, Annex II.

[359] Art 2(3) of Dir 2000/43/EC implementing the principle of equal treatment between persons irrespective of racial or ethnic origin, OJ 2000, L180/22.

[360] Art 2(3) of Dir 2000/78/EC establishing a general framework for equal treatment in employment and occupation, OJ 2000, L303/16. Art 1 provides that the scope of this Directive includes combating discrimination on the grounds of religion or belief, disability, age or sexual orientation.

[361] For an overview, see J Gregory, 'Sexual Harassment: the Impact of EU Law in the Member States' in M Rossilli (ed) *Gender Policies in the European Union* (Peter Lang, New York, 2000) 175–91.

nature, is forbidden, to provide support to victims, to set up a complaints procedure and to establish disciplinary sanctions for offenders.[362] In France the Labour Code was amended to provide statutory protection to victims and witnesses of 'the abuse of authority at work in sexual matters' and also grants them a right to a legal remedy if they suffer discrimination in employment as a result. In addition the Penal Code has been amended to make sexual harassment a criminal offence.[363] In Ireland a Code of Practice has been drawn up by the Employment Equality Agency.[364] The Irish Code builds on the Commission's Code by providing for a formal procedure for complaints to be investigated and pursued involving assistance from an outside expert where necessary.[365] Perhaps the most significant impact of this formalistic approach is that it encourages preventative action to be taken by employers before any question of unequal treatment contrary to the Directive arises. In the UK the statutory Equal Opportunities Commission has issued a guide on the subject to employers, trade unions and employees advocating both formal and informal methods of conflict resolution. Further, a criminal law measure has been adopted by the UK Parliament that renders *intentional* racial, sexual, or other forms of harassment in the street and at work a criminal offence punishable by imprisonment.[366]

What is the effect of the Recommendation and Code on labour courts and tribunals? Several cases of interest have arisen in the UK. Early signs were encouraging, following the advice given by the Employment Appeal Tribunal (EAT) in *Wadman v Carpenter Farrer Partnership*,[367] where it was held that tribunals determining cases of sexual discrimination might use the Code for interpretative assistance. The Code has been referred to in several subsequent cases. For example, in *Stewart v Cleveland Guest (Engineering) Ltd*,[368] a case concerning a display of 'pin-ups' in the workplace, the EAT found that, as both men and women might object, the overall effect was neutral. By contrast, in *British Telecommunications v Williams*[369] the EAT held that because sexual harassment was gender-specific there was no need for a comparison between the position of a man and a woman. In a similar

---

[362] Decree of 18 Sep 1992. For fuller details, see (1992) 227 *European Industrial Relations Review* 12.

[363] *Ibid.*

[364] For the full text see vol 59 *Equal Opportunities Review*, Jan/Feb 1995, pp 39–41.

[365] *Ibid* p 39.

[366] Criminal Justice and Public Order Act, 1994. For details, see vol 58 *Equal Opportunities Review*, Nov/Dec 1994, p 34. See also, the Protection from Harassment Act 1997, noted by B Barrett (1998) 27 *Industrial Law Journal* 330.

[367] [1993] IRLR 373.

[368] [1994] IRLR 440. Noted by A McColgan (1995) 24 *Industrial Law Journal* 181. See also, the note by M Rubenstein in vol 57, *Equal Opportunities Review*, Sept/Oct 1994, pp 24–6. Rubenstein cites the US case of *Robinson v Jacksonville Shipyards Inc* (DC Fla 1991, 57 FEP Cases 971) in which the District Court found that 'sexualisation of the workplace imposes burdens on women that are not borne by men', as evidence of a more sound approach.

[369] [1997] IRLR 668.

vein, the EAT in *Institu Cleaning v Heads*,[370] ruled that a derogatory remark by a manager about a woman employee's breasts subjected her to a detriment and, when the employer failed to satisfactorily investigate the complaint, the employee was justified in her decision to resign and claim constructive unfair dismissal.

Several conclusions can be drawn from these developments. The Recommendation and Code have prompted some Member States to act unilaterally to improve standards rather than wait for a Community-level measure offering only minimum requirements. In this way the resulting national legislation may be much stronger than a putative binding Community-level measure would have been. In addition, in certain circumstances, the national courts can draw upon the Equal Treatment Directive and apply it to unacceptable sexual harassment where it causes unlawful sex discrimination outlawed by the Directive. While such developments can be seen as positive it must be recognised that several Member States have not responded with national legislation or codes of conduct and the Commission has no power to bring infringement proceedings. Moreover, the interpretative obligation rests with national courts rather than the Court of Justice. Indeed a recent survey has shown that while all Member States have responded to the Recommendation and Code to a greater or lesser degree, there are still numerous gaps in national laws and an absence of effective procedures for implementing them.[371] Evidence suggests that action has been least effective in precisely those Member States where, for societal reasons, such behaviour is most prevalent and awareness is at the lowest level.[372]

The Commission Recommendation, together with parallel institutional declarations,[373] has created a momentum for binding legislation in this area. Rubenstein has noted that 'it was necessary to test the adequacy of existing national remedies in the courts before a new Directive could be considered'.[374] By 1995 the Commission had formed the view that it was necessary to bring forward a 'binding Community instrument on sexual harassment at work' based on the 1991 Recommendation.[375] This was not a view shared by the Council, which made no reference to such a proposal in its ensuing decision on an action programme for 1996–2000.[376] In order

---

[370] [1994] IRLR 4. See also, *Bracebridge Engineering v Derby* [1990] IRLR 3; cf *Porcelli v Strathclyde Regional Council* [1986] IRLR 134.

[371] Gregory, n 361 above at 181.

[372] *Ibid* at 188.

[373] See Council Declaration of 19 Dec 1991 on the implementation of the Recommendation and Code of Practice, OJ 1992, C27/1; European Parliament Resolution of 22 Oct 1991 on the protection of the dignity of men and women at work, OJ 1991, C305/36; and an Opinion of the Economic and Social Committee of 30 Oct 1991, OJ 1992, C14/4.

[374] See the note by M Rubenstein (1992) 21 *Industrial Law Journal* 70 at 70.

[375] COM(95) 381, n 352 above, p 27.

[376] Dec 95/593/EC, OJ 1995, L335/37.

to revitalise this idea the Commission embarked on a new study of sexual harassment in the workplace.[377]

In its study the Commission concluded that, firstly, despite the existence of the Recommendation and Code, there is no universal definition of what constitutes sexual harassment and this has made it more difficult to objectively measure and quantify. Secondly, the percentage of female employees who have received unwanted sexual proposals, and therefore experienced some form of sexual harassment, can be estimated at between 40 per cent and 50 per cent. Thirdly, the level of awareness of this phenomenon in the Member States is very poor. This lack of awareness is illustrated by the lack of proper legislation addressing the issue in most Member States.[378] Following on from a series of parallel consultations starting in 1996, the Commission have published proposals to revise Directive 76/207,[379] which, for reasons of coherence with the Article 13 EC directives,[380] and taking the definition in the Code as the point of reference, defines sexual harassment in a similar way. Hence Article 1a of the draft Directive contains the following definition:

Sexual harassment shall be deemed to be discrimination on the grounds of sex at the workplace when an unwanted conduct related to sex takes place with the purposes or effect of affecting the dignity of a person and/or creating an intimidating, hostile, offensive or disturbing environment, in particular if a person's rejection of, or submission to, such conduct is used as a basis for a decision which affects that person.

Thus soft law has served a transitional purpose and the stage of hard law legality approaches.[381]

(3) Commission Opinion on an Equitable Wage

The Commission's Opinion on an Equitable Wage, issued on 1 September 1993,[382] is, by contrast, an example of soft law-making falling within the

---

[377] *Sexual Harassment at the Workplace in the European Union* (European Commission, Brussels, 1999).

[378] See the Commission's Explanatory Memorandum accompanying its proposal of 7 June 2000 for a Directive of the European Parliament and of the Council amending Council Dir 76/207/EEC on the implementation of the principle of equal treatment for men and women as regards access to employment, vocational training and promotion, and working conditions, COM(2000) 334, para 15. The Commission have also noted that several non-EU countries have legislation prohibiting sexual harassment on their statute books viz: Title VII of the USA Civil Rights Act of 1964, 42 U.S.C. § 2000e-2(a)(1); Canadian Charter of Human Rights and Freedoms, s 10.1; and s 27 of the Australian Sex Discrimination Act, 1984.

[379] COM(2000) 334, *ibid* and COM(2001) 321 of 25 Sept 2001. The revised proposal was issued after the Council adopted Common Position 32/2001, OJ 2001, C307/5, on 23 July 2001.

[380] *Ibid* para 18.

[381] See Wellens and Borchardt, n 348 above at 282.

[382] COM(93) 388.

weakest category of soft law, comprising of broad statements of principle in areas on the fringes or even outside of Community competence where there is no realistic prospect, nor any clear intention, of bringing forward binding legislative proposals in the foreseeable future. Although point 5 of the Social Charter had called for 'all employment to be fairly remunerated' and for workers to be 'assured of an equitable wage', the Action Programme merely promised a non-binding opinion.[383] Indeed, by the time the Opinion was issued, the majority of Member States had agreed, by virtue of Article 2(6) of the Agreement on Social Policy that 'pay' was to be excluded altogether from the new legal bases in Article 2(2) and 2(3) thereof, a point later reinforced by the inclusion of an identical clause in the revised Article 137(6) EC. At the very least, this has precluded the Community from adopting binding legislation on pay as part of mainstream social policy.

In the preamble to the Opinion the Commission's limited horizons are made transparent thus:

... the Commission intends neither to enact legislation nor to propose binding instruments on pay. It does, though, take the view that it would be apposite to pinpoint a number of basic principles regarding equitable pay ...

Therefore the Commission admits that it is merely asserting the fact that low pay is an 'important problem for a significant proportion of the working population'. This air of caution permeates the entire document. The Commission is reduced to generalities. Hence, the concept of an 'equitable wage' for workers is defined in the Opinion as:[384]

... a reward for work done which in the context of the society in which they live and work is fair and sufficient to enable them to have a decent standard of living.

There is no prospect therefore of either a fixed Community minimum wage, which would almost certainly be impractical, or even guidance on a target reference wage. Instead all operational definitions are left to national, regional or sectoral levels and Member States are encouraged to take measures to establish negotiated minima. Moreover, in an important rhetorical commitment, all workers should receive an equitable wage 'irrespective of gender, disability, race, religion, ethnic origin or nationality'. While this commitment may appear to be platitudinous it can be seen as a helpful guideline for the non-discrimination guarantee that was to emerge in the Article 13 EC anti-discrimination directives that, because they fall outside the social policy provisions, are not affected by the exclusion in Article 137(6) EC. Hence, Article 3(1)(c) of the Race Equality Directive[385] extends the principle of non-discrimination to include 'employment and working

---

[383] *Social Europe* 1/90, p 59.
[384] Point 1 of the Opinion.
[385] Dir 2000/43, OJ 2000, L180/22.

conditions, including dismissals and pay'. An identical clause can be found in Article 3(1)(c) of the Framework Employment Directive.[386]

In order to provide a further justification for straying into the area of wages, the Opinion draws upon the commitment of the Community to reinforce economic and social cohesion arising, in particular, from disparities of income affecting particular regions and groups in society.[387] In the preamble the Commission merely note 'the persistence of very low wage levels raises problems of equity and social cohesion which could be harmful to the effectiveness of the economy in the long term'. An opportunity was missed, however, to draw a direct link with the wider goals of social cohesion encompassing the agenda pursued through the separate Commission Communication on Social Exclusion[388] and the Council Recommendation on common criteria concerning sufficient resources and social assistance in social protection systems.[389] In the absence of a link with related soft law instruments emanating from the Social Charter and the Action Programme, the Opinion on an Equitable Wage is left rudderless.

The Opinion also fails to directly address the issue of 'social dumping' arising, in part, from persistent low pay. Indeed the Commission state that measures should not have 'a negative impact on job creation'. This would appear to give credence to the statistically unproven argument that a minimum wage, or indeed improved pay and conditions in general, are inimical to employment creation and retention.[390] Evidence from the UK, where a minimum wage was introduced in 1998, indicates otherwise,[391] confirming the predictions of those who had suggested that a minimum wage would not harm employment, or cause competitive disadvantage and would alleviate poverty.[392]

As an isolated statement the Opinion is laudable but, without any firm linkage with the Treaty and other Community instruments, and in the absence of strict guidelines or machinery for monitoring its effect, it is very difficult to discern any practical impact. Indeed, early evidence suggested that several Member States were ignoring the Opinion altogether. For example, the UK initially proceeded to abolish all of its sectoral wage setting machinery outside of agriculture,[393] while Spain reduced its minimum wage for young workers and, in the Netherlands, the minimum wage was

---

[386] Dir 2000/78, OJ 2000, L303/16.

[387] See Art 158 EC [ex 130a EEC].

[388] COM(92) 542. See also, the Opinion of the Economic and Social Committee on Social Exclusion, OJ 1993, C352/48.

[389] Council Recommendation 92/441/EEC, OJ 1992, L245/46.

[390] For a counter-argument, see S Deakin and F Wilkinson, 'Rights vs Efficiency? The Economic Case for Transnational Labour Standards' (1994) 23 *Industrial Law Journal* 289.

[391] See Incomes Data Services (IDS) Report 802, Feb 2000: <www.incomesdata.co.uk>.

[392] See Issue 29, *New Review of the Low Pay Unit* (Sept/Oct 1994) pp 8–12.

[393] *Ibid.*

frozen.[394] Although the UK has now embraced the concept of a minimum wage there is no evidence to suggest that this is remotely connected with the Commission's Opinion.

In a follow-up report,[395] the Commission acknowledged that most Member States had the basic planks of legislation towards an equitable wage in place before the Opinion was issued, but were opposed to intervention in wage setting. In some Member States there had been a widening of wage inequalities, particularly as a result of changes in the ways that wages are determined (growth in performance-related pay, decline in traditional forms of collective bargaining) and of changes in the labour market (growth in non-standard forms of employment and casual employment). These developments have reduced control over monitoring and maintaining an equitable wage, as well as the ability of governments to influence wage policy. Some Member States have even questioned the value of Community-wide data on this subject, citing the problem posed by differences in standards of living, wage rates and non-wage costs.

To conclude, the Commission's Opinion on an Equitable Wage represents an ineffective form of soft law. Lacking any clear point of reference in the Treaty, and detached from other soft law programmatic activity, it has failed to have a dynamic effect on either the laws or the behaviour of the Member States or the social partners. Moreover, the Community's commitment to an equitable wage is vague and ambiguous. When the Community eventually returns to this question, perhaps imminently now that the Euro has made pay differentials more transparent, a completely fresh start will be required.

V CONCLUSION

In this chapter we have seen how a variety of legislative and non-legislative methods, at times bold and imaginative, were applied between 1989 and 1994 to deliver the Social Charter Action Programme at a time when consensus was lacking and the revised EEC Treaty offered only limited pathways for social policy measures. Article 118a EEC guided the selected health and safety measures, placing an emphasis on specific risks in the workplace for certain groups, such as pregnant workers and young workers, while allowing Member States a wide discretion on implementation consistent with the flexibility required by that provision. With the exception of the basic rights to maternity leave, set at a low threshold, and paid annual leave, an enhancement in several Member States, these directives have failed to

---

[394] See the Commission's report on the European Employment Strategy: Recent Progress and Prospects for the Future, COM(95) 465, p 29.
[395] *Equitable wages—A progress report*, COM(96) 698, issued on 8 Jan 1997.

provide uniform exercisable rights for workers. Despite the fact that Article 118a EEC introduced an autonomous legal base for social policy, analysis of the legislative output in this period does not support the Commission's assumption of a 'solid base of European social legislation'.[396]

Equally, while the Employee Information (Contract or Employment Relationship) Directive offers helpful additional information to employees about their terms of employment which, in certain circumstances, can be relied upon in legal proceedings, it does not intrinsically strengthen the framework of legal regulation of the individual employment relationship in the Member States. Given the requirement for unanimity under Article 100 EEC [now 94 EC], and the exclusion of social policy from internal market measures under Article 100a(2) EEC [now 95(2) EC], this is hardly surprising, but as with the employment protection directives in the first Social Action Programme, it further underlines the limitations of the market approximation route.

Moreover, by evaluating two examples of soft law adopted under the Action Programme, it has been demonstrated that, although such instruments fulfil a variety of purposes consistent with the Community's integrationist goals, filling gaps, sometimes strengthening the application of related legislation, and prompting action at national level, ultimately, they are not a satisfactory substitute for binding legislation designed to ensure a fair and genuine platform of rights available to the Community worker as envisaged by the Social Charter. Indeed the Community's heavy reliance on non-binding measures to secure a significant proportion of the measures identified in the action programme only serves to reveal the difficulties faced by the Community institutions in fulfilling the aims of the Social Charter, at all levels, notwithstanding the Commission's superficially impressive tick-list of achievements. Rather soft law, in all its various forms, should be understood as being wholly transitional, legitimising and encouraging conduct at national level to conform to a Community norm which, if it is not effectively carried out through legislative action or judicial interpretation at a national level, must be achieved through binding Community law at a later date.

Indeed it was precisely for this reason that, at Maastricht, the majority of Member States sought to amend Articles 117–122 EEC and replace them with a new Social Chapter in order to address 'the wide gap between the powers available under the current legal bases and the ambitions set out in the Charter'.[397]

---

[396] COM(94) 333. Introduction, para 22.
[397] Working Document submitted to the Intergovernmental Conference on Political Union, SEC(91) 500 of 30 March 1991, p 84.

6

The Treaty on European Union: Transition or Transformation?

Maastricht, delightful town though it is, did not nurture the lucid expression of straightforward ideas.[1]

I INTRODUCTION

WITH THE INK barely dry on the Single European Act, the Community's leaders convened at Hanover in June 1988 to contemplate the next stage of Europe's navigation towards the uncertain destination of 'ever closer union'.[2] Two divergent conceptual journeys were being mapped. The first route would involve sailing through stormy waters in pursuit of full political union based on a federal constitutional model and, even more adventurously, the possibility of arriving at a union founded on the fundamental rights of its citizens. The second course would entail proceeding steadily through apparently becalmed seas towards full economic and monetary union and thereby to complete the construction of Europe's economic constitution.[3] In this second conception of Europe's journey, a separate vessel would set sail on a cautious passage towards a kind of political union always following in the slipstream of the main voyage towards economic and monetary union. In the event, the European

[1] G Lyon-Caen, 'Subsidiarity' in P Davies, A Lyon-Caen, S Sciarra and S Simitis (eds) *European Community Labour Law: Principles and Perspectives* (Clarendon Press, Oxford, 1996) 49–62 at 62.
[2] See A Shonfield, *Europe: Journey to an Unknown Destination* (Harmondsworth, London, 1973); E Wellenstein, 'Unity, Community, Union—What's in a Name?' (1992) 29 *Common Market Law Review* 205; R Dehousse, 'From Community to Union' in R Dehousse (ed) *Europe After Maastricht: An Ever Closer Union?* (Law Books in Europe, Munich, 1994) 5–15.
[3] See M Streit and W Mussler, 'The Economic Constitution of the European Community: From 'Rome' to 'Maastricht'' (1995) 1 *European Law Journal* 5; C Joerges, 'European Economic Law, the Nation-State and the Maastricht Treaty' in Dehousse, *ibid* 29–62; N Walker, 'European Constitutionalism and European Integration' [1996] *Public Law* 266; M Poiares Maduro, *We the Court: The European Court of Justice and the European Economic Constitution* (Hart, Oxford, 1998).

Council chose the second option even though this too was fraught with many hidden dangers.

Once the European Council had set the course, a Committee for the Study of Economic and Monetary Union (EMU) was assembled, chaired by the Commission President Jacques Delors.[4] The Committee recommended a three-stage process towards EMU: closer co-ordination of national economic and monetary policies; establishment of an independent European Central Bank; and replacement of national currencies by a single European currency.[5] The Committee advised that Treaty amendments would be required[6] and it followed that full economic integration had to be accompanied by fundamental institutional reform, including subsidiarity[7] and deeper political integration, to balance economic and monetary union. For 'Social Europe' the stakes could not have been higher. EMU would require a tightening of public expenditure, reform of welfare systems, wage flexibility and greater labour mobility.[8] Delors recognised the need for countervailing policies[9] and, in the context of the negotiations for the planned Intergovernmental Conference (IGC) on EMU, a two-pronged approach to social policy was required to, firstly, complete the Social Charter Action Programme through the adoption of a robust Social Chapter, replacing Articles 117–122 EEC and, secondly, to flank macroeconomic policy with a Community-wide strategy to combat unemployment and social exclusion through active labour market and anti-poverty programmes.[10] Further development of the process of social dialogue was regarded as a central plank linking both elements. The challenge that lay ahead was to balance the Community's ambitions for employment rights for individual workers with a wider agenda aimed at opening up markets to create employment. In the remaining chapters we will trace the evolution of these two interlinked elements of social policy as they have developed in the 1990s and 2000s.

---

[4] *Report on Economic and Monetary Union in the Community* ('Delors Committee') (European Communities, Luxembourg, 1989). The Committee was set up by the European Council in June 1988 and was composed of central bank governors and independent experts.

[5] See T Paddoa-Schioppa, *The Road to Monetary Union in Europe: the Emperor, the Kings and the Genies*, revised edn (OUP, Oxford, 2000) pp 113–25; F Snyder, 'EMU—Metaphor for European Union? Institutions, Rules and Types of Regulation' in Dehousse, n 2 above, 63–99; J-V Louis, 'A Monetary Union for Tomorrow?' (1989) 26 *Common Market Law Review* 301.

[6] Arts 102a–109m [now 98–124] EC.

[7] Delors Committee, n 4 above, p 14 (para 19).

[8] *Ibid* p 19 (para 29). See P Teague, 'Monetary Union and Social Europe' (1998) 8 *Journal of European Social Policy* 117.

[9] *Ibid* p 18 (para 29).

[10] The term 'flanking policies' denotes areas where the Community contributes to the policies of the Member States but does not possess a competence to harmonise laws. See T Hervey, *European Social Law and Policy* (Longman, Harlow, 1998) p 26.

II THE NEXT STAGE OF THE PROCESS

In the period between June 1988, when the IGC process was launched, and December 1991, when the negotiations were completed at Maastricht, a cascade of events transformed the post-war configuration of Europe. The Berlin Wall fell, the two Germanys were united, the Soviet Union imploded and the Yugoslav crisis escalated in a roller coaster of change that induced a dynamic effect on the process of political integration. In the post-Cold War era a new and accelerated phase of European integration was needed to prepare for a reconstructed and enlarged European political space. In April 1990 the leaders of France and Germany had published a joint letter calling for a second IGC on political union with the objective of strengthening the democratic legitimacy of the proposed union, rendering its institutions more efficient and implementing a common foreign and security policy.[11] By the end of 1990 both the Dutch Government[12] and the European Parliament[13] had issued detailed proposals for political union and four European Council meetings[14] had been held to carry forward the momentum for faster and deeper integration.

In the run up to the parallel IGCs, the Community's leaders were presented with two competing models for a 'European Union'.[15] One model, supported by political integrationists, envisaged the Union growing endogenously, like a tree sprouting new branches from a single supranational trunk. This model would preserve and reinforce the unitary structure of the European Communities while allowing for the development of new competences in areas such as justice and home affairs. An alternative model, favoured by intergovernmentalists, presented the Union in the form of an imaginary Ionic temple supported by three columns. The central column or pillar would represent a strengthened supranational element building on the Community *acquis* while the two remaining columns would preserve and develop intergovernmental co-operation in areas of home and foreign affairs that had hitherto been the subject of *ad hoc* arrangements. The European Council would be positioned on the entablature of the temple representing the institutional apex of the Union. While the Dutch Presidency favoured the arboreal paradigm they ultimately had to submit to a model closely resembling the temple-like superstructure preferred by France

---

[11] 'Kohl-Mitterand letter' of 20 April 1990. The Dublin European Council of 25/26 June 1990 formally agreed to convene a parallel IGC on political union. See R Corbett, *The Treaty of Maastricht* (Longman, Harlow, 1993) p 126.

[12] Memorandum of May 1990, *Possible Steps Towards European Political Union*. *Ibid* pp 127–33.

[13] The 'Martin II Report' of 11 July 1990: Rapporteur David Martin MEP. *Ibid* pp 112–19.

[14] In Dublin (April and June) and Rome (October and December). *Ibid* pp 97–103.

[15] See *Europe After Maastricht*, Second Report, House of Commons Foreign Affairs Committee, HC 642-I, Session 1992–93 (HMSO, London, 1993) paras 25 and 26; H Young, *This Blessed Plot: Britain and Europe from Churchill to Blair* (Macmillan, London, 1998) p 427.

and the UK. Shorn of any reference to federalism, the Treaty that emerged represented a transition rather than a transformation[16] of the European constitution.[17] As a statement of political intent the Member States established 'among themselves' a European Union 'as a *new stage in the process* of creating an ever closer union among the peoples of Europe' in which decisions were to be taken 'as openly as possible and as closely as possible to the citizen'.[18] Nominally the Union was established, but the mechanisms contained within the Treaty were not yet capable of fully realising the objective. Rather, as Everling has noted, they were a stage along the road towards it.[19] Hence the Union is a political construct that builds upon but does not displace the Community legal order.[20]

The emergent Union would be served by a 'single institutional framework'[21] but only in the sense that the Community institutions were to be put at the disposal of the Union without any concomitant role in its functioning. By creating two distinct but interdependent legal regimes, with the European Council as the guiding institution, Maastricht represented a historic compromise between the supranational and intergovernmental methods of European integration.[22] While the formal presentation of the concept of a single institutional framework was intended to provide consistency and continuity, while respecting and building upon the Community's *acquis*,[23] this failed to hide the fact that, even within the Community pillar, this was a threadbare compromise with several 'opt outs' and reservations that, although intended to be transitional,[24] validated an ongoing process of differentiated integration.[25] Indeed, in the absence of either a political consensus or a coherent constitutional blueprint for political union,

---

[16] See in the context of the '1992 process', J Weiler, 'The Transformation of Europe' (1991) 100 *Yale Law Journal* 2403; cf P Allott, 'The European Community is Not the True Community' (1991) 100 *Yale Law Journal* 2485.

[17] The Court of Justice has described the EEC Treaty as a 'constitutional charter' in Case 294/83, *Parti Ecologiste 'Les Verts' v European Parliament* [1986] ECR 1339, para 23. See also, *Opinion 1/91* [1991] ECR 6079, paras 21 and 46.

[18] Art A [now 1] TEU.

[19] See U Everling, 'Reflections on the Structure of the European Union' (1992) 29 *Common Market Law Review* 1056 at 1059; 'Editorial Comments, 'Post-Maastricht'' (1992) 29 *Common Market Law Review* 199, where the editors, at 202, refer to the new Treaty as a 'house half-built . . . suddenly abandoned by the builders'.

[20] Art A [now 1] of the Treaty on European Union (TEU) 1993, states that the 'Union shall be founded on the European Communities, supplemented by the policies and forms of cooperation established by this Treaty'.

[21] Art C [now 3] TEU. See P Demaret, 'The Treaty Framework' in D O'Keeffe and P Twomey (eds) *Legal Issues of the Maastricht Treaty* (Wiley Chancery, London, 1994) 3–11.

[22] See Dehousse, n 2 above at 12.

[23] Art C [now 3] TEU.

[24] Art N.2 TEU obliged the Member States to review the Treaty by means of an IGC by 1996 at the latest.

[25] See generally C-D Ehlermann, 'Increased Differentiation or Stronger Uniformity' in J Winter, D Curtin, A Kellermann and B de Witte (eds) *Reforming the Treaty on European Union—The Legal Debate* (Kluwer, The Hague, 1996) 27–50; A Stubb, 'Differentiated Inte-

the outcome was a hybrid Treaty with a fragmented *acquis* aptly described by Curtin as a 'Europe of bits and pieces'.[26] Nowhere was this more apparent than in the social provisions contained in the annexed Protocol and Agreement on Social Policy.

III ELEVEN MARCH AHEAD

During 1990 and 1991, as the process of drafting a Treaty on European Union unfolded, a concerted attempt was made to strengthen the social provisions in the revised Treaty. The European Parliament's Resolution on the IGC of 11 July 1990[27] endorsed the inclusion in Article 3 EEC of common action in the field of social affairs and employment and deletion of the single market derogation in Article 100a(2) EEC. Parliament proposed the extension of Article 118a EEC to cover the continued improvement of living standards and social provisions, equal opportunities, training, minimum levels of social security, and provisions for union law and collective bargaining. It was envisaged that these social rights would be extended to persons from third countries. Article 119 EEC was to be strengthened to include the objective of equal opportunities at work and in society. The procedures for social dialogue in Article 118b EEC were to be developed by the adoption of a legal framework for European 'collective bargaining'. Memoranda supporting this approach were issued by Denmark[28] and the Netherlands[29] and, once the IGC process began in earnest, proposals to strengthen the Social Chapter were published by several Member States[30] and the Commission.[31] Even at this stage, however, the Commission proposed that the Community's role should be limited to complementing and supporting the action of the Member States through laying down minimum standards.[32] Belgium suggested the idea of legally binding framework agreements at Community level between management and labour. This concept was taken forward by the social partners who negotiated an accord on a revised draft of Articles 118, 118a and 118b[33]

---

gration' (1996) 34 *Journal of Common Market Studies* 283; F Tuytschaever, *Differentiation in European Union Law* (Hart, Oxford, 1999); J Usher, 'Variable Geometry or Concentric Circles: Patterns for the EU' (1997) 46 *International and Comparative Law Quarterly* 243.

[26] D Curtin, 'The Constitutional Structure of the Union: A Europe of Bits and Pieces' (1993) 30 *Common Market Law Review* 17.

[27] See Corbett, n 11 above, pp 112–19.

[28] 4 Oct 1990. *Ibid* pp 159–64.

[29] 26 Oct 1990. *Ibid* pp 173–86.

[30] Belgium, France and Italy. *Ibid* p 50.

[31] *European Commission proposal on the social dimension and the development of human resources*. See Corbett, *ibid* pp 235–40.

[32] *Ibid* pp 50–51.

[33] The agreement was signed by the European Trades Union Confederation (ETUC) the Union of Industrial and Employers' Confederations of Europe (UNICE) and the European Centre of Enterprises and Public Participation (CEEP). See *Social Europe* 2/95, p 149. For

EEC that was to form the basis for the final text presented to the IGC held at Maastricht on 9/10 December 1991.

When the European Council convened at Maastricht the draft Social Chapter, hitherto an issue of secondary importance was to prove the biggest sticking point. John Major, the UK's new Prime Minister,[34] was personally inclined to reach a deal but he pulled back in the face of a threat of resignation from his Employment Secretary.[35] After six hours of resistance, one against 11, it was clear that the whole Treaty was in jeopardy and, at the behest of the Dutch Prime Minister, Ruud Lubbers, a messy solution was reached whereby the social policy provisions in Articles 117–122 EEC were left essentially unaltered[36] but, instead, all 12 Member States approved a separate Protocol on Social Policy[37] which was appended together with the draft 'Social Chapter' now converted into an annexed Agreement on Social Policy[38] applicable only to 11 Member States with the UK wholly excluded. The Maastricht compromise led to a bifurcation of Community social policy. Two autonomous regimes were created—one for a Community of 12, bounded by social provisions in the body of the revised and renamed European Community (EC) Treaty, another for a Community of 11, governed by the Agreement and two separate Declarations. Each regime would be based on its own freestanding range of policy objectives and legislative routes. Remarkably, the 11 were prepared to undermine the essential unity of the treaties, as an expression of their combined will to 'implement the 1989 Social Charter'[39] even if this meant that the UK was to be left behind for a temporary but indeterminate period. For the 11, the option of a twin-stream approach to Community social policy appeared, despite its attendant risks, to offer a more attractive prospect than a further period of stagnation. Moreover, by using the ingenious device of the Protocol, they had created for themselves the capacity to apply a form of Community law, or majority *acquis*, that would extend beyond the limited scope of Article 118a EEC, albeit at the expense of 26 million workers based in the UK who were to be exempted from the Agreement's territorial effects.[40] From the perspective of the UK, isolation and opprobrium at European level was

comment, see B Bercusson, 'Maastricht: a fundamental change in European labour law' (1992) 23 *Industrial Relations Journal* 177 at 177.

[34] Major succeeded Margaret Thatcher in an internal party coup in November 1990.

[35] Michael Howard MP. See Young, n 15 above, pp 431–32.

[36] Apart from an amendment to Art 118a EEC allowing for legislation to be adopted in accordance with the co-operation procedure. Arts 123–27 [now 146–50] EC concerning the European Social Fund, education, vocational training and youth, contain enhancements and new Community competences.

[37] Protocol No 14 on Social Policy.

[38] See the Final Act of the Intergovernmental Conferences.

[39] Protocol on Social Policy, point 1.

[40] See the Commission's 1994 report on *Employment in Europe*, COM(94) 381, p 184. This figure is based on the total number of EU nationals working in the UK at the time when the Maastricht Treaty came into force in Nov 1993.

preferable to any compromise that might further divide an increasingly fractious and Euro-sceptic governing party. Indeed the Major Government promoted the Maastricht deal on the questionable assumption that the UK could opt-out from or delay any future Commission proposals that ran counter to their own deregulatory approach to social policy.[41]

Four interlocking functions were performed by the Protocol. The first was purely mechanistic. Without the Protocol, contracted to by the 12, it would not have been possible for the 11 to have recourse to the 'institutions, procedures and mechanisms' of the Treaty 'for the purposes of taking among themselves' and 'applying as far as they are concerned' the 'acts and decisions' required to give effect to the Agreement.[42] This procedure raises a whole raft of questions. How can 11 use procedures designed for 12? Is such an Agreement part of 'Community law'? What is the legal status of any 'acts and decisions'? What happens if there is a conflict of interpretation between measures adopted under the two different legislative routes? In the discussion below I will attempt to answer these questions in the context of the academic literature.

Secondly, the Protocol operated to exempt the UK from the 'deliberations' and 'adoption by the Council' of Commission proposals made on the basis of the Protocol and the Agreement.[43] Within the Council of Eleven a qualified majority would consist pro rata as 52 out of 76 votes instead of 62 out of 86.[44] Any acts adopted by the 11 and any financial consequences thereof, other than administrative costs entailed by the institutions, would not be applicable to the UK.[45] One bizarre but logical consequence of this arrangement was that, outside the arena of the Council, representatives or appointees from the UK, whether members of the Commission, the European Parliament or the Economic and Social Committee, or sitting as judges at the Court, or as social partners negotiating under the procedure in the Agreement,[46] were able to fully participate at all operative stages under the Agreement because they were supranational not intergovernmental actors.[47] It should be added that there was no specific procedure laid down in the Protocol for the UK to accede to the Agreement and reunite the combined *acquis* at a future date. This matter would have to be resolved

---

[41] Major rather over egged his apparent 'victory'. His spokesman declared that it was 'game, set and match' to the British. Such triumphalism was short-lived. Ratification was only achieved in July 1993 after Major had threatened his rebellious backbenchers with a no confidence vote and near certain electoral defeat. See Young, n 18 above, pp 432–4.

[42] Protocol on Social Policy, point 1.

[43] *Ibid* point 2, para 1.

[44] *Ibid* point 2, para 2.

[45] *Ibid* point 2, para 3.

[46] Under the procedure in Art 4 of the Agreement discussed below.

[47] In support of this view, see P Watson, 'Social Policy After Maastricht' (1993) 30 *Common Market Law Review* 481 at 503–5; G Brinkmann, 'Lawmaking under the Social Chapter of Maastricht' in P Craig and C Harlow (eds) *Lawmaking in the European Union* (Kluwer, London, 1998) 239–61 at 243.

if, and indeed when, the UK decided that it wished to 'sign up' to the Agreement. The most logical procedure would involve a Treaty amendment with transitional arrangements, the route eventually chosen in 1997,[48] although it was suggested at the time that it might be possible for the UK to adhere directly to the Agreement without amending the Protocol.[49]

Thirdly, the Protocol determined the relationship between the Agreement and the social policy provisions that were preserved in Articles 117–122 EC [ex EEC]. The first paragraph of the Protocol provided that the Protocol and Agreement were *'without prejudice'*[50] to the provisions of the EC Treaty 'particularly those relating to social policy which constitute an integral part of the *acquis communautaire'*. The words 'without prejudice' appeared to give primacy to the whole Community route. Once the Agreement came into effect, on 2 November 1993, the Commission swiftly issued a Communication on its application.[51] According to the Commission, the Agreement would operate as follows. All social policy proposals were to be formally introduced under the mainstream Treaty bases. The Agreement would only be brought into play 'on a case by case basis'[52] at a later stage as a fall-back device where the UK opposed the measure in question in circumstances where Article 118a [now 137] EC was inapplicable and Articles 100 or 235 [now 94 and 308] EC inappropriate.[53] From the perspective of the Commission this 'twin-track'[54] approach would be wholly complementary and serve to minimise the potentially disintegrative effects of the Protocol. The Commission's principal objective was:[55]

. . . to promote the development of a European social policy *which will benefit all the citizens of the Union* and will therefore enjoy, as far as is possible, the support of all the Member States.

It was for precisely this reason that the Commission chose not to follow the advice of the Economic and Social Committee (ECOSOC) which had suggested, in its Opinion on the Communication,[56] that the effect of the

---

[48] See ch 8.

[49] See B Bercusson, 'The Dynamic of European Labour Law after Maastricht' (1994) 23 *Industrial Law Journal* 1 at 5. See also, Brinkmann, n 47 above at 243; cf M Weiss, 'The Significance of Maastricht for European Community Social Policy' (1992) 8 *International Journal of Comparative Labour Law and Industrial Relations* 3 at 3.

[50] Emphasis added.

[51] See the Commission's Communication concerning the application of the Agreement on Social Policy, COM(93) 600 final of 14 Dec 1993.

[52] *Ibid* para 8.

[53] In light of the application of the principle of subsidiarity in Art 3b [now 5] EC, discussed below.

[54] See J Shaw, 'Twin-track Social Europe—the Inside Track' in O'Keeffe and Twomey, n 21 above, 295–311.

[55] COM(93) 600, para 8. Emphasis added.

[56] OJ 1994, C397/40, para 1.4.4.

Protocol was to give priority to the Agreement in order to guarantee the consultation rights of management and labour under the Agreement.[57] In order to reassure ECOSOC on this point, the Commission resolved to consult management and labour on all proposals, in accordance with the procedure in Article 3 of the Agreement,[58] irrespective of the route being followed.[59]

Fourthly, the Protocol was 'annexed' to the EC Treaty[60] and the Agreement was annexed to the Protocol.[61] Both the methodology and the terminology used were the subject of a vigorous debate in the contemporary academic literature concerning the legal status of both the Protocol and the Agreement. The arguments were far from clear-cut. Indeed, as the Commission observed at the time, 'this situation has never occurred in the Community before'.[62] Unlike the annexed EMU Protocols,[63] which allowed for exemptions for the UK and Denmark from the new provisions concerning monetary union and therefore kept all formal decision-making within the ambit of the main Treaty provisions, the Social Protocol took those decisions outside this central arena and, by virtue of the Agreement, created an extraneous decision-making arrangement operating in parallel with the retained social provisions in the EC Treaty.

Barnard has persuasively argued that although the Protocol was valid as an agreement in international law it breached the essential unity that underpins Community law and, by allowing a majority of Member States to pursue their own course, it was contrary to the fundamental principles of the Community because it would create a barrier to free movement of persons, undermine fundamental rights and positively distort competition.[64] The potential for social dumping as a direct or indirect consequence of the Agreement was vividly demonstrated in 1993 when, for reasons based on

---

[57] For a comprehensive case in support of the ECOSOC view, see B Bercusson and J van Dijk, 'The Implementation of the Protocol and Agreement on Social Policy of the Treaty on European Union' (1995) 11 *International Journal of Comparative Labour Law and Industrial Relations* 3. Van Dijk was the Rapporteur for the ECOSOC Opinion. Bercusson was the Expert to the Rapporteur.

[58] The first stage of consultation under the Agreement, discussed below.

[59] *Commission Communication on the Development of the Social Dialogue at Community Level*, COM(96) 448, Annex 1, p iv. See Brinkmann, n 47 above at 245.

[60] Protocol on Social Policy, point 3.

[61] *Ibid* first para.

[62] *Ibid* p 1 of the summary.

[63] Protocols No 11 and 12.

[64] C Barnard, 'A Social Policy for Europe: Politicians 1:0 Lawyers' (1992) 8 *International Journal of Comparative Labour Law and Industrial Relations* 15 at 18–21. See also, the editorial in (1993) 30 *Common Market Law Review* 445, where, at 448, the Agreement was described as an 'institutionalised invitation to social dumping'. See further, C McGlynn, 'An Exercise in Futility: The Practical Effects of the Social Policy Opt-out' (1998) 49 *Northern Ireland Law Quarterly* 60.

labour costs, Hoover[65] and Digital Equipment[66] switched production to the UK from, respectively, France and Ireland. In fact these cases, whilst they raised understandable fears, pre-dated the ratification of Maastricht and, moreover, as British trade unionists would quickly point out, traffic in the other direction had been just as frequent, not least because of the ease with which employers were able to sack staff under UK employment laws and retreat to their continental bases.

Weatherill,[67] while not entering the debate about the legality of the Protocol and/or Agreement, has starkly portrayed its inherent contradictions:[68]

The Protocol is not an attempt to manage diversity within a basic Community framework in the manner of minimum harmonization. It arises from objections to the existence of a Community framework. It does not share competence, it denies it. It envisages a particular State competing against other States outside the control of even a minimum Community rule.

Other authors, notably Everling[69] and Vogel-Polsky,[70] have specifically questioned the legality of the Agreement on the basis that it was not part of the Protocol and therefore fell outside the corpus of Community law. This argument has been developed by Curtin who refers directly to Article 239 [now 311] EC, where it is stated that protocols annexed to the Treaty 'by *common accord* of the Member States shall form an *integral part thereof*'.[71] Therefore the Social Protocol, along with 16 other protocols,[72] would become part of Community law on ratification of the Treaty.[73] Curtin subtly

---

[65] The 'Hoover affair' aroused considerable political debate. On 25 Jan 1993 the president of Hoover Europe announced the closure of the company's factory near Dijon with the loss of 600 out of 700 jobs. These activities were shifted to an existing plant near Glasgow in Scotland where wages and associated labour costs were lower. Martine Aubrey, the French Minister of Labour at the time, said that 'it is probably not a coincidence that Great Britain has not signed the agreement by the eleven'. For John Major, the UK Prime Minister, the position was starkly simple. On 2 Feb 1993 he reminded Parliament that Jacques Delors had, as President of the Commission, warned that the UK's opt-out had made Britain a 'paradise for foreign investment'. Rejecting the view that Britain was becoming the 'sweatshop of Europe' he declared, 'industry will locate where it can be most efficient and most competitive'. See *European Industrial Relations Review* 230, March 1993, pp 14–20.

[66] For comment, see Watson, n 47 above at 512.

[67] S Weatherill, 'Beyond Preemption? Shared Competence and Constitutional Change in the European Community' in O'Keeffe and Twomey, n 21 above, 13–33.

[68] *Ibid* at 29.

[69] Everling, n 19 above at 1066.

[70] E Vogel-Polsky, *Evaluation of the social provisions of the Treaty on European Union agreed by the European summit at Maastricht*, DOC en/cm/202155 PE 115.405/I, p 3. For comment, see E Szyszczak, 'Social Policy: a Happy Ending or a Reworking of the Fairy Tale?' in O'Keeffe and Twomey, n 21 above, 313–27 at 323.

[71] Emphasis added. See Curtin, n 26 above at 45.

[72] For example, in the social policy context, Protocol No 2 concerning Art 119 EC. On the legality of this Protocol, see T Hervey, 'Legal Issues concerning the *Barber* Protocol' in O'Keeffe and Twomey, n 21 above, 329–37 at 335–6.

[73] In accordance with Art 236 EEC, now repealed.

argues, however, that while the Protocol was valid as Community law, the status of the Agreement was less certain. As Curtin explains, notwithstanding the statement in the Protocol that it was 'without prejudice' to the provisions of the Treaty, the Agreement would, in practice, be capable of undermining the cohesiveness of Community law and therefore any 'directives' adopted under its provisions would not be synonymous with directives as defined in Article 189 [now 249] EC.[74] Although Curtin does not fully resolve the conundrum concerning the legal status of the Agreement, her argument, if accepted, would have allowed for the preservation of the hegemony of mainstream Community law directives and therefore avoided the 'hijacking' of the *acquis*.[75] Such second-class 'directives' would, however, not be legally binding and would depend on the goodwill of the Member States concerned for their implementation.[76]

Watson[77] presents a compelling case for the legality of the Protocol *and* the Agreement. While also relying on Article 239 [now 311] EC, Watson argues that the Agreement could not be excised from the Protocol on the basis that the Final Act of the IGCs annexed it to the Protocol and therefore both the Protocol and the Agreement were integral to the EC Treaty.[78] The references in the Protocol to the Community institutions and directives and indeed to 'Community action' and dialogue 'at a Community level' in Articles 3 and 4 of the Agreement would have no meaning if the Agreement were to be merely intergovernmental.[79] In addition, the implementation of the Agreement was founded upon the *acquis* and was therefore the basis for binding Community laws applying to the 11, subject to the scrutiny of the Court.

Ultimately Watson's argument, supported by Whiteford[80] and Falkner,[81] has proved the most convincing. From an integrationist perspective, the Protocol and Agreement conformed to the technical requirements for amending the EC Treaty and the operative novelty of the Agreement was capable of being accommodated within the Community system on the basis that it was transitional, would be extended to acceding States[82] and would apply only in situations where progress at a whole Community level was not

---

[74] Curtin, n 26 above at 57–8.

[75] *Ibid* at 57.

[76] *Ibid* at 58.

[77] Watson, n 47 above.

[78] *Ibid* at 489–91.

[79] *Ibid* at 493.

[80] See E Whiteford, 'Social Policy After Maastricht' (1993) 18 *European Law Review* 202 at 203–4.

[81] See G Falkner, 'The Maastricht Protocol on Social Policy: Theory and Practice' (1996) 6 *Journal of European Social Policy* 1.

[82] Austria, Finland and Sweden joined the 11 other signatories on accession to full EU membership on 1 Jan 1995. They had already been committed to its provisions by virtue of their membership of the European Economic Area established in 1993.

possible. Moreover, as Ehlermann explains,[83] the Protocol and Agreement represented a clear case of 'variable geometry' and any directives adopted would be binding as Community law among the 11 as reviewable acts consistent with the '*ERTA* doctrine'[84] in the sense that they would be 'designed to lay down a course of action binding on both the institutions and the Member States'[85] concerned. In its 1993 Communication on the application of the Agreement, the Commission, perhaps overstating the case, concluded that the Agreement was 'soundly based in law' and considered the Community nature of any directives adopted under the Agreement as 'beyond doubt'.[86] Such directives would be 'territorial' in the sense that they would not be applicable to the territory of the UK, but in every other respect they would be indistinguishable, in a formal sense, from other Community laws. Hence, a UK national or a subsidiary of a British company, based in another Member State, would be subject to its provisions.[87] In practice these formal arguments were to lead the Community institutions to accept the Agreement as a parallel form of Community law creating, for the purposes of social law, a separate Community of Eleven, later Fourteen, sitting alongside a Community of Twelve, later Fifteen.[88]

Paradoxically, the last minute deal unhappily cobbled together at Maastricht ultimately suited all of the major players, the Community institutions, the social partners and the 11/14, on the limited number of occasions when they sought to take advantage of the Agreement as a 'fast track',[89] and the UK which, until a change of Government in May 1997, was quite content with its 'splendid isolation'. The general view was that the Court would be unlikely to tamper with a constitutional arrangement negotiated between the Member States and the greatest danger would be a hypothetical one arising from a potential conflict of interpretation between directives adopted via the two different routes.[90] The outcome was what Falkner has aptly described as a kind of 'pragmatic normalisation'[91] of these novel arrangements. The fact that the Agreement violated the principle of non-discrimination, by creating two categories of Union citizens and an unfair competitive advantage for the UK within a notional Single Market, was an

---

[83] Ehlermann, n 25 above at 36.
[84] Case 22/70, *Commission v Council 'ERTA'* [1971] ECR 263.
[85] *Ibid* para 53.
[86] COM(93) 600, paras 7 and 8.
[87] *Ibid* para 8.
[88] Including Austria, Finland and Sweden from 1 Jan 1995.
[89] See M Rhodes, 'The Social Dimension after Maastricht: Setting a New Agenda for the Labour Market' (1993) 9 *International Journal of Comparative Labour Law and Industrial Relations* 297 at 324.
[90] See B Fitzpatrick, 'Community Social Law after Maastricht' (1992) 21 *Industrial Law Journal* 199 at 203.
[91] Falkner, n 81 above at 3.

inconvenience, but 'a price worth paying' for many social integrationists, even if one consequence, as Curtin rightly warned, has been the consolidation of a differentiated approach to integration in the Amsterdam and Nice Treaties. As Brinkmann wryly observes, the result was a kind of 'unconstitutional constitutional law'.[92] Indeed the Court's capacity for legal sidestepping in line with the emerging pragmatic consensus was amply demonstrated when, in *UEAPME*,[93] the first case concerning the legality of a directive adopted under the Agreement,[94] the Court of First Instance (CFI)[95] held that such a directive was a legislative measure for the purposes of Community law without any need to directly address the legal status of the Agreement.[96] In the absence of any plea on this point by the parties, the CFI merely chose to note that the Agreement was annexed to the Protocol that, in turn, was annexed to the EC Treaty.[97] It followed that there was an umbilical link between the Agreement and the Treaty.

In the remaining sections of this chapter several aspects of the Maastricht settlement will be addressed. The first element consists of an analysis of the broad Treaty framework within which both the retained social provisions in the EC Treaty and the clauses in the annexed Agreement on Social Policy would now operate. In the second part consideration will be given to the particular implications for social policy arising from the principle of subsidiarity referred to in Article 3b [now 5] EC. The third section contains an analysis of the substantive social provisions contained in Articles 1, 2 and 6 of the Agreement [now 136, 137 and 141 EC]. In the fourth part there will be an explanation of the innovative procedures in Articles 3 and 4 of the Agreement [now 138 and 139 EC] concerning the social partners, with a focus on the issue of the representativeness of the parties and the democratic legitimacy of the process as a whole. Finally, there will be a qualitative assessment of three cross-sectoral agreements negotiated by the social partners and now converted into directives. In chapter 7 there will be an analysis of wider social policy developments during the period from Maastricht to Amsterdam arising, in particular, from Commission 'white papers' and European Council initiatives published in the context of rapidly deteriorating socio-economic conditions in the early to mid-1990s.

[92] See Brinkmann, n 47 above at 240.
[93] Case T–135/96, *Union Européenne de l'Artisant et des Petits et Moyennes Entreprises (UEAPME) v Council* [1998] ECR II–2335.
[94] Dir 96/34/EC on the framework agreement on parental leave concluded by UNICE, CEEP and the ETUC, OJ 1996, L145/4.
[95] From 1993 the CFI has been granted jurisdiction over all direct actions brought by natural and legal persons under Art 230 [ex 173] EC. See OJ 1993, L144/21 and OJ 1994, L66/29. Discussed by A Arnull, *The European Union and its Court of Justice* (OUP, Oxford, 1999) pp 14–18.
[96] Case T–135/96, *UEAPME v Council* [1998] ECR II–2335, para 67.
[97] Para 2.

IV THE TREATY FRAMEWORK

The preamble of the Treaty on European Union (TEU) indicates that any advances in economic integration are to be accompanied by parallel progress in other fields.[98] This commitment is reinforced by the first objective contained in Article B [now 2] TEU calling for the promotion of 'economic and social progress which is balanced and sustainable'. Such progress is to be achieved through the creation of an area without internal frontiers, the strengthening of economic and social cohesion and the establishment of economic and monetary union. While this language serves to carry forward the rhetoric of equality between the economic and social dimensions of European integration, it is the economic imperative that is reinforced by the reference to 'balanced and sustainable' progress.[99] The parameters for such progress would now be set by the apparently strict deflationary convergence criteria required by EMU[100] and, in the longer term, by the interest rate policy of a European Central Bank established in order to maintain price stability.[101]

An additional objective central to the TEU involves the protection of the rights and interests of nationals of the Member States through the introduction of a citizenship of the Union, although the detailed provisions[102] amount only to a modest extension of the existing rules on free movement of persons.[103] Moreover, the human rights clause inserted into Article F [now 6] TEU[104] merely restates the jurisprudential reasoning of the Court

---

[98] 7th recital of the preamble of the TEU.

[99] See Shaw, n 54 above at 298.

[100] See Protocol No 6 on the convergence criteria referred to in Article 109j(1) [now 121(1)] EC. The criteria are:

—Price stability—inflation must not exceed 1.5% above the average of the three best performing Member States;
—Budget deficits—not exceeding 3% of GDP and a public debt to GDP ratio of less than 60% of GDP;
—Exchange rate—staying within the normal fluctuation margins of the ERM (currently 2.5%) for at least two years;
—Interest rates—must not exceed 2% above the three best performing Member States over the previous year.

[101] Art 105 [ex 105] EC.

[102] Art 8–8e [now 17–22] EC.

[103] By virtue of Art 8 [now 17] EC, Union citizenship is extended to every person holding the nationality of a Member State. Union citizenship complements but does not replace national citizenship. Art 8a [now 18] EC grants the 'right to move and reside freely' within the territory of the Member States to all Union citizens. Other provisions are concerned with the right to stand and vote in municipal and European elections, to diplomatic and consular protection in third-countries and to petition the European Parliament (Arts 8b–8d [now 19–21] EC). For discussion, see C Closa, 'The Concept of Citizenship in the Treaty on European Union' (1992) 29 *Common Market Law Review* 1137; D O'Keeffe, 'Union Citizenship' in O'Keeffe and Twomey, n 21 above, 87–107; J Shaw, 'The Many Pasts and Futures of Citizenship of the European Union' (1997) 60 *Modern Law Review* 554.

[104] Art 6(1) declares that the Union 'is founded on the principles of liberty, democracy,

in cases where, for example, the European Convention on Human Rights has been taken into account as a means of interpreting Community law within the framework of the structure and objectives of the Community.[105] Strictly speaking this did not amount to a codification of this jurisprudence because the clause was explicitly excluded from the jurisdiction of the Court.[106] Noteworthy also is the absence of any direct reference in the TEU either to the European Social Charter or to international standards laid down by the United Nations and the International Labour Organisation. The Maastricht construct of the TEU was to be a 'political union' without any pretension towards social citizenship or a foundation of human rights.[107]

Title II of the TEU amends the EEC, now EC, Treaty. In particular Article 2 EC, setting out the task of the Community, is expanded to include, inter alia, a commitment to:

... a high level of employment and social protection, the raising of the standard of living and quality of life, and economic and social cohesion and solidarity among Member States.

Among the activities of the Community set out in Article 3 EC can be found a policy in the social sphere comprising a European Social Fund and the strengthening of economic and social cohesion. The specific goal of securing a 'high level of employment' is further reinforced by a refinement of the social provisions in chapters 2 and 3 of the new Title VIII [now XI] EC on Social Policy, Education, Vocational Training and Youth. Articles 123–125 [now 146–148] EC, concerning the European Social Fund, shift the focus of the Fund from facilitating the free movement of workers to improving 'employment opportunities for workers in the internal market'.[108] The aim is to help workers to adapt to industrial changes and changes in production systems, in particular through vocational training and retraining. Articles 126–127 [now 149–150] EC contain strengthened provisions on education and vocational training intended to promote co-operation

respect for human rights and fundamental freedoms, and the rule of law, principles which are common to the Member States'. Art 6(2) resolves that the Union 'shall respect fundamental rights, as guaranteed by the European Convention for the Protection of Human Rights and Fundamental Freedoms . . . and as they result from the constitutional traditions common to the Member States, as general principles of Community law'.

[105] For example, Case 11/70, *Internationale Handelsgesellschaft v Einfuhr-und Vorratsstelle Getreide* [1970] ECR 1125, para 4; Case 44/79, *Hauer v Land Rheinland-Pfalz* [1979] ECR 3727, paras 14–16.

[106] See Art L TEU—but see the Court's limited jurisdiction 'with regard to the action of the institutions' under all three pillars now contained in Art 46 TEU.

[107] See Hervey, *European Social Law and Policy*, n 10 above, p 27; P Twomey, 'The European Union: Three Pillars without a Human Rights Foundation' in O'Keeffe and Twomey, n 21 above, 121–32; M Rodríguez-Piñero and E Casas, 'In Search of a European Social Constitution' in Davies *et al*, n 1 above, 23–48 at 26–8.

[108] Art 123 [now 146] EC. For discussion, see J Kenner, 'Economic and Social Cohesion— The Rocky Road Ahead' [1994] *Legal Issues of European Integration* 1 at 20–30.

between Member States in the development of 'quality education' and implement a Community vocational training policy aimed at facilitating the integration and reintegration of workers generally and young people in particular into the labour market.[109] Hence, even without a fully-fledged 'Social Chapter' to replace Articles 117–122 EC, the balance of the main Treaty provisions on social policy in the revised Title VIII marked a shift in the policy emphasis from employment protection to employment creation and retention.

One recurring feature of both the revised social policy provisions in Articles 123–127 [now 146–150] EC and the annexed Agreement on Social Policy is the supplementary role accorded to the Community vis-à-vis the Member States. For example, in respect of both education and vocational training, the Community's task is to make a contribution by supporting and supplementing the action of the Member States who retain overall responsibility for the content and organisation of teaching and training.[110] Moreover, a subsequent European Council proclamation has explicitly ruled out harmonisation in these areas.[111] Under Article 2(1) of the Agreement [now 137(1) EC] the Community's role is to 'support and complement the activities of the Member States' with a view to achieving the objectives set out in the Agreement.[112] Therefore, the principle of subsidiarity, which has been both an implicit and informal governing rule in the area of Community social policy, is fully reflected in these provisions, but now, with the incorporation of Article 3b [now 5] EC into the Treaty, it was being made explicit, reinforcing the presumption in favour of action at the national level. But, did the formalisation of the principle of subsidiarity make any difference in the social policy context?

V THE PRINCIPLE OF SUBSIDIARITY—*PLUS ÇA CHANGE, PLUS C'EST LA MÊME CHOSE?*

Subsidiarity is a natural by-product of the expansion of the Community's competences and the establishment of the wider Union post-Maastricht. It marks a development of the idea of allocative efficiency first mooted in the 1970s by Tindemans.[113] In essence, subsidiarity provides a guiding principle

---

[109] See generally, J Shaw, 'From the Margins to the Centre: Education and Training Law and Policy' in P Craig and G de Búrca (eds) *The Evolution of EU Law* (OUP, Oxford, 1999) 555–95; and M Freedland, 'Vocational Training in EC Law and Policy—Education, Employment or Welfare?' (1996) 25 *Industrial Law Journal* 110.

[110] Arts 126(1) and 127(1) [now 149(1) and 150(1)] EC.

[111] Presidency Conclusions of the Edinburgh European Council, 11/12 Dec 1992, Part I, point 4, note 4. (*Bulletin of the European Communities* 12/92, pp 25–6).

[112] Art 1 of the Agreement [now 136 EC], discussed below.

[113] COM(75) 481. For comment, see D Cass, 'The Word that Saves Maastricht? The Principle of Subsidiarity and the Division of Powers within the European Community' (1992) 29 *Common Market Law Review* 1107 at 1112–116.

for determining the distribution of powers between the Community and the Member States. On the one hand, it is a centralising concept permitting action at Community level, but only where that is the most efficient method of fulfilling the Community's objectives. On the other hand, it creates a presumption in favour of decentralisation by placing responsibility for achieving the Community's objectives at the national level under Article 3b [now 5] EC or, in a broader conception derived from the common provisions of the TEU, at the point closest to the citizen.[114] Therefore, as the Community's reach expands, subsidiarity operates as a process for managing interdependence between sub-national, national and supranational actors.[115] Subsidiarity can be presented positively as a tool for enhancing integration within an overall process of federalisation.[116] The prime motivation for the EC Treaty amendment, however, was negative, amounting to a desire by the Member States to protect their national policy prerogatives against what they saw as unnecessary and undesirable Community interference.[117]

Article 3b [now 5] EC sandwiches the principle of subsidiarity between two established Community concepts: attribution of powers[118] and proportionality.[119] Paragraph 2 defines subsidiarity as follows:

In areas which do not fall within its exclusive competence, the Community shall take action, in accordance with the principle of subsidiarity, only if and in so far as the objectives of the proposed action cannot be sufficiently achieved by the Member States and can therefore, by reason of the scale and effects of the proposed action, be better achieved by the Community.

Subsidiarity applies to all facets of Community social policy because this is an area where the Community has concurrent competence with the Member States in a limited number of fields while, in a majority of fields, such as

---

[114] Art A [now 1] TEU, which refers to the central goal of a Europe 'in which decisions are taken as openly as possible and as closely as possible to the citizen'. For discussion, see G de Búrca, 'Reappraising Subsidiarity's Significance after Amsterdam', *Harvard Jean Monnet Working Paper 7/99*, pp 10–12; G Berman, 'Taking Subsidiarity Seriously' (1994) 94 *Columbia Law Review* 332 at 340–2. Berman explains the distinction, in the US context, between executive and democratic federalism. In the EU context, de Búrca notes at 12, Art A [now 1] TEU indicates a preference for democratic federalism, protecting citizens' rights, while Art 3b [now 5] EC emphasises the prerogatives of the Member States.

[115] See R Dehousse, *Does Subsidiarity Really Matter?* EUI Working Paper LAW No 92/32 (EUI, Florence, 1993) p 29.

[116] See the address by J Delors to the College of Europe in Bruges on 17 Oct 1989. Discussed by Cass, n 113 above at 1120–121.

[117] See de Búrca, n 114 above, p 6. See also, G Lyon-Caen, n 1 above at 56, who describes Art 3b [now 5] EC as an 'outburst of resentment' against the Court and the Commission.

[118] Para 1: 'The Community shall act within the limits of the powers conferred upon it by this Treaty and of the objectives assigned to it therein'. For an analysis of the scope of this provision, see A Dashwood, 'The Limits of European Community Powers' (1996) 21 *European Law Review* 113.

[119] Para 3: 'Any action by the Community shall not go beyond what is necessary to achieve the objectives of this Treaty'. For discussion, see N Emiliou, *The Principle of Proportionality in European Law* (Kluwer, London, 1996); G de Búrca, 'The Principle of Proportionality and its Application in EC Law' (1993) 13 *Yearbook of European Law* 105.

the organisation of education, health and social protection systems, the Member States have exclusive competence. By contrast, the Community's exclusive competence arises where the EC Treaty clearly and precisely places the sole responsibility for action on the Community and, consequently, Member States lose the right to act unilaterally.[120] Subsidiarity applies, therefore, to all areas of the EC Treaty except those centred around the four fundamental freedoms and certain common policies essential to, or a corollary of, the establishment of the internal market.[121]

At the core of the subsidiarity clause is a requirement for the Community to demonstrate that there is a legitimate need for each new initiative.[122] In the Presidency Conclusions issued after the Edinburgh European Council of December 1992 this requirement was explained in the following terms:[123]

> *For Community action to be justified* the Council must be satisfied that both aspects of the subsidiarity criterion are met: the objectives of the proposed action cannot be sufficiently achieved by the Member States' action and can therefore be better achieved by the Community.

In order to satisfy this rule specific guidelines must be used including an examination of whether the issue in question has transnational aspects which cannot be satisfactorily regulated by action by Member States; and/or, where action by the Member States alone or lack of Community action would conflict with the requirements of the Treaty. The Council must be satisfied that action at Community level would produce clear benefits by reason of its scale and effects compared with action at the level of the Member States.[124] The European Council concluded that harmonisation should only take place where it is necessary to achieve the Community's objectives and the reasons for taking action must be substantiated by both qualitative and, where possible, quantitative indicators.[125]

Following on from the Edinburgh European Council, the Commission, in an influential report issued in November 1993,[126] presented subsidiarity

---

[120] Commission Communication to the Council and the European Parliament, SEC(92) 1990.

[121] *Ibid.* The Commission lists the following areas: the removal of barriers to the free movement of goods, persons, services and capital; the common commercial policy; the general rules on competition; the common organisation of the agricultural markets; the conservation of fishing resources; the essential elements of transport policy.

[122] *Commission Report to the European Council on the Adaptation of Community Legislation to the Subsidiarity Principle*, COM(93) 545.

[123] Presidency Conclusions. Part II, para (i). Emphasis added. For discussion, see the following editorial comment: 'Subsidiarity: Backing the Right Horse?' (1993) 30 *Common Market Law Review* 241; cf A Toth, 'The Principle of Subsidiarity in the Maastricht Treaty' (1992) 29 *Common Market Law Review* 1079.

[124] *Ibid* Part II, para (ii)

[125] *Ibid* Part II, paras (iii) and (v).

[126] COM(93) 545.

as a kind of 'rule of reason' designed to regulate the exercise of powers and justify their use in a particular case.[127] In the age of subsidiarity, Community action is not the rule but the exception. Although the primary aim is to decentralise, a secondary function is to act as an impulse for integration 'where effectiveness demands that a problem be solved in a common framework'.[128] In each case where action is contemplated three questions must be answered:[129]

—What is the Community dimension of the problem?
—What is the most effective solution, given the means available to the Community and to Member States?
—What is the real added value of common action compared with isolated action by the Member States?

Subsidiarity would be developed as a 'dynamic concept' to be applied in the light of Treaty objectives, allowing Community activity to be expanded so long as 'added value' can be demonstrated or, conversely, restricted or discontinued if it is no longer necessary.[130] Although the UK trumpeted the inclusion of subsidiarity at Maastricht as a great triumph, a memorandum submitted to an influential House of Commons Committee warned that it would in practice 'prove of little use as a means of checking intrusive social policy measures'.[131] This point had been reinforced at Edinburgh where it was determined that directives based on Article 118a EEC/EC would not 'warrant re-examination' in the light of subsidiarity but rather the Community's priority was to 'supplement them by implementing all the provisions of the Charter on the Fundamental Social Rights of Workers'.[132] This somewhat confusing statement suggests a direct link between the Charter and Article 118a EEC/EC notwithstanding the distinction between the two arising from the Protocol. When, in November 1993, the Council sidestepped the UK's veto and adopted the Working Time Directive[133] under Article 118a EEC/EC, the UK, believing that its opt-out was being undermined, instantaneously mounted a legal challenge.

In the *Working Time*[134] case the UK presented a wide-ranging submission seeking to question not only the legal base of the Directive but also both the necessity for the Community to act and the intensity of the action. While

---

[127] *Ibid* point 1, para 2.
[128] *Ibid.*
[129] *Ibid* point 1, para 1.
[130] Edinburgh European Council Presidency Conclusions, Dec 1992. Part I, point 4.
[131] Memorandum submitted by M Howe to the House of Commons Foreign Affairs Committee, 1992, para 1.4. See D Pollard and M Ross, *European Community Law: Text and Materials* (Butterworths, London, 1994) pp 57–64.
[132] Presidency Conclusions, Dec 1992. Annex 2, Part A. See Watson, n 47 above at 497; Shaw in O'Keeffe and Twomey, n 21 above at 300.
[133] Dir 93/104/EC, OJ 1993, L307/18.
[134] Case C–84/94, *UK v Council* [1996] ECR I–5755.

the UK did not expressly invoke disregard of subsidiarity as one of its grounds for seeking annulment of the Directive, it regularly made reference to the principle during the course of the proceedings.[135] AG Léger lightly scolded the UK for equating subsidiarity with proportionality.[136] In his view the principles operate in turn, at two different levels of Community action.[137] Subsidiarity determines whether Community action is to be taken, whereas proportionality defines its scope. Therefore subsidiarity comes into play *before* the Community takes action while proportionality comes into play *after* such action has been taken. It follows that the question of competence operates at a different level from that of its exercise.[138] The principle that the Community can act in the area cannot be called into question because of the objective of harmonisation in Article 117 [now 136] EC. It would be illusory to expect the Member States alone to achieve the harmonisation envisaged, since it necessarily involves supranational action.[139]

The Court was equally dismissive in its judgment finding that:[140]

... it is the responsibility of the Council, under Article 118a, to adopt minimum requirements so as to contribute, through harmonisation, to achieving the objective of raising the level of health and safety protection of workers which ... is primarily the responsibility of the Member States. *Once the Council has found it necessary* to improve the existing level of protection as regards the health and safety of workers and to harmonise the conditions in this area while maintaining the improvements made, *achievement of that objective through the imposition of minimum requirements necessarily presupposes Community-wide action, which otherwise* ... *leaves the enactment of the detailed implementing provisions largely to the Member States.*

From the perspective of the Court, subsidiarity comes into play as a guiding principle for the Community legislature in the *exercise of its power* and not as a principle for determining whether or not that power exists,[141] which is a question of the attribution of powers,[142] nor for deciding on the intensity of the action, which is governed by the principle of proportionality.[143] This approach was subsequently supported by the Member States who, by virtue of the Treaty of Amsterdam, have annexed Protocol No 8 to the EC Treaty, where it is stated that 'the principle of subsidiarity does not call into question the powers conferred on the European Community by the Treaty, as inter-

---

[135] Opinion of AG Léger, para 124.
[136] *Ibid.*
[137] *Ibid* para 126.
[138] *Ibid.* For a critique, see A Dashwood, 'The Working Time Judgment in a Wider Perspective' in C Barnard, A Dashwood and B Hepple, *The ECJ's Working Time Judgment: The Social Market Vindicated* (CELS Occasional Paper No 2, Cambridge, 1997) 23–31 at 30–1.
[139] Judgment, para 129.
[140] *Ibid* para 47.
[141] See de Búrca, *Harvard Jean Monnet Working Paper* 7/99, n 114 above, p 31.
[142] Art 3b [now 5] EC, first paragraph.
[143] *Ibid* third paragraph.

preted by the Court of Justice'.[144] Thus the Court can ultimately determine the matter in the context of the Treaty powers in question.[145] In the area of social policy, where the terminology of Article 118a EEC has been subsumed within, first, the Agreement on Social Policy, and now Article 137 EC, the principle of subsidiarity is directed at the Community's legislative institutions, which have considerable latitude when it comes to the exercise of the powers granted to them under the Treaty.

In practice, subsidiarity has been reduced to its core political dimension and it is here that it has made a difference. Subsidiarity has reinforced the powers of the Member States at the expense of the Community by creating an assumption that, in areas of shared competence, the appropriate level of action is national. The role of the Community is complementary and supportive which may, in certain circumstances, require binding legislation where the Treaty powers so allow and the European Council's guidelines on justification are complied with, but equally, in accordance with the principle of proportionality, if the objective can be achieved by other less intensive means, such as programmatic action or soft law, then that is to be preferred.[146] Thus, when the Commission issued its White Paper on Social Policy in July 1994,[147] at a time when no binding legislation had been adopted under the Agreement on Social Policy, it was decided that legislation would only be proposed 'when strictly necessary to achieve the objectives of the Union and when the issues addressed cannot be solved at Member State level'.[148] Paradoxically, just as the Agreement was entering into force, as an expression of the will of the 11 to 'implement' the Social Charter through an expansion of legal competences and the broad exercise of qualified majority voting (QMV), it was being simultaneously neutered by the operation of the principle of subsidiarity.[149] It is with this context in mind that we shall now examine the substantive provisions of the Agreement.

VI THE AGREEMENT ON SOCIAL POLICY—A WAY OUT OF THE IMPASSE?

Between November 1993, when the Protocol on Social Policy entered into force, and May 1999, when it was repealed,[150] the Community conducted

---

[144] Para 3 of Protocol No 8.

[145] See de Búrca, *Harvard Jean Monnet Working Paper* 7/99, n 114 above, p 31.

[146] See Edinburgh European Council Presidency Conclusions, Dec 1992. Part II, para (v).

[147] *European Social Policy: A Way Forward for the Union*, COM(94) 333.

[148] *Ibid*. Introduction, para 22.

[149] See generally, J Kenner, 'The Paradox of the Social Dimension' in P Lynch, N Neuwahl and W Rees (eds) *Reforming the European Union: From Maastricht to Amsterdam* (Longman, Harlow, 2000) pp 108–29.

[150] The Protocol was repealed when the Treaty of Amsterdam entered into legal force on 1 May 1999.

a unique experiment. Two competing typologies of 'Social Europe' coexisted. For the Community of 12/15 the parameters were set by Articles 117–122 EC marking a continuum of the 'social dimension' of the internal market. QMV was available only through the channel of Article 118a EEC/EC, while the social partners were limited to the peripheral role accorded to them under Article 118b EEC/EC. For the transitional Community of 11/14, however, a new challenge was presented by the separate '*acquis*' of the Agreement on Social Policy signifying an apparently decisive shift from an integrated market to a social justice rationale for the development of the law in this area.[151] In the view of the Commission, the Agreement represented an opportunity for the social dimension to progress at the same pace as the economic aspect of the construction of Europe.[152] Indeed the immediate practical purpose of the Agreement was to 'implement' the Social Charter on the basis of the new *acquis*. To secure this objective, the Community of 11/14 were now able to utilise a wide-range of legal bases for QMV. Meanwhile the social partners, who had previously been passive bystanders, were now active players in the legislative process, able to reach agreements capable of being converted into binding 'Community' legislation. Thus, having invented the Protocol as a device for ending the impasse over social policy, the 11/14 and, more specifically, the Commission and the social partners, were now presented with a series of strategic political and legal questions. To what extent was the new *acquis* capable of securing the implementation of the Charter? How far and how fast should they move towards a two-speed 'Social Europe'? How would the new procedures involving the social partners operate within the Community's legislative system? With these questions in mind, the substantive and procedural elements of the Agreement will now be analysed.

During the period of its operation, the Agreement was brought into play without prejudice to the main Treaty provisions and, therefore, as a supplemental procedure subject to the specific framework provided by the Treaty, including the overarching ambition in Article 2 EC of promoting a high level of employment and social protection.[153] Once triggered the Agreement performed three specific tasks.[154] First, it redefined and extended the shared social policy objectives of the Community and the Member States, in the context of the Community of 11/14. Second, it set out specific rules for the adoption of laws in this context. Third, it developed the role of the social partners in the consultative and legislative process.

Article 1 of the Agreement [now replaced by Article 136 EC] laid down the revised social policy objectives in the following context:[155]

---

[151] See Fitzpatrick, n 90 above at 211.
[152] COM(93) 600. Introduction, para 3.
[153] *Ibid*. Introduction, para 5.
[154] *Ibid*. Introduction, para 6.
[155] Emphasis added.

The Community and the Member States shall have as their objectives the promotion of employment, improved living and working conditions, proper social protection, dialogue between management and labour, the development of human resources with a view to lasting high employment and the combating of exclusion. To this end the *Community and the Member States* shall implement measures which take account of the diverse forms of national practices, in particular in the field of contractual relations, and the need to maintain the competitiveness of the Community economy.

Whereas Article 117 EEC was presented in the form of a contract between the Member States to pursue their national social policies in a coordinated fashion, Article 1 of the Agreement placed responsibility for the development and implementation of policies at both national and Community levels. This approach did not, however, signify a shift of responsibility to the Community.[156] Rather it represented an application of the horizontal provisions in points 27–30 of the Social Charter, where the primary responsibility for implementation lies with the Member States, while the Commission's role is to submit legislative proposals and to monitor progress through annual reporting, a function reinforced by Article 7 [now 143 EC].[157] Article 2(1) [now 137(1) EC] reasserted the leading role of the Member States in social policy both under the Treaty and Agreement, where it was stated that, with a view to achieving the objectives listed in the first sentence of Article 1, the Community 'shall support and complement the activities of the Member States'. This clause was cited by the Edinburgh European Council as a specific application of the idea of subsidiarity.[158]

The second sentence of Article 1 was more nuanced. When compared with the text of Article 117 EEC, it is immediately apparent that the 'Community' would no longer favour the harmonisation of social systems in a formal sense. Indeed, by emphasising diversity, the signatories of the Agreement were seeking to assert the individuality of their national laws and practices and, by implication, a preference for less formalised, more programmatic Community intervention and, more specifically under Article 2(2) [now 137(2) EC], in those cases where directives were the appropriate means of complementary Community activity, these should provide for 'minimum requirements for gradual implementation, having regard to the conditions and technical rules obtaining *in each of the Member States*'.[159] Furthermore, the primary role of the Commission under Article 5 [now 140 EC] was, first, to 'encourage' co-operation between the Member States and, second, to 'facilitate' their action in all social policy fields under the Agreement. This was broadly consistent with the function of Article 118 EEC but

---

[156] See Brinkmann, n 47 above at 244.
[157] The Commission decided to combine the annual reports on the Charter and the Protocol.
[158] Presidency Conclusions, Dec 1992. Part 1, point 3, note 3.
[159] Emphasis added.

with the overall objective of harmonisation removed. Hence the variation from harmonisation to minimum standards, first tested by the addition of Article 118a EEC, was now being extended to the whole schema of the Agreement. Improvements beyond the Community minimum would be left to the individual Member States under Article 2(5) [now 137(5) EC], extending the approach introduced in Article 118a(3) EEC. The experience of Article 118a EEC/EC in practice demonstrates that this approach leads to a reductionist interpretation of social standards rather than upward harmonisation.[160]

While the reference to diversity, particularly in the field of contractual relations, was neutral in policy terms, the inclusion of a competitiveness test served to provide an economic anchor to restrict the apparently freestanding social provisions that followed in Articles 2 and 6 [now 137 and 141 EC]. As Falkner has noted, any social directive may to some extent create additional distortions of competition.[161] Measures designed to improve living and working conditions may, directly or indirectly, increase labour costs that may, without productivity savings, render the 'European economy' less competitive and, potentially, undermine the EMU project. Moreover, the test is subjective and capable of being used as a political weapon by opponents of transnational social regulation.[162] Therefore the appearance of an autonomous social policy under the Agreement was illusory, as Majone explained:[163]

But even if they no longer have to be justified in functional terms, measures proposed by the Commission in the social field must be compatible with the 'economic constitution' of the Community, that is, with the principles of a liberal economic order. This requirement creates an ideological climate quite unlike that which made possible the development of the welfare state in the Member States.

It followed that any progress would have to be linked to the Community's overall economic objectives and, as Shaw noted, would be hinged 'on a coincidence of political will and normative competence, both of which are relatively weak in the Social Policy field'.[164] The scope of that 'normative competence' under the Agreement was to be found in Articles 2 and 6.

Article 2 [now 137 EC] provided a framework within which the objectives in Article 1 could be achieved. In a similar fashion to Article 118 EEC, this had the effect of circumscribing the social policy objectives set out therein.[165] The legislative system in Article 2 was divided into three parts.[166]

---

[160] For an excellent analysis, see S Simitis and A Lyon-Caen, 'Community Labour Law: A Critical Introduction to its History' in Davies *et al*, n 1 above, 1–22 at 18–19.

[161] Falkner, n 81 above at 11.

[162] See Weiss, n 49 above at 9.

[163] G Majone, 'The European Community Between Social Policy and Social Regulation' (1993) 31 *Journal of Common Market Studies* 153 at 156.

[164] Shaw in O'Keeffe and Twomey, n 54 above at 299.

[165] See Szyszczak, n 70 above at 316.

[166] See Fitzpatrick, n 90 above at 201.

The first part, Article 2(1), enumerated specific fields where the Community 'shall support and complement' the activities of the Member States allowing, under Article 2(2), for directives to be adopted by the Council by QMV.[167] The fields covered by Article 2(1) were as follows:

—improvement, in particular, of the working environment to protect workers' health and safety;
—working conditions;
—the information and consultation of workers;
—equality between men and women with regard to labour market opportunities and treatment at work;
—the integration of persons excluded from the labour market . . .

Following the rubric laid down in Article 118a EEC, these directives had to be based on 'minimum requirements for gradual implementation, having regard to the conditions and technical rules' in each of the Member States. Such directives needed to 'avoid imposing administrative, financial and legal constraints in a way which would hold back the creation and development of small and medium-sized undertakings'.[168]

The second part, Article 2(3), listed other residual areas where Community action was possible, not specifically in the form of directives, but only on a unanimous vote in the Council.[169] These areas were:

—social security and social protection of workers;
—protection of workers where their employment contract is terminated;
—representation and collective defence of the interests of workers and employers, including co-determination, subject to paragraph 6;
—conditions of employment of third-country nationals legally residing in Community territory;
—financial contributions for promotion of employment and job-creation, without prejudice to the provisions relating to the Social Fund.

The final part, Article 2(6), was negative, excluding several areas from the content of any measures adopted under paragraphs (1) and (3). The areas in question were 'pay, the right of association, the right to strike or the right to impose lock-outs'.

Article 2(4) and (5) dealt with implementation issues. Article 2(4) permitted Member States to entrust management and labour, at their joint request, with the implementation of directives adopted under paragraphs (2) and (3). Responsibility for guaranteeing the results imposed by those directives remained with the Member States. Article 2(4) was drafted on the basis of the accord signed by the social partners in advance of the Treaty negotiations.[170] It was drawn from point 27 of the Social Charter, itself inspired by

---

[167] Art 2(2). The co-operation procedure in Art 189c [now 252] EC applied.
[168] Art 2(2).
[169] Subject to consultation with the European Parliament and the Economic and Social Committee.
[170] For discussion in the context of Art 2(4), see S Sciarra, 'Collective Agreements in the Hierarchy of European Community Sources' in Davies *et al*, n 1 above, 189–212 at 197–8;

the case law of the Court.[171] Article 2(5) incorporated the clause contained in Article 118a(3) EEC whereby, notwithstanding the content of any measures adopted, a Member State would not be prevented 'from maintaining or introducing more stringent protective measures compatible with the Treaty'. By implication, this incorporated the principle of non-retrogression of social laws outlined in the preamble of the Social Charter.[172]

In the aftermath of the Maastricht settlement there was considerable uncertainty about, first, the relationship between the legal bases in Article 2 and the internal market provisions in Article 100a [now 95] EC, second, the implications of the clause in Article 2(2) concerning small and medium-sized enterprises (SMEs) and third, the interplay between paragraphs (1) (3) and (6).

On the first point, many queried whether it was possible for Article 2(1) and (3) to trump the derogation in Article 100a(2) [now 95(2)] EC concerning 'the rights and interests of employed persons'? Weiss was confident that these new demarcations overrode the 'blockade' established by that derogation.[173] Szyszczak contended that the exemption would be narrowed down or might become 'an embattled chess piece in future litigation'.[174] In the event the matter was effectively settled by the *Working Time* case[175] where the Court held that the existence of other provisions in the Treaty did not have the effect of restricting the scope of Article 118a EEC/EC.[176] Article 2 directly replaced and extended Article 118a EEC/EC in the context of the *acquis* applying to the 11/14. It followed that, where the Agreement came into play, Article 2 had to be used providing the principal aim of the measure in question fell within the enumerated legal bases taking into account the objectives in Article 1.[177]

Moreover, with regard to the scope of the SME clause,[178] the Court, when interpreting the provisions in the Working Time Directive, has taken a

---

B Bercusson, 'Social Policy at the Crossroads: European Labour Law after Maastricht' in Dehousse, n 2 above, 149–86 at 168–71. The practical issues are summarised by the Commission at: COM(93) 600, paras 43–8.

[171] Case 143/83, *Commission v Denmark* [1985] ECR 427. At 434–5 the Court held that Member States 'may leave the implementation of the principle of equal pay in the first instance to representatives of management and labour'. Member States remain ultimately bound to guarantee the principle of equality if the agreement is inadequate. For discussion, see ch 2.

[172] 16th recital.

[173] Weiss, n 49 above at 7.

[174] Szyszczak, n 70 above at 316–17.

[175] Case C–84/94, *UK v Council (Working Time Directive)* [1996] ECR I–5755.

[176] *Ibid* paras 12 and 13.

[177] *Ibid* para 21.

[178] The Commission has attempted to define SMEs in Recommendation 96/280/EC, OJ 1996, L107/4. An SME is an 'independent enterprise' with fewer than 250 employees and either an annual turnover not exceeding ECU 40 million or an annual balance sheet not exceeding ECU 27 million (Art 1(1)). An 'independent enterprise' is normally one that is not owned as to 25% or more of the capital or the voting rights by one enterprise, or jointly by several

narrow view of the identical provision in Article 118a EEC/EC.[179] The Court has laid down the following test. When considering the validity of a directive, the Court only has to satisfy itself that the directive in question takes account of the SME clause in the framing of its provisions.[180] In those circumstances clauses in national legislation not permitted by the relevant directive will be struck down even if they are designed to exempt, protect or promote SMEs.[181]

Turning to the third point, there seemed to be considerable potential for overlap between the legal bases requiring either QMV or unanimity. The role of the Commission would be pivotal in determining not only when to activate the Agreement but also the choice between paragraphs (1) and (3) and the drafting of provisions to avoid the exclusion in paragraph (6). This would also be a factor for the social partners to take into account when negotiating 'framework agreements' under Article 4 [now 139 EC].

How would proposals concerning 'information and consultation of workers' under Article 2(1) be distinguished from those regarding 'representation and collective defence of the interests of workers' under Article 2(3)? Weiss suggested that this distinction might lead to incongruous outcomes.[182] For example, a measure merely concerning worker involvement, such as the 'Vredeling' proposal of the 1980s,[183] would fall under the QMV provisions, whereas if the structure of worker representation was altered, as in the case of the then proposed European Works Council (EWC) Directive,[184] this would require unanimity. In the event the revised Commission proposal,[185] and the EWC Directive subsequently adopted,[186] were justified

enterprises (Art 1(3)). The ILO, by contrast, defines SMEs as enterprises with up to 50 employees. See ILO, *The Promotion of Small and Medium-sized Enterprises*, Report IV, International Labour Conference. 72nd session (ILO, Geneva, 1986) p 4. For discussion see J-M Servais, 'Labour Law in Small and Medium-Sized Enterprises: An Ongoing Challenge' (1994) 10 *International Journal of Comparative Labour Law and Industrial Relations* 119.

[179] See Case C–84/94, *UK v Council (Working Time Directive)* [1996] ECR I–5755; and Case C–173/99, *R v Secretary of State for Trade and Industry, ex parte Broadcasting, Entertainment, Cinematographic and Theatre Union (BECTU)* [2001] ECR I–4881, para 60.

[180] This approach is also consistent with Declaration No 1 annexed to the Agreement, which states 'that the Community does not intend, in laying down minimum requirements for protection of the safety and health of employees, to discriminate in a manner unjustified by the circumstances against employees in small and medium-sized undertakings'. The legal status of the declarations annexed to the Agreement is uncertain but, unlike the declarations accompanying the Single European Act (SEA) these declarations are contained in the list of protocols to be annexed to EC Treaty in the Final Act of the IGC, suggesting that they may have the same legal status as the Agreement itself. See Whiteford, n 80 above at 210; and, on the SEA, see A Toth, 'The Legal Status of the declarations annexed to the Single European Act' (1986) 23 *Common Market Law Review* 803.

[181] C–173/99, *R v Secretary of State for Trade and Industry, ex parte Broadcasting, Entertainment, Cinematographic and Theatre Union (BECTU)* [2001] ECR I–4881, paras 57–60.

[182] Weiss, n 49 above at 7–8.

[183] OJ 1980, C297/3 and OJ 1983, C217/3.

[184] OJ 1991, C39/10.

[185] OJ 1994, C135/8 and C199/10.

[186] Dir 94/45/EC on the establishment of a European Works Council or a procedure in

on the basis of 'information and consultation' even though, it could be argued that both the EWC[187] and the Special Negotiating Body[188] procedure laid down in the Directive involved representation, if not collective defence, of workers' interests.

Further questions were raised concerning the open-ended term 'working conditions' in Article 2(1).[189] For example, one area under consideration by the Commission in its 1994 White Paper on Social Policy was a proposal for a measure to grant workers the right to payment of wages on public holidays and during illness.[190] Would such a measure be primarily concerned with 'working conditions' under Article 2(1) or 'social protection' under Article 2(3)? From the perspective of the worker these rights would logically fall under the former heading, but for many Member States the bulk of the administration and cost of such a scheme would have to be met by their social welfare budgets. Also, if such a measure had been pursued, would it have been caught by the exclusion in Article 2(6) concerning 'pay'? Although the Court has favoured the most democratic method when presented with a choice of legal bases,[191] indicating a potential preference for the co-operation procedure applicable under Article 2(1), the exclusion in Article 2(6) would have been more difficult to overcome. The White Paper only referred to 'legislative action'[192] rather than a directive in this area and, in the event, the idea has not been pursued. Significantly, the Parental Leave Directive,[193] the first measure arising from the negotiation of a framework agreement between the social partners,[194] makes no provision for paid leave.

While Articles 117–122 EEC/EC have been repeatedly criticised for their limitations, the original social provisions did not specifically exclude any area of social policy or labour law from the Community's horizons. Article 2(6) [now 137(6) EC], by contrast, placed within a structure designed to implement the Social Charter, specifically denied two of its fundamental freedoms: fair remuneration and freedom of association. The exclusion of pay created a further variation in the Community's geometry as Streeck explained:[195]

For a while it was believed that the British 'opt-out' would give a strong boost to Union social policy by setting it free from the threat of a British veto. But this over-

---

Community-scale undertakings and Community-scale groups of undertakings for the purposes of informing and consulting employees, OJ 1994, L254/64.

[187] *Ibid.* Art 1(2) and the Annex.
[188] *Ibid.* Art 5.
[189] See Weiss, n 49 above at 7.
[190] COM(94) 333, ch 3, para 13(iv).
[191] For example, see Cases C–65/90 and C–295/90, *European Parliament v Council* [1992] ECR I–4593 and I–4193.
[192] COM(94) 333, ch 3, para 13(iv).
[193] Dir 96/34/EC, OJ 1996, L145/4, as amended by Dir 97/75/EC, OJ 1998, L10/24.
[194] Signed on 14 Dec 1995 and annexed to the Directive.
[195] W Streeck, 'Neo Voluntarism: A New European Social Policy Regime?' (1995) 1 *European Law Journal* 31 at 46.

looked the fact that the exemption is now likely to become a routinely accepted device to reconcile the desire of some countries to have, for whatever reasons, a common minimum standard, with the desire of others to remain below that standard. One consequence of this will be further fragmentation of European social policy, with different subjects being dealt with by differently demarcated 'sub-unions' under varying decision-rules.

Moreover, while Article 2(3) [now 137(3) EC] appeared to allow for legislation in the area of 'collective defence of the interests of workers and employers' with 'co-determination' as an option, any proposal would be very difficult to frame in the light of this exclusion.[196] Not surprisingly no such proposal has been forthcoming.

One explanation for Article 2(6) has been to regard it as a strict application of subsidiarity.[197] But Article 2(6) amounted to what Bercusson has aptly described as 'autoexclusion'.[198] The Community denied itself competence precisely in the area where collective bargaining is at its most meaningful, when the parties are contemplating the exercise of their traditional weapons of industrial conflict.[199] Moreover, this exemption cannot be explained away as an attempt to entice the UK to endorse the draft of the Social Chapter, because the Commission's proposal to include the right to strike in the list of areas where unanimity is required, was rejected in the first Luxembourg draft of the Treaty and never reinstated, well in advance of the British objections.[200] Rather, as Ryan explains, Article 2(6) entrenched a policy of systematic exclusion of pay and trade union rights from Community employment law.[201] While the need to respect diversity may inhibit the Community's desire to act in the field of collective labour law, this argument is less tenable in the area of pay where instrumentation is well established at international level.[202] As Sciarra observes, this lacuna has meant that no broad interpretation or 'far-sighted initiative' of the social partners can compensate for the lack of a solid constitutional basis on which to found the development of collective rights at Community level.[203] The Community is therefore not directly concerned either with the countervailing power of labour, or the reaction to it by management. For the Community, social dialogue—even if it is sometimes described as a form

---

[196] See B Ryan, 'Pay, Trade Union Rights and European Community Law' (1997) 13 *International Journal of Comparative Labour Law and Industrial Relations* 305 at 311–13.

[197] Lyon-Caen, n 1 above at 61; cf Ryan, *ibid* at 319–20.

[198] Bercusson in Dehousse, n 118 above at 185.

[199] *Ibid.*

[200] See Ryan, n 196 above at 308. For the Commission's proposals of 4 April 1991, see *Bulletin of the European Communities Supplement* 2/91, pp 126–31. The Luxembourg draft was circulated to the Member States on 12 April 1991.

[201] *Ibid* at 324.

[202] *Ibid* at 320–4. For example ILO Convention No 26 of 1928 on Minimum Wage-Fixing Machinery.

[203] See S Sciarra, 'Collective Agreements in the Hierarchy of European Community Sources' in Davies *et al*, n 1 above 189–212 at 194–5.

of collective bargaining[204]—has become a substitute for collective labour law.

Article 6 [now revised as Article 141 EC] appears altogether more straightforward, but it also bears some intriguing internal contradictions. Article 6 was originally drafted as a replacement for Article 119 EEC on equal pay between men and women. Hence, Article 6(1) simply reasserted the principle of 'equal pay for equal work' while Article 6(2) repeated the definition of 'pay' in Article 119 EEC verbatim. The principle of equal treatment, derived from the Equal Treatment Directive[205] was, somewhat incongruously, not incorporated into Article 6 even though the Social Charter proclaims that 'equal treatment for men and women must be assured'.[206] This cautious approach avoided any conflict between the two *acquis*, although this was incidental as even the draft Treaty had left out the equal value concept.[207] As a result there was no obvious purpose to Article 6(1) and (2).[208] There was no legal base for implementing equal pay and yet, in the context of the minimum standards provisions in Article 2 there was a legal base for supportive and complementary directives in the field of equality between men and women 'with regard to labour market opportunities and equal treatment at work'. While the repetition of Article 119(1) and (2) EEC can be explained by the last minute decision to negotiate the Protocol, the exclusion of equal value and equal treatment from what was now Article 6 of the Agreement reflected the limited ambition of the draft 'Social Chapter', a fact implicitly recognised when, in the Treaty of Amsterdam, this was the one provision in the Agreement that underwent whole scale revision before emerging as the new Article 141 EC.

The confusion surrounding Article 6 was compounded by paragraph 3, which provided that:[209]

This Article *shall not prevent any Member State from maintaining or adopting measures providing for specific advantages* in order to make it easier for *women* to pursue a vocational activity or to prevent or compensate for disadvantages in their professional careers.

Bizarrely, having excluded the principle of equal treatment from Article 6, the Community of 11 were now seeking to incorporate an exception to that

[204] See Bercusson (1994, *Industrial Law Journal*) n 49 above; A Lo Faro, *Regulating Social Europe: Reality & Myth of Collective Bargaining in the EC Legal Order* (Hart, Oxford, 2000) pp 54–60; cf Lord Wedderburn, 'Consultation and Collective Bargaining in Europe: Success or Ideology?' (1997) 26 *Industrial Law Journal* 1 at 29.

[205] Dir 76/207/EEC, OJ 1976, L39/40.

[206] Point 16 of the Social Charter.

[207] Luxembourg Presidency 'Draft Treaty on the Union', 18 June 1991; Dutch Presidency draft 'Towards European Union', 24 Sept 1991. See Corbett, n 11 above, pp 303–4.

[208] See Watson, n 47 above at 499.

[209] Emphasis added.

principle drawn from Article 2(4) of the Equal Treatment Directive.[210] Not only did this clause create a potential for conflict between the parallel *acquis*,[211] because no similar provision was located in Article 119 EEC/EC, but also, it provided a national vehicle for positive action specifically for women without adding the necessary Community policy rationale for such a significant and apparently contradictory amendment.[212] Watson suggested that a range of measures might be justifiable to 'prevent or compensate' women for disadvantages that make it difficult for them to compete on equal terms with men in the workplace.[213] For example, payments to cover childcare costs; grants for vocational training; increased paid holidays to care for children; and notional contributions to occupational pension schemes.[214] Curtin, while agreeing that the clause created a permanent foundation for what she described as 'so-called "positive action"',[215] argued that Article 6(3) went much further than the stated position of the Court as judicially elaborated,[216] concluding that the tension was likely to be resolved in favour of the Community norm, the unamended Article 119 EEC/EC.[217] In the event, Article 6(3) was not directly adjudicated upon, but the Court, in its first judgment on Article 2(4) of the Equal Treatment Directive after the Agreement entered into force,[218] interpreted the provision narrowly, perhaps reflecting a desire to avoid a widening conflict between the related provisions in advance of a further revision of the treaties. On reflection the addition of Article 6(3) in isolation was premature and, as we shall see in chapters 8 and 10, the conflict was eventually resolved by the inclusion of

[210] Dir 76/207/EEC, OJ 1976, L 39/40. Art 2(4) states that the Directive 'shall be without prejudice to measures to promote equal opportunity for men and women, in particular by removing existing inequalities which affect women's opportunities in the areas referred to in Article 1(1)'. These areas are: access to employment, including promotion; vocational training; working conditions and social security (arising from the implementation of Dir 79/7/EEC, OJ 1979, L6/24).

[211] See Curtin's critique, n 26 above at 61.

[212] See Whiteford, n 80 above at 206–7. Whiteford notes, at 207, that Art 9(2) of the Directive obliges Member States to assess the remaining social relevance of such exceptions to the principle of equal treatment. This suggests that when such distinctions are no longer appropriate they should be removed, albeit without any temporal limitation. No such test appears in Art 6(3) of the Agreement.

[213] Watson, n 47 above at 499.

[214] *Ibid.*

[215] Curtin, n 26 above at 61.

[216] See Case 318/86, *Commission v France* [1988] ECR 3559, para 15, where the Court held that positive action measures under Art 2(4) of the Equal Treatment Directive must be of a specific rather than a general nature applying only to those areas where existing inequalities are demonstrated by the Member State in question.

[217] Curtin, n 26 above at 61.

[218] Case C–450/93, *Kalanke v Freie Hansestadt Bremen* [1995] ECR I–3051; cf Case C–409/95, *Marschall v Land Nordrhein-Westfalen* [1997] ECR I–6363. In *Marschall* the Court adopted a more liberal interpretation of a positive action clause concerning appointment and promotion at a time when it was known that a Treaty change was being prepared. See ch 10 for discussion of the Court's jurisprudence in this area and developments post-*Marschall*.

both the principle of equal treatment and an amended positive action clause in the new Article 141 EC.

VII ARTICLES 3 AND 4—REPRESENTATIVENESS AND DEMOCRATIC LEGITIMACY—TWO SIDES OF THE SAME COIN?

(1) The Social Partners Move to Centre Stage

In the field of employment law there is as much interest in the process, the more Byzantine the better, as there is in the product, which tends to be meagre. Articles 3 and 4 of the Agreement [now 138 and 139 EC] exemplify this point. In their landmark agreement of 31 October 1991,[219] the ETUC, UNICE and CEEP,[220] an élite self-selected group of European 'social partners', fashioned a novel consultative and, potentially, quasi-legislative architecture for Community social policy. The provisions in the Agreement, reproducing the concordat of the social partners in almost identical terms,[221] have taken the tentative conception of 'relations based on agreement' in Article 118b EEC onto a new plane. What may have first appeared as perhaps little more than a laboratory experiment within a narrowly confined legal space, has metamorphosised into a more substantial prototype systematically disrupting the established rhythm of the legislative cycle and the Community's fiercely contested institutional balance. Fundamental issues have been raised about the representativeness of the parties and the democratic legitimacy of introducing a corporatist[222] law-making process where private actors make public policy without any direct form of accountability.[223] In a nutshell: *who should participate on behalf of whom?*[224]

Under Article 3 of the Agreement [now 138 EC] the Commission have a general obligation *at Community level* to promote the consultation of 'management and labour' and to take 'any relevant measure' to facilitate their dialogue by ensuring balanced support for the parties.[225] Therefore the

---

[219] See *Social Europe* 2/95, p 149.

[220] The European Trades Union Confederation (ETUC) the Union of Industrial and Employers' Confederations of Europe (UNICE) and the European Centre of Enterprises and Public Participation (CEEP).

[221] See COM(93) 600. Summary, para 5.

[222] See Falkner, n 81 above at 5; and D Obradovic, 'Accountability of Interest Groups in the Union Lawmaking Process' in Craig and Harlow, n 47 above, 354–85. According to Obradovic, at 355, corporatism involves organisations representing monopolistic functional interests in a role that combines interest representation and policy implementation through delegated self-enforcement.

[223] Obradovic, *ibid* at 355–6.

[224] See L Betten, 'The Democratic Deficit of Participatory Democracy in Community Social Policy' (1998) 23 *European Law Review* 20 at 30. Betten asks a slightly narrower question: 'who participates on behalf of whom?'.

[225] Art 3(1) [now 138(1) EC].

Commission have been assigned a dynamic role to act as both champion and adjudicator for the social partners. Further, within the specific context of the social policy provisions in the Agreement [now Articles 136–145 EC], Article 3 [now 138 EC] creates an obligatory two-stage consultative process involving the social partners that may lead to negotiations and, ultimately, to agreements capable of being converted into binding Community legislation. First, the Commission must consult 'management and labour' at the pre-legislative stage 'on the possible direction of Community action' in the social policy field.[226] At this stage the Commission retains the power to act or not to act. Secondly, if the Commission decides to make a proposal, it is obliged to consult management and labour—or the social partners[227]— on its content and they, in turn, are required to forward an opinion or recommendation to the Commission.[228] It is at this stage that the social partners can activate the negotiation process in Article 4 [now 139 EC] by informing the Commission[229] that they wish to embark upon a process of 'dialogue' that 'should they so desire . . . may lead to contractual relations, including agreements'.[230] The duration of the negotiations should not exceed nine months, unless management and labour and the Commission agree to an extension.[231] Once this process begins the conventional legislative process is frozen[232] and, in effect, privatised.[233] Where the parties decide to reach an 'agreement' Article 4(2) [now 139(2) EC] comes into play as follows:

Agreements concluded at Community level shall be implemented in accordance with the procedures and practices specific to management and labour and the Member States or, in matters covered by Article 2, at the joint request of the signatory parties, by a Council decision on a proposal from the Commission.

The Council shall act by qualified majority, except where the agreement in question contains one or more provisions relating to the areas referred to in Article 2(3) in which case it shall act unanimously.

---

[226] Art 3(2) [now 138(2) EC]. In their Communication concerning the application of the Agreement, COM(93) 600, at para 19, the Commission state that the initial consultation period should not exceed 6 weeks.

[227] The two terms are used interchangeably by the Commission and, more generally, in the academic literature, although the Agreement only refers to 'management and labour'.

[228] Art 3(3) [now 138(3) EC]. This phase should also not exceed six weeks. See COM(93) 600, para 19.

[229] Art 3(4) [now 138(4) EC].

[230] Art 4(1) [now 139(1) EC].

[231] Art 3(4) [now 138(4) EC]. The Commission will assess the chances of an agreement within the requested extension period. While respecting the independence of the social partners, the Commission will be keen to prevent any prolongation of fruitless negotiations that would ultimately block the Commission's ability to regulate. See COM(93) 600, para 32.

[232] See E Whiteford, 'W(h)ither Social Policy?' in J Shaw and G More (eds) *New Legal Dynamics of European Union* (Clarendon Press, Oxford, 1995) 111–45 at 111.

[233] See N Bernard, 'Legitimising EU Law: Is the Social Dialogue the Way Forward? Some Reflections Around the UEAPME Case' in J Shaw (ed) *Social Law and Policy in an Evolving European Union* (Hart, Oxford, 2000) 279–302 at 279.

With the insertion of these two brief paragraphs 'management and labour' were presented with the tantalising prospect of being transformed from passive interlocutors engaged in dialogue, into active, nay decisive, bargainers in the Community's legislative process in the areas covered by Article 2 [now 137 EC]. It takes two to tango and, at first, there was some understandable scepticism about whether the social partners would have the necessary 'desire' both to reach agreements *and* seek their implementation into national or Community norms. Questions were also raised about the manner in which the Commission would exercise its role as an intermediary.[234]

When, shortly after the new procedure came into operation, the Commission circulated its proposal for a draft directive on European Works Councils (EWCs),[235] which had earlier been deadlocked in the Council,[236] the portents were not encouraging. From the perspective of the trade unions, the text, derived from a joint opinion of 1987,[237] was broadly acceptable. For the employers, however, there was little incentive to reach agreement when they had every reason to believe that if the negotiations failed the other partner had more to lose.[238] It seemed inevitable that one party would always have a vested interest in the failure of the process.[239] In the case of the EWC proposal, there was added piquancy to the eventual breakdown of the negotiations because the withdrawal of the Confederation of British Industry was one of the main reasons for the impasse.[240] As Rhodes pithily observed, the employers now had a means to replace the UK's veto with their own.[241] In practice, however, the position was not so straightforward. The Commission, faced with the breakdown of negotiations, called the employers' bluff by launching a fresh proposal, which was swiftly converted into the EWC Directive,[242] the first legislative measure adopted under the Agreement.[243]

The Commission's strategy in the case of the EWC Directive provided ample evidence that, once the social partners received the Commission's proposal they were, to apply Bercusson's memorable phrase, 'bargaining in the shadow of the law' for:[244]

---

[234] See P Lange, 'Maastricht and the Social Protocol: Why Did They Do It?' (1993) 21 *Politics and Society* 5 at 13.

[235] OJ 1994, C135/8. For the revised proposal, see OJ 1994, C199/10.

[236] OJ 1990, C39/10.

[237] The signatories to the Joint Opinion of March 1987 were the ETUC, UNICE and CEEP.

[238] See Whiteford in Shaw and More, n 232 above at 122; and Streeck, n 195 above at 37.

[239] Whiteford, *ibid* at 123.

[240] See Brinkmann, n 47 above at 258. For a detailed account, see M Gold and M Hall, 'Statutory European Works Councils: The Final Countdown?' (1994) 25 *Industrial Relations Journal* 177.

[241] Rhodes, n 89 above at 300.

[242] Adopted in accordance with Art 2(2) of the Agreement as Dir 94/45/EC, OJ 1994, L254/64.

[243] Although the original proposal was revised the substance was largely retained. See C Barnard, *EC Employment Law*, 2nd edn (OUP, Oxford, 2000) pp 527–9.

[244] Bercusson (1992, IRJ) n 33 above at 185.

Experience from many countries demonstrates that there will be pressures on the social partners to negotiate and agree to avoid an imposed standard which pre-empts their autonomy and which may be also a less desirable result.

Following another failed attempt to consult on a proposal concerning the burden of proof in sex discrimination cases,[245] an area that the social partners regarded as beyond their remit,[246] further pressures were brought to bear by the Commission in its proposals for cross-sectoral directives concerning parental leave and atypical work.[247] On each occasion the Commission warned in its consultation papers that any fresh proposal would be more comprehensive. For the employers, framework agreements now seemed the lesser evil.[248] The trade unions, meanwhile, wanted to demonstrate that the new procedures were workable. This cumulative pressure secured the desired result: three negotiated framework agreements[249] later annexed to directives.[250] The mere existence of the agreements does not, however, herald the successful introduction of a new system of European industrial relations, for the agreements themselves are less important than the content,[251] to be discussed separately in Section VIII below. First, we need to consider the wider institutional implications of the process.

(2) Reinventing Europe's Social Policy Architecture—A Question of Democratic Legitimacy

Just as the social partners have had to adjust to new roles so too have the other *dramatis personae*, the Community's institutions. Let us consider the

---

[245] See COM(96) 340. The Commission proposal was taken forward using the conventional legislative route and was eventually adopted as Dir 97/80/EC, OJ 1997, L14/16, as amended by Dir 98/52/EC, OJ 1998, L205/66.

[246] This was a unanimous view reflecting the fact that the content would affect court procedures outside the scope of the social partners. See B Keller and B Sörries, 'The New Social Dialogue: Procedural Structuring, First Results and Perspectives' in B Towers and M Terry (eds) *Industrial Relations Journal European Annual Review 1997* (Blackwell, Oxford, 1998) 77–98 at 87.

[247] Respectively, COM(96) 26 and COM(90) 533 (the latter forming the basis for the start of consultations on 27 Sept 1995).

[248] See M Schmidt, 'Representativity—A Claim Not Satisfied: The Social Partners' Role in the EC Law-Making Procedure for Social Policy' (1999) 15 *International Journal of Comparative Labour Law and Industrial Relations* 259 at 262–3.

[249] Concluded by the ETUC, UNICE and CEEP on, respectively, 14 Dec 1995 (parental leave) 6 June 1997 (part-time work) and 18 March 1999 (fixed-term work). See further, Barnard, *EC Employment Law*, n 243 above, pp 94–6.

[250] Dir 96/34/EC on the framework agreement on parental leave concluded by UNICE, CEEP and the ETUC, OJ 1996, L145/4; Dir 97/81/EC concerning the framework agreement on part-time work concluded by UNICE, CEEP and the ETUC, OJ 1998, L 14/9; Dir 99/70/EC concerning the framework agreement on fixed-term work concluded by UNICE, CEEP and the ETUC, OJ 1999, L175/43.

[251] See B Keller and B Sörries, 'The New European Social Dialogue: Old Wine in New Bottles?' (1999) 9 *Journal of European Social Policy* 111 at 123.

changes affecting the Commission, the Council and the European Parliament sequentially.

The Commission lose control of the right of initiative once the second stage of negotiation commences.[252] Where the parties fail to reach an agreement, as in the first test case on EWCs, the Commission's proposal can be unfrozen and relaunched under the conventional legislative route. Where, however, an agreement is signed the parties have two choices. Either they can jointly request the Commission to propose that the Council adopt a decision to implement the agreement, or they may prefer to implement the agreement in accordance with the procedure and practices specific to management and labour and to the Member States. Where the social partners opt for the latter method a second Declaration annexed to the Agreement comes into play. The Declaration states:

. . . this arrangement implies no obligation on the Member States to apply the agreements directly or to work out rules for their transposition, nor any obligation to amend national legislation in force to facilitate their implementation.

While this Declaration has been criticised for stripping Article 4(2) [now 139(2) EC] of much of its potential for producing national legislation as a result of the social dialogue[253] and undermining the obligation to implement,[254] it is no more than a statement of the obvious in the sense that any agreement between the social partners at Community level will only be given normative effect by national practice and procedure which, in the absence of binding Community legislation, must be understood as purely voluntary. Moreover, the Declaration helps to avoid the problem that may arise where the national affiliates of the Community-wide social partners have been outvoted but, as independent voluntary organisations, would not expect to have such a decision imposed on them.[255] In practice, however, any coherent implementation would be extremely unlikely due to major legal and institutional differences between national industrial relations systems and the need to ensure 100 per cent coverage.[256] The Commission, aware of the limitations of this method, have merely called for information and monitoring procedures to ensure 'effective implementation' at national level.[257] Therefore this route has limited utility,[258] but it offers an alternative for sectoral agreements that may not be suitable for conversion into

---

[252] Betten, n 224 above at 29, describes this as a 'hijacking' of the Commission's initiative.
[253] See Whiteford (1993, *European Law Review*) n 80 above at 210.
[254] See Bercusson (1992, *Industrial Relations Journal*) n 33 above at 187–8.
[255] See E Franssen, 'Implementation of European Collective Agreements: Some Troublesome Issues' (1998) 5 *Maastricht Journal* 53 at 58.
[256] See Keller and Sörries (1999, *Journal of European Social Policy*) n 251 above at 119.
[257] *Adapting and Promoting the Social Dialogue at Community Level*, COM(98) 322, para 5.4.1.
[258] See B Hepple, *European Social Dialogue—Alibi or Opportunity* (Institute of Employment Rights, London: 1993) p 31; Brinkmann, n 47 above at 256.

binding Community directives, or agreements concerning areas falling outside Article 2 [now 137 EC] such as pay. When this route was tested for the first time in July 1997 the agreement in question had precisely these characteristics.[259]

Where the social partners opt for the former method, the Commission, as part of its overall responsibility to ensure 'balanced participation' of management and labour, must make a value judgment on the representative status of the contracting parties,[260] their mandate and the 'legality' of each clause in the agreement in relation to Community law including the clause on SMEs.[261] At this stage, it has been suggested that the Commission's role can be likened to that of a 'waitress' serving up the agreement in the form of a proposal to the Council.[262] This is not strictly correct. The Commission retains the right not to propose a measure in accordance with Article 155 [now 211] EC. As a matter of policy, however, the Commission has declared that, following the formal examination of the agreement, it will propose its adoption 'as concluded'.[263] In practice the Commission has proposed a draft directive with the sole purpose of putting into legal effect the agreement negotiated by the social partners, which is attached as an annex.[264] With respect to the implementation of agreements between the social partners, the Commission has twice proposed the insertion of a non-discrimination clause in the main body of the draft directive to which the agreement has been annexed.[265] This approach might suggest that the Commission is concerned with the wider public interest and wants to fend off the accusation that special interest groups have captured the legislative

---

[259] The agreement concerned pay levels and the reduction of working time in the agricultural sector. Two further sectoral agreements have been reached on the organisation of working time in maritime transport and railways, both in Sept 1998. For further details on the sectoral dialogue see the Commission's *Report on Industrial Relations in Europe—2000*, COM(2000) 113, pp 6–7.

[260] See E Franssen & A Jacobs, 'The Question of Representativity in the European Social Dialogue' (1998) 35 *Common Market Law Review* 1295 at 1306. In Case T–135/96, *UEAPME v Council* [1998] ECR II–2335, the CFI held, at paras 88–9, that both the Council and the Commission are under a duty to verify that the signatories to the agreement are truly representative.

[261] See COM(93) 600, para 39. Where the Commission considers that it should not present a proposal for a Council decision to implement an agreement to the Council, it will immediately inform the parties of the reasons for its decision.

[262] See Weiss, n 49 above at 12; cf Betten, n 224 above at 33.

[263] COM(93) 600, paras 38–39. This is consistent with the wording of the Oct 1991 agreement between the social partners. See *Social Europe 2/95*, p 149.

[264] See for example, Art 1 of the Parental Leave Dir, 96/34/EC, OJ 1996, L145/4.

[265] See COM(96) 26, the Commission proposal concerning the agreement on parental leave. Art 2(5) of the draft directive read: 'When the Member States adopt the provisions . . . they shall prohibit any discrimination based on race, sex, sexual orientation, colour, religion or nationality'. See also COM(97) 392 concerning the agreement on part-time work. Art 3 of the draft read: 'When Member States adopt the provisions to implement this Directive, these shall prohibit any discrimination based on sex, race, ethnic origin, religion or beliefs, disability, age or sexual orientation'.

process.[266] In practice, however, the Commission's room for manoeuvre is limited and, although this addition would not have affected the substance of the text agreed by the social partners, on each occasion the Council rejected the proposed clause. Nevertheless, the Commission retains a degree of discretion over its proposal, providing the agreement between the parties remains untouched.[267]

Turning now to the position of the Council. On a literal reading of the first paragraph of Article 4(2) [now 139(2) EC] it might appear that the Council, the Community's most powerful institution, loses all of its discretion in this area. On the face of it, following a proposal by the Commission, an agreement negotiated by the social partners *'shall be implemented . . . by a Council decision'*. Further guidance may, however, be gleaned from the somewhat obtuse wording of the second paragraph. Although this paragraph does not explicitly refer to a right to reject an agreement negotiated by the social partners, such a right must exist by implication because Article 4(2) [now 139(2) EC] directly refers to the requirements for QMV and unanimity under Articles 2(2) and 2(3) [137(2) and 137(3) EC] respectively. Moreover, the discretion of the Council to reject an agreement will not be fettered, for it ultimately has the power of decision under Article 145 [now 202] EC. Therefore an agreement under Article 4(1) [139(1) EC] may fail, not because the Council has not attempted to act with a view to its implementation, but because the necessary majority has not been achieved.[268] Under these circumstances an agreement between the social partners would, at most, have contractual force between them as signatories but it would not have normative effect.[269] The Commission, in its Communication on the application of the Agreement, have determined that where the Council rejects a proposal under this procedure they will withdraw it and examine whether a legislative instrument in the area in question would be appropriate.[270] In theory, the social partners could seek to amend their own agreement to make it acceptable to the Council but this would normally require the entire Article 4 [139 EC] process to be restarted.[271]

Having established that the Council has the power to reject a Commission proposal to implement an agreement signed by the social partners, a further question arises concerning the Council's power to make amendments. According to the Commission, the Council has no opportunity to amend such an agreement.[272] Instead the Council's decision must be limited

---

[266] See Obradovic, n 222 above at 371.

[267] See Franssen, n 255 above at 57–8.

[268] See G Britz and M Schmidt, 'The Institutionalised Participation of Management and Labour in the Legislative Activities of the European Community: A Challenge to the Principle of Democracy under Community Law' (2000) 6 *European Law Journal* 45 at 54.

[269] *Ibid* at 52.

[270] COM(93) 600, para 42.

[271] See Franssen, n 255 above at 59.

[272] COM(93) 600, para 38.

to making the provisions of the agreement binding, so the text of the agreement would not form part of the decision, but would be annexed thereto.[273] Although the Council has accepted that it cannot modify an agreement,[274] some Member States, who were concerned about the content of the first agreement on parental leave, expressed the view that certain matters were the responsibility of national authorities or raised procedural or institutional issues.[275] Several scholarly writers have endorsed the Commission's view.[276] The Council does, however, have an overriding power under Article 189a [now 250] EC to make amendments on a legislative proposal from the Commission, providing unanimity can be secured. Franssen suggests that the Council may amend the Commission's proposal but not the annexed agreement.[277] An alternative view is that the Council has the power *de jure* to amend an agreement under Article 250 EC but will not exercise this power in practice because of the political consequences.[278] Indeed if the Council were to make amendments to agreements negotiated between the social partners it would undermine the balance of power between the organisations represented in the social dialogue and destroy confidence in the very system constructed by Articles 3 and 4 [now 138 and 139 EC].[279] The Commission, who regard the text of an agreement between the social partners as sacrosanct, went so far as to warn the Council that, if it amended the agreement on parental leave, the proposal would be withdrawn.[280] The Council has taken heed of this advice. To date five proposals for directives have been adopted unamended—three cross-sectoral[281] and two sectoral.[282] None have been rejected.

---

[273] *Ibid* para 41.

[274] Opinion of 31 March 1994. Council Document 6116/94. See Brinkmann, n 47 above at 254.

[275] See *Commission Communication concerning the Development of the Social Dialogue at Community Level*, COM(96) 448, para 68.

[276] See Betten, n 224 above at 33; Britz and Schmidt, n 268 above at 55; Watson, n 47 above at 66.

[277] See Franssen, n 255 above at 58.

[278] See Franssen and Jacobs, n 260 above, who note, at 1306, that the Council 'seems to refrain from amending the text and to restrict itself to adopting or rejecting the agreement'.

[279] On this point, see Franssen, n 255 above at 58.

[280] COM(96) 26, point 30.

[281] Dir 96/34/EC on the framework agreement on parental leave concluded by UNICE, CEEP and the ETUC, OJ 1996, L145/4; Dir 97/81/EC concerning the framework agreement on part-time work concluded by UNICE, CEEP and the ETUC, OJ 1998, L 14/9; Dir 99/70/EC concerning the framework agreement on fixed-term work concluded by UNICE, CEEP and the ETUC, OJ 1999, L175/43.

[282] Dir 99/63/EC concerning the Agreement on the organisation of working time of seafarers concluded by the European Community Shipowners' Association (ECSA) and the Federation of Transport Workers' Unions in the European Union (FST), OJ 1999, L167/33; Dir 2000/79/EC concerning the European Agreement on the Organisation of Working Time of Mobile Workers in Civil Aviation concluded by the Association of European Airlines (AEA) the European Transport Workers' Federation (ETF) the European Cockpit Association (ECA) the European Regions Airline Association (ERA) and the International Air Carrier Association (IACA), OJ 2000, L302/57.

An alternative option available to the Council would be to adopt a 'decision' to implement an agreement negotiated by the social partners by issuing another Community instrument instead of a directive. This raises the possibility that the Council may choose a non-binding instrument such as a recommendation because a 'decision' in the context of Article 4(2) [now 139(2) EC] is a generic term that encompasses a range of legislative and non-legislative options available to the Council.[283] Such an approach would, however, frustrate the will of the signatories of an agreement who are seeking to give it legal effect.[284] The Commission, seeking to avoid such an outcome, has stressed that a 'decision' refers to one of the binding legislative instruments in Article 189 [now 249] EC and that the Commission should choose the appropriate measure.[285] There would be a stronger case for the Council to adopt a non-binding measure where the subject matter is concerned with areas covered by Article 2(3) [now 137(3) EC], where the form of instrument is left open, than Article 2(2) [now 137(2) EC], where directives are specified. The Council has not pursued the non-legislative option to date, although it may offer a way out where it does not wish to be seen to reject an agreement outright.

For the European Parliament the effect has been even more unsettling. As soon as negotiations between the parties commence, Parliament is effectively locked out of the process, a position that is only retrieved if the negotiations are unsuccessful. Where the negotiations result in an agreement, Article 4(2) [now 139(2) EC] assigns no role for the Parliament, pre-empting its right to involvement under the co-operation, and now co-decision, procedures provided for under, respectively, Article 2(2) of the Agreement and now Article 137(2) EC. The Commission, aware of the sensitivity of excluding the Community's only directly elected representative institution, has determined that, although it is not legally obliged to consult the Parliament, it will, nevertheless, inform them at all stages and send them the text of the agreement, together with its proposal for a decision and the explanatory memorandum, so that Parliament may, 'should it consider it advisable', deliver its opinion to the Commission and the Council.[286]

While critical of its time-consuming and cumbersome operation,[287] Parliament has not expressly objected to the Article 4(2) [now 139(2) EC] procedure because it is generally supportive of the participation of civil

---

[283] See Bercusson (1994, *Industrial Law Journal*) n 49 above at 28. As Bercusson notes the reference to a 'decision' is not to be confused with a 'decision' under Art 189 [now 249] EC which is a specific legislative instrument binding on those to whom it is addressed, as distinct from a directive that is addressed only to Member States.

[284] See Bercusson, *ibid*.

[285] COM(96) 26, p 7. See Barnard, *EC Employment Law*, n 243 above, p 93.

[286] COM(93) 600, para 40.

[287] See European Parliament Report on the Framework Agreement on Parental Leave [1996] A4–0064/96, p 8. Discussed by Obradovic, n 222 above at 366.

society in Union policy formation.[288] Where, however, the Council may be considering rejecting an agreement of the social partners, Parliament has insisted on its prior right to be consulted and issue an opinion.[289] The Committee on Employment and Social Affairs has been more forthright, calling for Parliament to be granted the power of co-decision in the form of a simple power to reject or approve, putting Parliament on a par with the Council in the framework of the legislative procedure arising from Article 4(2) [now 139(2) EC].[290] In reserving the right to intervene, Parliament is asserting its institutional prerogative to play an actual part in the legislative process of the Community.[291] Parliament's participation has been recognised by the Court as a fundamental democratic principle that the peoples should take part in the exercise of power through the intermediary of a representative assembly.[292]

In the *UEAPME*[293] case, discussed in more detail in the next section, the CFI reiterated the democratic principle[294] but noted that, in the framework of the Agreement on Social Policy, democratic legitimacy derives from Parliament's participation in the conventional legislative procedure under Article 2(2) [now 137(2) EC].[295] In contrast, where the procedure under Article 4(2) [now 139(2) EC] is activated, the CFI found that there is no provision for the participation of Parliament.[296] Nevertheless, the fundamental principle of democracy, which is a foundation for the Union under Article F.1 [now 6(1)] TEU,[297] requires that 'the participation of the people be otherwise assured'.[298] The CFI concluded that, in order to make sure that the requirement of democracy is complied with, the Commission and the Council are 'under a duty to verify that the signatories to the agreement are truly representative'.[299] Unless the parties are 'sufficiently representative' the Commission and the Council must refuse to implement the agreement at Community level.[300] Therefore, for the CFI, the issues of democratic

---

[288] See European Parliament Resolution on the new social dimension of the European Union, OJ 1994, C77/30. Discussed by Obradovic, *ibid* pp 363–66.

[289] *Ibid.*

[290] Report on the Commission Communication concerning the development of the social dialogue at Community level [1997] A4–0226/97. Discussed by K Armstrong, 'Governance and the Single European Market' in Craig & de Búrca, n 109 above, 745–89 at 769–70.

[291] Case 138/79, *Roquette Frères v Council* [1980] ECR 3333, para 33.

[292] *Ibid.* See also, Case C–300/89, *Commission v Council* [1991] ECR I–2867, para 20; Case 139/79, *Maizena v Council* [1980] ECR 3393, para 34.

[293] Case T–135/96, *UEAPME v Council* [1998] ECR II–2335.

[294] Para 88.

[295] *Ibid.*

[296] Para 89.

[297] Art 6(1) TEU provides that: 'The Union is founded on the principles of liberty, democracy, respect for human rights and fundamental freedoms, and the rule of law, principles which are common to the Member States'.

[298] Para 89.

[299] *Ibid.*

[300] Para 90.

legitimacy and representativeness are inextricably linked and yet, even if the parties are deemed to be 'sufficiently representative' according to objective criteria laid down by the Commission,[301] can the democratic principle be satisfied when only a fraction of workers in the European Union are represented in this law-making procedure[302] and an even smaller proportion of the population as a whole?[303] Furthermore, unlike a democratically elected parliament the decisions of the social partners are formulated in closed sessions by 'representatives' whose decisions are not traceable back to the people.[304] An exploration of the background to the *UEAPME* case may help us to unpick this problem.

(3) Representativeness—Testing the Criteria

When considering the issues of representativeness and democratic legitimacy two related questions keep recurring. Who are management and labour and, assuming that they can be identified, why should they have a stake in the legislative process in the area of social policy?

Representativeness is the key criterion for determining the identity of 'management and labour'.[305] This is hardly a new issue. Indeed representativeness has proved to be a thorny problem ever since the foundation of international tripartitism in 1919. The International Court of Justice was asked to determine the question in the context of the International Labour Organisation as early as 1927.[306] Within the Community arena the issue had to be addressed at the outset with the appointment of representatives to the Consultative Committee of the European Coal and Steel Community[307] and the Economic and Social Committee (ECOSOC).[308] By the time

---

[301] COM(93) 600, para 24. Discussed below.

[302] In 1990 the share of organised employees ranged from 80% in Denmark to as low as 18% in Greece and 10% in Spain and France. The available evidence suggests that trade union membership has declined during the 1990s. Moreover, atypical workers and women workers are under-represented within unions. For further details, see Schmidt, n 248 above at 265–66.

[303] On this point, see Betten, n 224 above at 32.

[304] See Schmidt, n 248 above at 260; Britz & Schmidt, n 268 above at 65–6.

[305] See Bercusson & van Dijk, n 57 above at 12–13.

[306] See the *Serrarens* case, *Recuil International de Jurisprudence du Travail*, Geneva, 1927. See Franssen and Jacobs, n 260 above at 1312.

[307] Under Art 18 ECSC the Committee consists of an equal number of producers, workers, consumers and purveyors. The Council has responsibility both for assigning the representative organisations to serve on the Committee and appointing the members from the list of candidates nominated by the organisations. In the 1970s this system was challenged by the French trade union CFDT, which had not been included among the new appointments despite being the second largest confederation of trade unions in France. The legal challenge failed on the grounds of admissibility because the ECSC Treaty did not permit private actors to bring annulment proceedings—Case 66/76, *CFDT v Council* [1977] ECR 305. See Franssen and Jacobs, *ibid* at 1296–97.

[308] Art 195(3) [now 259(3)] EC provides that before appointing members of ECOSOC the Council may consult 'representative' European organisations. See Franssen and Jacobs, *ibid* at 1296.

of the TEU there was already a well established procedure for involving the three largest Community-wide organisations in the social dialogue process namely: the ETUC,[309] representing affiliated trade union confederations; and UNICE and CEEP,[310] representing affiliated employers' organisations in, respectively, the private and public sectors. The Commission, in its 1993 Communication, was inclined to favour the status quo on the grounds that there was a 'substantial body of experience' already in place among these organisations.[311] In fact the elevated position of each of these organisations has been, and remains, fiercely contested.[312] The Commission, aware of the sensitivity of the issue and its duty to ensure 'balanced participation', conducted a study of the representativeness of the social partners at all-industry level in advance of its 1993 Communication.[313] The Commission drew two main messages from the study:[314]

(a) the diversity of practice in the different Member States is such that there is no single model which could be replicated at European level, and
(b) the different Member States' systems having all taken many years to grow and develop, it is difficult to see how a European system can be created by administrative decision in the short term.

Despite these obvious drawbacks the Commission proceeded to draw up three criteria for organisations to be consulted. They should:[315]

—be cross industry or relate to specific sectors or categories and be organised at European level;
—consist of organisations which are themselves an integral and recognised part of Member State social partner structures and with the capacity to negotiate agreements, and which are representative of all Member States, as far as possible;
—have adequate structures to ensure their effective participation in the consultation process.

The Commission appended a list of 29 organisations that complied broadly with these criteria.[316] Each of these organisations would be consulted at the

---

[309] For a comprehensive assessment of the ETUC, see K Abbott, 'The European Trade Union Confederation: Its Organisation and Objectives in Transition' (1997) 35 *Journal of Common Market Studies* 465.
[310] See F Traxler, 'Employers and Employer Organisations' in Towers and Terry, n 246 above, 99–111.
[311] COM(93) 600, para 25.
[312] On the trade union side there are two rival European organisations—CESI (*Confédération Européenne des Syndicats Indépendants*) and CEC (*Confédération Européenne des Cadres*). On the employers side UEAPME (*Union Européenne de l'Artisan et des Petits et Moyennes Entreprises*) claim to be the most representative organisation for SMEs. Other groups who claim to be under-represented include the civil service (who are not affiliated to CEEP, which only represents public enterprises), agricultural employers, hoteliers and the liberal professions. See Franssen and Jacobs, n 260 above at 1299.
[313] COM(93) 600. Annex 3.
[314] *Ibid* para 23.
[315] *Ibid* para 24.
[316] COM(93) 600. Annex 2. For an updated list, see COM(98) 322. Annex I.

first stage but, while not wishing to take a restrictive view of the issue, the Commission was conscious of the practical problems posed by a multiplicity of potential actors. They concluded that only the organisations themselves would be in a position to develop their own dialogue and negotiating structures.[317] Therefore, the Commission was prepared to grant autonomy to the social partners at the critical negotiation stage even though this inevitably favoured the established actors. The Commission, having rejected the idea of establishing an umbrella liaison committee,[318] was only prepared to offer a vague promise to those organisations left out in the cold to promote wider involvement and pay 'special attention' to the 'due representation' of SMEs.[319]

The Commission's criteria have been widely criticised. Bercusson and van Dijk object to the use of representativeness as the main criterion when it is not necessarily the most straightforward method of identifying management and labour.[320] The criteria were too closely linked to the representativeness of Member States rather than the direct link between the organisations concerned and their members. The ECOSOC Opinion on the Commission's Communication focused on the need to ensure the involvement of European social partners who, by reaching agreement, would be capable of binding national social partners and affecting directly, or by extension, all workers and employees in the Member States.[321] The European Parliament stressed the need for the social partners to have a mandate from their members to represent them in the context of Community social dialogue and to demonstrate their representativeness.[322] While both of these suggestions offer potential for wider and more representative involvement, they still fail to overcome the Commission's concerns about diversity and the need to avoid imposing a system on the social partners.

In its 1996 Communication, the Commission responded to these criticisms by agreeing to examine each agreement to determine 'whether those affected by the agreement have been represented' and 'whether those involved in the

---

[317] *Ibid* para 26.
[318] *Ibid* para 27.
[319] *Ibid* para 26.
[320] Bercusson and van Dijk, n 57 above at 14–17.
[321] OJ 1994, C397/40, para 2.1.12. At para 2.1.9. ECOSOC proposed two alternative criteria for determining representativeness:

(a) designate as representative EC level social partners those organisations recognised by national social partners deemed representative by national law and practice;
(b) the social partners at EC level are to be selected having regard to the nature of the process and of the outcome of EC social dialogue. These would indicate transnational criteria linked to national social partners and organisational capacity.

[322] Report of the Committee on Social Affairs, Employment and the Working Environment, on the Application of the Agreement on Social Policy [1994] A3–0269/94, PE 207.928-/fin.

negotiations have a genuine interest in the matter and can demonstrate significant representation in the domain concerned'.[323] Unfortunately the Commission did not add or redefine the criteria to assist them in this process.[324] Ultimately, the Commission maintained that it cannot select the negotiators and must leave it to the social partners to decide who satisfies the criteria.[325] When reviewing the position again in 1998, the Commission simply reaffirmed the original three criteria.[326] This creates a serious inconsistency for, as Schmidt notes, the Commission's criteria are strictly formal, relating only to the associations' organisational structure, and say nothing about whether the agreement in question adequately addresses the interests that it affects and supposedly represents.[327] This criticism strikes at the kernel of the representativeness question for, as Betten observes, 'UNICE, CEEP and ETUC . . . may be the most representative of all organisations, but they still do not represent a majority of employers and workers'.[328] It was precisely this problem that was brought to a head when the first Framework Agreement on Parental Leave was signed in December 1995.

On 5 September 1996, UEAPME,[329] which claimed to represent the largest number of small and medium-sized employers at a pan-European level, challenged the Parental Leave Directive[330] before the Court of First Instance (CFI) because it claimed to have been 'systematically excluded from the negotiations' which led to the adoption of the Framework Agreement 'even though it had on several occasions expressed the wish to be included and given reasons why it should be'.[331] While accepting that it had been involved in the first stage consultations, UEAPME's case was that, regardless of the subject matter, the same trinity of 'European social partners' acted as a 'closed shop' at the negotiation stage.[332] UEAPME applied for judicial review under Article 173 [now 230] EC seeking to annul the whole Directive, or to annul it with respect solely to its application to SMEs as referred to in Article 2(2) [now 137(2) EC].[333] While a series of arguments[334] were put forward in support of their claim, the critical issue was admissibility. The fourth paragraph of Article 173 [now 230] EC states:

---

[323] COM(96) 448, para 16.
[324] See Schmidt, n 248 above at 263.
[325] COM(96) 448, para 14.
[326] COM(98) 322.
[327] Schmidt, n 248 above at 264.
[328] Betten, n 224 above at 32.
[329] *Union Européenne de l'Artisant et des Petits et Moyennes Entreprises.*
[330] Dir 96/34/EC, OJ 1996, L 145/4.
[331] OJ 1996, C318/21.
[332] See Betten, n 224 above at 31.
[333] Case T–135/96, *UEAPME v Council* [1998] ECR II–2335, para 19.
[334] Annulment was sought on five grounds: (i) infringement of Arts 3(1) and 4(1) [now 138(1) and 139(1) EC]; (ii) breach of the principle *patere legem quam ipse fecisti*; (iii) discrimination between the various representative organisations; (iv) infringement of Art 2(2) [now 137(2) EC] and; (v) breach of the principles of subsidiarity and proportionality.

Any natural or legal person may ... institute proceedings against a decision addressed to that person or against a decision which, although in the form of a regulation or a decision addressed to another person, is of direct and individual concern to the former.

On this point the CFI noted that the mere fact that the contested measure was a directive was not sufficient to render such an action inadmissible.[335] The Community institutions could not, merely through their choice of legal instrument, deprive individuals of the judicial protection offered by Article 173 [now 230] EC.[336] Notwithstanding the fact that the Directive was a legislative act rather than an individual 'decision' it was still possible for UEAPME to be individually concerned if it could show that it affected them by reason of circumstances which differentiated them from all other persons.[337] Therefore, UEAPME would have to establish that they possessed special rights in the context of the procedural measures for the adoption of the Directive.[338]

The CFI found that the SME clause in Article 2(2) [now 137(2) EC] did not convey an automatic right for the representatives of SMEs to participate in the negotiations.[339] It followed that they did not have a general right to participate in the negotiation stage or an individual right to participate in the negotiation of a framework agreement.[340] However, that was not sufficient to render the action inadmissible. In view of the particular features of the procedure it was also necessary to determine whether UEAPME's rights had been infringed as a result of any failure on the part of either the Commission or the Council to fulfil their obligations under that procedure.[341] The representativeness test bites at this point because both the Commission and Council have a duty to verify the representativeness of the signatories to the agreement because they are responsible for 'endowing an agreement concluded between management and labour with a Community foundation of a legislative character'.[342] This obliges them to ascertain whether 'having regard to the content of the agreement in question', the signatories are 'sufficiently representative'.[343] Where that degree of representativeness is lacking:[344]

---

[335] *UEAPME*, para 63. See Case C–298/89, *Gibraltar v Council* [1993] ECR I–3605.

[336] *UEAPME*, para 63. See Case T–122/96, *Federolio v Commission* [1997] ECR II–1559, para 50.

[337] *UEAPME*, para 69. See Case 25/62, *Plaumann v Commission* [1963] ECR 95 at 107; Case T–12/93, *CCE de Vittel and Others v Commission* [1995] ECR II–1247, para 36; and Case T–122/96, *ibid* para 59.

[338] *UEAPME*, para 70.

[339] Para 80.

[340] Para 82.

[341] Para 83.

[342] Para 88.

[343] Para 90.

[344] *Ibid*. Emphasis added.

... the representatives of management and labour which were consulted by the Commission ... but which were not parties to the agreement, and *whose particular representation*—again in relation to the content of the agreement—*is necessary in order to raise the collective representativity of the signatories to the required level*, have the right to prevent the Commission and the Council from implementing the agreement at Community level by means of a legislative instrument.

In those circumstances the non-signatory representatives of management and labour would have the necessary direct and individual concern to bring an annulment action.[345]

Was UEAPME's participation in the negotiations necessary to achieve the required level of 'collective representativity'? The CFI answered in the negative for the following reasons. First, the Framework Agreement was based on minimum requirements for all employment relationships whatever their form and therefore all signatories had to represent all categories of undertakings and workers at Community level. UNICE met these requirements in the private sector because its membership included SMEs.[346] CEEP has a general mandate across the public sector.[347] Secondly, the proportion of SMEs represented, respectively, by UNICE and UEAPME, could not be regarded as a decisive criterion because the Directive was concerned with the employment relationship and two-thirds of the employees concerned worked for SMEs linked with UNICE.[348] Thirdly, UEAPME were involved at the consultation stage and the Framework Agreement did take account of the SME clause in Article 2(2) [now 137(2) EC].[349] The action was therefore inadmissible because the Commission and the Council, acting in conformity with their obligations, in particular those derived from the fundamental democratic principle, had properly taken the view that the collective representativeness of the signatories was sufficient in relation to the Framework Agreement's content for its implementation at Community level as a Directive.[350]

The most remarkable feature of the CFI judgment is, perhaps deliberately, understated. In essence, Articles 3 and 4 of the Agreement [now 138 and 139 EC] operate in accordance with a specific application of the fundamental democratic principle that replaces representation of the people by the European Parliament with representation of employers and workers by social partners deemed to be cumulatively representative by the Commission and the Council. Franssen and Jacobs support the approach of the CFI because it judges the representativeness of the totality of the signatory

---

[345] *Ibid.*

[346] Paras 98–9.

[347] Para 100.

[348] Paras 102–4.

[349] Paras 105–9. The CFI cited clause 2.3(f) of the Framework Agreement which states that the Member States and/or management and labour may, in particular: 'authorise special arrangements to meet the operational and organisational requirements of small undertakings'.

[350] Para 110.

parties rather than any single organisation.[351] This argument is superficially attractive but it rests on two misconceived assumptions. Firstly, it equates what the CFI describes as 'collective representativity' with democratic legitimacy, when the latter is derived from the people, usually, but not exclusively, through the prism of a parliamentary system of governance. The CFI, and indeed the Commission criteria, ignore the fact that, as Britz and Schmidt observe, democratic legitimacy and representativeness are two very different animals.[352] Secondly, while the social dialogue offers an alternative mode of involvement in decision making by citizens,[353] the CFI has favoured a narrow representation-based model of democracy that, as Bernard contends, is concerned with the procedural aspects of the social dialogue, rather than a wider participatory model that legitimates on the basis of outcomes.[354]

Consider, for example, the subject matter of the framework agreements on parental leave, part-time and fixed-term work. If we take, as a starting point, the fact that trade unions and employers' organisations are per se the most representative bodies of workers and employers, despite the evidence of declining membership and affiliations, the representativeness deficit is compounded when one considers that the proportion of part-time, fixed-term and temporary workers who are unionised is considerably lower than the proportion within the workforce.[355] In particular women are under-represented, a fact recognised both by the ETUC[356] and the Commission.[357] Those most concerned with the outcome of these agreements, predominantly female carers and atypical workers, were largely disconnected from the process. Precisely the same argument applies to employers' organisations like UEAPME. As Bernard notes, UNICE may represent many SMEs because of its broad coverage of employers of all sizes, but UEAPME constitutes a different 'voice' because it exists exclusively to represent and advocate for SMEs.[358]

An alternative critique of the judgment in *UEAPME* has been put forward by Bercusson who persuasively argues that the autonomy of the

---

[351] Franssen and Jacobs, n 268 above at 1309.

[352] Britz and Schmidt, n 260 above at 66.

[353] See Bernard, n 233 above at 281.

[354] *Ibid* at 284.

[355] See Schmidt, n 248 above at 265.

[356] An ETUC study found that the presence of women in trade union decision-making bodies across Europe had risen from 23% to 28% in the period from 1993–1998: *The Second Sex of European Trade Unionism* (ETUC and Catholic University of Louvain, Brussels, 1999).

[357] See the Commission proposal for a Council Decision on the Programme relating to the Community framework strategy on gender equality (2001–2005), COM(2000) 335. Para 3.2 states that the 'persistent under-representation of women in all areas of decision making marks a fundamental democratic deficit which requires Community level action'. See also, Council Recommendation 96/694/EC on the balanced participation of women and men in the decision-making process, OJ 1996, L319/11.

[358] Bernard, n 233 above at 288.

social partners has been compromised by the additional supervision require-ments on the Commission, the Council and, ultimately, the Court.[359] In his view the CFI has chosen the wrong conceptual framework by equating the social dialogue with the legislative process.[360] These are dual processes of creating Community labour law brought together by the 'amalgam' of Article 4(2) [now 139(2) EC] which allows for either Member State or Com-munity level *erga omnes* extension of collective agreements reached between private organisations.[361] The constitutional law paradigm of democratic legitimacy, institutional scrutiny and judicial review is, therefore, inappro-priate for the social dialogue that has its conceptual roots mainly in indus-trial relations.[362] Bercusson concludes that this conceptual problem can be bridged by treating both the mechanisms in Article 4(2) [now 139(2) EC] as functionally equivalent with two possible routes for achieving an *erga omnes* effect.[363] He proposes to tackle the democratic legitimacy question by promoting the idea of an agreement between the social partners and the European Parliament on a framework of negotiating rules and principles which would satisfy the 'sufficient representativity' test of the social part-ners while preserving the autonomy of the social partners.[364]

Bercusson's argument underlines both the strengths and weaknesses of involving private actors generally, and the social partners in particular, in the legislative process. While Bercusson is right to distinguish between the two different conceptual frameworks that underpin social dialogue and the conventional legislative process, his analysis does not address the fact that the process first established by the Agreement on Social Policy is a com-promise between these two conceptions that inevitably limits the autonomy of both the social partners *and* the Community institutions. In this context the social dialogue must be understood as an alternative form of lawmak-ing[365] and therefore fundamentally different from collective bargaining. Moreover, the notion of the social dialogue as national collective bargain-ing transposed into a Community framework is attractive as an abstracted view of the process but the comparison is inaccurate for three reasons. First, the notion of parallel procedures each allowing for an *erga omnes*

---

[359] See B Bercusson, 'Democratic Legitimacy and European Labour Law' (1999) 28 *Indus-trial Law Journal* 153 at 159–63. At 163, Bercusson cites Council Document 10218/98 issued by the Legal Service of the Council in the aftermath of the judgment. The Legal Service expressed concern at the degree of control retained by the Court which it regarded as exces-sive and damaging to the Council's institutional prerogatives because it amounted to a denial of its normal degree of discretion, particularly in the area of social policy.

[360] *Ibid* at 163–64.

[361] *Ibid* at 168.

[362] *Ibid* at 164–65.

[363] *Ibid* at 169.

[364] *Ibid* at 170.

[365] See Bernard, n 233 above at 287; S Fredman, 'Social Law in the European Union: The Impact of the Lawmaking Process' in Craig and Harlow, n 47 above 386–411 at 408; and Keller and Sörries (1999, *Journal of European Social Policy*) n 251 above at 120.

extension of 'collective agreements' does not match the reality because the *erga omnes* approach is not available in several Member States.[366] Second, to describe the trilateral social dialogue as akin to bilateral free collective bargaining is a misnomer because of the absence of any economic pressure, particularly in the form of industrial action or threats thereof.[367] Hence, the employers' side can refrain from the entire process with impunity, either because they oppose regulation in the area concerned, or would rather rely on initiatives at national level, citing the principle of subsidiarity.[368] Third, there is the problem of accountability. While grassroots organisations will usually be accountable to their members, there is no evidence that the power granted to management and labour at Community level has been exercised in a way that is accountable to those over whom it is wielded in a comparable manner.[369]

One advantage of promoting sectoral rather than cross-sectoral agreements is that the former are negotiated by organisations that are more directly accountable for their actions, a factor which has led the Commission to develop a specific strategy in this regard.[370] Sectoral dialogue committees have been established across 24 sectors as forums to promote social dialogue with the capacity to negotiate sectoral agreements.[371] In each case the sectoral social partners must submit a joint request and be 'sufficiently well organised with a meaningful European presence in line with the established criteria of representativeness'.[372]

Even if one accepts, at least terminologically, both Bercusson's conceptualisation of the social dialogue as a form of European 'collective bargaining' and the Commission's rhetoric of 'representativity',[373] we are still left with the related question that I posed earlier. Why should the social partners have a stake in the legislative process in the area of social policy? While this question can be addressed by measuring the essential features of social dialogue against a variety of models of representative, participative and associative democracy,[374] it cannot be separated from the debate about the role and future of the European Union which has increasingly focused

[366] For example, Denmark, Italy and the UK. See Keller and Sörries, *ibid* at 119–120; Hepple, n 258 above, pp 28–30.

[367] See Bernard, n 233 above at 286.

[368] As in the case of the proposal for information or consultation of workers or their representatives at national level, COM(98) 612. See E Szyszczak, 'The New Parameters of European Labour Law' in D O'Keeffe and P Twomey (eds.) *Legal Issues of the Amsterdam Treaty* (Hart, Oxford, 1999) 141–55 at 150.

[369] See Obradovic, n 222 above at 356.

[370] See Commission Dec 98/500/EC on the establishment of Sectoral Dialogue Committees Promoting the Dialogue between the social partners at European level, OJ 1998, L225/27.

[371] COM(2000) 113, p 6.

[372] Art 1 of Commission Dec 98/500/EC, OJ 1998, L225/27. For further discussion, see Barnard, *EC Employment Law*, n 243 above, pp 102–4; and B Keller and B Sörries, 'Sectoral Social Dialogue: New Opportunities or Impasses?' (1999) 30 *Industrial Relations Journal* 330.

[373] See Britz & Schmidt, n 268 above at 69.

[374] See generally, Bernard, n 233 above; and Fredman, n 365 above at 408–11.

on its legitimacy as an entity.[375] Indeed, following on from the referenda in Denmark, France and Ireland in 1992–93,[376] fundamental questions were asked about the lack of consent among the peoples of Europe for the concept of a Union, leading to an ongoing legitimacy crisis.[377]

The 'Reflection Group',[378] established to report to the institutions in the run-up to the planned 1996 IGC, addressed the twin concerns of openness and accountability, an approach echoed in the institutional responses,[379] which sought to bring 'Europe closer to the people'[380] and to make it the 'business of every citizen'.[381] Only in this way would it be possible to enhance the Union's credibility and to 'ensure grassroots involvement in the integration process'.[382] These reports emphasised the *social aspect* of legitimacy rooted in popular consent[383] with the Treaties as a form of 'social contract' between EU citizens.[384] Paradoxically, the social dialogue, despite its limitations when measured against both the representative and participative models of democracy, helps to fill a gap in the Union's system of governance by giving private citizens, broadly representing the 'two sides of industry', a stake in both the construction and implementation of European labour law. Moreover, these are roles to which they appear to be ideally suited because of their intimate knowledge of the realities of the workplace.[385] For the Commission, the social dialogue is the 'ideal instrument for the harmonious development of the Commission's social policy'.[386] This linkage between the citizen and the Union can also be presented as an expression of a form of 'horizontal subsidiarity'[387] at the Community level

[375] See G de Búrca, 'The Quest for Legitimacy in the European Union' (1996) 59 *Modern Law Review* 349; D Curtin, 'Betwixt and Between: Democracy and Transparency in the Governance of the European Union' in Winter *et al*, n 25 above, 95–121; and J Weiler, U Haltern and F Mayer, 'European Democracy and its Critique' (1995) 18 *Western European Politics* 4.

[376] On 2 June 1992, 50.7% of the Danish electorate voted *nej* to the TEU, a vote that was reversed following concessions to Denmark, with 56.8% voting in favour, on 18 May 1993. Referendums in Ireland, on 18 June 1992, and France, on 20 Sept 1992, were hard fought with a very close *oui* vote in France. See D Curtin and R van Ooik, 'Denmark and the Edinburgh Summit: Maastricht without Tears' in O'Keeffe and Twomey (1994) n 21 above, 349–65.

[377] See de Búrca (1996, *Modern Law Review*) n 375 above at 349.

[378] The Reflection Group was established in June 1994 and was composed mainly of Member State representatives. *Bulletin of the European Communities* 6–94, I.25.

[379] See de Búrca (1996, *Modern Law Review*) n 375 above at 355.

[380] Report of the Council on the Functioning of the Treaty on European Union (Council of the European Union, Brussels, 1995) p 6.

[381] Commission Report on the Operation of the Treaty on European Union, SEC(95) 731, preface, p 1.

[382] Report of the Economic and Social Committee on the 1996 Intergovernmental Conference (Brussels, 4 May 1995) I.2.

[383] See de Búrca (1996, *Modern Law Review*) n 375 above at 349.

[384] See Weiler *et al* (1995, *Western European Politics*) n 375 above at 21.

[385] See Fredman, n 365 above at 409–10.

[386] See the preface by former Commissioner Flynn in 'Social Dialogue—The Situation in the Community in 1995', *Social Europe*, 2/95, p 5.

[387] See further, Bercusson and van Dijk, n 57 above at 9–12; cf Lyon-Caen, n 1 above at 59.

arising from the choice of options in Article 4(2) [now 139(2) EC]. As the Commission explains:[388]

The Agreement confirms the fundamental role of the social partners . . . in the implementation of the social dimension at Community level. In conformity with the fundamental principle of subsidiarity . . . there is thus recognition of a *dual form of subsidiarity in the social field*: on the one hand, subsidiarity regarding regulation at national and Community level; on the other, subsidiarity as regards the choice, at Community level between the legislative approach and the agreement-based approach.

Therefore the social dialogue process creates a form of 'stakeholder democracy' that has the potential to directly connect people who will be affected by Community laws with the law making process. This potential will, however, only be realised if the process becomes more transparent, more internally democratic, more representative and more accountable. A wider range of 'stakeholders' drawn from civil society need to be represented in order to take account of other voices both inside and outside the workplace, including the unemployed and groups who are socially marginalised or excluded.[389] Otherwise the existing corporatist élite will perpetuate a consensus that excludes the majority and accentuates the sense of popular alienation associated with the persisting legitimacy crisis. While such a consensus can be superficially presented, in accordance with consociational theory,[390] as a means of gradually broadening ultimate consent to government and stabilising potentially conflicting social interests, it inevitably isolates social forces that are not fully recognised, particularly new minorities, and reinforces the status quo.[391]

VIII THE FRAMEWORK AGREEMENTS—A QUALITATIVE ASSESSMENT

In this penultimate section we will concern ourselves with the output of the Agreement on Social Policy, focusing on the quality of the legislation arising from cross-sectoral framework agreements on parental leave, part-time work and fixed-term work. When evaluating the content of these agreements, account will be taken of the inevitable compromises involved in reaching agreement during the negotiations and the broad policy parameters within which the social partners were operating.

---

[388] COM(93) 600, para 6c. Emphasis added.

[389] Only tentative steps have been taken in this direction. For example an informal and quite separate European 'civil dialogue' was launched in 1996 bringing together around 1,000 representatives including NGOs, churches and other social actors in regional and local governments. See Hervey, *European Social Law and Policy*, n 10 above, p 75.

[390] See H Daalder, 'The Consociational Democracy Theme' (1974) 26 *World Politics* 606.

[391] See Weiler *et al* (1995, *Western European Politics*) n 375 above at 30–1.

(1) Parental Leave

Directive 96/34 on Parental Leave[392] was the first measure adopted as a Council 'decision' on the basis of a Framework Agreement negotiated between the social partners under the procedure in Article 4(2) [now 139(2) EC].[393] Once the Commission had satisfactorily completed its tests to ensure the representativeness of the parties, their mandate and the legality of the clauses,[394] the Directive, having been unanimously adopted by the 'Council of the Fourteen', served simply as a wraparound mechanism to 'put into effect the annexed agreement on parental leave'[395] with an implementation date of 3 June 1998.[396] The Directive and, more particularly, the Framework Agreement, is of symbolic importance not just because of its novelty, but also because of its lengthy gestation period dating back to the Commission's first attempt to pilot a proposal in 1983 at the tail end of the first Social Action Programme,[397] by which time the UK had become well versed in wielding the veto in the social policy arena.[398] The Commission's idea was kept alive in the Social Charter[399] and, in February 1995, the Commission consulted the social partners with the aim of encouraging them to negotiate an agreement on the reconciliation of family and professional life.

In part, the Commission was seeking to promote equal opportunities in recognition of the fact that it is predominantly women who bear the dual burden of work and care,[400] but the proposal was also inextricably linked to the Community's labour market objectives centred on expanding employment levels through greater 'flexibility' in work and family life.[401] Such

---

[392] OJ 1996, L145/4, amended by Dir 97/75/EC, OJ 1998, L10/24. The amendment extends the Directive to the territory of the UK. For discussion, see M Schmidt, 'Parental Leave: Contested Procedure, Creditable Results' (1997) 13 *International Journal of Comparative Labour Law and Industrial Relations* 113.

[393] Framework Agreement concluded by ETUC, UNICE and CEEP on 14 Dec 1995. A joint letter sent by these organisations on 5 July 1995 initiated the process.

[394] See the general considerations, point 13. The Commission also informed the European Parliament and the Economic and Social Committee before submitting the proposal to the Council (general considerations, points 14 and 15).

[395] Art 1 of Dir 96/34.

[396] *Ibid.* Art 2(1). Art 2(2) allows for a maximum additional period of one year, if this is necessary to take account of special difficulties or implementation by a collective agreement. Art 2(1a) inserted by Dir 97/75, provides for an implementation date of 15 Dec 1999 for the UK.

[397] COM(1983) 686, OJ 1983, C333/6, as revised by COM(1984) 631, OJ 1984, C316/7.

[398] See E Ellis, 'Parents and Employment: An Opportunity for Progress' (1986) 15 *Industrial Law Journal* 97 at 108.

[399] Point 16 on equal treatment for men and women provides, inter alia, that 'measures should also be developed enabling men and women to reconcile their occupational and family obligations'.

[400] See T Hervey and J Shaw, 'Women, Work and Care: Women's Dual Role and Double Burden in EC Sex Equality Law' (1998) 8 *Journal of European Social Policy* 43.

[401] See the Commission's *Medium Term Social Action Programme 1995–1997*, COM(95) 134, para 5.1.2.

flexibility is double-edged for, to apply Deakin and Reed's paradigm,[402] it has both a demand side; the 'flexible firm', where employers may wish to vary labour inputs according to the state of external demand, leading to greater casualisation, and a supply side; 'family friendly' policies, where changes in labour supply reflect new lifestyle choices and responses to the changing division of labour within the household.[403] It was precisely because this delicate balance had to be struck that this topic appeared ideally suited for a negotiated compromise between the social partners. Before examining the content of the Framework Agreement let us first consider the issues that provide its backcloth.

From the early 1990s the Commission actively pursued the broad goal of 'reconciling work and family life'. This aphorism encompasses a range of policy objectives including high quality affordable care for children and dependants, parental and other family leave, job sharing, career breaks, and a reduction in the gender gap in working hours and employment participation.[404] The gender gap in employment rates is just under 20 per cent, increasing to 40 per cent when there is a child under the age of six in the household.[405] The gender gap in terms of full-time employment is significantly higher because 80 per cent of part-time workers are women.[406] In fact, notwithstanding the persisting gender gap, the trend towards an increase in the participation of women in the labour market during the 1990s has magnified the need for Community action in this area.[407] In turn, these factors have a knock on effect on the gender gap in pay because there is an inextricable link between pay, childcare and opportunities for employment and promotion.[408] All of these issues had been recognised by 1992 when a non-binding Recommendation on Childcare was adopted by the Council to urge Member States to '*take and/or progressively encourage initiatives to enable women and men to reconcile their occupational, family*

---

[402] S Deakin and H Reed, 'The Contested Meaning of Labour Market Flexibility: Economic Theory and the Discourse of European Integration' in Shaw, n 233 above, 71–99.

[403] *Ibid* at 73–5.

[404] See the Commission reports on *Reconciliation between work and family life* (European Commission DGV, Brussels, 1998); and *Gender and working time policies* (European Commission, DGV, Brussels, 1998).

[405] *Towards a Community Framework Strategy on Gender Equality (2001–2005)*, COM(2000) 335, Annex I, pp 18–19. In 1998, 51% of women were in employment compared with 71% of men. For the 20–44 age group with children under the age of five the comparative figures were 52% and 91%.

[406] *Employment in Europe 2000* (European Commission, Brussels, 2000) p 30.

[407] See generally, E Caracciolo di Torella, 'The 'family-friendly' workplace: the EC position' (2001) 17 *International Journal of Comparative Labour Law and Industrial Relations* 325; and S Fredman, 'Labour Law in Flux: the Changing Composition of the Workforce' (1997) 26 *Industrial Law Journal* 337.

[408] EUROSTAT figures for June 1999 reveal that women earn on average 28% less than men in the EU. See COM(2000) 335, p 21.

and upbringing responsibilities arising from the care of children'.[409] Four areas were identified for such initiatives:[410]

1) The provision of children-care services[411] while parents are working, are following a course of education or training in order to obtain employment, or are seeking a job or a course of education or training in order to obtain employment.
2) Special leave for employed persons with responsibility for the care and upbringing of children.
3) The environment, structure and organisation of work, to make them responsive to the needs of workers with children.
4) The sharing of occupational, family and upbringing responsibilities arising from the care of children between women and men.

While not specifying any precise period or indicating any level of payment for special leave, the Recommendation refers to both men and women having leave where they desire to 'properly discharge their occupational, family and upbringing responsibilities . . . with some flexibility as to how leave may be taken'.[412]

The Recommendation on Childcare is, intrinsically, a weak form of soft law falling within a grouping of soft laws that serve as prompters to maintain the momentum of existing programmes or, alternatively, as reminders of the Community's unfulfilled ambition.[413] Member States are merely encouraged to take initiatives that would not necessarily involve wider state provision of childcare. However, at the time of its adoption, the TEU was not yet in force, and therefore the Recommendation helped to fill a gap and provide a foundation upon which hard law could be constructed at a later date once Treaty powers were available and exercisable.[414]

As a follow-up to the Recommendation, the Commission has produced baseline data on childcare infrastructure and services in the Member States.[415] The Commission's studies have revealed disparate levels of provision in childcare in general and parental leave in particular. For example, a Commission survey of 1997[416] reported that Belgium, the UK, Ireland and

---

[409] Art 1 of Council Recommendation 92/241/EEC on childcare, OJ 1992, L123/16.

[410] Art 2.

[411] Art 2(1) defines 'children care services' as any type of childcare, whether public or private, individual or collective.

[412] Art 4.

[413] For a categorisation of Community soft law, see ch 4.

[414] See further, F Beveridge and S Nott, 'A Hard Look at Soft Law' in Craig and Harlow, n 47 above, 285–309 at 306–8.

[415] COM(94) 333, p 43. See Barnard, *EC Employment Law*, n 243 above, pp 278–80.

[416] *Equal Opportunities for Women and Men in the European Union* (European Commission, Brussels, 1997) p 64. For analysis, see G Bruning and J Plantenga, 'Parental Leave and Equal Opportunities: Experiences in Eight European Countries' (1999) 9 *Journal of European Social Policy* 195 at 196–98.

Luxembourg had no national regulations on parental leave. In the Netherlands, Spain, Greece and Portugal there was no right to paid leave. In all
other EU countries payment was made to partially compensate for loss of
earnings varying from fixed sums to a proportion of the salary.[417] The
maximum duration of leave ranged from three and half months in Greece
to three years in France and Spain. Generally leave was only available in
blocks of time and as a family right rather than an individual right. Where
leave was a family right the evidence suggested that fewer fathers took leave,
for example just 1.5 per cent in Germany in 1986.[418] In the majority of
countries leave was only available to care for children under the age of
three.[419]

There is a direct correlation between payment for leave and take-up rates.
Although parental leave was available in the majority of Member States
before the Directive was implemented, figures for 1995 show that just 5 per
cent of men in the EU exercised their right to take leave.[420] A survey of
banks in the UK where unpaid parental leave was offered, revealed that just
42 men, out of 130,000 who were eligible, had taken leave over a five-year
period.[421] Significantly, take up is highest in Denmark, Finland and Sweden
where the payment is earnings related, with Sweden having a 50 per cent
take up rate among men, a fact that has been made possible because leave
arrangements are very flexible.[422]

Therefore, when embarking on negotiations, the social partners were
faced with a number of considerations on the substance of any agreement.
An opportunity had been presented to address the reconciliation of work
and family life broadly by including provisions concerning not just parental
leave, but also more general childcare provisions, incorporating ideas
from the Childcare Recommendation, and other 'family friendly' initiatives
such as flexible working hours, career breaks and job-sharing. Several questions arose. Was it possible to cover a wide range of these areas in the
context of the principle of subsidiarity? To what extent should account be
taken of the needs of SMEs by allowing for derogations? What was the
appropriate level for 'minimum standards' and how much flexibility should
be left to the Member States on implementation? Should parental leave be
an individual right or a transferable family right? In particular, the social

[417] For example in Finland 66% of the salary was paid. In Germany there was a flat rate
of DM600 per month.
[418] See Schmidt (1997, *International Journal of Comparative Labour Law and Industrial
Relations*) n 392 above at 120.
[419] The exceptions were the Netherlands and Sweden (8) and Denmark (9).
[420] *European Network, Family and Work* 2/98 (European Commission, Brussels, 1998)
p 3.
[421] House of Commons 1998–99 Session, *Social Security Implications of Parental Leave*,
HC 543. Submission by Ruth Kelly MP: ⟨www.official-documents.co.uk/⟩. Discussed by A
McColgan, 'Family Friendly Frolics? The Maternity and Paternity Leave etc. Regulations 1999'
(2000) 29 *Industrial Law Journal* 125 at 139.
[422] See (1996) 66 *Equal Opportunities Review* 22. See McColgan, *ibid* at 140.

partners were faced with a dilemma over the issue of paid parental leave. On the one hand, they were free to negotiate an agreement on 'matters covered by Article 2', including the field of 'equality between men and women with regard to labour market opportunities'. The evidence suggested that this would only be meaningful if leave was paid. On the other hand, Article 2(6) specifically excluded the subject of 'pay'. Did this necessarily exclude paid leave in the context of the objective in Article 2(1)? These questions were particularly acute for the ETUC who wanted to make the new arrangement work but may have gained more from a directive steered by the Commission, with the support of the European Parliament and, ultimately, agreed by the Council on the basis of a compromise among the Member States.[423]

An examination of the Framework Agreement helps us to answer some but not all of these questions. The general considerations preceding the main clauses in the Agreement encapsulate four broad themes: the balancing of work and family life; equal opportunities for men and women; women's participation in the workforce; and the assumption of a more equal share of family responsibility by men.[424] Flexibility is addressed in a brief anodyne paragraph:[425]

Whereas measures to reconcile work and family life should encourage the introduction of new flexible ways of organising work and time which are better suited to the changing needs of society and which should take the needs of both undertakings and workers into account.

Clause 1 prescribes the purpose and scope of the Framework Agreement, which is to lay down minimum requirements 'designed to facilitate the reconciliation of parental and professional responsibilities for working parents'.[426] Therefore its nomenclature, as an agreement on *parental leave*, is perplexing when account is taken of the wider purpose it purports to espouse. To add to the sense of confusion, the Agreement not only grants leave to working parents[427] who have an employment contract or employment relationship,[428] but also, quite separately, gives rights to all employees to take time off work on grounds of *force majeure* for urgent 'family' reasons.[429]

Clause 2(1) grants men and women workers an individual right to parental leave on the grounds of the birth or adoption of a child to enable

---

[423] See Brinkmann, n 47 above at 258.

[424] Dir 96/34, Annex. General considerations, points 3–5 and 7–8. See McColgan, n 421 above at 140.

[425] General considerations, point 6.

[426] Clause 1(1).

[427] Clause 2.

[428] Clause 1(2) provides that the agreement 'applies to all workers, men and women, who have an employment contract or employment relationship as defined by the law, collective agreements or practices in force in each Member State'.

[429] Clause 3.

them to take care of that child, for *at least* three months, until a given age *up to* eight years to be defined by Member States and/or management and labour. The individual nature of the right is reinforced by Clause 2(2), which states that, in order to promote equal opportunities between men and women, the parties to the Agreement consider that the right to parental leave should 'in principle' be granted on a non-transferable basis. Therefore, in principle, both parents can take leave at the same time. The Agreement is, however, silent on the question of pay and gives only general guidance on the detailed application of the right beyond the minimum requirements. Clause 2(3) provides that:

The conditions of access and detailed rules for applying parental leave shall be defined by law and/or collective agreement in the Member States, as long as the minimum requirements of this agreement are respected.

Standard clauses allow for the application or introduction of 'more favourable provisions'[430] and non-retrogression,[431] although, to add to the ambiguity, the Framework Agreement allows Member States and/or management and labour to develop different legislative, regulatory or contractual positions, 'in the light of changing circumstances', including the introduction of non-transferability, as long as the minimum requirements are complied with.[432] Moreover, management and labour 'at the appropriate level' may conclude agreements 'adapting and/or complementing the provisions of this agreement in order to take account particular circumstances'.[433] It follows that the Member States and the national social partners are given a virtual *carte blanche* to deal not only with such matters as entitlement, if any, to pay, the period of leave and the age of the child, but also, specific areas listed in Clause 2(3) which will allow for more flexibility including:

(a) granting parental leave on a full-time or part-time basis, in a piecemeal way or in the form of a time-credit system;
(b) making the entitlement to parental leave subject to a work or service qualification up to a period of one year;
(c) adjustment of the conditions of access and detailed rules for applying parental leave to the 'special circumstances of adoption';
(d) establishing notice periods to be given by the worker to the employer when exercising the right to parental leave, specifying the beginning and end of the period of leave;

---

[430] Clause 4(1).
[431] Clause 4(2), which states, in its first sentence, that implementation of the agreement 'shall not constitute valid grounds for reducing the general level of protection afforded to workers in the field covered by this agreement'.
[432] Clause 4(2) second sentence.
[433] Clause 4(3).

(e) defining circumstances where, subject to consultation rights, parental leave can be postponed for 'justifiable reasons related to the operation of the undertaking' (e.g. where work is of a seasonal nature, where a replacement cannot be found within the notice period, where a significant proportion of the workforce applies for parental leave at the same time, where a specific function is of strategic importance).[434]

(f) In addition to (e) authorising special arrangements 'to meet the operational and organisational requirements of small undertakings'.[435]

What distinguishes this Agreement from mainstream Community legislation adopted hitherto, such as the Working Time Directive,[436] is that flexibility applies not just to particular groups of workers or undertakings but across the board. The thirteenth and final point in the general considerations helps to explain the rationale for this development and is indicative of the new legislative method flowing from the social dialogue process:

> Whereas management and labour are best placed to find solutions that correspond to the needs of both employers and workers and must therefore have conferred on them a special role in the implementation and application of the present agreement.

The remainder of Clause 2 offers core protection to employees who wish to exercise their right to apply for and take parental leave. Under Clause 2(4) Member States and/or management and labour shall take the necessary measures to protect workers against dismissal 'in accordance with national law, collective agreements or practices'. Clause 2(5) grants workers the right to return to the same job at the end of a period of parental leave but 'if that is not possible, to an equivalent or similar job consistent with the employment contract'. Clause 2(6) provides that rights 'acquired or in the process of being acquired by the worker on the date on which parental leave starts shall be maintained as they stand until the end of parental leave'.[437] Clause 2(7) gives some leeway to Member States and/or

---

[434] Any problem arising from the application of this provision 'should be dealt with in accordance with national law, collective agreements and practices'.

[435] Point 12 of the general considerations makes specific reference to account being taken of the SME clause in Art 2(2) of the Agreement on Social Policy [now 137(2) EC].

[436] Dir 93/104/EC, OJ 1993, L307/18.

[437] The scope of rights acquired or in the process of being acquired under Clause 2(6) has been considered by the Court in Case C–333/97, *Lewen v Denda* [2000] ECR I–7243. In this case, the employee, Mrs Lewen, took extended parenting leave in accordance with German law which states that such leave is voluntary and may last up to three years after the birth of a child during which time the contract of the employee is suspended. Mrs Lewen was excluded from the employer's Christmas bonus scheme because her contract of employment was suspended. The Court held that the bonus did not constitute a right acquired or in the process of being acquired by the worker on the date on which parental leave started since it was paid voluntarily after the start of that leave. This is a very narrow interpretation of Clause 2(6) that effectively excludes certain payments and fringe benefits that may arise only during the parental leave period. For discussion, see E Caracciolo di Torella, 'Childcare, Employment and Equality in the European Community: First (False) Steps of the Court' (2000) 25 *European Law Review* 25.

management and labour to define employment status for the period of parental leave. Clause 2(8) leaves all related matters of social security entirely to the Member States 'taking into account the importance of the continuity of the entitlements to social security cover under the different schemes, in particular health care'.[438] The general considerations indicate that Member States may take account of their 'budgetary situation'.[439]

Clause 3(1) of the Framework Agreement grants an entitlement to workers to time off from work on grounds of *force majeure* for urgent family reasons in cases of sickness or accident 'making the immediate presence of the worker indispensable'. This right applies to all workers whether or not they are parents and there can be no service qualification. Typically, a worker would be taking time off in an emergency situation concerning a partner, a child, or an elderly or dependant relative. There is no obligation on the employer to pay the worker who is taking time off. Once again Member States and/or management and labour may specify the conditions of access and detailed rules and, moreover, they may limit the exercise of this right to a certain amount of time per year or per case.

The Parental Leave Directive marks a step in the direction of reconciling work and family life,[440] but the social partners have taken that step very gingerly. The right to time off in cases of *force majeure* is fairly straightforward and offers a modicum of reassurance for an employee who has an unsympathetic employer. While the availability of parental leave is an advance, there is little in the content of the Framework Agreement to suggest that it will be widely exercised, particularly by men. Although the right to take parental leave is an individual right, consistent with the equal opportunities objective, this has to be set against the areas of discretion, such as the service qualification, which, where they are taken up by a Member State, are antithetical to that right. A survey of the implementation measures taken by the Member States,[441] reveals that several have not introduced paid leave[442] while others have applied only the minimum period of three months leave.[443] Without extended and flexible periods of paid leave it is extremely unlikely that the equality objective can be furthered, it may even be hindered.[444]

To what extent is the relative weakness of the Directive a reflection both on the procedure of legislation via social dialogue and the representativeness, or lack thereof, of the social partners involved? The evidence is not

---

[438] Point 10 of the general considerations states that Member States should maintain entitlement to benefits in kind under sickness insurance during the minimum period of parental leave.

[439] General considerations, point 11.

[440] See Schmidt (1997, *International Journal of Comparative Labour Law and Industrial Relations*) n 392 above at 124–25.

[441] *Reconciliation between work and family life* (European Commission DGV, Brussels, 1998). Discussed by McColgan, n 421 above at 143.

[442] UK, Greece, Ireland, Netherlands, Portugal and Spain.

[443] UK, Belgium, Greece and Ireland.

[444] See McColgan, n 421 above at 143.

conclusive. For a start, although the Commission proposed the Directive under Article 2(1) of the Agreement on Social Policy, as an equal opportunities measure, there was some doubt about the legal base because of the inclusion of clauses concerning termination of employment and social security.[445] In the event the Council did not need to decide whether unanimity was required since there was consensus to adopt the agreement.[446] Even if the social partners had agreed on the need for paid leave, there appears to have been no leeway for the Directive to be adopted solely on the basis of the equal opportunities objective and therefore it would not have been possible to bypass the exemption in Article 2(6) of the Agreement [now 137(6) EC].[447] Moreover, while the flexibility clauses are remarkable because of the wide discretion granted to national actors, they reflect a general trend being actively pursued by the Commission by the mid-1990s, to adapt and simplify legislation in line with the principle of subsidiarity[448] and the need to avoid placing obstacles in the way of employment and competitiveness.[449] Significantly, the Commission funded a 1995 study by UNICE into regulation and competitiveness which emphasised alternatives to Community legislation.[450] In the case of the Parental Leave Directive, the legislation reflected the 'lowest common denominator' for the social partners.[451] For the employers, or at least those employers' organisations present, they achieved a result that they could live with while avoiding the risk of more regulatory measure. For the ETUC, they demonstrated that there was no employers' veto while securing an outcome that would not necessarily have been bettered had the conventional legislative route been pursued.

(2) Part-time Work

Directives 97/81[452] on part-time work and Directive 99/70[453] on fixed-term work have a common lineage. As with parental leave, attempts to legislate

---

[445] Clauses 2(4) and 2(8).

[446] See Brinkmann, n 47 above at 255.

[447] On this point, see Ryan, n 196 above at 313–14.

[448] See COM(93) 545.

[449] See the Commission 'White Paper', *Growth, Competitiveness and Employment: The Challenges and Ways Forward into the 21st Century, Bulletin of the European Communities Supplement* 6/93; and the Report of the Independent Experts on Legislative and Administrative Simplification (the 'Molitor Report') COM(95) 288. For discussion, see Armstrong, n 290 above at 756–67.

[450] *Releasing Europe's Potential Through Targeted Regulatory Reform* (UNICE, 1995). See Armstrong, *ibid* at 759–61.

[451] See Schmidt (1999, *International Journal of Comparative Labour Law and Industrial Relations*) n 248 above at 261–62.

[452] Dir 97/81/EC concerning the framework agreement on part-time work concluded by UNICE, CEEP and the ETUC, OJ 1998, L14/9, as amended by Directive 98/23/EC, OJ 1998, L131/10. The amendment extends the Directive to the territory of the UK.

[453] Dir 99/70/EC concerning the framework agreement on fixed-term work concluded by UNICE, CEEP and the ETUC, OJ 1999, L175/43.

in this area had floundered in the early 1980s.[454] While the Commission saw legislation as a means to promote alternative work arrangements and provide a modicum of protection for workers, there was little appetite among the Member States for binding Community measures. Once again the Social Charter was to prove a catalyst for action.[455] When, in 1990, an attempt was made to simultaneously launch three proposals using different legal bases,[456] only the proposal based on Article 118a EEC was successful.[457] More contentious 'horizontal' measures concerning the working conditions of both part-time and fixed-term workers remained in draft form despite several attempts by the Commission to offer concessions and to highlight them in its annual reports on the implementation of the Charter.[458]

Once the TEU came into force the Commission switched gear. In its 1994 White Paper on Social Policy the Commission proposed a new 'vertical' directive on part-time work to be introduced as a first step.[459] Moreover, they noted that there had been dramatic changes in the labour market, both in the model of production and the service sector, leading to more flexible forms of work contract (fixed-term, temporary and part-time). In a subtle shift of emphasis, the Commission observed that this had occurred not only because management wanted to increase flexibility, but also because the workers involved quite often preferred alternative work patterns.[460] They concluded that, if these flexible forms of work were to be generally accepted, this would require legislation to ensure that such workers were given 'broadly-equivalent working conditions to standard workers'.[461]

By the end of 1994 the UK had made it clear that it would not support any Community legislation on atypical work and would veto any proposals from the Commission.[462] Once again the Commission was presented with an

---

[454] See COM(82) 155, OJ 1982, C62/7 and OJ 1982, C128/2 as amended by OJ 1983, C18/5 and COM(84) 159. See further, M Jeffery, 'The Commission's Proposals on 'Atypical Work': Back to the Drawing Board . . . Again' (1995) 24 *Industrial Law Journal* 296.

[455] The Charter contains several references to atypical or non-standard workers. For example, point 5 provides that workers subject to terms of employment other than an open-ended full-time employment contract should benefit from an equitable reference wage. Point 6 requires an improvement of living and working conditions as regards in particular 'the duration and organisation of working time and forms of employment other than open-ended contracts, such as fixed-term contracts, part-time working, temporary work and seasonal work'.

[456] COM(90) 228, OJ 1990, C224/8, as amended by COM(90) 533, OJ 1990, C305/12. For discussion on the legal base issues, see ch 3. See generally, R Blanpain (ed) *Temporary Work and Labour Law* (Kluwer, Deventer, 1993).

[457] Dir 91/383/EEC supplementing the measures to encourage improvements in the safety and health of workers with a fixed-duration employment relationship or a temporary employment relationship, OJ 1991, L206/19.

[458] COM(92) 562, para 13 and COM(93) 668, p 8.

[459] COM(94) 333 at 31.

[460] *Ibid* at 30.

[461] *Ibid*.

[462] See Jeffery, n 454 above at 299.

opportunity to activate the procedures under the Agreement on Social Policy. The first consultation on 'flexibility of working time and security for workers (forms of employment other than full-time, open-ended employment)' commenced in September 1995 and in June 1996 the social partners announced that they would begin negotiations.[463] One year later, following an extended period of negotiations,[464] a Framework Agreement was signed by the ETUC, UNICE and CEEP on 6 June 1997. The Commission's proposal swiftly followed[465] and Directive 97/81 was adopted on 15 December 1997.[466] While the Directive's sole stated purpose is to 'implement' the annexed Framework Agreement,[467] a secondary objective, conveyed mainly through the Commission's Explanatory Memorandum, is to reinforce the references in the Framework Agreement to SMEs at a time when the litigation brought by UEAPME was pending.[468] The Council, consistent with its minimalist approach to implementation, deleted a proposed non-discrimination clause[469] and a provision concerning effective sanctions.[470] The implementation date of the Directive was 20 January 2000.[471]

Before evaluating the Framework Agreement, two highly influential developments must be taken into account. Firstly, in June 1994 the ILO adopted Convention No 175 and Recommendation No 182 concerning part-time work.[472] The form and content of the Framework Agreement has been inspired by the ILO Convention, which formed the basis for the Commission's proposals and heavily influenced the ETUC's negotiating position.[473] The significance of the ILO Convention, however, is that it marks a shift away from the ILO's traditional social justice philosophy.[474] The

---

[463] See the Commission's Explanatory Memorandum, COM(97) 392, paras 9 and 11.

[464] On 12 March 1997 the social partners asked the Commission for a further three months in accordance with Art 3(4) of the Agreement [now 138(4) EC]. The Commission concurred. *Ibid* para 9.

[465] COM(97) 392 was issued on 23 July 1997, just six weeks after the Framework Agreement was signed.

[466] OJ 1998, L14/9.

[467] Art 1.

[468] COM(97) 392, paras 24–29. For example, point 7 of the general considerations to the Framework Agreement declares that: 'whereas this agreement takes into consideration the need to improve social policy requirements, to enhance the competitiveness of the Community economy and to avoid imposing administrative, financial and legal constraints in a way which would hold back the creation and development of small and medium-sized undertakings'.

[469] *Ibid* draft Art 3.

[470] *Ibid* draft Art 4, which stated that penalties 'must be effective, commensurate with the infringement, and must constitute a sufficient deterrent'.

[471] 7 April 2000 was the implementation date for the UK. Dir 98/23, OJ 1998, L131/10.

[472] Text available at: <www.ilo.org>. For discussion, see J Murray, 'Social Justice for Women? The ILO's Convention on Part-time Work' (1999) 15 *International Journal of Comparative Labour Law and Industrial Relations* 3.

[473] See further, Murray, *ibid* at 4; and M Jeffery, 'Not Really Going to Work? Of the Directive on Part-Time Work, 'Atypical Work' and Attempts to Regulate It' (1998) 27 *Industrial Law Journal* 193 at 200.

[474] Murray, *ibid*.

Convention breaks new ground because, as Murray notes,[475] it qualifies rights already enshrined within core ILO conventions and seeks to increase employment in ways that may result in the lowering of working conditions in ratifying Member States.[476] The focus of the Convention is on equal treatment rather than positive rights for part-time workers.[477] Significantly, the latter are largely to be found in the advisory Recommendation.[478] The Convention seeks to guarantee the 'same protection as that accorded to comparable full-time workers' in respect of: the right to organise; to bargain collectively; and act as workers' representatives; to occupational health and safety; and non-discrimination in employment and occupation.[479] Part-time workers should receive the same proportionate 'basic wage' as full-time workers engaged in the same or similar work.[480] There should also be equal treatment in respect of, inter alia, maternity protection, termination of employment, paid annual leave, and sick leave, although a Member State may be able to exclude workers whose hours of work or earnings are 'below specified thresholds'.[481] Article 3(2), however, allows Member States, after consultation with the social partners at national level, to exclude from the operation of the Convention 'particular categories of workers or establishments when its application to them would raise particular problems of a substantial nature'.[482] Finally, Articles 9 and 10 are concerned with the promotion of part-time work including the 'voluntary' transfer of workers from full-time to part-time work and vice versa.[483]

[475] Murray, *ibid*.

[476] Art 2 offers some protection against this eventuality because it states that the Convention does not affect 'more favourable' provisions in other ILO conventions.

[477] Murray, n 472 above at 6.

[478] For example, rights to consultation on the introduction or extension of part-time working; to be informed of the specific conditions of employment; to social security benefits and employment compensation schemes; and paid educational, parental and dependant leave; access to training, career opportunities and occupational mobility (points 4,5, 9, 10, 13 and 15).

[479] Art 4.

[480] Art 5 and Art 1(c)(i). This is narrower than ILO Convention No 100 on Equal Remuneration for Men and Women Workers for Work of Equal Value, both because it is restricted to equal work rather than equal value, and it only covers the basic wage and not, as in Convention No 100 'any additional emoluments whatsoever possible directly or indirectly, whether in cash or in kind'. See Murray, n 472 above at 10–11.

[481] Art 8(1). This exemption also covers equal treatment in social security schemes under Art 6. The Convention gives little guidance on the criteria for setting these thresholds except that they shall be 'sufficiently low as not to exclude an unduly large percentage of part-time workers' (Art 8(2)). Member States availing themselves of these thresholds are to consult the social partners, periodically review them and report to the ILO (Art 8(3) and (4)).

[482] As Murray notes, n 472 above at 9–10, this conflicts with ILO Conventions Nos 87 and 98, which grant 'workers' rights to freedom of association and to organise. Convention No 98 does, however, contain a derogation concerning the armed forces, the police and public servants.

[483] Art 10. Murray, *ibid* notes, at 13, that voluntary transfer is only 'where appropriate', implying that there may be unspecified situations where a forced transfer may be permitted contrary to ILO Convention No 29 on Forced or Compulsory Labour.

Secondly, in April 1997, at a critical stage in the negotiations between the social partners on part-time work, the Commission issued its seminal Green Paper on *Partnership for a New Organisation of Work*,[484] which sought to elicit a debate about changes in the labour market from full-time to part-time work, from permanent to fixed-term contracts, from manufacturing to service sectors, from office to home working and, to a lesser extent, from male to female employment as a proportion of the workforce.[485] In particular, the number of part-time workers in the EU was 24 million and rising fast, while up to 40 per cent of new jobs were on temporary contracts. In the post-modern labour market the 'typical' worker had become 'atypical'. The Commission explained its rationale for action on part-time work thus:[486]

This form of work represents both opportunities and risks. From the employer's point of view it provides the flexibility which is necessary to meet changing consumer demands, especially in services. From the worker's point of view it also provides a flexibility that makes it easier to combine work with other responsibilities, for example studies or housework. The problem is that conditions of employment, for example social protection, for part-time workers are often limited when compared with those for full-time work. This crystallises the benefits for both sides and could lead to the integration of part-time workers into the labour market, in particular by making their work less precarious . . . *A European agreement on this would make an important contribution to the development of flexibility and security in working life.*

The Framework Agreement draws heavily from the ILO Convention while emphasising the balance in the Green Paper between 'flexibility and security'. Indeed the first sentence of the preamble declares that the Framework Agreement is a 'contribution to the overall European strategy on employment'. This is reinforced in point 4 of the general considerations, following on from the preamble, which directly refers to the employment promotion objectives of the Essen European Council of December 1994, which called for measures aimed at:[487]

. . . increasing the employment intensiveness of growth, *in particular by more flexible organisation of work* in a way which fulfils both the wishes of employees and the requirements of competition.

This balance is reflected in the dual purpose presented in Clause 1. First, the Framework Agreement seeks to provide for the removal of discrimination against part-time workers and to improve the quality of part-time

---

[484] COM(97) 128.

[485] *Employment in Europe 1999* (European Commission, Brussels, 1999) p 7.

[486] COM(97) 128, para 52. Emphasis added.

[487] Emphasis added. This is the second of five employment priorities agreed at the Essen European Council held on 9/10 Dec 1994. For discussion, see ch 7.

work.[488] Secondly, it strives to facilitate the development of part-time work on a voluntary basis and to contribute to the flexible organisation of working time in a manner that takes into account the needs of employers and workers.[489] The latter forms the basis for specific measures in Clause 5 whilst also satisfying the SME clause in Article 2(2) of the Agreement on Social Policy [now 137(2) EC].

Before addressing the principle of non-discrimination, the Framework Agreement seeks to determine its scope and define who is a 'part-time worker' and a 'comparable full-time worker'. The scope of the Agreement is limited to part-time workers with an employment contract or employment relationship in accordance with national law.[490] Moreover, Member States *may*, after consultation with national social partners, wholly or partly exclude part-time workers 'who work on a casual basis'.[491] Such exclusions 'shall be reviewed periodically to establish if the objective reasons for making them remain valid'.[492] There is no definition of a 'casual' part-time worker, although it is implicit that this is a matter for national law.

Clause 3 defines a 'part-time worker' as an employee whose normal hours of work, calculated on a weekly or annual basis, are less than those of a 'comparable full-time worker'—defined as a full-time worker in the same establishment with the same type of employment contract or relationship—'who is engaged in the same or similar work/occupation' with 'due regard' being given to other considerations including seniority and qualifications/skills. In the absence of a comparable full-time worker, reference may be made to collective agreements, national legislation, or practice. No attempt is made to define full-time work, although there is a side reference to the principle of *pro rata temporis* that shall apply 'where appropriate'.[493]

The principle of non-discrimination is set out in Clause 4(1) as follows:[494]

In respect of employment conditions, part-time workers shall not be treated in a less favourable manner than comparable full-time workers *solely* because they work part-time *unless different treatment is justified on objective grounds*.

The Agreement does not flesh out the meaning of the term 'employment conditions'. Unlike the ILO Convention, it makes no direct reference to areas such as health and safety, organisation and representation, pay, social security, maternity, dismissal, paid leave and sick leave.[495] While it

---

[488] Clause 1(a).
[489] Clause 1(b).
[490] Clause 2(1).
[491] Clause 2(2).
[492] *Ibid.*
[493] Clause 4(2).
[494] Emphasis added.
[495] See Jeffery (1998, *Industrial Law Journal*) n 473 above at 200.

would have been desirable to expressly include these areas, it should be noted that the term 'employment conditions' is capable of broad interpretation by the Court to include each of these areas, with the exception of social security, providing that they are part of the employment contract or relationship of the comparable full-time worker. Although the exclusion of social security is regrettable, it is logical because this is not an area that would normally fall within the remit of the social partners and it raises wider issues that should be addressed by separate measures taken at national level or, if necessary, a specific Commission proposal pursued through the conventional legislative route. By contrast, the express inclusion of pay would have posed difficulties because of the operation of Article 2(6) [now 137(6) EC], although the issue of pay in the context of the principle of non-discrimination, rather than positive rights, is quite different from that envisaged by the exemption. Moreover, although Directive 91/383[496] does not refer explicitly to the health and safety of part-time workers, the scope of the framework Directive on Health and Safety encompasses all workers.[497]

An additional factor, when interpreting the scope of the principle of non-discrimination in the context of part-time work, is that sex discrimination and discrimination against part-time workers is regarded as mutually exclusive for the purposes of the Directive. Once again, this can be explained by reference to the ILO Convention, which also separates out these two issues. Within the framework of Community law, this is remarkable given the Court's case law on sex discrimination and part-time workers and the fact that 80 per cent of part-time workers are female, a significant factor when explaining the gender gap in pay and other conditions of employment. In practice, however, the distinction makes sense because the Directive may provide a useful fallback for women who are unable to prove sex discrimination in the context of Article 119 [now 141] EC and the Equal Treatment Directive.[498] The Directive is, by virtue of Clause 6(4) 'without prejudice to any *more specific Community provisions*, and in particular . . . concerning equal treatment or opportunities for men and women'.[499] It follows that, under Clause 4(1), female and/or male part-time workers, individually or as a group, will have to show that discrimination arises 'solely' because they are part-time workers who can be compared with full-time workers in the same establishment performing the same or similar work, whereas, in a sex discrimination case, it is necessary for women to leap the initial hurdles of showing that not only are substantially more part-time workers in the enterprise women, but also,

---

[496] OJ 1991, L206/19.
[497] OJ 1989, L183/1.
[498] Dir 76/207/EEC, OJ 1976, L39/40.
[499] Emphasis added.

women part-time workers should be compared with full time, predominantly male, workers.

The reference to 'objective justification' in Clause 4(1) is more complex. Although there is now a codification of the Court's case law on objective justification in Directive 97/80 on the burden of proof in sex discrimination cases,[500] adopted on the same day as the Part-time Work Directive,[501] that Directive does not cover the part-time work or fixed-term work directives which have identical provisions.[502] Clause 4(1) of the Framework Agreement makes no distinction between direct and indirect discrimination, whereas Directive 97/80 specifically defines indirect discrimination.[503] The orthodox position is that there can be no objective justification for direct sex discrimination.[504] Theoretically, the same objective reason could be given to defeat a case mounted on the grounds of both sex discrimination and part-time/fixed-term work discrimination with different rules in operation regarding the burden of proof.[505] More problematically, if direct discrimination against part-time workers can be justified this may act as a barrier to women seeking to rely on the Part-time Work Directive as an alternative to a sex discrimination claim.

Moreover, to further muddy the waters between part-time work and sex discrimination cases, Clause 4(4) provides that Member States, where justified by objective reasons, 'may, where appropriate', and subject to consultation, make access to particular conditions of employment subject to a period of service, time worked, or earnings qualification. These qualification rules are to be 'reviewed periodically' having regard to the principle of non-discrimination 'as expressed' in Clause 4(1). This is an odd clause, wider than the derogation in Article 8(1) of the ILO Convention, and explainable only as a compromise between the social partners. Any such review would inevitably lead to the conclusion that these qualifying

---

[500] Dir 97/80/EC, OJ 1997, L14/16.

[501] 15 Dec 1997.

[502] See Clause 4(1) of the Framework Agreement annexed to Dir 99/70/EC, OJ 1999, L175/43.

[503] Art 2(2) of Dir 97/80/EC, OJ 1997, L14/16.

[504] See generally, T Hervey, 'Justification of Indirect Sex Discrimination in Employment: European Community Law and UK Law Compared' (1991) 40 *International and Comparative Law Quarterly* 807; T Hervey, *Justifications for Sex Discrimination in Employment* (Butterworths, London, 1993) ch 8; and Barnard, *EC Employment Law*, n 243 above, pp 213–20.

[505] By analogy with sex discrimination cases, the appropriate question in each case would be: what are 'objective factors unrelated to part-time work'? For example, in Case C–167/97, *R v Secretary of State for Employment, ex parte Seymour-Smith* [1999] ECR I–623, the UK argued that a reduction in the national two-year qualifying period for unfair dismissal claims would act as a deterrent to recruitment. The Court, having accepted that the encouragement of recruitment was a legitimate social policy aim, considered whether such an aim could objectively justify indirect sex discrimination and stated that it 'must also be ascertained, in the light of all the relevant factors and taking into account the possibility of achieving the social policy aim in question by other means, whether such an aim appears to be unrelated to any discrimination based on sex and whether the disputed rule, as a means to its achievement, is capable of advancing that aim' (para 72).

rules are, intrinsically, discriminatory against part-time workers, and yet, they may be saved by arguments founded on objective justification.

Provisions in Clause 5 deal with the second objective of facilitating the development of part-time work and the flexible organisation of working time. While these are not conventional provisions in a Community directive on employment protection or non-discrimination, the inclusion of Clause 5 is a direct consequence of the framework of the ILO Convention rather than the involvement of the social partners in the pre-legislative process.

Clause 5(1) broadly following Article 9 of the ILO Convention, places obligations on the Member States and the social partners to review obstacles that may limit the opportunities for part-time work and 'where appropriate' eliminate them. Any steps taken must be consistent with the principles of non-discrimination and non-retrogression[506] and the overall objectives of the Directive. In practice this will allow for a measure of deregulation consistent with the balance between 'security and flexibility', because the principle of non-retrogression is a qualified one. While implementation of the Framework Agreement shall not constitute valid grounds for reducing the general level of protection afforded to workers, this does not prejudice the right of Member States and/or social partners to 'develop different legislative, regulatory or contractual provisions, *in the light of changing circumstances*' and, specifically, does not prejudice the employment promotion objectives of Clause 5(1) as long as the principle of non-discrimination 'as expressed' in Clause 4(1) is complied with. Therefore, at national level, the application of the Framework Agreement is dynamic and may allow for deregulation over time,[507] particularly where there is objective justification including, for example, justifications used in sex discrimination cases, such as economic factors relating to the needs of the undertaking,[508] or state measures deemed to be within a margin of discretion and capable of achieving the aims of social and employment policy.[509]

Clause 5(2) is more direct:[510]

A worker's refusal to transfer from full-time to part-time work or *vice-versa* should not *in itself* constitute a valid reason for termination of employment, without prejudice to termination in accordance with national law, collective agreements and practice, *for other reasons such as may arise from the operational requirements of the establishment concerned.*

---

[506] Clause 6(2).
[507] See Jeffery (1998, *Industrial Law Journal*) n 473 above at 197.
[508] See Case 170/84, *Bilka Kaufhaus v Weber* [1986] ECR 1607; and Case 127/92, *Enderby v Frenchay HA* [1993] ECR I–5535.
[509] See Case C–317/93, *Nolte v Landesversicherungsanstalt Hannover* [1995] ECR I–4625; and Case C–444/93, *Megner and Scheffel v Innungskrankenkasse Rheinhessen-Pfalz* [1995] ECR I–4741.
[510] Emphasis added.

This is a double-edged sword for employees who may, under current national legislation, be under no obligation at all to switch to, or from, part-time work. While there is a reference in Clause 1(a) to the development of part-time work 'on a voluntary basis', the provision in Clause 5(2) may undermine existing national protection by introducing a presumption that, where such a change is necessary for a genuine 'operational' reason within an enterprise, an employee who refuses to agree may be fairly dismissed. For example, Jeffery suggests that this might include an offer of part-time work as an alternative to, or in mitigation of, redundancy.[511]

Finally Clause 5(3) addresses many of the areas covered by the ILO Recommendation, but there is no onus on Member States to make them obligatory or for employers to act on them. Rather, as far as possible, employers should give consideration to:

(a) requests by workers to transfer from full-time to part-time work that becomes available in the establishment;
(b) requests by workers to transfer from part-time to full-time work or to increase their working time should the opportunity arise;
(c) the provision of timely information on the availability of part-time and full-time positions in the establishment in order to facilitate transfers from full-time to part-time or vice versa;
(d) measures to facilitate access to part-time work at all levels of the enterprise, including skilled and managerial positions, and where appropriate, to facilitate access by part-time workers to vocational training to enhance career opportunities and occupational mobility;
(e) the provision of appropriate information to existing bodies representing workers about part-time working in the enterprise.

Therefore, only the heavily circumscribed non-discrimination provisions offer additional rights for part-time workers and, for many women workers, they may only duplicate rights that already exist.[512]

The Directive is unlikely to achieve its first objective of removing discrimination against part-time workers.[513] It would be wrong, however, to blame the vacuity of the Directive on the social partners. They were hardly likely to negotiate a stronger binding text at the level of the Community than had been agreed by their colleagues at the ILO. Although the ILO text is broader in its coverage, the derogations are not dissimilar. Furthermore, in the light of the preceding Green Paper, and the overriding importance of the employment promotion agenda by the mid-1990s, there is no evidence to suggest that a more concrete measure would have ensued had the social partners failed to negotiate an agreement.[514] Indeed, as former Commis-

---

[511] Jeffery (1998, *Industrial Law Journal*) n 473 above at 198.
[512] See Schmidt (1999, *International Journal of Comparative Labour Law and Industrial Relations*) n 248 above at 262.
[513] See Jeffery (1998, *Industrial Law Journal*) n 473 above at 196.
[514] See however, the criticisms of the European Parliament in its response: [1997] A4–1-0352/97.

sioner Flynn noted, the proposal envisaged by the Member States in 1994 had excluded social security and replaced positive rights with the principle of non-discrimination leaving only 'the minimum of the minimum, below which nothing is conceivable in social protection'.[515]

(3) Fixed-term Work

On 23 March 1998, the social partners (UNICE, CEEP and the ETUC) announced their intention to start negotiations on fixed-term work. After an extended period of negotiations,[516] the three organisations concluded a Framework Agreement on 18 March 1999.[517] In the meantime, UEAPME had reached an accommodation with UNICE which allowed it to have an input into the negotiation stage as part of the UNICE delegation.[518] As with the proposal on part-time work, the Commission, in its Explanatory Memorandum,[519] sought to include provisions concerning non-retrogression and sanctions.[520] Once again the Council deleted these provisions, although non-retrogression is provided for in the body of the Framework Agreement.[521] Council Directive 99/70 was adopted on 28 June 1999,[522] the first measure enacted under the revised social provisions made effective by the ratification of the Amsterdam Treaty.[523] The implementation date was 10 July 2001.[524]

The Framework Agreement on Fixed-term Work mirrors its predecessor on part-time work in a number of respects, although there are some important differences. In particular, the employment promotion objective is made even more explicit. The first paragraph of the preamble proclaims:

This framework agreement illustrates the role that the social partners can play in the European employment strategy . . . and, following the framework agreement on part-time work, represents a further contribution towards achieving a better balance between 'flexibility in working time and security for workers'.

Whereas, as recently as 1998, the ETUC had declared that temporary work was essentially a low quality form of employment and should be strictly

---

[515] *Agence Europe*, 8 Dec 1994. Cited by Jeffery (1998, *Industrial Law Journal*) n 473 above at 201.
[516] The Commission agreed to the extension in accordance with the procedure in Art 3(4) of the Agreement [now 138(4) EC].
[517] For a full summary of the background, see the Commission's Explanatory Memorandum, COM(99) 203.
[518] *Ibid* para 17.
[519] *Ibid*.
[520] *Ibid* draft Arts 2 and 3.
[521] Clause 8(3).
[522] OJ 1999, L175/43.
[523] The legal base was Art 137(1) EC concerning 'working conditions' [ex Art 2(1) of the Agreement], although this is not directly referred to in the Directive.
[524] Art 2.

limited in its application,[525] it was now prepared to recognise that fixed-term contracts respond, in certain circumstances, to the needs of employers and workers.[526] While expressing a preference for employment contracts of an indefinite duration, the regulatory effect of the Framework Agreement is to normalise fixed-term contracts entered into directly by employers and workers.[527]

Clause 1 sets out the two-fold purpose of the Framework Agreement, which is to:

(a) improve the quality of fixed-term work by ensuring the application of the principle of non-discrimination;
(b) establish a framework to prevent abuse arising from the use of successive fixed-term employment contracts or relationships.

Hence, the merits of fixed-term work are undisputed, but what really matters is its 'quality'—a concept that has been developed as the central plank of the Commission's Social Policy Agenda of 2000.[528] Moreover, the need to improve the quality of work and prevent abuse is linked directly to the equality objective because more than half of the fixed-term workers in the EU are women.[529] The purpose of the measure is far narrower than the Framework Agreement on Part-time Work, and yet, from a social justice perspective, it is marginally stronger. There is no suggestion that promotion of fixed-term work should be a positive Community objective. Rather, fixed-term work is accepted, or at least condoned, but requires not only the application of a near identical non-discrimination clause, but also an element of standardisation to prevent 'abuse', while allowing for considerable flexibility in particular sectors and occupations, including seasonal activities.

Clause 2, read in conjunction with the preamble and general considerations, determines the scope of the Framework Agreement. Member States can limit its application to fixed-term workers with a contract of employment or employment relationship.[530] Unlike the Part-time Work Agreement, there is no exemption available for 'casual' workers, although there is an oblique reference to the need to 'take account of the situation in each Member State and the circumstances of particular sectors and occupations, including the activities of a seasonal nature'.[531] Temporary agency workers 'at the disposition of a user enterprise', are excluded by a short paragraph in the preamble,[532] a

[525] See J Murray, 'Normalising Temporary Work' (1999) 28 *Industrial Law Journal* 269 at 270–71.
[526] Preamble, para 2.
[527] Murray (1999, *Industrial Law Journal*) n 525 above at 271.
[528] COM(2000) 379, approved at the Nice European Council, 7/9 Dec 2000, Presidency Conclusions, Annex I. See further, ch 11.
[529] Point 9 of the general considerations.
[530] Clause 2(1).
[531] Point 10 of the general considerations.
[532] Para 4.

point reinforced in Clause 3(1) which, when defining who is a 'fixed-term worker', refers only to 'contracts entered into directly between an employer and a worker'. In the preamble the social partners declared that they intended to reach a separate agreement on temporary agency work at a later date.[533] Further, after consultation with national social partners, Member States can exclude, first, initial vocational training and apprentice schemes and, second, employment contracts and relationships concluded within the framework of a specific public or publicly-supported training, integration and vocational retraining programme.[534] Therefore, the State is able to exempt itself and its contractors entirely where projects are linked with the 'employability' and 'adaptability' criteria that underpin the European Employment Strategy, to be discussed later in chapters 7 and 11.

Clause 3 defines the terms 'fixed-term worker' and 'comparable permanent worker' in a manner that mirrors the approach adopted for part-time and comparable full-time work under the Part-time Work Agreement. A 'fixed-term worker' is a person with a direct employment contract or relationship with an employer where the end of that contract or relationship is determined by 'objective conditions such as reaching a specific date, completing a specific task, or the occurrence of a specific event'.[535] By contrast, a 'comparable permanent worker' is a worker with an employment contract or relationship of 'indefinite duration' in the same establishment, engaged in the same or similar work/occupation, due regard being given to qualifications/skills. In the absence of a comparable permanent worker in the same establishment, reference shall be made to the applicable collective agreement or in accordance with national law and practice.[536]

The principle of non-discrimination is contained in Clause 4(1) providing:

> In respect of employment conditions, fixed-term workers shall not be treated in a less favourable manner than comparable permanent workers solely because they have a fixed-term contract or relationship unless different treatment is justified on objective grounds.

Therefore, as with part-time work, both direct and indirect discrimination can be objectively justified and, where appropriate, the principle of *pro rata temporis* shall apply.[537] In the case of fixed-term work, however, the worker faces additional disadvantages arising from lack of recognition of relevant prior service and related factors that are not fully taken into account.[538] However, Clause 4(4) represents a shift of emphasis from the parallel provision concerning part-time work, providing that:

---

[533] *Ibid.*
[534] Clause 2(2).
[535] Clause 3(1).
[536] Clause 3(2).
[537] Clause 4(2).
[538] See Murray (1999, *Industrial Law Journal*) n 525 above at 274–75.

Period-of-service qualifications relating to particular conditions of employment shall be the same for fixed-term workers as for permanent workers except where different length-of-service qualifications are justified on objective grounds.

Therefore, the assumption is that such qualification rules are discriminatory, whereas, under Clause 4(4) of the Part-time Work Agreement, they amount to derogations available to Member States subject only to consultation and periodic review. There is also no reference to derogations on the basis of 'time worked' or an 'earnings qualification'. This suggests that the ETUC toughened up their negotiating position or, more likely, the employers were prepared to be more flexible because the economic cost of regulating part-time work is far greater, particularly as national law protects fixed-term workers in a similar fashion in the majority of Member States.[539]

Clause 5 enumerates the measures intended to 'prevent abuse arising from the use of successive fixed-term contracts or employment relationships'.[540] There is no definition of 'abuse' in this context although such workers are often placed in an extremely vulnerable position under national law. Further, the Court is somewhat reluctant to intervene in matters concerning the construction and termination of the contract of employment or employment relationship under national law. This point has been highlighted by the Court's judgment in *Jiménez Melgar*,[541] a case where the non-renewal of the contract of a pregnant worker who had been employed under successive fixed-term contracts was deemed not to be a 'dismissal' for the purposes of the protective provisions in Article 10(1) of the Pregnancy and Maternity Directive.[542] In such circumstances there may still be a violation of the Equal Treatment Directive, but would such treatment amount to an 'abuse' under the Fixed-term Work Directive and what responsibility, if any, would fall on the State to take preventative action? Clause 5 does little to assuage any fears that the Fixed-term Work Directive would be of limited use in such circumstances.

Clause 5(1) provides that Member States shall, after consultation with the social partners, and in the absence of equivalent legal measures to prevent abuse, introduce 'in a manner which takes account of the needs of specific sectors and/or categories of workers' *one or more* of the following measures:

(a) objective reasons justifying the renewal of such contracts;
(b) the maximum total duration of successive fixed-term employment contracts or relationships;
(c) the number of renewals of such contracts.

---

[539] See generally, the survey of national law in Volume 15/2 (1999) *International Journal of Comparative Labour Law and Industrial Relations* 81–209.
[540] Clause 5(1).
[541] Case C–438/99, *Jiménez Melgar v Ayuntamiento de Los Barrios* [2001] ECR I–6915. For full discussion, see ch 5, pp 165–67.
[542] Dir 92/85/EEC, OJ 1992, L348/1. See para 45, *ibid*.

Discretion is granted to Member States to determine under what conditions fixed-term contracts shall be regarded as 'successive' and shall be deemed to be contracts of 'indefinite duration'.[543] This is an extremely flexible provision that would, for example, if only (b) is introduced, allow fixed-term contracts to be renewed for many years without limiting the number of renewals or providing for objective justification. Therefore, the extent to which 'abuse' will be prevented is almost entirely dependent upon the approach taken by Member States, with scope for variations for SMEs and particular areas where fixed-term contracts are common, such as research jobs and the holiday trade. As Murray notes, Clause 5 amounts to little more than a platform for national bargaining around loosely defined terms.[544]

Clause 6 provides limited additional rights to information and training. Employers are obliged to inform fixed-term workers about vacancies in the establishment or undertaking and must ensure that these workers have the same opportunities to secure permanent positions as other workers.[545] As far as possible, employers should facilitate access by fixed-term workers to appropriate training opportunities to enhance their skills, career development and occupational mobility.[546] While the main aim of this Clause is employment promotion, it is perhaps significant that these rights are stronger than the equivalent provisions in Clause 6 of the Part-time Work Agreement.

Other provisions in the Framework Agreement ensure that fixed-term workers are included for information and consultation purposes.[547] As with the Part-time Work Agreement, there are matching provisions allowing for the maintenance or introduction of 'more favourable provisions',[548] and for the Framework Agreement to operate without prejudice to any more specific Community provisions, including equal treatment.[549] Clause 8(3) is a straightforward non-retrogression statement with no scope for qualifications 'in the light of changing circumstances'.[550] Finally, Clause 8(4) allows the national social partners to conclude agreements adapting or complementing the provisions in the Framework Agreement.

The Fixed-term Work Agreement is a more precise measure than the earlier agreements on Part-time Work and Parental Leave, suggesting a gradual maturation of this method of negotiating quasi-legislative agreements at Community level. For former Commissioner Flynn this was 'by

---

[543] Clause 5(2).
[544] Murray (1999, *Industrial Law Journal*) n 525 above at 275.
[545] Clause 6(1).
[546] Clause 6(2).
[547] Clause 7(1).
[548] Clause 8(1).
[549] Clause 8(2).
[550] Cf Clause 6(2) of the Part-time Work Agreement.

far the most politically sensitive and technically difficult issue'[551] that the social partners had tackled in formal negotiations. Certainly it is the case that there is a huge variation among the Member States, particularly concerning the rules on the length of fixed-term contracts and renewal.[552] In essence, however, the legal effects of the measure are largely limited to the establishment of the non-discrimination principle with considerable scope for elaboration at national level.[553] For the ETUC, the outcome fell significantly short of their bargaining position which was to secure firm limits on recourse to fixed-term contracts, on the maximum length of such contracts and the number of renewals.[554] For UNICE, this is a balanced agreement that will improve employment perspectives because fixed-term work is a necessary form of work in flexible labour markets.[555] The rather limited nature of the measure may be explained by the fact that the incidence of fixed-term contracts across the EU is just 12.2 per cent, with only Spain exceeding 20 per cent.[556] The majority of Member States will have to make little or no changes to their existing national laws.[557]

In conclusion, an opportunity to regulate the area of temporary work, including the most insecure form of agency work, has been missed. In particular, what is lacking is a portability of basic employment and social protection entitlements for temporary workers.[558] The sensitivity of this issue has been highlighted by the failure of the social partners to negotiate an agreement on temporary agency work within the required time period and the recent decision of the Commission to pilot its own proposal through the conventional legislative route.[559] Such a measure will need to provide a higher level of protection because, although the needs of part-time and temporary workers may appear complementary, and indeed many workers are both, the reality is that temporary workers are faced with, by the very nature of their employment contracts, greater job insecurity. This is compounded by the fact that there may be concurrent discrimination against women on the grounds of gender whether they have full-time, part-time, indefinite or fixed-term contracts. The application of the discrimination test

---

[551] See (1999) 304 *European Industrial Relations Review* 14 at 15.

[552] See generally (1999, *International Journal of Comparative Labour Law and Industrial Relations*) n 539 above.

[553] See Murray (1999, *Industrial Law Journal*) n 525 above at 271.

[554] See (1999) 304 *European Industrial Relations Review* 14 at 14. See also the criticism of the European Parliament's Committee on Employment and Social Affairs [1999] A4–0261/99.

[555] *Ibid* at 17.

[556] *Employment in Europe 1998* (European Commission, Brussels, 1998). Based on statistics for 1997.

[557] See (1999) 304 *European Industrial Relations Review* 14 at 16. In those Member States where fixed-term workers have very limited protection the Directive is viewed more positively. See P Lorber, 'Regulating Fixed-term Work in the UK: A Positive Step towards Workers' Protection?' (1999) 15 *International Journal of Comparative Labour Law and Industrial Relations* 121.

[558] See Murray (1999, *Industrial Law Journal*) n 525 above at 274.

[559] For the draft directive, see COM(2002) 149.

in sex discrimination cases suggests that the extension of non-discrimination to the fields of part-time and fixed-term work will not be a panacea for workers facing multi-dimensional discrimination.[560] Therefore, as Murray observes,[561] the benign references in the Framework Agreement to symmetrical needs between employers and workers in relation to fixed-term work paint a false picture.

XI CONCLUSION

When the Agreement on Social Policy was terminated on the entry into force of the Treaty of Amsterdam,[562] it had been fully activated, from consultation through to legislation, on just four occasions.[563] For those who had striven for a political compromise to break the social policy impasse at Maastricht, this was a derisory outcome. In part, this paucity can be explained by the sheer technical complexity of the process combined with the operation of the Agreement 'without prejudice' to the mainstream Treaty provisions. Even allowing for these difficulties, however, greater reliance on the Agreement on a 'case by case basis' might have been expected had there been the commensurate political will among the signatory parties to make full use of the wide range of legal bases and legislative procedures available to implement the Social Charter and secure the overarching objective of economic and social progress which is balanced and sustainable.

In practice, throughout this transitional period, the Community institutions and the social partners were only prepared to utilise the Agreement reluctantly and incrementally.[564] Moreover, the legislation that emerged, after lengthy negotiations between the social partners, provided only limited Community 'added value' in those Member States, frequently a minority, where the prevailing standards were below the minimum levels prescribed in the agreements. Such an outcome is hardly surprising when one considers the distance, in terms of representativeness, between the social partners and the intended beneficiaries of these agreements, a fact compounded by the gaping deficit in the democratic legitimacy of the whole process. It would be unfair and, more importantly, inaccurate, however, to blame the social partners for the minimalism of these agreements when, as the analysis in Section VIII above has demonstrated, the parameters within which

---

[560] Murray (1999, *Industrial Law Journal*) n 525 above at 275.

[561] *Ibid* at 274.

[562] 1 May 1999.

[563] Two directives arising from framework agreements (Dir 96/34/EC on Parental Leave, OJ 1996, L145/4; Dir 97/81/EC on Part-time Work, 1998, L14/9); and two directives adopted by the conventional legislative route (Dir 94/45/EC on European Works Councils, OJ 1994, L254/64; Dir 97/80/EC on the burden of proof in sex discrimination cases, OJ 1997, L14/16).

[564] See Falkner, n 81 above at 11.

they were operating had been preordained at both Community and international levels.

In order to understand these quantitative and qualitative shortcomings, we must conclude by taking cognisance of several more fundamental factors:

1) The Member States' preference for monetary union over political union, and the pillared structure of the new edifice, has served to reinforce rather than recalibrate the imbalance between the Union's economic and social objectives. In particular, the limited conception of citizenship and the absence of a human rights foundation in the TEU have diminished the potential for the development of a European 'social citizenship' in place of 'market citizenship'.

2) Subsidiarity has guided the exercise of power at Community level by creating a presumption that national measures are to be preferred and, even in areas where the legal bases for Community measures have been expanded, programmatic activity or soft law should be considered as a first step and, where binding Community action is deemed necessary, it should lay down minimum standards with plenty of scope for elaboration by national actors.

3) The UK's 'opt-out' inevitably acted as a brake on progress, as desire to utilise the Agreement was matched by fear of social dumping, although in practice it was somewhat futile as the UK was not able to fully insulate itself from the spill over effect of the Agreement.[565]

4) The Agreement had internal contradictions that belied its packaging by the Protocol as a mechanism for implementing the Social Charter. In particular, the requirements of diversity and competitiveness, coupled with the SME clause, anchored the social provisions to the imperatives of the Community's 'economic constitution'. Moreover, the exemptions in Article 2(6) [now 137(6) EC] not only undermined the fulfilment of the Social Charter's cherished objectives, but also, served to strip bare the pretence that the social dialogue is a form of 'collective bargaining' in the absence of the countervailing power that is an essential precondition for balanced industrial rule-making.

5) Finally, as we shall discover in the next chapter, Europe's global competitiveness plummeted in the period between Maastricht and Amsterdam and the objective of employment promotion emerged as the Union's pre-eminent social policy ambition subsuming all other priorities and leading to, first, a questioning and, ultimately, a reshaping of the 'European social model'.

---

[565] See Brinkmann, n 47 above at 260; McGlynn, n 64 above at 60. For example, in the case of Dir 94/45/EC on European Works Councils (EWCs), OJ 1994, L254/64, 58 out of the first 386 agreements to establish EWCs or equivalent information and consultation bodies were signed by British multinationals. See Barnard, *EC Employment Law*, n 243 above, p 535.

7

From Maastricht to Amsterdam— Reshaping the European Social Model

I SEARCHING FOR EUROPE'S SOCIAL SOUL

ARTICLE N2 OF the TEU blandly provided for an Intergovernmental Conference (IGC) to be convened in 1996 to revise the Treaty in accordance with its objectives. This timetable, already tight when the Treaty was exhaustively negotiated at Maastricht in December 1991, was even more challenging by the time it belatedly entered into force in November 1993. Almost immediately, the Union embarked on an intensive period of *fin de siècle* introspection. Green papers and white papers abounded, committees of the wise and expert groups were established, and an aptly named 'Reflection Group' was appointed to examine and elaborate ideas for Treaty changes and other possible improvements 'in a spirit of democracy and openness'.[1] By December 1995, when the Reflection Group's Report was submitted to the Member States,[2] its focus had been sharpened by a deepening legitimacy crisis,[3] a steep decline in Europe's global competitiveness and, above all, by escalating levels of unemployment. The Report recommended making the Union more relevant to its citizens, improving its efficiency and democracy, preparing it for enlargement, and giving it greater capacity for external action. The Presidency Conclusions at the Madrid European Council contained a probing, almost physiological, self-examination of the Union's ills. In their opening paragraph the Member States humbly confessed that:[4]

---

[1] Presidency Conclusions of the Corfu European Council, June 1994. Bull EU 6/94, I.25. The Reflection Group was comprised of personal representatives of the Member States with two observers from the European Parliament. The Spanish representative Carlos Westendorp chaired the Group. For a critique, see F Dehousse, 'The IGC Process and Results' in D O'Keeffe and P Twomey (eds) *Legal Issues of the Amsterdam Treaty* (Hart, Oxford, 1999) 93–108.

[2] *The Reflection Group Report*, 5 Dec 1995, SN 520/95 (REFLEX 21).

[3] See D Chalmers, *European Union Law Volume One: Law and EU Government* (Dartmouth, Aldershot, 1998) p 66.

[4] Madrid European Council, Dec 1995. Bull EU 12/95, I.98. Emphasis added.

Men and women of Europe today, more than ever, feel the need for a common project. And, yet, for a growing number of Europeans, *the rationale for Community integration is not self-evident*. This paradox is a first challenge.

For Europe's leaders it was a deeply perplexing fact that, in their view, public disaffection with the European integration project was growing in inverse proportion to the Union's success in contributing to an unprecedented period of peace and prosperity.[5] The answer to this quandary was somehow to find a means to bring the Union closer to its citizens by nurturing a sense of collective identification with Europe as a socio-political unit based on shared values.[6]

In the contested field of European social policy, however, the demand for a convincing and truly cohesive rationale for integration was, if anything, even more intense and challenging. Common social values were needed to underpin a European social policy that had been constructed upon economic foundations.[7] Market integration alone could not sustain social policy in the absence of mutually shared criteria for achieving social justice.[8] In the age of globalisation and flexible labour markets, the challenge for the Union was to pre-empt the emergence of a dystopian neo-Hobbesian order[9] where employment law might be dismantled layer by layer.[10] As the Commission poignantly asked in its 1993 Green Paper on Social Policy, 'what sort of a society do Europeans want?'[11]

Post-Maastricht, Europe's struggle for its 'social self'[12] formed the backdrop for a fundamental reappraisal of the parameters of Community social policy and its essential purpose. Within a period of nine months after the ratification of the TEU, the Commission's Directorate General on Employment, Industrial Relations and Social Affairs had published a Green Paper, intended to stimulate a wide-ranging and intensive debate on the future of

[5] Madrid European Council, Dec 1995. Bull EU 12/95, I.98. Emphasis added.

[6] See D Obradovic, 'Policy Legitimacy and the European Union' (1996) 34 *Journal of Common Market Studies* 191 at 208. For a stimulating discussion of the dilemma of European identity, see P Allott, 'The Concept of European Union' (1999) 2 *Cambridge Yearbook of European Legal Studies* 31.

[7] See B Hepple, 'Social Values and European Law' (1995) *Current Legal Problems* 39 at 40; and M Kleinman and D Piachaud, 'European Social Policy: Conceptions and Choices' (1993) 3 *Journal of European Social Policy* 1 at 3.

[8] See Hepple, *ibid* at 43; and M Poiares Maduro, 'Europe's Social Self: 'The Sickness Unto Death'' in J Shaw (ed) *Social Law and Policy in an Evolving European Union* (Hart, Oxford, 2000) 325–49 at 331.

[9] See M Rhodes, *Globalisation, Labour Markets and Welfare States: A Future of 'Competitive Corporatism?'* EUI Working Paper No 97/36 (EUI, Florence, 1997) p 2. Hobbes (1588–1679) classically depicted a world where there was: 'No arts; no letters; no society; and which, worst of all, continual fear and danger of violent death; and the life of man, solitary, poor, nasty, brutish and short'. See *The Concise Oxford Dictionary of Quotations*, 2nd edn (OUP, Oxford, 1981) p 120.

[10] For an insightful analysis of the dangers of a 'refeudalisation' of European society, see A Supiot, 'The Dogmatic Foundations of the Market' (2000) 29 *Industrial Law Journal* 321 at 323–4.

[11] *Green Paper on European Social Policy: Options for the Union*, COM(93) 551, p 14.

[12] See Poiares Maduro, n 8 above.

European social policy,[13] and a White Paper to respond to that debate by setting out the means by which the ideal of a 'European social model' was to be preserved and developed into the 21st Century.[14] Sandwiched in between was a searing analysis of the relative global weakness of the European economies in the form of the Commission's landmark White Paper on Growth, Competitiveness, Employment.[15]

These publications triggered and shaped an ongoing dynamic and interactive discourse on the content and direction of Europe's economic and social values. Indeed, within three years, the Commission had published a medium-term Social Action Programme (SAP)[16] and a Green Paper on the Organisation of Work.[17] Over the same period the Council adopted a Resolution on Union Social Policy,[18] a Decision on an Action Programme on Equal Opportunities for Men and Women[19] and launched the 'European Employment Strategy' by publishing a series of priorities for job creation directed at the Member States.[20] Meanwhile, an ad hoc *Comité des Sages* proposed a European 'bill of rights' encompassing indivisible civic and social rights.[21] This Chapter will draw on these documents and identify five emerging themes that have refashioned European social policy over the last decade, specifically:

(i)   promoting employment;
(ii) reorganising work;
(iii) combating social exclusion;
(iv) mainstreaming gender equality; and
(v)   consolidation, compliance and enforcement of social legislation.

II PROMOTING EMPLOYMENT

(1) Growth, Competitiveness, Employment

Why this White Paper?
The one and only reason is unemployment. We are aware of its scale, and of its consequences too. The difficult thing, as experience has taught us, is knowing how to tackle it.

---

[13] COM(93) 551. For comment, see J Kenner, 'European Social Policy—New Directions' (1994) 10 *International Journal of Comparative Labour Law and Industrial Relations* 56.

[14] *European Social Policy: A Way Forward for the Union*, COM(94) 333, p 7.

[15] *Growth, Competitiveness, Employment: The Challenges and Ways Forward into the 21st Century, Bulletin of the European Communities* Supplement 6/93.

[16] *Medium Term Social Action Programme 1995–1997*, COM(95) 134.

[17] *Partnership for a New Organisation of Work, Bulletin of the European Union* Supplement 4/97. See also COM(97) 127.

[18] Council Resolution on certain aspects for a European Union social policy: a contribution to economic and social convergence in the Union, OJ 1994, C368/3.

[19] Decision 95/593/EC on a medium-term Community action programme on equal opportunities for men and women (1996 to 2000) OJ 1995, L335/37.

[20] Presidency Conclusions, Essen European Council, 9/10 Dec 1994.

[21] *For a Europe of Civic and Social Rights* (European Commission, Luxembourg, 1996).

With this concise but sharp rhetorical exchange the Commission launched its 1993 'White Paper' on *Growth, Competitiveness, Employment: The Challenges and Ways Forward into the 21st Century*.[22] Whereas the Community's outlook had traditionally been introverted, concerned with integration and the establishment of an 'internal' market, the 'Growth White Paper' represented a turning point for a new Union that was in a hurry to assert itself as a global player. As Sciarra has noted,[23] the global bearing of unemployment and the 'impossibility of conceiving of growth for Europe without looking beyond its borders' is the philosophy that inspired the White Paper. Hence, the Commission's first task was to snuff out complacency, although it should be noted that, as in 1980,[24] the Economic and Social Committee (ECOSOC), in its Opinion on Employment in Europe,[25] had already sounded the warning bells. Radical rethinking was required to balance the desire to remain faithful to the 'ideals which have come to characterise and represent Europe' while finding a 'new synthesis of the aims pursued by society'—work as a factor of social integration, equality of opportunity—and the requirements of the economy—competitiveness and job creation.[26] Moreover, by placing the promotion of employment at the top of the Union's global agenda, the Commission was also subverting the widely perceived dichotomy between employment protection and employment creation objectives within European social policy.

Between 1991 and 1993 there had been a reduction of two million in total employment in the Community, the first ever recorded decline. Unemployment levels, endemic in the Community since the 1970s, but steady at 12 million by the late 1980s, had now reached 17 million with a projected rise to 20 million in 1994, comprising 12 per cent of the labour force.[27] The growth of cyclical, structural and technological unemployment was now recognised as both a consequence and a cause of Europe's declining global competitiveness.[28] The employment rate in the EU stood at 60 per cent compared with 70–75 per cent in the US and Japan, the Union's global competitors. To return unemployment rates to 1980s levels by 2000 would

---

[22] *Bulletin of the European Communities Supplement* 6/93, p 9.

[23] S Sciarra, *How 'Global' is Labour Law? The Perspective of Social Rights in the European Union*, EUI Working Paper No 96/6 (EUI, Florence, 1996) p 8.

[24] See the introduction of ch 3.

[25] OJ 1993, C161/34. ECOSOC warned that unemployment threatened to become the 'key problem of the 1990s and to destabilise Europe's democratic structures' (para 1.1). Reference was made to an earlier Council Resolution of 21 Dec 1992, OJ 1993, C49/3, which acknowledged the need to tackle the 'serious and deteriorating situation' concerning unemployment in the Community but did not actually lead to any new progress (para 1.2.4).

[26] *Bulletin of the European Communities Supplement* 6/93, p 3.

[27] Reported to the Copenhagen European Council, 21/22 June 1993. See further, *Employment in Europe 1993*, COM(93) 341.

[28] *Bulletin of the European Communities Supplement* 6/93, pp 10–11.

require the creation of at least 15 million new jobs.[29] The Growth White Paper also pointed to a relative decline over 20 years in the growth of the European economy from around 4 per cent to 2.5 per cent a year; a fall in the investment ratio of five percentage points; and a worsening of Europe's competitive position in relation to the US and Japan as regards export share, research and development and launching new products.[30] Moreover, any return to growth needed to be employment-intensive for, as ECOSOC had warned, Europe's existing production system based on a market economy open to international competition was likely to be able to absorb only part of the pool of unemployed.[31]

How then to tackle mass unemployment? Was there a route back to full employment and, if so, was such a path compatible with both higher social standards and stronger global competitiveness? The established wisdom, derived from a highly influential report of the OECD,[32] was that high unemployment and the lack of job creation were caused by 'rigidities' in the labour market. Rules deemed restrictive and hidebound would be likely to discourage employers from taking on new workers, particularly young ones.[33] Such rigidities could only be removed by systematic deregulation of employment law and modernisation of social protection systems to create more 'flexibility' in order to attract entrepreneurs into the Single Market.[34] From this perspective, flexibility is solely concerned with the labour market from the employer's standpoint and the employee's distinct needs for flexibility are overlooked.[35] Moreover, other forms of flexibility: capital; managerial expertise; or technological ability, are not taken into account.[36] Instead employers would seek to utilise a 'peripheral' workforce of part-time, temporary and, increasingly, 'externalised' sub-contracted workers.[37] Not surprisingly, the narrow view that flexibility is a byword for labour

---

[29] See Commission Recommendation for the Broad Guidelines of the Economic Policies of the Member States and of the Community, COM(93) 629.

[30] *Bulletin of the European Communities Supplement* 6/93, p 9.

[31] *Opinion on growth, competitiveness and employment: medium-term considerations. Priority for employment within the context of the European socio-economic system*, OJ 1993, C352/9, para 10.2.

[32] *Labour Market Flexibility*. Report by a High Level Group of Experts (OECD, Paris, 1986). See E Szyszczak, 'The Evolving European Employment Strategy' in Shaw, n 8 above, 197–220 at 200–1.

[33] See ECOSOC *Opinion on growth, competitiveness and employment*, OJ 1993, C352/9, para 4.3.

[34] See H Siebert, 'Labor Rigidities: at the Root of Unemployment in Europe' (1997) 11 *Journal of Economic Perspectives* 43. For a critique, see S Deakin and H Reed, 'The Contested Meaning of Labour Market Flexibility: Economic Theory and the Discourse of European Integration' in Shaw, n 8 above, 71–99.

[35] See G More, 'The Acquired Rights Directive: Frustrating or Facilitating Labour Market Flexibility?' in J Shaw and G More (eds) *New Legal Dynamics of European Union* (Clarendon Press, Oxford, 1995) 129–45 at 137–8.

[36] *Ibid*.

[37] *Ibid*.

market deregulation was strongly supported by European employers' organisations.[38] Ominously, ECOSOC, in an Opinion issued in advance of the White Paper,[39] leaned towards deregulation, or at least amending social laws so as to permit the more efficient organisation of production processes and services,[40] although the 'removal of restrictions must not *unacceptably impair* the legal situation of workers'.[41]

An alternative view, advanced by Deakin and Wilkinson,[42] is that transnational social standards dynamically interact with economic integration to produce a continuous upwards movement in social and economic outcomes. Labour markets and social welfare systems should be *adapted* rather than deregulated through active measures designed to ensure macroeconomic stability and high employment levels.[43] This would avoid the trap of a low paid, low skilled and relatively under-productive labour market as typified by the US,[44] a cycle that elements within the Clinton administration were seeking to break.[45] 'Flexibility', in this context, is to be achieved through an 'active labour market policy' encompassing enhanced vocational training, assisted job searches and targeted public expenditure and subsidies to enterprises, encouraging employers to retain and take on workers.[46] An active labour market policy is an antidote for passive protectionism[47] that could help to overcome 'rigidities', real or imaginary, by creating a climate for employment-intensive growth where social policy, far from being an obstacle to job creation and the operation of the labour market, serves as an 'input' into economic development.[48] Therefore, a flexible economy would be in a better position to create jobs and wealth, *and* to procure the

---

[38] See for example, the views of employers expressed in ECOSOC's *Opinion on growth, competitiveness and employment*, OJ 1993, C352/9. ECOSOC noted that: 'employers are dismayed at the way in which industry has increasingly subjected to often burdensome and sometimes unjustified charges, and hamstrung by constraints of all kinds. Restrictive rules and regulations have prevented them from organising their production processes efficiently (and some of these regulations come from the EC) . . . Employers therefore call for early action to free firms from these constraints' (paras 2.2–2.3).

[39] *Ibid.*

[40] *Ibid* para 2.4.

[41] *Ibid* para 2.6. Emphasis added.

[42] See S Deakin and F Wilkinson, 'Rights vs Efficiency? The Economic Case for Transnational Labour Standards' (1994) 23 *Industrial Law Journal* 289 at 308.

[43] See Rhodes, n 9 above at 5.

[44] See Deakin and Wilkinson, n 42 above at 298.

[45] See in particular the policies put forward by Robert Reich, Clinton's Labor Secretary: R Reich, *The Work of Nations* (Vintage, London, 1992); and R Reich, *The Next American Frontier* (Penguin, London, 1984). Discussed by S Sciarra, 'Social Values and the Multiple Sources of European Social Law' (1995) 1 *European Law Journal* 60 at 73–6.

[46] See Deakin and Reed, n 34 above at 83–4.

[47] See A Supiot, *Beyond Employment: Changes in Work and the Future of Labour Law in Europe* (OUP, Oxford, 2001) p 199. Supiot argues that it is no longer possible to manage predictable risks and therefore the focus must be to manage all forms of uncertainty by offering freedom of action and a range of choices for employers and workers.

[48] See Deakin and Reed, n 34 above at 83.

means for greater security than a rigid economy.[49] In other words, there is mutual dependency between flexibility and security, a theme later developed in the 1997 Green Paper on the Organisation of Work.[50]

In the Growth White Paper the Commission eschewed ideologically driven 'miracle cures' such as protectionism, public spending sprees, reductions in working hours or drastic cuts in wages to align labour costs with those of competitors in developing countries.[51] While accepting that the unemployment level was, in part, a legacy of the depressed rate of economic growth and 'rigidities in the labour market',[52] the Commission avoided repeating the explicitly deregulatory language used by ECOSOC and sought instead to reconcile both sides of the flexibility debate by targeting policies aimed at:[53]

... *a thoroughgoing reform of the labour market*, with the introduction of greater flexibility in the organisation of work and the distribution of working time, reduced labour costs, a higher level of skills, and pro-active labour market policies.

Such an overhaul of the labour market, while it would address the issue of direct and indirect labour costs,[54] would be focused mainly on improving education and training and reviewing the way work is organised. For example, steps could be taken to remove obstacles that make it more difficult or costly to employ part-time or fixed-term workers, an approach later taken up by the social partners when negotiating agreements covering these areas. At the same time, social protection systems should be maintained and priority given to combating social exclusion and unemployment among young people and the long-term unemployed.[55] Action was also required to strengthen equal opportunities policies for men and women in employment.[56]

Labour flexibility needed to be examined from two angles.[57] First, *external flexibility* to make it possible for more unemployed people to meet the identified requirements of business. This would involve improvements to geographical mobility, greater vocational training and 'sometimes radical' initiatives tested in several Member States, such as reducing unemployment benefits, cutting taxes for low paid workers and making it easier to lay off

---

[49] Supiot, *Beyond Employment: Changes in Work and the Future of Labour Law in Europe*, n 47 above, p 191.

[50] *Bulletin of the European Union Supplement* 4/97. For an earlier reference, see the Commission's 'European Pact of Confidence for Employment', *Action for Employment in Europe*, COM(96) 485, para 3.13.

[51] *Bulletin of the European Communities Supplement* 6/93, p 9.

[52] *Ibid* p 127.

[53] *Ibid* p 124.

[54] *Ibid* pp 130–1.

[55] *Ibid* p 124.

[56] *Ibid* p 134.

[57] *Ibid* p 17.

workers on unlimited contracts.[58] Secondly, *internal flexibility* arising from the 'optimum management of a company's human resources',[59] or what would be later described as the 'flexible firm'.[60] The aim was to 'adjust the workforce without making people redundant wherever this can be avoided'.[61] For example, companies might improve internal flexibility by means of staff versatility, the integrated organisation of work, flexible working hours and performance-related pay.[62] Hourly wage increases would need to be kept below the growth of productivity.[63] Both aspects of flexibility required decentralisation and the involvement of the social partners.[64]

Pro-active labour market measures were presented as an alternative to the traditional inactive approach that treats the unemployed as passive recipients of benefit with little to occupy their time.[65] The catalyst for change would be to reform education and training systems.[66] This would involve job training and placements together with an overhaul of employment services to meet these objectives.[67] Anyone leaving the school system before the age of 18 without a meaningful vocational qualification would be entitled to a 'Youthstart' in the form of a training and employment experience.[68]

Reforming the labour market, as envisaged by the Growth White Paper, would involve a fundamental shift in the orientation of employment law and social policy in two ways. First, employment law and social protection systems that had been designed to guarantee stability would now have to be adapted to create flexibility.[69] Secondly, the 'European social model' which had been tailored towards the 'standard' employment relationship[70]—where employees, usually male, typically work full-time on a permanent basis for the same concern for their entire career—would have to be reshaped to reflect the increase in 'non-standard' employment—predominantly female, part-time, fixed-term and temporary work. Rather, European social policy had to transcend such outmoded distinctions and

---

[58] *Bulletin of the European Communities Supplement* 6/93, p 9.
[59] *Ibid.*
[60] See *Partnership for a New Organisation of Work*, *Bulletin of the European Union Supplement* 4/97, paras 18–19.
[61] *Bulletin of the European Communities Supplement* 6/93, p 17.
[62] *Ibid.*
[63] *Ibid* p 130.
[64] *Ibid* pp 17–18.
[65] *Ibid* pp 18–19.
[66] *Ibid* pp 117–22.
[67] *Ibid* pp 18–19.
[68] *Ibid* p 19. For a comprehensive discussion of this area, see J Shaw, 'From the Margins to the Centre: Education and Training Law and Policy' in P Craig and G de Búrca (eds) *The Evolution of EU Law* (OUP, Oxford, 1999) 555–95.
[69] See Sciarra, *How 'Global' is Labour Law? The Perspective of Social Rights in the European Union*, n 23 above, p 4.
[70] See U Mückenberger, 'Non-standard Forms of Work and the Role of Changes in Labour and Social Security Regulation' (1989) 17 *International Journal of the Sociology of Law* 381.

other traditional bipolarities such as the differentiation between working time and leisure time.[71] As Whiteford observes,[72] the sub-text was the dismantling of the frameworks built up in the past for the legal protection of workers—or at least 'standard' workers—but there was no certainty or clear consensus about the shape of Union social policy in the future.

(2) The Green Paper on European Social Policy

Many of these themes had already emerged in the preceding Green Paper on European Social Policy of November 1993.[73] In his introduction, former Commissioner Flynn, aware of the broad thrust of the proposals to be presented in the Growth White Paper, revealed the essentially defensive standpoint of the Directorate General for Employment, Industrial Relations and Social Affairs when he explained that:[74]

The premise at the heart of this Green Paper is that the next phase in the development of European social policy cannot be based on the idea that social progress must go into retreat in order for economic competitiveness to recover.

Flynn sought to steer the debate towards solutions that would enable economic success and high social standards to go hand in hand. Europe's social policy was influenced by the operation of free markets, especially free labour markets, and by the development of social ground rules. The Commission identified two important elements in this concept:[75]

... on the one hand *a defensive mechanism* to ensure that there is a minimum floor below which social standards should not fall in certain key areas, and on the other hand *a more pro-active concept* aimed at ensuring convergence through social progress.

While acknowledging that the social consensus that lay behind this statement was now open to question, the Commission proceeded to set out its stall as follows:[76]

Although it is a fact that in times of fierce competition enterprises need flexibility and that high unemployment reduces the bargaining power of workers, competition within the Community on the basis of *unacceptably low social standards*, rather than productivity of enterprises, will undermine the economic objectives of the Union.

---

[71] See Supiot, *Beyond Employment: Changes in Work and the Future of Labour Law in Europe*, n 47 above, pp 58–93.
[72] See E Whiteford, 'W(h)ither Social Policy?' in Shaw and More, n 35 above, 111–28 at 126.
[73] COM(93) 551.
[74] *Ibid* p 6.
[75] *Ibid* p 59. Emphasis added.
[76] *Ibid* pp 59–60. Emphasis added.

Therefore, although the Commission was endorsing high social standards as an integral part of a competitive model of economic development,[77] the driving motivation for this assertion was to equate low social standards with 'unfair competition' and warn against the threat of a deregulatory 'race to the bottom',[78] rather than to present a case for common social values distinct from the integration process. This essentially negative approach was firmly reinforced by the ensuing White Paper on European Social Policy where the Commission, echoing the Ohlin Report,[79] stated that:[80]

The establishment of a framework of basic minimum standards . . . provides a bulwark against using low social standards as an instrument of unfair economic competition and protection against reducing social standards to gain competitiveness, and is also an expression of the political will to maintain the momentum of social progress.

In the Green Paper, the Commission, recognising that changes were taking place that were comparable with the industrial revolution,[81] suggested a range of responses to technological and structural change; including: life-long education and training, greater labour market adaptability to match jobs with skills; more wage variety to reflect economic conditions; and greater incentives to work through more effective targeting of social benefits. The Commission also highlighted other factors affecting the role of work in society and the future of the welfare state:[82] rapid technological progress; the demise of the 'Fordist' model of production;[83] changes in family structures; the massive entry of women into the labour market; and demographic trends, notably the ageing of the population.[84] Ultimately this

---

[77] COM(93) 551, p 60. See also the Commission's Explanatory Memorandum on its Opinion on an Equitable Wage which sought to encourage firms to 'replace low-wage, low-productivity employment with high-wage, high-productivity employment', COM(93) 388. See C Barnard and S Deakin, 'Social Policy in Search of a Role: Integration, Cohesion and Citizenship' in A Caiger and D Floudas (eds) *1996 Onwards: Lowering the Barriers Further* (Wiley, Chichester, 1996) 177–95 at 186.

[78] This expression can be traced back to Judge Brandeis in *Ligett v Lee* [1933] US 557. Judge Brandeis used the phrase to describe the competition between states to reduce regulatory requirements so as to attract business. See B Hepple, 'New Approaches to International Labour Regulation' (1997) 26 *Industrial Law Journal* 353 at 355–6. See generally, C Barnard, 'Social Dumping and the Race to the Bottom: Some Lessons for the EU from Delaware' (2000) 25 *European Law Review* 57.

[79] 'Social Aspects of European Economic Co-operation' (1956) 74 *International Labour Review* 99. See ch 1 for discussion.

[80] COM(94) 333. Introduction, para 19.

[81] COM(93) 551, p 19.

[82] *Ibid* pp 19–22.

[83] Supiot describes this concept as, typically, large industrial businesses engaging in mass production based on a narrow specialisation of jobs and competencies and pyramidal management (hierarchical structure of labour, separation between product design and manufacture). See Supiot, *Beyond Employment: Changes in Work and the Future of Labour Law in Europe*, n 47 above, p 1.

[84] The Commission estimated that by 2020 the ratio of people of age 65 or older to those in working age, ie 15–64 would increase by about 50% raising implications for the costs on employed workers to guarantee maintenance of pension levels and universal health care.

would lead to a realignment of the functions of the State, the enterprise and the family.[85] Most importantly, the Green Paper, while it made a general case for social justice and equal opportunity, stressed the need for a new paradigm of Union social policy beyond the world of work, a theme taken up in the White Paper when it was published in July 1994.

(3) The White Paper on European Social Policy

The White Paper sought to address 65 questions raised in the Green Paper[86] by taking account of extensive consultations contained in a separate technical annex. Whilst the Commission sought to respond to the broad themes of the Green Paper, its new document was more cautious, reflecting the influence of the intervening Growth White Paper and the publication of annual Economic Guidelines by the Council intended to co-ordinate the economic policies of the Member States.[87] The Guidelines for 1993 had stressed price and exchange rate stability as well as pay moderation as methods of stimulating job creation. Emphasis was also placed on controlling indirect labour costs.[88]

Dispensing with any reference to social justice, the Commission sought to establish a consensus around a synergy of 'shared values which form the basis of the European social model' encapsulated in the Social Charter.[89] These included:[90]

... democracy and individual rights, free collective bargaining, the market economy, equality of opportunity for all and social welfare and solidarity.

The purpose of the White Paper was to preserve and develop the 'European social model' by developing guiding principles and applying a range of instruments for action.[91] The Commission's rhetoric was coded. By unveiling the concept of a 'European social model', or perhaps more accurately, a north European social model,[92] the Commission was seeking to identify

---

[85] COM(93) 551, p 19.

[86] *Ibid* pp 74–9.

[87] Council Recommendation 94/7/EC on the broad guidelines of the economic policies of the Member States and of the Community, OJ 1994, L7/9. The guidelines, issued in accordance with Art 103(2) [now 99(2)] EC, are intended to co-ordinate the economic policies of the Member States as a matter of 'common concern'. The Council Recommendation broadly echoed the themes in the Growth White Paper while placing special emphasis on reducing the indirect cost of labour with the objective of promoting the twin aims of job-creation in services responding to society's new needs and pay moderation to save jobs in sectors exposed to international competition by curbing the replacement of labour by capital and the relocation of activity.

[88] *Ibid* p 11. See Sciarra (1995, *European Law Journal*) n 45 above at 64.

[89] COM(94) 333. Introduction, para 3.

[90] *Ibid.*

[91] *Ibid.* Introduction.

[92] See Kleinman and Piachaud, n 7 above at 12. For example, Szyszczak notes that government expenditure on social welfare is one-third of GDP in Sweden and only one-sixth in Portugal. See E Szyszczak, *EC Labour Law* (Longman, Harlow, 2000) p 165.

the confines within which the Community actors were prepared to operate. In other words, the 'European social model' was being presented both positively, as an assertion of Europe's collective social identity,[93] and negatively, as an alternative to the politically unacceptable models of the US and Japan.[94] The crux of the matter was somehow to find a policy mix and *modus operandi* that would enable Europe to maintain a social consensus and yet be able to adapt its social policies through greater flexibility in the labour market and close the employment and competitiveness gap with its global competitors. By investing in a 'world-class' labour force[95] it would still be possible to encourage high standards in a competitive Europe.[96] Sciarra explains the evolution of employment law in the following terms:[97]

Its new genetic structure is produced by the combination of the 'old' protective guarantees with the 'new' measures aimed at integrating in the labour market. Labour law in the European context does not—and could not—pursue an abstract idea of solidarity among job holders; it should rather be thought of as a new tool to favour and create occupations, differentiating—when necessary—individual and collective guarantees, and yet entitling all employees to basic essential rights . . .

The new structure would not involve exchanging social rights for the needs of business but modulating them in accordance with the needs of workers for flexibility.[98] With this task in mind, the Commission presented four guiding principles and objectives for the future role of the Union. First, employment was the key to social and economic integration. Without new jobs, high social standards and the capacity to compete in world markets would not be reconcilable.[99] Secondly, competitiveness and solidarity were two sides of the same coin. Maintenance of social standards would be dependant on continuing productivity gains.[100] Thirdly, the Commission extended the notion of convergence from macroeconomic policy to employment policy by linking convergence to diversity. It followed that total harmonisation of social policies would not be an objective of the Union. However, in a tilt towards a programmatic soft law oriented approach, the Commission recommended the convergence of goals and policies by fixing common objectives that would permit the coexistence of different national systems progressing in harmony towards the fundamental objectives of the Union.[101] Fourthly, there should be a level playing field of common minimum

---

[93] For discussion on the ideals of social models from More to Rousseau, see Allott, n 6 above at 52–3.
[94] See Szyszczak, *EC Labour Law*, n 92 above, pp 164–5.
[95] COM(94) 333. Ch II.
[96] *Ibid.* Ch III.
[97] Sciarra (1995, *European Law Journal*) n 45 above at 66. Emphasis contained in the original.
[98] *Ibid* at 67.
[99] COM(94) 333. Introduction, para 16.
[100] *Ibid* para 17.
[101] *Ibid* para 18.

standards that would take account of the relative economic strength of the different Member States. Minimum standards should not over-stretch the economically weaker Member States, and they should not prevent the more developed Member States from implementing higher standards.[102]

Post-1994 these four principles have guided the development of Community employment law and social policy. In each case the achievement of a high level of employment and social protection in line with the objective in Article 2 EC, has provided the rationale for Community action. The emphasis was now on social goals to be achieved through technocratic support and soft law rather than social rights furthered by harmonisation.[103] In order to reinforce this new approach the Council adopted a Resolution on Union Social Policy in December 1994.[104]

(4) The Council Resolution on Social Policy

The Council Resolution sought to merge three strands of policy drawn from the Commission's documents. First, the Council envisaged the further development of the social dimension and the strengthening of the role of the two sides of industry as an essential precondition for combining 'market freedom and social balance'.[105] Secondly, emphasising the need for strong and sustainable growth, the Council sought to improve the 'efficiency of the labour market' by means of specific measures to facilitate renewed growth that would create as many jobs as possible.[106] Thirdly, the Union's international competitiveness had to be strengthened so that 'in the framework of firm competition as regards the location of undertakings' any economic success would be used for the purpose of sustainable social progress.[107]

In order to reconcile these policy strands, the Council resolved that proposals for minimum standards in social legislation would have to include an assessment of the impact on employment and on small and medium-sized enterprises.[108] Progress would be at a cautious pace, with an emphasis on specific proposals designed to build up instrumentally a core of minimum standards in a pragmatic and flexible manner to facilitate a 'gradual convergence', respecting both the economic capabilities of Member

---

[102] *Ibid* para 19.
[103] See H Cullen and E Campbell, 'The future of social policy-making in the European Union' in P Craig and C Harlow (eds) *Lawmaking in the European Union* (Kluwer, London, 1998) 262–84 at 263.
[104] Council Resolution of 6 Dec 1994 on certain aspects for a European Union social policy: a contribution to economic and social convergence in the Union, OJ 1994, C368/3.
[105] *Ibid* point 9.
[106] *Ibid.*
[107] *Ibid.*
[108] *Ibid* point 14.

States and helping to meet the expectations of workers, while calming fears about social dismantling and dumping in the Union.[109] Convergence rather than unification of social systems was to be preferred, not just because of the principle of subsidiarity, but also because the latter would reduce the chances of disadvantaged regions in the competition for location.[110] The Council aimed to achieve this 'gradual convergence' by aligning national goals with due regard for the economic strength of the Member States.[111]

(5) The 'Essen Process'

Within a week of the adoption of the Council Resolution, the European Council met at Essen and sought to apply the notion of 'gradual convergence' by introducing an experimental process to monitor and co-ordinate employment policies in the Member States, intensifying activities to exchange information and promote best practice.[112] In particular, a series of five key areas for job creation were identified based on active labour market measures. The priorities were set out as follows:

(1) Improving employment opportunities for the labour force by promoting investment in vocational training.[113]
(2) Increasing the employment-intensiveness of growth.[114]
(3) Reducing non-wage labour costs extensively enough to ensure that there is a noticeable effect on decisions concerning the taking on of employees and in particular of unqualified employees.[115]
(4) Improving the effectiveness of labour-market policy.[116]

---

[109] Council Resolution of 6 Dec 1994 on certain aspects for a European Union social policy: a contribution to economic and social convergence in the Union, OJ 1994, C368/3, points 10 and 11.

[110] *Ibid* point 18.

[111] *Ibid* point 19.

[112] Presidency Conclusions, Essen European Council, 9/10 Dec 1994. Bull EU 12/94.

[113] To that end a key role would fall to the acquisition of vocational qualifications, particularly by young people. As many people as possible should receive initial and further training which enables them through life-long learning to adapt to changes brought about by technological progress, in order to reduce the risk of losing their employment.

[114] In particular through: more flexible organisation of work in a way which fulfils both the wishes of employees and the requirements of competition; a wage policy which encourages job-creating investments and in the present situation requires moderate wage agreements below increases in productivity; and, finally, the promotion of initiatives, particularly at regional and local level, that create jobs which take account of new requirements, e.g. in the environmental and social services spheres.

[115] The problem of non-wage labour costs could only be resolved through a joint effort by the economic sector, trade unions and the political sphere.

[116] The effectiveness of employment policy would be increased by avoiding practices, which are detrimental to readiness to work, and by moving from a passive to an active labour market policy. The individual incentive to continue seeking employment on the general labour market must remain. Particular account must be taken of this when working out income-support measures. The need for and efficiency of the instruments of labour-market policy would be assessed at regular intervals.

(5) Improving measures to help groups which are particularly hard hit by unemployment.[117]

The European Council, having set out these detailed priorities, proceeded to establish a co-ordinated 'European Employment Strategy' (EES) albeit without specific Treaty powers and by means of non-binding legal instruments. The idea behind Essen was based on both horizontal and vertical conceptions of interdependence. First, at the Union level, macroeconomic and employment policy priorities had to be reconciled if the Union's strategic priorities for global economic competitiveness and internal cohesion were to be fulfilled. For example, attempts were swiftly made to reconcile the Economic Guidelines with the Essen priorities to help overcome the danger of a 'two track' approach arising from any conflict with the EMU convergence criteria.[118] Second, in an increasingly integrated European economy, there would be greater interdependence between national and local actors,[119] to the extent that the employment policies of one state would be increasingly the 'common concern' of all[120]—a point graphically demonstrated by the 'Hoover affair'.[121]

Under the machinery of the emergent EES, each Member State was made responsible for transposing the key areas of action into their individual employment policies by producing a multi-annual employment programme having regard to the specific features of their economic and social situation.[122] Progress was to be reported annually to the Commission and the Councils responsible for Employment and Social Affairs and Economic and Financial Affairs. In order to promote best practice, a benchmarking exercise was conducted focusing on long-term unemployment, youth unemployment and equal opportunities. This strategy was developed by way of joint reports on the employment situation from the Commission and the Council to successive end of year summits in Madrid and Dublin.[123] The 'Essen process' was designed as an operational means for the Member States

[117] In particular: helping young people, especially school leavers who have virtually no qualifications, by offering them either employment or training; fighting against long-term unemployment must be a major aspect of labour-market policy; varying labour-market policy measures are necessary according to the very varied groups and requirements of the long-term unemployed; and special attention should be paid to the difficult situation of unemployed women and older employees.

[118] See European Commission, *Follow-up to the Essen European Council on Employment*, COM(95) 74, para 5. For discussion on the broader social policy implications of the convergence criteria, see T Hervey, *European Social Law and Policy* (Longman, Harlow, 1998) pp 29–30.

[119] See W Streeck, 'Neo-Voluntarism: A New European Social Policy Regime?' (1995) 1 *European Law Journal* 31 at 54–5.

[120] See the later reference to promoting employment as a 'common concern' in Art 126(2) EC, introduced by the Treaty of Amsterdam.

[121] See p 224 above.

[122] COM(95) 74, para 2.

[123] Dec 1995 and Dec 1996 respectively.

to develop, monitor, assess and report on their employment policies within the framework of an integrated strategy agreed by the European Council.[124] The Commission's role was to monitor and report rather than develop policy.

Essen represented a technocratic alternative to harmonisation driven by the European Council. After Essen, the initiative was firmly with the European Council. This top-down but multi-level approach was indicative of the political rather than legal orientation of employment policy[125] and was to provide a blueprint for the Employment Guidelines, essentially a reiteration of the five priorities, and the associated reporting, monitoring and surveillance procedures of the EES later formalised in the Amsterdam Employment Title.[126]

The 'Essen process' was accompanied by a raft of other activities and 'flanking policies' promoted in the Social Policy White Paper and applied in the Commission's medium-term SAP for 1995–1997,[127] including: an expansion of the policy content of the Commission's annual *Employment in Europe* reports;[128] strengthening of the employment observatory system and databases on labour market measures—in particular, to improve the quality of comparative statistical information;[129] and consolidation of the European Employment Service (EURES) set up to inform, counsel and place job-seekers across Europe.[130] The Standing Employment Committee, first established in 1970,[131] was to be revised and updated as the main institutional forum for dialogue between the Council, the social partners and the Commission on the Union's employment strategy.[132] The Structural Funds, particularly the European Social Fund, were to be adapted and strengthened to contribute in a complementary way to promote employment.[133] In respect of education and training, the 'Youthstart' initiative was to be

---

[124] See Presidency Conclusions, Dublin European Council, 13/14 Dec 1996, para 36.

[125] See Cullen and Campbell, n 103 above at 271; and S Sciarra, 'The Employment Title in the Amsterdam Treaty. A Multi-language Legal Discourse' in O'Keeffe and Twomey (1999) n 1 above, 157–70 at 160.

[126] Title VIII, Art 125–30 EC. Discussed in ch 11.

[127] COM(95) 134.

[128] COM(94) 333. Ch I, para 22. In the Action Programme, *ibid* the Commission proposed to focus these reports on the five Essen priorities and consider also the employment potential of the information society, the emergence of new approaches to work organisation, and local employment initiatives (para 1.1.4.). See further, *A European Strategy for Encouraging Local Development and Employment Initiatives,* COM(95) 273; and *Job Opportunities in the Information Society: Exploiting the Potential of the Information Revolution,* COM(98) 590.

[129] COM(94) 333. In the Action Programme, *ibid* the Commission proposed to rationalise these instruments in order to develop closer and more structured employment research programmes (para 1.2.2.).

[130] COM(94) 333. Ch I, para 22.

[131] Decision 70/532/EEC, OJ 1970, L273/25 (subsequently modified in 1972 and 1975).

[132] COM(95) 134, para 1.2.5.

[133] *Ibid* para 1.3.1. During the period 1994–1999, 141 mn ECU was to be committed for this purpose.

underpinned by a 'Union-wide guarantee' that no young person should be unemployed under the age of 18.[134] Targets were to be established to, inter alia, eliminate basic illiteracy, raise the status of initial vocational education and training, extend the scope and range of existing apprenticeship schemes and introduce tax incentives for firms and individuals to invest in their continuing training.[135] Further, the 'Leonardo' and 'Socrates' action programmes were established in tandem to harness activities in these areas.[136] Finally, a new series of Community initiatives was launched including Employment, designed to improve access to employment for disadvantaged groups, and ADAPT, intended to assist workers at risk of unemployment through industrial change to adapt to new working practices and methods.[137]

Despite all these efforts, by 1996, when the Commission launched a 'Confidence Pact' for Employment,[138] an air of crisis was pervading. Aggregate employment had fallen by 4 per cent since 1991 and such a persistent fall was 'undermining society and placing millions of men and women in precarious situations'.[139] A climate of confidence had to be restored as a prior condition for the recovery of investment and consumption.[140] The 'Confidence Pact' was primarily aimed at 'full mobilisation' of *all the actors*— public authorities and social partners alike—in a comprehensive strategy at macro-economic level and in the internal market.[141] Only in this way would it be possible to deliver the aims of an active labour market policy. Hence, in the relatively brief period from Maastricht to Amsterdam, the Union's strategy for combating unemployment through promoting active labour market measures and surveillance of national policies had become the *raison d'être* for the Union's social policy, first pervading and then eclipsing all other priorities in both ex-Articles 117–122 EC and the Agreement on Social Policy. All of this was made possible by a battery of high-level soft law initiatives—what Streeck has described as 'governance by persuasion'[142]—shattering the myth, actual or potential, of an autonomous, insulated European social policy.

---

[134] COM(94) 333. Ch II, para 12. Young persons should be provided with either a place on an education and training system or in a linked work and training placement.

[135] *Ibid.*

[136] 'Leonardo', the action programme on vocational training (1995–1999) was based on Art 127 [now 150] EC, Decision 94/819/EC, OJ 1994, L340/8. 'Socrates', the education action programme covering the same period, was based on Arts 126 and 127 [now 149 and 150] EC, Decision 95/819/EC, OJ 1995, L87/10. For discussion, see Hervey, n 118 above, pp 112–19.

[137] COM(94) 333. Ch II, para 24.

[138] *Action for Employment in Europe*, COM(96) 485.

[139] *Ibid* para 1.

[140] *Ibid.*

[141] *Ibid* para 5. The broad aims of the Pact were incorporated into the 'The Jobs Challenge: Dublin Declaration on Employment' issued at the Dublin European Council, 13/14 Dec 1996.

[142] See Streeck, n 119 above at 49.

III REORGANISING WORK

While the main thrust of the 'Essen process' was directed at addressing the structural problem of unemployment in the Union through a reform of national employment systems, the 'Confidence Pact' envisioned an equally ambitious parallel process, already trailed in the Growth White Paper,[143] whereby a new concept of the content and role of work in society needed to be devised.[144] This would entail two strands of policy development: firstly, reorganisation of work in firms, diversification of individual working times and statuses *to facilitate a new balance between flexibility and security*; and, secondly, the transformation of the link between working life, education and training throughout active life.[145] The Commission's mission, mapped out in the 1997 Green Paper on the Organisation of Work, was to rise above the sterile flexibility debate because:[146]

... while much has been written about the need for flexibility of the labour market and its regulation, much less has been said about the need for flexibility and security in the workplace ...

An improved organisation of work will not of itself solve the unemployment problem, but it can make a valuable contribution, firstly, to the competitiveness of European firms, and, secondly, to the improvement of the quality of working life and the employability of the workforce.

Once again the Commission was seeking a 'third way' to reconcile apparently conflicting themes, just as it had done in the 1980s with the inter-departmental Working Party on *The Social Dimension of the Internal Market*.[147] Whereas the Working Party had sought to reconcile the decentralised and normative (deregulatory/regulatory) approaches to social policy integration, the Green Paper addressed the hitherto opposing concepts of flexibility and security.[148] By early 1997 the notion of a third or middle path, as a means of overcoming conventional bipolar thinking, was very much in vogue with the emergence of 'modernising', putatively social democratic, leaders like President Clinton and his 'New Democrats' in the US and, imminently, Tony Blair and 'New Labour' in the UK.[149] Giddens, whose writings

---

[143] *Bulletin of the European Communities Supplement* 6/93, p 17.
[144] COM(96) 485, para 3.1.2.
[145] *Ibid.*
[146] *Bulletin of the European Union Supplement* 4/97, paras 3–4.
[147] *Social Europe*, Special Edn (European Communities, Luxembourg, 1988). See ch 3 for analysis.
[148] National developments along these lines were already taking place. For example, in the Netherlands a 'Flexibility and Security Agreement' was signed by the social partners in 1996 to address the needs of part-time and temporary workers. See Rhodes, n 9 above at 18.
[149] See for example, T Blair, *The Third Way: New Politics for the New Century* (Fabian Society, London, 1998). For discussion, see J Kenner, 'The EC Employment Title and the 'Third Way': Making Soft Law Work?' (1999) 15 *International Journal of Comparative Labour Law and Industrial Relations* 33.

have profoundly influenced Blair, has posited the 'Third Way' as a means of responding to fundamental challenges and dilemmas such as globalisation, individualisation and the breakdown of the Left/Right dichotomy.[150] In particular, advocates of the 'Third Way' regard globalisation not just as an economic phenomenon but as the *transformation of time and space in our lives*,[151] a refrain that carries echoes of the earlier demands of the European Parliament for an ergonomic approach to the concept of the 'working environment',[152] a plea largely heeded by the Court in the *Working Time* case.[153] Giddens argues that Europe needs to respond to globalisation by developing social, political and economic institutions that 'stretch above the nation-state and reach down to the individual'.[154]

In the 1997 Green Paper the Commission sought to address this transformation as manifested in what Supiot had described as the gradual erosion of the distinction between the two domains of 'working time'— largely male, and characterised by subordination within the employment relationship, and 'free time'—mainly female, typically unpaid household work and child rearing.[155] The Commission suggested a range of 'working lifetime policies' that may reduce unemployment and improve the quality of life by '*humanising* the world of work and, above all, its compatibility with private life'.[156] Among the suggestions were a reduction in working time, calculation of working time on an annual basis, greater part-time work and flexible leave arrangements.[157]

The Council Recommendation on Childcare[158] and the Framework Agreements on Parental Leave[159] and Part-time Work,[160] although limited in both scope and legal effectiveness, were indicative of this approach, possessing the dual aims of furthering a 'family friendly' agenda based on a sharing of responsibilities between working parents, and offering both 'flexibility of working time and security for workers'.[161] Most significantly, while

---

[150] See A Giddens, *The Third Way* (Polity Press, Cambridge, 1998) pp 27–68; and, generally, A Giddens, *Beyond Left and Right: The Future of Radical Politics* (Polity Press, Cambridge, 1994).

[151] Giddens, *The Third Way*, *ibid* pp 30–1. See further, F Snyder, 'Europeanisation and Globalisation as Friends and Rivals: European Union Law in Global Economic Networks' in F Snyder (ed) *The Europeanisation of Law: The Legal Effects of European Integration* (Hart, Oxford, 2000) 293–320.

[152] *The Concept of the Working Environment and the Scope of Article 118a of the EEC Treaty*, 'Salisch Report', PE DOC A 2–226/88, 21 Oct 1988. See ch 3 for discussion.

[153] Case C–84/94, *United Kingdom v Council (Working Time Directive)* [1996] ECR I–5755.

[154] Giddens, *The Third Way*, n 150 above, p 142.

[155] See Supiot, *Beyond Employment: Changes in Work and the Future of Labour Law in Europe*, n 47 above, pp 58–93.

[156] *Bulletin of the European Union Supplement* 4/97, para 54. Emphasis added.

[157] *Ibid* paras 48–54.

[158] Council Recommendation 92/241/EEC, OJ 1992, L123/16.

[159] Dir 96/34/EC, OJ 1996, L 145/4.

[160] Dir 97/81/EC, OJ 1998, L 14/9.

[161] See the Commission's Explanatory Memorandum concerning the draft directive on part-time work, COM(97) 392, paras 9 and 11.

the main thrust of the Working Time Directive has tended to reinforce the traditional dichotomy between mutually excusive periods of 'working time' and 'rest',[162] it also contains specific provisions, such as the somewhat amorphous Article 13, which is intended to 'humanise' the workplace where work is organised according to a 'certain pattern' by obliging Member States to take account of the 'general principle of adapting work to the worker', in particular, by alleviating monotonous work and work at a pre-determined work rate, especially as regards breaks during work time.

The Green Paper was intended to build on these tentative developments as part of an overall philosophy, later developed in the 'Supiot Report',[163] that time must be envisaged as an individual subjective experience, that is to say, as time in workers' lives.[164] From this starting point of greater autonomy, the Commission proceeded to respond to the impact of globalisation by arguing that job security was no longer possible without flexibility. It was necessary to break out from conventional thinking because the organisation of work was no longer solely based on 'Fordist' hierarchical, top-down management with a high degree of specialisation and simple, often repetitive jobs.[165] Rather, a more fundamental change in the organisation of work was emerging in the 'post-Fordist' age—the 'flexible firm'. In this new entrepreneurial environment firms were shifting from fixed systems of production to flexible open-ended processes of organisational development offering new opportunities for lifelong learning, innovation and increased productivity.[166] Innovative methods piloted by highly productive 'flexible firms' were to be encouraged because, on the one hand, they would meet the requirements of employers for a reliable workforce with interchangeable skills and adaptable work patterns capable of coping with fluctuations in demand for their goods and services, while, on the other hand, it was hoped that employees would have greater job satisfaction, higher skills and long-term employability.[167] In particular, 'flexible firms' would be best placed to respond to rapid changes arising from, amongst other things, the emergence of a better-educated and trained workforce, more demanding consumers and, above all, the technological revolution.[168] In this new climate the buzzwords were 'adaptability' and 'employability'—later to emerge as central tenets of the Employment Guidelines post-Amsterdam.

The Green Paper was imbued with notions of rights *and* responsibilities. The worker who accepts more responsibility in order to be flexible will be

---

[162] Art 2(1) and (2) of Dir 93/104/EC, OJ 1993, L307/18.
[163] See Supiot, *Beyond Employment: Changes in Work and the Future of Labour Law in Europe*, n 47 above. Supiot's expert report to the Commission was first published in French in 1999.
[164] *Ibid* p 84.
[165] *Bulletin of the European Union Supplement* 4/97, para 13.
[166] *Ibid* para 18.
[167] *Ibid* para 31.
[168] *Ibid* paras 19–20.

rewarded with greater security. Moreover, security comes at a price. For society to afford security with flexibility, there would, over time, have to be a review of the basic foundations of systems of labour law, industrial relations, wage regulation and social security.[169] In particular, traditional labour law did not appear to have the answers to the diversification of work in the form of downsizing, outsourcing, subcontracting, teleworking and joint ventures.[170] As Streeck has argued, the idea was to renew the 'European social model' through a strategy of 'competitive solidarity' in which social policy interventions would be aimed at enabling individuals, sectors and, indeed, nation states to survive in an internationally competitive economy.[171] Ultimately, therefore, Community employment law, to be effective, must address the individualisation and heterogeneous nature of working time.[172]

The Green Paper identified several elements of this debate including, inter alia: lifelong learning[173] and training; mainstreaming equal opportunities policies;[174] integrating people with disabilities;[175] modernising the public sector;[176] reforming taxation;[177] and adapting social security systems.[178] In each case the Commission urged the Member States and the social partners to adapt systems, such as contributory pension schemes,[179] which are based on outdated models of employment that assume that the normal pattern of work is lifelong, full-time and permanent and therefore serve to perpetuate the work/family life distinction.

One of the problems for the Commission was that, in many of these areas, touching on social policies beyond the traditional confines of 'employment', competence rested mainly with the Member States. The potential for Community 'added value' justified under the subsidiarity principle was therefore

---

[169] *Ibid* paras 41–61.

[170] *Ibid* para 41.

[171] W Streeck, 'Competitive Solidarity: Rethinking the 'European Social Model'', MPIfG Working Paper 99/8 (Max-Planck-Institut für Sozialforschung, Cologne, 1999) p 3. Discussed by Deakin and Reed, n 34 above at 72.

[172] See Supiot, *Beyond Employment: Changes in Work and the Future of Labour Law in Europe*, n 47 above, p 84.

[173] *Bulletin of the European Union Supplement* 4/97, paras 39–40. See also, the White Paper, *Teaching and Learning: Towards the Learning Society*, COM(95) 590; the Green Paper on *Living and Working in the Information Society: People First* (European Commission, Brussels, 1996); and the follow-up Communication, COM(97) 397. The White Paper on Teaching and Learning defines 'lifelong learning' as 'the on-going access to the renewing of skills and the acquisition of knowledge'. See also, the Council Conclusion on Lifelong Learning, OJ 1997, C7/6.

[174] *Ibid* paras 65–7. See Section IV of this chapter.

[175] *Ibid* para 69.

[176] *Ibid* para 74. See further, COM(98) 641, *Modernising Public Employment Services to support the European Employment Strategy*.

[177] *Ibid* paras 55–7.

[178] *Ibid* paras 58–61. See also, COM(99) 347, *A Concerted Strategy for Modernising Social Protection*.

[179] *Ibid* para 58.

strictly limited. One area where Community action was possible was the labour market under the guise of the redefined European Social Fund which, under Article 123 [now 146] EC was intended to make the 'employment of workers easier' by facilitating their 'adaptation to industrial changes and to changes in production systems, in particular through vocational training and retraining'. The ADAPT Community initiative, introduced in the programming period 1994–1999 under the revised Objective 4,[180] carried a budget of 4 billion ECU, directing resources at training and re-training in an overall context of industrial change within and among companies. The Commission proposed to refocus ADAPT on work organisation with priority given to those willing to make improvements.[181]

Ultimately the success of the Commission's vision of a new organisation of work would depend on 'partnership',[182] a theme taken forward in the Commission's follow-up Communication on Modernising the Organisation of Work.[183] National and local actors, most importantly the social partners, were encouraged to accept a 'sense of ownership' of changes aimed at modernising the organisation of work and improving levels of employment.[184] The Final Report of the European Council's High Level Group on the economic and social implications of industrial change, the Gyllenhammer Report,[185] noted that all economic partners—the business community, employee representatives and public authorities—needed to anticipate and prepare for industrial change on a continuous basis.[186] This would only be possible if there was a high level of trust based on regular, transparent and comprehensive dialogue.[187] The Commission's group of experts set up to analyse and assess systems of participation in companies, the 'Davignon Group' explained the challenge that lay ahead in the following terms:[188]

Globalisation of the economy and the special place of European industry raises fundamental questions regarding the power of the social partners within the company. The type of labour needed by European companies—skilled, mobile, committed, responsible, and capable of using technical innovations and of identifying with the objective of increasing competitiveness and quality—cannot be expected to simply obey the employers' instructions. Workers must be closely and permanently involved in decision-making at all levels of the company.

---

[180] For the general framework, see Reg 2081/93/EEC, OJ 1993, L193/95; and for the detailed scheme, see the amended Social Fund Regulation, 2084/93/EEC, OJ L193/39.
[181] *Bulletin of the European Union Supplement* 4/97, paras 70–3.
[182] Hence the full title of the Green Paper: 'Partnership for a New Organisation of Work'.
[183] COM(98) 592.
[184] See C Barnard, *EC Employment Law*, 2nd edn (OUP, Oxford, 2000) p 508.
[185] Brussels: European Commission, 1998. Available at: <http://europa.eu.int/comm/dg05/soc-dial/gyllenhammer/gyllen-en.pdf>.
[186] *Ibid* p 9.
[187] *Ibid*. See further, Barnard, *EC Employment Law*, n 184 above, p 508.
[188] 'The Group of Experts on European Systems of Worker Involvement', Final Report, May 1997, para 19: <http://europa.eu.int/comm/employment_social/soc-dial/labour/davignon/davi_en.htm>.

The Community had already sought to establish trust through voluntary agreements. One example is the 'PEPPER' Recommendation on the promotion of employee participation in profits and enterprise results,[189] which is regarded as a shared responsibility of management and labour. In practice most national governments have not created a legal framework where such schemes can prosper.[190]

Another example is Article 13 of the European Works Councils Directive.[191] Under this provision the Directive would not apply where employers and employees' representatives in large transnational enterprises[192] had reached voluntary agreements in advance of the formal deadline for implementation provided such agreements covered the entire workforce and guaranteed transnational information and consultation of employees.[193] By September 1996, when the deadline had expired, 386 agreements had been signed, including 58 by British companies who were not technically bound by the Directive when it came into force.[194] Even within the framework of the Directive, every effort is made to create trust through the process of negotiation with the details of any agreement being left to the parties providing a consensus is reached within a stipulated timeframe.[195]

Further steps were now required to help create a workplace environment in which workers would be prepared to accept change while firms would be able to demonstrate their 'corporate social responsibility'. As we shall see in Chapter 11, these efforts have focused on the revival of the 'European Company Statute',[196] dormant since the early 1980s, a Directive on a General Framework for Improving Information and Consultation Rights of Employees,[197] and a Green Paper on a European framework for Corporate Social Responsibility.[198]

---

[189] Council Recommendation 92/443/EEC, OJ 1992, L243/53. See further, Barnard, *EC Employment Law*, n 184 above, pp 550–1.

[190] See the follow-up Communication, COM(96) 697.

[191] Dir 94/45/EC, OJ 1994, L254/64.

[192] Under Art 2(1) the Directive covers either: 'Community-scale undertakings', defined as undertakings with at least 1000 employees within the Member States and at least 150 employees in at least two Member States, or: 'Community-scale groups of undertakings', which are groups with at least 1000 employees in the Member States; at least two group undertakings—a controlling undertaking and its controlled undertaking—in different Member States; and, at least one group undertaking with at least 150 employees in one Member State and at least one other group undertaking with at least 150 employees in another Member State.

[193] Information should, under Art 6(3) relate to transnational questions that significantly affect workers' interests. Under Art 2(2) 'consultation' is defined as the 'exchange of views and establishment of dialogue' between employees' representatives and management.

[194] British firms not covered by the original Directive were not bound to comply until 15 Dec 1999 when the 'UK extension' Directive came into force: Dir 97/74/EC, OJ 1998, L10/22.

[195] See Arts 5–7 of Dir 94/45.

[196] Reg 2157/2001/EC on the Statute for a European Company (SE) OJ 2001, L294/1; Dir 2001/86/EC supplementing the Statute for a European company with regard to the involvement of employees, OJ 2001, L294/22.

[197] Dir 2002/14/EC, OJ 2002, L80/29.

[198] COM(2001) 366.

IV COMBATING SOCIAL EXCLUSION

(1) Reconceptualising Social Solidarity

Promoting employment rests side by side, but not always comfortably, with the interlocking but discrete aim of combating and, ultimately, eradicating social exclusion. Unemployment and social exclusion represent visible man-ifestations of situations that reflect, by their very existence and scale, the need to combine the Union's economic and political ambitions with a concern for its internal cohesion and social dimension.[199] The Social Charter left much unfinished business, not least the unsatisfactory resolution of the 'citizen / worker' debate. As was shown in chapter 4, the Social Charter protects workers who are not citizens but not citizens who are not workers. The Member States drew back from a broad inclusive conception of social citizenship and, in the process, excised or diluted all references from the Commission's draft to combating unemployment and social exclusion. Hence, when the TEU introduced limited citizenship provisions, a 'market citizenship' orientation to the concept was reinforced.[200] 'Social solidarity', an apparently all-embracing cornerstone of the 'European social model', was mere empty rhetoric for the increasingly large number of Europeans who were not 'worker citizens' and therefore excluded. As Kleinman and Piachaud perceptively observe:[201]

Solidarity can be understood as a mechanism of inclusion, but one that depends on identification with a particular group and hence paradoxically, on the exclusion of those deemed to be outside the group.

Social exclusion is a multifaceted phenomenon arising from a variety of incidences of poverty and marginalisation, including: long-term unemploy-ment; the impact of industrial change on poorly skilled workers; the break-down of family structures; homelessness; rural and urban deprivation; racism and xenophobia; and inaccessible social services.[202] By the early 1990s, Member States, who had traditionally regarded poverty as a resid-ual state of affairs that would disappear with progress and growth,[203] were finding these problems increasingly intractable and, therefore, politically sensitive. While Community anti-poverty programmes had been ongoing

[199] See *Towards a Europe of Solidarity: Intensifying the fight against social exclusion, fostering integration*, COM(92) 542, p 4.
[200] See now Arts 17–22 [ex 8–8e] EC. See further, M Everson, 'The Legacy of the Market Citizen' in Shaw and More, n 35 above, 73–90.
[201] See n 7 above at 7.
[202] See generally, COM(92) 542, and ECOSOC's Opinion on Social Exclusion, OJ 1993, C352/48.
[203] COM(92) 542, p 7.

from the 1970s,[204] there was general agreement that a fresh approach was needed and that many of the mechanisms causing social exclusion were structural.[205] Moreover, exclusion was linked with the wider legitimacy crisis as demonstrated by rising disillusion with the political process and growing social tensions, including disruptive behaviour involving violence or drugs and racial attacks, often founded on insecurity and fear for the future.[206] In the wake of escalating unemployment and homelessness,[207] widening income disparities,[208] demographic changes and pressures on social protection systems, the challenge for the Union was to reconceptualise social solidarity and develop policies capable of transcending the citizen/worker dichotomy.

In the Green Paper on Social Policy the Commission accepted this challenge and sought to carry forward a debate that had first been launched with the publication of the 'Poverty 3' Action Programme in 1989[209] followed by a Council Resolution on combating social exclusion.[210] The Commission's aim, developed in its 1992 Communication on Social Exclusion,[211] was to break out from the contested discourse over narrow and somewhat futile definitions of 'poverty'[212] and simultaneously develop a new, less stigmatised terminology because:[213]

The concept of social exclusion is a dynamic one, referring both to processes and consequent situations . . . More clearly than the concept of poverty, understood far too often as referring exclusively to income, it also states out the multidimensional

[204] See Council Resolution of 21 Jan 1974, OJ 1974, C13/1; Decision 75/458/EEC ('Poverty 1') OJ 1975, L199/34; Decision 85/8/EEC ('Poverty 2') OJ 1985, L2/24; and Decision 89/457/EEC ('Poverty 3') OJ 1989, L224/10.

[205] COM(92) 542, p 7.

[206] COM(93) 551, p 21.

[207] See COM(92) 542, p 3, where it was recorded that 35% of the long-term unemployed had never worked and it was estimated that there were three million homeless people in the Community.

[208] 50 million people were recorded as 'poor' in 1985 on the basis that poverty, statistically, is based on a person living in a household for which the disposable income per adult equivalent is less than half the average disposable income per adult equivalent in the Member State in which that person lives. EUROSTAT, Rapid Reports, Population and Social Conditions 1990.7. By 1994 this figure had increased to 52 million. See COM(94) 333. Ch VI, para 14.

[209] Decision 89/457/EEC establishing a medium-term Community action programme concerning the economic and social integration of the economically and socially less privileged groups, OJ 1989, L224/10. See Hervey, n 118 above, p 165.

[210] OJ 1989, C277/1. See also, Council Recommendation 92/441/EEC on common criteria concerning sufficient resources and social assistance in social protection systems, OJ 1992, L245/46.

[211] COM(92) 542. The report was based on the work of an independent group of experts operating as the 'Observatory of policies for combating social exclusion'—see the Annex.

[212] In 'Poverty 1' people living in poverty were defined as 'persons, families or groups of persons, whose resources (material, cultural and social) are so limited as to exclude them from the minimum acceptable way of life in the Member State in which they live': Decision 85/8/EEC, OJ 1985, L2/24. See Hervey, n 118 above, p 161.

[213] COM(92) 542, p 8.

nature of the mechanisms whereby individuals and groups are excluded from taking part in the social exchanges, from the component practices and rights of social integration and of identity. Social exclusion does not only mean insufficient income, and it even goes beyond participation in working life: it is felt and shown in the fields of housing, education, health and access to services.

Within the framework of the implementation of the principle of subsidiarity, the areas of policy that impinge upon social exclusion are mainly the responsibility of the Member States not the Community. In particular, at the time of the TEU, there was no specific power for the Community to act to combat racism and xenophobia or address the exclusion of the disabled through anti-discrimination legislation. In its Communication, the Commission justified Community action on the basis that the problems were cumulative and interdependent and, therefore, it would be futile to tackle any one of the dimensions of social exclusion in isolation.[214] Moreover, because social exclusion affects both individuals and groups subject to discrimination and segregation, it highlights the risks of cracks appearing in the social fabric, suggesting something more than social inequality and, concomitantly, carries with it the risk of a two-tier or fragmented society.[215] The Community's role, therefore, was to provide 'added value' by identifying best practice, creating support networks and contributing to a deeper understanding of the debate.[216] The impact of Community policies on social exclusion would be analysed and transnational problems addressed. Further, the Community would seek to contribute towards the 'affirmation values common to all Member States: with special reference to respect for human dignity'.[217] A series of proposals for social policies to integrate people into society were set out both in the Communication and elsewhere, including the Green Paper, the White Paper and the medium term SAP.

(2) The Community's Structural Funds

An immediate aim was to gear the Community's Structural Funds[218] to combat social exclusion and interact with the labour market agenda.[219] The resources available were far from negligible. In the period between 1987 and 1993 these funds had doubled to an annual 14 billion ECU and a further increase of 72 per cent was planned for 1994–1999.[220] For example,

---

[214] COM(92) 542, p 8.

[215] *Ibid.*

[216] *Ibid* p 4.

[217] *Ibid* p 5.

[218] The European Social Fund (ESF); the European Regional Development Fund (ERDF); and the European Agricultural Guidance and Guarantee Fund (EAGGF).

[219] See *From the Single Act to Maastricht and beyond: the means to match our ambitions*, COM(92) 2000; and *Community Structural Assistance and Employment*, COM(96) 109.

[220] For details see *Community Structural Policies—Assessment and Outlook*, COM(92) 84.

the European Social Fund, which largely benefited the 'included'—helping skilled, mainly male, full-time workers to be geographically mobile—was now converted into an instrument for cohesion, targeting extra resources at the long-term unemployed and integrating young people into work mainly in the less developed and declining regions.[221] Specific initiatives were launched such as 'NOW', promoting equal opportunities for women in employment and vocational training,[222] and 'HORIZON', addressing the educational and vocational needs of disabled people with specific job access difficulties.[223] More generally, enterprises were to be encouraged to introduce 'anthropocentric production systems' aimed at preventing exclusion.[224]

(3) Expanding Community Action

The Green Paper makes a specific link between social exclusion and new or expanded Treaty competences in areas such as education, vocational training and youth,[225] culture[226] and public health.[227] For example the 'SOCRATES' decision on education emphasised the elimination of social exclusion and the reduction of racism and xenophobia in the EU.[228] Vocational training initiatives would be targeted at young people and the long-term unemployed to help prevent exclusion or reintegrate the 'non-active' population through a 'trampoline effect' enabling people to bounce back from adversity to an acceptable standard of living.[229] Also, under the umbrella of social exclusion, neighbourhood-housing programmes within cities have been supported through the 'URBAN' initiative.[230] In relation to health care, policies have focused on the need for convergence of best practice in the Member States based on securing the right to health care for all as an element of the European social protection model.[231]

---

[221] The criteria for the ESF were redefined as priority Objectives 3 and 4 as broadly set out in the Structural Funds 'Framework' Regulation, 2081/93/EEC, OJ 1993, L193/95; and detailed in the amended Social Fund Regulation, 2084/93/EEC, OJ L193/39. See J Kenner, 'Economic and Social Cohesion—The Rocky Road Ahead' [1994] *Legal Issues of European Integration* 1 at 16–17.

[222] OJ 1990, C327/5.

[223] OJ 1990, C327/9.

[224] COM(92) 542, p 20.

[225] Arts 126–7 [now 149–50] EC.

[226] Art 128 [now 151] EC.

[227] Art 129 [now 152] EC.

[228] Decision 95/819/EC, OJ 1995, L87/10. See Cullen and Campbell, n 103 above at 270.

[229] COM(93) 551, pp 43–5.

[230] COM(94) 61. The criteria are satisfied where there is an accumulation of factors such as, high unemployment, low education attainment, poor housing, environmental decay and high crime rates.

[231] See for example, the Council Resolution on future action in the field of public health, OJ 1993, C174/1; and COM(94) 333, ch VII. See further, Hervey n 118 above, pp 135–57.

(4) Social Protection

Action was also required to converge economic policy with social protection objectives.[232] In 1992 the Council had adopted two recommendations on common criteria for guaranteed resources and benefits in social protection systems which sought to combine the need for financial support for the most deprived with all the measures necessary for their social and economic integration.[233] The Member States recognised that they had common problems, such as unemployment, ageing, changing family structures, and rising costs for social protection[234] and health care, but at the same time, they were determined to maintain hegemony over their economic and social protection policies.[235] The Commission instituted bi-annual reports on Member States' social protection systems but there was no obligation on States to take heed of them.[236]

In 1995, following a proposal in the medium-term SAP,[237] the Commission issued a Communication intended to spark a European debate on the future of social protection.[238] Emphasis was placed on social protection as an essential vector of social cohesion.[239] Social protection was presented as an example of solidarity resulting from the aim of universal coverage and the absence of a proportional link between contributions levied to finance the system and the individual vulnerability of the persons concerned.[240] Although the Commission sought to recognise the need to contain costs and replace 'the old rigidities with more flexibility',[241] the report heavily stressed the need to root out inequalities, including systemic bias against women, and proposed, for example, full social protection for part-time and temporary workers, and increased help for carers.[242] There was little enthusiasm

---

[232] See *The Future of Social Protection: A Framework for a European Debate*, COM(95) 466, where, at para 1.1, the Commission defines 'social protection' broadly as 'all the collective transfer systems designed to protect people against social risks'. The Commission note that, while there is significant diversity among national systems, all Member States provide specific maintenance benefits to cover the classic risks of old age and retirement, the death of the provider, disability, sickness, maternity, dependant children and unemployment. Some Member States also cover other contingencies, such as the cost of caring for the frail elderly, disabled or sick relatives, and sole parenthood.

[233] Recommendation 92/441/EEC on common criteria concerning sufficient resources and social assistance in social protection schemes, OJ 1992, L245/46; and Recommendation 92/442/EEC on the convergence of social protection objectives and policies, OJ 1992, L245/49.

[234] Amounting to one quarter or even one third of the GDP of individual Member States. See COM(94) 333. Ch VI, para 7.

[235] See COM(92) 542, p 20.

[236] See *Social Protection in Europe*, COM(95) 547.

[237] COM(95) 134, para 6.1.1.

[238] COM(95) 466.

[239] *Ibid* para 2.1.

[240] *Ibid* para 1.1.

[241] *Ibid*.

[242] *Ibid* para 2.1.

in the Council for taking forward the Commission's suggestions. Instead, the Member States focused narrowly on those elements of social protection strategies most closely tied to active labour market policies compatible with the budgetary constraints required for EMU. Moreover, parallel attempts to take this strategy further in the proposed 'Poverty 4' programme[243] were firmly rebuffed by, at least, the UK and Germany, on the grounds that the Commission's proposals were too invasive of national sovereignty in these areas.[244] The Commission continued to finance anti-poverty projects, some of which had originally been intended for 'Poverty 4' and, following a legal challenge by the UK, the Court later upheld the Commission's decisions on the grounds of legal certainty.[245] In the meantime, the Commission believed that such reticence on the part of Member States would be temporary because both the level and financing of social protection were likely to become more sensitive political issues in the future, especially as demand for protection against social risks rose.[246]

(5) Integrating the Disabled and Older People

In addition to the above, specific action programmes were launched with the aim of ensuring the societal integration of disabled people and older people. While the programmes in question were, in part, a by-product of the Social Charter, they were now brought fully within the strategies for combating social exclusion and promoting employment. For example, 'Helios II', the Third Community Action Programme to assist Disabled People (1993–1996),[247] was concerned, on the one hand, with principles for implementing a vocational training policy and promoting employment[248] and, on the other, with measures, including those to promote functional rehabilitation, educational integration, social integration and an

---

[243] COM(93) 435.

[244] See Cullen & Campbell, n 103 above at 270–1.

[245] Case C–106/96, *United Kingdom v Commission (Poverty 4)* [1998] ECR I–2729; noted by T Hervey (1999) 36 *Common Market Law Review* 1053. The UK contended that the Commission had no authority to fund these projects and therefore breached Art 4 [now 7] EC on the grounds that each institution can only act within the limits of its powers. The Court agreed that the Commission was not competent to fund the expenditure (paras 31–5) but applied its power under Art 174 [now 231] EC to preserve the validity of payments made or undertakings given by the Commission in order to preserve legal certainty (paras 39–42).

[246] COM(95) 466, para 2.7.

[247] Decision 93/136/EEC, OJ 1993, L56/30. 'Helios' stands for 'Handicapped People Living Independently in an Open Society'.

[248] For example, the 'Handynet' computerised information and documentation system had been introduced during 'Helios I' (1988–1992) to meet the training needs of disabled people so as to enable them to enter or re-enter the labour market. See *ibid*. Annex, point 3.

independent way of life for disabled people.[249] These measures included the development of a policy at Community level of co-operation with the Member States and the organisations and associations concerned with the integration of disabled people based on the 'best innovative and effective experience and practice in the Member States' involving, where appropriate, voluntary organisations.[250] Perhaps the most important element of 'Helios II' was the establishment of the European Disability Forum representing the Commission and NGOs[251] acting on behalf of disabled people and their families.[252] The Forum was to report to an Advisory Committee of government representatives chaired by the Commission.[253] The Commission would be obliged to take account of opinions issued by the Advisory Committee.[254] Although the consultative procedure was somewhat convoluted, the establishment of the Forum was a small but significant step towards enhanced civil dialogue and indicated a trend in favour of a more participatory approach to policy development.

Despite these positive features, the Council's Decision on 'Helios II' was marked by caution. References in the Commission's drafts to the development of a 'comprehensive Community integration policy' and a 'Community disability policy' were deleted from the final text.[255] However, the Commission, subjected to extensive lobbying, proceeded to launch a Communication in 1996 designed to integrate disability policies into mainstream Community policies and promote further initiatives for the integration of disabled people in working life as part of the 'Essen process'.[256] Just as significant as the move towards mainstreaming was, paradoxically, the Commission's decision not to proceed with its plans for a new multi-annual programme after 1996 on the grounds that there was no longer political support for such a measure. The Commission's reasoning was that programmatic activity in this area would be partly based on Article 235 [now 308] EC and was therefore deemed inimical to the principle of subsidiarity by some Member States.[257] This, in turn, threw a spotlight on the need for

---

[249] Annex Art 3. Art 2 defines disabled people as 'people with serious impairments, disabilities or handicaps resulting from physical, including sensory, or mental or psychological impairments which restrict or make impossible the performance of an activity or function considered normal for a human being'. Approximately one tenth of the total population are disabled, approximately 37 million in 1996, and about half of all disabled people are of working age. See *Equality of Opportunity for People with Disabilities*, COM(96) 406, p 3.

[250] *Ibid.* Art 3(c). 37mn ECU was set aside for these activities during the lifetime of the programme (Art 5(2)).

[251] Non-governmental organisations.

[252] Decision 93/136/EEC, OJ 1993, L56/30, Art 9.

[253] *Ibid.* Art 8(1).

[254] *Ibid.* Art 8(2).

[255] COM(91) 350 and COM(92) 482. See L Waddington, *Disability, Employment and the European Community* (Maklu, Antwerp, 1995) pp 123–8.

[256] See COM(96) 406, pp 12–13.

[257] In the case of 'Helios II' reliance was also placed on Art 128 EEC on vocational training.

a Treaty amendment encompassing disability discrimination for which the establishment of the Disability Forum was a catalyst.[258]

Programmatic activity in relation to older people in this period was more piecemeal. The Commission identified the broad challenge in terms of maintaining a high level of integration of the older population as Europe ages.[259] Following on from the European Year of Older People and Solidarity between Generations in 1993,[260] Council resolutions were adopted on flexible retirement arrangements[261] and the employment of older workers.[262] In both cases the Council was seeking to encourage actions by Member States to open up the labour market to those older workers who wished to continue working and be retrained while continuing to provide the security offered by retirement benefits. In the White Paper the Commission sought to build on these initiatives by establishing a framework for Community support for actions in favour of older people,[263] but, despite matching calls from ECOSOC[264] and the European Parliament,[265] the Council did not proceed with the proposal.

(6) Tackling Racism and Xenophobia

Lastly, but perhaps most importantly, soft law proclamations designed to combat racism, discrimination and xenophobia issued before Maastricht,[266] were now supplemented by stronger declarations within the framework of combating social exclusion.[267] This was a logical policy progression, for

---

[258] Calls for a Treaty amendment dated back to 1993 and were focused around the annual European Day of Disabled Persons. See M Bell & L Waddington, 'The 1996 Intergovernmental Conference and the Prospects of a Non-Discrimination Treaty Article' (1996) 25 *Industrial Law Journal* 320 at 327–8.

[259] COM(94) 333. Ch VI, para 25. According to EUROSTAT the number of people aged over 65 was expected to grow by 23 million or 45% by 2020 while the overall population was likely to fall. See *The demographic situation in the Community*, COM(94) 595.

[260] Decision 92/440/EEC, OJ 1992, L245/43.

[261] OJ 1993, C188/1.

[262] OJ 1995, C228/1.

[263] COM(94) 333. Ch VI, para 26. For the proposal, see COM(95) 53 and OJ 1995, C115/6.

[264] OJ 1993, C343/1.

[265] OJ 1994, C77/24.

[266] See the European Parliament's Committee of Enquiry (the Evrigenis Report, Strasbourg, 1986) and the ensuing 1986 Joint Declaration against Racism and Xenophobia of the European Parliament, the Council and the Commission, OJ 1986, C158/1. See also, the Council Resolution of 29 May 1990 on the struggle against racism and xenophobia, OJ 1990, C157/1; and the Declaration on Racism and Xenophobia issued at the Maastricht European Council on 9/10 Dec 1991. For further discussion, see ch 9.

[267] For example, the Council Resolution of 5 Oct 1995 on the fight against racism and xenophobia in the fields of employment and social affairs, OJ 1995, C296/5; ECOSOC Resolution on Racism, Xenophobia and Religious Intolerance, ESC 1387/92; the Joint Declaration of the Social Partners on the Prevention of Racial Discrimination and Xenophobia and the Promotion of Equal Treatment at the Workplace; and the European Parliament's Resolutions on Racism and Xenophobia, B4–0261/94, and Racism, Xenophobia and Anti-Semitism, B4–1239/95.

heightened incidents of racism, race discrimination and xenophobia are based on 'heterophobia', the fear of 'others' who are in some way different from or outside the majority.[268] Moreover, as Hervey notes,[269] public policy, including action at Union level,[270] may, consciously or not, serve to perpetuate assumptions that these 'others' are not full members of a particular society. For example, structural discrimination in national employment and education systems may make the acquisition of necessary skills disproportionately difficult for members of racial minorities.[271]

In the context of rising social tensions and internal policy contradictions, it was now widely recognised that rhetorical commitments and sporadic activities to combat racism and xenophobia were no longer sufficient. What was required, according to the Commission in the Green Paper, was comprehensive anti-discrimination legislation as part of an integrated and coherent approach to combating racism, discrimination and xenophobia, whether founded on colour, race, ethnicity or national origin, religion, beliefs or culture.[272] Moreover, the Commission called for full integration of third-country nationals including equal opportunities in employment, education, training and housing.[273] In the White Paper, the Commission recommended further steps to integrate migrant workers,[274] codes of practice on race discrimination,[275] and improved systems for monitoring racial harassment[276] but, instead of recommending anti-discrimination legislation, they merely pressed for specific powers to be included in the Treaty,[277] a wish later fulfilled with the inclusion of Article 13 EC by the Treaty of Amsterdam.

In the meantime, the momentum for further action to combat racism in the Member States was growing.[278] The Council set up an expert Consul-

---

[268] See T Hervey, 'Putting Europe's House in Order: Racism, Race Discrimination and Xenophobia after the Treaty of Amsterdam' in O'Keeffe and Twomey (1999) n 1 above, 329–49 at 330.

[269] *Ibid.*

[270] For example, under the 'Third Pillar' on Justice and Home Affairs, Title VI TEU (now mainly incorporated along with the 'Schengen acquis' into Title IV EC). See however, Joint Action 96/443/JHA adopted by the Council on the basis of Article K.3 [now 31] TEU concerning action to combat racism and xenophobia, OJ 1996, L185/5.

[271] See Hervey in O'Keeffe and Twomey (1999) n 268 above at 337; and E Szyszczak, 'Racism: The Limits of Market Equality' in B Hepple and E Szyszczak (eds) *Discrimination: The Limits of the Law* (Mansell, London, 1992) 125–47 at 127.

[272] COM(93) 551, p 49. See also, the European Parliament Resolution on the White Paper, OJ 1995, C43/63.

[273] *Ibid* p 47.

[274] COM(94) 333. Ch IV, paras 18–21. Proposed measures included ratification by the Member States of the International Convention on the protection of all migrant workers and members of their families adopted by the UN on 18 Dec 1990.

[275] *Ibid* para 24. See also, COM(95) 134, para 6.5.2.

[276] *Ibid.* At the Cannes European Council, 26/27 June 1995, the Council agreed to consider the feasibility of a European Monitoring Centre on Racism and Xenophobia.

[277] *Ibid* para 25. The Commission strongly reinforced the case for a Treaty amendment in its Communication on Racism, Xenophobia and Anti-Semitism, COM(95) 653, at para 2.3.7.

[278] See M Bell, 'The New Article 13 EC Treaty: A Sound Basis for European Anti-discrimination Law?' (1999) 6 *Maastricht Journal* 5 at 19.

tative Commission on racism and xenophobia in June 1994,[279] the Kahn Commission, which called for the elimination of all forms of discrimination against persons, or groups of persons, *whether citizens of the union or not.*[280] In the view of the Kahn Commission:

The Union has an imperative obligation to combat racism and racial discrimination. Indeed, as long as immigrants from non-EU countries are denied Community residential status, the process of their integration will be retarded and their segregation prolonged.

The ensuing Council Resolution on the fight against racism and xenophobia in the fields of employment and social affairs[281] called for account to be taken of the Kahn Commission's recommendations and agreed to make progress towards the following common objectives:[282]

(a) guaranteeing protection for persons against all forms of discrimination on grounds of race, colour, religion or national or ethnic origin;
(b) promoting employment and vocational training as significant means of integrating persons legally resident in the Member State concerned;
(c) fighting all forms of labour discrimination against workers legally resident in each Member State;
(d) promoting equal opportunities for the groups most vulnerable to discrimination;
(e) promoting adherence to democratic principles and human rights, and the principle of cultural and religious diversity;
(f) stimulating co-operation and the exchange of experience between Member States on working methods and arrangements to promote social cohesion.

Significantly, the Member States were seeking to restrict their commitment to those *legally resident* according to national laws—effectively excluding those most vulnerable to exploitation and discrimination such as asylum seekers and migrant workers performing 'undeclared work'.[283] Also absent was any commitment to amending the Treaty to enable comprehensive Community anti-discrimination legislation to be adopted. Nevertheless, the Council Resolution provided a route map for these objectives to be pursued through specific actions, such as the designation of 1997 as the European Year against Racism,[284] and within the IGC process, by individual Member

---

[279] *Bulletin of the European Union* 6–94, point I.29. The Commission included representatives of the Member States and two MEPs. See further, Bell and Waddington, n 258 above at 321–2.

[280] European Commission Consultative Commission on Racism and Xenophobia, 'Final Report' Ref 6906/1/95, p 59. See Bell, n 278 above for discussion.

[281] OJ 1995, C296/5. A separate Council Resolution was issued on the response of the educational systems to the problems of racism and xenophobia, OJ 1995, C312/1.

[282] *Ibid* point 7.

[283] For a discussion of these issues, see S Peers, 'Towards Equality: Actual and Potential Rights of Third Country Nationals in the EU' (1996) 33 *Common Market Law Review* 7.

[284] OJ 1996, C237/1. The Commission proposal, COM(95) 653, sought approval for a Council Decision based on Art 235 [now 308] EC but the Council was only prepared to agree to a soft law Resolution.

States, the Community institutions and 'citizen's movements and organisations' actively committed by democratic means to the fight against racism
and xenophobia.[285]

(7) The Participatory Approach to Combating Exclusion

The growth of these 'citizen's movements and organisations' was perhaps
the most important development of the early to mid-1990s in this area, not
just because they provided a means of lobbying for more effective action
against racial discrimination, but also because of the part they played in
establishing networks and linking together a range of organisations
concerned about social exclusion and discrimination.[286] For example, the
Starting Line Group, formed in 1991, drew up a proposal for an
anti-discrimination directive in 1993[287] and, when this was rejected by the
Commission on the grounds of lack of legal competence, they formed an
effective and influential lobbying coalition of over 250 European organisations by 1996, all seeking a Treaty amendment.[288]

Starting with the Green Paper on Social Policy, and taking its cue from
an obscure Declaration annexed to the TEU,[289] the Commission now strove
to gradually institutionalise a process of 'civic dialogue' whereby NGOs
would be consulted and have an input into EU policy making as part of a
movement towards democratising the process of social change at a time
when the move towards globalisation was being paralleled by a growth in
regionalism and localism.[290] The Commission was firmly of the view that
in the next stage of European construction it would be necessary to involve
the 'grass roots' more as part of a dynamic approach to citizenship, both
for reasons of democratic functioning and for effectiveness.[291]

Further inspiration was to follow in 1995 with the Declaration of the
Copenhagen 'World Summit' on Social Development,[292] which called for a

---

[285] OJ 1995, C296/5, point 8(c).

[286] See generally, Bell and Waddington, n 258 above.

[287] See A Dummett, 'The Starting Line: A Proposal for a Draft Council Directive Concerning the Elimination of Racial Discrimination' (1994) 20 *New Community* 530.

[288] See Bell and Waddington, n 258 above at 323.

[289] Declaration No 23 on Co-operation with Charitable Associations. The Declaration states
that: 'This Conference stresses the importance, in pursuing the objectives in [ex Article 117
EC] of co-operation between [the Community] and charitable associations and foundations
as institutions responsible for social welfare establishments and services'.

[290] COM(93) 551, p 71.

[291] *Ibid*. See also, the Communication on Promoting the Role of Voluntary Organisations
and Foundations in Europe, COM(97) 241, s 9.7. For discussion, see R Atkinson and S
Davoudi, 'The Concept of Social Exclusion in the European Union: Context, Development
and Possibilities' (2000) 38 *Journal of Common Market Studies* 427 at 430–1.

[292] Held on 6/12 March 1995. For EU input into the summit, see COM(94) 669; the
ECOSOC Opinion, OJ 1995, C110/12; and the European Parliament Resolution, B4–0367/95.

participatory strategy to combat social exclusion and poverty and the creation of a 'participatory infrastructure'.[293] Hence, 'civil dialogue' provides
a vehicle for addressing the heterogeneous nature of European society
whereby diverse peoples can challenge exclusionary policies on their own
terms using the language of citizenship to seek recognition of their identity
and an equal place in society.[294] Moreover, through diversity and assertive-
ness it is possible for social exclusion to be challenged without simply
ghettoising categories of people under a new label.[295]

In the medium-term SAP the Commission set out a new pluralistic ethos
of 'opportunities for all' in the following terms:[296]

Community action in the social field cannot be restricted to the world of work.
There is already a wide degree of public support for a strong European social policy
across the Union. Further support for the future construction of Europe will be
forthcoming only through action which is credible and visible, in which *all of the
citizens of the Union* feel involved. This means that, through mutually supporting
economic and social policies, Europe should aim to provide 'opportunities for all'
to play an active part in society in the years ahead and to engage in building Europe
together. The role of civic and voluntary bodies has to be recognised, as well as the
wide range of organisations representing firms, and the different sectors both public
and private.

This vision of a transformed mode of governance for the Union, although
short on detail, was pursued, albeit tentatively, with the establishment of a
European Forum on Social Policy[297] to debate fundamental and social rights
in the Union. The Forum comprised the platform of European social NGOs,
the established social partners and representatives of national, regional and
social partners. While not all such organisations can be described as 'grass
roots', the establishment of the Forum provided a totem for a more uni-
versalistic view of citizenship founded on the notion of inclusiveness as an
essential component of Europe's identity. Further, universal inclusion brings
with it a sense of mutuality or shared ownership that engenders both
individual rights and responsibilities.

This inclusive conception of citizenship was carried forward through the
umbrella of the Forum by the March 1996 report of a *Comité des Sages*[298]
set up by the Commission. Outwardly the *Comité des Sages* was not
groundbreaking. After all, it was just another expert committee. However,
in its recommendations, the *Comité* embraced the need for a fully participatory process for *negotiating* a 'bill of rights' encompassing indivisible

---

[293] See R Lister, 'Citizenship, Exclusion and "the Third Way" in Social Security Reform:
Reflections on T.H. Marshall' (2000) 7 *Journal of Social Security Law* 70 at 86.
[294] *Ibid* at 73.
[295] Atkinson and Davoudi, n 291 above at 437.
[296] COM(95) 134, p 3. Italicised emphasis added.
[297] *Ibid* para 6.0.4.
[298] *For a Europe of Civic and Social Rights* (European Communities, Luxembourg, 1996).

civic and social rights. Institutions or experts could no longer have a monopoly of discussion on subjects such as fundamental rights that affect the day-to-day life of individuals.[299] It was proposed that an initial set of civic and social rights and duties should have immediate effect followed by a second stage five years later.[300] Although not immediately acted upon, the report of the *Comité* was to provide the kernel of an idea that was be developed and reformulated, albeit through another expert drafting 'Convention', as the EU Charter of Fundamental Rights.[301]

V MAINSTREAMING GENDER EQUALITY

By 1995, when the Community was contemplating a Fourth Action Pro-gramme on Equal Opportunities for Men and Women,[302] there was a widely held view, at least among the Community institutions, that in the field of gender equality in the labour market, the Community had provided a strong legal framework from a narrow legal basis and limited financial resources,[303] arising from a combination of legislation, case law and soft law programmes, that had delivered 'significant achievements' for women.[304] The Community's 'upbeat rhetoric',[305] based in part on a surge in the activity rate of women in the labour market,[306] was tempered by recognition that actual inequalities in employment persisted obdurately and numerous barriers to women's participation on equal terms with men in both employment and society remained.[307] In particular, women continued to hold the largest proportion of low-paid, low-qualified and insecure jobs, often part-time, with a high degree of occupational segregation in services and the public sector.[308] Moreover, as the economic position deteriorated,

[299] *For a Europe of Civic and Social Rights* (European Communities, Luxembourg, 1996) p 53.

[300] *Ibid* pp 16–18.

[301] OJ 2000, C364/1. See ch 12.

[302] See COM(95) 381 and Decision 95/593/EC on a medium-term Community action pro-gramme on equal opportunities for men and women (1996 to 2000) OJ 1995, L335/37. For an overview, see C Hoskyns, 'A Study of Four Action Programmes on Equal Opportunities' in M Rossilli (ed), *Gender Policies in the European Union* (Peter Lang, New York, 2000) 43–59.

[303] See COM(94) 333. Ch V, para 1.

[304] See COM(95) 134, para 5.0.1.

[305] See J Shaw, 'Law, Gender and the Internal Market' in T Hervey and D O'Keeffe (eds) *Sex Equality Law in the European Union* (Wiley, Chichester, 1995) 283–99 at 288.

[306] Between 1983 and 1991 the activity rate of women aged 25–49 increased in every Member State. See COM(93) 551, p 24. Among women as a whole, the percentage in work rose from under 30% in 1960 to over 40% in 1992. See *Employment in Europe 1994* (European Commission, Brussels, 1994) p 45.

[307] COM(93) 551, p 25.

[308] *Ibid*. See also, J Rubery and C Fagan, 'Occupational Segregation of Women and Men in the European Community', *Social Europe*, Supp 3/93; C Hakim, 'Segregated and Integrated Occupations: A New Approach to Analysing Social Change' (1993) 9 *European Sociological Review* 289; and B Hepple, 'Equality and Discrimination' in P Davies, A Lyon-Caen, S Sciarra and S Simitis (eds) *European Community Labour Law: Principles and Perspectives* (Clarendon Press, Oxford, 1996) 237–59 at 240–6.

there was evidence that women were disproportionately affected because there was a higher level of unemployment among women than men.[309] In addition, apparently gender-neutral policies, such as the establishment of the internal market, had adverse, or at least uncertain, consequences for women because women were more vulnerable to restructuring, particularly in the service sectors.[310] The Community's existing strategies had proved inadequate to tackle the structural causes of inequality in the labour market.[311]

Beveridge, Nott and Stephen have identified four interlinked Community equalities strategies.[312] First, there is a guarantee, developed through the case law of the Court, of a fundamental right of equality within the limited confines of Community employment law.[313] Second, the Community has adopted a broad range of anti-discrimination legislation concerning employment and, to a lesser extent, social security. Third, from 1982, the Community launched a series of action programmes to build on its achievements and adapt its policies in the light of economic and social development.[314] The purpose of the first Action Programme was to set up schemes, including discretionary programmes for positive action,[315] which allowed women access to employment and wider social opportunities where they were not well represented.[316] While each of these strategies has helped to promote equality, at least on a case-by-case basis, none of them has systematically addressed the structural causes of discrimination both in employment and society in general.[317] A fourth Community strategy, 'mainstreaming', was now presented as a means of tackling head-on deep-rooted and pervasive gender inequality in an all-encompassing fashion.[318]

Article 2 of the Council Decision establishing the Fourth Equalities Action Programme (1996–2000) defines 'mainstreaming' as the principle of

[309] EUROSTAT figures for 1995 show unemployment at 12.5% among women compared with 9.5% among men and 10.7% overall. *Unemployment* No 2 (European Communities, Luxembourg, 1996) pp 10–11. For an overview, see J Neilson, 'Equal Opportunities for Women in the European Union: Success or Failure?' (1998) 8 *Journal of European Social Policy* 64.

[310] See *The Impact of the Completion of the Internal Market on Women in the European Community*, DGV Working Document V/506/90 (1990). Discussed by Shaw in Hervey and O'Keeffe, n 305 above.

[311] See F Beveridge, S Nott and K Stephen, 'Addressing Gender in National and Community Law and Policy-making' in Shaw, n 8 above, 135–54 at 138–41.

[312] *Ibid.*

[313] See, in particular, Case 149/77, *Defrenne v Sabena III* [1978] ECR 1365, paras 26–7.

[314] *A New Community Action Programme on the Promotion of Equal Opportunities for Women 1982–1985*, COM(81) 758, para 1. For the Second Action Programme (1986–1990) see COM(85) 801; and the Third Action Programme (1991–1995) see COM(90) 449.

[315] See Council Resolution of 12 July 1982 on the promotion of equal opportunities for women, OJ 1982, C186/3.

[316] See Beveridge, Nott and Stephen, in Shaw, n 311 above at 140.

[317] *Ibid.*

[318] *Ibid.*

integrating equal opportunities for women and men 'in the process of preparing, implementing and monitoring all policies and activities of the European Union and the Member States, having regards to their respective powers'.[319] While the terminology was recent, derived from the *Global Platform for Action* adopted at the Fourth UN Conference on Women held in Beijing,[320] the concept was not. Indeed, as early as 1982, a Council Resolution on the promotion of equal opportunities for women had indicated that account should be taken of the equal opportunities dimension in 'preparing and implementing Community policies likely to affect it'.[321] In the Third Equalities Action Programme (1991–1995) the Commission had called for the integration of equality into general mainstream policy in the 'formulation and implementation of all relevant Community policies and action programmes at Community and the Member State level'.[322] While this commitment appeared far-reaching, it is important to note that the fundamental objective of the Third Action Programme was limited to participation by women in the labour market.[323]

Mainstreaming was taken forward and given substance in the White Paper on Social Policy where a commitment was made to publish an annual 'Equality Report' to review developments at Member State and Union-level and serve as a monitoring instrument for equality policies.[324] The Commission also agreed to examine how to build monitoring by gender into all relevant Union policies and 'make it a requirement of their evaluation'.[325] Significantly, the Commission was using similar, but not identical, language to the Women's Rights Committee of the European Parliament and feminist authors who were calling for a system of 'gender auditing' to assess the potential gender impact of all Community action.[326] The Council, in its response to the White Paper, was more circumspect when, in its Resolution on Union Social Policy, it called for the development of an 'ongoing process' of including 'specific matters relating to women and men and to equal

---

[319] See COM(95) 381 and Decision 95/593/EC, OJ 1995, L335/37.

[320] Issued on 15 Sept 1995. The Conference defined mainstreaming as the promotion by 'Governments and other actors' of 'an active and visible policy of mainstreaming a gender perspective into all policies and programmes so that, before decisions are taken, an analysis is made of the effects on women and men respectively'. The UN had previously used the term in its international development programmes; see Beveridge, Nott and Stephen, in Shaw, n 311 above at 148. On Beijing, see further, the Commission's background document, COM(95) 221; and the European Parliament's response, B4–1194/95, OJ 1995, C269/146.

[321] Council Resolution of 12 July 1982 on the promotion of equal opportunities for women, OJ 1982, C186/3. See also the second Council Resolution of 24 July 1986 on the promotion of equal opportunities for women, OJ 1986, C203/2.

[322] COM(90) 449. Introduction, para 16.

[323] *Ibid*. Introduction, para 12.

[324] COM(94) 333. Ch V, para 15. The first annual report was published in 1996, COM(96) 650.

[325] *Ibid* para 16.

[326] See S Beveridge and F Nott, 'Gender Auditing—Making the Community Work for Women' in Hervey and O'Keeffe, n 305 above, 383–98.

opportunities for them, in the definition and implementation of all Community policies'.[327]

Several piecemeal examples of 'mainstreaming' were to follow, mainly in the form of soft laws and programmatic action.[328] In the context of employment policy, the Council issued two resolutions in 1994. The first was concerned with the promotion of equal opportunities for men and women through the employment-related Objective 3 of the European Social Fund.[329] Building on a commitment in the Regulation implementing the Structural Funds,[330] the Resolution invited the Member States to, inter alia, help to ensure that specifically funded measures targeted at women would be laid down to promote equal opportunities 'in every sector of economic activity and in all areas linked directly or indirectly to the labour market' by making use, in particular, of the flagship 'NOW' vocational training initiative.[331] The second Resolution sought to promote equal participation by women in the 'employment-intensive economic growth strategy' within the Union.[332] While this Resolution was presented in the form of a benign attempt to promote equality, it was even more explicitly linked to the employment agenda derived from the earlier Growth White Paper and the contemporaneous Essen priorities. The Resolution identified 'the growing number of highly educated women' as a 'hitherto insufficiently exploited source of skills and innovative capacity which will have to be developed and used more intensively'.[333] Moreover, 'equal opportunities *depend* on men and women being able to support themselves by taking up paid employment'.[334] A variety of objectives were espoused including,[335] inter alia: facilitating access by women to the labour market and career progression through education and training opportunities; overcoming the sex-based segregation of the labour market; and promoting the employment of women in decision-making posts. Therefore, the success of the European Employment Strategy was contingent upon progress towards equal opportunities and vice versa.

Following the European Councils at Essen and Cannes,[336] where the Member States declared that promoting equal opportunities and the fight

---

[327] OJ 1994, C368/6.
[328] Examples in other policy areas include separate Commission Communications on integrating gender issues into development co-operation and the external dimension of human rights policy, COM(95) 423 and COM(95) 567.
[329] OJ 1994, C231/1.
[330] Art 1(1)(d) of Reg 4255/88/EEC laying down provisions for implementing Reg 2052/88/EEC as regards the European Social Fund, OJ 1988, L374/21.
[331] OJ 1994, C231/1, point 6(c). For the 'NOW' initiative, see OJ 1990, C327/5.
[332] OJ 1994, C368/3.
[333] *Ibid* point 2(c).
[334] *Ibid* point 2(a). Emphasis added.
[335] *Ibid* point 4.
[336] Dec 1994 and June 1995.

against unemployment were now the priority tasks of the Community and the Member States, the Fourth Equalities Action Programme, and an ensuing Commission Communication,[337] were issued to drive forward and bring coherence to the Community's mainstreaming initiatives. A new group of Commissioners, chaired by the President, was established to oversee the 'horizontal' approach to gender issues.[338] The strategy was intended to, on the one hand, provide the highest level political commitment to promoting equality in all areas and at all levels and, on the other, to provide a set of tools for appraising and monitoring policies for their positive and negative effects on equal opportunities.[339] While equality was to be integrated into all areas and all actors were to be 'mobilised', the programme was intended to support Member States' efforts mainly in areas linked to the labour market. For example, the aims included:[340]

—promoting equal opportunities for men and women in a changing economy, especially in the fields of education, vocational training and the labour market;
—reconciling working and family life for men and women;
—promoting a gender balance in decision making and;
—making conditions more conducive to exercising equality rights.

A variety of tools would be utilised to implement these objectives including:[341] exchange of information and experience of good practice or 'benchmarking'; observing and monitoring relevant policies and conducting studies in the field; and rapid dissemination of the results of the initiatives embarked upon. Under the medium-term SAP, Community legislation would be considered in two areas: reconciling family and professional life;[342] and the burden of proof in sex discrimination cases where it was difficult or sometimes impossible for complainants to prove discrimination.[343] The Commission also envisaged soft law guidance in the form of a Code of Practice on Equal Pay,[344] designed to eliminate direct and indirect sex discrimination in grading, classification and job evaluation systems. An

---

[337] *Incorporating Equal Opportunities for Men and Women into All Community Policies and Activities*, COM(96) 67. See also, the European Parliament Resolution on Mainstreaming, OJ 1997, C307/50.
[338] COM(95) 26, para 3.2. See Beveridge and Nott, n 326 above at 384.
[339] C Booth, 'Gender Mainstreaming in the European Union. Toward a New Conception and Practice of Equal Opportunities', *ESCR Seminar Series: The Interface Between Public Policy and Gender Equality* (Centre for Regional Economic and Social Research, Sheffield Hallam University, 1999). See Beveridge, Nott and Stephen, in Shaw, n 311 above at 148.
[340] Art 2(c)–2(f) of Decision 95/593/EC, OJ 1995, L335/37.
[341] *Ibid*. Art 4 and the Annex.
[342] COM(95) 134, para 5.1.2. Followed up by the Framework Agreement and Directive 96/34/EC on Parental Leave, OJ 1996, L145/4.
[343] *Ibid* para 5.1.4. Followed up by Directive 97/80/EC on the Burden of Proof in Sex Discrimination Cases, OJ 1997, L14/16.
[344] *Ibid* para 5.1.5. See COM(96) 336 for the Code.

evaluation report was planned on the Recommendation on the protection of the dignity of men and women at work.[345] A separate Recommendation would be proposed concerning the greater participation of women in decision-making processes in both public and private sectors.[346]

In order for mainstreaming to be effective, sufficient resources need to be devoted to it along with trained personnel, transparency at all levels and a separate agency to oversee the process.[347] The Council Decision, however, strictly limited the scope of the Commission's original proposal, by requiring that only 'existing structures' should be used for monitoring and appraisal[348] and restricting the budget for the Action Programme to a paltry ECU 30 million over five years.[349] Moreover, the Commission had proposed a revamped Advisory Committee on Equal Opportunities consisting of representatives from Member States, national equalities bodies, the social partners and the European Women's Lobby, with enhanced powers of monitoring and scrutiny.[350] The Council restricted the Committee's representation to the Member States with the Commission in the Chair.[351] The Committee's role was limited to issuing an opinion on the Community's general guidelines, annual work programme and evaluation procedures.[352] The reaction from the Member States to mainstreaming was initially mixed. For example, no specific mechanisms were established in Spain and Portugal. By contrast, in Sweden and the Netherlands combating gender discrimination was incorporated into all fields of activity through the use of gender impact assessment tools and the development of expert resources.[353]

Mainstreaming represents an ambitious pluralistic approach to gender equality that, despite the limitations inherent in the Council Decision, has, firstly, provided a springboard for Union action directed from the highest level in the specific area of the Community's Structural Funds,[354] and in a variety of general areas including, inter alia: employment and the labour

---

[345] *Ibid* para 5.1.7.

[346] *Ibid* para 5.1.6. See Council Recommendation 96/694/EC, OJ 1996, L319/11.

[347] See Beveridge, Nott and Stephen, in Shaw, n 311 above at 148.

[348] Decision 95/593/EC, OJ 1995, L335/37, Art 4(1). In COM(95) 381, the Commission had proposed, in its draft Art 3(b) the 'setting up of facilities for observing and monitoring relevant policies with regard to equal opportunities and conducting of studies on all the economic, social and legal issues arising in connection with equal opportunities'.

[349] *Ibid*. Art 10(1). See the Commission's complaint in its Communication on mainstreaming, COM(96) 67, p 4.

[350] Commission Decision 95/420/EC amending Decision 82/43/EEC relating to the setting up of an Advisory Committee on Equal Opportunities for Women and Men, OJ 1995, L249/43.

[351] Decision 95/593/EC, OJ 1995, L335/37, Art 9(1).

[352] *Ibid* Art 9(2).

[353] See Beveridge, Nott and Stephen, in Shaw n 311 above at 150–51; and *Commission Annual Report on Equal Opportunities for Men and Women in the European Union—1998*, COM(1999) 106, Section 1.

[354] See the Council Resolution of 2 Dec 1996 on mainstreaming equal opportunities for men and women into the European Structural Funds, OJ 1996, C386/1.

market; the status of women entrepreneurs; education and training; fundamental rights of persons; external relations; and information awareness.[355]
Secondly, following the adoption of the Recommendation on balanced participation,[356] the drive for mainstreaming has been directly linked with
wider issues of citizenship and democratic systems of governance because:[357]

... a balanced sharing of power and responsibilities between women and men will
improve the quality of life of the whole population; the representation of all parts
of society is indispensable if the problems of European society are to be addressed.

Thirdly, the momentum for mainstreaming created by Beijing and the
Fourth Equalities Action Programme was to spill-over directly into the IGC
process leading to agreement at Amsterdam for a general commitment to
'equality between men and women' among the Community's tasks in Article
2 EC—extending beyond the sphere of the labour market—and, in Article
3(2) EC, a specific 'horizontal' clause formalising mainstreaming whereby,
in all the Community's activities referred to in Article 3(1) [ex 3] EC, 'the
Community shall aim to eliminate inequalities, and to promote equality,
between men and women'. Fourthly, and finally, reliance on soft law has
served to respect the diversity of Member States, while reflecting the fact
that there is no single meaning to sex equality,[358] and has allowed for an
evolutionary approach to gender impact assessment at both Union and
national levels.

VI CONSOLIDATION, COMPLIANCE AND ENFORCEMENT OF COMMUNITY SOCIAL LEGISLATION

(1) Introduction

One of the underlying themes of the social policy discourse of the mid-
1990s was the contrast between the Community's self-acclaimed achievement of a 'solid base' of social legislation[359] and the practical reality that,
if such legislation was to have a meaningful impact on the lives of individuals in Europe, it was essential for it to be correctly transposed *and*
properly applied.[360] Over the period of the 1989 Action Programme the

---

[355] See COM(96) 67, p 5.
[356] Council Recommendation 96/694/EC, OJ 1996, L319/11.
[357] See the 'Charter of Rome' signed on 17 May 1996 at the European Conference on
'Women for the Renewal of Politics and Society'. Reproduced in the *Annual Report on Equal
Opportunities for Men and Women—1996*, COM(96) 650, s 4.4.
[358] See I Ward, 'Beyond Sex Equality: The Limits of Sex Equality Law in the New Europe'
in Hervey and O'Keeffe, n 305 above 369–82 at 372. For discussion, see Beveridge, Nott and
Stephen, in Shaw, n 311 above at 152.
[359] See COM(94) 333. Introduction, para 22.
[360] *Ibid* Ch X, para 1.

Commission expended considerable energy on delivering its 47 flagship proposals, a task largely achieved through a variety of legislative and non-
legislative means,[361] but afforded a relatively low priority to qualitative
reform of existing laws, more effective monitoring of the application of
directives by Member States, and exercising their powers of enforcement in
accordance with Article 155 [now 211] EC.[362] In the meantime the Court
had the difficult task of interpreting social legislation designed in the
1970s and applying it in a rapidly changing labour market environment.
The White Paper on Social Policy and the ensuing medium-term SAP
foreshadowed a change in the relationship of reciprocity between the
Community and the Member States in the area of employment law and
social policy. While the Community would now accept a greater onus to be
accountable by reviewing and justifying its actions, present and past,
the Member States would be expected to give a higher priority to the full
implementation and enforcement of the Community's rules.[363] In this
section we will consider these twin challenges as follows: first, consolidation and legislative review; and second, compliance and enforcement.

(2) Consolidation and Legislative Review

The White Paper on Social Policy needs to be understood in the context of
the Union's broader response to applying the principle of subsidiarity and,
arising from the Growth White Paper, the growing demands of business
for a reduction in the quantity and complexity of Community regulation
deemed to be anti-competitive. What emerged from this process was not a
radical deregulation agenda, but rather a less threatening and more technocratic review exercise that did not directly tamper with the Community's
system of governance.[364] The Community would 'do less, but do it better'.[365]
As a first step the Union embarked upon a drive to clarify and simplify legislation to make it more transparent and accessible to its citizens.[366] These

---

[361] At the time of the Green Paper 29 proposals identified by the Commission for legislative action had been referred to the Council and 16 of these had been adopted. COM(93) 551,
p 10.

[362] *Ibid* para 2. Under Art 211 the Commission shall 'ensure that the provisions of this
Treaty and the measures taken by the institutions pursuant thereto are applied'.

[363] See COM(94) 333. Ch X.

[364] See generally, I Maher, 'Legislative Review by the EC Commission: Revision without
Radicalism' in Shaw and More, n 35 above, 235–51; and K Armstrong, 'Governance and the
Single European Market' in Craig and de Búrca (1999) n 68 above, 745–89 at 757.

[365] See the Commission's 'Better Lawmaking' reports: COM(95) 580; COM(96) 7; and
COM(97) 626. Discussed by Armstrong, *ibid* at 757.

[366] Declarations were issued at the Edinburgh European Council of December 1992 on:
Making New Community Legislation Clearer and Simpler, and *Transparency: Making Existing Community Legislation More Accessible*, Bulletin of the European Communities 12/1992,
pp 18–20.

moves coincided with the publication of the influential Sutherland Report[367] which, while it was confined to examining the internal market, recommended a variety of measures to improve the quality of the law, including consolidation of laws and post-legislative assessment to ensure that laws were still compatible with their original objectives, an approach taken up by the Commission in its follow-up Communication.[368] In the wake of these developments, guidance was issued on improving the drafting of legislation[369] and the procedure for consolidating laws was simplified.[370] Further, the Commission's report on the adaptation of Community legislation to the subsidiarity principle indicated a fresh desire to stabilise the volume of permanent legislation, as a form of quality control, by reducing both the quantity of laws to be enacted and the number of laws within the statute book, the latter aim to be achieved by recasting the law through applying simplifying techniques involving consolidation, codification and updating.[371]

An additional factor for consideration was the effect of Community legislation and national regulation on competitiveness and employment. In 1994, the Commission, following a Council mandate, established a group of independent experts chaired by Dr Bernhard Molitor to look into this question.[372] At the same time, the Commission funded a parallel study by the employers' group UNICE looking into the relationship between regulation and competitiveness.[373] Therefore the concern of both studies was the impact of Community legislation on the competitiveness of European businesses.[374] Social values were outside the framework of reference although a majority of the 'Molitor Group' supported a call for fundamental social rights to be enshrined in the TEU.[375] In its report, UNICE recommended

---

[367] *The Internal Market after 1992: Meeting the Challenge*, Report to the Commission by the High Level Group on the Operation of the Internal Market, SEC(92) 2277. For discussion Maher, see Maher, in Shaw and More, n 364 above; Armstrong, in Craig and De Búrca, n 364 above; and T Burns, 'Better lawmaking? An evaluation of lawmaking in the European Community' in Craig & Harlow, n 103 above, 435–53.

[368] COM(93) 361.

[369] Council Resolution on Drafting Quality, OJ 1993, C66/1. The Resolution called for the wording of acts to be 'clear, simple, concise and unambiguous'. 'Community jargon' and 'excessively long sentences' should be avoided.

[370] By virtue of an inter-institutional agreement on official codification of Community legislation, OJ 1995, C43/41 and OJ 1996, C102/2. See also, the earlier European Parliament Resolution on simplification, clarification and codification of Community law, OJ 1989, C158/386.

[371] COM(93) 545, p 8. See generally, R Bieber and C Amarelle, 'Simplification of European Law' in Snyder, n 151 above, 219–41; and C Timmermans, 'How can one improve the Quality of Community Legislation?' (1997) 34 *Common Market Law Review* 1229.

[372] COM(95) 288. The group was made up of non-lawyers. Molitor was the former head of policy at the German Economics Ministry.

[373] *Releasing Europe's Potential through Targeted Regulatory Reform* (UNICE, 1995).

[374] See Armstrong, in Craig and De Búrca, n 364 above at 759.

[375] See the Commission's separate report, SEC(95) 2121, p 39. See Barnard and Deakin, n 77 above at 192.

alternatives to Community legislation including non-binding agreements between business and governments. The 'Molitor Group' were broadly in tune with UNICE, concluding that the 'volume, complexity and rigidity' of Community law was an obstacle to growth, competitiveness and job creation, although, in the absence of consensus within the Group, they did not explicitly recommend deregulation. Among Molitor's recommendations was a call for greater flexibility in the interpretation of the reference period for the calculation of working hours in the Working Time Directive[376] and, more controversially, a suggestion that the standard of care for employers with regard to health and safety at work might be lowered on the basis of a strict cost/benefit analysis.[377] These proposals reveal that the Molitor Group had a preconceived view that equated simplification with deregulation when no empirical or scientific evidence had been presented to support this concept.[378] The Commission, in a withering response, criticised the absence of criteria for evaluating such a cost/benefit analysis and noted that the benefits of social policy are mostly qualitative and therefore impossible to express in monetary terms.[379] More generally, the Commission pointed to an absence of analytical discussion by the Group of the relationship between simplification and competitiveness.[380] Nevertheless, the Molitor Report was to spur the Commission to launch the Simpler Legislation for the Internal Market (SLIM) initiative,[381] as an attempt to develop a methodology through which to examine the operation of Single Market legislation, and the Business Environment Simplification Taskforce (BEST) to identify regulatory barriers to competitiveness and employment opportunities.[382]

Set against the background of this evolving process of consolidation, codification, simplification and deregulation in all policy areas, the Commission, in the Social Policy White Paper, recommended that 'in order to adapt to a changing world' all social legislation should be regularly reviewed and, if necessary, amended or even repealed.[383] For example, the proposed

---

[376] COM(95) 288, proposal 9.

[377] *Ibid* proposal 23. See further, Burns, in Craig and Harlow n 367 above at 451.

[378] See Bieber and Amarelle, n 371 above at 239; and Armstrong, in Craig and De Búrca, n 364 above at 759–61. See also, the European Parliament's Resolution on the report of the group of independent experts on simplification of Community legislation and administrative provisions ('Deregulation') [A4–0201/96], OJ 1996, C211/23, which declared, at point 2.9, that the 'provisions of labour law and those governing health and safety at work must not be impaired, and need to be made more transparent for those concerned. The report's contention (which reflects the opinion of the majority of the Group of Experts) that deregulation in this area will improve competitiveness and employment, is totally unsubstantiated'.

[379] SEC(95) 2121, p 16.

[380] *Ibid* p 2.

[381] COM(96) 204.

[382] See the Report issued at the Special Employment Summit held in Luxembourg in Nov 1997. For discussion of SLIM and BEST, see Armstrong, in Craig and De Búrca, n 364 above at 761–67.

[383] COM(94) 333. Ch X, para 13.

chemical agents directive,[384] now adopted as Directive 98/24,[385] was intended to replace three earlier directives on specific health and safety risks,[386] a good example of 'simplification'. Revision clauses would be incorporated into future directives, providing a basis for ascertaining when, and to what extent, legislation should be revised.[387] In particular, legislation needed to be kept under review in the light of the Court's judgments, either to consolidate the legislation to take account of judgments, or to review legislation in cases 'where the Court's interpretations raise the issue of the real intentions of the legislator',[388] providing a basis for proposals to codify judicial law-making. As in other policy areas, the Commission sought to approach legislative review purely as a technocratic housekeeping exercise. Apparently there was no need to audit all social legislation to take account of the strengthened social policy objectives in the Agreement on Social Policy and the as yet unfulfilled ambitions of the Social Charter. Rather, the whole process was to be conducted in a manner that was devoid of social values. Administrative convenience was to provide a convenient foil for the Community's decision *not* to pursue a wide-ranging legislative programme even though legal powers were now available under the Agreement.[389] The schism over the Agreement had created a political and legislative vacuum that could now be partially filled by a rolling programme of review pending the completion of the IGC process and, if there were to be a change of power in the UK, repatriation of the social policy provisions in the Treaty. During the period of the medium-term SAP several proposals for simplification and codification—followed, where necessary, by consolidation—were put forward mainly in the areas of employment protection and sex equality.

(3) Employment Protection

In the White Paper the Commission cited the revision of the Collective Redundancies Directive in 1992[390] as an example of a legislative amendment that would ultimately require consolidation.[391] This truism masked the fact that the motivation for reviewing the Directive was not simplifica-

---

[384] COM(93) 155.
[385] OJ 1998, L131/11.
[386] Dir 80/1107/EEC, OJ 1980, L327/8; Dir 82/605/EEC, OJ 1982, L247/12; and Dir 88/364/EEC, OJ 1988, L179/44.
[387] COM(94) 333. Ch X, para 15.
[388] *Ibid.*
[389] *Ibid.* Introduction, para 22.
[390] Dir 92/56/EEC, OJ 1992, L245/3, amending Dir 75/129/EEC, OJ 1975, L48/29. Now consolidated in Dir 98/59/EC, OJ 1998, L 225/16. For background discussion of the employment protection directives, see ch 2.
[391] COM(94) 333. Ch X, para 13.

tion or tidying up, but policy oriented, specifically to fulfil a commitment in the Social Charter to provide improved information and consultation rights to workers where the collective redundancy decision in question is taken by an undertaking located in another Member State irrespective of where, and at what level, that decision is taken.[392]

The amended Collective Redundancies Directive, 92/56,[393] also sought to mitigate the effects of the *Nielsen* decision where the Court had rejected the Danish trade union's argument that the employer was liable for failure to consult where he ought reasonably to have contemplated dismissals.[394] Under Article 2(4) account would not be taken of 'any defence on the part of the employer on the ground that the necessary information has not been provided to the employer by the undertaking which took the decision leading to collective redundancies'. Moreover, in order to make the Directive more effective, consultation would now have to take place 'in good time'[395] and include written notification of the criteria for selecting workers for redundancy and the employer's own method for calculating redundancy payments.[396] Also, voluntary redundancies in the form of early retirement would, depending on the precise circumstances, now be capable of falling within the scope of the Directive.[397] Hence, the Community's aim was to respond to 'accelerating corporate restructuring'[398] by adding a transnational dimension designed to expand and strengthen the protective goals of the original legislation.[399] Further, by addressing the transnational element in a proactive fashion the Community was helping to create conditions that

---

[392] *Social Europe* 1/90, ch 2, points 17 and 18. The first paragraph of Art 2(4) of the amended Dir, 92/56, OJ 1992, L245/3, provided that: 'The obligations laid down . . . shall apply irrespective of whether the decision regarding collective redundancies is being taken by the employer or by an undertaking controlling the employer'.

[393] *Ibid.*

[394] Case 248/83, *Dansk Metalarbejderforbund v Nielsen and Son Maskin-fabrik A/S* [1985] ECR 553, para 16. The Court's reasoning was that such an interpretation would cause employers to incur penalties for failing to have foreseen the collective redundancies when Art 1(2)(d) of Dir 75/129 had excluded from the scope of the Directive collective redundancies caused by 'the termination of an establishment's activities where that is the result of a judicial decision'. Art 1 of Dir 92/56 deleted this exemption—effectively undercutting any resurrection of this defence in future cases. See further, Barnard, *EC Employment Law*, n 184 above, p 493.

[395] Art 2(3).

[396] Art 2(3)(v) and (vi).

[397] The revised Art 1 states that 'terminations of an employment contract which occur on the employer's initiative for one or more reasons not related to the individual workers concerned shall be assimilated to redundancies, provided that there are at least five redundancies'.

[398] See the Commission's Explanatory Memorandum, COM(91) 292, paras 8–10. For example, the Commission referred to the increasing number of mergers in the Community. Between 1983 and 1989 national mergers had risen from 101 to 233 (an increase of 233%) while mergers between a Community-based undertaking and a third-country undertaking rose from 25 to 62 (up 248%) and mergers between undertakings situated in different Community Member States rose from 29 to 187 (up 697%). For discussion, see C Bourn, 'Amending the Collective Dismissals Directive: A Case of Rearranging the Deckchairs?' (1993) 9 *International Journal of Comparative Labour Law and Industrial Relations* 227 at 230.

[399] See B Bercusson, *European Labour Law* (Butterworths, London, 1996) p 230.

were conducive to the adoption within two years of a more general directive on transnational information and consultation, namely the European
Works Council Directive.[400] Therefore the amendment to the Collective
Redundancies Directive, and its eventual consolidation in 1998,[401] may have
been administratively convenient but such benefits were incidental to the
primary social policy objective.

Following on from the review of the Collective Redundancies Directive,
the White Paper also highlighted plans to modify or replace the related
directives concerning Insolvency and Acquired Rights.[402] Turning first to the
Insolvency Directive, 80/987,[403] several reports and studies were instituted
by the Commission[404] and, in 1997, an ad hoc group of government experts
was set up to consider the main difficulties in enforcing the Directive. The
original Directive had been carefully drafted to avoid, or rather disengage
from, the conflict at national level between the rights of creditors and the
rights of employees in an insolvency scenario. The Community's solution
was to place a social policy obligation on the Member States to establish
institutions guaranteeing employees whose employer had become insolvent
the payment of their outstanding claims for remuneration over a specific
period. Therefore, any further attempt to address gaps or shortcomings in
national insolvency laws by reinforcing employment rights was bound to
be controversial.[405] The issue was not progressed during the period of the
next SAP, 1998–2000,[406] and it was not until the advent of a new 'Social
Policy Agenda' in 2000 that a decision was taken by the Commission to
revise the Directive in line with case law and the changing world of work.[407]

The Commission's proposal, published in May 2001,[408] seeks to broaden
the concept of insolvency while ensuring greater consistency with other
Community directives. Under the present definition of a state of insolvency
the scope of the Directive is limited to cases where employers are subject
to proceedings involving liquidation of their assets to satisfy collectively the
claims of creditors.[409] Thus, employees of insolvent employers not subject
to liquidation proceedings or their equivalent will not be protected under
Community law even though they may have outstanding pay claims against

---

[400] Dir 94/45/EC, OJ 1994, L254/64.
[401] Dir 98/59/EC, OJ 1998, L225/16.
[402] COM(94) 333. Ch X, para 13. Respectively, Dir 80/987/EEC, OJ 1980, L283/23 and
Dir 77/187/EEC, OJ 1977, L61/26.
[403] *Ibid.*
[404] See COM(95) 164 and COM(96) 696.
[405] For background to the revision process, see the Explanatory Memorandum, COM(2000)
832.
[406] COM(98) 259.
[407] COM(2000) 379.
[408] OJ 2001, C154/109.
[409] Art 2 of Dir 80/987 as interpreted by the Court in Case C–479/93, *Francovich II v Italy*
[1995] ECR I–3843.

employers who have ceased to trade. The Commission note, however, that many Member States use a wider definition of the concept of insolvency which is now reflected in Article 1(1) of Regulation 1346/2000 on insolvency proceedings.[410] The Commission therefore propose the following definition in draft Article 2(1):

For the purposes of this Directive, an employer shall be deemed to be in a state of insolvency where a request has been made for the opening of collective proceedings, as provided for under the laws, regulations and administrative provisions of a Member State, based on insolvency of the employer and involving the partial or total divestment of the employer's assets and the appointment of a liquidator and the authority which is competent pursuant to the said provisions has:
(a) either decided to open the proceedings,
(b) or established that the employer's undertaking or business has been definitively closed down and that the available assets are insufficient to warrant the opening of the proceedings.

Moreover, in line with other recent directives,[411] while the definition of 'employee' remains a matter for national law,[412] the proposal seeks to insert a provision stating that Member States may not exclude part-time or fixed-term workers,[413] or workers with a temporary employment relationship.[414] Also, the Commission propose to dispense with the widely criticised Annex, which allows Member States to exclude certain workers from its scope on the grounds that these exemptions are incompatible with social policy. Nevertheless, the draft of the revised Article 1 retains an exemption for domestic servants employed by natural persons and share-fishermen.[415] Furthermore, Member States may exclude claims by 'certain categories of employee' by virtue of 'the existence of other forms of guarantee if it is established that these offer the persons concerned a degree of protection equivalent to that resulting from this Directive'.[416]

Under the present Directive there is a complex process whereby the Member States may impose a time-limit on the guaranteed pay claim involving three alternative dates marking the beginning of the reference period for claims.[417] In the interests of simplification the Commission propose to lay down a minimum period of three months pay under Community law and leave it to Member States to fix a date and a reference period.[418] Not only would this be consistent with the principle of subsidiarity, but also it

---

[410] Reg 1346/2000/EC, OJ 2000, L160/1. Effective from 30 June 2000.
[411] See Dir 98/50/EC, OJ 1998, L201/88, discussed below.
[412] Art 2(2).
[413] Within the meaning of Dir 97/81/EC and 99/70/EC on part-time and fixed-term work, respectively, OJ 1998, L14/9 and OJ 1999, L175/43.
[414] Within the meaning of Dir 91/383/EEC on health and safety at work, OJ 1991, L206/19.
[415] Draft Art 1(3).
[416] Draft Art 1(2).
[417] Art 4(2) of Dir 80/987.
[418] Draft Art 4(2).

would enable Member States to cover claims arising after the reference date where the business operation of the firm continues and wages are still payable.[419] The revised provision would continue to allow Member States to set a ceiling on payment made by the guarantee institution providing they inform the Commission of the methods used to set the ceiling.[420]

The final issue addressed in the Commission's proposal concerns the absence of any provision in the Directive regarding the issue of cross-border insolvencies. Problematic scenarios have arisen where employees are affected by insolvency proceedings instituted in another Member State, or where an insolvent company has establishments in several Member States. In either of these circumstances there has been uncertainty about which State's guarantee institution is responsible. In *Mosbœk*[421] a British company with an employee in Denmark became insolvent. The company was neither established nor registered in Denmark. The Court held that the guarantee institution responsible must be the institution of the State where, either it is decided to open the proceedings for the collective satisfaction of creditors' claims, or it has been established that the employer's undertaking or business has been definitively closed down.[422] Therefore, on the facts, the UK guarantee institution had the responsibility to make the payment. By contrast, in *Everson*[423] the Court distinguished *Mosbœk*. An Irish company with establishments in several Member States had been established and registered in the UK where the employees who had brought the proceedings were employed. In those circumstances the guarantee institution of the Member State where the employee was employed was responsible.[424]

Following on from these cases, and the adoption of the Regulation on insolvency proceedings,[425] which provides for automatic recognition of insolvency proceedings initiated in another Member State, the Commission proposed to codify the law broadly in line with *Mosbœk* and *Everson*. Providing an undertaking has 'establishments' in the territories of at least two Member States, draft Article 8a(1) would, if adopted, provide that the com-

---

[419] See however, Case C–125/97, *Regeling v Bestuur van de Bedrijfsvereniging voor de Metaalnijverheid* [1998] ECR I–4493, where, at para 23, the Court held that claims made during the reference period took precedence over payment due before that period.

[420] Draft Art 4(3). Note, however, that this provision does not imply that the duty to inform the Commission gives rise to a Community procedure for monitoring the methods chosen by the Member State, or that the Member State's exercise of the option to set a ceiling is subject to the express or implied agreement of the Commission. The obligation is simply to inform the Commission whether or not the Member State has exercised the option. Failure to give prior notice will not render the ceilings adopted unlawful: Case C–235/95, *AGS Assedic Pas-de-Calais v Dumon and Froment* [1998] ECR I–4531, paras 29–30.

[421] Case C–117/96, *Mosbœk v Lønmodtagernes Garantifond* [1997] ECR I–5017.

[422] *Ibid* para 20.

[423] Case C–198/98, *Everson and Barrass v Secretary of State for Trade and Industry and Bell Lines Ltd* [1999] ECR I–8903.

[424] *Ibid* paras 23–24.

[425] Reg 1346/2000/EC, OJ 2000, L160/1.

petent guarantee institution will be that of the State where the employee habitually works even where the opening of insolvency proceedings has been requested in another Member State. In the Explanatory Memorandum the Commission determined that in order to be established an employer must have a sufficient business presence in the territory where the employees work, including remuneration of employees in that country, dealings with the administrative authorities in that State and responsibility for social security contributions.[426]

The Commission's proposal to amend the Insolvency Directive strikes a careful balance between procedural simplification, including the removal of several loopholes, and expansion of protection for the employees affected, arising from a combination of codification of the case law concerning cross-border insolvencies and, most importantly, a broader interpretation of the concept of insolvency, aided by parallel developments in company law at national and Community level. The Commission have demonstrated a reflective approach to reviewing the Directive, in contrast with its hasty attempts to revise the Acquired Rights Directive, considered below, and the result has been a well-rounded proposal that will, if adopted, further the social policy aims of the original measure.

Now let us consider the Acquired Rights Directive, 77/187,[427] originally introduced in the 1970s as a partial harmonisation measure intended to safeguard the rights of employees in the event of a change of their employer. The Commission, in a report to the Council in 1992, had pointed to the inflexibility of the Directive in the event of the transfer of insolvent businesses and in covering transnational transfers.[428] As with the review of collective redundancies, the context for this report had been the completion of the internal market and references in the Social Charter to improvements in living and working conditions and enhanced worker involvement in undertakings in connection with corporate restructuring.[429] An added dimension, however, was the quantity of what the Commission described as 'emergency case law' arising from references to the Court covering areas of uncertainty in the Directive.[430] As a consequence, the revision of the Directive was to become an increasingly politicised battleground between those who viewed the process of amendment as a straight-forward updating exercise, notably the trade unions and the European Parliament, and others, including employers' organisations and certain Member States,[431] who were fighting a rearguard action to reverse the effects of what they

---

[426] COM(2000) 832, para 4.3.
[427] Dir 77/187/EEC, OJ 1977, L61/26.
[428] SEC(92) 857.
[429] See the Commission's draft text contained in COM(94) 300 and OJ 1994, C274/10. Reference is made to points 7,17 and 18 of the Charter.
[430] COM(94) 300.
[431] In particular, Germany and the UK.

regarded as the Court's increasingly 'protectionist' interpretation of the Directive, particularly its application to the contracting-out of services.[432] The publication of the Commission's draft text—presented as a replacement of the Directive rather than an amendment—threw a spotlight on the apparent contradiction between the original employment protection aims pursued by the Directive and the desire of both the Community and Member States to promote business flexibility, including competitive restructuring, in pursuit of the objectives set out in the Growth White Paper.[433]

After considering a series of national expert reports, the Commission controversially proposed to end what they regarded as the main area of uncertainty by excluding contracting-out from the scope of the Directive in the second sentence of the draft Article 1(1), as follows:[434]

> *The transfer of only an activity of an undertaking* . . . whether or not it was previously carried out directly, does not *in itself* constitute a transfer within the meaning of the Directive.

From the Commission's perspective this new clause was a necessary clarification that merely served to codify case law as part of the post-Maastricht legislative review process.[435] The Commission's reference point was *Spijkers* where the Court had identified a range of possible factors to determine the central question of whether a business, or part of a business, retains its identity as a stable economic entity?[436] In answering this question the national court would take account of those factors that indicate whether its operation is actually continued or resumed by the new employer with the same or similar activities.[437] From this standpoint it would be logical to argue that the mere transfer of an activity would not 'in itself' establish a transfer, as it is only one element of the overall equation to be considered by the national court. This was a narrow and somewhat disingenuous

---

[432] See J Hunt, 'Success at last? The amendment of the Acquired Rights Directive' (1999) 24 *European Law Review* 215 at 216–17. See generally, S Hardy and R Painter, 'The New Acquired Rights Directive and its Implications for European Employee Relations in the Twenty-First Century' (1999) 6 *Maastricht Journal* 366. For application of the Directive in contracting out cases, see Case C–209/91, *Rask and Christensen v ISS Kantinservice* [1993] ECR I–5755; and Case C–392/92, *Schmidt v Spar und Leikhasse* [1994] ECR I–1311.

[433] See further, More, n 35 above, 129–45.

[434] OJ 1994, C274/10, Art 1(1). Emphasis added. The Commission's reasoning was set out in the seventh recital of the proposal which asserted that: 'considerations of legal security and transparency . . . demand, in the light of the case law of the Court . . . that a clear distinction be made between transfers of undertakings, businesses or parts of businesses and the transfer of only an activity of an undertaking'.

[435] See the Commission's background report, ISEC/B2/95, p 5.

[436] Case 24/85, *Spijkers v Gebroeders Benedik Abbatoir CV* [1986] ECR 1119, para 12. These factors include: the type of business concerned; whether its tangible assets have been transferred; the value of those assets at the time of transfer; the retention of employees and customers; and continuation of similar activities.

[437] *Ibid* paras 11–14.

explanation as, in the more recent cases of *Rask*[438] and *Schmidt*,[439] the Court had applied and, effectively, updated the *Spijkers* test to cover contracting-out cases where the activity transferred was only an ancillary activity of the transferor or part of a service performed by a single employee with no transfer of assets.

The Commission premise was therefore incorrect because, as Bercusson has explained,[440] the Directive also covers the transfer of 'part of a business', a fact not diminished by the Court's gloss of an 'economic entity' test, which was not to be determined solely by reference to 'an activity' but rather should reflect the objective of the Directive, which is the protection of employees' rights, not the protection of employers who transfer activities. Therefore, through their selective interpretation of *Spijkers*, the Commission were proposing an amendment that would, in practice, have excluded many contracting-out 'transfers' for commercial reasons, thereby losing sight of the employment safeguarding aims of the Directive.

The Commission's 1994 proposal was heavily criticised by the European Parliament, where all the political groups opposed the draft of Article 1(1) on the grounds that it did not improve legal certainty and, on the contrary, introduced new sources of uncertainty that might prove detrimental to the rights of workers and the interests of firms.[441] Chastened perhaps by the strength of opposition, the Commission informed the Parliament in February 1996 that it would be willing to accept amendments 'designed to transform its proposal' by deleting the offending clause.[442] In the meantime, however, the timing of the proposal, coinciding with growing opposition in France and Germany to *Schmidt*,[443] was to have a cautionary effect on the Court in its ensuing judgments in *Rygaard*[444] and *Süzen*.[445]

Both cases concerned sub-contracting. In *Rygaard* a company (SP) that was contracted to build a canteen sub-contracted the work to another building company (SMA) which, as part of the deal, agreed to buy building

---

[438] Case C–209/91 [1993] ECR I–5755, para 17.

[439] Case C–392/92 [1994] ECR I–1311, paras 13–17.

[440] Bercusson, *European Labour Law*, n 399 above, pp 243–46.

[441] Resolution B4–0033/96 of 18 Jan 1996. See the Explanatory Memorandum to the Commission's revised proposal, COM(97) 60. See also, the critical view taken by ECOSOC in its Opinion of 9 Mar 1995, CES 317/95. ECOSOC complained that the draft 'undermines employees' rights in respect of the Directive's declared aims'. See further, Hunt, n 432 above at 218.

[442] PV (96) 1279. See the Explanatory Memorandum to the Commission's revised proposal, COM(97) 60.

[443] See P Davies, 'Taken to the Cleaners? Contracting Out of Services Yet Again' (1997) 26 *Industrial Law Journal* 193 at 197.

[444] Case C–48/94, *Rygaard v Strø Mølle Akustik* [1995] ECR I–2745.

[445] Case C–13/95, *Süzen v Zehnacker Gebäudereinigung GmbH Krankenhausservice* [1997] ECR I–1259. On this point, see C de Groot, 'The Council Directive on the Safeguarding of Employees' Rights in the Event of Transfers of Undertakings: An Overview of Recent Case Law' (1998) 35 *Common Market Law Review* 707 at 715; Hunt, n 432 above at 219.

materials from SP. Rygaard was informed by SP that SMA would continue to pay him until the end of his employment relationship. SMA subsequently dismissed him. Significantly, the Court decided to use this case as an opportunity to extensively review its case law before deciding that its earlier judgments presupposed 'that the transfer relates to a stable economic entity whose activity is not limited to performing one specific works contract'.[446] The transfer of one building works contract would only come within the terms of the Directive if it included the transfer of a body of assets enabling the activities in question to be carried out in a stable way. Where an undertaking merely makes available to the new contractor certain works material for carrying out the works there would be no transfer of assets.[447] Therefore, the transfer of a body of assets, just one factor to be considered according to *Spijkers*,[448] and not regarded as essential in *Schmidt*,[449] was now regarded as a prerequisite in a case involving a transfer under a subcontract. The workers themselves were not deemed to be assets in this context.

In *Süzen* a company (Z) had contracted with a school (A) to clean the school buildings. Süzen (S) and other cleaners were transferred from the employ of A to Z. Later, A terminated the contract with Z and negotiated a new cleaning contract with another company (LG)—a so-called 'second generation' contract. Z sacked S and her colleagues. The Full Court held that, notwithstanding the reference to the 'same or similar activities' in *Spijkers*, the mere fact that the service provided by the old and new awardees of the contract was similar did not support the conclusion that an economic entity had been transferred.[450] According to the Court, the term 'entity' refers to 'an organised grouping of persons and assets facilitating the exercise of an economic activity which pursues a specific objective'.[451] Using language strikingly similar to that contained in the Commission's proposed clause, the Court went on to conclude that an entity 'cannot be reduced to the activity entrusted to it'.[452] Its identity emerges from other factors, such as its workforce, management staff, the way in which work is organised, its operating methods or the operational resources made available to it.[453] Hence 'the mere loss of a service to a competitor cannot . . . by itself indicate the existence of a transfer within the meaning of the directive'.[454] In those circumstances, the service does not, on losing a customer, cease to fully exist and cannot be considered to have transferred

[446] Case C–48/94 [1995] ECR I–2745, para 20.
[447] *Ibid* paras 21–2.
[448] Case 24/85 [1986] ECR 1119, para 12.
[449] Case C–209/91 [1993] ECR I–5755, para 17.
[450] Case C–13/95 [1997] ECR I–1259, para 15.
[451] *Ibid* para 13.
[452] *Ibid* para 15.
[453] *Ibid*.
[454] *Ibid* para 16.

to the new awardees of the contract.[455] By contrast, in certain labour-intensive sectors, such as services, a group of workers may themselves constitute an economic entity because the new employer will have to take on a major part of the workforce to perform whatever task is required.[456]

Although *Schmidt* was not directly overruled in *Süzen*,[457] the scope of the Court's earlier ruling was effectively limited to first-generation contracts except where a body of assets was transferred or the workers themselves were—collectively—deemed to be intrinsic to the economic entity. The Court's reasoning provides no logical explanation for making a distinction between first and second-generation contracts as the Court conceded that the absence of a direct contractual relationship is not conclusive evidence against a transfer.[458] Moreover, business certainty, or indeed flexibility, was not aided because, as Davies observes, the transferee of the original contract would have to take on the transferor's workforce but might have to retain them if they subsequently lost the contract.[459]

Paradoxically, the outcome was a form of reverse codification. The Court was bringing its jurisprudence into line with the projected view of the Member States, as presented by the Commission and, in the process, adapting the Directive in a manner that accorded with the broader labour market flexibility agenda. In determining whether or not a transfer had taken place, the Court's principal concern was the status of the business concerned as an 'economic entity'—a commercial test of its own invention—rather than the employment test they had applied a decade earlier in *Ny Moelle Kro*[460]— has there been a change in the natural or legal person who is responsible for carrying on the business and who by virtue of that fact incurs the obligations of an employer? The effect of applying a commercial test was to deem the employee expendable once the direct connection with the original employer had been severed even though the Directive had been designed to protect them in the event of a change of their employer.

In order to end the uncertainty that it had inadvertently helped to create, the Commission, having accepted the view of the European Parliament,[461] published a revised proposal in February 1997[462] followed by a separate Memorandum based on its assessment of the Court's cumulative case law on acquired rights.[463] After a brief hiatus, to allow for a change of

---

[455] *Ibid.*

[456] *Ibid* paras 18–21. Applied in Case C–234/98, *Allen and others v Amalgamated Construction Co Ltd* [1999] ECR I–8643.

[457] For a critique, see Davies (1997, *Industrial Law Journal*) n 443 above.

[458] Case C–13/95 [1997] ECR I–1259, paras 11–12. See Davies, *ibid* at 195.

[459] *Ibid.*

[460] Case 287/76 [1987] ECR 5465, para 12.

[461] OJ 1997, C33/81.

[462] COM(97) 60. The proposal was to be followed by a consolidated text in accordance with the inter-institutional agreement on codification, OJ 1995, C43/41 and OJ 1996, C102/2.

[463] COM(97) 85.

Government in the UK in May 1997, Directive 77/187 was amended by Directive 98/50,[464] which was unanimously adopted at the culmination of the British Presidency on 29 June 1998.[465] Implementation was due by 17 July 2001 and, in the meantime, both directives have been consolidated in Directive 2001/23.[466]

Directive 98/50, and now Directive 2001/23, retains the core definition of a 'transfer' in Article 1(1)(a)[467] while adding two further clauses in paragraphs (b) and (c) although 'such clarification does not alter the scope of Directive 77/187/EEC as interpreted by the Court of Justice'.[468] Article 1(1)(b) provides that, subject to the other provisions in Article 1:

... there is a transfer of an economic entity which retains its identity, meaning an organised grouping of resources which has the objective of pursuing an economic activity, whether or not that activity is central or ancillary.

Notwithstanding the rider regarding the Court's previous interpretation of the Directive, by codifying the 'economic entity' test in *Süzen*,[469] Article 1(1)(b) now superimposes additional commercial criteria absent from the original text for the purpose of determining whether or not employees are safeguarded when restructuring takes place. While the absence of the transfer of a body of assets will not necessarily preclude the existence of a transfer, as the Court acknowledged in *Süzen*, the requirement that there should be an 'organised grouping of resources' with the objective of 'pursuing an economic activity' strictly restricts the Court's scope for a teleological interpretation of the safeguarding objective in future cases. In effect, notwithstanding the withdrawal of the contracting out clause, *Süzen* has been crystallised.

The Court's post-1998 case law takes *Süzen* as a starting point but indicates greater flexibility of interpretation, fully respecting the *Spijkers* criteria, perhaps reflecting the absence of a specific contracting out exclusion in the final text of the Directive. For example, in *Vidal*[470] a company terminated a cleaning contract and decided to carry out the work in-house instead. Having referred to the definition of 'economic entity' in *Süzen* and

[464] OJ 1998, L201/88.
[465] The legal base for the Directive was Art 100 [now 94] EC requiring unanimity. For an account of the process leading up to the adoption of the amended Directive, see Hunt, n 432 above at 219–25.
[466] OJ 2001, L82/16.
[467] Formerly Art 1(1) which states that: 'This Directive shall apply to any transfer of an undertaking, business, or part of an undertaking or business to another employer as a result of a legal transfer or merger'.
[468] Fourth recital of the preamble of Dir 98/50. See also, the eighth recital of the preamble of Dir 2001/23.
[469] Case C–13/95 [1997] ECR I–1259, para 13.
[470] Cases C–127/96, C–229/96 & C–74/97, *Hernández Vidal SA v Gómez Pérez and others* [1998] ECR I–8179.

the limited interpretation of an 'activity' in *Rygaard*,[471] the Court distinguished those cases and added a further refinement concluding that:[472]

Whilst such an entity must be sufficiently structured and autonomous, it will not necessarily have significant assets, tangible or intangible. Indeed, in certain sectors such as cleaning, these assets are often reduced to their most basic and the activity is essentially based on manpower. Thus an organised group of wage earners who are specifically and permanently assigned to a common task may, in the absence of other factors of production, amount to an economic activity.

In other words 'wage earners' such as cleaners[473] were capable of being 'resources'—to use the language in the revised Article 1(b)—in sectors where a test based on 'manpower' was appropriate. Furthermore, in a judgment issued on the same day the Court in the joined cases of *Sánchez Hidalgo* and *Ziemann*,[474] held that the Directive is capable of applying to 'second generation' contracting out involving public bodies providing, respectively, home-help and surveillance services, so long as the operation is accompanied by the transfer of an economic entity between the two undertakings.[475] There is no need for a direct contractual relationship between the transferor and the transferee.[476] Likewise, in the private sector context, the Court has held in *Temco*[477] that, providing the economic entity test is satisfied, it is immaterial whether the transferor is the original contractor or their subcontractor 'since it is sufficient for that transfer to be part of the web of contractual relations even if they are indirect'.[478]

In *Allen*[479] the Court was asked to consider whether the Directive covered a transfer of employees within the same group of mining companies. The Court held that the Directive could apply to a transfer between two subsidiary companies in the same group where the companies are distinct legal persons each with specific employment relationships with their employees.[480] Although driving in underground tunnels, the main work carried out by the employees in question, could not be considered an activity based essentially on manpower, as in *Vidal*, since it required a significant amount

---

[471] *Ibid* para 26. See *Süzen*, para 13; and *Rygaard*, para 20.
[472] *Ibid* para 27.
[473] See also, Case C–51/00, *Temco Service Industries SA v Imzilyen and others* [2002] ECR I (nyr) judgment of 24 Jan 2002.
[474] Cases C–173/96, *Sanchez Hidalgo ea v Asociacion de Servicios Aser and Sociedad Cooperativa Minerva*, and C–247/96, *Horst Ziemann v Ziemann Sicherheit GmbH and Horst Bohn Sicherheitsdienst* [1998] ECR I–8237.
[475] *Ibid* para 34.
[476] *Ibid* para 23. See also, Cases C–171–172/94, *Merckx and Neuhuys* [1996] ECR I–1253, paras 28 to 30.
[477] Case C–51/00, *Temco Service Industries SA v Imzilyen and others* [2002] ECR (nyr) judgment of 24 Jan 2002.
[478] *Ibid* para 32.
[479] Case C–234/98, *Allen and others v Amalgamated Construction Co Ltd* [1999] ECR I–8643.
[480] *Ibid* para 17.

of plant and equipment, it was clear that, in the mining sector, it was common for the essential assets required for driving work to be provided by the mine owner itself. In the circumstances, the fact that there was no transfer of assets was held not to be decisive.[481]

In a shift of emphasis, therefore, the Court, in *Vidal, Hidalgo, Allen* and *Temco*, whilst endorsing *Süzen* and *Rygaard*, was allowing itself, and most importantly national courts, an opportunity to distinguish these cases on the facts. There are, however, limits to the Court's post-*Süzen* flexibility. In *Liikenne*[482] the Court distinguished *Allen* and applied *Süzen* and *Vidal* strictly. *Liikenne* concerned the re-engagement of bus drivers on less favourable terms following the tendering out of bus routes in Helsinki. The Court held that in a sector such as scheduled public transport by bus, where the tangible assets contribute significantly to the performance of the activity, the absence of a transfer to a significant extent from the old to the new con-tractor of such assets, which are necessary for the proper functioning of the entity, led the Court to conclude that the entity did not retain its identity.[483]

In addition to the 'economic entity' test in Article 1(1)(b), the applica-tion of the Directive to both the public and private sectors is confirmed in Article 1(1)(c).[484] However, the definition of 'employee' in Article 2(1)(d) remains a matter for Member States.[485] In *Collino*[486] the Court referred directly to this provision, citing the revised Directive,[487] and confirmed that, where the workers in question are subject to public-law status and not employment law, the Directive may not be applicable to them as this is a matter for national law.[488] Article 1(1)(c) also codifies the Court's ruling in *Henke*,[489] which excludes transfers where there is merely an administrative reorganisation of public administration authorities, or a transfer of admin-istrative functions between such authorities.[490]

---

[481] Case C–234/98, *Allen and others v Amalgamated Construction Co Ltd* [1999] ECR I–8643, para 30.

[482] Case C–172/99, *Oy Liikenne Ab v Liskojärvi and Juntunen* [2001] ECR I–745. See P Davies, 'Transfers—The UK Will Have to Make Up Its Own Mind' (2001) 30 *Industrial Law Journal* 231.

[483] *Ibid* para 42.

[484] The first sentence of Art 1(c) of Dir 2001/23 states that: 'This Directive shall apply to public and private undertakings engaged in economic activities whether or not they are operating for gain'.

[485] Art 2(1)(d).

[486] Case C–343/98, *Collino and Chiappero v Telecom Italia SpA* [2000] ECR I–6659.

[487] *Ibid* para 39.

[488] *Ibid* paras 36–41. See also, Case 105/84, *Foreningen af Arbejdsledere i Danmark v Danmols Inventar* [1985] ECR 2639, para 27.

[489] Case 298/94, *Henke v Gemeinde Schierke and Verwaltungsgemeinschaft 'Brocken* [1996] ECR I–4989.

[490] *Henke* was distinguished in Case C–343/98, *Collino and Chiappero v Telecom Italia SpA* [2000] ECR I–6659, paras 32–35, where the Court held that the Directive applies to a situation in which an entity operating telecommunications services for public use and managed by a public body within the State administration is, following decisions of the public author-ities, the subject of a transfer for value, in the form of an administrative concession, to a private-law company established by another public body which holds its entire capital.

Other changes provide for some enhancements of both the scope of the Directive and the specific provisions concerning the information and consultation of employees. For example, Article 2(2) of Directive 2001/23 prohibits Member States from excluding employees solely because they are part-time, fixed-term or temporary workers.[491] Article 6 provides for information and consultation rights for employees in the event of bankruptcy or insolvency proceedings. Under Article 7(4) the information and consultation provisions shall apply regardless of whether the decision resulting in the transfer is taken by the immediate employer or by an undertaking controlling the employer. Employees also must also be informed, inter alia, of the reasons for a transfer and its legal, social, and economic implications, even where there is no employee representative.[492]

Undoubtedly the most novel feature of the Directive, as revised, is the flexibility that has been introduced through the inclusion of optional provisions.[493] Perhaps the most significant changes can now be found in Article 5 of the consolidated Directive. As a general rule the Directive codifies the case law concerning transfers of insolvent undertakings. Although the Directive is silent on the question, the Court in *Abels*[494] held that the Directive is inapplicable where the transferor is bankrupt or analogous insolvency proceedings have been instituted. In effect Community law is pre-empted, in those circumstances, by national insolvency laws that will normally give priority to the property rights of creditors. Hence, the chances of the business being saved and some jobs preserved have been deemed by the Court to override the acquired rights provisions in the Directive.[495] At the pre-insolvency stage, however, even where proceedings have been launched,[496] or where a company has gone into voluntary liquidation,[497] the Directive may still apply.[498] It is only at that stage that employees' rights trump creditors' rights.

In order to offer some room for manoeuvre, however, Article 5(1) now provides that, where the core acquired rights provisions in Articles 3 and

---

[491] Within the meaning of, respectively, Dirs 97/81/EC, OJ 1998, L14/9; 99/70/EC, OJ 1999, L175/43; and 91/383/EEC, OJ 1991, L206/19.

[492] Art 7(6).

[493] See Hunt, n 432 above at 228–29.

[494] See Case 135/83, *Abels v Bedrijfsvereniging voor de Metaalindustrie en de Electrotechnische Industrie* [1985] ECR 469. See also, Case C–362/89, *d'Urso v Ercole Marelli Elettromeccanica Generale* [1991] ECR I–4105.

[495] See P Davies, 'Acquired Rights, Creditors' Rights, Freedom of Contract and Industrial Democracy' (1989) 9 *Yearbook of European Law* 21 at 45.

[496] See Case C–472/93, *Spano and others v Fiat Geotech and Fiat Hitachi* [1995] ECR I–4321.

[497] See Case C–399/96, *Europièces v Sanders and Automotive Industries Holding Company SA* [1998] ECR I–6965.

[498] The test is based on the purpose of the procedure in question in so far as it means that the undertaking continues or ceases trading. See Case C–319/94, *Déthier Equipment v Dassy* [1998] ECR I–1061. For further discussion, see Barnard, *EC Employment Law*, n 184 above, pp 469–75.

4 apply to a transfer during insolvency proceedings, Member States may promulgate laws permitting the transferee to be indemnified against the transferor's debts as long as the employees concerned receive compensation consistent with the Insolvency Directive rather than acquired rights under Article 3(1).[499] This would separate the issue from the complexities of employment law and allow the State in question to socialise the costs of the employees' claims.[500] An alternative option is available in such circumstances, and also where the transferor is in a situation of serious economic crisis short of liquidation proceedings or bankruptcy. This would allow for negotiation between the transferor, transferee, and the employees' representatives, with a view to agreeing to changes in the employees' terms and conditions of employment designed to safeguard employment opportunities by ensuring the survival of the undertaking or part thereof.[501] As an additional safeguard for employees, Member States will be under an obligation to take measures to prevent the misuse of insolvency proceedings in such a way as to deprive employees of their rights under the Directive.[502]

When the Community first decided to review the Acquired Rights Directive the context was the 'Social Dimension' of the internal market and fulfilling the ambitions of the Social Charter. In this context there was a powerful case, notwithstanding the UK's opposition, for considerably strengthening the Directive by limiting the scope for dismissals to be made on economic grounds and protecting the rights of employees *after* the transfer rather than merely *upon* transfer.[503] In the eight years from conception to birth, however, the orientation of the review shifted to codification, reflecting—not entirely successfully—the commercial emphasis of recent case law, and 'adaptability', a central priority of the employment and competitiveness agenda of the second half of the 1990s.[504] In the process, notwithstanding the enhancements to the information and consultation provisions, the substantive safeguarding goals of the original Directive have been balanced, or even overtaken, by the perceived need for both the public and private sectors to have more flexibility to restructure in order to be globally competitive.

(4) Sex Equality

Over the period of the medium-term SAP the Commission introduced several relatively uncontroversial proposals to legislate in the area of sex

---

[499] Art 5(2)(a).
[500] See Davies (1989, *Yearbook of European Law*) n 495 above at 53.
[501] Art 5(2)(b).
[502] Art 5(4).
[503] See More, n 35 above at 145.
[504] See Hunt, n 432 above at 229–30.

equality as a direct response to the case law of the Court. In the area of equal treatment for men and women in occupational social security schemes, an unsatisfactory example of politically contrived codification had already been enacted in the form of the 'Barber Protocol' annexed to the revised EC Treaty. The Protocol declares that benefits under occupational pensions schemes shall not be considered as remuneration if and in so far as they are attributable to periods of employment prior to 17 May 1990.[505] The purpose of this financially driven Protocol was to apply the narrowest possible interpretation to the Court's pronouncement that, while periodic payments under occupational pension schemes were 'pay' for the purpose of Article 119 [now 141] EC,[506] for 'overriding considerations of legal certainty'[507] individuals cannot rely on the direct effect of the equal pay provisions to claim entitlement to benefits prior to that date unless legal proceedings had already been initiated or an equivalent claim had been raised under the applicable national law.[508] In effect the extension of the principle of equal pay, covering the full period of the occupational pension (or any benefit relating to service before 17 May 1990)[509] was deferred for 40 years,[510] an interpretation of *Barber* that the Court, showing awareness of the political sensibilities, was prepared to endorse in *Ten Oever*.[511] Moreover, the Court has taken an extremely broad view of the range of 'benefits' caught by the Protocol, which applies even when the benefits in question are deemed to be 'pay' under Article 119 [now 141] EC.[512] The

---

[505] Protocol 2. 17 May 1990 being the date of the judgment in *Barber*. For analysis of the Protocol, see T Hervey, 'Legal Issues concerning the *Barber* Protocol' in D O'Keeffe and P Twomey (eds) *Legal Issues of the Maastricht Treaty* (Wiley, London, 1994) 329–37.

[506] Case C–262/88, *Barber v Guardian Royal Exchange* [1990] ECR 1889, para 34. For full discussion of *Barber* and the surrounding case law, see E Whiteford, 'Occupational Pensions and European Law: Clarity at Last?' in Hervey and O'Keeffe, n 305 above, 21–34; B Fitzpatrick, 'Equality in Occupational Pensions—the New Frontiers after *Barber*' (1991) 54 *Modern Law Review* 271; and S Fredman, 'The Poverty of Equality: Pensions and the ECJ' (1996) 25 *Industrial Law Journal* 91.

[507] *Barber, ibid* para 44.

[508] *Ibid* para 45.

[509] See Case C–110/91, *Moroni v Collo GmbH* [1993] ECR I–6591, para 33; Case C–200/91, *Coloroll Pension Trustees Ltd v Russell* [1994] ECR I–4389, para 71. For discussion, see Barnard, *EC Employment Law*, n 184 above, pp 359–63.

[510] Hervey in O'Keeffe and Twomey (1994) n 505 above at 330.

[511] Case C–109/91, *Ten Oever v Stichting Bedrijfspensioenfonds voor het Glazenwassers- en Schoonmaakbedrijf* [1993] ECR I–4879.

[512] Case C–166/99, *Defreyn v Sabena SA* [2000] ECR I–6155. In *Defreyn* the Court was asked to determine the status of an additional pre-retirement payment provided by a collective agreement, rendered compulsory under national law. Ms Defreyn and the Commission had argued that that this was 'pay' under Art 119 [now 141] EC and therefore that provision took precedence over the Protocol, allowing backdating to 8 April 1976, the date of the Court's earlier time-limited judgment on Art 119 EEC in Case 43/75, *Defrenne v Sabena II* [1976] ECR 455. The Court, which in an earlier case had found that the payments in question were not a social security benefit (Case C–173/91, *Commission v Belgium* [1993] ECR I–673) held that, although the payments were caught directly by the Treaty principle, that finding did not foreclose the application of the Protocol if the payments were deemed to constitute a 'benefit'

only exception to the Protocol arises from the right to join an occupational pension scheme which had been established in the earlier case of *Bilka*,[513] and therefore, the Court has subsequently found that the issue of legal certainty arising from *Barber* does not apply.[514] The Member States, driven primarily by financial considerations, favoured a static view of equality that ignored the continuing effects of past discrimination[515] and, in the process, effectively placed a straightjacket on the Court, setting an unfortunate precedent for codification of Community social laws.

Barber was also to have direct legislative repercussions.[516] Directive 86/378 on equal treatment in occupational social security schemes[517] contained two sweeping derogations in Article 9(a) and (b) allowing Member States to defer the principle of equal treatment concerning the determination of pensionable ages and survivors' pensions until equality is achieved in statutory schemes or a further Directive is adopted requiring equality. The Commission had challenged these derogations at the time, on the grounds that they were incompatible with Article 119 [now 141] EC[518] and, following the judgments of the Court in *Barber* and *Ten Oever*, it was now established that, notwithstanding the Directive, the principle of equal pay applied to occupational pensions and survivors' benefits[519] under occupational schemes, rendering the specific derogations in Article 9(a) and (b) otiose, a point specifically confirmed by the Court in *Moroni*.[520] Moreover,

---

under an *occupational* social security scheme for the purposes of the Protocol (para 27). The Court then proceeded to find, at para 28, that the Protocol applied because the payments provided protection against the risk of unemployment by guaranteeing benefits intended to supplement benefits paid under the state social security scheme, thereby falling within the definition of occupational security schemes in Dir 86/378 as amended by Dir 96/97 (see below).

[513] Case 170/84, *Bilka Kaufhaus v Weber von Hartz* [1986] ECR 1607.

[514] See Case C–246/96, *Magorrian and Cunningham v EHSSB and DHSS* [1997] ECR I–7153, para 28. Further, the Court has held in Case C–50/96, *Deutsche Telekom AG v Schröder* [2000] ECR I–743, at paras 47–50, that the limit on retroactivity under *Defrenne II* does not preclude *national provisions* which lay down a principle of equal treatment by which part-time workers are entitled to retroactive membership of an occupational pension scheme and to receive a pension under that scheme as the obligation on Member States to apply Art 119 EEC dated back to 1 Jan 1962.

[515] See Fredman (1996, *Industrial Law Journal*) n 506 above at 105.

[516] See D Curtin, 'Scalping the Community Legislator: Occupational Pensions after *Barber*' (1990) 27 *Common Market Law Review* 475.

[517] OJ 1986, L225/40.

[518] Dir 86/378 was adopted just two months after the Court had held in Case 170/84, *Bilka Kaufhaus v Weber von Hartz* [1986] ECR 1607, that access to an occupational pension scheme was an element of 'pay' within the scope of Art 119 [now 141] EC. See E Cassell, 'The Revised Directive on Equal Treatment for Men and Women in Occupational Social Security Schemes— The Dog that Didn't Bark' (1997) 26 *Industrial Law Journal* 269 at 269.

[519] In Case C–109/91, *Ten Oever v Stichting Bedrijfspensioenfonds voor het Glazenwassers-en Schoonmaakbedrijf* [1993] ECR I–4879, the Court held, at paras 13–14, that the survivor was the person asserting the employee's right. See also Case C–147/95, *DEI v Evrenopoulos* [1997] ECR I–2057, para 22; and Case C–50/99, *Podesta v CRICA* [2000] ECR I–4039, para 27.

[520] Case C–110/91, *Moroni v Collo GmbH* [1993] ECR I–6591, para 24.

exemptions in Article 2(2) of the Directive, relating to individual contracts, single member schemes and individual insurance schemes were also invalidated.

Self-evidently, Directive 86/378 had to be amended because the Treaty takes precedence. The Commission's response was to issue a proposal that was 'purely declaratory' of the case law.[521] Although the Commission's proposal was heavily criticised by the Women's Rights Committee of the European Parliament,[522] which called for the express application of the Directive to atypical workers[523] and removal of the remaining derogations,[524] the amending Directive, 96/97,[525] was adopted with only minor amendments taking effect from 1 July 1997.

Article 1 of the revised Directive removes the exemptions in Articles 2(2) and the derogations in Article 9(a) and (b) of Directive 86/378, in respect of occupational social security schemes for employees,[526] but retains them for the self-employed.[527] In strict accordance with the case law, however, specific derogations have been now been included exempting Additional Voluntary Contributions (AVCs) deemed not to be 'pay' in *Coloroll*,[528] and, following *Birds Eye Walls*,[529] supplementary bridging pensions payable to employees who have retired early on the grounds of ill-health but who are not yet entitled to a state pension.[530] While the removal of these derogations appears, superficially at least to be a victory for 'equality', there is no accompanying commitment to levelling-up entitlements notwithstanding the fact that statistical evidence demonstrates that women are at a distinct

[521] OJ 1995, C218/5.

[522] C4–0422/95. Discussed by Cassell, n 518 above at 271–5.

[523] In the view of two AGs the Directive and Art 119 [141] EC provide adequate protection for part-time workers. See the Opinions of AG Van Gerven in Case C–57/93, *Vroege v NCIV Instituut voor Volkhuisvesting BV and Stichting Pensionfonds VCIV* [1994] ECR I–4541, para 17; and AG Cosmas in Case C–435/93, *Dietz v Stichting Thuiszorg Rotterdam* [1996] ECR I–5223, para 25. Discussed by Cassell, *ibid* at 272–3.

[524] For example, the derogation in Art 9(c) permitting the use of different actuarial factors in calculating entitlements, and Art 9(a) concerning the equalisation of the State retirement age.

[525] OJ 1996, L46/20.

[526] Art 2(1) as amended by Art 1(1) of Dir 96/97, defines 'occupational social security schemes' as 'schemes not governed by Dir 79/7/EEC [concerning statutory social security schemes] whose purpose is to provide workers, whether employed or self-employed, in an undertaking or group of undertakings, area of activity, occupational sector or group of sectors with benefits intended to supplement the benefits provided by statutory social security schemes or to replace them, whether membership of such schemes is compulsory or optional'.

[527] Arts 2(a) and 9 as amended.

[528] Case C–200/91, *Coloroll Pension Trustees Ltd v Russell* [1994] ECR I–4389, para 92. On the grounds that AVCs are paid into a separate fund administered by occupational pension schemes, but operating as secure benefits separate from the employment relationship.

[529] Case C–132/92, *Birds Eye Walls Ltd v Roberts* [1993] ECR I–5579. See Whiteford in Hervey and O'Keeffe, n 506 above at 29–33.

[530] Art 2(3) as amended. In Case C–132/92, *Birds Eye Walls Ltd v Roberts* [1993] ECR I–5579, the Court, at paras 17–20, adopted a narrow formalistic view of equality, determining that there was no discrimination under such schemes because men and women were not starting from identical positions.

disadvantage compared with men in their ability to secure an adequate independent pension in their old age.[531] Indeed, in *Smith*[532] the Court endorsed an employer's post-*Barber* scheme to adjust the pensionable age of women from 60 to 65 to achieve notional 'equality' with men on the grounds of consistency, without directly addressing the argument that equality was not to be achieved by withdrawing rights from women.

Under the amended Article 3, the Directive applies to survivors in accordance with *Ten Oever*.[533] The 'Barber Protocol' is incorporated into Article 2 of the new Directive. In the case of workers who have initiated a claim prior to 17 May 1990, the retroactive effect is limited to 8 April 1976, the date of the Court's earlier judgment in *Defrenne II*.[534]

In a minor concession to the European Parliament, the amended Article 6(1)(i) allows employers to make higher contributions for women either in the case of defined-contributions schemes,[535] if the aim is to equalise the amount of the final benefits or to make them more nearly equal for both sexes, or defined-benefit schemes,[536] to ensure the adequacy of the funds necessary to cover the cost of the benefit. Moreover, while differential sex-based actuarial factors will, in general, continue to be tolerated under the revised Directive, in accordance with the case law of the Court,[537] the Annex contains examples of inequalities, deemed contrary to the principle of equal treatment.[538] These inequalities relate to 'certain elements' in defined-benefit schemes arising from the use of actuarial factors differing according to sex at the time when the scheme's funding is implemented.[539] Finally, after consultation with the European Parliament, a small gesture towards greater flexibility can be found in a new Article 9a, inserted by Article 1(6) of Directive 96/97, which allows men and women to claim a 'flexible pensionable

---

[531] See Fredman (1996, *Industrial Law Journal*) n 506 above at 91.

[532] Case C–408/92, *Smith v Advel Systems* [1994] ECR I–4435. See also, Case C–28/93, *Van den Akker v Stichting Shell Pensionenfonds* [1994] ECR I–4527. Discussed by Fredman, *ibid* at 97–8.

[533] Case C–109/91, *Ten Oever v Stichting Bedrijfspensioenfonds voor het Glazenwassers-en Schoonmaakbedrijf* [1993] ECR I–4879, paras 13–14.

[534] Case 43/75, *Defrenne v Sabena II* [1976] ECR 455. Subject to the exceptions in *Magorrian* and *Schröder*, n 514 above.

[535] Schemes where a fixed percentage of the salary is paid. The lump sum is used to purchase a pension when the employee retires.

[536] Schemes where the employee pays a fixed contribution and the employer agrees to pay benefits set in accordance with a formula.

[537] See Case C–200/91, *Coloroll Pension Trustees Ltd v Russell* [1994] ECR I–4389; and Case C–152/91, *Neath v Hugh Steeper Ltd.* [1993] ECR I–6935. See the contrary opinion of AG Van Gerven in *Coloroll*. See further, B Jones, 'Sex Equality in Pension Schemes' in J Kenner (ed) *Trends in European Social Policy* (Dartmouth, Aldershot, 1995) 85–144.

[538] Art 6(1)(h).

[539] The Annex gives the following examples of possible inequalities arising from: conversion into a capital sum of a periodic pension; transfer of pension rights; a reversionary pension payable to a dependant in return for the surrender of part of a pension; and a reduced pension where the worker opts to take early retirement.

age' under the same conditions. This approach was strongly supported by the European Parliament, which was concerned about the discriminatory effects for women of upward equalisation of the retirement age.[540]

Directive 96/97 is an extremely limited consolidation measure. Its purpose is reactive and minimalist. The Commission, wary of the political sensitivity of the Member States in this area, and conscious of the need for unanimity, opted to dispense with its obligation to make policy and chose instead to react cautiously to the development of the law by the Court. The Community has settled for running repairs on Directive 86/378 instead of starting afresh by addressing the underlying issues of equal treatment in occupational pensions.[541]

While Directive 96/97 is an example of a piece of reactive, essentially defensive legislation, the Burden of Proof Directive, 97/80,[542] stemmed from a longstanding concern, first articulated in the Equal Opportunities Action Programme of 1981,[543] that there was a disparity in the evidential rules concerning the burden of proof in sex discrimination cases across the Member States and, following the recommendations of an expert report in 1984,[544] it was proposed in the Second Action Programme to put forward a legal instrument to reverse the burden of proof applying to all equal opportunities measures in order to ensure improved application of existing sex equality laws.[545]

First proposed in 1988, the draft directive was regarded by the Court as a consolidation of its existing case law.[546] In successive cases, the Court has established the principle that the burden of proving sex discrimination under Article 119 [now 141] EC and the sex equality directives rests with the complainant.[547] Where, however, the employer's system is completely lacking in transparency, the Court has held, in *Danfoss*,[548] that complainants would be deprived of any effective means of enforcing the principle of equal pay before the national courts if the effect of adducing such

---

[540] See Cassell, n 518 above at 273.

[541] *Ibid* at 275.

[542] OJ 1998, L14/16, amended by Dir 98/52/EC, OJ 1998, L205/66.

[543] COM(81) 758.

[544] *A comparative analysis of the provisions for legal redress in Member States of the European Economic Community in respect of Art 119 of the Treaty of Rome and the Equal Pay, Equal Treatment and Social Security Directives*, V/564/84–EN.

[545] Second Action Programme on Equal Opportunities for Women (1986–1990) COM(85) 801, para 19(c).

[546] Case 109/88, *Handels- og Kontorfunktionaerernes Forbund i Danmark v Danfoss* [1989] ECR 3199, para 14. See R Nielsen and E Szyszczak, *The Social Dimension of the European Community*, 2nd edn (Handelshøjskolens Forlag, Copenhagen, 1993) p 162.

[547] Case 170/84, *Bilka Kaufhaus v Weber von Hartz* [1986] ECR 1607; *Danfoss, ibid*; Case C–127/92, *Enderby v Frenchay Health Authority* [1993] ECR I–5355; and Case C–400/93, *Dansk Industri (Royal Copenhagen) v Specialarbejderforbundet i Danmark* [1995] ECR I–1275.

[548] *Ibid* para 13. See also, Case 318/86, *Commission v France* [1988] ECR 3559, para 27.

evidence was not to impose on the employer the burden of proving that his practice in the matter of wages was not in fact discriminatory.

This reasoning was applied in *Enderby*,[549] a case in which public hospital speech therapists in the UK—predominantly female—sought equal pay with pharmacists—predominantly male. The Court held that:[550]

The onus may shift when that is necessary to avoid depriving workers who appear to be the victims of discrimination of any effective means of enforcing the principle of equal pay. *Accordingly, when a measure distinguishing between employees on the basis of their hours of work has in practice an adverse impact on substantially more members of one or other sex, that measure must be regarded as contrary to the objective pursued by [Article 119 [now 141] EC] . . . unless the employer shows that it is based upon objectively justified factors unrelated to any discrimination on grounds of sex.*

Directive 97/80, which largely resurrects the blocked 1988 proposal, codifies and extends the evidential rule in the areas of equal pay, equal treatment in employment (but not social security) and, in so far as sex discrimination is concerned, maternity rights, and parental leave.[551] The aim of the Directive, set out in Article 1, is to ensure that the measures taken by the Member States to implement the principle of equal treatment are made more effective. This is to be achieved by enabling 'all persons who consider themselves wronged' because the principle of equal treatment has not been applied to them 'to have their rights asserted by judicial process after possible recourse to other competent bodies'. From the standpoint of the Community this is a highly ambitious objective as matters of judicial procedure, including evidential rules, are delegated to the national courts under the principal of procedural autonomy, to be considered in the next section. The primary tool in the Directive is Article 4(1) which reformulates the obligation on national courts as follows:

Member States shall take such measures as are necessary, in accordance with their national judicial systems, to ensure that, when persons who consider themselves wronged because the principle of equal treatment has not been applied to them establish, before a court or other competent authority, facts from which it may be presumed that there has been direct or indirect discrimination, it shall be for the respondent to prove that there has been no breach of the principle of equal treatment.

In practice the effect of Article 4(1) is to establish an obligation on Member States to provide for rules of evidence for courts and other legal bodies that ensure that the burden of proof switches from the claimant to the respondent once a prima facie case of sex discrimination has been established.[552]

---

[549] Case C–127/92, *Enderby v Frenchay Health Authority* [1993] ECR I–5355, para 19.
[550] *Ibid* para 14 (emphasis added).
[551] Art 3(1)(a).
[552] Art 4(3) provides that the reversal of the burden of proof need not be applied to proceedings in which it is for the court or the competent body to investigate only the facts of the case.

Furthermore, Article 4(2) provides that the Directive shall not prevent Member States from introducing rules of evidence that are *more favourable* to plaintiffs.[553] Whereas the case law of the Court has been effective in ensuring, through judicial dialogue, the reversal of the burden of proof in individual cases, and more generally in systems where active litigation strategies and a willingness on the part of the national courts to refer have coincided, the application of the Court's evidential rule has been far from uniform in the less active Member States.[554] Therefore the Commission's role in monitoring the implementation of the Directive will be critical. Member States were due to implement the Directive by 1 January 2001,[555] or, in the case of the UK, 22 July 2001.[556]

Article 4(1) is to be read together with the definitions of equal treatment and discrimination in Article 2. First, Article 2(1) defines equal treatment as meaning that 'there shall be no discrimination whatsoever based on sex, either directly or indirectly'. While Article 4(1) refers to the reversal of the burden of proof in cases of both direct and indirect sex discrimination, Article 2(2) refers to 'objective justification' only in the context of indirect discrimination as follows:

For the purposes of the principle of equal treatment . . . indirect discrimination shall exist where an apparently neutral provision, criterion or practice disadvantages a substantially higher proportion of the members of one sex unless that provision, criterion or practice is appropriate and necessary and can be justified by objective factors unrelated to sex.

Hence, while the burden of proof shifts in *all* cases where a prima facie case is established on the facts, the separate question of justification only applies in those cases where discrimination is indirect. Article 2(2) tends to reinforce the conventional position of the Court that direct sex discrimination cannot be justified because the detrimental treatment is based on sex leaving no scope for justification. By contrast, as Ellis has explained,[557] in cases of indirect discrimination the cause of the detrimental treatment is unclear and the defendant is entitled to show that there is an objective reason for different treatment unrelated to sex. For example, in *Dekker*[558] discrimination

---

[553] Further reinforcement is provided by a non-regression clause in Art 6.

[554] For an excellent overview, see C Kilpatrick, 'Gender Equality: A Fundamental Dialogue' in S Sciarra (ed) *Labour Law in the Courts: National Judges and the European Court of Justice* (Hart, Oxford, 2001) 31–130. Kilpatrick identifies Germany and the UK as the most active for litigation and referral in the area of Community equality law, whereas Spain and Italy are the least active.

[555] Art 7.

[556] Art 7, as amended by Art 2 of Dir 98/52/EC, OJ 1998, L205/66.

[557] E Ellis, 'The Definition of Discrimination in European Community Sex Equality Law' (1994) 19 *European Law Review* 563.

[558] Case 177/88, *Dekker v Stichting Vormingscentrum voor Jong Volwassenen* [1990] ECR I–3941.

on the grounds of pregnancy was found to be directly discriminatory and therefore incapable of objective justification. In subsequent cases, the Court has found that dismissals for reasons of pregnancy or as a consequence of pregnancy amount to automatic direct sex discrimination.[559] Nevertheless, submissions of the Commission,[560] pronouncements of AGs[561] and ambiguous paragraphs in judgments of the Court[562] have raised the possibility that there may be circumstances where direct discrimination can be justified. While the Directive is silent on this point—indicating that only indirect discrimination can be justified—the absence of a specific exclusion has kept the door open for a resurrection of this debate in the future.

Additional problems arise from the definition of indirect discrimination in the Directive. Article 2(2) emphasises narrow proportional factors based on statistical evidence within the context of the workplace rather than a broader disadvantage test, that takes account of wider social factors, such as the higher proportion of women who are lone parents and responsible for a child, or the fact that more women than men are employed on short-term contracts.[563] As we shall see in chapter 9, a disadvantage test has been applied in the more recent anti-discrimination directives.[564] The Court, however, has generally favoured the proportional approach. For example, in *Seymour-Smith and Perez*[565] the Court defined indirect discrimination as follows:[566]

---

[559] See Case C–32/93, *Webb v EMO Air Cargo* [1994] ECR I–3567; Case C–179/88, *Hertz* [1990] ECR I–3979. For a contrary view, see R Wintemute, 'When is Pregnancy Discrimination Indirect Sex Discrimination' (1998) 27 *Industrial Law Journal* 23.

[560] See Case C–132/92, *Birds Eye Walls Ltd v Roberts* [1993] ECR I–5579; and *Webb, ibid*. See further, E Szyszczak, 'Community Law on Pregnancy and Maternity' in Hervey and O'Keeffe, n 305 above, 51–62 at 57.

[561] For example, AG Van Gerven in *Birds Eye Walls, ibid* who was concerned that it may be difficult in certain cases to distinguish between direct and indirect discrimination on the facts. He concluded that the possibility 'must not be ruled out' that direct discrimination might nevertheless be justified 'having regard to the specific circumstances of the case'.

[562] For example, the Court in Case C–32/93, *Webb v EMO Air Cargo* [1994] ECR I–3567, at para 27, rejected the arguments put forward by the employer for justifying a pregnancy dismissal without directly excluding the possibility of justification. See Szyszczak in Hervey and O'Keeffe, n 560 above at 58.

[563] See C Barnard & B Hepple, 'Indirect Discrimination: Interpreting *Seymour-Smith*' (1999) 58 *Cambridge Law Journal* 399 at 405–7.

[564] Dir 2000/43/EC implementing the principle of equal treatment between persons irrespective of racial or ethnic origin, OJ 2000, L180/22; and Dir 2000/78/EC establishing a general framework for equal treatment in employment and occupation, OJ 2000, L303/16.

[565] Case C–167/97, *R v Secretary of State for Employment ex parte Seymour-Smith and Perez* [1999] ECR I–623.

[566] *Ibid* para 65 (emphasis added). In *Jørgensen*, a complex Danish case involving the calculation of medical fees based on the turnover of medical practices, the Court held that a separate assessment must be made of each key element of the conditions governing the exercise of professional activity in so far as those key elements constitute in themselves specific measures based on their own criteria of application and affecting a significant number of persons belonging to a determined category (Case C–226/98, *Jørgensen v Foreningen af Speciallæger* [2000] ECR I–2447).

... in order to establish whether a measure adopted by a Member State has disparate effect as between men and women to such a degree as to amount to indirect discrimination for the purposes of [Article 119 [now 141] EC], the national court must verify whether the statistics available indicate that a *considerably smaller* percentage of women than men is able to fulfil the requirement imposed by that measure. If that is the case, there is indirect sex discrimination, unless that measure is justified by objective factors unrelated to any discrimination based on sex.

The Court determined that the question of whether a two-year qualifying rule for unfair dismissal claims, then operative in the UK, produced a disparate impact on women could be determined by an examination of statistical evidence—77.4 per cent of men and 68.9 per cent of women could comply with the rule at the time when it was introduced—which suggested 'on the face of it' that the number of women affected was not *considerably smaller* than the number of men during the relevant period of time.[567] The Court rejected the submission of the Commission, which favoured a broader interpretation of the concept of 'disparate impact' that took account of social factors.[568] The effect of the Directive, therefore, if it is applied literally by the national courts, is to reinforce the proportional approach and, potentially, to restrict the scope of the Court to develop the law on indirect discrimination to tackle the hidden obstacles that stand in the way of women at work and in society.[569]

Article 2(2) codifies the concept of 'justification' based on 'objective factors unrelated to any discrimination based on sex'. Justification limits the application of the concept of equal treatment because it places those differently situated beyond the reach of Community law and yet, as Hervey observes,[570] the range of justifications accepted by the Court unduly emphasises market factors which fail to take sufficient account of the fact that women's domestic and parental roles differ from those of men leading, for example, to a greater proportion of women part-time workers. For example, in *Bilka*[571] the Court held that a justification based on a 'real need on the part of the undertaking' to pay full-time workers more than part-timers in order to encourage full time-work[572] related to the objective pursued and was proportionate.

---

[567] *Ibid* para 64. The Court had been more sympathetic to claimants in earlier cases where working hours were linked to promotion—Case C–1/95, *Gerster v Freiestaat Bremen* [1997] ECR I–5253; and Case C–100/95, *Kording v Senator für Finanzen* [1997] ECR I–5289—but not pay—see Cases C–399, 409 and 425/92 and C–34, 50 and 78/93, *Stadt Lengerich v Helmig* [1994] ECR I–5727. See further, E Ellis, 'Recent Developments in European Community Sex Equality Law' (1998) 35 *Common Market Law Review* 379 at 382–6.

[568] *Ibid* para 57. For a critique see Barnard and Hepple, n 563 above.

[569] See Ellis (1998, *Common Market Law Review*) n 567 above at 383.

[570] T Hervey, 'The Future of Sex Equality Law in the European Union' in Hervey and O'Keeffe, n 305 above, 399–413 at 405–6. See further, T Hervey, *Justifications for Sex Discrimination in Employment* (Butterworths, London, 1993).

[571] Case 170/84 [1986] ECR 1607.

[572] In order to ensure that retail premises were staffed throughout opening times.

In *Enderby*[573] the Court accepted the 'state of the employment market' as a justification by the State for pay differentials where there are staff shortages. From this standpoint it is possible to argue, in the broader context of the European Employment Strategy, that the encouragement of recruitment and other legitimate social policy aims are capable of objectively justifying indirect sex discrimination, an approach that has increasingly found favour with the Court.[574] Moreover, in *Jørgensen*,[575] although the Court held that budgetary considerations cannot, in themselves, justify discrimination by the State on the grounds of sex, measures intended to ensure sound management of public expenditure on specialised medical care and to guarantee people's access to such care may be justified if they meet a legitimate objective of social policy, are appropriate to attain that objective and are necessary to that end.[576]

Having opened the floodgates so wide, the Court has limited the scope for Member States to justify sex discrimination to a certain extent by insisting that mere generalisations and assertions about part-time workers will be insufficient in the absence of strong evidence.[577] Moreover, in *Seymour-Smith* the Court emphasised that, while a broad margin of discretion is left to the Member States, such justifications 'cannot have the effect of frustrating the implementation of a fundamental principle of Community law such as that of equal pay for men and women'.[578] An example of this approach can be found in *Krüger*,[579] a case where a part-time employee on child-care leave was denied a Christmas bonus. The Court rejected the employer's justification based on a collective agreement and national law on part-time work,[580] on the grounds that women who work while on child-care leave and who are raising children are put in a worse position than women who have given up work to care for their children.[581]

On one level, the Burden of Proof Directive provides a welcome contrast with the revised Occupational Social Security Directive. Unlike the latter, it

---

[573] Case C–127/92 [1993] ECR I–5355.

[574] See for example, Case C–317/93, *Nolte v Landesversicherungsantsalt Hannover* [1995] ECR I–4625; Case C–444/93, *Megner and Scheffel v Innungskrankenkasse Rheinhessen-Pfalz* [1995] ECR I–4741; Case C–457/93, *Kuratorium für Dialyse und Nierentransplantation e V v Lewark* [1996] ECR I–243; Case C–278/93, *Freers and Speckmann v Deutsche Bundespost* [1996] ECR I–1165.

[575] Case C–226/98, *Jørgensen v Foreningen af Speciallæger* [2000] ECR I–2447. Applied in Case C–322/98, *Kachelmann v Bankhaus Hermann Lampe KG* [2000] ECR I–7505.

[576] *Jørgensen, ibid* para 42.

[577] See Case C–243/95, *Hill and Stapleton v Revenue Commissioners* [1998] ECR I–3739.

[578] Case C–167/97, *Seymour-Smith and Perez* [1999] ECR I–623, para 75.

[579] Case C–281/97, *Krüger v Kreiskrankenhaus Ebersberg* [1999] ECR I–5127.

[580] The same rule had been upheld as a *State aim* in Case C–317/93, *Nolte v Landesversicherungsantsalt Hannover* [1995] ECR I–4625; and Case C–444/93, *Megner and Scheffel v Innungskrankenkasse Rheinhessen-Pfalz* [1995] ECR I–4741. These cases were distinguished because the right to the allowance in this case was determined by a separate collective agreement.

[581] Case C–281/97, *Krüger v Kreiskrankenhaus Ebersberg* [1999] ECR I–5127, para 9.

was introduced as a positive measure designed to address the difficulties that women face when seeking to rely on Community equality law before national courts that operate according to a wide array of procedural rules. Codification of the Court's case law on the reversal of the burden of proof is designed to achieve a systematic change in national rules of evidence that the Court's jurisprudence—applied on a case-by-case basis—cannot secure alone. Codification brings about legal certainty and transparency providing the law is sufficiently clear.[582] At another level, however, as an example of the wider updating process arising from the White Paper, the Directive exhibits a tendency towards an over fussy approach to codification that imperils equality by leading to an ossification of the law, contradicting the evolutionary character of Community law[583] by impeding further refinement by the Court of its tests on indirect discrimination and justification to take fuller account of substantive equality goals.

(5) Enforcement of Community Social Legislation

On 27 February 1997 the French car manufacturer, Renault, announced the closure of its Belgian plant at Vilvoorde with the loss of 3,000 jobs.[584] Vilvoorde was highly productive and regarded as an exemplar of flexible work organisation. Industrial relations appeared to be excellent both locally and across the company, with a fully functioning European Works Council (EWC) for transnational information and consultation in place. Renault's 'final decision', however, had been taken without prior consultation with the local works council at Vilvoorde or the EWC. An unprecedented wave of co-ordinated protest was to follow in both France and Belgium and, in the meantime, Renault's decision was challenged separately in the Belgian and French courts on the grounds that it had violated the information and consultation procedures set out in the directives concerning Collective Redundancies and EWCs.[585] Neither directive creates the capacity to challenge the managerial prerogative—indeed Renault was able to close the plant in July 1997—but the ensuing legal actions raised fundamental questions about the enforcement of Community law rights by national courts and, in particular, the effectiveness of national systems of sanctions against blatant violations of the Community's social legislation.

---

[582] See J Schwarze, 'The Convergence of the Administrative Laws of the EU Member States' in Snyder, n 151 above, 163–82 at 178.

[583] *Ibid* at 177.

[584] For full accounts of the events at Vilvoorde, see *European Industrial Relations Review* 289, February 1998, pp 22–5; and *European Works Councils Bulletin*, Issue 9, May/June 1997.

[585] Dir 92/56/EEC, OJ 1992, L245/3 amending Dir 75/129/EEC, OJ 1975, L48/29, now consolidated in Dir 98/59/EC, OJ 1998, L 225/16; and Dir 94/45/EC, OJ 1994, L254/64, now amended by Dir 97/74/EC, OJ 1998, L10/20.

In Belgium the Collective Redundancies Directive had been implemented by a collective agreement that was binding in national law. Under the collective agreement consultation with the local works council was required before any announcement was made and before any decisions were taken. Potential sanctions for breaching these procedures amounted to a maximum of 30 days imprisonment and a fine of BFr4 million (£65,953).[586] The Brussels Labour Tribunal found that Renault had breached three separate collective agreements and two royal decrees but no sanctions were imposed. Instead the Tribunal's solution was to demand that Renault should restart the consultation procedure with a view to reducing the number of redundancies and mitigating their effects. In the event a 'Social Plan' was hastily cobbled together allowing for limited redeployment and early retirement, but 2,900 jobs were lost when the plant was eventually closed. At the political level new legislation was introduced in Belgium in January 1998 to strengthen the procedural obligations on employers and, where litigation takes place, to switch the burden of proof and guarantee payment of wages and related benefits during the information and consultation period.

France was the headquarters of Renault under the EWC agreement. Members of the EWC therefore brought separate proceedings under French law before the Nanterre District Court. The Court found that Renault had violated the transnational information and consultation arrangements in the EWC agreement and ordered them to pay the EWC a total of Fr15,000 (£1,525) plus expenses.[587] The Court's decision was later upheld in a condemnatory appeal judgment. However, from the perspective of the workers involved and the trade unions in Belgium and France this was a pyrrhic victory.

The Vilvoorde saga illustrated the limitations of Community social law in the field of information and consultation, spurring strong demands for further legislation in this area, including the previously stalled proposal for a national-level worker information and consultation directive.[588] Most significantly, while the Commission applauded the legal actions pursued at national level, they expressed caution about proposals to strengthen existing legislation and to impose heavier fines on those breaching Community law. The Commission's caution was a reflection of the delicate balance that has to be struck between Community rights and national remedies. The effectiveness of the Community system is ultimately dependent on the dynamic interrelationship between Community law and national law and,

---

[586] *European Industrial Relations Review* 289, February 1998, p 22.
[587] *Ibid* p 24.
[588] Now adopted as Dir 2002/14/EC, OJ 2002, L80/29. For the Commission's original proposal, see COM(98) 612, OJ 1999, C2/3. Revised by COM(2001) 296, OJ 2001, C240/133.

in the field of legal remedies, a lack of homogeneity threatens to undermine the Community's social policy ambitions.[589]

The events at Vilvoorde brought a fresh focus to the debate about the effective application of Community social law. In its White Paper on Social Policy[590] the Commission recognised that, while the psychological impact on a Member State of an infringement ruling under Article 169 [now 226] EC,[591] or even a fine or penalty payment under the new procedure added by Article 171(2) [now 228(2)] EC,[592] should not be underestimated,[593] several Member States were apparently willing to sign up for legislative initiatives so long as enforcement remained lax or protracted.[594] Indeed, by the end of 1993, only Portugal and, somewhat ironically, the UK had transposed over 90 per cent of the 37 applicable employment and social policy directives.[595] Italy and Luxembourg had transposition rates of less than 60 per cent and several other Member States were faring little better.[596] In the

---

[589] For discussion see W Van Gerven, 'Bridging the gap between Community and national laws: towards a principle of homogeneity in the field of legal remedies' (1995) 32 *Common Market Law Review* 679; C Harlow, 'A Common European Law of Remedies' in C Kilpatrick, T Novitz and P Skidmore (eds) *The Future of Remedies in Europe* (Hart, Oxford, 2000) 69–83; A Tash, 'Remedies for European Community Law Claims in Member State Courts: Towards a European Standard' (1993) 31 *Columbia Journal of Transnational Law* 377; B Fitzpatrick, 'The Effectiveness of Equality Law Remedies: A European Community Law Perspective' in Hepple and Szyszczak, n 271 above, 67–85; and G Tesauro, 'The Effectiveness of Judicial Protection and Co-operation between the Court of Justice and National Courts' (1993) 13 *Yearbook of European Law* 1.

[590] COM(94) 333.

[591] Art 155 [now 211] EC places an obligation on the Commission to 'ensure' that Treaty provisions and legislative measures are applied and, under Art 169 [now 226] EC, if the Commission considers that a Member State has failed to fulfil a Treaty obligation it shall first pursue a process of *administrative enforcement* by delivering a reasoned opinion on the matter after giving the State concerned the opportunity to submits its observations. The Commission's discretionary power to seek *judicial enforcement* only arises if the State concerned does not comply with the opinion within the period designated by the Commission. At this stage the Commission may bring the matter before the Court of Justice.

[592] Under Art 171(1) [now 228(1)] EC the Court is empowered to issue a ruling that the State concerned must 'take the necessary measures' to comply with the judgment. Under the pre-TEU procedure, if the State concerned failed to take these measures, the Commission would have to restart the whole procedure even though no direct sanction was available. The TEU, in an important move towards improving the effectiveness of Community law, added Art 171(2) [now 228(2)] EC permitting the Commission, when bringing a repeat case of non-compliance before the Court, to specify a lump sum or penalty payment to be paid by the Member State concerned, and placing with the Court the power to impose the lump sum or penalty payment it considers to be appropriate.

[593] See A Arnull, *The European Union and its Court of Justice* (OUP, Oxford, 1999) p 29. In the first case brought under Art 171(2) [now 228(2)] EC, Greece has been fined for failing to comply with directives on toxic waste over a period of 20 years: Case C–387/97, *Commission v Greece* [2000] ECR I–5047.

[594] See F Snyder, 'The Effectiveness of European Community Law: Institutions, Processes, Tools and Techniques' (1993) 56 *Modern Law Review* 19 at 53.

[595] COM(94) 333. Ch X, Table 1.

[596] *Ibid*. Respectively, 21 and 22 out of 37. Other notable defaulters were: Greece, 24; Spain, 25; the Netherlands, 26; and Germany, 27.

high profile area of health and safety at work, where the framework Directive[597] was designed to provide a basis for systematic implementation of detailed directives, the Commission noted that by mid-1994 only one Member State, France, had transposed all of the Directives in force, while five had not yet notified measures to transpose the framework Directive itself.[598]

The Commission's efforts to throw a spotlight on non-compliance were only partly motivated by the potential award of a fine or penalty payment against Member States which, although representing an important addition to the Court's armoury, is relatively limited—essentially a power of last resort—when compared with the much broader principle of state liability that had recently been established in *Francovich*[599] as an alternative route for individuals to bring proceedings against a defaulting state before their national courts.[600]

Francovich represents a copybook case of non-compliance. By 1988 Italy had failed to implement 278 out of 622 Community directives. 196 had passed their implementation date and, in the case of 48, that date had expired more than five years previously.[601] The Insolvency Directive,[602] adopted unanimously on 20 October 1980, required implementation by 23 October 1983. Although the Commission contacted Italy one month after the expiry of the implementation period, a reasoned opinion was not issued until 19 March 1986. Having rejected an Italian request for more time, the Commission moved from the administrative to the judicial phase on 29 January 1987. The Court eventually ruled against Italy on 2 February 1989.[603] Two months later, 35 employees brought proceedings against Italy claiming compensation for arrears of salary arising from the insolvency of their former employer in 1985. The Italian Preture asked two questions. First, can a directive be enforced against the State in the absence of implementing measures? Second, is a private individual who has been adversely

---

[597] 89/391/EEC, OJ 1989, L183/1.

[598] COM(94) 333. Ch X, Table 2. The five Member States were Germany, Greece, Spain, Ireland and Luxembourg.

[599] Cases C–6/90 and C–9/90, *Francovich and Bonifaci v Italian Republic* [1991] ECR I–5357.

[600] The academic literature on *Francovich* is extensive and includes the following: C Harlow, 'Francovich and the Problem of the Disobedient State' (1996) 2 *European Law Journal* 199; D Curtin, 'State Liability under Community Law: a New Remedy for Private Parties' (1992) 21 *Industrial Law Journal* 74; C Lewis and S Moore, 'Duties, Directives and Damages in European Community Law' [1993] *Public Law* 151; R Caranta, 'Government Liability after Francovich' (1992) 52 *Cambridge Law Journal* 272; J Steiner, 'From direct effects to Francovich: Shifting Means of Enforcement of Community Law' (1993) 18 *European Law Review* 3; P Craig, 'Francovich, Remedies and the Scope of Damages Liability' (1993) 109 *Law Quarterly Review* 595; and M Ross, 'Beyond Francovich' (1993) 56 *Modern Law Review* 55.

[601] See Bercusson, *European Labour Law*, n 399 above, p 101.

[602] Dir 80/987/EEC, OJ 1980, L283/23.

[603] Case 22/87, *Commission v Italian Republic* [1989] ECR 143.

affected by the failure of the State to implement the directive entitled to claim reparation for the loss and damage sustained as a result?

On 19 November 1991—more than 11 years after the adoption of the Directive—the Court answered no to the first question, on the basis that the compensation provisions were insufficiently precise to be directly effective, but gave a qualified yes to the second question, finding that irrespective of the absence of direct effect, the full effectiveness of Community rules would be impaired and the protection of the rights they grant weakened if individuals were unable to obtain redress when their rights have been infringed by a breach of Community law for which a Member State could be held responsible.[604] It follows that there is a general 'right to reparation', a right that is inherent in the system of the Treaty[605] and is also derived from the obligations of Member States under Article 5 [now 10] EC.[606] The 'right to reparation' for failure to implement a directive in breach of Community law operates on the basis of national rules of liability[607] and is subject to three conditions. First, the result prescribed by the directive should entail the grant of rights to individuals. Second, it should be possible to identify the content of those rights on the basis of the provisions of the directive. Third, there must be a causal link between the breach of the State's obligation and the loss and damage suffered by the injured parties.[608]

In *Francovich* the breach arising from non-implementation was self-evident and the case for reparation was unambiguous. Would a less culpable Member State be equally liable? This question was particularly resonant in the light of the Court's case law concerning non-contractual liability of the institutions under Article 215 [now 288] EC.[609] In the joined cases of *Brasserie* and *Factortame*,[610] the Court, at the behest of the submissions

---

[604] Para 33.

[605] Para 35. Derived from the principle of effective protection of rights conferred on individuals—see Case 106/77, *Amministrazione dello Finanze dello Stato v Simmenthal* [1978] ECR 629, para 16; Case C–213/89, *R v Secretary of State for Transport, ex parte Factortame* [1990] ECR I–2433, para 19. See A Arnull, 'Does the Court of Justice have inherent jurisdiction?' (1990) 27 *Common Market Law Review* 683.

[606] Para 36. See Case 6/60, *Humblet v Belgium* [1960] ECR 559.

[607] Paras 42–3.

[608] Para 40.

[609] The second paragraph of Art 288 [ex 215] EC provides that: 'In the case of non-contractual liability, the Community shall, in accordance with the general principles common to the laws of the Member States, make good any damage caused by its institutions or by its servants in the performance of their duties'.

[610] Case C–46/93, *Brasserie du Pêcheur SA v Federal Republic of Germany* and Case C–48/93, *R v Secretary of State of Transport, ex parte Factortame Ltd* [1996] ECR I–1029. For discussion see: E Deards, 'Curioser and Curioser? The Development of Member State Liability in the Court of Justice' (1997) 3 *European Public Law* 117; N Emiliou, 'State Liability under Community Law: Shedding More Light on the *Francovich* Principle?' (1996) 21 *European Law Review* 399; N Gravells, 'State Liability in Damages for Breach of European Community Law' [1996] *Public Law* 567; and P Craig, 'Once more unto the breach: The Community, the State and Damages Liability' (1997) 113 *Law Quarterly Review* 67.

of the Commission and several governments,[611] took the opportunity to reconcile the *Francovich* principle with its own jurisprudence on non-contractual liability of the institutions[612] and the general principles of tort liability in the Member States. In particular, the Court ruled that account has to be taken of the complexity of situations to be regulated, difficulties in the application or interpretation of the texts and, more particularly, the margin of discretion left to the author of the act in question.[613] The Court concluded that where the Member State has a wide margin of discretion the breach must be 'sufficiently serious' to give rise to liability.[614] A breach would be 'sufficiently serious' where the Member State concerned 'manifestly and gravely disregarded the limits of its discretion'.[615] In applying this test a competent court would take a range of factors into consideration including: the clarity and precision of the rule breached; the measure of discretion left by that rule to the national or Community authorities; whether the infringement and the damage caused was intentional or involuntary; whether any error of law was excusable or inexcusable; the fact that the position taken by a Community institution may have contributed towards the omission; and the adoption or retention of national measures or practices contrary to Community law.[616] Where the Court had already found an infringement, the breach would be per se sufficiently serious[617] and, as the Court subsequently found in *Dillenkofer*,[618] the same applied in a case of non-implementation of a directive, although it must be emphasised that causation must still be established.[619] However, where there is mis-implementation rather than non-implementation of a directive, as in *British Telecom*,[620] a Member State may be able to raise the defence that it acted 'in good faith' on the basis of arguments that the wording of the directive in question was ambiguous and there was no clear guidance from the Community institutions.

---

[611] Para 40.

[612] Para 41.

[613] Para 43.

[614] Para 51.

[615] Para 55. This was in line with the Court's case law on Art 215 [288] EC—Cases 83 and 94/76 and 4, 15 and 40/77, *HNL v Council and Commission* [1978] ECR 1209, paras 5–6.

[616] Para 56.

[617] Para 57.

[618] Cases C–178–179 and 188–190/94, *Dillenkofer and others v Federal Republic of Germany* [1996] ECR I–4845.

[619] On the problem of causation, see Case C–319/96, *Brinkmann Tabakfabriken GmbH v Skatteministeriet* [1998] ECR I–5255; and Case C–140/97, *Rechberger and Greindl v Austria* [1999] ECR I–3499. Discussed by M Dougan, 'The *Francovich* right to reparation: The contours of Community remedial competence' (2000) 6 *European Public Law* 103; and T Tridimas, 'Liability for Breach of Community Law: Growing Up and Mellowing Down?' (2001) 38 *Common Market Law Review* 301.

[620] Case C–392/93, *R v HM Treasury, ex parte British Telecommunications plc* [1996] ECR I–1631. See also, Cases C–283, 291 and 292/94, *Denkavit International BV and others v Bundesamt für Finanzen* [1996] ECR I–5063.

In the context of Community directives in the area of employment and social law, it is important to distinguish between examples of blatant non-compliance and cases involving other forms of behaviour where, as the case law on Article 215 [now 288] EC has shown,[621] it can be extremely difficult to establish liability.[622] What if the Court's interpretation of a directive, although not entirely conclusive, throws into doubt the veracity of a Member State's implementing legislation? How clear does a provision have to be before it generates liability?[623] Even if these hurdles can be overcome in a given case, the fact remains that state liability remains a poor substitute for the absence of horizontal direct effect of directives for employees who have to bring an action against the Member State in default rather than the private employer who cannot be held responsible for the State's default,[624] notwithstanding the fact that individuals in other Member States are able to rely on the directive in question. As AG Van Gerven observed in his Opinion in *Marshall II*,[625] the development of state liability although, in principle, favourable, does not create equality before the law because it:[626]

... does not remedy the fact that individuals who are operating in a Member State which implemented the directive correctly and are therefore bound by the obligations ... are disadvantaged in comparison with individuals (perhaps their competitors) who are operating in a Member State which has not yet correctly implemented the directive.

As Ryan[627] observes, an employee may strongly prefer their employer to respect the substance of a given Community law right—capable of enforcement through a direct contractual claim—rather than receive monetary compensation, at a much later date, from the State. Moreover, the employee's non-contractual claim against the State may be hindered on procedural grounds for, as the Court acknowledged in both *Francovich* and

---

[621] See Case 5/71, *Aktien-Zuckerfabrik Schöppenstedt v Council* [1971] ECR 975; Cases 83 and 94/76 and 4, 15 and 40/77, *HNL v Council and Commission* [1978] ECR 1209; Cases 103 and 145/77, *Royal Scholten Honig* [1978] ECR 2037; Cases 116 and 124/77, *Amylum v Council and Commission* [1979] ECR 3497; Case C–152/88, *Sofrimport v Commission* [1990] ECR I–2477; and Cases C–104/89 and 37/90, *Mulder v Council and Commission* [1992] ECR I–3061.

[622] See T Hervey and P Rostant, 'After *Francovich*: State Liability and British Employment Law' (1999) 25 *Industrial Law Journal* 259 at 261.

[623] See Chalmers, n 3 above, p 418.

[624] See Case 152/84, *Marshall v Southampton and South-West Hampshire AHA I* [1986] ECR 723; Case C–91/92, *Dori v Recreb* [1994] ECR I–3325.

[625] Case C–271/91, *Marshall v Southampton and South-West Hampshire AHA II* [1993] ECR I–4367.

[626] *Ibid*. Opinion, para 12.

[627] B Ryan, 'The Private Enforcement of European Union Labour Laws' in Kilpatrick *et al*, n 589 above, 141–63 at 155.

Brasserie/Factortame, applying earlier case law,[628] while there is a Community right to reparation, under the principle of national procedural autonomy, it is for the domestic legal system of each Member State to set the criteria for determining the procedure to be followed[629] and the extent of the reparation, subject to two overriding principles. Firstly, procedural conditions, such as time limits for bringing proceedings or launching appeals, must not be less favourable than those relating to similar actions of a domestic nature—*the principle of equivalence*—and, secondly, they must not be framed so as to render virtually impossible or excessively difficult the exercise of rights conferred by Community law—*the principle of effectiveness*. It follows, therefore, that national courts, acting as Community courts,[630] have responsibility for providing an effective remedy for individuals deprived of their Community law rights within the framework of their national procedures. Hence, so long as it is possible to bring a claim in accordance with national procedural rules, such as time limits, and the rule in question is equivalent as between Community law and national law,[631] Community law does not preclude reliance on such limits even where the

---

[628] See Case 33/76, *Rewe v Landwirtschaftskammer Saarland* [1976] ECR 1989, para 5; Case 45/76, *Comet v Produktschap voor Siergewassen* [1976] ECR 2043, para 13; Case 199/82, *Amministrazione delle Finanze dello Stato v San Giorgio* [1983] ECR 3595, para 12; Case C–208/90, *Emmott v Minister for Social Welfare* [1991] ECR I–4269, para 16; Cases C–6/90 and C–9/90, *Francovich and Bonifaci v Italian Republic* [1991] ECR I–5357, para 43; Case C–338/91, *Steenhorst Neerings v Bestuur van de Bedrijfsvereniging voor Detailhandel, Ambachten en Huisvrouwen* [1993] ECR I–5475, para 15; Case C–410/92, *Johnson v Chief Adjudication Officer II* [1994] ECR I–5483, para 21; Case 312/93, *Peterbroeck v Belgian State* [1995] ECR I–4599, para 12; Cases C–430–431/93, *Van Schijndel* [1995] ECR I–4705, para 17; and Cases C–46/93, *Brasserie du Pêcheur SA v Federal Republic of Germany* and C–48/93, *R v Secretary of State for Transport, ex parte Factortame Ltd* [1996] ECR I–1029, para 83. For discussion, see FG Jacobs, 'Enforcing Community Rights and Obligations in National Courts: Striking the Right Balance' in J Lonbay and A Biondi (eds) *Remedies for Breach of EC Law* (Wiley, Chichester, 1997) 25–36; W Van Gerven, 'Of rights, remedies and procedures' (2000) 37 *Common Market Law Review* 501; and A Biondi, 'The Court of Justice and certain national procedural limitations: not such a tough relationship' (1999) 36 *Common Market Law Review* 1271.

[629] See Case C–54/96, *Dorsch Consult Ingenieurgesellschaft mbH v Bundesbaugesellschaft Berlin mbH* [1997] ECR I–4961, para 40. For example, in the UK the employee would have to pursue a claim through the ordinary courts rather than the more accessible employment tribunals. See Ryan, n 627 above at 157. See further, Hervey and Rostant, n 622 above; J Convery, 'State Liability in the United Kingdom after *Brasserie du Pêcheur*' (1997) 34 *Common Market Law Review* 603; and R Craufurd Smith, 'Remedies for Breaches of EC Law in National Courts: Legal Variation and Selection' in Craig and de Búrca, n 68 above, 287–320.

[630] See I Maher, 'National Courts as European Community Courts' (1994) 14 *Legal Studies* 226.

[631] In Case C–326/96, *Levez v Jennings (Harlow Pools) Ltd* [1998] ECR I–7835, the Court was asked to consider the meaning of the phrase 'similar domestic actions'. The Court ruled, at paras 42–7, that the principle of equivalence is not to be interpreted as requiring Member States to extend their most favourable rules to all actions brought in the field of employment law. In order to determine whether the principle of equivalence has been complied with the national court must consider both the purpose and the essential characteristics of allegedly similar domestic actions. Furthermore, whenever it falls to be determined whether a proce-

relevant directive has not been implemented in national law.[632] Reasonable time limits can be reconciled with effectiveness on the basis that they constitute an application of the fundamental principle of legal certainty.[633] In return for this latitude, national courts are under a positive obligation to guarantee judicial protection and the full force and effect of Community law.[634] In particular, Member States must ensure that national courts apply a system of sanctions that is effective, dissuasive and proportionate.[635]

The Court is extremely sensitive when adjudging the scope of national procedural rules, tempering their natural inclination for active judicial protection of Community law rights with restraint. Article 6 of the Equal Treatment Directive provides that:[636]

Member States shall introduce into their national legal systems *such measures as are necessary* to enable all persons who consider themselves wronged by failure to apply to them the principle of equal treatment . . . *to pursue their claims by judicial process after possible recourse to other competent authorities.*

Manifestly this clause grants individuals no more than a basic right of access to bring their case before a court or other competent body capable of

---

dural rule of national law is less favourable than those governing similar domestic actions, the national court must take into account the role played by that provision in the procedure as a whole, as well as the operation and any special features of that procedure before the different national courts. Accordingly, the fact that the same procedural rules applied to two comparable claims, one relying on a right conferred by Community law, the other on a right acquired under domestic law, was not enough to ensure compliance with the principle of equivalence, since one and the same form of action is involved. Applied in Case C–78/98, *Preston v Wolverhampton Healthcare NHS Trust and others* and *Fletcher and others v Midland Bank plc* [2000] ECR I–3201.

[632] See Case C–338/91, *Steenhorst Neerings v Bestuur van de Bedrijfsvereniging voor Detailhandel, Ambachten en Huisvrouwen* [1993] ECR I–5475; and Case C–410/92, *Johnson v Chief Adjudication Officer II* [1994] ECR I–5483; cf Case C–208/90, *Emmott v Minister for Social Welfare* [1991] ECR I–4269. Discussed by Jacobs, n 628 above at 29. For examples of more recent cases where a time limit has been overturned on application of these criteria, see Case C–246/96, *Magorrian and Cunningham v EHSSB and DHSS* [1997] ECR I–7153; and *Preston, ibid.* See L Flynn, 'Whatever Happened to Emmott? The Perfecting of Community Rules on Time Limits' in Kilpatrick *et al*, n 589 above, 51–67.

[633] See Case C–261/95, *Palmisani v Istituto Nazionale della Previdenza Sociale* [1997] ECR I–4025, para 28. Applied in *Preston, ibid* paras 33–5.

[634] Case 106/77, *Amministrazione dello Finanze dello Stato v Simmenthal* [1978] ECR 629. See for example, Case C–185/97, *Coote v Granada* [1998] ECR I–5199, which involved alleged victimisation of an ex-employee. The Court ruled that, having regard to the fundamental nature of the right to effective judicial protection, employees enjoy such protection even after the employment relationship has ended. See M Dougan, 'The Equal Treatment Directive: Retaliation, Remedies and Direct Effect' (1999) 24 *European Law Review* 664.

[635] See for example, Cases C–382 and C–383/92, *Commission v United Kingdom* [1994] ECR I–2435 and [1994] ECR I–2479.

[636] Dir 76/207/EEC, OJ 1976, L39/40. Emphasis added. By comparison note that, while Art 2 of the Equal Pay Dir (75/117/EEC, OJ 1975, L45/19) contains an identical clause, Art 6 of that Directive creates a more precise obligation on the Member States to: 'take the measures necessary to ensure that the principle of equal pay is applied. They shall see that *effective means* are available to take care that this principle is observed' (emphasis added).

granting an effective judicial remedy.[637] In *Von Colson*,[638] however, the Court furnished Article 6 with a more explicit meaning by ruling that, although Member States are free to choose between different suitable solutions, and, therefore, while there is no directly effective right to a remedy arising from Article 6,[639] necessary measures must 'guarantee real and effective judicial protection' and must also have a 'real deterrent effect on the employer'.[640] As the Court explained in *Marshall II*,[641] Article 6 places an implied obligation on Member States to provide a minimum guarantee that the measures in question should be sufficiently effective to achieve the equality objective and should be capable of being effectively relied upon by the persons concerned before national courts.[642] It followed that, where financial compensation is the measure adopted, it must be adequate, in that it must enable the loss and damage actually sustained as a result of discrimination to be made good in full in accordance with national applicable rules.[643] Consequently, an arbitrary financial ceiling on compensation levels and the absence of any power to award interest, as an essential component of compensation, was deemed inadequate.[644]

Marshall II represents a high point of the Court's interventionism.[645] In subsequent cases the Court has sought to strike a balance by exercising judicial restraint.[646] For example, in the context of Article 6 of Directive 79/7 on equal treatment in social security,[647] a near identical 'aggrieved

[637] See Case 222/84, *Johnston v Chief Constable of the RUC* [1986] ECR 1651, para 58.
[638] Case 14/83, *Von Colson and Kamann v Land Nordrhein Westfalen* [1984] ECR 1891. For discussion, see D Curtin, 'Effective Sanctions and the Equal Treatment Directive: The *Von Colson* and *Harz* Cases' (1985) 22 *Common Market Law Review* 505; Fitzpatrick in Hepple and Szyszczak, n 589 above; J Shaw, 'European Community judicial method: its application to sex discrimination law' (1990) 19 *Industrial Law Journal* 228; and, generally, Craufurd Smith, n 629 above.
[639] *Von Colson, ibid* para 35. There is, however, a directly effective *right of access* to a remedy. See Case 222/84, *Johnston v Chief Constable of the RUC* [1986] ECR 1651, para 58. Discussed by Fitzpatrick, *ibid* at 74–6.
[640] *Von Colson, ibid* para 23.
[641] Case C–271/91 [1993] ECR I–4367.
[642] *Ibid* para 22.
[643] *Ibid* para 26.
[644] *Ibid* paras 33–5. As anticipated by Fitzpatrick in Hepple and Szyszczak, n 589 above at 79–80.
[645] See P Craig and G de Búrca, *EU Law: Text, Cases and Materials*, 2nd edn (OUP, Oxford, 1998) p 229.
[646] See M Hoskins, 'Tilting the Balance: Supremacy and National Procedural Rules' (1996) 21 *European Law Review* 365; A Ward, 'Effective Sanctions in EC Law: a Moving Boundary in the Division of Competence' (1995) 1 *European Law Journal* 205; G de Búrca, 'National Procedural Rules and Remedies: The Changing Approach of the Court of Justice' in Lonbay and Biondi, n 628 above, 37–46; C Himsworth, 'Things Fall Apart: The Harmonisation of Community Judicial Protection Revisited' (1997) 22 *European Law Review* 291; and E Szyszczak, 'Making Europe More Relevant to its Citizens: Effective Judicial Process' (1996) 21 *European Law Review* 351.
[647] OJ 1979, L6/24.

claimant'[648] clause to Article 6 of Directive 76/207, the Court, wary perhaps of interfering with the structure and organisation of national social systems and conscious also of the associated cost implications, has exercised caution by permitting rules that restrict retroactive claims.[649] Moreover, in *Sutton*,[650] the Court distinguished *Marshall II* when asked to determine whether a backdated award of a social security benefit in the UK should include interest.[651] The Court held that, although the Member State was under a duty to compensate for the loss caused by the breach, they enjoyed discretion as to the calculation of damages subject to the principles of effectiveness and equivalence. As the payment in question was a benefit and not compensation under national law the payment of interest on that benefit was not part of the right of reparation.[652]

In a similar vein, extending the logic of *Sutton* to the application of Directive 76/207, the Court in *Draehmpaehl*[653] ruled that a national rule setting a maximum of three months salary might be adequate where the candidate who had been discriminated against would not have been appointed to the job in question because the other candidate was better qualified. Therefore, notwithstanding the emergence of state liability, considerable legal uncertainty arises from the unpredictable nature of national legal rules and the Court's increasing tendency towards non-interventionism has left a chasm between Community rights and national remedies.

One method of bridging the gap, suggested by the Commission in the medium-term SAP, was to replace general 'judicial process' clauses in social legislation with a more specific obligation on Member States to impose sanctions that are effective, proportionate and dissuasive.[654] The Commission's attempts to codify the principle in *Von Colson* and *Marshall II* were not initially successful. For example, the Commission's proposal on fixed-term work, arising from the framework agreement signed by the social partners, included the following draft clause:[655]

Member States shall determine the range of penalties applicable for infringements of national provisions made in implementation of this Directive and shall take all necessary steps to ensure that they are enforced. The penalties must be effective, commensurate with the infringement, and must constitute a sufficient deterrent.

---

[648] See Fitzpatrick in Hepple and Szyszczak, n 589 above at 71.

[649] See Case C–338/91, *Steenhorst Neerings v Bestuur van de Bedrijfsvereniging voor Detailhandel, Ambachten en Huisvrouwen* [1993] ECR I–5475; and Case C–410/92, *Johnson v Chief Adjudication Officer II* [1994] ECR I–5483; cf Case C–208/90, *Emmott v Minister for Social Welfare* [1991] ECR I–4269.

[650] Case C–66/95, *R v Secretary of State for Social Security, ex parte Sutton* [1997] ECR I–2163.

[651] *Ibid* para 23.

[652] *Ibid* paras 24 and 27.

[653] Case C–180/95, *Draehmpaehl v Urania Immobilienservice* [1997] ECR I–2195.

[654] COM(95) 134, para 11.1.8.

[655] COM(1999) 203. Draft Art 3.

In the final text of the Directive this clause had been deleted and replaced with a rather insipid general obligation on Member States to 'take any necessary measures to enable them at any time to guarantee the results imposed by this Directive'.[656] The Member States, anxious to preserve the autonomy of their national procedures and social systems, appeared to have slammed the door on the Commission's attempts to codify the Court's more interventionist rulings on remedies. Another explanation, however, for the reticence of the Member States lay with their reluctance to interfere with framework agreements between the social partners, as discussed in Chapter 6. There was still a chink of light and, when the Commission later proposed a similar but stronger clause in the draft Race Equality Directive[657] it was adopted in the final text as follows:[658]

Member States shall lay down the rules on sanctions applicable to infringements of the national provisions adopted pursuant to this Directive and shall take all measures necessary to ensure that they are applied. The sanctions, which may comprise the payment of compensation to the victim, must be effective, proportionate and dissuasive.

The adoption of this clause,[659] with its direct reference to compensation, can be interpreted as a more extensive form of codification of the Court's existing approach but, as an expression of legislative will, it emphasises, for the first time, the paramountcy of the effectiveness principle. The ultimate test, however, will rest with the Member States and their national courts, which will have, in the context of the Article 13 EC anti-discrimination directives,[660] a clear and unambiguous responsibility to introduce and apply effective sanctions.

Unless and until the Member States and, just as importantly, the national courts, as part of their inherent jurisdiction, accept their part in ensuring the full effectiveness of Community law rights on the ground, the jigsaw of judicial protection of individuals will remain incomplete.[661] While the creation of Community social law, piece by piece, helps to build a body of social standards, rendered increasingly certain and transparent through codification, this new legal order can only prove successful if it is enforced by the Member States as uniformly as possible, pursuant to common standards.[662]

---

[656] Art 2 of Dir 99/70/EC, OJ 1999, L175/43.

[657] COM(1999) 564.

[658] Art 15 of Dir 2000/43/EC, OJ 2000, L180/22.

[659] See also, Art 16 of Framework Dir on Equal Treatment, 2000/78/EC, OJ 2000, L303/16.

[660] See ch 9 for further discussion.

[661] See D Curtin, 'The Constitutional Structure of the Union: A Europe of Bits and Pieces' (1993) 30 *Common Market Law Review* 17 at 55.

[662] See Schwarze, in Snyder n 582 above at 181; cf C Harlow, 'European Administrative Law and the Global Challenge' in Craig and de Búrca (1999) n 68 above, 261–85.

8

The Treaty of Amsterdam— An Overview

I A MODEST ACHIEVEMENT?

WHEN THE INTERGOVERNMENTAL Conference (IGC) was formally convened in March 1996[1] the Union was still suffering from its post-Maastricht melancholia. Less than three years on from ratification of the TEU, the popular backlash against what was widely seen as an élite-driven integration process was in full swing.[2] According to a 'EUROBAROMETER' survey of public opinion, just 48 per cent considered the European Union to be a 'good thing' compared with 72 per cent six years earlier.[3] Reviewing the Treaties seemed far less important than the far more challenging task of renewing the Union's legitimacy. In such inauspicious circumstances it was hardly surprising that the Union's leaders swiftly dispensed with any grandiose constitutional dreams, real or imaginary, and concentrated instead on the need to respond both symbolically and practically to the legitimacy crisis. In particular, the Maastricht referenda and popular concerns over the Single Currency had highlighted the fact that, as Arendt had observed 40 years earlier, people only feel part of a polity if they feel that they have played a role in its construction.[4] Against this backdrop the immediate challenges for the Union were twofold: firstly, to become demonstrably more democratic, transparent and accountable in both its formal and informal methods of consultation, decision-making and 'governance' and; secondly, to address what Poiares Maduro has described

[1] At the Turin European Council on 29 Mar 1996.
[2] See P Lynch, N Neuwahl and W Rees, 'Conclusions: Maastricht, Amsterdam and beyond' in P Lynch, N Neuwahl and W Rees (eds) *Reforming the European Union: From Maastricht to Amsterdam* (Longman, Harlow, 2000) 235–50 at 239.
[3] *Public Opinion in the EU, Report No 46, Autumn 1996* (European Communities, Luxembourg, 1997). See further, D Chalmers, *European Union Law Volume One: Law and EU Government* (Dartmouth, Aldershot, 1998) p 70.
[4] See H Arendt, *The Human Condition* (University of Chicago Press, Chicago, 1958). Discussed by I Ward, 'Amsterdam and the Continuing Search for Community' in D O'Keeffe and P Twomey (eds) *Legal Issues of the Amsterdam Treaty* (Hart, Oxford, 1999) 41–55 at 49.

as Europe's 'social deficit',[5] by developing a more inclusive notion of citizenship that elevates shared European social values within an evolving European constitutional framework.

Set against these expectations, the Treaty of Amsterdam,[6] when it eventually emerged 15 months later, appeared, *at first sight*, to have neither bark nor bite.[7] This was, perhaps, inevitable because, as Shaw notes, the 'Reflection Group'[8] and the IGC process offered only a top-down, managerial vision of legitimacy that was incapable of delivering more than a rather passive form of citizen consent.[9] The leaders of the European Union, increasingly aware of their own fallibility, rejected a 'sign now, pay later' approach to Treaty building on this occasion. Pressed with the immediate need to prepare for eastwards enlargement by revamping the Union's institutional architecture,[10] Europe's leaders postponed their decision and, by means of a Protocol, paved the way for yet another IGC in 2000.[11] Presented with the opportunity to fundamentally redefine the tri-pillared structure of the 'European Union', they chose instead to reinforce the historic compromise reached at Maastricht between the supranational and intergovernmental methods of European integration. While there was much fanfare for the establishment of an area of 'freedom, security and justice'[12] and the 'Communitarisation' of the so-called 'Schengen *acquis*',[13] a series of Protocols concerning Denmark, the UK and Ireland allowed for strategic opt-outs.[14] 'Variable geometry', road-tested by the Social Protocol at

---

[5] M Poiares Maduro, 'Europe's Social Self: "The Sickness Unto Death"' in J Shaw (ed) *Social Law and Policy in an Evolving European Union* (Hart, Oxford, 2000) 325–49 at 341.

[6] OJ 1997, C340/1.

[7] Ward, n 4 above at 41.

[8] See *The Reflection Group Report*, 5 Dec 1995, SN 520/95 (REFLEX 21).

[9] See J Shaw, 'The Treaty of Amsterdam: Challenges of Flexibility and Legitimacy' (1998) 4 *European Law Journal* 63 at 83.

[10] Applications had been received from the Czech Republic, Hungary, Poland, Estonia, Latvia, Lithuania, Slovenia, Rumania, Bulgaria, Slovakia, Cyprus and Malta.

[11] Protocol No 7, annexed to the TEU, EC, ECSC and Euratom Treaties, on the Institutions with the Prospect of Enlargement of the European Union. For discussion, see R Dehousse, 'European Institutional Architecture After Amsterdam: Parliamentary System or Regulatory Structure?' (1998) 35 *Common Market Law Review* 595; B de Witte, 'The Pillar Structure and the Nature of the European Union: Greek Temple or French Gothic Cathedral?' in T Heukels, N Blokker and M Brus (eds) *The European Union After Amsterdam: A Legal Analysis* (Kluwer, The Hague, 1998) 51–68; and L Gormley, 'Reflections on the Architecture of the European Union after the Treaty of Amsterdam' in O'Keeffe and Twomey (1999) n 4 above, 57–70.

[12] Title IV EC, Arts 61–69, concerning a common visa, immigration and asylum policy (formerly part of the 'Third Pillar'). Measures to establish the area of 'freedom, security and justice' would be introduced over a five-year period.

[13] Protocol No 2 annexed to the TEU and EC Treaty. The 'Schengen' *acquis* is based on the Schengen Agreement on external border controls of 1985, the implementing convention of 1990 and decisions taken thereunder.

[14] Protocols Nos 3–5, annexed to the TEU and EC Treaty, concerning, respectively: the UK and Ireland: Border Controls; UK and Ireland: Visas, Asylum etc; Denmark: Border Controls and Defence. For comment, see A Toth, 'The Legal Effects of the Protocols Relating to the United Kingdom, Ireland and Denmark' in Heukels *et al*, n 11 above, 227–52.

Maastricht, was now formalised as a wide-ranging general technique of flexibility, or 'closer cooperation', perpetuating the trend towards differentiated integration or a 'multi-speed' Europe.[15] Just as Maastricht emphasised subsidiarity rather than centralisation, so Amsterdam placed flexibility ahead of uniformity.[16] Indubitably, for those seeking to unpick the compromises of Maastricht and intensify the integration process ahead of enlargement without fracturing the Community *acquis*,[17] the long night of Amsterdam ended on a note of disquiet, even bitter disappointment.[18] Even worse, at least for academic lawyers, the Treaties were to be renumbered as a means of 'simplification' once the Amsterdam Treaty entered into force on 1 May 1999, shortly after the Danish electorate had signified their approval at the first time of asking.[19]

When examined more circumspectly, however, these failures were modest, and perhaps inevitable, taking account of the restrictive effect of national vetoes and the absence of a radical reforming agenda but, as Weiler has observed,[20] there were modest achievements too. Several small steps were taken towards greater democracy and openness. Among the institutions the European Parliament was the big winner,[21] securing a dramatic extension of the legislative co-decision procedure,[22] thereby reducing but not eliminating the democratic deficit within the Community pillar. The horizontal principle of open decision-making in Article 1[ex A] TEU was given some substance by a transparency clause inserted as Article 255 EC, providing a

---

[15] For discussion see, generally, Shaw (1998, *European Law Journal*) n 9 above; G de Búrca and J Scott (eds) *Constitutional Change in the EU: From Uniformity to Flexibility* (Hart, Oxford, 2000); F Tuytschaever, *Differentiation in European Union Law* (Hart, Oxford, 1999); and M den Boer, A Guggenbühl and S Vanhoonacker (eds) *Coping with Flexibility and Legitimacy after Amsterdam* (EIPA, Maastricht, 1998).

[16] See P Craig and G de Búrca, *EU Law: Text, Cases and Materials*, 2nd edn (OUP, Oxford, 1998) pp 47–8.

[17] On the status and scope of the Community *acquis* post-Amsterdam, see S Weatherill, 'Safeguarding the *Acquis Communautaire*' in Heukels *et al*, n 11 above, 153–78. See also, D Curtin and I Dekker, 'The EU as a 'Layered' International Organization: Institutional Unity in Disguise' in P Craig and G de Búrca (eds) *The Evolution of EU Law* (OUP, Oxford, 1999) 83–136. Curtin and Dekker argue that flexibility arises within the context of a 'layered' international organisation with an overall unitary legal and institutional system.

[18] See for example, the foreword by the then serving Italian Prime Minister, Lamberto Dini, in A Duff (ed) *The Treaty of Amsterdam: Text and Commentary* (Federal Trust, London, 1997) pp xxvii–xxix.

[19] 55% were in favour, a higher ratio than in either of the Maastricht referendums.

[20] See J Weiler, 'Prologue: Amsterdam and the Quest for Constitutional Democracy' in O'Keeffe and Twomey (1999) n 4 above, 1–20 at 1; and the editorial comments in the *Common Market Law Review*, 'Neither a bang nor a whimper' (1997) 34 *Common Market Law Review* 767.

[21] See K St C Bradley, 'The European Parliament and Treaty Reform: Building Blocks and Stumbling Blocks' in O'Keeffe and Twomey, *ibid* 123–39; and P Dankert, 'What Parliament for Europe?' in Heukels *et al*, n 11 above, 131–8.

[22] Co-decision under Art 251 [ex 189b] EC replaced the co-operation procedure in all areas except Economic and Monetary Union. In many key areas, however, including the new anti-discrimination clause in Art 13 EC, only the weaker consultation procedure was provided.

limited right of access to European Parliament, Council and Commission documents.[23] Further, a Protocol on Subsidiarity and Proportionality, which codifies post-Maastricht 'soft law' on subsidiarity, obliges the Commission to consult widely before proposing legislation and, where appropriate, publishing consultation documents.[24] Most significantly, while the proposal of the *Comité des Sages* for a European 'bill of rights'[25] was not taken up at this stage, the revised Article 6(1) [ex F] TEU now proclaims that:

The Union is founded on the principles of liberty, democracy, respect for human rights and fundamental freedoms, and the rule of law, principles which are common to the Member States.

In part this clause serves to act as an insurance policy, providing a condition for accession of new Member States[26] and, as a post-accession fallback, a basis for a new mechanism to suspend Treaty rights in cases of a 'serious and persistent breach' by a Member State of the principles in Article 6(1).[27] Nevertheless, when taken together with the accompanying horizontal obligation on the Union in Article 6(2) [ex F.2] TEU to respect fundamental rights including the ECHR[28]—now subject to strictly limited judicial supervision[29]—and the evolving conception of Union citizenship,[30] Amsterdam represented an incremental advance, if not a huge leap, towards a fully-fledged human rights policy for the Union.[31]

Amsterdam marked the first Treaty revision where economic integration was not a central part of the process.[32] Social values, distinct from economic

---

[23] See further, Reg 1049/2001/EC regarding public access to European Parliament, Council and Commission documents, OJ 2001, L145/43. The Reg is designed, according to the fourth recital of the preamble, to give the 'fullest possible effect' to the right of public access to documents in Art 255(2) EC. See also, Protocol No 9, annexed to the TEU, EC, ECSC and Euratom Treaties, on the Role of National Parliaments in the European Union. This Protocol requires all Commission proposals and consultation documents to be forwarded for consideration by national parliaments. For a critique of developments in this area, see D Curtin, 'The Fundamental Principle of Open Decision-making and EU (Political) Citizenship' in O'Keeffe and Twomey (1999) n 4 above, 71–91.

[24] Protocol No 30 annexed to the EC Treaty. The Commission's obligation to consult applies in all cases except where there is particular urgency or confidentiality.

[25] *For a Europe of Civic and Social Rights* (European Communities, Luxembourg, 1996).

[26] Art 49 [ex O] TEU.

[27] Art 7 [ex F.1] TEU.

[28] The European Convention for the Protection of Human Rights and Fundamental Freedoms, 1950.

[29] Art 46(d) [ex L] TEU extends jurisdiction to the Court over Art 6(2) 'with regard to the action of the institutions, insofar as the Court has jurisdiction under the Treaties establishing the European Communities and this Treaty'. See further, B de Witte, 'The Past and Future Role of the European Court of Justice in the Protection of Human Rights' in P Alston (ed) *The EU and Human Rights* (OUP, Oxford, 1999) 859–97 at 884–5.

[30] Arts 17–22 [ex 8–8e] EC. The citizenship provisions were not amended but the concept remains inherently dynamic.

[31] See further, J Weiler and S Fries, 'A Human Rights Policy for the European Community and Union: The Question of Competences' in Alston, n 29 above, 147–65.

[32] See Chalmers, n 3 above, p 69.

objectives, helped to fill the Treaty void. Following the timely election of a Labour administration in the UK, some six weeks before the Amsterdam meeting, agreement was reached to abolish the Social Protocol and incorporate an updated version of the Agreement on Social Policy into the first Chapter of Title XI, Articles 136–145 EC, replacing *in toto* Articles 117–122. Hence, in the area of social policy, repatriation of the provisions in the Agreement bucked the general trend towards greater differentiation.[33] Further, a new Title VIII on Employment, Articles 125–130 EC, has brought the nascent 'European Employment Strategy' within the formal scope of the EC Treaty and, moreover, within the overarching Union framework by virtue of Article 2 [ex B] TEU, which now includes both the promotion of economic and social progress and a 'high level of employment' among the Union's objectives.[34]

Perhaps the most important and surprising feature of Amsterdam, however, was the inclusion of new horizontal clauses in the 'Principles' section of the revised EC Treaty. Article 2 EC adds 'equality between men and women' to the Community's tasks, while Article 3(2) EC mainstreams the aim of eliminating inequalities and promoting equality between men and women in each area of the Community's activities.[35] These mainstreaming provisions dynamically interact both with extended provisions in Article 141 [ex 119] EC, concerning equality between men and women in working life, and the broader anti-discrimination clause in Article 13 EC which states that:[36]

Without prejudice to the other provisions of this Treaty and within the limits of the powers conferred upon it by the Community, *the Council*, acting unanimously on a proposal from the Commission and after consulting the European Parliament, *may take appropriate action to combat discrimination* based on sex, racial or ethnic origin, religion or belief, disability, age or sexual orientation.

The simultaneous emergence of mainstreamed provisions intended to promote equality and combat discrimination within a pluralistic and diverse

---

[33] Although other forms of 'softer' flexibility, such as optional clauses in directives, would continue to be promoted within the revised Social Chapter. For discussion, see C Barnard, 'Flexibility and Social Policy' in de Búrca and Scott, n 15 above, 197–217.

[34] See also Art 3 EC which includes the co-ordination of employment policies among the Community's activities.

[35] See generally, F Beveridge, S Nott and K Stephen, 'Addressing Gender in National and Community Law and Policy-making' in Shaw, n 5 above, 135–54.

[36] Emphasis added. There is a wealth of academic literature on Art 13 EC and the surrounding issues. For excellent sources, see: M Bell, 'The New Article 13 EC Treaty: A Sound Basis for European Anti-Discrimination Law?' (1999) 6 *Maastricht Journal* 5; L Waddington, 'Testing the Limits of the EC Treaty on Non-discrimination' (1999) 28 *Industrial Law Journal* 133; C Barnard, 'Article 13: Through the Looking Glass of Union Citizenship' in O'Keeffe and Twomey (1999) n 4 above, 375–94; L Flynn, 'The Implications of Article 13 EC—After Amsterdam Will Some Forms of Discrimination be More Equal Than Others?' (1999) 36 *Common Market Law Review* 1127; and T Hervey, 'Putting Europe's House in Order: Racism, Race Discrimination and Xenophobia after the Treaty of Amsterdam' in O'Keeffe and Twomey (1999) n 4 above, 329–49.

society sprung from a combination of soft laws, programmatic action and, as explained in chapter 7, multi-faceted civil dialogue.

Hence, Article 13 EC provides the capacity for an autonomous instrumental response to the totality of discrimination, in the areas within its scope, with the *potential* to reverse the trend towards a segmented, hierarchical and market-driven approach to inequality.[37] However, it places no 'imperative obligation'[38] on the institutions of the Union to 'take appropriate action'[39] and, even where a proposal is put forward, permits national vetoes and marginalises the prime instigator of the provision, the European Parliament. In the absence of such an obligation, Article 13 EC is not directly effective and therefore, by contrast with the nationality discrimination clause in Article 12 [ex 6] EC[40] and provisions in other constitutions,[41] does not automatically give rise to an exercisable right to non-discrimination, contrary to the recommendations of the Council's expert commission on racism.[42] Inclusion of the phrase 'Without prejudice to the other provisions of this Treaty' allows for a clear delineation between measures under Article 13 EC and more specific sex equality initiatives in the employment field under Article 141 [ex 119] EC, where QMV and co-decision are required, thus avoiding any overlap but raising the spectre of a hierarchy of equalities laws. Equally, while Article 13 EC is without prejudice to internal market measures under Article 95 EC, its place in the general provisions of the Treaty allows for its application as a horizontal instrument to combat discrimination rather than a mechanism for purely economic integration.

Furthermore, reference to the 'limits of powers', which equates with competences, is narrower than the term 'Within the scope of application of this Treaty' in the general non-discrimination clause, Article 12 [ex 6] EC, reflecting the fact that the latter was initially concerned with maximising the effects of market integration.[43] Hence, once a social right is regarded as being instrumental to the guarantee of free movement it must be

---

[37] See U O'Hare, 'Enhancing European Equality Rights: A New Regional Framework' (2001) 8 *Maastricht Journal* 133 at 142.

[38] See the European Council Consultative Commission on Racism and Xenophobia, the 'Kahn Commission', 'Final Report' Ref 6906/1/95, p 59.

[39] In the absence of a specific reference to any legal instrument the presumption must be that all such instruments are available, by contrast with Art 137(2) EC which refers only to directives. See Waddington, n 36 above at 137.

[40] For a broad interpretation of Art 12 EC, see Case C–85/96, *Martinez Sala v Freistaat Bayern* [1998] ECR I–2691. Discussed by J Shaw, 'Citizenship of the Union: First Steps in the European Court of Justice' (1998) 4 *European Public Law* 533.

[41] See for example, s 15 of the Canadian Charter of Rights and s 9 of the South African Constitution. Discussed by Barnard in O'Keeffe and Twomey (1999) n 36 above.

[42] *Ibid*. See Bell, n 36 above at 8.

[43] See further, G de Búrca, 'The Role of Equality in European Community Law' in A Dashwood and S O'Leary (eds) *The Principle of Equal Treatment in E.C. Law* (Sweet & Maxwell, London, 1997) 13–34.

applied in a non-discriminatory fashion.[44] This would suggest that Article 13 EC should not be regarded as a basis for a general Community anti-discrimination law extending beyond the areas of Community competence.[45] It should also be noted that while Article 13 EC creates the potential for the development of a more inclusive non-statist model of European citizenship[46] founded on notions of 'solidarity', it contains no express reference to third-country nationals, unlike Article 137(3) EC, leaving open the possibility of measures concerning racism and xenophobia which, paradoxically, extend only to Union citizens and thereby exclude 'others' who are deemed 'non-European'.[47]

Notwithstanding these constraints and uncertainties, the significance of Article 13 EC as a mechanism for tackling discrimination should not be understated. Indeed, in many respects, the extended reach of Article 13 EC surpassed expectations during the negotiations[48] and, as we shall see in the next chapter, has provided a catalyst for wide-ranging, if not comprehensive, programmatic and legislative action flowing from earlier soft law initiatives. Moreover, these provisions form the basis for a more secure foundation for human rights in the Treaties[49] which, in the context of employment and social law, must be construed together with the principle of equality in Article 141 EC and the revised Article 136 [ex 117] EC, which identifies 'fundamental social rights', derived from both the European Social Charter (ESC) and the Community Social Charter,[50] as the inspiration for social policy.

While the rhetoric of fundamental social rights at Amsterdam can be seen as a counterweight to the economic imperative of the TEU, we need to

---

[44] See Poiares Maduro, n 5 above at 335. For example, see Case C–85/96, *Martínez Sala v Freistaat Berlin* [1998] ECR I–2691 where, at para 63, the Court held that unequal treatment within the scope of Art 12 [ex 6] EC would include a situation where a decision was made by a Member State to delay or refuse to grant a child allowance on the grounds that the claimant was not in possession of a document which nationals of the same State were not required to have.

[45] For example, see Case C–152/82, *Forcheri v Belgian State* [1983] ECR 2323, a case concerning access to education and vocational training courses, where the Court distinguished between the 'scope' of the Treaty and the 'competences' of the Community by holding, at para 17, that although 'educational and vocational training is not as such part of the areas which the Treaty has allotted to the competence of the Community institutions, the opportunity for such kinds of instruction falls within the scope of the Treaty'. Discussed by Bell, n 36 above, at 12–14. See generally, S O'Leary, 'The Principle of Equal Treatment on Grounds of Nationality in Article 6 EC: A Lucrative Source of Rights for Member State Nationals?' in Dashwood and O'Leary, n 43 above, 105–36.

[46] See further, Barnard in O'Keeffe and Twomey (1999) n 36 above.

[47] By contrast the Kahn Commission, n 38 above at 59, called explicitly for the elimination of discrimination irrespective of Union citizenship. See Bell, n 36 above, p 19. See further, Hervey in O'Keeffe and Twomey (1999) n 36 above.

[48] See Flynn, n 36 above at 1129–32.

[49] *Ibid* at 1127.

[50] In this context the eighth recital of the Social Charter calls for the combating of 'every form of discrimination' (*Social Europe* 1/90, ch 2).

determine whether there is substance behind these emerging social values and a realignment of economic freedom and social rights in the EU.[51] In the next two sections of this chapter there will be a brief outline of the main provisions in the Social Chapter and Employment Title to provide a framework within which to undertake, over the next three chapters, a fuller analysis of three main strands of employment law and social policy post-Amsterdam:

(i) Combating discrimination—new concepts, new laws and new hierarchies?
(ii) Reconceptualising sex equality and market integration in the Court of Justice.
(iii) Employment and labour market policy—reinventing social policy governance?

Finally, in chapter 12, we conclude with an assessment of the *potential* of the EU Charter of Fundamental Rights[52] to act as a catalyst for the emergence of a European 'social citizenship' based on common values.

II ARTICLES 136–145 EC—RE-UNIFYING SOCIAL POLICY?

The termination of the Social Protocol was much more straightforward than its conception.[53] At a stroke, the Agreement on Social Policy, now redefined in Articles 136–145 EC, was to revert to its intended place in the scheme of the Treaties and the Protocol would be no more. Several steps were necessary, however, to deal with the consequences of having separate streams for social law in the interregnum between Maastricht and Amsterdam. No immediate solution to the gap in the 'social *acquis*' was offered at Amsterdam, but it was agreed in the Presidency Conclusions that a 'means would have to be found' to give legal effect to the wish of the Member States to re-unify social policy before the new Treaty entered into force. Article 100 [now 94] EC, for so long a vital conduit for Community employment laws in a much earlier age of social policy consensus, was to prove, once again, to be a convenient means for very short-term ends.

Over the next 18 months brief 'extension' directives were adopted covering the entire legislative output of the Agreement, specifically, European Works Councils, Parental Leave, Part-time Work and the Burden of Proof in Sex Discrimination Cases.[54] With striking uniformity, the preamble of

---

[51] See M Poiares Maduro, 'Striking the Elusive Balance Between Economic Freedom and Social Rights in the EU' in Alston, n 29 above, 449–72.

[52] Adopted as an inter-institutional 'solemn proclamation' in advance of the Nice IGC on 7 Dec 2000: OJ 2000, C364/1.

[53] For discussion, see C McGlynn, 'An Exercise in Futility: The Practical Effects of the Social Policy Opt-out' (1998) 49 *Northern Ireland Legal Quarterly* 60.

[54] Respectively, Dir 97/74/EC, OJ 1998, L10/20; Dir 97/75/EC, OJ 1998, L10/24; Dir 98/23/EC, OJ 1998, L131/10; and Dir 98/52/EC, OJ 1998, L205/66.

each Directive justifies the use of Article 100 [now 94] EC on the basis that extending the 'social *acquis*' arising from the Agreement would improve the functioning of the Common Market by removing a source of distortion of competition linked to the application of different standards, or, in other words, 'social dumping'. The fact that the source of this distortion was the Agreement itself was conveniently overlooked.

For the sake of convenience, the Member States might have opted to insert the Agreement into the revised Treaty unamended. In practice, however, several alterations were deemed necessary, subtly reflecting policy shifts and the evolving case law of the Court in the intervening period. Article 136 EC differs from the preamble and Article 1 of the Agreement, which it replaces, in two important respects. First, whereas the express function of the Agreement was to 'implement the 1989 Social Charter', the first paragraph of Article 136 EC draws on the Charter as a *source of social rights* rather than a foundation for their implementation by declaring that:[55]

The Community and the Member States, *having in mind fundamental social rights such as those set out in the European Social Charter [and in the] Community Charter of the Fundamental Social Rights of Workers*... shall have as their objectives the promotion of employment, improved living and working conditions, so as to make possible their harmonisation while the improvement is being maintained, proper social protection, dialogue between management and labour, the development of human resources with a view to lasting high employment and the combating of exclusion.

While retaining the latent Community preference for a general 'harmonisation of social systems',[56] Article 136 EC, like its precursor, Article 117 EEC, serves as a reference point for interpreting other Treaty provisions without presupposing a rolling programme of social legislation. Moreover, as with Article 1 of the Agreement, the implementation of measures by the Community and the Member States shall take account of national diversity, in particular in contractual relations, and the competitiveness of the European economy.[57] Siren calls for either the formal incorporation of the two Charters,[58] or the negotiation of a hybrid 'social constitution' of Europe,[59] were firmly resisted by the Member States who were quite prepared to espouse social rights so long as there was no specific mechanism

---

[55] Emphasis added. Art 136 EC represents a more specific affirmation of a general statement of principle set out in the fourth paragraph of the preamble of the TEU inserted by the Amsterdam Treaty, whereby the Member States have confirmed their 'attachment to fundamental social rights as defined in the European Social Charter [and in the] Community Charter of the Fundamental Social Rights of Workers'.

[56] Art 136 EC, third paragraph.

[57] Art 136 EC, second paragraph.

[58] See B Bercusson, S Deakin *et al*, 'A Manifesto for Social Europe' (1997) 3 *European Law Journal* 189. See also, the report of the ad hoc *Comité des Sages* which called for the incorporation of a negotiated 'bill of rights' encompassing indivisible civic and social rights. *For a Europe of Civic and Social Rights* (European Communities, Luxembourg, 1996).

[59] See B Hepple, 'Social Values and European Law' (1995) *Current Legal Problems* 39.

for their exercise within the Community legal order. Nevertheless, the inclusion of direct references to the European Social Charter, noticeably absent from the Maastricht Treaty,[60] and the more nebulous concept of 'fundamental social rights', constitutes a basis for teleological interpretation by the Court. While Article 136 EC does not allow an individual to rely on any list of 'fundamental social rights' in a directly effective sense, even after the subsequent adoption of a non-binding EU Charter of Fundamental Rights,[61] it offers scope for the Court, when interpreting Community law, to strike down or prohibit any measure or activity which amounts to an arbitrary violation of clearly understood and accepted social rights.[62] Hence, there is the potential, as in the case of attempts to disregard the general principle of equality,[63] to challenge and seek to delimit or prohibit any future attempts to deregulate Community social laws.

There is a second important change from the Agreement within the first paragraph of Article 136 EC, which reinstates the direct link between the objective of 'improving living and working conditions' and the possibility of 'harmonisation while the improvement is being maintained'. The non-retrogression principle, strangely absent from Article 1 of the Agreement,[64] is retained in the form originally derived from Article 117 EEC and continues to act as a bulwark against deregulatory measures in the social policy field.

Democratisation, the 'big idea' behind the generally cautious Amsterdam amendments, is a feature of Article 137 EC which, in the main, replicates the legal bases and related provisions in Article 2 of the Agreement by dividing the scope of supplementary and complementary directives into two spheres subject to either qualified majority voting (QMV) or unanimity in the Council.[65] However, while the legal bases subject to the unanimity rule in Article 137(3) EC continue to require only consultation with Parliament, proposals in those areas listed in Article 137(1) EC are now subject to co-decision under Article 251 [ex 189b] EC,[66] where Council and Parliament act jointly as co-legislators, rather than mere co-operation under Article 252 [ex 189c] EC.

---

[60] See the earlier reference in the preamble of the Single European Act, discussed in ch 4.

[61] OJ 2000, C364/1.

[62] On the basis that 'measures incompatible with the protection of fundamental rights thus recognised and safeguarded [by the Court] cannot be accepted in the Community'—Case C–260/89, *ERT* [1991] ECR I–2925, paras 41–2.

[63] See Case C–13/94, *P v S and Cornwall CC* [1996] ECR I–2143, para 20. For further discussion, see ch 10.

[64] On this point, see B Bercusson, 'Trade Union Rights in EU Law' in F Snyder (ed) *The Europeanisation of Law: The Legal Effects of European Integration* (Hart, Oxford, 2000) 195–209 at 204.

[65] See the listing in Arts 2(1) and 2(3) of the Agreement, now 137(1) and 137(3) EC, on p 239.

[66] By virtue of Art 137(2) EC.

While this modest amendment has been generally welcomed, the exclusion of Parliament from the unaltered provisions concerning the involvement of the social partners in the legislative process is now even more glaring. The Member States, paying no heed to widely expressed criticisms concerning the deficiencies in the democracy and representativeness of 'management and labour',[67] directly transposed Articles 3–4 of the Agreement in Articles 138–139 EC, perpetuating the previously experimental legislative regime introduced at Maastricht.

Article 137 EC also retains provisions allowing for implementation of directives by national social partners[68] and maintaining and introducing more stringent protective measures compatible with the Treaty.[69] Article 137(6) EC replaces Article 2(6) of the Agreement, excluding pay and collective rights from legislation introduced under 'this Article'. Now that the Community seeks to affirm fundamental social rights under Article 136 EC, the exclusion of areas such as fair remuneration, the right of association and the right to strike from Article 137 EC directives, is even more incongruous. Nevertheless, Article 137(6) EC is capable of a narrow interpretation. While the exemption ring-fences legislation proposed under Article 137 EC it does not amount to a blanket exclusion of matters concerning pay or collective rights from the reach of Community law. For example, legislation may be permitted if its principal aim is the establishment and functioning of the common market under Article 94 [ex 100] EC.[70] Hence, in the context of Economic and Monetary Union, a powerful case can be presented for harmonising national laws on minimum wages in order to combat market distortions arising from variations between the Member States. However, in the absence of formal Treaty recognition of collective labour rights, the limitations of Community law have been made apparent by AG Jacobs in his opinion in *Albany International*,[71] a case concerning

[67] See ch 6.
[68] Art 137(4) EC. Subject to the proviso that the Member State in question will, at any time, be in a position to guarantee the results imposed by the directive.
[69] Art 137(5) EC.
[70] See paras 71–3 of AG Léger's opinion in Case C–84/94, *United Kingdom v Council (Working Time Directive)* [1996] ECR I–5755. This interpretation remains valid even after the Court's ruling in Case C–376/98, *Germany v European Parliament and Council (Tobacco Advertising)* [2000] ECR I–8419. In that case the Court narrowly defined the scope of Art 95 [ex 100a] EC concerning specific 'internal market' approximation measures but did not address the broader issue of the scope of more general 'common market' approximation under Art 94 [ex 100] EC. For comment, see ch 3.
[71] Case C–67/96, *Albany International v Stichting Bedrijfspensioenfonds Textielindustrie* [1999] ECR I–5751; Cases C–115–117/97, *Brentjens' Handelsonderneming BV v Stichting Bedrijfspensioenfonds voor de Handel in Brouwmaterialen* [1999] ECR I–6025; and Case C–219/97, *Maastschappij Drijvende Bokken BV v Stichting Pensioenfonds voor de Vervoer-en Havenbedrijven* [1999] ECR I–6121. For comment, see R Van den Bergh and P Camesasca, 'Irreconcilable Principles? The Court of Justice Exempts Collective Labour Agreements from the Wrath of Antitrust' (2000) 25 *European Law Review* 492; and S Vousden, 'Albany, Market Law and Social Exclusion' (2000) 29 *Industrial Law Journal* 181.

the compatibility of collective labour rights with Community competition law, discussed earlier both in that context and as part of the interpretation of the Community Social Charter.[72] Drawing on a wide range of international sources of social rights,[73] the AG concluded that the Community legal order protects the right to form and join trade unions and employers' associations at the heart of freedom of association.[74] It follows that the right to take collective action in order to protect occupational interests in so far as it is indispensable for the enjoyment of freedom of association is also protected by Community law.[75] However, there is insufficient convergence of national legal orders and international legal instruments to allow for the recognition of a specific fundamental right to bargain collectively.[76] Therefore, while Article 137(6) EC does not inhibit recognition of collective rights in the context of competition law, the scope for protection of such rights by the Community is circumscribed in the absence of specifically recognised collective rights within the social provisions of the Treaty.[77]

Article 141 EC radically reformulates both Article 119 EEC and the poorly drafted Article 6 of the Agreement. What emerges is a wide-ranging panoply of provisions which, when interpreted together with the gender mainstreaming objectives[78] and the anti-discrimination clause,[79] considerably strengthen the Community's powers to promote sex equality at work and in society. An immediate symbolic change can be found in Article 141(1) EC which makes explicit the concept of equal value, hitherto implied by the Court into Article 119 EEC by reference to ILO Convention No 100.[80] Drawing directly from Article 1(1) of the Equal Pay Directive[81] the principle has now been reformulated within the Treaty as 'equal pay for equal work *or work of equal value*'.[82] Rather more importantly, Article 141(3) EC furnishes the sex equality provisions with an autonomous legal base for the first time in order to facilitate the adoption of:

... measures to ensure the application of the principle of equal opportunities and equal treatment of men and women in matters of employment and occupation, including the principle of equal pay for equal work or work of equal value.

---

[72] In chs 1 and 4.

[73] Including Art 11 ECHR; Art 6 ESC; Art 22 of the International Covenant on Civil and Political Rights; Art 8 of the International Covenant on Economic, Social and Cultural Rights; and Convention Nos 87 and 98 of the ILO.

[74] Opinion, para 158.

[75] Para 159.

[76] Para 160. The AG concluded, at para 161, that the right to collective bargaining is sufficiently protected by the general principle of freedom of contract. The Court did not address the international instruments in its judgment although it too ultimately concluded that collective agreements per se fell outside the competition rules in Art 81 EC.

[77] See E Szyszczak, *EC Labour Law* (Longman, Harlow, 2000), p 48.

[78] Arts 2 and 3(2) EC.

[79] Art 13 EC.

[80] Art 2 of the Convention as applied in Case 43/75, *Defrenne v Sabena II* [1976] ECR 455, para 20.

[81] Dir 75/117/EEC, OJ 1975, L 45/19.

[82] Emphasis added.

As with Article 137(1) EC, the new legal base in Article 141(3) EC provides for QMV and co-decision. Somewhat confusingly, Article 141(3) EC partly duplicates the pre-existing legal base in Article 137(1) EC allowing for measures concerning 'equality between men and women with regard to labour market opportunities and treatment at work'.[83] Article 141(3) EC however, is more comprehensive, addressing three elements of the principle of equality—equal opportunities, equal treatment, equal value—and, perhaps most significantly, is beyond the legislative remit of the social partners, a tacit acknowledgment perhaps of the need to separate sex equality at work from the corporatist mode of social policy governance.

Most intriguingly, Article 141(4) EC replaces Article 6(3) of the Agreement with the following:[84]

With a view to ensuring full equality in practice between men and women in working life, the principle of equal treatment shall not prevent any Member State from maintaining or adopting measures providing for specific advantages in order to make it easier for the under-represented sex to pursue a vocational activity or to prevent or compensate for disadvantages in professional careers.

This amendment is notable for two reasons. First, by referring to the goal of 'full equality in practice' it extends the Community's area of concern beyond the notion of *formal equality*, comprising equal opportunity and equal access, and embraces the philosophy of *substantive equality* whereby a remedy is sought to redress the structural advantages perpetuating from inequality of outcome.[85] Secondly, by explicitly endorsing positive action, it is intended to mitigate the effects of the Court's judgment in *Kalanke*,[86] which appeared to outlaw quota systems favouring women in the German public service on the grounds that they violated the overriding principle of equal treatment in Directive 76/207.[87] In the longer term this provision may have a wider impact upon the approach of the Community to the concept of equality, a prospect that will be explored in Chapter 10. The first signs were detected with the clarification of *Kalanke* in the *Marschall*[88] case where the Court took account of substantive equality considerations, relying on a 1984 Council Recommendation on positive action for women,[89] and

---

[83] Previously contained in Art 2(1) of the Agreement.

[84] Emphasis added. See also, Declaration No 28 annexed to the Treaty which states that: 'When adopting measures referred to in Article 141(4) . . . Member States should, in the first instance, aim at improving the situation of women in working life'.

[85] For a detailed explanation of these terms, see S Fredman, 'European Community Discrimination Law: A Critique' (1992) 21 *Industrial Law Journal* 119; and H Fenwick and T Hervey, 'Sex Equality in the Single Market: New Directions for the European Court of Justice' (1995) 32 *Common Market Law Review* 443.

[86] Case C–450/93, *Kalanke v Freie Hansestadt Bremen* [1995] ECR I–3051.

[87] OJ 1976, L39/40.

[88] Case C–409/95, *Marschall v Land Nordrhein-Westfalen* [1997] ECR I–6363. Noted by G More (1999) 36 *Common Market Law Review* 443.

[89] Council Recommendation 84/635/EEC, OJ 1984, L331/34.

approved positive measures providing they contained a saving clause allowing individual circumstances to be considered.[90] While Article 141(4) EC was not applicable in *Marschall* it may well have had a subliminal influence on the Court's decision not to follow the AG's advice in his pre-Amsterdam opinion.[91]

III ARTICLES 125–130—EMPLOYMENT AS A MATTER OF COMMON CONCERN

Title VIII on Employment, Articles 125–130 EC, formalises the 'Essen process' and the emergent European Employment Strategy (EES). Strategically inserted immediately after the closely related provisions on Economic and Monetary Policy,[92] the Employment Title places the objective of employment promotion at the heart of the Union's endeavours. Moreover, building on the blueprint provided by the 1994 Council Resolution on Union Social Policy,[93] its working methods are based on gradual convergence not harmonisation, promoting interdependence between all actors, Community surveillance and benchmarking of best practice. We will evaluate these methods later in chapter 11, but let us first sketch out the main provisions.

The Employment Title is founded on a decentralising conception of subsidiarity in which the Community enables and the Member States deliver. Indeed, while placed within the Community pillar, the *modus operandi* of the Employment Title is essentially intergovernmental with the European Parliament marginalised and the Commission a supporting player. For example, Article 126(2) places responsibility on the Member States whom 'shall regard promoting employment as a matter of *common concern* and shall co-ordinate their action in this respect within the Council'.[94] This terminology is appropriated directly from Article 99(1) [ex 103(1)] EC whereby Member States 'shall regard their economic policies as a matter of common concern' also under the co-ordination of the Council. Congruence between economic and employment objectives is underlined by Article

---

[90] Hence *Marschall* was distinguished on these grounds in Case C–407/98, *Abrahamsson and Anderson v Fogelqvist* [2000] ECR I–5539.

[91] For post-Amsterdam application of *Marschall* see Case C–158/97, *Badeck and others v Hessischer Ministerpräsident* [2000] ECR I–1875. See ch 10 for full discussion of this case law.

[92] Title VII, Arts 98–124 [ex 102a–109m] EC. Under Art 98 [ex 102a] EC the Member States must conduct their economic policies with a view to contributing to the objectives defined in Art 2 EC which include the promotion of a 'high level of employment'. See further, J Kenner, 'Employment and Macroeconomics in the EC Treaty: A Legal and Political Symbiosis' (2000) 7 *Maastricht Journal* 375.

[93] OJ 1994, C368/3.

[94] Emphasis added.

126(1) EC which requires that employment and labour market policies shall be consistent with the broad economic guidelines issued annually.[95]

While the activity of the Member States is placed at the apex of the Employment Title, the Community's function is one of facilitation. Under Article 127(1) EC the Community's task is to encourage co-operation between Member States and to support and, if necessary, complement their action. It follows that, at a strategic level, the EES depends on shared ownership as made explicit in Article 125 EC which states:

Member States and the Community shall . . . work towards developing a coordinated strategy for employment and particularly for promoting a skilled, trained and adaptable workforce and labour markets responsive to economic change . . .

Shared commitment, or 'common concern', creates an onus on the Member States not only to co-ordinate their macroeconomic and employment policies but, ultimately, to make them fully compatible. Further, just as the notion of 'common concern' is designed to ensure that no single Member State can regard employment as a low priority,[96] a mainstreaming provision in Article 127(2) EC provides that the objective of a high level of employment shall be taken into consideration 'in the formulation and implementation of all Community policies and activities'.

Article 129 EC is the only provision in the Employment Title containing a specific legal base for the adoption of binding measures. Such measures are aimed at facilitating convergence by developing exchanges of information and best practice including pilot projects.[97] In particular, they 'shall not' include harmonisation of the laws and regulations of the Member States. Indeed, it is only in this severely circumscribed area that the European Parliament can exercise co-decision with the Council.

Article 130 EC provides for the establishment of an advisory Employment Committee with responsibility for co-ordinating and formulating opinions. The social partners, who have no power to adopt framework agreements under this Title, are merely bit part players who must be consulted by the Committee, which is made up of experts from the Member States and the Commission. The Employment Committee, formally established in 2000,[98] is quite separate from the reconstituted Standing Committee on Employment where the social partners are formally represented.[99]

---

[95] Under Art 99(2) [ex 103(2)] EC.

[96] See A Larsson, 'Employment is a Matter of Common Concern', *Employment and Industrial Relations International*, Aug 1997, p 18.

[97] In June 2001 the Council reached a common position on a Commission proposal to introduce a package of Community incentive measures, OJ 2001, C301/14.

[98] Decision 2000/98/EC, OJ 2000, L29/21. The Employment Committee replaces the Employment and Labour Market Committee previously established by Decision 97/16/EC, OJ 1997, L6/32.

[99] Decision 99/207/EC, OJ 1999, L72/33.

Article 128 EC incorporates the cyclical 'Essen process', mirroring the multilateral surveillance of economic policies in Article 99 [ex 103] EC. The cycle commences with the production of a joint report from the Commission and Council on the employment conditions in the Member States.[100] Next, based on the conclusions of the European Council, the Commission issues draft guidelines that Member States 'shall take into account in their employment policies'.[101] The Council adopts the guidelines after consulting the European Parliament, the Economic and Social Committee, the Committee of the Regions and the Employment Committee. As a prerequisite the employment guidelines must be synchronised with the economic guidelines.[102]

Once the employment guidelines have been issued, each Member State must produce an annual report, or National Action Plan, setting out the principal measures taken to implement its employment policies in order to comply with them.[103] Examination of these plans and any other evidence is a matter for the Council and not the Commission. There is an interface with the Employment Committee, whose views must be received, but there is no input at this stage from the European Parliament. While the Council may move to a qualified majority vote on a proposal from the Commission they are only empowered to adopt non-binding recommendations.[104] By contrast with macroeconomic policy, there is no scope for issuing sanctions against Member States whose policies are in conflict with the guidelines.[105] Finally, the cycle is completed by the next joint report to the European Council on the implementation of the employment guidelines and the employment situation in the Community.[106]

In addition to formalising the EES, the Amsterdam European Council issued resolutions on a 'Stability and Growth Pact' and 'Growth and Employment'.[107] A further statement, in the Presidency Conclusions, concerned 'Employment, Competitiveness and Growth.'[108] These declarations sought to reconcile employment policy with other strands of Community activity, notably EMU, and place them on the same footing. Most significantly, the Resolution on Growth and Employment contained a commitment to give immediate effect to the Employment Title, notwithstanding the Treaty ratification process. An emergency 'Jobs Summit' was swiftly convened in Luxembourg in November 1997 to kick-start the process.

---

[100] Art 128(1) EC.
[101] Art 128(2) EC.
[102] Art 128(2) EC.
[103] Art 128(3) EC.
[104] Art 128(4) EC.
[105] See in particular the sanctions available against Member States who persistently maintain an 'excessive' budgetary deficit under Art 104 [ex 104c] EC.
[106] Art 128(5) EC.
[107] OJ 1997, C236/1 and C236/3, respectively.
[108] Available at: <http://www.europa.eu.int/council/off/conclu/index.htm>.

In chapter 11 two elements of the EES will be explored in more depth. First, the substantive content of the employment guidelines will be considered in the context of the 'pillars' of adaptability, employability, entrepreneurship and equal opportunities, which can be seen as part of a wider agenda derived most immediately from the Green Paper on the Organisation of Work.[109] Secondly, in the absence of harmonisation and formal sanctions, the effectiveness of provisions that rely heavily on cyclical target-setting, surveillance and benchmarking, a form of soft law that has become known as the 'open method of co-ordination', will be evaluated in the context of the Union's Social Policy Agenda adopted at the Nice IGC in December 2000.[110] The new Agenda seeks to apply the 'open method' horizontally across social, employment and macroeconomic policies, marking a new phase in the social policy governance of the Union based on a combination of co-ordination, convergence and harmonisation.

[109] COM(97) 128.
[110] Presidency Conclusions, Annex I, p 3.

9

Combating Discrimination—New Concepts, New Laws, New Hierarchies?

I ARTICLE 13 EC—AN EMPTY VESSEL?

IN THE WEEKS and months after the summiteers had departed from Amsterdam there was much prognostication about the destiny of Article 13 EC. In the absence of any compulsion on the Council to act or take any prescribed form of action, those advocating legislation and programmes to combat discrimination had good reason to fear that the new provision would be an empty vessel, serving as a latent reminder of the capriciousness of Treaty negotiations. For the Commission, charged with the task of persuading the Council to take 'appropriate action', the immediate challenges presented by this enigmatic new provision were both practical and political.

On a practical level a strategic decision had to be made on the form, timing and material scope of any proposals for action. In the absence of any Treaty reference to a specific legal instrument should binding or non-binding measures be proposed? Was it 'appropriate' to blend harmonisation with programmatic action? What forms of discrimination should be combated? Above all, should action be vertical—specific to individual heads of discrimination—or horizontal? Acting horizontally would help to achieve a balance between equality and effectiveness.[1]

In relation to material scope, Article 13 EC is capable of a horizontal application in at least four respects. Firstly, it allows specific measures to 'combat' discrimination indivisibly across policy areas within the limits of powers conferred by the Treaty. The European Parliament suggested that a directive might cover 'the fields of employment, education, health care, social security, housing and public and private services'.[2] By acting

---

[1] See M Bell, 'Anti-discrimination Law after Amsterdam' in J Shaw (ed.) *Social Law and Policy in an Evolving European Union* (Hart, Oxford, 2000) 157–70 at 169.

[2] Resolution on racism, xenophobia and anti-Semitism and the results of the European Year Against Racism, OJ 1998, C56/35, point 8.

horizontally the Community would be able to transcend traditional legislative boundaries and remove artificial distinctions between discrimination in employment and wider society. Secondly, common anti-discrimination provisions can be introduced across the different listed grounds, an approach that is responsive to the fragmentary and complex nature of discrimination as actually experienced by individuals who do not easily fit into all too often stereotyped categories because, for example, they face prejudice because of their race, gender *and* social background[3] or their religious or other beliefs *and* sexual orientation. Unless multiple or 'intersectional'[4] discrimination is tackled, the result will be an inconsistent, fragmented and hierarchical corpus of legal protection. Indeed, as Bell[5] notes, measures which extend protection against certain grounds of discrimination, but not others, may be regarded as creating discrimination in law. Thirdly, Article 13 EC has created firm grounds for indirect measures, such as equal opportunities clauses in community legislation.[6] Fourthly, the term 'combat discrimination' indicates a need for the Community to take active, even pre-emptive, mainstreaming measures in all policy areas,[7] such as the internal market, where disability needs should be taken into account,[8] or police and judicial co-operation in criminal matters under the 'Third Pillar', where there is now an additional obligation to pursue actions aimed at 'preventing and combating racism and xenophobia'.[9]

---

[3]   See further, S Fredman and E Szyszczak, 'The Interaction of Race and Gender' in B Hepple and E Szyszczak (eds) *Discrimination: The Limits of Law* (Mansell, London, 1992) 214–26.

[4]   This term is used by North American writers who advocate a multidimensional approach to discrimination that transcends traditional stereotypical categorisations of disadvantaged groups within a rigid and unresponsive legal framework. See K Abrams, 'Complex Claimants and Reductive Moral Judgments: New Patterns in the Search for Equality' (1996) *University of Pittsburg Law Review* 337; and K Crenshaw, 'Demarginalizing the Intersection of Race and Sex: A Black Feminist Critique of Antidiscrimination Doctrine, Feminist Theory and Antiracist Politics (1989) *University of Chicago Legal Forum* 139.

[5]   Bell in Shaw, n 1 above at 158.

[6]   As proposed in the 1995 Commission Communication on Racism, Xenophobia and Anti-Semitism, COM(95) 693. See L Waddington, 'Testing the Limits of the EC Treaty Article on Non-discrimination' (1999) 28 *Industrial Law Journal* 133 at 143. An early example of this approach can be found in the Broadcasting Dir 89/552/EEC, OJ 1989, L298/23, which provides, inter alia, at Art 12 that television advertising must not include any discrimination on grounds of race, sex or nationality, nor offend any religious or political beliefs. See G de Búrca, 'The Role of Equality in European Community Law' in A Dashwood and S O'Leary (eds) *The Principle of Equal Treatment in E.C. Law* (Sweet & Maxwell, London, 1997) 13–34 at 29–30. See also, the Commission's proposal to amend Reg 1612/68 on free movement of workers, COM(98) 394, OJ 1998, C344/9, where it is noted, in draft Art 1a, that: 'Within the scope of this Regulation, all discrimination on grounds of sex, racial or ethnic origin, religion, belief, disability, age or sexual orientation shall be prohibited'.

[7]   See Waddington, *ibid* at 138.

[8]   See the Disability Declaration attached to the Amsterdam Treaty. See further, Waddington, *ibid* at 144.

[9]   Art 29 [ex K.1] TEU. On 15 July 1996 the Council adopted a Joint Action (96/443/JHA) under which Member States have undertaken to ensure effective judicial protection in respect of offences based on racist and xenophobic behaviour, OJ 1996, L185/5.

Setting political considerations to one side, the extent to which a horizontal approach is desirable may be determined by the level of detail in any proposed measure. Each ground for discrimination has specific characteristics which are not necessarily shared with all other grounds.[10] Bell has suggested horizontal framework directives setting out the basic rules forbidding discrimination to be followed up by vertical measures tailored to combat discrimination in specific areas.[11] Such an approach would be consistent with the principle of subsidiarity, allowing the Member States to exercise some discretion and flexibility on implementation.[12]

Ultimately, however, the question of what is 'appropriate action' must be politically determined by the Council and is unlikely to be amenable to judicial review.[13] For the Commission, the immediate political challenge was to produce a coherent package of legislative and programmatic measures—both horizontal and vertical—around which a consensus in the Council could be formed. Initially the prospects were uncertain. During the negotiations at Amsterdam there was general support for action to combat racism and xenophobia, as recommended by the Council's 'Kahn Commission',[14] but reservations were expressed about some of the other areas proposed in the draft clause, including disability and sexual orientation.[15] Indeed a reference to social origin had been dropped.[16] By adopting Article 13 EC, the Member States were able to respond to a highly effective lobbying exercise without accepting any obligation to *implement* non-discrimination outside the area of sex equality.[17]

Set against this backdrop, the Commission's initial moves were tempered by caution. In the Social Action Programme 1998–2000,[18] action under the Employment Title was placed at the top of the agenda and, within this framework, initial steps under Article 13 EC were posited as a contribution to promoting an inclusive society to underpin the Union's labour market strategy.[19] Action to combat discrimination and promote equality was required not simply to achieve social justice, but to enable all to

[10] Bell in Shaw, n 1 above at 158.

[11] *Ibid.*

[12] *Ibid* at 167.

[13] See L Flynn, 'The Implications of Article 13 EC—After Amsterdam Will Some Forms of Discrimination be More Equal Than Others?' (1999) 36 *Common Market Law Review* 1127 at 1136.

[14] European Council Consultative Commission on Racism and Xenophobia, the 'Kahn Commission', 'Final Report' Ref 6906/1/95

[15] Flynn, n 13 above at 1132.

[16] *Ibid.* Flynn suggests that this ground was intended to protect the travelling or gypsy community.

[17] See G More, 'The Principle of Equal Treatment: From Market Unifier to Fundamental Right?' in P Craig and G de Búrca (eds) *The Evolution of EU Law* (OUP, Oxford, 1999) 517–53 at 547.

[18] COM(98) 259.

[19] Part III.3.

participate in the economic well being of societies. In this context, the Commission sought to maximise the possibilities for success by proposing a vertical legislative measure to combat racial discrimination,[20] building on the momentum of the 1997 European Year against Racism and the establishment of the European Monitoring Centre on Racism and Xenophobia.[21] In the meantime, while awaiting ratification of the new Treaty, the Commission proposed to launch a broad debate on the use of Article 13 EC 'including the possibility of a framework programme to combat all forms of discrimination'.[22]

In July 1999, shortly after ratification of the Treaty, the Commission published a call for proposals to 'help prepare for *possible action* under a future Community programme to combat discrimination'.[23] Through a process of attrition the Commission hoped to pave the way for a multidimensional approach to tackling discrimination as opposed to the target-group specific policy of the past.[24] There was no immediate prospect of a horizontal proposal and yet, within a matter of weeks, the political landscape was transformed.

On 3 October 1999, the far-Right, anti-immigration, Freedom Party (FPO) won a share of power in Austria. Paradoxically, this dissonant event was to render progress under Article 13 EC more, not less, likely. The FPO's victory presented the EU with an immediate challenge to show that it meant business when asserting its commitment to 'respect for human rights and fundamental freedoms' in Article 6 [ex F] TEU. On the one hand, Member States who wished to be seen to act to isolate Austria diplomatically could hardly resist proposals designed to combat the kind of discrimination that the FPO was espousing. On the other hand, Austria's mainstream Christian-Democrat leadership, seeking to combat their isolation, had an opportunity to demonstrate their human rights credentials by supporting such proposals. Parallel developments added to the momentum.[25] In the Council of Europe agreement was reached to insert a general right to non-discrimination into the European Convention on Human Rights.[26]

---

[20] See also the Commission's earlier 'Action Plan Against Racism' where this strategy was outlined in more detail—COM(98) 183.

[21] Reg 1035/97/EC establishing a European Monitoring Centre on Racism and Xenophobia, OJ 1997, L151/1.

[22] COM(98) 259, Part III. 3.

[23] OJ 1999, C191/21, para II.

[24] *Ibid.*

[25] Developments at national level were also a factor. For example, in the UK, the Government agreed to implement a wide-ranging report into systemic failures arising from an investigation into a racist murder: Stephen Lawrence Inquiry (1999) *Report of an Inquiry by Sir William MacPherson of Cluny*, London, HMSO, Cm 3684.

[26] Protocol No 12 supplementing the non-discrimination clause in Art 14 ECHR. The Protocol, which was formally adopted by the Council of Ministers in June 2000, provides in Art 1 that: 'The enjoyment of any right set forth by law shall be secured without discrimination on any ground such as sex, race, colour, language, religion, political or other opinion, national

Meanwhile the Union wished to be portrayed positively at a forthcoming UN World Conference against Racism, Racial Discrimination, Xenophobia and Related Intolerance.[27]

The Commission was now under pressure from the Council to rapidly firm up its tentative proposals, redesigned as part of the Union's human rights strategy. An extraordinary European Council at Tampere, on 15/16 October 1999, invited the Commission to come forward as soon as possible with proposals to implement Article 13 EC as part of the fight against racism and xenophobia. Moreover, the timely publication of the Council's first Annual Report on Human Rights (1998–99)[28] placed action under Article 13 EC centre-stage, amounting to a 'huge opportunity' to promote fundamental rights and fight discrimination.[29] Having latched onto Article 13 EC as a vehicle for furthering a wider human rights agenda, the report concluded that progress in this area was essential as a means of championing diversity on the basis that racism, xenophobia and intolerance are the antithesis of what the EU stands for and, moreover, the principle of non-discrimination, as a general principle of Community law, is at the centre of the EU's understanding of human rights.[30]

Within a matter of weeks, on 25 November 1999, the legislative package was formally launched.[31] The Commission were acutely aware of the opening of a window of opportunity arising from the publication of the Annual Report and the launch of negotiations on a draft EU Charter of Fundamental Rights.[32] Echoing the language of the Court in *P v S and Cornwall CC*,[33] the primary justification for the package was to formally recognise that the right to equality before the law and the protection of all persons against discrimination constitutes a fundamental right and is

---

or social origin, association with a national minority, property, birth or other status'. The Parliamentary Assembly, in a debate on 27 January 2000, expressed reservations about the Protocol because of the absence of any reference to sexual orientation in the grounds listed. See the Council or Europe Press Release available at: <http:press.coe.int/>. For discussion, see U O'Hare, 'Enhancing European Equality Rights: A New Regional Framework' (2001) 8 *Maastricht Journal* 133 at 134–42.

[27] See UN General Assembly Resolution 52/111 of 12 Dec 1997. The Conference was held in Durban on 31 Aug–8 Sept 2001. Documentation is available at: <http://www.unhchr.ch/pdf/Durban.pdf>.

[28] The full report, covering the period from June 1998 to 30 June 1999, is available on the Council's website at: <http://ue.eu.int/pesc/human_rights/en/99main1.htm>.

[29] Point 3.5.

[30] *Ibid.*

[31] COM(99) 564.

[32] Presidency Conclusions, Tampere European Council, 15–16 Oct 1999, Annex.

[33] Case C–13/94 [1996] ECR I–2143. In a case concerning the right of a transsexual to rely on the principle of non-discrimination in Directive 76/207/EC on Equal Treatment between Men and Women (OJ 1976, L39/40) the Court held that: 'To tolerate [discrimination against transsexuals] would be tantamount, as regards such a person, to a failure to respect the dignity and freedom to which he or she is entitled, and which the Court has a duty to safeguard' (para 22). For further discussion, see ch 10.

essential to the proper functioning of democratic societies.[34] Such action would also help to address the crisis of legitimacy by associating all citizens with the ideals of the Union and showing that, in the context of enlargement 'principles must be more than simple words'.[35] The objectives of economic progress and a high level of employment were now secondary contributory reasons for acting. Significantly, the Commission was able to switch the emphasis of its proposals by relying heavily on international and national human rights standards[36] and a wealth of EU soft law pronouncements built up over many years.[37]

The Commission's package combined principle with pragmatism.[38] First, following through its original plan to mainstream anti-racism,[39] there was to be a far-reaching vertical directive offering a minimum framework of protection to prohibit discrimination on the grounds of racial or ethnic origin with a material scope encompassing the labour market and wider society.[40] Secondly, a general framework directive for equal treatment in employment and occupation was also proposed.[41] The framework directive would cover all grounds in Article 13 EC except sex discrimination, which would be subject to separate complementary action under Article 141 [ex 119] EC.[42] According to the Commission, horizontal action was consistent with the structure and apparent purpose of Article 13 EC because the 'absence of a qualitative hierarchy among the discretionary grounds is of particular importance in cases of multiple discrimination'.[43] Nevertheless, the draft directive allowed for additional protection in the case of disability discrimination and wide ranging exceptions concerning age and religious discrimination. The Commission's strategy was to carry a broad measure covering the span of Article 13 EC, including the more controversial areas,

---

[34] COM(99) 564, para 1.

[35] *Ibid.*

[36] In the international context the Commission refer, at para 2.1, to the right of non-discrimination as an autonomous right or associated with the exercise of other fundamental rights in the UN Covenants on Civil and Political Rights and Economic, Social and Cultural Rights; the UN Conventions on the elimination of all forms of discrimination against women and against racial discrimination; Art 14 ECHR and draft Protocol No 12; and, in the field of employment and occupation, ILO Convention No 111. For discussion on this point, see U O'Hare, 'Equality and Affirmative Action in International Human Rights Law and its Relevance for the European Union' (2000) 4 *International Journal of Discrimination and the Law* 3.

[37] Annex I contains 25 soft law instruments concerning human rights and fundamental freedoms. Annex II identifies 45 measures, most of which are non-binding, concerning disability, racial or ethnic origin, age and sexual orientation. No soft law instruments concerning religion or belief were listed.

[38] See Bell in Shaw, n 1 above at 168–70

[39] See 'An Action Plan Against Racism', COM(98) 183.

[40] COM(99) 566.

[41] COM(99) 565.

[42] At this stage discrimination on the grounds of race or ethnic origin was included in this proposal as a fallback should the vertical directive be unsuccessful.

[43] COM(99) 565, p 6.

in the slipstream of the vertical directive prioritised by the Council. The price to be paid was a limitation on the scope of the horizontal directive to employment and occupation for proportionality reasons, on the contestable basis that these areas constitute 'people's main guarantee' for social inclusion and enjoyment of basic human rights and freedoms.[44]

While the Commission offered only the thinnest veneer of justification for the special emphasis on combating racism,[45] it was made clear, however, that the horizontal directive was intended to be part of a step-by-step approach leading ultimately to a comprehensive framework of protection.[46] Somewhat unconvincingly, the Commission justified basing the proposal on Article 13 EC, rather than the specific employment legal base in Article 137(2) EC, on the grounds that its scope *rationae personae* was not limited to employed persons,[47] thereby avoiding the exclusion of pay in Article 137(6) EC. In the case of both draft directives the subsidiarity test was satisfied because the measures would lay down common protection to be enjoyed by all citizens of the Union, reinforcing and supplementing protection already existing in the Member States.[48] Thirdly, to complete the package, a Council decision was proposed to establish a six-year action programme to mainstream the Community's anti-discrimination initiatives as part of a co-ordinated and integrated strategy, recognising that practical action is just as important as legislation.[49] Once again the Commission sought to emphasise the non-hierarchical ranking of priorities in Article 13 EC and the concomitant need to address discrimination across the board.[50]

In the wake of events in Austria and the impending challenge of enlargement, the EU moved with remarkable alacrity to adopt the entire package by the end of 2000 as follows:

—Directive 2000/43/EC implementing the principle of equal treatment between persons irrespective of racial or ethnic origin (the Race Equality Directive);[51]
—Directive 2000/78/EC establishing a general framework for equal treatment in employment and occupation (the Framework Employment Directive);[52]
—Decision 2000/750/EC establishing a Community action programme to combat discrimination (2001–2006).[53]

---

[44] *Ibid.*
[45] See M Bell, 'Article 13 EC: The European Commission's Anti-discrimination Proposals' (2000) 29 *Industrial Law Journal* 79 at 80.
[46] COM(99) 565, p 6.
[47] *Ibid* p 7.
[48] COM(99) 566, p 4; COM(99) 565, p 6.
[49] COM(99) 567.
[50] *Ibid* pp 2–3.
[51] OJ 2000, L180/22.
[52] OJ 2000, L303/16.
[53] OJ 2000, L303/23.

For those who considered that the Commission had been too ambitious, flying Icarus-like too close to the sun, the outcome suggests that perhaps the strategy was not bold enough. The anti-discrimination package emerged largely unscathed and, in some respects, strengthened. Despite its obvious limitations, Article 13 EC had provided a basis for a broad extension of equalities protection, a reconfiguration of concepts of discrimination, a new hierarchy of Community equalities laws and an intensive focus on more effective methods of enforcement.[54] For the purposes of coherence, the Commission has published separate proposals in the area of sex equality to, first, amend the Equal Treatment Directive[55] under Article 141(3) EC and, second, to introduce a vertical measure under Article 13 EC broadly consistent with the Race Equality Directive.[56] Article 13 EC has also formed the legal basis for a separate Council Decision establishing a Community Framework Strategy on Gender Equality (2001–2005) complementing the Action Programme.[57] In the following sections we will discuss the scope of each of the directives and the Action Programme, explore key concepts and assess the effectiveness of the provisions on enforcement. The concluding section will include some suggestions about the future direction of this fast-moving policy area.

II THE ANTI-DISCRIMINATION PACKAGE—AN ANALYSIS

(1) Scope of the Article 13 EC Directives

The Race Equality Directive marks a new departure in Community equalities legislation. For the first time the Community has adopted a comprehensive equal treatment measure which seeks to provide protection to all Union citizens and, to a lesser extent, third-country nationals, through a foundation based on human rights not market integration.[58] Recitals 2–4 of the preamble draw inspiration not only from Article 6 TEU and the ECHR, but also from an array of international standards which establish that the 'right to equality before the law and protection against discrimination for all persons constitutes a universal right'.[59]

---

[54] For analysis see L Waddington and M Bell, 'More Equal than Others: Distinguishing European Union Equality Directives' (2001) 38 *Common Market Law Review* 587; and O'Hare (2001, *Maastricht Journal*) n 26 above.

[55] Dir 76/207/EEC, OJ 1976, L39/40. For the Commission's proposals, see COM(2001) 321, revising the original proposal contained in COM(2000) 334 after receipt of the Council's Common Position of 23 July 2001(32/2001) OJ 2001, C307/5.

[56] See COM(2000) 335, para 3.3.1.

[57] Council Decision 2001/51/EC, OJ 2001, L17/22.

[58] See further, S McInerney, 'Bases for Action Against Race Discrimination in EU Law' (2002) 27 *European Law Review* 72.

[59] Recital 3. See also, recital 4 of the Framework Employment Directive.

The Framework Employment Directive is also founded on human rights, restating the main reference points in the recitals of the Race Equality Directive,[60] but stressing also the mainstreaming provisions in Article 3(2) EC, in relation to the promotion of equality between men and women, and noting that women are often the 'victims of multiple discrimination'.[61] Further justification for the Directive's horizontal approach can be found in recital 6 where reference is made to the commitment in the Social Charter to combat every form of discrimination 'including the need to take appropriate action for the social and economic integration of elderly and disabled people'.

While the Equal Treatment Directive[62] provides the model for both directives, what is remarkable is the breadth of the scope of the Race Equality Directive. Article 3(1), although it incorporates a reference to the limits of the Community's conferred powers in Article 13 EC, extends the reach of the Directive to areas on the very fringes of the Community's competence where, previously, a link with market integration had been required before protection could be afforded.[63] The Directive applies to all persons as regards both the public and private sectors, including public bodies. The listed areas can be broken down into two groupings.

The first grouping is broadly concerned with employment and occupation and contains provisions that are common to both the Race Equality Directive and the Framework Employment Directive. The areas covered by this grouping are:

(a) conditions for access to employment, to self-employment and to occupation, including selection criteria and recruitment conditions, whatever the branch of activity and at all levels of the professional hierarchy, including promotion;
(b) access to all types and to all levels of vocational guidance, vocational training, advanced vocational training and retraining, including practical work experience;
(c) employment and working conditions, including dismissals and pay;
(d) membership of and involvement in an organisation of workers or employers, or any organisation whose members carry on a particular profession, including the benefits provided by such organisations;

Subparagraphs (a)–(c) are broadly comparable with the combined scope of the equal pay and equal treatment directives, with the exception of the reference in (b) to 'practical work experience'. However, with regard to (d), the earlier directives are silent,[64] a difference that will be rectified by the Commission's separate proposal to extend the Equal Treatment Directive.[65]

---

[60] Recitals 1, 4 and 5.
[61] Recital 3. See also recital 14 of the Race Equality Directive.
[62] Dir 76/207/EEC, OJ 1976, L39/40.
[63] See for example, Reg 1612/68/EEC on the free movement of workers, OJ 1968, L257/2.
[64] See Waddington and Bell, n 54 above at 590.
[65] COM(2001) 321, Art 3(1)(d) of the draft revised Directive.

The second grouping applies exclusively to the Race Equality Directive and includes:

(e) social protection, including social security and healthcare;
(f) social advantages;
(g) education;
(h) access to and supply of goods and services which are available to the public, including housing.

In its Explanatory Memorandum the Commission note that while the design and delivery of social protection, social security and health care are the responsibility of the Member States, subparagraph (e) requires that Member States must ensure that there is no discrimination based on racial or ethnic origin when implementing that responsibility.[66] Thus, despite the formal distinction between the legal scope of Articles 12 [ex 6] and 13 EC, Article 3(e) of the Race Equality Directive applies in a similar way to Article 12 EC, at least in the context of implementation by a Member State of its rules on social protection and social security, because, as the Court held in *Martínez Sala*,[67] once the unequal treatment in question comes within the scope of application of the Treaty it amounts to unlawful discrimination.

Article 3(f) is potentially even more wide-ranging. The concept of 'social advantages' is drawn from Article 7(2) of Regulation 1612/68 on free movement of workers in the context of Article 39 [ex 48] EC.[68] In *Even*[69] the Court held that the 'social advantages' in question are those which, whether or not linked to a contract of employment, 'are generally granted to national workers primarily because of their objective status as workers or by virtue of the mere fact of their residence'. The same concept is applied here, albeit in a quite different context. The Court has developed an expansive approach to the concept, which has been held to include concessionary travel on public transport,[70] language rights,[71] childbirth loans,[72] grants to the elderly,[73] and funding for attending training courses.[74] The effect of Article 3(f) is that once such advantages are granted by a state they must be applied without discrimination on the grounds of racial or ethnic origin.

Education is an area of strictly limited Community competence under Article 149 [ex 126] EC. While Article 149 EC does not permit harmoni-

---

[66] COM(99) 566, p 7. Note that Art 3(3) of the Framework Employment Directive explicitly excludes payments made by state schemes or similar, including state social security or social protection schemes. By virtue of recital 14 it is also made clear that the Framework Employment Directive shall be without prejudice to national provisions laying down retirement ages.
[67] Case C–85/96, *Martínez Sala v Freistaat Berlin* [1998] ECR I–2691, para 64.
[68] OJ 1968, L257/2. See COM(99) 566, p 7.
[69] Case 207/78, *Ministère Public v Even* [1979] ECR 2019, para 22.
[70] Case 32/75, *Christini v SNCF* [1975] ECR 1085.
[71] Case 137/84, *Mutsch* [1985] ECR 2681.
[72] Case C–111/91, *Commission v Luxembourg* [1993] ECR I–817.
[73] Case 261/83, *Castelli v ONPTS* [1984] ECR 3199.
[74] Case 24/86, *Blaizot v Université de Liège and others* [1988] ECR 379.

sation, the inclusion of 'education' as a heading in Article 3(g) can be justified in a similar fashion to Article 3(e) on the basis that Member States maintain responsibility for the organisation of their education systems but there should be no discrimination on the grounds of racial or ethnic origin in the award of grants and scholarships.[75]

Finally, Article 3(h) concerns public services and housing, areas where there are no express references elsewhere in the Treaty. Once again, however, the inclusion of this heading is necessary for the implementation of equality in practice. Article 3(h) can be equated with analogous rules in Regulation 1612/68 whereby:[76]

... the right to freedom of movement, in order that it may be exercised, by objective standards, in freedom and dignity, requires that the right to equality and treatment shall be ensured in fact and in law in respect of all matters relating to the actual pursuit of activities as employed persons and to eligibility for housing ...

Article 3(2) which is found in both directives, contains an important limitation whereby:

This directive does not cover difference of treatment based on nationality and is without prejudice to provisions and conditions relating to the entry and residence of third-country nationals and stateless persons on the territory of the Member States, and to any treatment which arises from the legal status of the third-country nationals and stateless persons concerned.

Therefore, although the directives protect legally resident third-country nationals, so long as the discrimination in question is within their scope[77] and violates one of the grounds in Article 13 EC,[78] Article 3(2) exempts Member States from the obligations therein when applying their immigration rules. This approach is reinforced by the 'fortress Europe' provisions in Title IV EC,[79] establishing an 'area of freedom, security and justice'. A Member State which, for example, admits white Zimbabweans without restriction but detains and ultimately expels black Zimbabweans as 'bogus' asylum seekers, will be able to maintain its policy stance. Such a derogation, which reflects the extreme sensitivity of Member States on immigration and asylum policy, runs counter to the professed desire of the Community's legislators to be seen to stand up to the anti-immigrant

---

[75] See COM(99) 566, p 8. See also, M Bell, 'The New Article 13 EC Treaty: A Sound Basis for European Anti-Discrimination Law?' (1999) 6 *Maastricht Journal* 5 at 16–17.

[76] OJ 1968, L257/2, 5th recital of the preamble. Art 9(1) provides that a migrant worker 'shall enjoy all the rights and benefits accorded to national workers in matters of housing, including ownership of the housing he needs'. Applied in Case C–305/87, *Commission v Greece* [1989] ECR 1461. See further, Bell, *ibid* at 18.

[77] See the Court's finding in Case C–230/97, *Awoyemi* [1998] ECR I–6781, where it was held that social legislation applies generally to all persons in the European Union. Discussed by Bell (2000, *Industrial Law Journal*) n 45 above at 84.

[78] In relation to sex discrimination, Art 141 EC contains no such limitation.

[79] Arts 61–9 EC.

policies of parties such as the Austrian FPO, and may, through a process of exclusion, actually engender or exacerbate racial discrimination and multiple discrimination.[80]

Finally, the Framework Employment Directive contains two additional paragraphs limiting its scope. First, in order to remove any doubt, the Directive does not apply to payments of any kind made by state schemes or similar, including state social security or social protection schemes.[81] Member States may also avail themselves of a blanket exclusion of the armed forces in relation to discrimination on the grounds of disability and age.[82] Somewhat confusingly, recital 19 appears to functionally limit this derogation to safeguarding the 'combat effectiveness' of the armed forces, an approach that would be more proportionate as there is surely no justification for discrimination where these employees can be redeployed to non-combat positions?[83]

(2) Grounds of Discrimination

In each of the directives, Article 1 sets out the general purpose to lay down a framework for combating discrimination on the applicable grounds with a view to putting into effect in the Member States the principle of equal treatment. In the first instance it is necessary to consider the concepts of 'racial or ethnic origin' in order to differentiate the forms of discrimination brought within the range of the Race Equality Directive from other grounds covered by the Framework Employment Directive, although in many cases there may be discrimination on overlapping grounds.

The Race Equality Directive contains no specific definition of the term 'racial or ethnic origin' although it is made clear in the recitals that the EU rejects theories that attempt to determine the existence of separate human races and use of the term 'racial origin' does not imply acceptance of such theories.[84] The Court will therefore have some leeway in interpreting the term 'racial or ethnic origin' as a single concept or to give specific conceptual meanings to the words 'ethnic origin' and 'racial origin'. Two possible approaches have been identified by Guild.[85] The first approach arises from the interpretation of the UK's Race Relations Act of 1976 by the House of Lords. The

---

[80] See T Hervey, 'Putting Europe's House in Order: Racism, Race Discrimination and Xenophobia after the Treaty of Amsterdam' in D O'Keeffe and P Twomey (eds) *Legal Issues of the Amsterdam Treaty* (Hart, Oxford, 1999) 329–49 at 334.

[81] Art 3(3).

[82] Art 3(4).

[83] See O'Hare (2001, *Maastricht Journal*) n 26 above at 153.

[84] Recital 6. The point here is to reject the 'separate but equal' philosophy upon which the US Supreme Court upheld racial segregation in the first half of the 20th Century following its ruling in *Plessey v Ferguson* [1896] 163 US 567.

[85] E Guild, 'The EC Directive on Race Discrimination: Surprises, Possibilities and Limitations' (2000) 29 *Industrial Law Journal* 416 at 418–19.

Lords have developed a 'distinct community' test whereby individuals can identify themselves as part of an ethnic or racial group so long as that group can be shown to have certain common characteristics such as shared history, culture and language.[86] Such a broad approach is capable of including some traveller communities.[87] One problem arising from this test is that some religious groups have been deemed to fall within this test, whilst others have not.[88] By contrast, Article 13 EC lists discrimination on the grounds of 'religion or belief' separately, and by including these heads of discrimination within the coverage of the Framework Employment Directive, it will be necessary to view the terms 'racial or ethnic origin' and 'religion or belief' as mutually exclusive in a Community context.[89] Nonetheless, the broad 'distinct community' model is preferable to an alternative approach based on 'immutable characteristics' established in the US.[90] Under the latter approach, the individual must conform to a particular norm for the group in question. Although this is advantageous, in terms of legal certainty, by helping to define racial or ethnic groups, it is inflexible[91] and requires comparisons to be made on the basis of an assumed societal norm. Anyone falling outside the designated norm is excluded from protection.[92]

The Framework Employment Directive is also silent on the definitions of 'religion or belief, disability, age or sexual orientation'. This is problematic, in part because of the difficulty of defining terms which are multidimensional and often strongly contested within society. For example, Member States may adopt their own definition of disability and leave its application to case law, as in the UK, where the emphasis is on the long-term adverse effects of a physical or mental impairment.[93] The Court may be asked to consider whether disability should cover a short-term or temporary disability, perhaps adopting the broad definition used in the US.[94] Even more radically, there is a case for an autonomy or self-identification model by

---

[86] *Mandla v Dowell Lee* [1983] 2 AC 548.

[87] *CRE v Dutton* [1989] IRLR 8 (CA).

[88] Sikhs and Jews but not Muslims.

[89] The UK will be expected to retain its present approach to the Race Relations Act, 1976, as Art 6(2) of the Race Equality Directive contains a 'non-retrogression' clause which makes it clear that implementation of the Directive shall under no circumstances constitute grounds for a reduction in the level of protection against discrimination already afforded by Member States in the fields covered by the Directive. See Guild, n 85 above at 418.

[90] See Guild, *ibid*.

[91] *Ibid*.

[92] Guild, *ibid* suggests that travelling communities might be excluded on the grounds that individuals could stop travelling and no longer come within the identity.

[93] S 1(1) of the Disability Discrimination Act 1995 defines disability as 'a physical or mental impairment which has a substantial and long term adverse effect on his ability to carry out his normal day to day activities'.

[94] Under S 3(2) of the Americans with Disabilities Act, 1990, an 'individual with a disability' includes a person with: '(a) a physical or mental impairment which substantially limits one or more of the major life activities of such an individual; (b) a record of such an impairment; or (c) being regarded as having such an impairment'. Discussed by L Waddington, *Disability, Employment and the European Community* (Maklu, Antwerp, 1995) pp 141–80.

which an individual can determine his or her own status. By contrast, legislation concerning sexual orientation discrimination is still rare among the Member States.[95] In part also, difficulties arise, as we shall see below, because of differing rules and derogations applying to particular heads of discrimination.

(3) Concepts of Discrimination

Article 2 in both directives marks a radical shift in the Community's conception of discrimination, placing an emphasis on the eradication of comparative disadvantage and encompassing both harassment and an instruction to discriminate. Both directives also provide more extensive protection against victimisation.[96]

Following the model in Article 2(1) of the Equal Treatment Directive,[97] each directive provides, in Article 2(1) that, for the purposes of putting into effect the principle of equal treatment, 'there shall be no direct or indirect discrimination whatsoever' on any of the applicable grounds. While retaining the requirement for a comparator, Article 2(2) of each directive departs from the definition of discrimination contained in the Burden of Proof Directive concerning sex equality cases.[98] Whereas the latter contains no definition of direct discrimination, Article 2(2)(a) of both the Race Equality Directive and the Framework Employment Directive states that, in respect of the specific grounds:[99]

... direct discrimination shall be taken to occur where one person is treated less favourably than another is, has been *or would be* treated in a comparable situation ...

This definition is more than merely a transplantation of a codified definition of direct discrimination in sex equality cases. As Guild observes, the comparison may be contemporary, historic or potential.[100] Difficulties may arise under each of the grounds both in determining unfavourable treatment and finding a suitable comparator. Disability and age discrimination may be particularly complex in this respect. However, the definition would appear to cover hypothetical situations in contrast with sex discrimination where the Court has rejected hypothetical comparators in pregnancy

---

[95] For a survey, see K Waaldijk, 'The Legal Situation in the Member States' in K Waaldijk and A Clapham (eds) *Homosexuality: A European Community Issue* (Nijhoff, Dordrecht, 1993) 71–130.

[96] See Art 9 of the Race Equality Directive and Art 11 of the Framework Employment Directive.

[97] Dir 76/207/EEC, OJ 1976, L39/40.

[98] Dir 97/80/EC, OJ 1997, L14/16. See ch 7, pp 357–63.

[99] Emphasis added.

[100] Guild, n 85 above at 419.

cases.[101] When applying the directives the possibility of a hypothetical comparator may serve to strengthen the case of an applicant who is unfavourably treated on one of the applicable grounds but is unable to find an actual comparator in relation to that ground.[102]

Under Article 2(2)(b) of the Race Equality Directive:[103]

... indirect discrimination shall be taken to occur where an apparently neutral provision, criterion or practice would put persons of a racial or ethnic origin *at a particular disadvantage compared with other persons*, unless that provision, criterion or practice is objectively justified by a legitimate aim and the means of achieving that aim are appropriate and necessary.

The Framework Employment Directive contains a similarly worded definition.[104] By contrast, under Article 2(2) of the Burden of Proof Directive, such a provision, criterion or practice must disadvantage 'a substantially higher proportion of members of one sex'. On the face of it a broad disadvantage test will be introduced in place of the proportional test based on a 'statistically significant' disproportionate impact which applies in sex discrimination cases.[105] For example, under the Race Equality Directive, there would be no need to show that other persons from racial or ethnic minorities have actually been discriminated against so long as it can be established that the effect of the relevant provision, criteria or practice has caused a disadvantage to the complainant when compared with other persons in society. The statistical requirement in sex equality cases is notoriously difficult to prove in cases where there is complex evidence not readily available to applicants.[106]

The alternative disadvantage test allows for societal factors to be taken into account by emphasising cyclical disadvantage rather than individualistic norms.[107] However, by including the requirement of an actual or

---

[101] Case 177/88, *Dekker v Stichting Vormingscentrum voor Jong Volwassenen* [1990] ECR I–3941; and Case C–32/93, *Webb v EMO Air Cargo* [1994] ECR I–3567. In this instance the Court's approach protects women who, because pregnancy is unique to women, do not have to seek a hypothetical male comparator in order to prove direct discrimination.

[102] See also, Waddington and Bell, n 54 above at 592.

[103] Emphasis added.

[104] The phrase 'at a particular disadvantage' replaces 'liable to affect adversely a person or persons' in the Commission's draft. The Commission's aim was to establish an effects-based test to replace the need for statistical comparisons following the jurisprudence of the Court in nationality cases where it is not necessary to establish that the provision in question affects a substantially higher proportion of migrant workers so long as it is 'liable to have that effect': Case C–237/94, *O'Flynn v Adjudication Officer* [1996] ECR I–2617 at 2639. See Bell (2000, *Industrial Law Journal*) n 45 above at 82; O'Hare (2001, *Maastricht Journal*) n 26 above at 146–47.

[105] Case C–167/97, *R v Secretary of State for Employment, ex parte Seymour-Smith* [1999] ECR I–623.

[106] See O'Hare (2001, *Maastricht Journal*) n 26 above at 147.

[107] For an interesting discussion, see N Lacey, 'From Individual to Group' in Hepple and Szyszczak, n 3 above, 99–124; cf B Hepple, 'Has Twenty-five Years of the Race Relations Acts in Britain Been a Failure' in Hepple and Szyszczak, n 3 above, 19–34. Hepple, at 26–7, argues that law is 'too *specific* and too *selective* in its choice of causes in the 'cycle of disadvantage' to be capable, in itself, of delivering real substantive equality rights' (emphasis in the original).

presumed comparator the objective of equality of results is, in practice, undermined in favour of the notion of formal equality between individuals.[108] Nevertheless, the new test signifies a shift in the perception of equality from a neutral concept based on unequal treatment, towards a more asymmetrical construct where equality is seen as a mechanism for correcting disadvantage.[109] In this sense the Community has taken a stride forward towards a broader effects-based conception of equality.

Just as the Community has taken a stride forward, however, it has also taken a step back. An identical paragraph in the recitals of both directives adds the rider that appreciation of the facts from which discrimination may be inferred is a matter for national courts in accordance with national laws or practices that 'may provide in particular for indirect discrimination to be established by any means including on the basis of statistical evidence'.[110] The result is an uncertain and messy compromise which will place both national courts and the Court of Justice in a predicament. What if statistical evidence does not conclusively establish a disadvantage for a particular individual but other evidence of disadvantage in society can be applied to that individual's situation? The purpose of recitals in the preamble of a Community directive is normally to form part of an overarching set of defining aspirations upon which the measure is based.[111] The Court has drawn upon recitals to give full effect to Community law and yet, in this instance, a set of unusually detailed and prescriptive recitals appear designed to have a narrowing effect on the definition of discrimination. Moreover, the specific reference to objective justification, which draws on the Burden of Proof Directive, provides plenty of scope for the Court to allow market-based justifications for discrimination, although it does not allow justifications based on the employer's subjective conception of morality.[112] While separate provisions allowing for agency or group litigation may help to overcome these difficulties, as O'Hare observes, there is a danger that mounting successful litigation will remain as problematic as it has been under Community sex equality laws.[113]

The most important innovation is perhaps to be found in Article 2(3) which, in essentially identical terms in each Directive, extends the concept

---

[108] See C Barnard and B Hepple, 'Substantive Equality' (2000) 59 *Cambridge Law Journal* 562 at 568.

[109] See S Fredman, 'European Community Discrimination Law: A Critique' (1992) 21 *Industrial Law Journal* 118 at 128–29.

[110] Recital 15 of the Race Equality Directive and recital 16 of the Framework Employment Directive.

[111] On this point, see B Fitzpatrick, 'Converse Pyramids and the EU Social Constitution' in Shaw, n 1 above, 303–24 at 305.

[112] See the opinion of AG Elmer in Case C–249/96, *Grant v South-West Trains* [1998] ECR I–621, where, at para 39, he rejected a justification for sex discrimination based on the employer's purely subjective view that homosexuals should be treated differently from heterosexuals. The Court found that there was no discrimination and therefore did not need to consider the issue of justification.

[113] O'Hare (2001, *Maastricht Journal*) n 26 above at 148.

of discrimination to include harassment, drawing heavily on the Commission's 1991 Recommendation on the protection of the dignity of women and men at work.[114] Harassment shall be deemed to be discrimination under the Race Equality Directive:

... when an unwanted conduct related to racial or ethnic origin takes place with the purpose or effect of violating the dignity of a person and of creating an intimidating, hostile, degrading, humiliating or offensive environment. In this context, the concept of harassment may be defined in accordance with the national laws and practice of the Member States.

Although the Commission Recommendation stressed that sexual harassment may, in certain circumstances, be 'contrary to the principle of equal treatment' the effectiveness of the Recommendation depends on the willingness of national courts to interpret the Equal Treatment Directive teleologically. Formal inclusion of harassment in the Race Equality Directive and Framework Employment Directive takes this process further, subject to the caveat in the final sentence. Immediately it is apparent that there is no requirement for a comparator for the unwanted conduct in question to be deemed to be harassment. Nor is there any reference to objective justification on the basis that 'unwanted' conduct must be judged from the perspective of the victim rather than by reference to objective standards.[115] The Commission makes no explicit theoretical explanation for this distinction in its Explanatory Memorandum, except for the generalisation that harassment 'seriously undermines people's rights in professional, economic and social spheres';[116] an argument that could be applied equally to other 'unwanted' forms of discrimination. Harassment is, however, deemed to be a more serious offence than other forms of discrimination because it has the 'purpose or effect' of, first, *violating* the *dignity* of the person *and*, second, creating an *intimidating, hostile, degrading, humiliating* or *offensive* environment. Whereas the Recommendation on Sexual Harassment stated that either limb must be satisfied,[117] under this definition it must be both. In theory it might be possible to create a hostile environment without violating a person's dignity but this seems unlikely. In particular, by emphasising the identity or personhood dimension of discrimination in Community legislation for the first time, Article 2(3) reinforces the importance of the individual's fundamental right to human dignity, which now forms Article 1 of the EU Charter of Fundamental Rights.[118]

---

[114] Recommendation 92/131/EC, OJ 1992, L49/1. Discussed in ch 5.

[115] See O'Hare (2001, *Maastricht Journal*) n 26 above at 149.

[116] COM(99) 566, p 7.

[117] An approach suggested by the Commission in the proposed draft Art 1(a) of the revised Equal Treatment Directive, COM(2001) 321.

[118] OJ 2000, C364/1 at 364/9: 'Human dignity is inviolable. It must be respected and protected'.

More problematic is the highly charged terminology in the second limb which, while it emphasises the multidimensional nature of harassment, may prove difficult to establish in practice. Moreover, the prospects for a coherent approach to defining these terms may be undermined by the reference in the final sentence to national laws and practice. Potentially this will detract from a consistent interpretation of harassment, one of the principal justifications for its inclusion.[119] Alternatively, a more benign explanation is possible, for it may simply provide a framework which allows limited discretion to Member States to flesh out the detail, while the Court of Justice retains its ultimate responsibility for consistent interpretation and application of Community law.[120]

Article 2(4), which is also essentially identical in both directives, refers to an 'instruction to discriminate' against persons on any of the applicable grounds which, as with harassment, shall be deemed to be discrimination without reference to the need for a comparator or the possibility of objective justification. The source of this clause, which was added following pressure from the European Parliament, is Article 4 of the UN Convention on the Elimination of Race Discrimination which prohibits incitement to racial and religious discrimination.[121] O'Hare suggests that this term could be interpreted as including not only express instructions but also may be implied from the culture and practice of an institution,[122] or what has become known as 'institutionalised discrimination', and may therefore provide an additional means of addressing this highly complex, and often less tangible, form of discrimination.

Fear of dismissal or other adverse treatment is one of the major obstacles that inhibit individuals from taking action to enforce the principle of equal treatment.[123] Under Article 7 of the Equal Treatment Directive, Member States are bound to take the necessary measures to provide protection against dismissal as a reaction to a complaint within an undertaking or legal proceedings aimed at compliance with the principle of equal treatment. Article 9 of the Race Equality Directive places a much broader obligation on Member States to protect individuals from victimisation in the form of 'any adverse treatment or adverse consequence' arising from an individual seeking to exercise her or his rights under the Directive. A similar clause in Article 11 of the Framework Employment Directive provides protection against 'dismissal or other adverse treatment by the employer' in those circumstances. An attempt by the European Parliament to include

---

[119] See Guild, n 85 above at 420.
[120] Under Art 220 [ex 164] EC.
[121] See O'Hare (2001, *Maastricht Journal*) n 26 above at 149.
[122] *Ibid.*
[123] See the Commission's Explanatory Memorandum to the Race Equality Directive: COM(99) 566, p 9.

protection for witnesses, who may be particularly vulnerable to victimisation, was unsuccessful.[124]

While the new directives are formally more extensive than the Equal Treatment Directive it should be noted that in practice these provisions are in line with the jurisprudence of the Court. In *Coote*[125] the applicant had brought an equal treatment claim against her employer alleging that she had been dismissed because of pregnancy. The claim was settled but, 12 months later, her employer refused to provide her with a reference with an employment agency which she regarded as unlawful victimisation. Was it possible for the Equal Treatment Directive to provide protection *after* the dismissal? The Court held that it was not the legislature's intention to limit protection solely to cases of dismissal because dismissal is not the only measure which may effectively deter a worker from making use of the right to judicial protection. Such deterrent measures include, inter alia, those which are taken as a reaction to proceedings brought against an employer and are intended to obstruct the dismissed employee's attempts to find new employment.[126]

(4) Reasonable Accommodation for Disabled Persons

Article 5 of the Framework Employment Directive provides that, in order to 'guarantee compliance with the principle of equal treatment' in relation to persons with disabilities 'reasonable accommodation shall be provided' by employers. The concept of 'reasonable accommodation', first recognised in the US, has been introduced into national legislation[127] and now forms part of the UN Standard Rules on the Equalisation of Opportunities for Persons with Disabilities.[128] In essence 'reasonable accommodation' is a modification or adjustment that is effective in enabling the disabled individual to perform the essential functions of the job.[129] Under Article 5 the precise obligation on the employer entails:

---

[124] See Doc A5–0264/2000: amendment no 45. Discussed by O'Hare (2001, *Maastricht Journal*) n 26 above at 150. In the Commission's revised proposal to amend the Equal Treatment Directive, COM(2001) 321, draft Art 7, if adopted, would protect 'employees and trade union delegates, whether as victims or witnesses, from dismissal or any other adverse treatment or adverse consequence, including the taking of judicial action against them, as a reaction to a complaint or to proceedings of any kind, aimed at enforcing compliance with the principle of equality of treatment for men and women'.

[125] Case C–185/97, *Coote v Granada* [1998] ECR I–5199.

[126] Para 27.

[127] See the UK Disability Discrimination Act, 1995; the Swedish Act on Discrimination of People with Disabilities, 1999; and the Irish Employment Equality Act, 1998.

[128] Adopted by UN Resolution 48/96, annex, of 20 Dec 1993. Available at: <www.un.org/esa/socdev/enable/dissre00.htm>.

[129] Waddington, *Disability, Employment and the European Community*, n 94 above, p 165.

... appropriate measures, where needed in a particular case, to enable a person with a disability to have access to, participate in, or advance in employment, or to undergo training, unless such measures would impose a disproportionate burden on the employer.

In practice Article 5 supplements existing obligations in Community health and safety legislation to adapt work to the individual.[130] In this instance, however, the aim is not merely protective but also forms part of a strategy to combat disadvantage. Where the specific 'appropriate measures' are laid down in national legislation, Article 2(2)(b)(ii) provides that the employer, or any person or organisation responsible, is obliged to take those measures in order to eliminate disadvantages and therefore this is deemed compatible with the definition of discrimination in the Directive. Recital 20 gives examples, such as adapting premises and equipment, patterns of working time, the distribution of tasks, or the provision of training or integration resources. It is important, however, to distinguish reasonable accommodation from positive action in that the former does not aim to create an opportunity where none would otherwise exist.[131] Instead, as Quinn explains, it serves to open up pathways to opportunities hitherto foreclosed.[132] Hence, the obligation to provide reasonable accommodation marks a substantive step towards equality for people with disabilities within the context of the employment relationship. While the specific measures in question are targeted at the employment relationship, the broader strategy underlying Article 13 EC allows for a mainstreaming of the 'reasonable accommodation' concept with a view to creating a barrier-free society for people with disabilities.[133]

Although there is no explicit reference in either Article 13 EC or the Framework Employment Directive to the need to take account of the needs of small and medium-sized enterprises, the defence of 'disproportionate burden' is likely to be most easily applied to smaller undertakings for whom the cost of taking measures deemed appropriate by the Member State may be prohibitive, a point emphasised by recital 21 which elaborates further on the type of measures that may constitute a disproportionate burden for such undertakings.[134] As an incentive to Member States to provide assistance to employers, the final sentence of Article 5 provides that the burden shall not be disproportionate when it is sufficiently remedied by measures

---

[130] Art 6(2)(d) of the Framework Directive on Safety and Health of Workers at Work, 89/391/EEC, OJ 1989, L183/1; and Art 5(1) of the Pregnant Workers Dir, 92/85/EEC, OJ 1992, L348/1.

[131] See G Quinn, 'Human Rights of People with Disabilities under EU Law' in P Alston (ed) *The EU and Human Rights* (OUP, Oxford, 1999) 281–326 at 291.

[132] *Ibid.*

[133] See COM(2000) 284, *Towards a Barrier-Free Europe for People with Disabilities.*

[134] Account should be taken in particular of the 'financial and other costs entailed, the scale and financial resources of the organisation or undertaking and the possibility of obtaining public funding or any other assistance'.

taken within the framework of the disability policy of the Member State concerned.[135] Despite this qualification, incorporation of the concept of reasonable accommodation represents a significant step towards recognition of the integrity and self-worth of persons with disabilities, now acknowledged as an integral part of their fundamental rights,[136] and helps to secure their participation and inclusion in the work environment.

(5) General Derogations to the Principle of Equal Treatment

Both directives permit derogations from the principle of equal treatment. Article 4 of the Race Equality Directive, which is essentially replicated in Article 4(1) of the Framework Employment Directive, allows a Member State to derogate on the grounds of genuine occupational requirements, broadly following Article 2(2) of the Equal Treatment Directive. Member States may provide that a difference in treatment based on a characteristic related to any of the applicable grounds shall not constitute discrimination where:

... by reason of the nature of the particular occupational activities concerned or the context in which they are carried out, such a characteristic constitutes a genuine and determining occupational requirement, providing that the objective is legitimate and the requirement is proportionate.

References to the Court on the interpretation of Article 2(2) of the Equal Treatment Directive have tended to arise where Member States have sought to exclude women from performing certain roles in the police and armed forces. Proportionality is not expressly referred to in that provision, although it has been inferred by the Court which has limited the exception to what is appropriate and necessary in order to achieve a particular aim and requires the principle of equal treatment to be reconciled, as far as possible, with the requirements of public security, viewed in the context in which the activities are performed.[137] For example, in *Sirdar*[138] a female British army chef was refused a transfer to the Royal Marines on the grounds that it was essential for 'combat effectiveness' for that corps to be all male. The Court accepted this explanation because the Royal Marines are a small force and all members, including chefs, may be required to serve

---

[135] For example, by providing financial, training or technical support. See Waddington and Bell, n 54 above at 596.

[136] Art 26 of the EU Charter of Fundamental Rights, OJ 2000, C364/1.

[137] Case 222/84, *Johnston v Chief Constable of the Royal Ulster Constabulary* [1986] ECR 1651, para 38.

[138] Case C–273/97, *Sirdar v The Army Board* [1999] ECR I–7403. For discussion, see P Koutrakos, 'Community law and equal treatment in the armed forces' (2000) 25 *European Law Review* 433.

as front-line commandos.[139] The exclusion was deemed to be proportionate and within the discretion allowed to the Member State. One caveat was that the Member State must assess the activities concerned periodically, to decide whether, in the light of social developments, such an exception is still justified.[140] By contrast in *Kreil*[141] the Court found that Germany's policy that women may 'on no account render service involving the use of arms' was disproportionate because such a prohibition may only be applied to specified activities.[142]

In the new directives the equivalent provision is more tightly defined. Member States must relate the justification closely to the nature of the job concerned and the context in which it is carried out.[143] In the case of the Framework Employment Directive, however, account must also be taken of the recitals. Recital 18 provides that the armed forces, police, prison or emergency services are not obliged to recruit or maintain in employment persons who do not have the range of functions that they may be called upon to perform with regard to the 'legitimate objective of preserving the operational capacity of those services'. This recital is somewhat ambiguous and may form a basis for reviving the argument that gays and lesbians should not be permitted to serve in certain units within the armed forces for 'operational reasons', a view advocated by the UK until it was rejected on privacy grounds by the European Court of Human Rights in 1999.[144]

Account should also be taken of Article 2(5) of the Framework Employment Directive which adds the following rider to the provisions on discrimination:

This Directive shall be without prejudice to measures laid down by national law which, in a democratic society, are necessary for public security, for the maintenance of public order and the prevention of criminal offences, for the protection of health and for protection of the rights and freedoms of others.

There is no equivalent clause in the Race Equality Directive. As Skidmore notes, unless the Court is vigilant this extra derogation could be used by Member States to perpetuate discrimination based on stereotypical assumptions which have historically been used to justify discrimination against minority religions, gays and lesbians, and people with disabilities.[145]

---

[139] Para 30.

[140] Para 31.

[141] Case C–285/98, *Kreil v Bundesrepublik Deutschland* [2000] ECR I–69.

[142] Para 27.

[143] COM(99) 565, p 10.

[144] On the basis of the right to private and family life under Art 8(2) ECHR. See Apps 33985/96 and 33986/96, *Smith and Grady v United Kingdom* [1999] IRLR 734. Discussed by P Skidmore, 'EC Framework Directive on Equal Treatment in Employment: Towards a Comprehensive Community Anti-Discrimination Policy?' (2001) 30 *Industrial Law Journal* 126 at 130.

[145] *Ibid.*

Finally, under recital 22, the Framework Employment Directive is 'without prejudice' to national laws on marital status and benefits dependant thereon. Hence, where national legislation provides for employment-related benefits or, indeed, tax breaks that favour marriage, as defined by national law, it would appear that Article 2(2) will be unavailable even though such laws may discriminate against same-sex couples who, in certain Member States, are unable to marry. This approach is consistent with the view of the Court in *Grant*[146] where it was held, prior to the adoption of the Directive, that according to the state of the law at the time, stable relationships between two persons of the same sex could not be regarded as equivalent to marriage.[147] More recently, in *D and Sweden v Council*[148] the Court has taken a static view of the law by upholding this distinction when ruling that a Swedish law on registered partnerships was distinct from marriage even though such legislation may have similar effects in law.[149] It followed that registered partners under this legislation were denied entitlement to a household allowance under the Community's Staff Regulations, which referred only to married couples.[150] The Court fell back on a separation of powers argument when ruling that amendment of the Regulations was the responsibility of the Council as legislator.[151] Significantly, the Court made reference to neither Article 13 EC nor the provisions of the EU Charter, although in the case of the latter, the Court may have been influenced by the reliance of the AG on an explanatory memorandum of the drafting Convention which states that there is no obligation to recognise same-sex

---

[146] Case C–249/96, *Grant v South-West Trains* [1998] ECR I–621.

[147] Para 35. The Court found, at paras 32–34, that in the majority of Member States a stable homosexual relationship was treated as equivalent to a stable heterosexual relationship outside marriage. Moreover, the European Court of Human Rights has interpreted Art 12 ECHR as applying only to the traditional marriage between two persons of the opposite biological sex—see *Rees* [1986] Series A no 106, p 19; and *Cossey* [1990] Series A no 184, p 17. For critiques, see R Wintemute, *Sexual Orientation and Human Rights: The United States Constitution, the European Convention and the Canadian Charter* (OUP, Oxford, 1995) ch 5; R Amy Elman, 'The Limits of Citizenship: Migration, Sex Discrimination and Same-Sex Partners in EU Law' (2000) 28 *Journal of Common Market Studies* 729; and I Canor, 'Equality for Lesbians and Gay Men in the European Community Legal Order—"they shall be male and female"?' (2000) 7 *Maastricht Journal* 273.

[148] Cases C–122/99P and C–125/99P [2001] ECR I–4139. On appeal the Court upheld the judgment of the Court of First Instance in Case T–264/97 [1999] ECR–SC I–A 1 and II–1. See the annotation by E Ellis (2002) 39 *Common Market Law Review* 151; and E Caracciolo di Torella and E Reid, 'The Changing Shape of the "European Family" and Fundamental Rights' (2002) 27 *European Law Review* 80.

[149] Paras 33–7 (ECJ). See paras 28–30 (CFI).

[150] The Regulations have been amended to require equal treatment of all officials regardless of their sexual orientation, but the new Regulation had not entered into force at the material time of the proceedings. See Reg 781/98/EC, OJ 1998, L113/4. On this point, see Ellis, n 148 above at 151.

[151] Para 12 (ECJ) and paras 31–2 (CFI); cf AG Tesauro in Case C–13/94, *P v S and Cornwall CC* [1996] ECR I–2143, who contended, at paras 9–13, in respect of the designation of gender on birth certificates, that it is permissible for a court to change civil status to keep up with social change.

couples as a result of the Charter.[152] The Court was also satisfied that the right for respect of private and family life under Article 8 ECHR was not affected by the Staff Regulations because the refusal to grant the allowance did not affect D's civil status.[153] While the Court can justly be criticised for outmoded social conservatism, the more problematic aspect of the judgment arises from its dismissive treatment of a legally recognised civil partnership intended to convey benefits equivalent to marriage for the precise purpose of removing discrimination against people who are legally unable to marry. Recital 22 may have the effect of denying justice to such individuals should the Court persist with such a narrow and inequitable approach to discrimination in future cases.

(6) Specific Derogations in the Framework Employment Directive: Religion or Belief, Age, Disability

The Framework Employment Directive contains a range of specific derogations concerning certain grounds of discrimination. Firstly, with regard to religion or belief, there is a separate territorial derogation concerning Northern Ireland[154] and an additional derogation regarding 'occupational activities' within churches and other public or private organisations the 'ethos' of which is based on religion or belief.[155] This is a particularly sensitive area for the Member States and was subject to a separate Declaration annexed to the Amsterdam Treaty.[156] The derogation is limited to national rules and practices in place at the date of the Directive's adoption. Where a person's religion or belief constitutes 'a genuine, legitimate and justified occupational requirement' in relation to the nature of these activities or the context in which they are carried out, it will not be discrimination to take into account the religion or belief of the person. Moreover, national law may allow these churches or organisations 'to require individuals who work for them to act in good faith and with loyalty to the

---

[152] On this point see Caracciolo di Torella and Reid, n 148 above at 83. Both the AG and the Court ignored Art 9 of the Charter which states that the 'right to marry and the right to found a family shall be guaranteed in accordance with the national laws governing the exercise of these rights'. For further discussion on the approach of the AG and the Court to the Charter in *D*, see ch 12.

[153] Para 59.

[154] Art 15 which, on the one hand, allows positive action to address under-representation of the Catholic community in the police service—promoting integration—while, on the other hand, disapplies the provisions on religion or belief for teacher recruitment—reinforcing segregation. Such contradictory steps are deemed necessary to promote peace and reconciliation between the communities (recital 34).

[155] Art 4(2).

[156] Declaration No 11 on the status of churches and non-confessional organisations (see recital 24). The Declaration states that the Treaty does not prejudice the status of churches and religious organisations under national law and it equally respects the status of philosophical and non-confessional organisations.

organisation's ethos'. Hence, the first limb of the derogation allows these organisations to restrict appointments for certain positions to members of the same religion or organisation. The second limb is more problematic as it may apply in relation to any employee of the relevant organisation regardless of their activities or the context in which they are carried out.[157] The derogation does not, however, permit derogations on any other ground and, therefore, would not allow discrimination against a teacher at a religious school who is lesbian or gay.[158]

Secondly, there are extensive derogations to the right to equal treatment on the grounds of age. Once again this is an acutely sensitive area for the Member States, although in this case the reasons are economic rather than ethical.[159] Uniquely within Community law, Article 6(1) allows for both indirect *and* direct age discrimination to be 'objectively and reasonably justified' by a 'legitimate aim' if the means of achieving that aim are 'appropriate and necessary'.[160] Significantly, Article 6(1) specifically refers to employment policy, labour market and vocational training objectives as legitimate aims. For example, reference is made to a non-exhaustive list of justifications including special employment schemes for young workers. More controversially, the list refers to the fixing of minimum conditions of age, professional experience or seniority in service for access to employment or to certain advantages linked to employment; and the fixing of a maximum age for recruitment based on the training requirements of the post or the need for a reasonable period of employment before retirement. These justifications apply 'notwithstanding Article 2(2)' which contains the detailed definitions of direct and indirect discrimination. It would appear that age discrimination founded on harassment or victimisation is not capable of justification.[161] Nonetheless, Member States will have a very wide discretion when implementing and applying national laws and, unless the courts strictly apply the tests of objective justification and proportionality, the provisions on age discrimination will be so heavily circumscribed as to be almost worthless.

Moreover, there is a second element of Article 6 that allows for an even broader derogation, in respect of retirement and also invalidity benefits and

---

[157] Skidmore, n 144 above at 131, gives the example of religious hospitals which may seek to discipline surgeons for performing 'unethical' operations.

[158] This example is discussed by Waddington and Bell, n 54 above at 600, who stress that account will also have to be taken of the fundamental right to respect for family and private life.

[159] On the 'demographic time bomb' see H Desmond, 'Older and Greyer—Third Age Workers and the Labour Market' (2000) 16 *International Journal of Comparative Labour Law and Industrial Relations* 235.

[160] Waddington and Bell, n 54 above at 599, point out that this enumeration closely matches the case law of the European Court of Human Rights under Art 14 ECHR, where any form of discrimination may be justified where the measure in question pursues a legitimate aim and is a proportionate means to achieving that aim.

[161] Arts 2(3) and 11.

the calculation thereof, than that contained in the Equal Treatment (Social Security) Directive, 79/7.[162] Article 6(2) provides that:

Notwithstanding Article 2(2) Member States may provide that the fixing for occupational social security schemes of ages for admission or entitlement to retirement or invalidity benefits, including the fixing under those schemes of different ages for employees or groups or categories of employees, and the use, in the context of such schemes, of age criteria in actuarial calculations, does not constitute discrimination on the grounds of age, provided this does not result in discrimination on the grounds of sex.

Member States, mindful of the Court's case law under Directive 79/7, are extremely worried about demographic trends and the potentially spiralling costs of social protection schemes for states, employers and wider society. The derogation seeks to ensure that the Court is bound to take a much more restrictive approach under Article 6(2) which amounts to a total derogation from Article 2(2) with no reference to the need for a legitimate aim or proportionality.

Thirdly, in addition to recitals 18 and 19 on the armed forces and emergency services, further difficulties in respect of age and disability discrimination, may arise from recital 17, which provides that:

This Directive does not require the recruitment, promotion or maintenance in employment or training of an individual who is not competent, capable or available to perform the essential functions of the post concerned or to undergo the relevant training, without prejudice to the obligation to provide reasonable accommodation for people with disabilities.

Recital 17 provides the basis for a lack of competence or capability defence that, notwithstanding the reference to reasonable accommodation, may, in practice, limit the scope for challenge on the grounds of disability, or indeed age discrimination, or both. Perhaps religious discrimination may be justified if the essential functions of a post have to be performed on a holy day? It seems unlikely that this is the intention of such a clause, the status of which is somewhat uncertain given its location in the recitals rather than the main provisions.

(7) Positive Action

Article 5 of the Race Equality Directive and Article 7(1) of the Framework Employment Directive are closely based on Article 141(4) EC on sex equality. Positive action by Member States is permitted with a view to 'ensuring

---

[162] OJ 1979, L6/24. Under Art 7(1)(a) Member States may exclude 'the determination of pensionable age for the purpose of granting old-age and retirement pensions and the possible consequences thereof for other benefits'.

full equality in practice' in the form of maintaining or adopting specific measures 'to prevent or compensate for disadvantages' related to the respective grounds of discrimination. Further, Article 7(2) of the Framework Employment Directive allows for additional health and safety measures by Member States to safeguard or promote the integration of disabled persons into the working environment.[163] To an extent the new realignment of discrimination laws is further underlined by the fact that while positive action under Article 141(4) EC and the Framework Employment Directive is limited to the field of employment, the Race Equality Directive permits positive action in all areas within its scope.

From the outset an asymmetrical approach to equality will be permitted to tackle both present and historical disadvantages and thereby address equality of outcomes.[164] This approach, which favours substantive equality and is consistent with the Court's more recent case law on Article 2(4) of the Equal Treatment Directive,[165] will, depending on the extent to which it is applied by Member States, fortify the disadvantage test for indirect discrimination in the new directives. Nevertheless, under the Equal Treatment Directive, positive action is only permitted where systems for selection or preference are not automatic or predetermined.[166] This test may present difficulties where, for example, Member States have obligatory quotas for the employment of people with disabilities or wish to establish exclusive training schemes for the members of a disadvantaged group.[167] Waddington and Bell suggest that the Court may regard the different social context for each head of discrimination as justification for a change in the scope of positive action.[168]

(8) Remedies, Enforcement, Compliance and Sanctions

The Race Equality Directive, when compared with earlier Community anti-discrimination and employment laws, contains more detailed and

---

[163] Waddington and Bell, n 54 above at 603, express concern that excessively protectionist measures may be introduced on this basis that could result in the exclusion or denial of equal treatment to people with disabilities.

[164] See O'Hare (2001, *Maastricht Journal*) n 26 above at 152.

[165] See Case C–409/95, *Marschall v Land Nordrhein-Westfalen* [1997] ECR I–6363; and Case C–158/97, *Badeck and others v Hessischer Ministerpräsident* [2000] ECR I–1875. In the view of the Commission the Directive has now been effectively superseded by Art 141(4) EC, a point borne out by the deletion of the original Art 2(4) in the draft of the revised text and its replacement with a biannual reporting duty on those Member States who adopt or maintain positive actions—see COM(2001) 321. For discussion of the concept of 'positive action' in the context of Art 141(4) EC and case law, see ch 10.

[166] See Case C–407/98, *Abrahamsson and Anderson v Fogelqvist* [2000] ECR I–5539.

[167] See Waddington and Bell, n 54 above at 603; and, generally, L Waddington, 'Reassessing the Employment of People with Disabilities in Europe: From Quotas to Anti-discrimination Laws' (1996) 18 *Comparative Labor Law Journal* 62.

[168] *Ibid.*

wide-ranging provisions on access to justice, effective remedies and enforcement of Community law in the national legal systems of the Member States. Articles 7–15 of the Directive will, cumulatively, erode the autonomy of national administrative and judicial procedures concerning *locus standi*, the burden of proof and assistance to victims, compliance and sanctions. Similar provisions in the Framework Employment Directive,[169] while not as extensive, are also designed to create a more effective framework of individual protection 'on the ground'.

From the perspective of the Commission, these intrusions into national procedural autonomy are necessary to guarantee the effectiveness of anti-discrimination legislation because each element is concerned with both the right of victims to a personal remedy against a person or body who has perpetuated discrimination, and the establishment of an appropriate mechanism in each Member State to ensure adequate levels of enforcement.[170]

Several reports in recent years have highlighted many problems faced by individual litigants seeking to rely on Community equal treatment legislation.[171] The Burden of Proof Directive,[172] covering the field of Community sex equality law, was intended as an aid to complainants who find it difficult or impossible to prove discrimination and who are hampered by a lack of resources, expertise and information.[173] In practice it has codified the existing case law of the Court which, for reasons of effective enforcement of the equality principle, places the burden on the employer to show that the practice in question was not in fact discriminatory.[174] Articles 3 and 4 of that Directive provide the model for identical provisions in the new directives.[175] Once the plaintiff has established a prima facie case of less favourable treatment caused by apparent discrimination the burden of proof switches to the defendant to prove that there has been no breach of the principle of equality of treatment.

The provisions on the burden of proof, which apply for both individual and group actions,[176] seek to preserve a modicum of autonomy for the national court which must apply this rule 'in accordance with their national

---

[169] Arts 9–14 and 16–17.

[170] COM(99) 567, p 9.

[171] See J Blom, B Fitzpatrick, J Gregory, R Knegt and U O'Hare, *The Utilisation of Sex Equality Litigation in the Member States of the European Community*, V/783/96-EN (European Commission, Brussels, 1996); and S Prechal, L Senden and B Koopman, *General Report 1997 of the Legal Experts Group on Equal Treatment of Men and Women* (European Commission, Brussels, 1999).

[172] Dir 97/80/EC, OJ 1997, L14/16. Discussed in ch 7.

[173] See O'Hare (2001, *Maastricht Journal*) n 26 above at 154.

[174] Case 109/88, *Handels- og Kontorfunktionaerernes Forbund i Danmark v Danfoss* [1989] ECR 3199, para 14; Case C–127/92, *Enderby v Frenchay Health Authority* [1993] ECR I–5355, para 19.

[175] Art 8 of the Race Equality Directive and Art 10 of the Framework Employment Directive.

[176] Art 8(3) and 10(3) respectively.

judicial systems'.[177] Moreover, as with the Burden of Proof Directive, Member States may introduce rules of evidence which are more favourable to plaintiffs. The provisions will not apply in cases where it is for the court or competent body to investigate the facts of the case.[178] Criminal proceedings are also excluded, which may be especially problematic when applying the Race Equality Directive as several Member States rely on criminal law sanctions for racial discrimination.[179]

Whilst all of this may seem very straightforward and fully consistent with the Burden of Proof Directive, an unhelpful paragraph in the recitals of the Framework Employment Directive may cause difficulties for plaintiffs. Recital 31, which curiously is not replicated in the Race Equality Directive, limits the burden on the respondent, who will not have to prove the plaintiff's 'particular' religion or belief, disability, age or sexual orientation. At one level this is logical, because there is no reason to assume that the employer is aware or should be aware of this information. Difficulties may arise, however, where an employer challenges an individual's assertion of, for example, their own sexual orientation or belief but is unwilling or unable to provide proof, perhaps to protect third parties. In such a case the Court may be provided with an opportunity to offer further guidance to national courts to uphold the individual's right to their own identity as part of their fundamental right of equality and privacy,[180] an approach favoured by AG Tesauro in *P v S and Cornwall CC*.[181] Recognition of an individual's right to their own identity is essential for the attainment of substantive equality because it shifts the focus from the particular characteristics of the individual, real or assumed, to the image in society of the group in question.

One of the most innovative features of the directives can be found in the provisions concerning institutional actors deemed to have a legitimate interest in ensuring national compliance with equal treatment legislation. Research has demonstrated that action by agencies can enable individuals to pursue their equality rights.[182] For example, in the UK, the statutory Equal Opportunities Commission has successfully pursued a two-stage strategy to test Community law by seeking references to the Court of Justice and to litigate in the public interest in judicial review proceedings by using Community law to strike down national law.[183] Under the new provisions individuals

---

[177] Art 8(1) and 10(1).

[178] Art 8(4) and 10(4).

[179] Waddington and Bell, n 54 above at 606, cite the examples of Spain, France and Luxembourg.

[180] For example, the right to respect for private life under Art 8 ECHR.

[181] Case C–13/94 [1996] ECR I–2143, opinion, para 22.

[182] See Blom *et al*, n 171 above. Discussed by O'Hare (2001, *Maastricht Journal*) n 26 above at 155.

[183] See C Barnard, 'A European Litigation Strategy: the Case of the Equal Opportunities Commission' in J Shaw and G More, *New Legal Dynamics of European Union* (Clarendon Press, Oxford, 1995) 253–72 at 265.

will have a general right of legal standing and access to justice[184] and, for the first time under Community law, both directives will oblige the legal orders of the Member States to grant *locus standi* to bodies that have a 'legitimate interest' in compliance to engage 'either on behalf or in support of the complainant', with his or her approval, in any judicial and/or administrative procedure providing for the enforcement of obligations thereunder.[185] Member States will, however, be able to determine whether these bodies have a legitimate interest in accordance with their own criteria, leaving some scope for a restrictive interpretation that may exclude certain organisations disapproved of by national governments. Moreover, while action for the enforcement of obligations under the directives may be brought even after the end of the relationship in which discrimination is alleged to have occurred has ended,[186] it shall be without prejudice to national time limits for bringing actions.[187] Contrary to the recommendations of the European Parliament, these provisions place no obligation on Member States to fund these bodies or to allow them to bring self-initiated test cases.[188]

Article 13 of the Race Equality Directive goes further. Member States are obliged to 'designate' a body or bodies for the promotion of equal treatment in respect of racial or ethnic origin.[189] Such bodies should be competent, inter alia, to provide independent assistance to victims, conduct independent surveys and publish independent reports concerning discrimination.[190] This approach follows the pattern in several Member States where independent equalities agencies are empowered to litigate on behalf of individuals,[191] but, whereas many of these bodies are also concerned with other grounds of discrimination, the Framework Employment Directive places no obligation on Member States to establish wider independent equal treatment bodies. The draft Equal Treatment Directive also provides for the designation of independent bodies,[192] adding to the divergence between Community equalities laws and holding back the creation and development of bodies capable of combating multiple discrimination.[193]

Essentially identical provisions on compliance and sanctions oblige Member States to, first, abolish national laws or other provisions contrary to the principle of equal treatment,[194] secondly, to override or render null

---

[184] Art 7(1) of the Race Equality Directive and Art 9(1) of the Framework Employment Directive.

[185] Arts 7(2) and 9(2) respectively.

[186] See Case C–185/97, *Coote v Granada* [1998] ECR I–5199.

[187] Arts 7(3) and 9(3).

[188] Doc A5–1036/2000. See further, O'Hare (2001, *Maastricht Journal*) n 26 above at 155.

[189] Art 13(1).

[190] Art 13(2).

[191] For example, the UK, Ireland, the Netherlands and Sweden. See Waddington and Bell, n 54 above at 608.

[192] COM(2001) 321. Draft Art 8a.

[193] See Waddington and Bell, n 54 above at 608.

[194] Art 14(a) of the Framework Employment Directive and Art 16(a) of the Race Equality Directive.

and void any discriminatory clauses in any contracts, corporate or institutional rules or collective agreements,[195] and third, to ensure that sanctions for infringements, which may comprise the payment of compensation to the victim, must be effective, dissuasive and proportionate.[196] Whilst these provisions are now regarded by the Commission as standard,[197] the combined effect of the requirements on remedies and enforcement will be to assist plaintiffs, a factor that will be particularly important in national jurisdictions where equalities law is relatively under-developed.

Finally, the implementation clause of the Framework Employment Directive carries a further sting in the tail, emphasising the emerging hierarchy of Community equalities laws. Whereas the Race Equality Directive must be implemented by 19 July 2003,[198] the Framework Employment Directive has an implementation date of 2 December 2003 with a further extension of three years "to take account of particular conditions" to implement the provisions on age and disability discrimination.[199] Hence, notwithstanding the wide-ranging derogations available to Member States in respect of these grounds, further allowance is made, almost certainly driven by cost considerations.

(9) The Anti-Discrimination Action Programme

In November 2000 the Council adopted a Decision establishing a five-year Community Action Programme to combat discrimination.[200] The Action Programme seeks to address all grounds listed in Article 13 EC except for sex discrimination, where a complementary strategy will be conducted over broadly the same period.[201] The Programme is resourced at a relatively modest €98.4 million over the six years. It supplements the directives as part of a 'comprehensive strategy' to combat all forms of discrimination.[202] Article 2 sets out the objectives which are to promote measures to prevent and combat discrimination whether based on one or on multiple factors, taking account of future legislative developments. It has three strands:[203]

---

[195] Arts 14(b) and 16(b) respectively.

[196] Arts 15 and 17.

[197] Note, however, that the revision of the Equal Treatment Directive, COM(2001) 321, would provide, in the draft amended Art 6(2), for the payment of interest and no upper limit on a claim for damages consistent with the Court's ruling in Case C–271/91, *Marshall v Southampton and South-West Hampshire AHA II* [1993] ECR I–4367.

[198] Art 16.

[199] Art 18.

[200] Decision 2000/750/EC, OJ 2000, L303/23. The operative period is 2001–2006. For the Commission's proposals, see COM(99) 567 and COM(2000) 649.

[201] Decision 2001/51/EC establishing a Community framework strategy on gender equality (2001–2005), OJ 2001, L17/22.

[202] Recital 5.

[203] Arts 2–3.

improved understanding of issues related to discrimination through evaluation of the effectiveness of policies and practice using studies and benchmarking; greater capacity to prevent and address discrimination effectively, in particular by strengthening organisations' means of action and, through networking, exchange of information and good practice among non-governmental organisations; and promoting and disseminating the values and practices underlying the fight against discrimination, including awareness-raising campaigns.

The Action Programme is to be implemented through a variety of measures listed in the Annex with the usual mix of annual reporting by Member States, monitoring by the Commission, consultation with interested parties and social dialogue. In addition a Committee will be established at Community level. The Programme will include practical measures to assist groups that are frequently victims of discrimination and will seek to involve these groups in the programme's design and implementation. Following the revision of the Commission's original proposal, the Programme will now give greater emphasis to the empowerment of self-help groups and combating forms of multiple discrimination cutting across the heads of discrimination listed in Article 13 EC. Above all, this Decision is intended to ensure both full implementation and application of the two directives and, also, mainstreaming of the equal treatment objective throughout all relevant activities at Community and national levels.

Following the practice established under the European Employment Strategy, now known as the open method of co-ordination (OMC),[204] the Action Programme will enable the Community to apply the established tools of the OMC—benchmarking, cyclical reporting, involvement of non-governmental organisations—as a means of developing a culture of non-discrimination and helping to overcome the different hurdles posed by national legal systems, a task not aided by the sliding-scale approach to equality created by the directives.

III THE FRAMEWORK STRATEGY ON GENDER EQUALITY: A WAY FORWARD?

The different forms of discrimination cannot be ranked: all are equally intolerable.[205]

With this bold sentiment the Commission seeks to compensate, at least through the delivery of the Action Programme, for the somewhat distorted set of priorities that has emerged from the first wave of Community legislation under Article 13 EC. Over the coming years Community equalities

---

[204] See ch 11 for analysis of the effectiveness of the OMC.
[205] Recital 5 of the Action Programme.

law will increasingly be shaped by the interpretation and application of the new directives and, perhaps to a lesser extent, by supplementary mainstreaming measures arising from the Action Programme and the Framework Strategy on Gender Equality.[206] While it is assumed that agreement on the amended version of the Equal Treatment Directive is imminent, such an amendment is likely to be in conformity with the Framework Employment Directive as the Commission aims to 'ensure coherence between secondary legislation on identical issues'.[207] The prospects for further directives based on Article 13 EC beyond the field of employment, whether on sex discrimination or the other listed grounds, remain less certain, not least because of the requirement of unanimity in the Council.

In the light of these developments Community equalities legislation increasingly resembles a patchwork quilt. While there is a degree of consistency between the directives, at least in terms of content if not scope, a clear hierarchy of equalities laws has been established.[208] Whereas inequality arises in ubiquitous forms both in employment and wider society, requiring a response that recognises multi-dimensional disadvantage, the law is developing along a hierarchical linear model which affords protection first to one category of persons and later extends protection, not necessarily to the same or similar extent of coverage, to other categories, in part due to societal recognition of disadvantage and in part in response to demands made by pressure groups and their coalitions of supporters.[209] In the absence of a general, indivisible, approach to equality, individuals must establish a premise of difference based on unitary or 'essentialist' classifications that assume, for example, a simple man/woman, white/black, straight/gay dichotomy. 'Essentialism' is a concept based on a desire to unite a disadvantaged group but it is double-edged in practice because it ignores the differences within groups and the simultaneous disadvantage that arises from multiple or cumulative discrimination.[210] As Fredman observes,[211] the law has been 'captured by categories' and there is now a need to

---

[206] Decision 2001/51/EC, OJ 2001, L17/22.

[207] See para 1 of the Explanatory Memorandum issued with the Commission's revised proposal, COM(2001) 321. The Council had reached a Common Position on the Commission's original proposal on 23 July 2001(32/2001) OJ 2001, C307/5. In the light of the Commission's revised proposal the European Parliament has proposed extensive amendments to the Council's Common Position at the second reading stage on 24 Oct 2001, A5–0358/2001.

[208] See Waddington and Bell, n 54 above at 610.

[209] See P Abrams, *Historical Sociology* (Open Books, Shepton Mallet, 1982) who notes, at p 15, that 'what any particular group of people get is not just a matter of what they choose to want but what they can force or persuade other groups to let them have'.

[210] For discussion see A Harris, 'Race and Essentialism in Feminist Legal Theory' (1990) 42 *Stanford Law Review* 581; T Higgins, 'Anti-essentialism, Relativism and Human Rights' (1996) 19 *Harvard Women's Law Journal* 1419; cf M Nussbaum, 'Human Functioning and Social Justice: In Defence of Aristotlean Essentialism' (1992) 20 *Political Theory* 202.

[211] See S Fredman, 'Equality: A New Generation?' (2001) 30 *Industrial Law Journal* 145 at 159.

reconceptualise the notion of difference which, instead of connoting 'absolute otherness', or deviance from a norm, is about relationships between and within groups. Ultimately, a single horizontal measure will be required to overcome simplistic and unfair distinctions between groups with some scope for special measures in respect of disability based on advancing rights rather than mere protectionism.[212]

Nevertheless, the directives mark an important turning point for Community equalities law which, as we shall see in the next chapter, is becoming increasingly less reliant on the market imperative. Moreover, the emphasis on group representation and the establishment of equalities bodies is indicative of a general trend towards positive action to promote equality rather than a negative obligation to refrain from discrimination.[213] Further, the directives require both the promotion of social dialogue[214] and the encouragement of dialogue with non-governmental organisations with a 'legitimate interest in contributing to the fight against discrimination' on any of the listed grounds.[215]

The next stage involves a much bolder step towards recognising so-called 'fourth generation' duties which move beyond the individualised fault-based model of existing anti-discrimination law and instead impose positive duties on states, public bodies, employers and other decision-makers to introduce equality measures and structural changes.[216] Mainstreaming of equalities policies and the establishment of group participation rights at all levels of decision-making form the centrepiece of this rapidly emerging approach. Positive duties subvert the existing paradigm because they do not depend on the need to prove individual discrimination based on a disparate impact of a specific criterion or practice and instead require evidence of structural discrimination or under-representation.[217]

In the short to medium-term, programmatic action at Union level will help to facilitate the development of this model at national level enabling knowledge to be gained from pioneering examples.[218] In particular, the Community's Framework Strategy on Gender Equality,[219] based on Article

[212] See the conclusions of Fredman, *ibid* at 159–60; and Bell in Shaw, n 1 above at 170.
[213] Fredman, *ibid* at 163.
[214] Art 11 of the Race Equality Directive and Art 13 of the Framework Employment Directive.
[215] Arts 12 and 14 respectively.
[216] See B Hepple, M Coussey and T Choudhury, *Equality: A New Framework*, Report of the Independent Review of the Enforcement of UK Anti-Discrimination Legislation (Hart, Oxford, 2000). Discussed by Fredman (2001, *Industrial Law Journal*) n 211 above at 163–64.
[217] See Fredman, *ibid* at 164.
[218] For example, in the UK, the Northern Ireland Act, 1998, places a positive duty on public authorities to have 'due regard to the need to promote equality of opportunity' when carrying out their functions. See Fredman, *ibid* at 165; and C McCrudden, 'The Equal Opportunity Duty in the Northern Ireland Act 1998: An Analysis' in *Equal Rights and Human Rights—Their Role in Peace Building* (Committee on the Administration of Justice Belfast, (Northern Ireland) 1999) 11–23.
[219] Decision 2001/51/EC, OJ 2001, L17/22.

13 EC, offers a way forward by seeking to encourage such innovation because:[220]

The persistence of structural, gender-based discrimination, double and often multiple discrimination faced by many women and persistent gender inequality justify the continuation and strengthening of Community action in this field and the adoption of new methods and approaches.

During the period of the Framework Strategy[221] the programme will co-ordinate, support and finance the implementation of horizontal activities under the 'fields of intervention' which are defined as 'economic life, equal participation and representation, social rights, civil life, gender roles and stereotypes'.[222] Building on the commitment to promote gender equality in Article 3(2) EC the strategy includes both gender mainstreaming policies and specific actions targeted at women.

Early signs of this approach can be seen in the Commission's revised proposal to amend the Equal Treatment Directive[223] which seeks to place an obligation on 'those responsible under national law' for access to training, employment or occupation, and the conditions relating thereto 'to introduce procedures to prevent sexual harassment which may include a system of confidential counsellors at the working place'.[224] Moreover, work related to equality of treatment should be pursued 'in a planned and systematic way, also at company level, where employers should be encouraged to establish annual equality plans'.[225]

At this stage these are tentative steps but they must be understood as part of a much bigger picture. Increasingly, as we shall see in chapters 11 and 12, the Union is responding to the legitimacy crisis and persistent structural problems, including inequality and disadvantage, by seeking to establish a multi-level framework of governance which involves participation by new actors, such as non-governmental equalities bodies, and embraces organisational and structural change.[226] Within this fluid environment there is considerable scope for the gradual, if piecemeal, development of an approach which shifts the emphasis of the law from individualised protection against discrimination to positive duties to promote equality.

[220] Recital 3.
[221] 2001–2005.
[222] Art 2(2).
[223] COM(2001) 321.
[224] Draft recital 4a.
[225] Draft recital 11.
[226] See generally, E Szyszczak, 'The New Paradigm for Social Policy: A Virtuous Circle?' (2001) 28 *Common Market Law Review* 1125.

10

Reconceptualising Sex Equality and Market Integration in the Court of Justice

I INTRODUCTION

OVER THE LAST decade the Court of Justice has been presented with several gilt-edged opportunities to reappraise the concept of equality in Community law.[1] For much of this period the Court has faced sustained criticism for failing to live up to its early promises to assert sex equality as a fundamental right[2] and tending to favour a strictly formal approach to equality when market forces are most clearly at stake.[3] Over the same period we have seen the gradual elevation of the principle of sex equality from a largely rhetorical commitment[4] to a constitutional principle,[5] mainstreamed in Articles 2 and 3(2) EC, and now expanded in Article 141 [ex 119] EC to include the notion of 'full equality in practice'. Moreover, Community sex equality law does not exist in a vacuum. The introduction of Union citizenship, Article 13 EC and the EU Charter of Fundamental Rights, has raised fresh questions about the values that drive the equality concept and its capacity to transcend stereotypical classifications of 'sex' and 'gender' and address the root causes of structural disadvantage.

---

[1] 106 references on gender equality in employment by national courts had been decided or were pending as of 1 Jan 2001. For a comprehensive overview, see C Kilpatrick, 'Gender Equality: A Fundamental Dialogue' in S Sciarra (ed) *Labour Law in the Courts: National Judges and the European Court of Justice* (Hart, Oxford, 2001) 31–130.

[2] See S Fredman, 'European Community Discrimination Law: A Critique' (1992) 21 *Industrial Law Journal* 119; and G More, '"Equal Treatment" of the Sexes in European Community Law: What Does 'Equal' Mean?' (1993) 1 *Feminist Legal Studies* 45.

[3] See H Fenwick and T Hervey, 'Sex Equality in the Single Market: New Directions for the European Court of Justice' (1995) 32 *Common Market Law Review* 443.

[4] G de Búrca, 'The Role of Equality in European Community Law' in A Dashwood and S O'Leary (eds) *The Principle of Equal Treatment in E.C. Law* (Sweet & Maxwell, London, 1997) 13–34 at 13.

[5] L Flynn, 'Equality Between Men and Women in the Court of Justice' (1998) 18 *Yearbook of European Law* 259 at 259.

In this chapter two groups of cases have been selected for the purpose of examining how far the Court has been able and willing to clarify and redraw the concept of sex equality. The first group of cases are concerned with the reach of discrimination based on, or on grounds of, 'sex' under Article 141 EC and the Equal Treatment Directive[6] and, in the light of the Court's jurisprudence on sex equality as a fundamental right, its possible extension to embrace wider conceptions of 'sexual identity'. In the second group of cases the Court has been asked to rule on positive action measures, such as quotas for appointment or promotion aimed at equality of results, and consider their compatibility with a conventional Community model which takes, as its starting point, a neutral assumption of equality between men and women. Finally, in a brief concluding section, there will be an analysis of the extent to which the mainstreaming of sex equality and the reformulation of Article 141 EC within the revised Social Chapter has been reflected by a dynamic shift in the Court's appreciation of the economic and social aims of Community equalities law.

II SEX EQUALITY AS A FUNDAMENTAL RIGHT—THE LIMITS OF THE LAW

Over dinner at a small restaurant in Cornwall early in 1992 a woman known as 'P' confided in her immediate employer 'S' that she had a rare medical condition known as Gender Identity Disorder[7] and intended to undergo surgery in order to change her biological sex (male) to suit her sexual identity (female).[8] This conversation set off a chain of events that ultimately took them both to the Court of Justice. P's employers were initially supportive and reassuring but, in the ensuing months, attitudes changed and, when she advised them that she would be returning to work dressed as a woman, she was instructed to work from home. P was later dismissed shortly before undergoing a final gender reassignment operation in December 1992. When the case came before the members of the Truro Industrial Tribunal they quickly realised that P had been discriminated against because she was a transsexual undergoing gender reassignment and asked the Court for guidance on whether her dismissal constituted a breach of the Equal Treatment Directive. For the UK and the Commission, the point of reference was discrimination against P, who remained a man under

---

[6] Dir 76/207/EEC, OJ 1976, L39/40.

[7] Based on P's own account issued in a press release by *Press for Change*, BM Network, London, April 1996. Gender Identity Disorder occurs where from childhood the brain develops a female inclination while the body's physical attributes are male, or vice versa. See L Flynn, 'The Body Politic(s) of EC Law' in T Hervey and D O'Keeffe (eds) *Sex Equality Law in the European Union* (Wiley, Chichester, 1996) 301–20 at 328.

[8] For a summary of the facts see paras 4–7 of the opinion of AG Tesauro in Case C–13/94, *P v S and Cornwall CC* [1996] ECR I–2143.

English law, and the Directive applied where a woman in a similar situation would not suffer adverse treatment. P, on the other hand, threw down the gauntlet by contending, from an anti-essentialist standpoint,[9] that Community law should apply to any person, regardless of whether they are male or female, who is discriminated against 'on grounds of sex'.[10]

For the Court in *P v S and Cornwall CC*[11] the safe option would have been to reassert the traditional man/woman dichotomy for, as AG Tesauro aptly observed: 'The law dislikes ambiguities and it is certainly simpler to think in terms of Adam and Eve'.[12] However, in an impassioned opinion, the AG challenged the Court to make a 'courageous' decision to construe the Directive in a broader perspective by including all situations in which sex appears as a discriminatory factor.[13] Conceptually, the AG was attracted by the notion that sex itself is a continuum, because men and women share characteristics, behaviour and roles, and therefore the law should protect those who are treated unfavourably precisely 'because of their sex and/or sexual identity'.[14] While conceding that such an approach would be a step too far—and rejecting the notion that transsexuals are a 'third sex'[15]—he advised that it was possible to protect those discriminated against 'by reason of sex' by applying the conventional comparator test once it was accepted that P's *sexual identity* was female, for, crucially, P would not have been dismissed if she had remained a man.[16] Hence the male comparator was, in effect, P's former self.[17] To suggest that she had been dismissed *only* because of her change of sex would, however, be a 'quibbling formalistic interpretation' because, for the purposes of this case, sex was important as a social parameter and thus:[18]

The discrimination of which women are frequently the victims is not of course due to their physical characteristics, but rather to their role, to the image society has of women. Hence the *rationale* for less favourable treatment is the social role which women are supposed to play and certainly not their physical characteristics. In the same way it must be recognised that the unfavourable treatment suffered by

---

[9] In the sense that the traditional 'essentialist' position requires every person to be formally categorised as 'male' or 'female'. See Flynn in Hervey and O'Keeffe, n 7 above at 318–19.

[10] Arts 2(1) and 5(1) of the Equal Treatment Directive, 76/207/EEC, OJ 1976, L39/40.

[11] Case C–13/94 [1996] ECR I–2143. See the annotations by L Flynn (1997) 34 *Common Market Law Review* 367; and C Stychin (1997) 2 *International Journal of Discrimination and the Law* 217.

[12] Opinion, para 17.

[13] Paras 23–24.

[14] Para 17.

[15] Para 22.

[16] Para 18.

[17] On this point, see R Wintemute, 'Recognising New Kinds of Direct Sex Discrimination: Transsexualism, Sexual Orientation and Dress Codes' (1997) 60 *Modern Law Review* 334 at 341; P Skidmore, 'Can Transsexuals Suffer Sex Discrimination?' (1997) 19 *Journal of Social Welfare and Family Law* 105 at 108; and A Sharpe, *Transgender Jurisprudence: Dysphoric Bodies of Law* (Cavendish Publishing, London, 2002) p 149.

[18] Para 20. Emphasis in the original.

transsexuals is most often linked to a negative image, a moral judgment which has nothing to do with their abilities in the sphere of employment.

In determining the rights of transsexuals the AG was mindful of developments in those Member States that have granted them the right to marry, adopt children and enjoy pension rights in accordance with their '*new sexual identity*'.[19] He warned that:[20]

... the law cannot cut itself off from society as it actually is, and must not fail to adjust to it as quickly as possible. Otherwise it risks imposing outdated views and taking on a static role. [It must] keep up with social change, and must therefore be capable of regulating new situations brought to light by social change and advances in science.

It followed that what was considered as 'normal' when the Directive was adopted in 1976 should now be construed more broadly taking account of its dual purpose of attaining the Treaty's economic goals and satisfying criteria for social justice by ensuring equal treatment between workers 'whenever sex is a discriminatory factor'.[21] The issue at stake was a universal fundamental value, namely: '*the irrelevance of a person's sex with regard to the rules regulating relations in society*'.[22]

In an extremely brief judgment the Court ruled in favour of P without referring explicitly to the challenge posed by its AG or the merits of his reasoning. Instead the Court focused narrowly on the fact that P had been dismissed while undergoing gender reassignment—the central issue raised by the Tribunal. The Court appeared to recognise P's female identity by referring, without comment, to a definition of the term 'transsexual' adopted by the European Court of Human Rights in *Rees*,[23] where it was noted that transsexuals who have been operated on 'form a fairly well-defined and identifiable group'. Implicitly P could be fitted in with this group as she had begun the gender reassignment process and therefore there was no need for the Court to consider the thorny question of whether P was or had been female as a matter of Community law. In addition to *Rees*, the Court drew support from repeated references in the Directive that there should be no discrimination 'on grounds of sex'.[24] Moreover, the Directive performs a wider function as an expression of the principle of equality as a fundamental principle of law and,[25] further, the right not to be discrimi-

---

[19] Para 10. The AG referred to legislation in Sweden, Germany, Italy and the Netherlands.
[20] Para 9.
[21] Para 23.
[22] Para 24.
[23] Judgment, para 16. *Rees v United Kingdom*, judgment of 17 Oct 1986, para 38, Series A No 106: 'the term 'transsexual' is usually applied to those who, whilst belonging physically to one sex, feel convinced that they belong to the other'.
[24] Para 17. Arts 2(1), 3(1) and 5(1).
[25] Para 18.

nated against 'on grounds of sex' is one of the fundamental human rights whose observance the Court has a duty to ensure.[26]

Having briskly completed its reasoning, the essence of the Court's judgment is contained in three consecutive paragraphs. First, the Court addressed the issue of scope:[27]

Accordingly, *the scope of the directive cannot be confined simply to discrimination based on the fact that a person is of one or other sex.* In view of its purpose and the nature of the rights which it seeks to safeguard, the scope of the directive is also such as to apply to discrimination arising, as in this case, from the gender reassignment of the person concerned.

Such discrimination is based, essentially, if not exclusively, on the sex of the person concerned . . .

Hence, in the specific case of gender reassignment, safeguarding the principle of equality requires an exception to the conventional male/female designation, because P had begun the anatomical process of changing sex.[28] This apparently open-ended statement indicated a broad conception of non-discrimination 'on grounds of sex', the logic of which raised the possibility that the same reasoning might apply in cases involving discrimination against transgendered persons who are not undergoing gender reassignment, or even in a case of discrimination based on sexual orientation.[29]

Secondly, the Court sought to fit its judgment within the formal equality model by observing that:[30]

Where a person is dismissed on the ground that he or she intends to undergo, or has undergone, gender reassignment, he or she is treated unfavourably by comparison with persons of the sex to which he or she was deemed to belong before undergoing gender reassignment.

For the Court, therefore, the comparator was a *male* who was not undergoing gender reassignment.[31] Gender Identity Disorder (GID) does not *exclusively* affect men and, it would appear, the same argument would have applied regardless of whether the person had been a male-female or

---

[26] Para 19. For support, see Case 149/77, *Defrenne v Sabena III* [1978] ECR 1365, paras 26–27; and Cases 75/82 and 117/82, *Razzouk and Beydoun v Commission* [1984] ECR 1509, para 16.

[27] Paras 20 and 21. Emphasis added.

[28] See Sharpe, n 17 above at 149.

[29] See N Bamforth, 'Sexual Orientation Discrimination after *Grant v South West Trains*' (2000) 63 *Modern Law Review* 694 at 695; Wintemute, n 17 above at 350. This reasoning was applied in the English courts in *R v Secretary of State for Defence, ex parte Perkins* [1997] IRLR 297 at 303, per Lightman J.

[30] Para 21.

[31] See Wintemute, n 17 above at 341–33, who suggests three different comparators: a non-transsexual male, a non-transsexual female, or P herself.

female-male transsexual.[32] The fact that P's sexual identity had arisen from her ongoing gender reassignment did not appear to affect the validity of the comparison with a non-transsexual male.[33] Indeed, on one reading, the Court's ambivalence about whether P was male or female left open the possibility that this comparison was between persons of the same sex.[34] In other respects the Court's reasoning lacked rigour. In particular, the Court did not address the intentions of the legislator[35] and offered no explanation for rejecting the UK's contention that a female employee should have been the comparator even though the Court did not dispute P's status as male under English law.[36]

Thirdly, while eschewing the social justice rationale of the AG, the Court indicated that the principle of equality has both an economic and moral foundation by declaring that:[37]

To tolerate such discrimination would be tantamount, as regards such a person, to a failure to respect the dignity and freedom to which he or she is entitled, and which the Court has a duty to safeguard.

Barnard has ventured that it might be possible to detect the introduction of a new moral dimension to the principle of equality, raising the principle to a higher plane, perhaps even taking precedence over treaties and secondary legislation.[38] Was this merely a rhetorical commitment to be utilised only in those cases where the Court is willing to use equality as a tool of interpretation for policy reasons? Unlike the AG, the Court did not construct its judgment upon a foundation of social justice or structural disadvantage based on sexual stereotyping. While the Court offered a discourse on fundamental rights before turning to the question of scope, a reversal of its conventional approach,[39] its application of fundamental rights as a safeguard was only possible once the formal requirement for a comparator

[32] See Flynn (1997, *Common Market Law Review*) n 11 above at 376–77, who distinguishes GID from pregnancy on the basis that the latter is a physiological condition unique to women rendering a comparison with a male, real or imaginary, unnecessary; cf M Bell, 'Shifting Conception of Sexual Discrimination at the Court of Justice: from *P v S* to *Grant v SWT*' (1999) 5 *European Law Journal* 63, who contends, at 67, that it is the absence of a genuine comparator that is relevant and therefore the logic of automatic sex discrimination should apply in this scenario—as in Case 177/88, *Dekker v Stichting Vormingscentrum voor Jong Volwassenen* [1990] ECR I–3941.

[33] See Bell, *ibid* at 67–68.

[34] See Flynn (1997, *Common Market Law Review*) n 11 above at 377

[35] *Ibid* at 375.

[36] *Ibid* at 377.

[37] Para 22. On this point see C Barnard, '*P v. S*: Kite Flying or a New Constitutional Approach?' in Dashwood and O'Leary, n 4 above, 59–79 at 69–73.

[38] *Ibid* at 72. See AG Tesauro's reference, at para 20, to equality as a 'fundamental and inalienable value'. See also the views of Mancini writing extra-judicially: G Mancini and D Keeling, 'Democracy and the European Court of Justice' (1994) 57 *Modern Law Review* 175 at 179.

[39] See Flynn (1997, *Common Market Law Review*) n 11 above at 384.

had been satisfied. In this sense the Court's judgment can be reconciled with contemporaneous jurisprudence where the Court had taken a strictly formalistic approach to equality.[40] The exact reach of the principle was left uncertain although, as Barnard concludes, the mechanics of its application were likely to undermine its effectiveness.[41]

The immediate significance of the judgment in *P v S* lay with its potential for extending protection under Community sex equalities law to other groups discriminated against on grounds of, or based on 'sex'.[42] Whereas P was dismissed because of her sexual identity as a transsexual undergoing gender reassignment, it would take a quantum leap for the same argument to be extended in a case of discrimination based on sexual orientation. Moreover, whereas *P v S* might be partly explained by the relatively small number of transsexuals,[43] the economic and political implications for the Member States of extending the reach of the Directive to homosexuals, who form a significant proportion of the population,[44] would be far more significant.[45] Remarkably, but perhaps not surprisingly,[46] the Court was shortly presented with an opportunity to address this question in *Grant v South-West Trains*.[47]

Lisa Grant, a clerical worker with South-West Trains (SWT), was entitled under her employer's contractual regulations to travel concessions for herself, her spouse and dependants. Concessions were granted to both a legal spouse and 'one common law opposite sex spouse' subject to a declaration that a 'meaningful relationship' had existed for two years or more. Ms Grant requested a travel concession for her female partner and submitted the declaration. SWT refused on the grounds that Ms Grant's partner was not of the opposite sex. SWT conceded that the travel concessions were 'pay' for the purposes of Article 119 [now 141] EC, but argued that there was no discrimination 'based on sex' within the meaning of that provision because a gay man seeking a travel concession for his partner would be

---

[40] *Ibid* at 378. For example, Case C–342/93, *Gillespie and others v NHSSB and others* [1996] ECR I–475, where, at para 16, the Court stated that 'it is well settled that discrimination involves the application of different rules to comparable situations or the application of the same rule to different situations'.

[41] Barnard in Dashwood and O'Leary, n 4 above at 73.

[42] Art 141 [ex 119] EC refers to discrimination 'based on sex'.

[43] According to figures supplied by P, 1 in 30,000 males and 1 in 100,000 females seek to change sex by means of surgery, AG's opinion, para 9. The transsexual pressure group, *Press for Change*, estimates that there are 40–50,000 transsexuals in Europe: 'Victory in the European Court of Justice', Press Release, BM Network, London, 30 Apr 1996.

[44] Approximately 30 million EU citizens according to AG Elmer in Case C–249/96, *Grant v South-West Trains* [1998] ECR I–621, para 42 of the opinion.

[45] See V Harrison, 'Using EC Law to Challenge Sexual Orientation Discrimination at Work' in Hervey and O'Keeffe, n 7 above, at 279.

[46] Stonewall, a UK-based gay and lesbian pressure group, had embarked on a strategic litigation strategy in the wake of the judgment in *P v S*. See further, Bell (1999, *European Law Journal*) n 32 above at 68.

[47] Case C–249/96 [1998] ECR I–621.

treated in the same way. In their view, the judgment in *P v S* related to the sex or sexual identity, male or female, to which a person belongs to or is being assigned and not, as in Ms Grant's case, to the worker's sexual orientation or sexual preference, which is a matter of behaviour or conduct. Ms Grant, relying on the AG in *P v S*, argued that there is discrimination whenever sex is a discriminatory factor and therefore the comparator was her male predecessor, Mr Potter, who had received the benefit in respect of his female partner. Furthermore, the term 'based on sex' should be interpreted as including a person's sexual orientation in cases where prejudicial treatment relates to the sexual behaviour normally expected of a person of a given sex. In the period between the reference and the Court's judgment, on 17 February 1998, the Amsterdam Treaty, including the draft of what is now Article 13 EC, had been signed but was awaiting ratification.

The first question at stake concerned whether or not there had been discrimination 'based on sex' contrary to Article 119 [now 141] EC?[48] AG Elmer, concurring with Ms Grant, considered that the Court in *P v S* had taken a 'decisive step' away from the traditional notion of equal treatment based on a comparison between a female and male employee.[49] The essential point was that the alleged discrimination against Ms Grant was based exclusively, or essentially, on *gender*.[50] By implication, the function provided by a comparator, in the traditional sense of establishing an existing sex-based criterion, was no longer necessary if other evidence could be adduced, such as SWT's regulations concerning the travel concessions.[51] Such an interpretation 'renders the principle appropriate for the cases of *gender discrimination* that come before the courts in present-day society'.[52] While this reasoning is superficially attractive it leaves open the question of who the comparator should be if discrimination is established?[53]

Nevertheless, the AG's emphasis on 'gender' rather than 'sex' was significant. As Flynn explains,[54] whereas *sex* connotes those 'irreducible, biological differentiations' between men and women, *gender*, which encompasses 'the assumptions, expectations, habits and usages which identify a particular individual to themselves and others as being a man or a woman, is socially constructed'. For the AG it was no longer appropriate to make a simplistic comparison between biological males and females, or the possession of

---

[48]   Para 24.

[49]   Opinion, para 15

[50]   *Ibid.*

[51]   See K Armstrong, 'Tales of the Community: sexual orientation discrimination and EC law' (1998) 20 *Journal of Social Welfare and Family Law* 455 at 459.

[52]   Para 15. Emphasis added.

[53]   See further, Armstrong, n 51 above at 460.

[54]   See L Flynn, 'Gender Equality Laws and Employers' Dress Codes' (1995) 24 *Industrial Law Journal* 255 at 256. See further, K Donovan, *Sexual Divisions in Law* (Wiedenfield & Nicholson, London, 1985) pp 60–77; J Squires, *Gender in Political Theory* (Polity Press, Cambridge, 1999) ch 2.

physical attributes—factors that had influenced the Court in *P v S*—but rather, it was necessary to take account of 'gender' in a way that includes beliefs or attitudes towards the social roles or behaviour associated with being one sex or the other.[55] Moreover, there was an additional dimension in this case because the wording of SWT's regulations switched attention to the gender of the employee's partner. On this point the AG was both creative and emphatic. Both the Equal Treatment Directive and Article 119 [now 141] EC should be construed as prohibiting discrimination in law or in fact against an employee not solely on the basis of the employee's own gender but also the gender of the employee's child, parent or other dependant.[56] It followed that, even though there was no reference in SWT's regulations to a specific sex, discrimination was exclusively gender-based.[57]

For the Court the answer to this question was straightforward and much narrower. First, based on a literal reading of SWT's regulations, the Court ruled that the travel concessions applied regardless of the sex of the worker concerned.[58] Travel concessions were refused to a male worker living with a person of the same sex, just as they were to a female worker in the same position—classic like-for-like Aristotelian equality. As the condition in question was formally equal it could not be interpreted as constituting discrimination based on sex. Both a lesbian and a gay man would be denied by SWT's policy of a right to the travel concession for their partner and—as they each suffered 'equal misery'—there was no discrimination.[59] The Court deemed it unnecessary to consider either the broader impact of SWT's regulations on Ms Grant and/or her partner, or the extent to which SWT's policies were influenced by sexual stereotyping and motivated by prejudice against lesbians and gay men. Moreover, while the rule appeared to be gender-neutral, its application was dependent on the employer's knowledge of the employee's sex and her relationship with her female partner—a sex-based criterion.[60] Nor was any attempt made to apply or indeed distinguish *P v S* on this point even though the UK had suggested, without success, that the comparator in that case was a female-male transsexual, also based on the logic of 'equal misery'.[61] Hence, sex discrimination was ruled out even before the issue of fundamental rights, or indeed the scope of Community law, was considered, an exact reversal of the line of reasoning in *P v S*. Ironically, this may be partly explained by the fact that here it was much easier to identify a comparator and dismiss the applicant's case, whereas in P the issue was more problematic and the

---

[55] Armstrong, n 51 above at 458.
[56] Para 16.
[57] Paras 23–25.
[58] Judgment, para 27.
[59] See Bell (1999, *European Law Journal*) n 32 above at 70.
[60] See Flynn (1998, *Yearbook of European Law*) n 5 above at 282.
[61] See Bell (1999, *European Law Journal*) n 32 above at 66.

Court's method of determining the comparator was both opaque and unconvincing. For the Court in *Grant* it was apparently an unproblematic fact that both Ms Grant and her putative gay comparator both faced discrimination because they had sexual preferences that departed from the assumed societal 'norm' for their sex.

Second, the Court examined whether Community law requires that all employers should regard stable relationships between two persons of the same sex as equivalent to marriage or stable relationships outside marriage between two persons of the opposite sex?[62] In fact Ms Grant and her partner were only seeking equivalence with other unmarried couples.[63] On the latter point, the Court conceded that cohabitation of same-sex couples is 'treated as equivalent to a stable heterosexual relationship outside marriage' in most Member States.[64] However, based on its own false premise, the Court noted that such equivalence had not been established at the level of the Community or under the ECHR,[65] and therefore, as the law stood at the time, there was no obligation on employers to treat such relationships as equivalent to either marriage or a stable relationship outside marriage with a partner of the opposite sex. The Court's analysis was highly selective and no consideration was given to the fact that eight out of 15 Member States had enacted relevant legislation prohibiting such discriminatory pay practices.[66] By contrast, the AG felt no need to pursue this point because he had already found that SWT's requirement that the cohabitee should be from the opposite sex was a discriminatory criterion derived from the sex of the employee.[67]

Third, the Court evaluated Ms Grant's alternative submission that differences of treatment based on sexual orientation were included in 'discrimination based on sex' under Article 119 [now 141] EC.[68] Support for this contention can be found in the observations of the UN Human Rights Committee on the interpretation of a similar provision in the International Covenant on Civil and Political Rights.[69] In a sweeping assessment, the

---

[62] Para 24.

[63] See Bell (1999, *European Law Journal*) n 32 above at 72.

[64] Para 32.

[65] The Court referred, at para 33, to the narrow interpretation of the right to respect for family life under Art 8 ECHR where the European Court of Human Rights had consistently held that stable homosexual relationships do not fall within the scope of that right: *X and Y v United Kingdom*, 3 May 1983, Appl No 9369/81; *S v United Kingdom*, 14 May 1986, Appl No 11716/85; and *Herkhoven and Hinke v The Netherlands*, 19 May 1992, Appl No 15666/89. Also, the European Court of Human Rights had held discrimination on the grounds of sexual orientation was not sex discrimination under Art 14 ECHR: *C and L M v United Kingdom*, 9 Oct 1989, Appl No 14753/89; and *B v United Kingdom*, 10 Feb 1990, Appl No 16106/90.

[66] Flynn (1998, *Yearbook of European Law*) n 5 above at 283.

[67] See Armstrong, n 51 above at 463.

[68] Para 37.

[69] The Committee had found that under Art 28 of the Covenant the term 'sex' is taken as including sexual orientation: Communication No 488/1992, *Toonen v Australia*, 31 Mar 1994, 50th session, point 8.7.

Court determined that, as the Committee is not a judicial body and its decisions have no binding force,[70] it followed that although the Covenant is one of the fundamental rights' instruments that it takes into account when applying the general principles of Community law, this observation did not reflect a generally accepted interpretation of the concept of discrimination based on sex and could not, in any case, provide a basis for the Court to extend the scope of Article 119 [now 141] EC.[71] In other words, even if the Court had accepted that Ms Grant's fundamental rights had been violated—behaviour which, by analogy with *P v S*, would have been deemed intolerable—it would have offered her no protection because Community law 'as it stands at present does not cover discrimination based on sexual orientation'.[72]

Ultimately the question boiled down to the issue of the scope of Community law. Drawing on its finding in *Opinion 2/94*,[73] concerning the Community's capacity to accede to the ECHR, the Court held that fundamental rights, in themselves, and the Court's observance thereof cannot have the effect of extending the scope of the Treaty provisions beyond the competences of the Community.[74] Hence, the scope of Article 119 [now 141] EC was to be determined only by having regard to its wording and purpose, its place in the scheme of the Treaty and its legal context.[75] In an astute example of 'judicial self-positioning'[76] the Court deferred to the Community legislature which would have the opportunity to take appropriate action under the new Article 13 EC once the Amsterdam Treaty was ratified.[77] However, the analogy with *Opinion 2/94* is unconvincing because the Court was not being asked to consider a new area of competence in *Grant* but rather to interpret Community law on equal pay, an area of existing competence.[78]

While the Court's judgment in *Grant* may seem somewhat otiose today, in the light of the subsequent adoption of the Framework Employment Directive, it remains important precisely because of what it reveals about the shallowness of the Court's commitment to the principle of equality when faced with a 'hard' case. The judgment in *P v S* may have appeared superficially 'courageous' but, rather than being a decision of potential

---

[70] Para 46. For criticism on this point see Flynn (1998, *Yearbook of European Law*) n 5 above at 284–85.

[71] Paras 46–47.

[72] Para 47. An outcome predicted several years earlier. See A Clapham and J Weiler, 'Lesbians and Gay Men in the Community Legal Order' in K Waaldijk and A Clapham (eds) *Homosexuality: A European Community Issue* (Nijhoff, Dordrecht, 1993) 11–69 at 21.

[73] [1996] ECR I–1759.

[74] Para 45.

[75] Para 47.

[76] Armstrong, n 51 above at 461.

[77] Para 48.

[78] See Bamforth, n 29 above at 711.

constitutional importance,[79] it represents an example of what de Búrca has aptly described as the Court's selective application of the equality principle,[80] a form of judicial 'gesture politics'. Transsexuals are a 'fairly well-defined and identifiable' group who are in the process of changing, or have changed, sex.[81] By finding in favour of P, the Court was able to use the language of rights to legitimate the position of transsexuals and further the integration process for this group,[82] adding a certain moral content to the law in this area, without necessarily, as *Grant* has revealed, opening the door for that same process to be applied to another group. Equally the vocabulary of rights can be divisive[83] if certain individuals and groups are deemed to be excluded by a Union that professes to uphold 'common values'.[84]

Nevertheless, while the judgment in *P v S* was not quite the 'decisive step' imagined by AG Elmer, it remains an important decision because it provides a basis for asserting the autonomy of the equality principle in new contexts.[85] The Court's unusual reasoning may be explained by the anomalous situation it was seeking to address.[86] *Grant*, on the other hand, was a case too far,[87] first, because lesbians and gay men are more numerous than transsexuals, a factor which should not affect the standard of protection they are afforded,[88] but raises the prospect of significant economic consequences for Member States and employers. Second, perhaps more importantly, the Court, if it had ruled in Ms Grant's favour, would have had to directly address wider gender issues such as sexual stereotyping and, more controversially, moral attitudes concerning sexual orientation.[89] Such issues, which strike at the core of an individual's sense of identity or personhood, challenge deeply entrenched values and moral assumptions about divisions in society and touch upon the national psyche. Not surprisingly, the more

---

[79] See Barnard in Dashwood and O'Leary, n 37 above, who, at 59, observed in the aftermath of the judgment that: 'In the annals of Community law history, the judgment in *P v. S* might be held as the *Van Gend en Loos*, or the *Costa v ENEL* of its time. Or it may not'.

[80] de Búrca in Dashwood and O'Leary, n 4 above at 15.

[81] *P v S*, para 16.

[82] See further, G de Búrca, 'The Language of Rights and European Integration' in J Shaw and G More, *New Legal Dynamics of European Union* (Clarendon Press, Oxford, 1995) 29–54 at 39–43.

[83] *Ibid* at 45–52.

[84] See the preamble of the EU Charter of Fundamental Rights, OJ 2000, C364/1. Discussed in ch 12.

[85] See for example, Case C–185/97, *Coote v Granada* [1998] ECR I–5199, where the Court applied fundamental rights, as expressed in *P v S*, as a basis for a broad interpretation of Art 6 of the Equal Treatment Directive. Discussed by Flynn (1998, *Yearbook of European Law*) n 5 above at 284.

[86] Flynn, *ibid* at 280.

[87] Nicholas Underhill QC, representing SWT declared that it was: 'a bridge too far and they [the Court] weren't going to cross it': *The Times*, 18 Feb 1998. See S Terry, 'A Bridge Too Far? Non-Discrimination and Homosexuality in European Community Law' (1998) 4 *European Public Law* 487 at 505.

[88] See Bell (1999, *European Law Journal*) n 32 above at 75.

[89] *Ibid* at 76.

contested the issue the greater the Court's reluctance to apply or elaborate fundamental rights.[90]

The Court's reference to the emergence of Article 13 EC was presented as almost an aside but it was, undoubtedly, an important component in its collective thought. Article 13 EC lists 'sex' and 'sexual orientation' separately and the Court would have been aware of potential pitfalls that might arise in a future scenario if these concepts overlapped. However, Ms Grant was not seeking to subsume sexual orientation discrimination within sex discrimination[91] but rather, as Wintemute has shown,[92] to ask whether:

... distinctions based on sexual orientation, when examined from a different angle, are in fact also or simultaneously 'on grounds of sex' because they are based on the sexes of the individuals concerned.

The Court did not address this question but if the scope of Community sex equalities law 'cannot be confined simply to discrimination based on the fact that a person is of one or other sex',[93] it must be capable of extension to encompass gender discrimination by reference to assumed norms of behaviour by persons of either sex.[94] The conservatism of the Court in *Grant* can now be seen as even more striking when contrasted with bolder steps in Strasbourg, where the European Court of Human Rights has now held, in *Smith and Grady v United Kingdom*,[95] that sexual orientation discrimination is a violation of the right to respect for private life guaranteed by Article 8 ECHR. Further, in *da Silva Mouta v Portugal*,[96] the Strasbourg Court held that sex discrimination is 'undoubtedly covered' by Article 14 ECHR,[97] although not on the basis that sexual orientation discrimination is sex discrimination, but rather because that provision contains a non-exhaustive enumeration.[98] It should also be noted that Article 14 ECHR only prohibits discrimination in conjunction with other substantive rights protected by the Convention. Nevertheless, these developments indicate that, should a further case be referred to Luxembourg, the Court will have to re-evaluate its analysis of case law under the Convention.[99]

---

[90] Hence the Court's equally conservative approach in a case involving the legality of the provisions on abortion under the Constitution of Ireland: Case C–159/90, *SPUC v Grogan* [1991] ECR I–4685.

[91] See Bamforth, n 29 above at 698.

[92] Wintemute, n 17 above at 344; cf J Gardner, 'On the Ground of Her Sex(uality)' (1998) 18 *Oxford Journal of Legal Studies* 167 at 179–83.

[93] *P v S*, para 20.

[94] See Bamforth, n 29 above at 701.

[95] Appl Nos 33985/96 & 33986/96 [2000] 29 EHRR 493.

[96] Appl No 33290/96 [2001] 31 EHRR 47.

[97] Para 28.

[98] *Ibid.* Under Art 14 ECHR: 'The rights and freedoms set forth in this Convention shall be secured without discrimination *on any ground such as* sex, race, colour, language, religion, political or other opinion, national or social origin, association with a national minority, property, birth or other status' (emphasis added).

[99] See Bamforth, n 29 above at 719.

Grant represents a missed opportunity for the Court to apply its reasoning in *P v S* within the context of 'sex' equality without prejudicing the right of the legislature to take appropriate action to combat discrimination based on sexual orientation under Article 13 EC. Further, as the judgment in *D and Sweden v Council* has shown,[100] the social conservatism expressed by the Court in *Grant* has become, if anything, more pervasive. For not only did the Court in *D* uphold a 15-year old authority on the meaning of the term 'spouse',[101] excluding same-sex partnerships, it ignored legislative developments in the Member States recognising such partnerships on the basis that they are akin to marriage.[102] The Court was also prepared to defer to the legislature even when interpreting outmoded terminology in the Community's own Staff Regulations.[103] The chasm between the rhetoric and the reality of the protection of rights,[104] as expressed by the Court, appears to be widening just as the EU is seeking to embrace fundamental rights as the centrepiece of a new constitutional paradigm.

III THE COURT OF JUSTICE AND POSITIVE ACTION—TOWARDS FULL EQUALITY IN PRACTICE?

Within the Community legal order 'positive action' is ambiguously situated. Under the revised Article 141(4) EC,[105] the principle of equal treatment 'shall not prevent' Member States from adopting measures providing for 'specific advantages' with a view to 'ensuring full equality in practice in working life' for members of the under-represented sex. Article 2(4) of the Equal Treatment Directive, adopted 20 years earlier, has served a similar but more modest purpose, seeking to promote 'equal opportunity between men and women' within the field of the Directive. Paradoxically, these provisions, although negatively expressed, are not conventional derogations in the sense that, far from lessening or impairing the objective of equality, they seek to give it strength and substance, albeit through non-mandatory action. A further paradox arises because, although such measures are designed

---

[100] Cases C–122/99P and C–125/99P [2001] ECR I–4139. Noted by E Ellis (2002) 39 *Common Market Law Review* 151. Discussed in chs 9 and 12.

[101] Case 59/85, *Netherlands v Reed* [1986] ECR 1283. Discussed by de Búrca, n 4 above at 19; and R Amy Elman, 'The Limits of Citizenship: Migration, Sex Discrimination and Same-Sex Partners in EU Law' (2000) 28 *Journal of Common Market Studies* 729 at 734–37.

[102] At the time of the judgment same-sex partnerships were legally recognised in the Netherlands, Denmark and Sweden. By Sept 2001, laws had also been adopted in Germany and Finland. See Ellis, n 100 above at 152.

[103] The Court would have been aware of the introduction of a new Regulation requiring equal treatment of all officials regardless of their sexual orientation. The new Regulation had not entered into force at the material time of the proceedings. See Reg 781/98/EC, OJ 1998, L113/4.

[104] See Armstrong, n 51 above at 466.

[105] Replacing Art 6(3) of the Agreement on Social Policy.

to boost de facto equality[106] for a collectively disadvantaged group, they may contravene equality in law. Indeed, the more ambitious the measure, designed to achieve equality of results, the more likely it will be deemed inconsistent or disproportionate with the non-discrimination principle and the 'right' of the individual to equal treatment.

Positive action is also ambiguous conceptually. While the terms 'positive action'[107] and 'affirmative action' may be used interchangeably, the aims and means of such action are much contested. The label of 'positive action' has been affixed to activities such as recruitment or outreach campaigns and, more readily, to various forms of 'reverse discrimination' based on targets, benchmarks or quotas.[108] While some measures seek to promote equal opportunities and 'merit' to improve the life chances of under-represented groups in society who wish to compete in the workplace, others are designed to systematically eradicate both past disadvantage and latent prejudice by eliminating obstacles affecting groups or persons in order to produce equality of outcomes.

While fierce battles have been waged over 'affirmative action' in the US for the last 40 years,[109] Germany has provided the setting for a series of more modest, but no less intensely fought, European skirmishes. From the mid-1980s quota systems have been introduced at both federal and regional level for the 'advancement of women' in areas of public employment to which women have traditionally been denied access.[110] Such measures are intended to be compatible with the aim of 'removing existing inequalities which affect women's opportunities' in the labour market under Article 2(4) of the Equal Treatment Directive,[111] as a means of achieving the aim of

---

[106] See the Commission's proposal for a Third Community Action Programme on Equal Opportunities for Women and Men (1991–1995), COM(90) 449: Introduction, para 2.

[107] 'Positive action' is a broad term which can be applied to a wide variety of equalities policies. It will be used here in preference to 'affirmative action' which, according to McCrudden, is used in the US specifically 'to refer to actions taken to identify and replace discriminatory employment practices, and to develop practices which result in the greater inclusion and participation in the workforce of women and minorities'. See C McCrudden, 'Rethinking Positive Action' (1986) 15 *Industrial Law Journal* 219 at 220–21.

[108] *Ibid* at 223–25.

[109] See especially, S Fredman, 'Reversing Discrimination' (1997) 113 *Law Quarterly Review* 575 at 590–96; C MacKinnon, 'Reflections on Sex Equality under Law' (1991) 100 *Yale Law Journal* 1281; and S Douglas-Scott, 'Affirmative Action in the US Supreme Court: the *Adarand* case—the Final Chapter' [1997] *Public Law* 43.

[110] For discussion, see J Shaw, 'Positive Action for Women in Germany: The Use of Legally Binding Quota Systems' in B Hepple and E Szyszczak (eds) *Discrimination: The Limits of Law* (Mansell, London, 1992) 386–411; N Colneric, 'Making Equality Law More Effective: Lessons from the German Experience' (1996) 3 *Cardozo Woman's Law Journal* 229; C Barnard and T Hervey, 'Softening the approach to quotas: positive action after *Marschall*' (1998) 20 *Journal of Social Welfare and Family Law* 333 at 333–34; and D Schiek, 'Positive Action in Community Law' (1996) 25 *Industrial Law Journal* 239 at 241–42. Schiek notes, at 241, that laws have been introduced in 14 *Länder* since 1989.

[111] Dir 76/207/EEC, OJ 1976, L39/40.

equal treatment under Article 2(1) thereof, and therefore, by legitimising preferential treatment, give legal substance to the rhetoric of sex equality derived from Community soft law.[112]

Schiek has identified four varieties of quotas in the German public sector.[113] First, in order to comply with the 'merit principle' in the Federal Constitution,[114] which requires an individual to be treated according to her or his own personal characteristics, a number of *Länder* introduced 'flexible' or 'weak' quotas which allow a systematic preference for women in jobs or training only when male and female candidates are equally qualified based on a fixed percentage—such as the proportion of women in the labour force as a whole.[115] Normally there will be a derogation clause which requires countervailing factors concerning the individual candidates to be taken into account.[116] Second, in some cases 'strict' quotas have been introduced which reserve a set percentage of positions for women. For example, in Berlin and Hessen 50 per cent of trainee places are reserved for women provided that enough women apply.[117] Third, 'result quotas' may be used whereby goals and timetables may be set in a plan to achieve a gender balance over a given period of time. In Hessen, where women are underrepresented, the plan requires that at least every second vacancy must be filled by a woman with a derogation where there are not enough women qualified for the position. Fourth, some systems combine 'result quotas' with 'flexible' and 'strict' quotas.

Quotas are the most contentious form of positive action precisely because, as Peters observes, they apply in situations where a single slot is available for one of the applicants and therefore 'the quota necessarily and immediately excludes the competitor'.[118] Hence, although quotas are incongruent with the liberal paradigm of equality in law, is it possible for unequal treatment to be justified in order to achieve a 'just' outcome in fact?[119] The Court was faced with precisely this challenge in a series of Article 234 [ex 177] EC references from German courts.

In the first case, *Kalanke*,[120] the issue at stake concerned the legality of a 'tie-break' system for promotions in the City of Bremen. In situations where

---

[112] Shaw in Hepple and Szyszczak, n 110 above at 387. In particular to give effect to soft law pronouncements such as Council Recommendation 84/635/EEC on the promotion of positive action for women, OJ 1984, L331/34.

[113] See D Schiek, 'Sex Equality Law After Kalanke and Marschall' (1998) 4 *European Law Journal* 148 at 149.

[114] Art 33(II).

[115] Shaw in Hepple and Szyszczak, n 110 above at 395.

[116] *Ibid* at 405.

[117] Schiek (1998, *European Law Journal*) n 113 above at 150.

[118] A Peters, 'The Many Meanings of Equality and Positive Action in Favour of Women under European Community Law—A Conceptual Analysis' (1996) 2 *European Law Journal* 177 at 178.

[119] *Ibid* at 184.

[120] Case C–450/93, *Kalanke v Freie Hansestadt Bremen* [1995] ECR I–3051.

women were under-represented in the relevant area, in this case horticultural managers, a woman would be given priority over an equally qualified man. Under-represented areas were those where less than 50 per cent of staff were women. Therefore, although this was not a 'strict' quota it nevertheless predetermined the result in this instance. The Court, in a taciturn judgment, was not prepared to countenance a quota system that gave automatic priority to women:[121]

National rules which guarantee women absolute and unconditional priority for appointment or promotion go beyond promoting equal opportunities and overstep the limits of the exception in Article 2(4) of the Directive.

Furthermore, in so far as it seeks to achieve equal representation of men and women in all grades and levels within a department, such a system substitutes for equality of opportunity as envisaged in Article 2(4) the result which is only to be arrived at by providing such equality of opportunity.

In order to explain the Court's reasoning and the highly contentious assumptions that underlie the judgment it is necessary to refer to the opinion of AG Tesauro. Firstly, the AG analysed the role of positive action *as a means of achieving equal opportunities.*[122] In particular, he asked whether the term 'equal opportunities' refers to starting points or points of arrival? Relying heavily on jurisprudence from the US, he asserted that equal opportunities means *putting people in a position to attain equal results* and hence restoring conditions of equality as regards starting points.[123] From this perspective both candidates had equal qualifications and therefore an 'equal footing at the starting block'. This helps to make sense of the Court's rather opaque reference to substituting the *result* of equal opportunity for equal opportunity itself as provided for by Article 2(4).[124] The equal starting points notion is, as Fredman astutely observes,[125] 'deceptively simple' if one views equal opportunities as merely a procedural requirement derived from an idealised liberal assumption of symmetry between individuals, but it disregards a more compelling substantive equality model which, by seeking equality of results, takes account of the extent to which in reality an individual's opportunities are determined by their social and historical status as a member of a disadvantaged group.[126]

Secondly, while recognising that the attainment of substantive equality, or equality of outcomes, is a legitimate aim of positive action,[127] the AG suggested that this could only be pursued under Article 2(4) of the

---

[121] Paras 22–23.
[122] Opinion, para 8.
[123] Para 13.
[124] Para 23. See further, L Senden, 'Positive Action in the EU Put to the Test: A Negative Score?' (1996) 3 *Maastricht Journal* 146 at 149.
[125] Fredman (1997, *Law Quarterly Review*) n 109 above at 579.
[126] *Ibid* at 578.
[127] Opinion, para 15.

Directive through measures designed to achieve an actual situation of equal opportunities.[128] Hence, as the Court had previously held, Article 2(4) authorises treatment which, although discriminatory in appearance, is 'in fact intended to eliminate or reduce actual instances of equality which may exist in the reality of social life'.[129] Interpreting this statement narrowly, the AG advised that, although positive action may be used to raise the starting threshold of the disadvantaged category, it could not be applied 'as a means of remedying, through discriminatory measures, a situation of impaired equality in the past'.[130] The logic of this reasoning is that the position of the male is the norm in the sense that substantive equality can be understood as placing women in a position to reach the same results as men.[131] As Peters explains,[132] the compensatory rationale is unhelpful and an obfuscation because a broader conception of substantive equality requires account to be taken not only of past discrimination but also of the reality of latent prejudices and internalised role expectations which are reflected in the organisation of the workplace and family life. When these factors are taken into account it is obvious that a test which assumes individual merit derived only from equal qualifications is inadequate and renders the commitment to 'removing existing inequalities' in Article 2(4) vacuous.

Thirdly, while the AG recognised that Article 2(4) is concerned with effectiveness and does not operate as a genuine derogation, he applied a proportionality test that effectively limited its scope as a basis for national measures. Ultimately the measure went beyond what was deemed necessary to achieve equality of opportunities for women because it aimed to confer the results on them directly.[133] Moreover, once that conclusion had been reached it followed that the Bremen law was a violation of the fundamental right of equality.[134]

The Court went further by treating Article 2(4) as a derogation that must be interpreted strictly.[135] Such an interpretation undermines the very purpose of Article 2(4) which seeks to further the objective of equality that underlies the Directive and not restrict it. Paradoxically, as Szyszczak notes,[136] the Court had turned its face against forms of positive action which bring about immediate and concrete equality. An alternative approach would recognise that measures aimed at rectifying existing inequalities cannot be regarded as discriminatory as they are designed to establish equal-

---

[128] Opinion, para 15.
[129] Case 312/86, *Commission v France* [1988] ECR 6315, para 15.
[130] Opinion, para 19.
[131] Peters, n 118 above at 191.
[132] *Ibid.*
[133] Opinion, para 25.
[134] Paras 27–28.
[135] Judgment, para 21.
[136] E Szyszczak, 'Positive Action After *Kalanke*' (1996) 59 *Modern Law Review* 876 at 883.

ity and therefore form part of the equality principle.[137] Moreover, neither the AG nor the Court were able to provide a satisfactory explanation for upholding Mr Kalanke's claim despite the fact that it was an assumed fact that there was no difference between the two candidates on individual merit.[138] Random selection by spinning a coin was, by implication, acceptable but automatic selection by quota was not.[139]

Not surprisingly the judgment in *Kalanke* generated considerable opposition, not least in Germany and among academics,[140] but it also turned a spotlight on the limitations of the liberal equality model and provoked much discussion about the prospects for an alternative approach that might legitimise positive action, including quotas, where such measures contribute to the achievement of equality in practice. In the immediate aftermath of *Kalanke* the Commission swiftly issued a Communication that emphasised the fact that the Court had not formally outlawed quotas.[141] Many positive action measures remained lawful so long as they did not give automatic and unconditional preference to women. Moreover, the Commission proposed an amendment to the Directive on the interpretation of Article 2(4) in order to clarify the legal position.[142] In the meantime the Court was given an early opportunity to reconsider its stance.

In *Marschall*[143] the Court was asked to rule, once again, on a quota system based on a 'tie-break' rule between equally qualified male and female candidates for promotion in the public service in Germany, in this instance in the *Land* of North Rhine-Westphalia. Where there were fewer women than men in the relevant sector of the authority, women were to be given priority for promotion 'in the event of equal suitability, competence and professional performance, *unless reasons specific to an individual [male] candidate tilt the balance in his favour*'.[144] Did the addition of this 'saving clause' enable the Court to distinguish *Kalanke* and permit the rule under Article 2(4) of the Directive?

---

[137] *Ibid.*
[138] See S Fredman, 'Affirmative Action and the European Court of Justice: A Critical Analysis' in J Shaw (ed) *Social Law and Policy in an Evolving European Union* (Hart, Oxford, 2000) 171–95 at 178.
[139] *Ibid.*
[140] See the observations of AG Jacobs in Case C–409/95, *Marschall v Land Nordrhein-Westfalen* [1997] ECR I–6363, at para 11 of his opinion.
[141] COM(96) 88.
[142] *Ibid.* The draft amendment provided that: '4. This Directive shall be without prejudice to measures to promote equal opportunity for men and women, in particular by removing existing inequalities which affect the opportunities of the under-represented sex in the areas referred to in Article 1(1). Possible measures shall include the giving of preference, as regards access to employment or promotion, to a member of the under-represented sex, provided that such measures do not preclude the assessment of the particular circumstances of an individual case'.
[143] Case C–409/95, *Marschall v Land Nordrhein-Westfalen* [1997] ECR I–6363.
[144] Judgment, para 3 (emphasis added).

AG Jacobs warned the Court not to make such a distinction on 'narrow technical grounds' which would, in his view, lead to confusion as to the law and a proliferation of litigation with arbitrary results.[145] For the AG, the existence of the 'saving clause', which he regarded as unclear in scope,[146] merely displaced the rule giving priority to women in a particular case but did not alter the discriminatory nature of the rule in general.[147] Dispensing with any discussion of the desirability of positive action, which he regarded as a diversion from the central issue of the compatibility of the rule in question with Article 2(4),[148] he noted that there were also exceptions to the Bremen rule under consideration in *Kalanke*.[149] Applying a strictly liberal equality rationale, he concluded that the effect of the ruling in *Kalanke* was that 'any rule which goes beyond the promotion of equal opportunities by seeking to impose instead the desired result of equal representation is similarly outside the scope of Article 2(4)'.[150]

For the Court, however, the saving clause and, perhaps more importantly, the salience of the objectives that lay behind the *Land's* scheme, amounted to compelling reasons to distinguish *Kalanke*. Significantly, the Court relied heavily on the Council's 1984 Recommendation on the promotion of positive action for women which recognises the need for parallel action at national level 'to counteract the prejudicial effects on women in employment *which arise from social attitudes, behaviour and structures*'.[151] In *Kalanke* the Court had highlighted the role played by Article 2(4) as a derogation from the equal treatment principle subject to strict interpretation, placing the Recommendation in that context.[152] In *Marschall*, however, the Court switched emphasis by stressing the positive aspect of Article 2(4), referring to the arguments of the *Land* and several intervening governments who had stressed that where male and female candidates are equally qualified, male candidates tend to be promoted in preference to females 'particularly because of prejudices and stereotypes concerning the role and capacities of women in working life'.[153] Moreover, the Court also referred to the fear that women will interrupt their careers more frequently, that owing to household and family responsibilities they will be less flexible in their working hours, or that they will be absent from work more frequently because of pregnancy, childbirth and breastfeeding.[154] For these reasons:[155]

---

[145] Opinion, para 37.
[146] *Ibid* para 35.
[147] *Ibid* para 33.
[148] *Ibid* para 11.
[149] *Ibid* para 28.
[150] *Ibid* para 32.
[151] OJ 1984, L331/34 (emphasis added). Discussed at para 28.
[152] *Kalanke*, paras 20–21.
[153] *Marschall*, para 29.
[154] *Ibid*.
[155] Para 30.

. . . the mere fact that a male candidate and a female candidate are equally quali-fied does not mean that they have the same chances.

This short paragraph directly refutes the 'equal starting points' model of equal opportunities relied upon by AG Tesauro in *Kalanke*. Consequently policies that seek to correct imbalances in the workforce by quotas and targets and whose aim is one of equality of outcome may be granted legiti-macy.[156] It follows that a national rule may fall within the scope of Article 2(4) if it operates to counteract such attitudes and behaviour and thus 'reduce the actual instances of equality *which may exist in the real world*'.[157] In other words, societal discrimination outside the workplace provides a justification for an element of positive action in the employment sphere. Hence, in an important shift, the Court acknowledged the conceptual underpinning of the substantive equality model by upholding the values of factual equality. The objectivity of the merit principle would no longer be accepted at face value.[158] Other factors such as the 'glass ceiling' on women's promotion at work and broader societal factors that underlie preferential treatment programmes[159] were now a factor in the equation. However, having espoused the rhetoric of substantive equality[160] the Court proceeded to position its judgment within the formal equality model by upholding *Kalanke* and distinguishing a saving clause that does not exceed these limits *if*, in each individual case:[161]

. . . it provides for male candidates who are equally as qualified as the female can-didates a guarantee that the candidatures will be the subject of an objective assess-ment which will take account of all criteria specific to the individual candidates and will override the priority accorded to female candidates where one or more of these criteria tilt the balance in favour of the male candidate. In this respect, however, it should be remembered that those criteria must not be such as to discriminate against female candidates.

The warning conveyed in the final sentence is important because, ironically, one of the reasons why the legislature in Bremen had omitted such a formal proviso was, according to the referring court in *Kalanke*, because there was too great a risk that application of such an exception would lead to indi-rect discrimination against women.[162] *Land* North-Rhine Westphalia had similar concerns, regarding the saving clause as a 'sword of Damocles' to be rarely invoked.[163] This rather begs the question of whether it is ever

---

[156] See Fredman in Shaw, n 138 above at 175.
[157] Para 31 (emphasis added).
[158] See Fredman in Shaw, n 138 above at 178.
[159] See the note on *Marschall* by G More (1999) *Common Market Law Review* 443 at 450.
[160] See further, L Charpentier, 'The European Court of Justice and the Rhetoric of Affirmative Action' (1998) 4 *European Law Journal* 167.
[161] Para 33.
[162] See the AG's opinion in *Marschall*, para 36. See further the annotation on *Kalanke* by S Prechal (1996) 33 *Common Market Law Review* 1245 at 1257.
[163] *Ibid.*

possible to formulate an objective gender-neutral 'guarantee' that can 'tilt the balance' in favour of a male candidate?[164]

The Court's attempt to distinguish *Kalanke* is unconvincing. Both the Bremen and North-Rhine Westphalian laws allowed for consideration of individual candidates with only minor technical differences. Further, even if one accepts that the latter provided additional safeguards for individual male candidates,[165] it operated only as an exception to a general asymmetrical rule which leads to equality of results rather than equality of opportunities—reversing the presumption upon which the ruling in *Kalanke* was based. Nevertheless, that technical difference was of vital importance because, by acknowledging the presence of a male contender,[166] it provided cover for the Court to embark on a retreat from *Kalanke* without jettisoning the liberal ideal of equality. Formally, at least, the two main elements of an equal opportunities approach—recognition of the limits of equal treatment and endorsement of the primacy of the individual[167]—remained intact albeit within a system of limited group preference.[168] Hence the judgment in *Marschall* provides a rather unconvincing basis for the Court to reconcile certain 'tie-break' quota schemes targeted at disadvantaged groups within an individualised equal treatment framework, but leaves a question mark over the prospects for stricter quota systems aimed at achieving equal representation more rapidly by removing the premise of equal qualification.[169]

In part the Court's ambivalence towards positive action in *Marschall* can be explained by the timing of the judgment. In the two-year period between *Kalanke* and *Marschall* external pressure for legislative change and Treaty amendment was keenly felt.[170] Whereas AG Jacobs criticised the Commission for seeking to introduce an interpretative amendment which he regarded as 'more innovatory than the Commission suggests' and 'lacking in clarity',[171] he acknowledged that a proposed revision of the EC Treaty would allow for 'certain forms of affirmative action'.[172] The Court, however, was not immune to external events.[173] In the period between the opinion

---

[164] For discussion on this point, see L Betten and V Shrubsall, 'The Concept of Positive Sex Discrimination in Community Law—Before and After the Treaty of Amsterdam' (1998) 14 *International Journal of Comparative Labour Law and Industrial Relations* 65 at 68–70.

[165] For Schiek (1996, *Industrial Law Journal*) n 110 above at 243, this distinction is of critical importance.

[166] Charpentier, n 160 above at 185–86.

[167] See Fredman in Shaw, n 138 above at 177.

[168] See More (1999) *Common Market Law Review*, n 159 above at 451.

[169] Fredman in Shaw, n 138 above at 179.

[170] More (1999) *Common Market Law Review*, n 159 above at 451. More also suggests, at 452, that a change in the composition of the Count may have been a factor.

[171] Opinion, para 49.

[172] *Ibid* para 50.

[173] See further, G Mancini and S O'Leary, 'The New Frontiers of Sex Equality Law in the European Union' (1999) 24 *European Law Review* 331 at 346.

and the judgment the Amsterdam Treaty was negotiated and, with the introduction of Article 141(4) EC, the centre of gravity of the equal treatment debate shifted from 'equal opportunity' to 'full equality in practice', signalling a preference, but not an obligation, for positive action[174] intended to make it easier for the 'under-represented sex' to pursue a vocational activity or 'to prevent or compensate for disadvantages in professional careers'. This provision would appear to encompass schemes designed to address the whole panoply of 'prejudices and stereotypes' of women referred to by the Court in *Marschall* in the sense that these are compensatory—remedying past deficits—and distributive—representing a desired level of equality of representation that women would have had in the absence of societal discrimination.[175] Nevertheless uncertainty remained not only about the relationship between Article 141(4) EC and Article 2(4) of the Equal Treatment Directive, but also whether Article 141(4) EC derogates from the principle of equal treatment or forms part of its expression?[176] The Court's studied ambiguity in *Marschall* reflected this uncertainty.

Two years later in *Badeck*,[177] a third reference from Germany, the Court was presented with an opportunity both to reconcile its case law and address the issue of positive action in the context of the now operative Article 141(4) EC. *Badeck* concerned the legality of positive action measures in the *Land* of Hessen that were altogether stricter and embraced a more substantive view of equality than those in Bremen and North-Rhine Westphalia.[178] Whereas the latter provided for 'women's quotas' allowing for a decision on each individual appointment or promotion,[179] the Hessen Equal Rights Law established a 'flexible result quota' in the form of a women's advancement plan that contained binding targets, for two years at a time, for the proportion of women appointed and promoted, for increasing the proportion of women in sectors where women were under-represented. In these sectors more than half the posts were designated for women. In effect the system—and related schemes also under consideration[180]—was stricter than those previously considered by the Court because it placed the numerical result ahead of any requirement for formal qualifications between competing candidates. Moreover, unlike in *Marschall*, there

---

[174] On this point, see H Fenwick, 'From Formal to Substantive Equality: the Place of Affirmative Action in European Union Sex Equality Law' (1998) 4 *European Public Law* 507 at 515.

[175] See Charpentier, n 160 above at 192–93.

[176] For further discussion, see Betten & Shrubsall, n 164 above at 76–80.

[177] Case C–158/97, *Badeck and others v Hessischer Ministerpräsident* [2000] ECR I–1875.

[178] See K Küchhold, '*Badeck*—The Third German Reference on Positive Action' (2001) 30 *Industrial Law Journal* 116 at 116; and Fredman in Shaw, n 138 above at 180.

[179] Küchhold, *ibid* at 117.

[180] In addition to the main 'flexible result quota' the reference also sought to address the status of an 'academic flexible result quota', a 'strict training quota', an 'interview quota' and a 'quota for collective bodies'. See *ibid*.

was no saving clause allowing for the priority given to women to be disregarded on objective grounds. However, a separate provision provided that posts were only to be filled on the basis of 'suitability, capability and professional performance' including qualifications.[181] Factors to be taken into account in this assessment included childcare responsibilities and family work, while part-time work, leave and delays in completing training because of care of children and dependants were not allowed to have a negative effect nor to adversely affect progress in employment. Significantly, seniority and age, criteria which usually work in favour of men,[182] would only become decisive if and where they added to the specific qualification needed in the job or office advertised.

Once again the Court relied on its AG to provide the conceptual background within which to frame a narrowly reasoned judgment. In his opinion, AG Saggio sought, with admirable clarity, to define the scope of positive action within the Community legal order.[183] In his view the combined effect of Article 2(4) of the Directive and Article 141(4) EC was to enable States to adopt provisions designed to achieve equal treatment even if they appear contrary to the principle of non-discrimination and entail actual disadvantages for men.[184] For the AG, the dynamic effect of Article 141(4) EC was of central importance.[185] In the light of express references to forms of positive action in that provision, a strict interpretation of Article 2(4) would now be inconsistent with the development of Community law.[186] Article 141(4) EC had shifted the presumption in favour of positive action and, as a result, 'we cannot in principle hold national provisions involving the actual recruitment or promotion of female candidates to be precluded by Community law'.[187] Any other interpretation would deprive positive action of its substance and accord it the status of an auxiliary measure which would not always be effective in redressing social inequalities.[188] Departing from the polarised vision of the AGs in *Kalanke* and *Marschall*, who considered preference for the under-represented sex to be irreconcilable with the principle of equality,[189] AG Saggio concluded that such a dynamic approach would allow the principles of formal and substantive equality to be regarded as 'not antithetical but complementary'. Conflicts

---

[181] Para 10 of the Hessen Equal Rights Law.

[182] On this point, see D Schiek, 'Positive Action before the European Court of Justice—New Conceptions of Equality in Community Law? From *Kalanke* and *Marschall* to *Badeck*' (2000) 16 *International Journal of Comparative Labour Law and Industrial Relations* 251 at 257.

[183] Opinion, para 19.

[184] *Ibid* para 20.

[185] See Flynn (1998, *Yearbook of European Law*) n 5 above at 264.

[186] Opinion, para 26.

[187] *Ibid.*

[188] *Ibid* para 28.

[189] On this point see Schiek (2000, *International Journal of Comparative Labour Law and Industrial Relations*) n 182 above at 252.

would arise, however, in two situations: first, where a measure is 'arbitrary in its content', in the sense that it impinges excessively on the rights of individuals not belonging to the group to which it is addressed; and second, when it is disproportionate to the real needs of the disadvantaged group because the social realities do not justify the adoption of the law in question.[190]

On this basis the rule at issue in *Kalanke* was arbitrary, in the sense that the automatic operation of the quota made it extremely difficult for an employer to select a male candidate.[191] In *Marschall*, on the other hand, there was no automatic effect because of the saving clause and the rule itself was proportionate because it lessened the discriminatory effect of the quota.[192] The AG concluded that quotas for women would be lawful in the Community legal order where they allow:

... the employer to select the candidate with the most suitable professional profile. In no case must such action affect the assessment of the merits and qualifications of male candidates.

Applying these criteria, the AG advised that, notwithstanding the absence of a saving clause, the main Hessen provision was lawful because it 'explicitly requires priority to be given to the best qualified and most suitable candidate'. Most importantly, it was perfectly appropriate for women's dual burden of work and care[193] to be taken into consideration among the criteria for assessment of merit because:

The system merely provides a mechanism to facilitate the integration of women and further their careers by ensuring, in particular, that they are not penalised as a result of the work they have done within the family.

Positive action is compatible with Community law so long as it 'does not preclude male candidates from competing for any post' and 'does not require a fixed quota of female candidates to be employed regardless of candidates' suitability for the specific post to be filled'. This indicates that the AG was seeking to apply a loose standard of proportionality in contrast with the strict test of AG Jacobs in *Marschall*, which would render almost all positive action unlawful.[194] On this basis all of the quotas under the Hessen law were lawful with the exception of a 'quota for collective bodies' because this provided that half of the membership of internal administrative bodies must be women irrespective of their suitability for the

[190] Opinion, para 29.
[191] *Ibid* para 30.
[192] *Ibid* paras 31–2.
[193] See further, T Hervey and J Shaw, 'Women, Work and Care: Women's Dual Role and Double Burden in EC Sex Equality Law' (1998) 8 *Journal of European Social Policy* 43.
[194] See Schiek (2000, *International Journal of Comparative Labour Law and Industrial Relations*) n 182 above at 271.

position.[195] The key criterion, allowing ultimate priority to be given to the most suitable candidate, was missing.

In its judgment the Court sought to consolidate its case law without elaborating upon its conception of equality or the compatibility of the formal and substantive equality models. Significantly, while making several references to Article 141(4) EC, the Court shied away from a dynamic interpretation of that provision and instead ruled that it would only be material to the outcome in cases where it considered that the national legislation was not permitted under Article 2(4) of the Directive.[196] Therefore, Article 2(4) was to be considered in isolation and, by implication, remained subject to strict interpretation as in *Kalanke*. Theoretically a rule that was not compatible with the Directive might still be lawful under Article 141(4) EC, but the Court offered no further guidance on the basis upon which such a conclusion might be reached and, as it ruled that each element of the Hessen law was permitted under the Directive,[197] it was, perhaps conveniently, not necessary to consider the ambit of Article 141(4) EC in this context.[198]

Nevertheless, despite according Article 141(4) EC a subordinate role vis-à-vis the Directive, the Court followed its AG when setting out a general presumption in favour of quotas while seeking to reconcile *Kalanke* and *Marschall* by holding that:[199]

. . . a measure which is intended to give priority in promotion to women in sectors of the public service where they are under-represented *must be regarded* as compatible with Community law if
—it does not automatically and unconditionally give priority to women when women and men are equally qualified, and
—the candidatures are the subject of an objective assessment which takes account of the specific personal situations of all candidates.

On the basis of this formulaic approach[200] the Court was prepared to uphold the main 'flexible result quota' because it met both of these criteria.[201] The Court also noted that the legitimacy of the substantive equality factors to be taken into account in assessing the suitability of candidates was not challenged in the main proceedings.[202]

Badeck represents an advance on *Marshall* and *Kalanke* because it shifts the presumption in favour of positive action programmes and allows sub-

---

[195] Opinion, para 42.
[196] Judgment, para 14.
[197] Including the 'quota for collective bodies'—see paras 64–6. In the view of the Court this quota was a non-mandatory provision and therefore permitted, to some extent, other criteria to be taken into account.
[198] Para 67.
[199] Para 23 (emphasis added).
[200] Fredman in Shaw, n 138 above at 181.
[201] Para 38.
[202] Para 32.

stantive equality criteria to form part of the individual assessment of merit. Hence, schemes that are designed to guarantee equality of results may be permitted, even without a saving clause, so long as the ultimate assessment takes account of the merit of individual candidates. Most importantly, in a significant and yet underplayed endorsement of the central place that substantive equality has now assumed in Community equalities law, the Court inferred that in the context of national legislation, the merit principle, which is the cornerstone of the equal opportunity ideal,[203] may legitimately reflect the realities of society and, in particular, women's dual burden of work and care.

It followed that the priority given to women in the main Hessen provision was formally subordinate to the reconstituted merit principle and, indeed, had been found by the national court to be compatible with the Federal Constitution on that basis.[204] The importance of this point was borne out when, in *Abrahamsson*,[205] the first Swedish reference on a positive action scheme, the overriding nature of the merit principle formed the basis for the Court's judgment.

Under Swedish legislation a strict 'women's quota' was introduced aimed at increasing the number of female professors in universities. The scheme provided that a candidate belonging to an under-represented sex could be appointed in preference to a candidate from the opposite sex even if they were less qualified. The only proviso was that the difference in their respective qualifications was not so great that the application of the rule would be contrary to the requirement of objectivity in the making of appointments. The Court distinguished *Kalanke*, *Marschall* and *Badeck* on the basis that, in none of those cases was it possible for preference to be given to a less qualified applicant.[206] Whereas the scheme in *Badeck* was clear and sophisticated, incorporating a wide range of clear and well-defined substantive equality criteria upon which merit could be assessed, the Swedish legislation under consideration in *Abrahamsson* was opaque and ambiguous. In the absence of transparent criteria that were amenable to review, the scope and effect of the proviso could not be precisely determined and therefore the presumption in favour of positive action was rebutted because, ultimately, the Swedish quota scheme automatically and unconditionally gave priority to a candidate 'based on the mere fact of belonging to the underrepresented sex' even where 'the merits of the candidate so selected are inferior to those of a candidate of the opposite sex'.[207]

Following the logic of its reasoning in *Badeck*, the Court, having found the scheme incompatible with Article 2(4) of the Equal Treatment

---

[203] See generally, C McCrudden, 'Merit Principles' (1998) 18 *Oxford Journal of Legal Studies* 543.

[204] Opinion, para 36.

[205] Case C–407/98, *Abrahamsson and Anderson v Fogelqvist* [2000] ECR I–5539.

[206] Para 45.

[207] Paras 50–3.

Directive, now turned its attention to Article 141(4) EC. The Court had earlier noted, in reference to the substantive equality criteria in *Badeck* that:[208]

The clear aim of such criteria is to achieve substantive, rather than formal, equality by reducing *de facto* inequalities which may arise in society and thus, in accordance with Article 141(4) EC, to prevent or compensate for disadvantages in the professional career of persons belonging to the under-represented sex.

Hence Article 141(4) EC permits national laws which have substantive equality as their aim, but the Court held that the criteria under which those laws operate must be proportionate to that aim.[209] It followed that the selection method under the Swedish scheme was deemed disproportionate because of its arbitrary nature.[210] While it is self-evident that proportionality should be applied to Article 141(4) EC, the Court has been criticised for not taking full account of the level of under-representation of women among university professors in Sweden and the corresponding need for a strict quota.[211] Such criticism rather misses the point. The problem with the Swedish scheme lay with its lack of sophistication. Indeed, on a broad reading of the judgment, it is submitted that the scheme may have been upheld on the basis of Article 141(4) EC alone had the 'objectivity' proviso been backed up by a set of substantive equality criteria that satisfied the requirements of being 'transparent and amenable to review'.[212] In many respects the package of schemes in *Badeck* provided for a stricter results-oriented quota regime than the rather crude mechanism tested in *Abrahamsson*, and yet, the latter was outlawed not because of its substantive aims, but rather its procedural inadequacies.

After *Marschall* and *Badeck* the contours of Community equalities law have been reshaped. There is now a presumption in favour of positive action measures so long as they clearly provide for a fair and objective assessment of the ability of individual candidates and are proportionate to the aim of substantive equality. The requirement of formal equality may be satisfied by redefining the concept of 'individual merit' to take account of the specific social context that influences an individual's life chances.[213] Once it is accepted that positive action is capable of furthering rather than diminishing the principle of equality, it follows that the proportionality principle permits action which is shown to be necessary to ensure equality in practice.

---

[208] Para 48.

[209] Para 55.

[210] Paras 55–6.

[211] See A Numhauser-Henning, 'Swedish Sex Equality Law before the European Court of Justice' (2001) 30 *Industrial Law Journal* 121 at 125.

[212] Para 49.

[213] See Fredman in Shaw, n 138 above at 194.

The Court's cautious approach to Article 141(4) EC in *Badeck* and *Abrahamsson* was unfortunate. Article 141(4) EC should be taken into account in the interpretation of Article 2(4) of the Directive as AG Saggio suggests rather than being accorded a residual status which is inconsistent with its wider object of 'full equality in practice . . . in working life'. The proportionality test should be applied with this aim in mind. Indeed, the proposed revision of the Equal Treatment Directive goes even further.[214] Article 141(4) EC would be deemed to supersede Article 2(4), which would be deleted and replaced with an obligation on those Member States who maintain, adopt or implement positive actions to submit a biannual report to the Commission who will, in turn, review and publish a comparative assessment of these measures.[215] This amendment will enable the Court to adopt a more coherent approach to positive action in the fields of sex equality and anti-discrimination law where, under the Article 13 EC anti-discrimination directives, positive action measures will be allowed 'to prevent or compensate' for group disadvantage.[216]

Moreover, the Court's jurisprudence on positive action post-*Kalanke* has been mirrored by an increasing willingness on its part to recognise the importance of substantive equality in discrimination cases.[217] For example, in contrast with earlier cases where substantive equality factors were disavowed,[218] the Court in *Gerster*[219] ruled that a system of promotion in the public service which took insufficient account of hours worked by part-time workers was unlawful on the basis that such a provision would 'in practice . . . result in discrimination against women employees as compared with men and must in principle be regarded as contrary to [the Equal Treatment Directive]'.[220] Formally neutral rules on length of service or seniority must, therefore, take account of societal factors and the concept of equal opportunities is equally dynamic for, as AG La Pergola pointed out in his opinion:[221]

---

[214] COM(2001) 321.

[215] *Ibid*. Draft Art 2(4).

[216] Art 5 of the Race Equality Dir, 2000/43/EC, OJ 2000, L180/22, and Art 7(1) of the Framework Employment Dir, 2000/78/EC, OJ 2000, L303/16.

[217] See Mancini and O'Leary, n 173 above at 334–36.

[218] Examples include: Case 184/83, *Hofmann v Barmer Ersatzkasse* [1984] ECR 3047 (division of labour within the family); Case C–399/92, *Stadt Lengerich v Helmig* [1994] ECR I–5727 (domestic or care work outside the workplace); Case C–297/93, *Grau Hupka v Stadtgemeinde Bremen* [1994] ECR I–5535 (child rearing). See further, T Hervey, 'The Future for Sex Equality Law in the European Union' in Hervey and O'Keeffe, n 7 above, 399–413 at 402–3; and G More, 'Equality of Treatment in European Community Law: The Limits of Market Equality' in A Bottomley (ed) *Feminist Perspectives on the Foundational Subjects of Law* (Cavendish, London, 1996) 261–78 at 271–5.

[219] Case C–1/95, *Gerster v Freistaat Bayern* [1997] ECR I–5253. See also Case C–281/97, *Krüger v Kreiskrankenhaus Ebersberg* [1999] ECR I–5127.

[220] Para 34. On this point, see Schiek (1998, *European Law Journal*) n 113 above at 161, who argues that *Marschall* and *Gerster*, read together, will—if applied consistently—'help to revolutionise promotion procedures in public services'.

[221] Opinion, para 40.

Accordingly, the vital stage at which equality counts is the starting point from which a career develops, compensating for the disadvantage which women alone continue to face, by removing the practical obstacles to equal opportunity in the field of employment.

While it is too early to conclude that there has been a radical remodelling of Community equality law along substantive equality lines,[222] these developments are indicative of a transition from an individual to a collective vision of equality based on identifying and remedying group disadvantage.[223]

Finally, it should be noted that positive action is not a panacea. As AG Tesauro correctly observed in *Kalanke*, numerical equality 'will remain illusory and devoid of all substance unless it goes together with measures that are genuinely destined to achieve equality'.[224] Positive action measures often have only a limited impact.[225] Full equality in practice will only be possible once policies have been developed to address structural discrimination in both work and society and to create genuine equal opportunities. The Community Framework Strategy on Gender Equality (2001–2005)[226] signifies a step in this direction by referring to the need to co-ordinate effective gender mainstreaming[227] in order to, inter alia, reduce occupational segregation, challenge gender roles and stereotypes, make it easier to reconcile work and family life, in particular by increasing provision for childcare and care for the elderly.

IV THE AIMS OF ARTICLE 141 EC—FROM THE ECONOMIC TO THE SOCIAL?

Notwithstanding the recasting of the social provisions in Articles 136–145 [ex 117–122] EC, the principle of equal pay between men and women in Article 141 [ex 119] EC remains the most explicit example of a social right enshrined in the Treaties.[228] As the Court recognised in *Defrenne II*,[229] economic rather than social factors were the motivating force behind the inclusion of an obligation on the original Member States to apply the

---

[222] See C Barnard, 'The Principle of Equality in the Community Context: *P, Grant, Kalanke* and *Marschall*: Four Uneasy Bedfellows?' (1998) 57 *Cambridge Law Journal* 352 at 371–2.

[223] See Barnard and Hervey (1998, *Journal of Social Welfare and Family Law*) n 110 above at 339–41. See also the opinion of AG Tesauro in *Kalanke*, para 8.

[224] Para 28. See the critique of Betten & Shrubsall, n 164 above at 75–6.

[225] Fredman in Shaw, n 138 above at 195.

[226] Council Decision 2001/51/EC, OJ 2001, L17/22.

[227] Annex, points 1.3–1.5.

[228] See M Poiares Maduro, 'Striking the Elusive Balance Between Economic Freedom and Social Rights in the EU' in P Alston (ed) *The EU and Human Rights* (OUP, Oxford, 1999) 449–72 at 455.

[229] Case 43/75, *Defrenne v Sabena II* [1976] ECR 455. Discussed in ch 2.

principle of equal pay from 1 January 1962.[230] Hence the introduction and maintenance of the obligation from that point was intended, first and foremost, to avoid unequal conditions of competition between Member States who had established equal pay and those who had not.[231] Having identified the primacy of economic objectives, the Court declared that the Community was 'not merely an economic union' and the principle of equal pay derived some social content from its location in the social provisions of the Treaty,[232] providing a foundation for its later elevation as a 'fundamental right' that forms part of the principle of non-discrimination on grounds of sex.[233]

In *Defrenne II* the Court was seeking to reconcile the apparently irreconcilable by reflecting the social and political environment at a time when the Equal Pay Directive had recently been adopted.[234] Nevertheless, while expressing this 'double aim' as 'at once economic and social',[235] the Court revealed its economic bias when, in deference to economic fears concerning the possible costs for employers,[236] it applied a temporal limitation on its judgment which prevented retrospective claims based on its finding that the principle of equal pay had direct effect.[237] This was to set an unfortunate precedent for later concessions to similar arguments in *Barber* and *Ten Oever*.[238] Further evidence of the Court's willingness to give precedence to market factors over social rights can be found in its development of a test for objective justification which enables arguments concerning the economic needs of undertakings to trump the equality principle.[239]

---

[230] Marking the end of the first stage of the EEC transitional period. See C Barnard, 'The Economic Objectives of Article 119' in Hervey and O'Keeffe, n 7 above, 321–34 at 322.

[231] *Defrenne II*, para 9.

[232] Para 10.

[233] Case 149/77, *Defrenne v Sabena III* [1978] ECR 1365, paras 26–7; Cases 75/82 and 117/82, *Razzouk and Beydoun v Commission* [1984] ECR 1509, para 16; and Case C–13/94, *P v S and Cornwall CC* [1996] ECR I–2143, para 19.

[234] Barnard in Hervey and O'Keeffe, n 230 above at 331.

[235] Para 11.

[236] Paras 69–70. The Court may have been influenced by the fact that these fears were expressed by two new Member States, the UK and Ireland, who had not been granted a transitional period within which to implement equal pay.

[237] Paras 69–75.

[238] Case C–262/88, *Barber v GRE* [1990] ECR I–1889, paras 44–5; and Case C–109/91, *Ten Oever* [1993] ECR I–4879, para 20. In *Barber* and *Ten Oever* the Court restricted *ratione temporis* the effect of its finding that pensions paid by private occupational schemes were 'pay' under Art 119 [now 141] EC. In *Barber* the Court noted arguments by the UK concerning the serious financial consequences that would arise from the fact that many occupational pension schemes in the UK derogate from the principle of equal pay by providing for different pensionable ages (para 44). The Member States had sought to codify this interpretation by attaching a separate Protocol (No 2) to the EC Treaty at Maastricht. See ch 7 for comment.

[239] See Case 170/84, *Bilka Kaufhaus v Weber* [1986] ECR 1607; and Case 127/92, *Enderby v Frenchay HA* [1993] ECR I–5535. Discussed by T Hervey, *Justifications for Sex Discrimination in Employment* (Butterworths, London, 1993) ch 8; and C Barnard, *EC Employment Law*, 2nd edn (OUP, Oxford, 2000) pp 213–20.

On 10 February 2000, nearly 25 years on from *Defrenne II*,[240] the Court delivered a series of rulings in *Schröder*[241] and related references from the German courts[242] arising from the exclusion of part-time workers from supplementary occupational pension schemes. The central issues at stake struck at the heart of the economic/social aims of not just the principle of equal pay but the whole European integration project. Did provisions in national law that enshrined the principle of sex equality and prohibited discrimination against part-time workers entail a retrospective application of the principle of equal pay, notwithstanding the fact that such an interpretation would not only override collective agreements but also risk distortion of competition and have a detrimental economic impact on employers?[243]

In a dynamic interpretation, the Court in *Schröder* answered in the affirmative. The time was ripe to re-evaluate the twofold aim of Article 119 [now 141] EC now that the Amsterdam Treaty had entered into force although it was not applicable in the instant case.[244] In particular, the Court sought to give substance to its social rhetoric in *Defrenne III*[245] and *P v S*[246] when concluding that:[247]

> In view of that case-law, it must be concluded that the economic aim pursued by Article 119 of the Treaty, namely the elimination of distortions of competition between undertakings established in different Member States, is secondary to the social aim pursued by the same provision, which constitutes the expression of a fundamental human right.

It followed that, notwithstanding arguments that the principle of legal certainty and the doctrine of supremacy required Member States to adhere to the temporal limitation in *Defrenne II*, national rules which operated to give retrospective effect to the principle of equal pay and 'ensure a result which conforms with Community law' could be relied upon by individuals.[248] Germany, as one of the original Member States, was entitled to bring in laws which clarified or defined the scope of a rule as it must be or ought to have been understood and applied from the time of its coming into force

---

[240] 8 April 1976.

[241] Case C–50/96, *Deutsche Telekom AG v Schröder* [2000] ECR I–743. Noted by L Besselink (2001) 38 *Common Market Law Review* 437.

[242] Cases C–234–235/96, *Deutsche Telekom AG v Vick and Conze* [2000] ECR I–799; and Cases 270–271/97, *Deutsche Post AG v Sievers and Schrage* [2000] ECR I–929.

[243] This is a reformulation of the first part of the sixth question asked by the national court in *Schröder*.

[244] Mrs Schröder was seeking arrears of pension for the period 20 May 1975 to 31 March 1994.

[245] Case 149/77, *Defrenne v Sabena III* [1978] ECR 1365, paras 26–7. See *Schröder*, para 56.

[246] Case C–13/94, *P v S and Cornwall CC* [1996] ECR I–2143, para 19. *Schröder, ibid.*

[247] Para 57.

[248] Para 48.

which, in the case of equal pay, was 1 January 1962.[249] Hence the doctrine of legal certainty, which provided cover for the Court to capitulate to market-based arguments in *Defrenne II* and *Barber*, was not allowed to stand in the way of national legislation granting part-time workers the social right of retroactive membership of an occupational pension scheme once it had been established that the exclusion of part-time workers from the scheme amounted to discrimination based on sex.

At one level *Schröder* was a relatively straightforward judgment for the Court. The *status quo* on occupational pensions was unaffected. *Schröder* confirms that although part-time workers may join pension schemes, they cannot claim the right to a pension unless they have made the relevant contributions—a de facto temporal limitation.[250] The Court's judgment in *Schröder* also chimes with the politics of subsidiarity[251] and sovereignty because, as Shaw observes,[252] the 'hidden subtext' of the Court's judgment is the long-standing tension between the Court of Justice and the German courts on the issue of fundamental rights and the desire, on the part of the Court, to avoid a constitutional clash.

Nevertheless, even if it is accepted that the Court was only partially motivated by concerns about the status of the equality principle, *Schröder* is significant for two reasons. First, the Court's judgment reveals an acute awareness of the post-Amsterdam process of Europeanisation of social rights arising from the autonomy of the social provisions in Article 136–145 EC, the affirmation of 'fundamental social rights' in Article 136 EC, and the mainstreaming of sex equality in Articles 2 and 3(2) EC. Moreover, the ongoing negotiation of the EU Charter of Fundamental Rights provided an appropriate backdrop for the Court to uphold core social values. Hence, the Court's preparedness to re-evaluate the economic and social aims of Article 119 [now 141] EC forms part of a wider recognition of the equivalence of the social and economic objectives of the Treaty as a whole,[253] as demonstrated by its ruling in *Albany International*,[254] where the Court upheld the Dutch system of compulsory pension funds because of the social task that they perform by protecting all workers, notwithstanding the fact that the operation of such funds might violate Community competition law.[255] The Court

---

[249] Paras 43–7.

[250] See J Shaw, 'Gender and the Court of Justice' in G de Búrca and J Weiler (eds) *The European Court of Justice* (OUP, Oxford, 2001) 87–142 at 123.

[251] On the increasing influence of subsidiarity on the Court, see G de Búrca, 'The Principle of Subsidiarity and the Court of Justice as an Institutional Actor' (1998) 36 *Journal of Common Market Studies* 217.

[252] Shaw in de Búrca and Weiler, n 250 above at 123.

[253] See E Szyszczak, 'The New Paradigm for Social Policy: A Virtuous Circle?' (2001) 28 *Common Market Law Review* 1125 at 1154.

[254] Case C–67/96, *Albany International BV v Stichting Bedrijfspensioenfonds Textielindustrie* [1999] ECR I–5751. Discussed in ch 1.

[255] Paras 88–123.

justified its approach by referring to the 'whole scheme of the Treaty', paying particular attention to social provisions added to the original Treaty by later amendments.[256] However, as with *Schröder*, subsidiarity played a major part in a case where the Court was anxious to assuage national sensitivities concerning the organisation of national social security systems.

Second, the Court's paradigm shift from the economic to the social in *Schröder* provides a basis for a more fundamental reappraisal of the economic bias in the Court's sex equality jurisprudence. Early indications suggest that this process has begun but the Court remains cautious, particularly where Member States seek to justify indirect discrimination on the basis of economic arguments.

In *Jørgensen*[257] the Court was asked to determine whether considerations relating to budgetary stringency, savings or medical practice planning might be regarded as objective factors such as to justify a measure that adversely affects a larger number of women than men? The Court decided that although budgetary considerations may underlie a Member State's choice of social policy, and influence the nature and scope of the social protection measures that it wishes to adopt, they do not themselves constitute an aim pursued by that policy and cannot therefore justify sex discrimination.[258] However, the Court added the caveat that:[259]

As Community law stands at present, social policy is a matter for the Member States, which enjoy a reasonable margin of discretion as regards the nature of social protection measures and the detailed arrangements for their implementation . . . If they meet a legitimate aim of social policy, are suitable and requisite for attaining that end and are therefore justified by reasons unrelated to discrimination on grounds of sex, such measures cannot be regarded as being contrary to the principle of equal treatment . . .

Therefore, while budgetary considerations cannot, in themselves, justify discrimination on the grounds of sex, measures, as in *Jørgensen*, that are intended to ensure sound management of public expenditure on specialised medical care, and to guarantee people's access to such care, may be justified if they meet a legitimate objective of social policy, are appropriate to attain that objective and are necessary to that end.[260] Hence, the Court used the language of *social* aims to justify policy choices that were ultimately driven by *economic* considerations.

Jørgensen has been applied in *Kachelmann*,[261] a case concerning German legislation providing for 'social criteria' to be taken into account in the

---

[256] Paras 54–8.

[257] Case C–226/98, *Jørgensen v Foreningen af Speciallæger* [2000] ECR I–2447.

[258] Para 39. See also, Case C–343/92, *De Weerd and others* [1994] ECR I–571, para 35.

[259] Para 41. See also, Case C–229/89, *Commission v Belgium* [1991] ECR I–2205, paras 19, 22 and 26; and Case C–226/91, *Molenbroek* [1992] ECR I–5943, paras 13, 15 and 19.

[260] Para 42.

[261] Case C–322/98, *Kachelmann v Bankhaus Hermann Lampe KG* [2000] ECR I–7505.

selection of workers for dismissal. Ms Kachelmann was a qualified banker working part-time who was selected for redundancy. She sought to compare her position with that of a full-time employee performing equivalent duties and argued that she had the greatest need on the basis of 'social criteria'. However, the Federal Labour Court had established that, taking account of the employer's right to organise the business of his company, part-time and full-time workers were not comparable for this purpose.

In his opinion, AG Saggio advised that such an interpretation would lead to indirect discrimination because, if part-time workers were predominantly female, they would have less chance of benefiting from 'social criteria' that might favour women.[262] Moreover, referring explicitly to the reformulation of the aims of Article 141 [ex 119] EC in *Schröder*,[263] he observed that 'it is specifically this principle that constitutes the ground for asserting that it is unlawful to take into account only part-time workers for the purposes of the selection according to social criteria'.[264] In this context, the AG referred to the 'conflict of interest that will inevitably exist' between the needs of the company and the needs of part-time workers and therefore of women not to suffer discrimination.[265] In his view it was not possible to make a case for objective justification unrelated to sex on the basis of mere generalisations concerning certain categories of worker.[266]

On the main substantive issue the Court agreed with its AG that the lack of comparability of the social criteria might give rise to a difference of treatment to the detriment of part-time workers.[267] However, without reference to *Schröder* or its case law on equality as a fundamental right, the Court referred to its statement in *Jørgensen* regarding the margin of discretion left to Member States in the area of social policy and noted that the purpose of the legislation in question was to protect workers against dismissal whilst at the same time taking account of the operational needs of the undertaking.[268] In the light of these factors, the Court ruled that the difference in treatment was justified by objective reasons unrelated to sex because if job comparability between full-time and part-time workers were to be introduced in the selection process on the basis of social criteria under German law that would have the effect of placing part-time workers at an advantage, while putting full-time workers at a disadvantage. In the event of their jobs being abolished, part-time workers would have to be offered a full-time job, even if their employment contract did not entitle them to one.[269]

---

[262] Opinion, para 25.
[263] Para 33, note 12. The AG referred to para 57 of the related case of *Sievers and Schrage*, n 242 above which is identical to para 57 of *Schröder*.
[264] *Ibid.*
[265] Para 33.
[266] *Ibid.*
[267] Judgment, para 28.
[268] Paras 30–1
[269] Para 33.

According to the Court, the question of whether part-time workers should enjoy such an advantage was a matter for the national legislature, which alone must find a fair balance in employment law between the various interests concerned.[270]

Whereas *Jørgensen* represents a compromise between the economic and social objectives of Community sex equalities law, *Kachelmann* is a classic case of judicial deference in the face of national legislation that permits the economic interests of the employer to counterbalance the social rights of employees and operates in a manner which, by discriminating against part-time employees, doubly disadvantages women. Moreover, an argument that was essentially based on subsidiarity was used as a basis for denying a woman her 'fundamental right' to equality. In addition to selectively dis-applying the equality principle, the Court took no account of the substantive equality model in its evaluation of the German legislation. While the interpretation proposed by Ms Kachelmann may have benefited part-time workers at the expense of full-time workers, the Court accepted that this provided the necessary objective justification at face value without considering the extent to which societal factors had led to the numerical discrepancy between the numbers of women and men working part-time in Germany. Furthermore, this interpretation necessarily requires consideration of the compatibility of the German legislation with the positive action provisions in Article 2(4) of the Equal Treatment Directive and Article 141(4) EC on the basis that the advantage conferred on part-time workers would help to 'reduce the actual instances of equality which may exist in the real world'.[271]

Is the Court's realignment of the aims of Article 119 [now 141] EC in *Schröder* a chimera? Certainly the logic of the Court's reasoning, based on sex equality as a fundamental right, suggests that the social imperative applies no less forcefully to the Equal Treatment Directive, notwithstanding its origins as a market approximation measure. Furthermore, the reconstituted Article 141 EC not only reformulates the principle of equal pay, but also provides a base for equal treatment measures rooted in the autonomous social provisions in the revised Social Chapter. The mainstreaming of sex equality and the introduction of general non-discrimination directives founded on social values, also points to a more coherent approach that emphasises positive social rights over negative market integration.

Over the last decade the Court has gyrated from a narrow, formalistic and market-driven approach in *Kalanke*, *Grant* and *Kachelmann* to a broad substantive affirmation of the autonomy of sex equality as a fundamental social right in *P v S, Marschall, Badeck* and *Schröder*. Shaw points to the

---

[270] Para 34.
[271] Case C–409/95, *Marschall v Land Nordrhein-Westfalen* [1997] ECR I–6363, para 31.

fact that the Court tends to cloak itself in the politics of gender when seeking to reinforce its own legitimacy but, more often than not, 'the bare realities of legal interpretation' have reasserted themselves, leaving the 'highly formal legacy of an equal treatment principle based on notions of comparison rather than structural disadvantage and societally based inequity'.[272] The post-Amsterdam constitutional settlement will, no doubt, present the Court with further opportunities to choose between respecting and protecting social values, even where there is a conflict with market aims, or adhering to a system in which market integration and free competition is paramount.[273]

[272] Shaw in de Búrca and Weiler, n 250 above at 142.
[273] See T Hervey, 'Social Solidarity: A Buttress Against Internal Market Law?' in Shaw, n 138 above, at 47.

11

The European Employment Strategy—Reinventing Social Policy Governance?

I INTRODUCTION

THE AMSTERDAM IGC is perhaps most readily recalled by images of tortuous late-night negotiations and bicycling political leaders, but the most immediate concerns of the participants can be found in the somewhat arcane Presidency Conclusions in which the Member States once again expressed themselves determined 'to tackle the scourge of unemployment'.[1] The sense of urgency was palpable. Between 1991 and 1996, the EU economy registered its worst post-war performance in growth and employment over a five-year period.[2] Whereas the EU employment rate fell from 62 per cent to 60.5 per cent, the comparative rates for the US and Japan touched a record 75 per cent.[3] Most alarmingly unemployment among the under 25s had risen above 20 per cent, twice the adult level.[4] Moreover, there was considerable diversity between Member States, ranging from 3.3 per cent unemployment in Luxembourg to 22.1 per cent in Spain,[5] threatening the cohesion of the Union. The EU's leaders were faced with the twin challenge of responding to the scale of the unemployment problem while addressing the limitations of existing governmental methods.[6] Moreover, although there was now a consensus that the 'European social model'

---

[1] Amsterdam European Council Presidency Conclusions, 16/17 June 1997, 'Employment, Competitiveness and Growth'. All European Council Presidency Conclusions referred to in this chapter are available at: <http://ue.eu.int/en/Info/eurocouncil/index.htm>.

[2] *Employment in Europe 1997*, COM(97) 479, p 9.

[3] *Ibid* p 10.

[4] *Ibid* p 11.

[5] Eurostat, *Employment Monthly*, July 1997. See V Symes, *Unemployment and Employment Policies in the EU* (Kogan Page, London, 1998) p 5.

[6] See D Trubek and J Mosher, 'New Governance, EU Employment Policy, and the European Social Model' in C Joerges, Y Mény and J Weiler (eds) *Jean Monnet Working Paper No 6/01: Symposium: Mountain or Molehill? A Critical Appraisal of the Commission White Paper on Governance* (New York University School of Law, New York, 2001) Part 9, 1–25 at 4. Available at: <http://www.jeanmonnetprogram.org/papers/01/010601.html>.

would have to 'modernise' in order to survive[7] there was much debate about the form of modernisation required. With the launch of the Euro less than two years hence and, in the wake of the Renault/Vilvoorde affair,[8] there was a need to reconcile macroeconomic, monetary and employment policies[9] and 'sell' the new Employment Title as a unifying and popular project to increasingly cynical and pessimistic EU citizens.[10] To add momentum and breathe life into the Employment Title in advance of formal ratification of the Amsterdam Treaty, an 'extraordinary' European Council was convened in Luxembourg on 20/21 November 1997.

The nascent 'Luxembourg process' was intended to 'mark a new departure' in EU 'thinking and action'[11] after several years of 'soft law discourse'[12] stemming from the Commission's reflective Green and White Papers of the early 1990s.[13] In particular, the Commission's White Paper on Growth, Competitiveness, Employment[14] diagnosed unemployment as Europe's Achilles' heel and prescribed solutions based on radical structural reforms of the labour market. From December 1994, the iterative rhythm of the European Employment Strategy (EES) was established based on the priorities agreed at the Essen European Council.[15] The EES soon developed as a multi-annual and multi-level process for transnational co-ordination of national employment policies around mutually agreed priorities. The experimental working methods of the EES, based entirely on persuasive soft law and legitimated by a conception of subsidiarity where different spheres of action are interrelated,[16] reflected a desire to strike a balance between preserving diversity and a degree of flexibility for national and local actors in the area of employment policy while, simultaneously, emphasising the interdependence of the Union's economic and social objectives and the interconnectedness of nation states who wish to act together for reasons of scale, influence and increased effectiveness in an age of rapid globalisation.[17]

---

[7] See E Szyszczak, 'The New Paradigm for Social Policy: A Virtuous Circle?' (2001) 38 *Common Market Low Review* 1125 at 1126.

[8] See ch 7 for discussion.

[9] See E Szyszczak, 'The Evolving European Employment Strategy' in J Shaw (ed) *Social Law and Policy in an Evolving European Union* (Hart, Oxford, 2000) 197–220 at 199.

[10] See J Goetschy, 'The European employment strategy from Amsterdam to Stockholm: Has it reached its cruising speed?' (2001) 32 *Industrial Relations Journal* 401 at 401.

[11] Luxembourg European Council, Presidency Conclusions, para 1.

[12] See S Sciarra, 'The Employment Title in the Amsterdam Treaty: A Multi-language Legal Discourse' in D O'Keeffe and P Twomey (eds) *Legal Issues of the Amsterdam Treaty* (Hart, Oxford, 1999) 157–70.

[13] For discussion, see ch 7.

[14] *Growth, Competitiveness, Employment: The Challenges and Ways Forward into the 21st Century, Bulletin of the European Communities Supplements* 6/93.

[15] Presidency Conclusions, Essen European Council, 9/10 Dec 1994. See pp 306–7.

[16] See C de la Porte, P Pochet and G Room, 'Social benchmarking, policy making and new governance in the EU' (2001) 11 *Journal of European Social Policy* 291 at 294.

[17] See G de Búrca, *Reappraising Subsidiarity's Significance After Amsterdam*, Harvard Jean Monnet Working Paper 7/99, p 2. Available at: <http://www.jeanmonnetprogram.org/papers>.

This chapter is divided into two main parts. First, there will be an examination of the methodology and objectives of the evolving 'Luxembourg process' which has provided the blueprint for the implementation of a 'new mode of EU governance'[18] now known as the 'open method of co-ordination' (OMC).[19] Secondly, we will evaluate the EU's Social Policy Agenda[20] which, in the framework of the strategic goal of 'more *and* better jobs', has placed a fresh emphasis on the importance of policies that promote 'quality' in work, social policy and industrial relations, to be delivered through a mix of harmonisation, co-ordination, co-operation and partnership. To what extent is there now a fusion of the EU's economic, social and employment policy objectives?

II THE EUROPEAN EMPLOYMENT STRATEGY COMES OF AGE

(1) The 'Luxembourg Process'

Although the basic shape of the EES was soon evident, the 'Essen process' had a twilight existence prior to the Luxembourg 'Jobs Summit'. The priorities agreed at Essen were geared to reconciling the emergent EES with the criteria for EMU and the annual economic guidelines issued under the procedure in Article 99(2) [ex 103(2)] EC. Traditional methods for promoting employment, such as budgetary expansion and use of the exchange rate, were no longer an option.[21] The introduction of 'soft co-ordination'[22] of national strategies for combating unemployment was a pragmatic response by governments who no longer had freedom of manoeuvre in their own right but wished to retain their status as the dominant participants in the European integration process.[23] 'Europeanisation' of policy formulation and decision-making as a response to supranational political and economic considerations[24] was regarded as a desirable alternative to traditional 'hard law' methods of Community regulation through harmonisation. The

[18] See D Hodson and I Maher, 'The Open Method as a New Mode of Governance: The Case of Soft Economic Policy Co-ordination' (2001) 39 *Journal of Common Market Studies* 719.
[19] At the Lisbon European Council, 23/24 March 2000.
[20] COM(2000) 379, approved at the Nice European Council, 7/9 Dec 2000, Presidency Conclusions, Annex I.
[21] See M Gold, P Cressey and C Gill, 'Employment, employment, employment: is Europe working?' (2000) 31 *Industrial Relations Journal* 275 at 276.
[22] See Hodson and Maher, n 18 above who, at 735, distinguish between non-binding guidance and 'hard co-ordination' in the form of the sanctions available under the economic provisions in Art 104(11) [ex 104c(11)] EC.
[23] See C Carter and A Scott, 'Legitimacy and Governance Beyond the European Nation State: Conceptualising Governance in the European Union' in Z Bankowski and A Scott, *The European Union and its Order: The Legal Theory of European Integration* (Blackwell, Oxford, 2000) 131–47 at 131.
[24] *Ibid* at 139.

process was inherently dynamic and innovative, but the informal Essen priorities for stimulating employment were subsumed by the political priorities and tight budgetary demands of the obligatory EMU convergence criteria[25] driven by the parallel process of macroeconomic co-ordination.[26] Essen laid the methodological foundations for the EES but it did not provide a legal framework to implement the employment priorities.[27]

The introduction of Title VIII, Articles 125–130 EC, was spurred by a desire to correct this imbalance. Just as Article 2 EC seeks to reconcile the overarching objectives of 'economic and social progress and a high level of employment', the Employment Title now complements Title VII, Chapter 1 on Economic Policy, Articles 98–104 [ex 102a–104c] EC. Mirroring the economic provisions, employment is now a matter of 'common concern' among the Member States to be co-ordinated within the Council.[28] Thus if a Member State gives employment a low priority or embarks on systematic social dumping it is no longer only a national matter.[29] Both the macroeconomic and employment processes feature co-operation between Member States and complementary Community action including multilateral surveillance, annual guidelines, benchmarking, national reporting and, ultimately, the *political* sanction of recommendations to individual Member States.[30] The principal themes are those of reciprocal learning, shared responsibility, structured but unsanctioned guidance,[31] and a decentralising conception of subsidiarity in which the EU enables and the Member States deliver.[32] Indeed, within the Member States, delivery may be delegated to local actors and the social partners.

In order to encourage the synchronisation of the EU's macroeconomic and employment policies[33] simultaneous resolutions were issued at

[25] See Protocol No 6 on the convergence criteria referred to in Art 109j(1) [now 121(1)] EC. The criteria are: price stability—inflation must not exceed 1.5% above the average of the three best performing Member States; budget deficits—not exceeding 3% of GDP and a public debt to GDP ratio of less than 60% of GDP; exchange rate—staying within the normal fluctuation margins of the ERM (currently 2.5%) for at least two years; and interest rates—must not exceed 2% above the three best performing Member States over the previous year.

[26] See further, J Kenner, 'Employment and Macroeconomics in the EC Treaty: A Legal and Political Symbiosis?' (2000) 7 *Maastricht Journal* 375; and D Ashiagbor, 'EMU and the Shift in the European Labour Law Agenda: From 'Social Policy' to 'Employment Policy" (2001) 7 *European Law Journal* 311.

[27] See Szyszczak (2001, *Common Market Law Review*) n 7 above at 1136.

[28] Art 126(2) EC, closely following Art 99(1) [ex 103(1)] EC.

[29] See A Larsson, 'Employment is a Matter of Common Concern', *Employment and Industrial Relations International* (EIRI, Dublin, Aug 1997) 18–21 at 18.

[30] Compare Arts 127–9 EC with Articles 99(2)–(5) [ex 103(2)–(5)] EC. On this point, see M Biagi, 'The Implementation of the Amsterdam Treaty with Regard to Employment: Co-ordination or Convergence?' (1998) 14 *International Journal of Comparative Labour Law and Industrial Relations* 325 at 327.

[31] See Trubek and Mosher, n 6 above at 3.

[32] See J Kenner, 'The EC Employment Title and the 'Third Way': Making Soft Law Work?' (1999) *International Journal of Comparative Labour Law and Industrial Relations* 33 at 48.

[33] See further, Kenner (2000, *Maastricht Journal*) n 26 above at 386.

Amsterdam on the 'Stability and Growth Pact'[34] and 'Growth and Employ-ment'.[35] Whereas the former was concerned with enforcing tight budgetary discipline and, as a last resort, imposing sanctions on Member States with 'excessive' budget deficits,[36] the latter sought to offer a 'new impulse' for keeping employment firmly at the top of the political agenda.[37] References in the Pact to the sanctions available under the Economic Chapter highlight the fact that similar punishment cannot be meted out against recalcitrant states under the Employment Title. Moreover, of equal significance is the fact that whilst Article 128(2) EC places a duty on the EU institutions to take account of the economic guidelines when drawing up the employment guidelines, there is no corresponding obligation in the Economic Chapter.[38] This lacuna was addressed by the Resolution on Growth and Employment whereby:[39]

The Council is . . . *called upon* to take the multi-annual employment programmes . . . into account when formulating the broad [economic] guidelines, in order to strengthen their employment focus. The Council *may make* the necessary recom-mendations to the Member States, in accordance with [Article 99(4) [ex 103(4)] EC].

Added stimulus was provided in the Amsterdam Presidency Conclusions, which referred, for the first time, to 'full employment' as the ultimate goal but did not specify a precise target.[40] Whilst this might suggest an equiva-lence of political status for the twin objectives of economic stability and employment growth, the legal effectiveness of the employment guidelines is undermined by the lack of a specific 'hard law' obligation on the Council to act in accordance with the employment priorities and the absence of a matching Treaty commitment. Article 4 EC ensures that the economic activ-ities of both the Member States and the Community must be pursuant to the primary objective of maintaining price stability and an open market economy with free competition.[41] This entails compliance with the guiding principles of stable prices, sound public finances and monetary conditions and a sustainable balance of payments.[42] The Stability and Growth Pact is

---

[34] OJ 1997, C236/1.

[35] OJ 1997, C236/3.

[36] Under the procedure laid down in Art 104(11) [ex 104c(11)] EC. The Pact was swiftly reinforced on 7 July 1997 by Reg 1466/97/EC on the strengthening of the surveillance of bud-getary positions and the surveillance and co-ordination of economic policies, OJ 1997, L209/1; and Council Reg 1467/97/EC on speeding up and clarifying the implementation of the exces-sive deficit procedure, OJ 1997, L209/6. Discussed by S Ball, 'The European Employment Strategy: The Will but not the Way?' (2001) 30 *Industrial Law Journal* 353 at 361.

[37] Resolution on Growth and Employment, point 1.

[38] See Art 99(2) [ex 103(2)] EC.

[39] Point 5. Emphasis added.

[40] Presidency Conclusions, p 3.

[41] Art 4(2) EC.

[42] Art 4(3) EC.

the principal mechanism for guaranteeing such compliance. Hence, while the employment guidelines are to be taken into account in the formulation of the economic guidelines as a matter of policy, the economic imperative is more explicit in the EC Treaty and is ultimately paramount.

In the Presidency Conclusions at Luxembourg the European Council sought to closely align the two sets of guidelines on the basis that:[43]

> The idea is, while respecting the differences between the two areas and between the situations in the individual Member States, to create for employment, as for economic policy, *the same resolve to converge* towards jointly set, verifiable, regularly updated targets.

Unfortunately, this rhetorical commitment was not reflected in the detail of the Council Resolution approving the 1998 Employment Guidelines.[44] The Commission, seeking to add substance to the concept of 'full employment', attempted to introduce quantitative employment targets to match the EMU convergence criteria. The draft guidelines contained a long-term target of 70 per cent labour market participation broadly in line with the US and Japan.[45] In the Commission's view, a five-year target participation rate of 65 per cent was achievable, up from the 1997 level of 60.5 per cent. This would involve the creation of at least 12 million jobs. The Commission also sought to establish targets for reducing the gap between male and female employment. The European Council, viewing quantitative targets as a hostage to fortune, proposed merely to 'arrive at a significant increase in the employment rate in Europe on a lasting basis'.[46] Nevertheless, while the European Council preferred to limit the number of quantifiable targets, the Commission's proposed structure was endorsed and a cyclical process put in place that has been retained, largely untouched, throughout the first five years of the 'Luxembourg process'.

The architecture of the EES now consists of six horizontal objectives, four vertical pillars and approximately 20 individual guidelines. The horizontal objectives were first included in the 2001 Employment Guidelines and they will be placed in context once we have discussed the priorities introduced at the Lisbon European Council in March 2000. Before assessing the methodology and effectiveness of the process in more detail, let us first consider the policy impulses behind the guidelines. The four pillars are: improving *employability*; developing *entrepreneurship*; encouraging *adaptability*; and strengthening *equal opportunities*. Detailed examination of the 1998 Employment Guidelines reveals several contradictory influences reflecting many underlying and unresolved tensions inherited from the 'Essen priorities'.[47]

---

[43] Para 3. Emphasis added.
[44] Council Resolution of 15 Dec 1997, OJ 1998, C30/1.
[45] COM(97) 497.
[46] Presidency Conclusions, para 52.
[47] See Szyszczak in Shaw, n 9 above at 202.

First, the language used is laden with the revisionist terminology of the 'Third Way' policy agenda associated with Bill Clinton's 'New Democrats' in the US and the 'New Labour' administration of Tony Blair elected in the UK in May 1997. Seeking to transcend 'Old Left' statism and 'New Right' neo-liberalism,[48] the 'Third Way' has served as a *leitmotif* for a series of policy responses to fundamental changes and dilemmas posed by globalisation, individualism and the remoteness of government.[49] Hence, the emphasis of governmental activity has been switched from 'welfare to work'—or from passive to active labour market measures—and promoting public/private partnerships rather than traditional nationalisation. Under this model, social progress is founded upon individual empowerment and the vital role of governments is to foster 'competitive solidarity'[50] by enabling, not commanding, the individual and harnessing the power of the market to serve the public interest.[51] Notable among the first set of guidelines were specific commitments that closely resembled Blair's 'New Deal' for the unemployed and related strategies. Take, for example, the firm targets set in the pillar of employability under which Member States 'will ensure' that every unemployed person is offered a new start before reaching one year, or in the case of young persons, six months of unemployment, in the form of training, retraining, work practice, a job, or other employability measure.[52] Active labour market measures to secure employability include training for at least 20 per cent of the unemployed, more apprenticeships and the promotion of lifelong learning.[53]

Secondly, the guidelines were influenced by the highly contested but prevailing view of the OECD[54] and neo-liberal economists that 'labour market rigidities', such as business taxes, wage structures and 'benefit disincentives', are at the root of unemployment in Europe and have contributed to a widening of the employment gap with the US.[55] In particular, the pillar of entrepreneurship has a distinctly deregulatory edge and owes much to the North American model, which is perceived as highly mobile, flexible and business friendly. Commitments include: cutting burdens for businesses;

---

[48] See T Blair, *The Third Way: New Politics for the New Century* (Fabian Society, London, 1998). Discussed by Kenner (1999, *International Journal of Comparative Labour Law and Industrial Relations*) n 32 above.

[49] See generally, A Giddens, *The Third Way* (Polity Press, Cambridge, 1998) pp 27–68.

[50] See W Streeck, 'Competitive Solidarity: Rethinking the 'European Social Model'', MPIfG Working Paper 99/8 (Max-Planck-Institut für Sozialforschung, Cologne, September 1999) p 3.

[51] Blair, n 48 above, p 7.

[52] Guideline 1 in the 1998 Employment Guidelines, Council Doc 13200/97 adopted in a Council Resolution of 15 Dec 1997.

[53] *Ibid*. Guidelines 3–5.

[54] See for example, *The OECD Jobs Study: Evidence and Explanations. Part II: The Adjustment Potential of the Labour Market* (OECD, Paris, 1994).

[55] See H Siebert, 'Labor Market Rigidities: At the Root of Unemployment in Europe' (1997) 11 *Journal of Economic Perspectives* 37; cf S Nickell, 'Unemployment and Labour Market Rigidities: Europe versus North America' (1997) 11 *Journal of Economic Perspectives* 55.

reducing tax and social security obstacles to self-employment and setting up small businesses; and reversing the long-term trend towards higher taxes and charges on labour.[56] However, although the Commission sought to focus policy on 'correcting' the problems caused by such 'rigidities'[57] and recommended a guideline on wage moderation,[58] the Member States did not accept the full thrust of these arguments and the resulting guidelines were somewhat platitudinous.

Thirdly, the pillar of adaptability was a by-product of the Commission's Green Paper on Partnership for a New Organisation of Work[59] and earlier initiatives[60] which, as a counterpoint to the deregulatory thrust of the entrepreneurship pillar, sought to match flexibility with security by emphasising new forms of work organisation based on high skills, high trust and high quality 'flexible firms'.[61] 'Adaptability' offers the prospect of a distinctly European solution in which organisational innovation is the means to boost growth in employment within a framework capable of preserving decent labour standards and sustainable levels of social protection. From this perspective, globalisation, far from being a threat to the European economy, can be seen as an opportunity to be grasped.[62] The Green Paper emphasised the 'partnership' model whereby both sides of industry accept the challenge to fundamentally renew their organisation.[63] The guidelines on adaptability aim to modernise work organisation and forms of work primarily through sectoral and enterprise agreements.[64] The Commission's recent success in reviving the European Company Statute[65] and introducing a Directive on establishing a general framework for informing and consulting employees[66] must be understood in this context. Member States are also encouraged under the guidelines to introduce more adaptable types of employment contract.[67] Both the language and content of the ensuing

---

[56] 1998 Employment Guidelines 8–12.

[57] See *Employment In Europe 1997*, COM(97) 479, p 3.

[58] See Trubek & Mosher, n 6 above at 9.

[59] COM(97) 127. For the background, see ch 7.

[60] Such as the ADAPT Community initiative introduced in the Structural Funds' programming period 1994–1999 which, under Art 146 [ex 123] EC, is intended to facilitate workers' 'adaptation to industrial changes and changes in production systems, in particular through vocational training and retraining'. For details, see the Social Fund Reg 2084/93/EEC, OJ 1993, L193/39.

[61] See S Deakin and H Reed, 'The Contested Meaning of Labour Market Flexibility: Economic Theory and the Discourse of European Integration' in Shaw, n 9 above, 71–99 at 72.

[62] See A Supiot, *Beyond Employment: Changes in Work and the Future of Labour Law in Europe* (OUP, Oxford, 2001) p 193.

[63] COM(97) 127, para 82.

[64] 1998 Employment Guideline 13.

[65] Reg 2157/2001/EC on the Statute for a European Company (SE), OJ 2001, L294/1; and Dir 2001/86/EC supplementing the Statute for a European company with regard to the involvement of employees, OJ 2001, L294/22.

[66] Dir 2002/14/EC, OJ 2002, L80/29.

[67] 1998 Employment Guideline 14.

framework agreements on Part-time Work and Fixed-term Work[68] chime with this agenda.

Fourthly, the pillar on strengthening equal opportunities arose from the strategy of mainstreaming of gender equality in the Fourth Action Programme on Equal Opportunities for Men and Women[69] and the Community obligation to aim to eliminate inequalities and promote equality between men and women in Article 3(2) EC. The equal opportunities pillar stresses four interlinked themes:[70] tackling gender gaps in employment generally and particular sectors; reconciling work and family life, including adequate childcare provision; facilitating return to work after absence; and, as a by-product of the Helios II programme,[71] integrating people with disabilities into working life. The equal opportunities pillar also provides a platform for the Community initiative 'EQUAL' which utilises the structural funds to promote a horizontal approach to combating all forms of discrimination and integrating persons excluded from the labour market by means of 'transnational co-operation' under Articles 13 and 137 EC.[72]

Next, we need to examine the methodology of the EES. The annual cycle can be divided up into four stages:[73]

(1) The Council adopts employment guidelines on the basis of a recommendation from the Commission following consultation with Community institutions[74] and the Employment Committee.[75]
(2) Each Member State submits a national action plan outlining the employment situation and steps taken to implement the guidelines and comply with any recommendations after consulting national social partners.
(3) The Commission and Council issue a joint employment report consisting of a general section summarising the employment situation in the EU across the four pillars and a detailed assessment of the performance of each Member State taking account of any recommendations adopted by the Council.

---

[68] Respectively, Dir 97/81/EC, OJ 1998, L14/9, and Dir 99/70/EC, OJ 1999, L175/43.

[69] See COM(95) 381 and Decision 95/593/EC on a medium-term Community action programme on equal opportunities for men and women (1996 to 2000), OJ 1995, L335/37.

[70] 1998 Employment Guidelines 16–19.

[71] Decision 93/136/EEC, establishing a Third Community Action Programme to assist Disabled People, OJ 1993, L56/30.

[72] See COM(2000) 853.

[73] Following the procedure laid down in Art 128 EC.

[74] The European Parliament, the Economic and Social Committee and the Committee of the Regions must be formally consulted.

[75] Formally established, in accordance with Art 130 EC, by Decision 2000/98/EC, OJ 2000, L29/21. The Employment Committee replaces the Employment and Labour Market Committee previously established by Decision 97/16/EC, OJ 1997, L6/32. The social partners are represented on a separate Standing Committee on Employment set up under Decision 99/207/EC, OJ 1999, L72/33.

(4) Based on a proposal from the Commission, and after consultation with the Employment Committee and the Economic Policy Committee,[76] the Council may adopt recommendations directed at individual Member States with a view to correcting specific problems in their employment performance.

Each year the guidelines are revised, progress is closely monitored by reference to performance indicators or benchmarks, new ideas are introduced and goals are ratcheted up.[77] For the Member States, participating in the EES is akin to stepping onto a steadily moving escalator leading inexorably towards a *convergence of objectives*. Thus while the guidelines are normative in character and effect,[78] in the sense that it is mandatory for Member States to take them into account, they are not intended, nor have the capacity to produce, a settled framework of binding rules. Rather, the guidelines are intended to be transformative over the long-term, imparting a repetitive soft law narrative to be interpreted and reinterpreted by a multiplicity of actors leading, cumulatively, to a synthesis of policy approaches by Member States but no single model. The aim is to produce a cross-fertilisation of ideas and methods designed to channel an effective and socially protective response to global change by prioritising ends not means.

During the first cycle, 1998–99, the Commission's approach was to encourage and persuade rather than censor individual Member States.[79] Emphasis was placed on continuity and consistency based on the four pillars. By April 1998, all Member States had produced national action plans (NAPs) and, three months later, implementation reports based on the guidelines. The UK Minister for Europe, in an assessment of the British Presidency in the first six months of 1998, reiterated the view that employment policy would remain largely a matter for national governments.[80] The value of the exercise was regarded as one of 'peer review and exchange of best practice'. However, in the 1998 Joint Employment Report a number of shortcomings in the process were identified.[81] One factor had been the rush to produce NAPs before many Member States had thought through their strategies or reconciled the plans with their budgetary commitments.[82]

---

[76] This Committee, originally established in 1974, has been reconstituted to oversee all aspects of macroeconomic policy coordination: Decision 2000/604/EC, OJ 2000, L257/28.

[77] See Trubek and Mosher, n 6 above at 10.

[78] See Biagi, n 30 above at 160.

[79] For the Commission's detailed analysis, see COM(98) 316. For a comprehensive analysis of the early phases of the 'Luxembourg process', see J Goetschy, 'The European Employment Strategy: Genesis and Development' (1999) 5 *European Journal of Industrial Relations* 117.

[80] D Henderson, 'The UK Presidency: An Insider's View' (1998) 36 *Journal of Common Market Studies* 563 at 567.

[81] *Employment Policies in the EU and in the Member States* (European Communities, Luxembourg, 1999).

[82] *Ibid* p 15.

Moreover, although the involvement of multiple interlocutors at national and European levels was welcomed, it also raised concerns about making the whole process more complex and cumbersome.[83]

The shared approach of the Commission and Council in this early phase was to consolidate the existing guidelines and streamline the reporting procedures.[84] Nevertheless, several distinctive strands of the evolving EES were emerging. First, it was soon apparent that the EES was about more than mere 'state watching'.[85] Although the Commission held back at this stage from proposing any recommendations to individual Member States and sought to issue selective praise in roughly equal measure, it was noted that the 'challenge' to improve was greatest in Italy, Spain and Greece.[86] The ground was being prepared for the development of a cajoling and ultimately 'naming and shaming'[87] approach designed to spur competition between Member States.

Secondly, the Commission and Council used the joint employment report as a vehicle to initiate a monitoring system to assess the implementation of the guidelines by describing the starting position of each Member State, on a comparable basis, with respect to a number of key areas of labour market performance.[88] The method chosen was to highlight the top three States across eight performance indicators.[89] Hence, the best performances became the reference standard or 'benchmark' for those countries to retain and for others to emulate.[90] The aim was to promote change and achieve a continuous improvement in national policies through a process of mutual learning[91] and indirect coercion.[92] Significantly, the benchmarks chosen tended to reflect quantitative rather than qualitative factors—striving to achieve more jobs possibly at the expense of better jobs[93]—and reflected the overriding aim of catching up with the employment participation rate of the US.

Benchmarking has swiftly become the principal methodology of the EES. At one level 'benchmarking' leads to a 'Europeanisation' or policy

---

[83] *Ibid.*

[84] *Ibid.*

[85] Szyszczak in Shaw, n 9 above at 209.

[86] COM(98) 316, p 5.

[87] See Szyszczak (2001, *Common Market Law Review*) n 7 above at 1147.

[88] Joint Employment Report 1998, p 19.

[89] *Ibid* pp 19–26. The following performance indicators were used: employment growth; employment rate; employment gender gap; employment rate 50–64; unemployment rate; youth unemployment ratio; unemployment gender gap; and long-term unemployment share.

[90] Finland and Austria emerged as the top performers with four top three rankings each, followed by Sweden, Luxembourg and Finland with three, the UK, Ireland and the Netherlands with two, and Germany featured once. Six Member States failed to achieve a top three place in any category: France, Italy, Spain, Greece, Belgium and Portugal.

[91] See de la Porte *et al*, n 16 above at 292.

[92] See Hodson and Maher, n 18 above at 727.

[93] See Ball, n 36 above at 370.

transfer[94] of employment policies, with the Commission playing a vital co-ordinating role in seeking to engineer convergence, and yet, it can also be seen as a form of 'renationalisation'[95] whereby the process is driven by national best practice rather then rules 'imposed from Brussels'. The main weakness of benchmarking, as a tool of governance is that it is best suited to organisations that have identical, or similar, objectives.[96] Difficulties arise because of the diversity of the EU, differences in the social and political context of Member States being compared, and variations in the size and scale of the employment challenge.[97] Member States may prefer local solutions to fit with their own circumstances but the benchmarks are 'top-down' rather than 'bottom-up' and tend to reflect the inherent policy tensions within the guidelines. Moreover, even if the benchmarks can be agreed, the ways and means to pursue them are often hotly disputed.[98]

Thirdly, the social partners were involved, in varying degrees, in formulating and monitoring the first round of NAPs.[99] Inclusion of the social partners and, in the longer-term, other members of 'civil society', is regarded by advocates of a reformed European governance as crucial both for policy input, to ensure a grass roots contribution to the detailed analysis of Europe's employment ills, and as a means of involving relevant 'stakeholders' in the process of policy formulation at every level.[100] The development of partnership in policy formulation at national level, originally fostered as a tool of European governance when the Community's Structural Funds were reformed in 1988,[101] has become an increasingly important strand of the deliberative process of the EES. Over time, as we shall see in Section III of this chapter, this theme has emerged as a central element of the 'open method of co-ordination' and, as a means of increasing participation and improving transparency, a main plank of the Commission's White Paper on European Governance of July 2001.[102]

Further consolidation took place with the publication of the 1999 Employment Guidelines, which contained only minor modifications.[103] Significantly, the additional guidelines were of a qualitative nature and included: a review of the tax and benefit system to provide incentives for the unemployed and inactive to enhance their employability;[104] and pre-

---

[94] Hodson and Maher, n 18 above at 722.
[95] See Goetschy (2001, *Industrial Relations Journal*) n 10 above at 403.
[96] See de la Porte *et al*, n 16 above at 292.
[97] *Ibid*.
[98] *Ibid* at 295.
[99] Joint Employment Report 1998, p 6.
[100] See de la Porte *et al*, n 16 above at 293; cf P Allott, 'European Governance and the Re-branding of Democracy' (2002) 27 *European Law Review* 60.
[101] See J Scott, 'Law, Legitimacy and EC Governance: Prospects for 'Partnership" (1998) 36 *Journal of Common Market Studies* 175.
[102] COM(2001) 428.
[103] Council Resolution of 22 Feb 1999, OJ 1999, C69/2.
[104] *Ibid*. Guideline 4.

ventative and active policies to meet the employment integration needs of the disabled, ethnic minorities and other disadvantaged groups.[105]

The 1999 Joint Employment Report and the 2000 Employment Guidelines marked the end of the pre-Lisbon phase of the 'Luxembourg process'. For the first time the Commission proposed recommendations to individual Member States under the procedure in Article 128(4) EC.[106] In the Commission's view, the EU was failing to fulfil its employment potential and lacked a sufficiently vibrant entrepreneurial culture. The estimated 'full employment potential' of the Union—defined by the Commission as the level of employment that would be achieved if all Member States performed as well as the best, or as well as the US—was some 30 million people— twice the number of recorded unemployed.[107] Hence, although the EU had marginally improved its performance since 1995, the gap between the EU and US had widened considerably.[108] The Commission identified eight areas from across the four pillars where national implementation remained insufficient.[109] These were: the fight against youth unemployment; preventing long-term unemployment; tax reforms and unemployment benefit reforms; job creation in the service sector; making the tax system more friendly; modernising the organisation of work; the fight against gender inequalities; and improving indicators and statistical tools.

Significantly, the least criticised countries were those with high social standards, strong productivity levels and low unemployment (Denmark, Sweden and Finland). Other countries with low unemployment or a rapidly improving position were also praised (Luxembourg, the Netherlands, Portugal and Austria). Notably, the UK, which had attuned itself most closely with the North American model and had achieved a participation rate above 70 per cent, was criticised, nonetheless, for a gender gap in full-time employment and persisting long-term unemployment among older people, ethnic minorities, lone parents and deprived communities. However, the Commission reserved its strongest criticism for 'three laggards' who were responsible, in its view, for depressing the EU employment rate (Germany, France and Italy) through a combination of high labour costs and low participation rates.[110]

Not surprisingly, the Commission's suggestions met with a frosty response from several Member States who were irritated by excessive

---

[105] *Ibid.* Guideline 9.
[106] The Commission's proposals were issued on 8 Sep 1998:
http://europa.eu.int/comm/dg05/empl&esf/empl99.
[107] *Community Policies in Support of Employment* (Brussels, European Commission, 2000) p 2.
[108] The US Bureau of Labor Statistics estimated job growth of 14% in the US between 1996 and 2006, compared with 19% over the preceding 10 years: *Employment in Europe, 1999* (European Commission, Brussels, 1999) p 86.
[109] See further, Goetschy (2001, *Industrial Relations Journal*) n 10 above at 411.
[110] See *Employment in Europe 2000* (European Commission, Brussels, 2000) p 6.

'finger-pointing'[111] and regarded the EES as essentially a revolving process of information exchange between the European Council and national administrations. However, the Commission was tactically astute, identifying shortcomings in the performance of all Member States. Eventually a Council Recommendation on the implementation of the Member States' employment policies was adopted in February 2000.[112] The Council warned that 'recommendations should be used sparingly, should concentrate on priority issues and should be based on sound and accurate analysis'.[113] Nevertheless, of the 55 recommendations proposed by the Commission, 52 were finally approved. The adoption of the Recommendation was a coup for the Commission, which now regards specific recommendations to Member States as a central part of the annual process. This view appears to have been reluctantly accepted by the Council, which, by issuing further recommendations on the same basis in 2001[114] and 2002,[115] has regularised the process within the annual cycle.

Recommendations are effective as a means of applying political and peer pressure on Member States to converge towards a particular benchmark but the structural reforms that they require may be alien to the policy objectives or traditions of some countries.[116] Therefore, while compliance with the recommendations may lead to the transposition and diffusion of policies from one Member State to another,[117] the effectiveness of such action will vary according to the particular social and political context and the appropriateness of the policy solution. As Szyszczak notes, the real test, in the absence of a power to sanction, will be how far the recommendations are observed in practice.[118]

One other feature of the first phase was the introduction of parallel 'processes' designed to complement and mainstream the EES in accordance with Article 127(2) EC. For example, at Cardiff in June 1998 the European Council introduced a new process of co-ordination of economic reforms alongside the 'Luxembourg process'. The 'Cardiff process' involves cyclical co-ordination of structural reforms in services, products and capital markets. Further, at the Cologne European Council of June 1999, a third pillar of co-ordination was introduced in the form of 'macroeconomic dialogue' under the 'European Employment Pact',[119] effectively superseding the pre-Amsterdam 'Confidence Pact for Employment'.[120] 'Macroeconomic

---

[111] See de la Porte *et al*, n 16 above at 295.
[112] Recommendation 2000/164/EC, OJ 2000, L52/32.
[113] *Ibid* recital 3.
[114] OJ 2001, L22/27.
[115] OJ 2002, L60/70.
[116] See de la Porte *et al*, n 16 above at 295.
[117] See Szyszczak (2001, *Common Market Law Review*) n 7 above at 1145.
[118] Szyszczak in Shaw, n 9 above at 218.
[119] See paras 7–20 and Annex I of the Presidency Conclusions.
[120] *Action for Employment in Europe*, COM(96) 485.

dialogue' is intended to involve the social partners and employment, fiscal and monetary policy-makers within existing institutions. In the course of this dialogue, ideas are exchanged on how to co-ordinate the employment strategy and economic reforms.[121] The status of employment as the EU's highest policy priority is a precondition for such dialogue. Sensitive reforms in areas such as wages, social security reforms and taxation, can be pursued indirectly through dialogue as an alternative to explicit 'top-down' guidelines and recommendations that would almost certainly be unworkable. As with the earlier 'Confidence Pact', the main aim is to stimulate activity on the ground and, in particular, encourage the parties at national, regional and sectoral levels to sign up to 'social pacts' that allow structural reforms to go ahead at a pace that is acceptable to all actors.[122]

Each of these processes is aimed at building a consensus around economic and social policies leading to convergence through networking and multi-level co-ordination. The introduction of new processes is intended to create an atmosphere of 'continuous revolution' leading to organisational change and greater efficiency. Naming each process after European Council venues not only satisfies the hosts, but also emphasises the growing importance of the European Council rather than the Commission or the European Parliament in what is essentially an inter-governmental process where flexibility of procedure and choice of actors is, as Barnard observes,[123] being used to achieve labour market flexibility, in particular functional flexibility at micro level.[124]

Multi-dimensional and multi-annual policy co-ordination is attractive not only because it is driven by a desire to avoid conflict and seeks to be pluralistic but also, as an ongoing process, it offers the prospect of long-term depoliticised European solutions to seemingly intractable national problems. In the view of the Commission, it is vital to promote new forms of European governance to give people a greater say in how Europe is run and build new forms of partnership between the different levels of governance in Europe.[125] There are, however, a number of disadvantages. In particular, the involvement of a multiplicity of actors in myriad processes leads to organisational overload and complexity. Moreover, the ad hoc nature and remoteness of such processes, which may be regarded as little more than a circuitous dialogue between élites, runs counter to incessant demands for

---

[121] Annex I of the Presidency Conclusions, Council Resolution, paras 1–7.

[122] For examples, see Gold *et al*, n 21 above; and M Rhodes and Y Mény, *The Future of European Welfare: A New Social Contract* (Macmillan, Basingstoke, 1998) and M Rhodes, 'Globalization, Labour Markets and Welfare States: A Future of 'Competititve Corporatism'?' 178–203 at 189–94.

[123] See C Barnard, 'Flexibility and Social Policy' in G de Búrca and J Scott (eds) *Constitutional Change in the EU: From Uniformity to Flexibility* (Hart, Oxford, 2000) 197–217 at 215.

[124] See further Rhodes, n 122 above.

[125] *Strategic Objectives 2000–2005: 'Shaping the New Europe'*, COM(2000) 154, p 5.

greater transparency and legitimacy. Above all, in order to make such processes effective, clear long-term strategic goals are required together with a more systematic methodological approach to co-ordination that complements the traditional Community method of policy formulation and decision-making. It was with this task in mind that Europe's leaders gathered at Lisbon in March 2000 determined to make their mark on the new millennium.

(2) The 'Lisbon Process' and the Open Method of Co-ordination

In preparation for the Lisbon meeting the Commission published a Communication entitled 'Strategic Objectives 2000–2005: "Shaping the New Europe"'.[126] The Commission identified four strategic objectives to be pursued over a five-year period: promoting new forms of European governance; a stable Europe with a stronger voice in the world; a new economic and social agenda; and a better quality of life.[127] Taking up themes later echoed in its policy document on the Social Policy Agenda,[128] the Commission called for policies aimed at building a competitive and inclusive knowledge-based economy capable of promoting strong and sustained growth, full employment and social cohesion.[129] Each of the strategic objectives was intended to mark a distinctive European response to the challenge of globalisation for:[130]

Europe's challenge must be to make globalisation compatible with the common interest . . . We must maximise its potential and minimise the undesirable side-effects.

Over the space of just 41 paragraphs, the European Council at Lisbon sought to confront the 'quantum shift' arising from globalisation and the knowledge-driven economy.[131] Responding to the challenge posed by the Commission, the European Council initially observed that these changes were affecting every aspect of people's lives and would require a radical transformation of the European economy, before ambitiously declaring that the Union 'must shape these changes in a manner consistent with its values and concepts of society and also with a view to the forthcoming enlargement'.[132] In order to secure this ambition the European Council sought to strengthen employment, economic reform and social cohesion. Over the

---

[126] COM(2000) 154, p 5.
[127] *Ibid* p 5.
[128] COM(2000) 379.
[129] COM(2000) 154, p 9.
[130] *Ibid* p 8.
[131] Lisbon European Council Presidency Conclusions, 23/24 Mar 2000, para 1.
[132] *Ibid*.

next decade, the Union would set itself a new strategic goal 'to become the most competitive and dynamic knowledge-based economy in the world capable of sustainable economic growth with more and better jobs and greater social cohesion'.[133] Achieving this goal would require an overall strategy that would include: structural reforms for competitiveness and innovation; modernising the 'European social model', investing in people and combating social exclusion; and applying an appropriate macro-economic policy mix.[134] This strategy would be designed 'to enable the Union to regain the conditions for full employment and to strengthen regional cohesion' against a 'sound macroeconomic background' with an average economic growth rate of 3 per cent a 'realistic prospect'.[135]

Three significant steps taken at Lisbon to underpin this new strategy are worthy of particular note. First, a 'mid-term review' of the EES was to be conducted to give new impetus to the process.[136] Although the EES had enabled Europe to 'substantially reduce' unemployment there were still 15 million people out of work.[137] More concrete targets were now required and increased involvement of the social partners in drawing up, implementing and following up the guidelines. The review would address four key areas:[138] improving employability and reducing skills gaps; giving higher priority to lifelong learning; increasing employment in services; and furthering all aspects of equal opportunities including reconciliation between work and family life. New benchmarks would be set on lifelong learning and improved childcare provision. Most importantly, in an important shift, the Member States, having now firmly identified 'full employment' as the measure of success in achieving the strategic goal, were prepared to lay down precise targets to raise the average employment rate from 61 per cent to 70 per cent by 2010 and increase women's employment participation from 51 per cent to 60 per cent over the same period.[139]

Each Member State would now be expected to set national targets for an increased employment rate while recognising their different starting points. Enlarging the labour force would be the key to reinforcing the sustainability of social protection systems.[140] Hence, despite the professed commitment to achieving an increase in the quantity and quality of jobs, the new targets emphasised *more* rather than *better* jobs. Moreover, while the Presidency Conclusions repeatedly referred to countries developing their own solutions, the final paragraph steered the Member States towards 'Third Way'

---

[133] *Ibid* para 5.
[134] *Ibid.*
[135] *Ibid* para 6.
[136] *Ibid* para 28.
[137] *Ibid.*
[138] *Ibid* para 29.
[139] *Ibid* para 30.
[140] *Ibid.*

policies deemed necessary to achieve the strategic goal by relying 'primarily on the private sector' and 'public-private partnerships'.[141]

A second important step taken at Lisbon was to implement the 'open
method of co-ordination' (OMC) as part of a 'more coherent and systematic approach' to improving and extending the Luxembourg, Cardiff, and
Cologne processes and facilitating the achievement of the strategic goal.[142]
The OMC, which is designed to help Member States 'progressively develop
their own policies', involves the following:[143]

—fixing guidelines for the Union combined with specific timetables for
  achieving the goals that they set in the short, medium and long terms;
—establishing, where appropriate, quantitative and qualitative indicators
  and benchmarks against the best in the world and tailored to the needs
  of different Member States and sectors as a means of comparing best practice;
—translating these European guidelines into national and regional policies
  by setting specific targets and adopting measures, taking into account
  national and regional differences;
—periodic monitoring, evaluation and peer review organised as mutual
  learning processes.

The European Council would now assume a 'pre-eminent guiding and coor-
dinating role' by holding a meeting every spring devoted to economic and
social questions.[144] The spring meeting would consider an 'annual synthesis report' on progress based on agreed structural indicators relating to
employment, innovation, economic reform and social cohesion.[145]

An additional layer of the OMC would be the instigation of a 'High
Level Forum' bringing together institutions, social partners and other bodies
to 'take stock' of the Luxembourg, Cardiff and Cologne processes and the
contributions of the various actors to enhancing the European Employment
Pact.[146] Further, with a view to increasing the legitimacy of the OMC:[147]

A fully decentralised approach will be applied in line with the principle of subsidiarity in which the Union, the Member States, the regional and local levels, as
well as the social partners and civil society, will be actively involved, using variable
forms of partnership. A method of benchmarking best practices on managing change
will be devised by the European Commission networking with different providers
and users, namely the social partners, companies and NGOs.

One ambitious possibility for partnership under the OMC was highlighted.
The European Council issued a 'special appeal' to companies to assume a

---

[141] Lisbon European Council Presidency Conclusions, 23/24 Mar 2000, para 41.
[142] *Ibid* paras 35–40.
[143] *Ibid* para 37.
[144] *Ibid* para 36.
[145] *Ibid*.
[146] *Ibid* para 40.
[147] *Ibid* para 38.

'corporate sense of social responsibility' regarding best practices on lifelong learning, work organisation, equal opportunities, social inclusion and sustainable development.[148] In order to further this initiative the Commission has issued a Green Paper on a European framework for Corporate Social Responsibility.[149] Hence, corporate social responsibility may be regarded as a quid pro quo for pro-enterprise labour market and fiscal policies and an acceptance of more flexible working methods by trade unions. To put it another way, as Allott wryly observes, we are witnessing the governmentalising of the corporation and the corporatising of government.[150]

The OMC is a dynamic process that appears to know no bounds. According to Hodson and Maher, it may be seen as a 'new mode of governance' for three reasons.[151] Firstly, in areas such as economic and employment policy, the OMC has emerged as a mechanism for dealing with a specific issue by co-ordinating national responses within a framework of commonly agreed parameters. Secondly, as EU policy moves into politically sensitive areas, the traditional Community method of centralised policy formulation is more problematic due to difficulties in achieving policy convergence and popular dissatisfaction with the Union. New methods of 'Europeanisation' are required to overcome these problems. Thirdly, by proffering national co-ordination as an alternative to centralised harmonisation, the OMC provides a pragmatic rather than principled answer to the legitimacy question without fully overcoming problems of élitism and opacity. At this stage it is too soon to determine whether the OMC, as a systematised soft law method, will be embedded as a permanent feature of European governance or a transitional step to a transfer of competence to the EU.[152] For the time being the OMC, viewed as a radical form of subsidiarity,[153] appears to be uniquely suited as a vehicle for driving forward integration by legitimating new institutional practices, using softer more flexible forms of law and involving actors at subnational and transnational levels.[154]

The momentum for the OMC as a horizontal method of EU governance has swiftly gathered pace. At Lisbon the OMC was extended, in varying forms of intensity, to a wide range of areas including: research and development; the information society; economic reforms; social protection; social inclusion and enterprise policy. The Commission's Social Policy Agenda,[155] approved at the Nice European Council,[156] creates the potential for the extension of the OMC to all areas of social policy, an approach consistent

---

[148] *Ibid* para 39.
[149] COM(2001) 366.
[150] See Allott, n 100 above at 61.
[151] Hodson and Maher, n 18 above at 721–22.
[152] *Ibid.*
[153] *Ibid* at 719.
[154] See de Búrca, n 17 above at 8.
[155] COM(2000) 379.
[156] Presidency Conclusions, 7/9 Dec 2000, Annex I.

with amendments to the EC Treaty in the draft Treaty of Nice.[157] At Stockholm, the first annual spring European Council on economic and social questions, the OMC was extended to the areas of education and pensions.[158] In a further development, the OMC has been incorporated into the enlargement process in order to enable applicant countries to assimilate to the EES. Each applicant country is now required to draw up a NAP to prepare its labour market for EU membership and non-binding recommendations can be issued.[159] In a separate development the Baltic Sea region has launched a sectoral programme on labour market policy modelled on the European Employment Pact.[160]

A third significant development at Lisbon, arising as a natural consequence of the implementation of the OMC, has been a deepening of the process of 'Europeanisation' in the related areas of 'modernising social protection' and 'promoting social inclusion'. Action in these areas is regarded as essential for achieving the targets for full employment and as part of a wider programme to modernise the 'European social model' under the umbrella of the Social Policy Agenda, considered in the next section of this chapter.

Turning first to the area of social protection, the introduction of the OMC can be seen as an intensification of a soft law process instigated in the form of Council recommendations[161] and Commission communications in the 1990s.[162] Reform of national social protection systems is now regarded as essential both in the context of labour market participation, 'as part of an active welfare state to ensure that work pays',[163] and as a response to the 'demographic challenge' arising from the estimate that by 2010 the number of retired people will have increased rapidly while the share of the working-age population will have diminished.[164] Hence, action in this area is necessary to meet key benchmarks on raising employment rates and reducing public debt.[165] In a follow-up Communication, the Commission underlined

[157] Draft Art 137(2)(a) EC—subject to ratification, OJ 2001, C80/1. Discussed below at pp 499–500.

[158] Presidency Conclusions, 23/24 Mar 2001, paras 11 and 32.

[159] See Hodson and Maher, n 18 above at 725.

[160] The countries involved are Denmark, Estonia, Latvia, Lithuania, Poland and Russia. *Ibid* at 727.

[161] See Recommendation 92/441/EEC on common criteria concerning sufficient resources and social assistance in social protection schemes, OJ 1992, L245/46; and Recommendation 92/442/EEC on the convergence of social protection objectives and policies, OJ 1992, L245/49. See further, ch 7.

[162] *The Future of Social Protection: Framework for a European Debate*, COM(95) 466; and *Modernising and Improving Social Protection in the European Union*, COM(97) 102.

[163] Lisbon European Council Presidency Conclusions, para 31.

[164] Stockholm European Council Presidency Conclusions, para 7. According to the Commission the 'old-age dependency ratio'—the relationship between the working population and those beyond the retirement age—will more than double from 24% in 2001 to 49% by 2050. See *The Lisbon Strategy—Making Change Happen*, COM(2002) 14, p 16.

[165] Stockholm European Council Presidency Conclusions, para 7.

the growing sense of concern about demographic changes in the following terms:[166]

. . . the prospect of population ageing and the retirement of the 'baby boomer' generation represents a major challenge to [the EU's historic achievements]. Population ageing will be on such a scale that, in the absence of appropriate reforms, it risks undermining the European social model as well as economic growth and stability in the European Union.

The increasing importance of this issue is reinforced by the fact that, under the draft Treaty of Nice, the 'modernisation of social protection systems' is added to the list of areas of social policy where the Community supports and complements the activities of the Member States.[167] However, harmonisation will not be permitted in this area, which remains distinct from 'social security and social protection of workers'[168] where directives may be adopted. Further, an advisory Social Protection Committee, closely modelled on the Employment Committee, was established in June 2000 to promote co-operation on social protection policies between Member States and with the Commission.[169] The Social Protection Committee is formally recognised in the draft Treaty of Nice.[170] Despite the location of these provisions in the Social Chapter, it is clear that the desire to modernise social protection systems is founded on economic considerations. This is borne out by the publication of reports by a High-Level Working Party on Social Protection set up to examine the future of social protection as regards pensions, working in conjunction with the Economic Policy Committee, which has been studying the financial implications of an ageing population.[171] This process is now being taken a stage further with the publication of 'national strategy reports' on the reform of pensions in the framework of the OMC[172] with the triple aim of: safeguarding the capacity of systems to fulfil their social objectives; ensuring financial sustainability; and adapting their capacity to meet the new needs of society.

Despite these initiatives, the infrastructure of the OMC in the field of social protection is underdeveloped. Although the Commission proposed

---

[166] *The Future Evolution of Social Protection from a Long-Term Point of View: Safe and Sustainable Pensions*, COM(2000) 622. See also the follow-up Communication, *Supporting National Strategies for Safe and Sustainable Pensions through an Integrated Approach*, COM(2001) 362.

[167] Draft Art 137(k) EC.

[168] Draft Art 137(c) EC.

[169] OJ 2000, L172/26. The Committee has two members from each Member State and the Commission and meets monthly.

[170] Draft Art 144 EC.

[171] See the Joint Report of the Social Protection Committee and the Economic Policy Committee, November 2001. Available at: <http://europa.eu.int/comm/employment_social/soc-prot/social/index_en.htm>.

[172] Barcelona European Council Presidency Conclusions, 15/16 Mar 2002, Part I, para 25 and Part II, Employment and Social Policy, para 5.

applying the techniques of the EES to the area of social protection and creating a 'European model' based on the creation of central pillars,[173] the European Council has sought to avoid the imposition of benchmarks, guidelines and NAPs. Instead, the emphasis is on dialogue and co-operation rather than co-ordination.[174] In part, this can be explained by the inadequacy of national statistics making it difficult to formulate valid comparisons for benchmarking purposes and target setting.[175] However, this problem also affects the EES. More fundamentally, there are differences in the conception and arrangement of European welfare states within specific institutional structures[176] that have been painstakingly constructed and fought over for generations. Member States fear an intrusion by the EU into their cherished national social welfare systems[177] and are determined to preserve their basic ethos and structures as far as possible, even if they accept the need to modernise or talk the language of modernisation. Indeed, as a means of reinforcing Member States' independence of action in this area, the draft Treaty of Nice adds an additional safeguard whereby measures adopted under Article 137 EC:[178]

... shall not affect the right of Member States to define the fundamental principles of their social security systems and must not significantly affect the financial equilibrium thereof.

This statement amounts to no more than a codification of the established position of the Court that, while Member States are willing to share objectives and co-operate with each other on social welfare issues at the level of the European Council, they remain determined to ensure that 'Community law does not detract' from their powers to organise their social security systems.[179]

By contrast with the rather selective approach to the OMC in the area of social protection, the co-ordination of policies for promoting social inclusion and combating social exclusion and poverty,[180] one of the original Essen priorities, is closer to the Lisbon model but is, nonetheless, much

---

[173] See *A Concerted Action for Modernising Social Protection*, COM(99) 347. The four pillars proposed by the Commission were employment, health care, old age and social exclusion. The Council added equal opportunities and the constructive use of technologies but accepted the pillars only within a framework of co-operation. See the Conclusions of the Employment and Social Affairs Council, 29 Nov 1999. See further, Szyszczak (2001, *Common Market Law Review*) n 7 above at 1143.

[174] See de la Porte *et al*, n 16 above at 297.

[175] *Ibid.*

[176] *Ibid.*

[177] *Ibid.*

[178] Draft Art 137(4) EC.

[179] See Case 238/82, *Duphar* [1984] ECR 523, para 16. See T Hervey, 'Social Solidarity: A Buttress Against Internal Market Law?' in Shaw, n 9 above, 31–47 at 31.

[180] The positive terminology of 'promoting social inclusion' is used interchangeably in the various documents and reports with more negative references to 'combating social exclusion'.

weaker than the EES. Significantly, 'the combating of social exclusion' has also been added to the list of areas in Articles 137 EC by the draft Treaty of Nice,[181] although as with the modernisation of social protection systems, legislative harmonisation will not be permitted. The OMC in this area was initiated by the publication of 'common objectives' on poverty and social exclusion at the Nice European Council in December 2000.[182] Not surprisingly, at this exploratory stage, the common objectives are rather vague and much less specific than the employment guidelines. The objectives are: to facilitate participation in employment and access by all to resources, rights, goods and services; to prevent the risks of exclusion; to help the most vulnerable; and to mobilise all relevant bodies. Gender equality is to be mainstreamed in all actions aimed at achieving the objectives.

In the light of these broad objectives, the Member States were invited to submit NAPs on social inclusion during June 2001, indicating their priorities and efforts over a bi-annual cycle. Following the Commission's assessment of the NAPs,[183] the Council and Commission approved a Joint Inclusion Report at the Laeken European Council in December 2001.[184] The Joint Inclusion Report contains a set of common indicators and examples of best practice based on a report of the Social Protection Committee, although the Commission notes a general lack of rigorous evaluation of policies and programmes by the Member States.[185] Moreover, cyclical activity under the OMC has now been supplemented by more conventional Community action under Article 137(2) EC in the form of a European Parliament and Council Decision establishing a programme to encourage co-operation between Member States to combat social exclusion.[186] This is consistent with the objective of mainstreaming the objective of fighting poverty and social exclusion into relevant strands of policy, at both national and Community level.[187]

The common indicators are neither guidelines nor benchmarks. Rather the objective is to use the indicators to monitor progress towards the general goal set at Lisbon of making a 'decisive impact' on the eradication of poverty by 2010.[188] Under the indicators, which will not be harmonised at EU level,[189] a 'low income' threshold has been set at 60 per cent of median

---

[181] Draft Art 137(j) EC.
[182] Annexed to the Presidency Conclusions.
[183] COM(2001) 565.
[184] Presidency Conclusions, 14/15 Dec 2001, para 28 and Annex IV.
[185] COM(2001) 565, Executive Summary, Part I, para 5.
[186] Decision 50/2002/EC, OJ 2002, L10/1. The action programme is financed to the tune of €75 million.
[187] Lisbon Presidency Conclusions, para 33.
[188] *Report on Indicators in the Field of Poverty and Social Exclusion* (Social Protection Committee, Brussels, Oct 2001) p 2.
[189] *Ibid* p 3.

incomes and related primary indicators concern the most important elements deemed to lead to social exclusion.[190] In 1997, more than 60 million people—18 per cent of the EU population—were living in households with an income below the threshold.[191] Whilst these methodological variations may be deemed consistent with the inherent flexibility and dynamism of the OMC, they also reflect the fact that the Treaty provides no framework for co-ordinating an approach to the highly complex and multidimensional phenomenon of social exclusion/inclusion.[192] In due course, this process will almost certainly lead to benchmarking and, over time, the indicators may be converted to non-binding guidelines with some involvement of 'stakeholders' in the process based on partnerships of all concerned.[193] However, in the short to medium-term this issue remains extremely sensitive,[194] a point underlined when, at the spring 2002 European Council in Barcelona, proposed targets for halving the number of people at risk of poverty by 2010[195] were rejected in favour of the general goal agreed at Lisbon.[196]

Increasingly, post-Lisbon, the EU's heightened activity in the areas of social protection and social exclusion revolves around the twin objectives of economic growth and social cohesion. Full employment is posited as the best safeguard against unacceptable levels of poverty and exclusion and the most effective means of sustaining social protection systems in an ageing Europe. Moreover, to highlight the interdependence of the Lisbon priorities, the aims of modernising social protection and promoting social inclusion have been mainstreamed in the 2001 Employment Guidelines.[197] However, the EU is not primarily concerned with eradicating poverty as a matter of fairness or equality, or as a means of closing the income gap, or as an act of social solidarity. Rather, as the European Council note, the creation of a society with greater cohesion and less exclusion is regarded, primarily, as a 'precondition for better economic performance'.[198] However,

---

[190] *Report on Indicators in the Field of Poverty and Social Exclusion* (Social Protection Committee, Brussels, Oct 2001) p 2. The primary indicators include: distribution of income; persistence of low income; median low income gap; regional cohesion; long-term unemployment; people living in jobless households; early school leavers not in education or training; life expectancy at birth; and self-perceived health status. The report also lists secondary indicators that support the lead indicators and describe other dimensions of the problem.
[191] COM(2001) 565, Executive Summary, Part I, para 10.
[192] See further, *Towards a Europe of Solidarity: Intensifying the fight against social exclusion, fostering integration*, COM(92) 542. Discussed in ch 7.
[193] See Art 2(3) of Council Decision 2002/50/EC, OJ 2002, L10/1.
[194] See de la Porte *et al*, n 16 above at 298.
[195] COM(2002) 14, p 16. The target would have been based on the average level in 1997 (the latest available year) of 18% of the EU population considered to be at risk of poverty after account is taken of support from welfare systems. There is considerable variety among the Member States with the share of the population below the threshold ranging from 8% to 23%.
[196] Presidency Conclusions, 15/16 Mar 2002, para 24.
[197] Decision 2001/63/EC, OJ 2001, L22/18, recital 6 of the preamble.
[198] Nice Presidency Conclusions, Annex II, p 2.

paid work does not automatically provide a passport to social inclusion.[199] Whether or not it does so depends on the quality of work offered[200] because, as Lister observes,[201] to the extent that the unemployed are moving into or staying in low paid and insecure jobs at the bottom of an increasingly polarised labour market, they will continue to occupy a marginalised position which is inconsistent with full and genuine inclusion. Slowly, however, as the EES adapts post-Lisbon, the importance of the *quality* of work is rising up the agenda as it becomes increasingly clear that higher productivity depends on 'decent' employment as well as full employment.[202]

III THE SOCIAL POLICY AGENDA—FROM ECONOMIC TO SOCIAL, FROM SOCIAL TO ECONOMIC?

(1) Quality, Quality, Quality

Shortly after the Lisbon meeting the Commission proceeded with the publication of its Social Policy Agenda (SPA),[203] subsequently approved at the Nice European Council in December 2000.[204] Over the course of the same long weekend, the draft Treaty of Nice was negotiated and the EU Charter of Fundamental Rights[205] was issued as a non-binding 'solemn proclamation', providing a new framework of EU 'common values' based on 'solidarity and justice'.[206] We will explore the potential of the EU Charter in chapter 12, but for now it is important to appreciate the immediate significance of the SPA.

The primary purpose of the SPA is to meet the challenge of the new strategic goal by highlighting the 'essential linkage' between Europe's economic strength and its social model. While this approach can be traced back to the White Paper on Social Policy of the mid-1990s,[207] the SPA marks a break from the deregulatory strategies advanced in the earlier, more influential,

---

[199] See R Lister, 'Citizenship, Exclusion and "the Third Way" in Social Security Reform: Reflections on T.H. Marshall' (2000) 7 *Journal of Social Security Law* 70 at 83.

[200] See A Atkinson, 'Preface' in A Atkinson & J Hills (eds) *Exclusion, Employment and Opportunity* (Centre for Analysis of Social Exclusion, London, 1998) p 1. See Lister, *ibid*.

[201] *Ibid.*

[202] See Ball, n 36 above at 373.

[203] COM(2000) 379. For discussion see Szyszczak (2001, *Common Market Law Review*) n 7 above; C Barnard, S Deakin and R Hobbs, 'Capabilities and Rights: An Emerging Agenda for Social Policy?' (2001) 32 *Industrial Relations Journal* 464; and P Syrpis, 'Smoke Without Fire: The Social Policy Agenda and the Internal Market' (2001) 30 *Industrial Law Journal* 271.

[204] Presidency Conclusions, para 13.

[205] OJ 2000, C364/1.

[206] Presidency Conclusions, Annex I, para 11.

[207] COM(94) 333. See Barnard *et al* (2001, *Industrial Relations Journal*) n 203 above at 476.

White Paper on Growth, Competitiveness, Employment.[208] Traditionally, Community-level social policy has been perceived as a beneficial by-product of economic integration and as a complement to national social legislation. European social legislation has been motivated by a desire to manage structural change and provide a minimum level of employment and social protection against economic vicissitudes in circumstances where it is not possible, or deemed counterproductive, to find national solutions.

In the SPA, the Commission rebuts the conventional passive view of European social policy and proposes instead that the new 'guiding principle' will be 'to strengthen the role of social policy as a productive factor'.[209] Social policy is productive because it represents an investment in human resources with beneficial economic effects. Therefore, according to the Commission, there is a 'positive correlation' between social expenditure and levels of productivity.[210] Viewed from this perspective, an improved and modernised 'European social model' is capable of underpinning economic dynamism and employment growth.[211] Moreover, recognition of fundamental social rights by means of the EU Charter can be seen as a means of facilitating individuals to fulfil their economic potential.[212] This runs counter to the argument that social regulation of the employment relationship necessarily entails economic 'costs' that must be weighed against the social gains achieved.[213] It follows that economic, employment and social policies must be understood as mutually reinforcing and, with the right policy mix, can create a 'virtuous circle' of economic and social progress.[214]

In order to create this 'virtuous circle' the Commission calls for economic policies founded on competitiveness and dynamism, social policies based on quality and cohesion, and employment policies that promote full employment and quality of work.[215] Hence, the promotion of *quality* is presented as the driving force for a thriving economy, more and better jobs, and an inclusive society because:[216]

Quality of work includes better jobs and more balanced ways of combining working life with personal life . . . Quality of social policy implies a high level of social protection, good social services available to all people in Europe, real opportunities for all, and the guarantee of fundamental social rights . . . Quality in industrial relations is determined by the capacity to build consensus on both diagnosis and ways and means to take forward the adaptation and modernisation agenda.

---

[208] *Bulletin of the European Communities Supplement* 6/93.
[209] COM(2000) 379, p 5.
[210] *Ibid* pp 5–6.
[211] *Ibid* p 7.
[212] See Barnard *et al* (2001, *Industrial Relations Journal*) n 203 above at 466. See further, Supiot, n 62 above, pp 190–214.
[213] COM(2000) 379, p 7.
[214] *Ibid* p 6.
[215] *Ibid*.
[216] *Ibid* pp 13–14.

When approving the SPA at Nice, the European Council focused on attaining 'quality in work' because of its importance for growth and as *an incentive to work*.[217] Policies on 'quality in work' should address 'working conditions, health and safety, remuneration, gender equality, balance between flexibility and job security, social relations'.[218] In order to make the rhetoric of quality more meaningful a fresh set of indicators on quality should be produced by the Employment Committee.[219]

In a separate Communication on Quality,[220] the Commission have attempted to put some flesh on the bones. According to the Commission, 'quality reflects the desire, not just to defend minimum standards, but to promote rising standards and ensure a more equitable sharing of progress'.[221] Quality also depends on retaining the 'European social model' of mainly public social spending in preference to the 'US model', which relies heavily on private expenditure with benefits unevenly spread among the population.[222] In seeking to define 'quality in work', or better jobs, the Commission emphasise not only the existence of the job but also the *characteristics of employment*.[223] In order to provide a framework for the analysis of quality in work and develop appropriate indicators, the Commission has divided the main characteristics into two dimensions:[224]

Job characteristics: objective and intrinsic characteristics, including: job satisfaction, remuneration, non-pay rewards, working time, skills and training and prospects for career advancement, job content, match between jobs characteristics and worker characteristics;

The work and wider labour market context: gender equality, health and safety, flexibility and security, access to jobs, work-life balance, social dialogue and worker involvement, diversity and non-discrimination.

The two dimensions have been sub-divided into ten areas with detailed indicators under each heading.[225] Both the Employment Committee and the European Council have approved the Commission's proposals.[226] It has

---

[217] Presidency Conclusions, Annex I, Part I(c).
[218] *Ibid.*
[219] *Ibid.*
[220] *Employment and Social Policies: A Framework for Investing in Quality*, COM(2001) 313.
[221] *Ibid* p 3.
[222] *Ibid* p 5. The Commission highlight the fact that 40% of the US population does not have access to primary health care, even though spending per head as a proportion of GDP is higher than in Europe.
[223] *Ibid* p 7.
[224] *Ibid* p 8.
[225] *Ibid*. Annex II. The ten areas are: intrinsic job quality; skills, lifelong learning and career development; gender equality; health and safety at work; flexibility and security; inclusion and access to the labour market; work organisation and work-life balance; social dialogue and worker involvement; diversity and non-discrimination; overall work performance.
[226] Council Document 14913/01, annexed to the Laeken Presidency Conclusions.

become quickly apparent, however, that compiling the indicators is problematic and the subject matter is extremely sensitive for certain Member
States. Many of the Commission's draft indicators refer to the unavailabil-
ity of data. Indeed the Commission have warned about the need to avoid
interpreting the indicators in a simplistic way and have advised Member
States to relate them closely to policy objectives and standards.[227] As if
to underline the sensitivity of the indicators, Spain has issued a statement
objecting to a separate indicator on 'industrial accidents' because a methodology for collecting data does not exist.[228] Hence, while 'quality' is now
a central part of the overall policy equation, the success of the SPA will
depend on whether there is the necessary political will—at all levels—to
establish an effective system for defining, monitoring and implementing the
indicators.

Nonetheless, the importance of the quality indicators should not be
underestimated. By focusing on characteristics of employment, in the broad-
est sense, they offer a vision of the concept of 'quality' that includes the
quality of the work experience from the perspective of the worker. Thus
quality in work addresses not only issues such as pay and rising standards,
both at work and in the wider environment, but also the personal and
professional development of the worker. Such an approach, if followed
through, would take arguments concerning ergonomics and humanising the
world of work—which have tended to be advanced from an objective standpoint—to a new stage.

One method of implementing the quality indicators by means of the
OMC is through the employment guidelines. Following the endorsement of
both the working methods and importance of the EES at Lisbon, the 2001
Employment Guidelines were revamped. Adopted for the first time in the
form of a binding Council Decision,[229] the Guidelines were prefaced by a
set of overarching horizontal objectives superimposed above the four pillars
and vertical guidelines around which Member States should articulate their
responses as part of a 'coherent overall strategy' for achieving full employment.[230] Further, following a decision of the Stockholm European
Council,[231] it was agreed that 'quality in work' should be included as a specific horizontal objective in the 2002 Employment Guidelines.[232] The new
Horizontal Objective B incorporates both of the quality in work dimensions drawn from the Commission's Communication, which are put
forward as 'areas for consideration' for Member States who 'will endeav-

---

[227] COM(2001) 313, p 10.
[228] Council Document 14913/01, addendum. The relatively high level of industrial accidents
in the Spanish construction industry have been highlighted in Commission reports on health
and safety over many years.
[229] Decision 2001/63/EC, OJ 2001, L22/18, recital 6 of the preamble.
[230] *Ibid.* Annex.
[231] Presidency Conclusions, para 27.
[232] Decision 2002/177/EC, OJ 2002, L60/60.

our to ensure that policies across the four pillars contribute to maintaining and improving the quality of work'.[233] In addition, references to quality have been integrated into specific 'thematic guidelines'.[234]

Other horizontal objectives also emphasise quality factors. For example, Member States are obliged to develop comprehensive and coherent strategies for lifelong learning[235] that will include national targets for increasing human resources and participation in further education and training.[236] Further, Member States shall develop a comprehensive partnership with the social partners for the implementation, monitoring and follow-up of the EES.[237] The shift of emphasis is also detectable in the detailed 2002 Employment Guidelines which include: developing policies for 'active ageing';[238] promoting social inclusion by access to employment while being aware of the danger of marginalising the 'working poor';[239] encouraging the take-up of entrepreneurial activities;[240] modernising work organisation;[241] and supporting adapatability in enterprises as a component of lifelong learning.[242] The guidelines on gender mainstreaming have also been considerably strengthened. Member States are now obliged to address: equal pay; the gender impact of tax and benefit systems; consultation with gender equality bodies; gender impact assessments under each guideline; and separate indicators to measure progress in gender equality in relation to each guideline.

While the incorporation of quality into the guidelines and horizontal objectives is a significant development, tension between the objectives of job creation and the provision of decent work remain.[243] Thus, although the 2001 and 2002 Employment Guidelines are inculcated with the 'quality' agenda, the quantitative aspects of the Lisbon priorities remain to the fore. Indeed the pressure for quantitative outcomes has been accentuated by the decision of the Stockholm European Council to set interim targets for the overall employment rate of 67 per cent (57 per cent for women) by 2005,[244] and add a new long-term target employment rate of 50 per cent for 'older

---

[233] *Ibid*. Annex.

[234] Explanatory Memorandum to the draft 2002 Employment Guidelines, COM(2001) 511, p 3.

[235] Decision 2002/177/EC, OJ 2002, L60/60, Horizontal Objective C.

[236] See for example, Guideline 4, *ibid* which includes targets for: halving by 2010 the number of 18–24 year olds with only lower-secondary level education who are not in further education or training; and increasing the proportion of the adult working age population (25–64 year olds) participating at any given time in education and training.

[237] *Ibid*. Horizontal Objective D. Discussed below at pp 503–505.

[238] *Ibid*. Guideline 3.

[239] *Ibid*. Guideline 7.

[240] *Ibid*. Guideline 9.

[241] *Ibid*. Guidelines 13–14.

[242] *Ibid*. Guideline 15.

[243] See Ball, n 36 above at 374.

[244] Presidency Conclusions, para 9. According to the latest data, there is an 18% gender gap in employment between men and women. Significantly, there is also a 14% gender pay gap but no specific target for its reduction was referred to at Stockholm. See COM(2002) 89, p 4.

persons' (aged 55–64) by 2010.[245] These new targets have been incorporated into the first horizontal objective in the 2002 Employment Guidelines.[246] Quality in work forms the second horizontal objective. Although separate horizontal objectives direct Member States to set priorities in a balanced manner across the pillars and objectives, respecting the integrated nature and equal value of the guidelines,[247] and adhere to the quality indicators,[248] the clear message is more jobs first, better jobs second.

More generally, by emphasising quality, in all its aspects, the Commission has provided a rationale for reviving dormant legislative proposals under the cover of the SPA. For example, the primary aim of the draft directive on working conditions for temporary workers[249] is 'to improve the quality of temporary work by ensuring that the principle of non-discrimination is applied to temporary workers'.[250] This is reinforced by the secondary aim, which is 'to establish a suitable framework for the use of temporary work to contribute to the smooth functioning of the labour and employment market'.[251] While the proposal has been launched under Article 137(2) EC, its centre of gravity lies with the Employment Title and the link between the quality of work and economic performance. The Commission has sought to underline this link by explicitly presenting the draft directive as an example of 'productive' social policy on the basis that it will stimulate the creation of quality jobs, promote diverse forms of employment and help reconcile flexibility and security.[252] References to the rights of every worker to decent working conditions, derived from the Social Charter[253] and the Charter of Fundamental Rights[254] are confined to the preamble.

Similar considerations lie behind the revival of proposals for worker involvement which can be seen as contributing to improving partnership, managing change, promoting quality in industrial relations and quality in corporate decision-making. In March 2002, Directive 2002/14 on establishing a general framework for informing and consulting employees in the European Community was finally adopted after four years of debate.[255] The

---

[245] Presidency Conclusions, para 9. In 2001 the estimated rate of employment participation among this group was 38.3%—COM(2002) 89, p 4.

[246] Decision 2002/177/EC, OJ 2002, L60/60, Horizontal Objective A.

[247] *Ibid.* Horizontal Objective E.

[248] *Ibid.* Horizontal Objective F.

[249] COM(2002) 149. The Commission published the proposal on 20 Mar 2002 after the social partners had failed to reach agreement within the timescale provided for under Art 138(4) EC.

[250] Draft Art 2(a).

[251] Draft Art 2(b).

[252] Explanatory Memorandum, p 2. See also, draft recital 3.

[253] Draft recital 2.

[254] Draft recital 1.

[255] Dir 2002/14/EC, OJ 2002, L80/29. Under Art 11(1) the implementation date is 23 Mar 2005. For the original proposal see OJ 1999, C2/3; and for the revised proposal, COM(2001) 296.

Directive applies to all companies with 50 employees or more, representing just 3 per cent of all EU companies but, significantly, 50 per cent of all employees.[256] Originally envisaged as an instrument that would help facilitate change in times of crisis and avoid or mitigate the effects of corporate restructuring, as vividly demonstrated by the 'Renault affair',[257] the thrust of the Directive, as adopted, is closer to the wider aims of the EES and the SPA. In particular, the Directive is now based on the concepts of 'anticipation', 'prevention' and 'employability' that are to be incorporated into the policies of individual undertakings 'by strengthening the social dialogue with a view to promoting change compatible with preserving the priority objective of employment'.[258] Indeed, the assimilation of the aims of the Directive with those of the EES has made it easier for Member States to sell this measure to a somewhat sceptical corporate audience.

Likewise the European Company Statute (ECS), now introduced as a Regulation[259] and accompanying Directive,[260] has been repositioned—after 30 years on the drawing board—as a measure that will combine greater freedom for transnational companies in the internal market with employee influence over decision-making.[261] In the context of the SPA and the EES, the ECS is presented as a means of improving the quality of work and industrial relations by involving workers more in managing changes in the economy and labour market arising from globalisation.[262]

Ultimately, the successful *delivery of quality* in work, social policy and industrial relations in the EU will depend, on the one hand, on the correlation between economic competitiveness, productivity and employment growth and, on the other, the capacity of national and European actors to

---

[256] See the Commission Press Release, 'New Worker Information and Consultation Directive "a modern business tool"', 17 Dec 2001. Available at:
<http:europa.eu.int/comm./employment_social/news/>.

[257] See ch 7 for discussion.

[258] Recital 10 of the preamble.

[259] Reg 2157/2001/EC on the Statute for a European company (SE), OJ 2001, L294/1. Under Art 2(4) a public limited-liability company registered in one Member State with a subsidiary company in another Member State for at least two years may voluntarily transform itself into a European Company. The purpose, according to recital 1 of the preamble, is to enable the company to plan and reorganise its business on a Community scale. In return, the company must abide by the rules governed by the Reg (Art 9).

[260] Dir 2001/86/EC supplementing the Statute for a European company with regard to the involvement of employees, OJ 2001, L294/22. Art 1(2) provides for obligatory employee involvement in the European Company. While the original proposals sought to establish a uniform method of employee involvement in the European Company, Art 2(h) allows for diversity based on a negotiated procedure. Employee involvement may include 'any mechanism', including information, consultation and participation, through which employees' representatives may 'exercise an influence on decisions to be taken by the company'. The legal base for both measures was Art 308 [ex 235] EC, the general powers provision. Under Art 14(1) the implementation date is 8 Oct 2004.

[261] See the Nice Presidency Conclusions, Annex I, Part II(a).

[262] *Ibid.*

develop and utilise an effective range of legislative and non-legislative means. It is to this question that we shall now turn.

(2) Delivering the Social Policy Agenda—Harmonisation, Co-ordination, Co-operation and Partnership

When the SPA was published in June 2000 it was quickly apparent that this was not a conventional 'action programme'. Whereas the Social Action Programme 1998–2000 had contained a familiar list of proposals for Community legislation to 'complete and consolidate the framework of minimum social standards',[263] the ambitious vision of the SPA is to be achieved primarily through the OMC and the activity of 'all stakeholders and actors' based on an 'improved form of governance'.[264] Indeed, notwithstanding the explicit objective in favour of harmonisation in Article 136 [ex 117] EC, the Commission declared that:[265]

The new Social Policy Agenda does not seek to harmonise social policies. It seeks to work towards common European objectives and increase co-ordination of social policies in the context of the internal market and the single currency.

In other words, the EU's objectives can be achieved *without* harmonisation of social policies. The combined effect of the Amsterdam Treaty, the Luxembourg process and the Lisbon strategic goal, has been to move social policy from the margins to the centre of the EU's endeavours. Within this 'new paradigm'[266] it is possible for policies and actions to be fashioned across the full range of social policy fields—which may or may not lead to harmonisation—without the need for strict reference to Community or national competences, so long as the ultimate aim is the achievement of the strategic goal. Thus to fulfil the EU's ambitious priorities of full employment, more and better jobs, lifelong learning and closing the gender gap, a combination of 'all existing means' will be applied—the OMC, legislation, social dialogue, structural funds, programmes, mainstreaming—all underpinned by policy analysis and research.[267] Moreover, consistent with a dynamic approach to subsidiarity, the level at which action is taken is less important than the action itself and its effectiveness. The only criterion for determining the intensity of the action and which level is appropriate is one of *outcome* rather than process[268]—in other words, ends not means.

---

[263] COM(98) 259, p 1.
[264] COM(2000) 379, p 14.
[265] *Ibid* p 7.
[266] See Szyszczak (2001, *Common Market Law Review*) n 7 above at 1125.
[267] COM(2000) 379, pp 14–15.
[268] See de Búrca, n 17 above at 15.

Significantly, the purpose of legislation as a technique under the SPA is to develop or adapt standards 'to ensure the respect of fundamental social rights and to respond to new challenges'.[269] Legislation is regarded as ongoing rather than merely programmatic or simply concerned with minimum standards. Moreover, the OMC may lead to co-operation, convergence, or even harmonisation. As a malleable method for furthering the SPA, the OMC is best understood as a refined soft law technique which, through a range of tools—high-level pronouncements, peer pressure, task forces, guidelines, performance indicators, benchmarking, scoreboards and recommendations—may induce compliance with EU objectives, even without binding legislation or formal sanctions, in areas that may be wholly within the competence of the Member States. Barnard and Deakin have aptly described the OMC in the context of social policy as an example of 'reflexive harmonisation',[270] a technique where a range of transnational instruments are deployed to set parameters for the laws and/or policies of the Member States, each combining to 'steer' national laws and practices in the direction of EU objectives.[271]

In the draft Treaty of Nice, the Member States have attempted to bring the Social Chapter into line with the de facto development of the OMC and their ambitions for the SPA. Draft Article 137 EC, as revised, will consolidate the existing fields of permitted legislative activity, adding only the Lisbon priorities of combating social exclusion and modernising social protection systems.[272] Article 137(2)(a) EC, as drafted, will add the following:

[The Council] may adopt measures designed to encourage cooperation between Member States through initiatives aimed at improving knowledge, developing exchanges of information and best practices, promoting innovative approaches and evaluating experiences, excluding any harmonisation of the laws and regulations of the Member States.

This provision will apply to all listed areas of activity in the Social Chapter. It precedes the retained legal base under which the Community may continue to adopt directives,[273] although this does not necessarily indicate an order of preference in the choice of methods. Legislative action short of harmonisation will also be possible in all areas, in which case qualified majority voting and the co-decision procedure will apply.[274] Most activities falling

---

[269] COM(2000) 379, p 14.

[270] C Barnard and S Deakin, 'In Search of Coherence: Social Policy, the Single Market and Fundamental Rights' (2000) 31 *Industrial Relations Journal* 331.

[271] See Barnard *et al* (2001) n 203 above at 478.

[272] Draft Art 137(1)(j) and (k) EC, OJ 2001, C80/1. The only other substantive change is the deletion of the final field listed in the current Art 137(3) EC—'financial contributions for promotion of employment and job creation'—a duplication of Art 129 EC in the Employment Title.

[273] Draft Art 137(2)(b) EC, which will replace Art 137(2)EC.

[274] In accordance with the procedure under Art 251 [ex 189b] EC.

under the umbrella of the OMC would appear to be covered by this provision, but the reference to 'cooperation' rather than 'coordination' suggests caution on the part of the Member States who are, perhaps, unwilling to constitutionalise the dynamic and flexible OMC in the Treaty.

When approving the SPA at Nice, the European Council sought to emphasise the importance of outcomes rather than processes by inviting the Commission to present an annual 'scoreboard' on the progress of implementation.[275] Scoreboards are a means of measuring performance delivery across a whole policy area at regular intervals. However, unlike the 'Internal Market Scoreboard', which the Commission uses to 'name and shame' Member States who have 'implementation deficits',[276] the SPA 'Scoreboard' is a much tamer affair, amounting to little more than a progress report with a very similar format to earlier annual reports on the implementation of the Social Charter Action Programme. Nevertheless, although the Scoreboard does not 'name names', it is now synchronised with the publication of an expanded list of 'EU Best Performance Indicators'[277] which provide 'league tables' of the top three states in areas such as employment, productivity, economic growth, education and training and poverty. This information feeds into the 'annual synthesis report' submitted to the European Council at its economic and social meeting every spring.

In the second annual SPA Scoreboard published in February 2002[278] the full range of planned legislation, areas for the development of the OMC, action programmes, structural fund activity and social dialogue, has been presented. Legislation is highlighted in fields such as worker involvement, temporary work and non-discrimination. In most areas, apart from the EES and social exclusion, the OMC is at a very early stage of development. One area where the OMC has been formally introduced is pensions where, in response to heightened concerns about the budgetary impact of 'ageing', common objectives have been set and national reporting will follow.[279] Other activities which may ultimately lead to the introduction of the OMC include: the establishment of a High-Level Task Force on skills and mobility;[280] a new health and safety strategy with an emphasis on monitoring and preventing occupational accidents and diseases;[281] the introduction of long-

---

[275] Nice Presidency Conclusions, Annex I, p 5. The first scoreboard was issued in February 2001, COM(2001) 104.

[276] The Internal Market Scoreboard was introduced in May 1997. For the November 2001 Scoreboard see: <http://europa.eu.int/comm/internal_market/en/update/score/score9.htm>.

[277] Updated online on: <http://europa.eu.int/comm/eurostat>. For a summary see COM(2002) 14, pp 8–9.

[278] COM(2002) 89.

[279] *Ibid* p 20. Approved by the Laeken European Council, Dec 2001.

[280] Final report, 14 Dec 2001: <http://europa.eu.int/comm/employment_social/general/index_en.htm>. See also, Recommendation 2001/613/EC on mobility within the Community for students, persons undergoing training, young volunteers, teachers and trainers, OJ 2001, L215/30.

[281] *A New Community Strategy on Health and Safety at Work (2002–2006)* COM(2002) 118.

term objectives on health care;[282] new targets on the provision of child-care;[283] and the publication of indicators on the gender pay gap.[284]

These developments reveal both the inherent dynamism of Community soft law and the potential of the OMC to develop and extend its tentacles across the breadth of social policy. However, much of this activity is unco-ordinated, unpredictable and lacks clear direction or purpose. The OMC—or at least some of its elements—is most likely to be extended to those areas most closely linked to meeting the targets on employment and ensuring the viability of social protection systems in the light of the budgetary require-ments of the Stability and Growth Pact—pensions, social exclusion, care for the elderly and childcare. In the majority of areas, where Community legislation is not an option and the OMC is unlikely to develop, evidence from the Scoreboard suggests that delivery of the SPA in general and the drive for quality in particular, will depend on co-operation backed up by influential, but not coercive, soft law. Ultimately, therefore, much will depend on the capacity of national, local and sectoral actors to ensure that the Member States maintain the political will and the capacity to deliver their strategic objectives.

For this reason the reinforcement of the social dialogue and attempts to involve other 'partners' and 'stakeholders' from civil society[285] in the overall delivery and governance of the SPA are of particular significance. Accord-ing to the Commission:[286]

'Governance' means rules, processes and behaviour that affect the way in which powers are exercised at European level, particularly as regards openness, participa-tion, accountability, effectiveness and coherence.

---

[282] *The Future of Health Care and Care for the Elderly: Guaranteeing Accessibility, Quality and Financial Viability*, COM(2001) 723. The Communication proposes three generalised long-term objectives: ensuring that everyone has access to health care; improving the quality of health care systems; maintaining the financial stability of care systems.

[283] Barcelona European Council Presidency Conclusions, 15/16 Mar 2002, para 32. The purpose of childcare targets is to 'remove disincentives for female labour force participation'. The European Council has agreed that Member States should 'strive' to provide childcare by 2010 to at least 90% of children between 3 years old and the mandatory school age and at least 33% of children under 3 years of age.

[284] *Framework Strategy on Gender Equality Work Programme for 2001*, COM(2001) 119. See also, the European Parliament's own-initiative report, A5/2001/275.

[285] According to the Economic and Social Committee, 'civil society' includes the following: trade unions and employer's organisations ('the social partners'); non-governmental organisa-tions; professional associations; charities; grass roots organisations; organisations that involve citizens in local and municipal life with a particular contribution from churches and religious communities. See the Opinion of the Economic and Social Committee on 'The Role and Con-tribution of Civil Society Organisations in the Building of Europe', OJ 1999, C329/30. For discussion, see K Armstrong, 'Civil Society and the White Paper—Bridging or Jumping the Gaps?' in Joerges, n 6 above, Part 10; cf Allott, n 100 above who, at 62, traces the origins of the term 'civil society' back to writings of Adam Ferguson a leading light of the 'Scottish Enlightenment' in the 18th Century.

[286] *European Governance: A White Paper*, COM(2001) 428, p 8.

Concerns about the way in which the EU exercises its power lie at the heart of the Commission's White Paper on European Governance.[287] In essence, the theory goes that by laying the foundations of 'good governance'[288] through reaching out to its citizens and involving them in shaping policy, the EU will reap the benefits in the form of better policies, regulation and delivery. As Armstrong explains,[289] the appeal of the concept of 'European civil society' lies in the hope that it can provide 'an intermediating civic sphere to connect society to transnational governance'. In other words, *European* civil society can offer an equally important but differentiated voice from the 'ethnically national *demos*'[290] and may ultimately lead to what Preuß describes as a '*societas civilis sive politica*', ie a civil society beyond the physical boundaries of the nation-states.[291] This can also be seen as a response to the growth of increasingly effective transnational protest movements seeking to roll back or restrain globalisation. The Commission's hope is that citizens will increasingly grow to accept the EU rather than protest against it.[292] For some critics, writing from the perspective of liberal democracy, such notions are extremely dangerous and anti-democratic because they 'separate the people from *their government*'.[293] In effect what is being contemplated is, to apply Streeck's apposite term, 'neo-voluntarism',[294] a process through which the EU is filtering decision-making through civil society by using the concept of 'partnership' to secure consensus or a plurality of support for, and ownership of, its objectives at the 'grass roots'.

In the White Paper, the Commission is mainly concerned with facilitating the development of a structured European civil society by helping to foster a 'reinforced culture of consultation and dialogue', in which the European Parliament will play a prominent role.[295] Suggestions include: a code of conduct setting minimum standards on what to consult on, when, whom and how to consult; and partnership arrangements with organisations in civil society who will have be more extensively consulted.[296] In return, the selected organisations would be expected to tighten up their

---

[287] *European Governance: A White Paper*, COM(2001) 428, p 3. For an excellent set of critical contributions, see Joerges *et al*, n 6 above.

[288] *Ibid* p 10. The Commission identifies five principles that underpin 'good governance': openness, participation, accountability, effectiveness and coherence.

[289] Armstrong, n 285 above at 3.

[290] See J Weiler, 'Epilogue: The European Courts of Justice: Beyond "Beyond Doctrine" or the Legitimacy Crisis of European Constitutionalism' in A-M Slaughter, A Stone Sweet and J Weiler (eds) *The European Courts and National Courts: Doctrine and Jurisprudence* (Hart, Oxford 1998) 365–91 at 384.

[291] See U Preuß, 'Problems of a Concept of European Citizenship' (1995) 1 *European Law Journal* 267.

[292] *Ibid* at 7.

[293] See Allott, n 100 above at 60.

[294] W Streeck, 'Neo-Voluntarism: A New European Social Policy Regime?' (1995) 1 *European Law Journal* 31 at 52.

[295] COM(2001) 428, p 16.

[296] *Ibid*.

internal structures, furnish guarantees of openness and representativeness, and prove their capacity to relay information or lead debates in the Member States.[297] The main problem with this approach is that it ignores the multi-level and multi-dimensional nature of civil society and focuses narrowly on managing existing relationships.[298] The Commission is offering different levels of involvement, or at the most consultation by way of 'partnership arrangements', in return for the acceptance of responsibility and imposed 'norms' of governance.[299] In practice, therefore, despite the rhetoric of the White Paper, the Commission is extremely cautious about opening up discourse and extending genuine and unconditional involvement to a wider plurality of actors and, therefore, these proposals only scratch at the surface of the legitimacy crisis.

The EU is on safer ground when dealing with the European social partners. Indeed, one of the main threads running through the SPA is the need for the social partners to play a pro-active role in anticipating and managing change and adapting to the new working environment.[300] According to the Commission and the European Council,[301] the best way to 'manage' corporate change and, if necessary, restructuring, which is regarded as essential for modernisation, is through dialogue in order to anticipate the need to change, take preventative action and find solutions that are consistent with the pillars of 'employability' and 'adaptability'. The general framework Directive for informing and consulting employees[302] will be of critical importance in this respect but there are several other strands of this policy. For example, there is an explicit link here with the notion of quality in industrial relations. In the SPA the Commission proposed to consult the social partners on, first, modernising and improving employment relations and, second, on the need to establish, at European level, voluntary mechanisms on mediation, arbitration and conciliation for conflict resolution.[303] This consultation has been taking place in parallel with the establishment of a European Monitoring Centre on Change and the convening of a High-Level Group on industrial relations and managing change, which is paying specific attention to the issue of industrial relations in an enlarged Union.[304] Further input into policy development arises at an annual 'Social Summit', which is convened by the Commission on the eve of each spring European Council.[305]

---

[297] *Ibid.*
[298] Armstrong, n 285 above at 7.
[299] *Ibid* at 7–9.
[300] COM(2000) 379, p 17.
[301] See the Barcelona European Council Presidency Conclusions, para 22.
[302] Dir 2002/14/EC, OJ 2002, L80/29.
[303] COM(2000) 379, p 17.
[304] See the 2002 Scoreboard, COM(2002) 89, p 14.
[305] See 'Social Summit: Commission calls on social partners to play their full part in the Lisbon strategy', European Commission, 14 Mar 2002: <http://europa.eu.int/comm/employment_social/news/>.

Within the context of the EES, the social partners were initially invited to negotiate agreements to modernise the organisation of work under the adaptability pillar of the employment guidelines.[306] The involvement of the social partners in the process was further reinforced when, in June 2000, the European Council invited them to 'play a more prominent role in defining, implementing and evaluating the employment guidelines', focusing particularly on modernising work organisation, lifelong learning and increasing the employment rate, particularly for women'.[307] 'Partnership' now features as Horizontal Objective D, which includes the following statement:[308]

Within the overall framework and objectives set by these guidelines, the social partners are invited to develop, in accordance with their national traditions and practices, their own process of implementing the guidelines for which they have the key responsibility, identify the issues upon which they will negotiate and report regularly on progress, in the context of the national action plans if desired, as well as the impact of their actions on employment and labour market functioning. The social partners at European level are invited to define their own contribution and to monitor, encourage and support efforts undertaken at national level.

As Goetschy[309] notes, the social partners are expected to create a 'process within a process', in effect their own sphere of action. Thus, within the adaptability pillar, the social partners are given sole responsibility for the guidelines concerning modernising work organisation,[310] and supporting adaptability in enterprises as a component of lifelong learning.[311] In relation to the latter, the social partners are invited to conclude agreements that will facilitate adaptability and innovation. However, in the area of modernising work organisation, delegation to the social partners is more substantial. The social partners are invited to 'negotiate and implement' agreements on such matters as, inter alia, new technologies, new forms of work, the reduction of working hours and overtime, the development of part-time working and access to career breaks. In return, for reasons of accountability, they must report annually on which aspects of modernising work organisation have been covered by the negotiations as well as the status of their implementation and the impact on employment and labour market functioning.

Goetschy suggests a number of possibilities arising from the strengthening of the social dialogue within the EES.[312] First, social partners at

---

[306] *Modernising the Organisation of Work*, COM(98) 592, p 4. This proposal was incorporated as Guideline 16 in the 1999 Employment Guidelines.

[307] Santa Maria da Feira European Council Presidency Conclusions, 19/20 June 2000, para 34.

[308] Decision 2002/177/EC, OJ 2002, L60/1. Originally introduced as Horizontal Objective C in the 2001 Employment Guidelines.

[309] Goetschy (2001, *Industrial Relations Journal*) n 10 above at 408.

[310] Guideline 13.

[311] Guideline 15.

[312] Goetschy (2001, *Industrial Relations Journal*) n 10 above at 409.

European and national levels could decide on areas suitable for benchmarking and define their own criteria. Secondly, actions under the guidelines may lead to sectoral or cross-industry agreements, which may tie in with areas of negotiation under the Social Chapter. Thirdly, the social partners may seek to elaborate new guidelines of their own which may be adopted by the Council. Fourth, the European social partners can actively monitor the participation of their national affiliates in the drawing up and implementation of NAPs and promoting ideas such as 'social pacts'.[313]

In chapter 6, the issue of the representativeness and democratic legitimacy of the social partners was discussed in the context of their role in the legislative process under the provisions in the Social Chapter.[314] A number of problems were identified including lack of accountability, élitism and levels of representation in the workplace. Moreover, the involvement of the social partners in the legislative process undermines the institutional role of the European Parliament. Indeed, the further expansion of the role of the social partners into the sphere of the Employment Title might be regarded as a form of 'neo-syndicalism' in which the power of the state is gradually replaced by the social power of corporate entities.[315] In the context of the adaptability pillar of the employment guidelines, however, and specifically in the area of modernisation of work, the role of the social partners is much more clearly defined and relevant. The social partners are the principal 'stakeholders' who will be most directly affected by changes in the organisation of work and who are most likely to have practical solutions for 'managing change'. Further, the requirement for an annual report, which is not contained in the Social Chapter, strengthens the accountability and transparency of the process, consistent with the notion of 'good governance' in the White Paper.

IV THE SAME RESOLVE TO CONVERGE?

From the above analysis it is far from clear that the legislative and non-legislative techniques available to the EU, particularly the OMC, are robust enough to successfully 'Europeanise' social policy and deliver a revamped 'European social model' based on the concept of 'quality'. The 'partnership' principle holds the prospect of a more 'imagining' and 'responsive' form of EU governance[316] but, in its present inchoate state, there is a danger that the OMC and other forms of co-operation will reinforce a trend towards minimum government and deregulation.[317] In the Governance

---

[313] See further, Rhodes, n 124 above.
[314] Arts 138 and 139 EC.
[315] See Allott, n 100 above at 64.
[316] See Scott, n 101 above at 176.
[317] *Ibid.*

White Paper the Commission propose that more use should be made of 'primary' legislation limited to 'essential elements'—basic rights and obligations and conditions to implement them.[318] The European Parliament, in a generally favourable response to the SPA, warned that in seeking to apply 'all existing means' the Union should not lose sight of that fact that binding legislation:[319]

... will often be the most effective tool in the Union's areas of competence because it guarantees enjoyment of social rights, aims to establish minimum social standards at Community level and at the same time maintains democratic parliamentary influence and judicial control over the Union's decisions.

Undoubtedly, Community legislation *will often* be the most effective method of giving substance to an evolving conception of European 'fundamental social rights' for *individuals*. All too often, however, there is confusion between ends and means.[320] Invariably, whenever social legislation is adopted at Community level, the completion of the process is hailed as a great victory, not least for the EU institutions, but the benefits for individuals may be less tangible. Soft law has many advantages over hard law, not only because it is easier to achieve,[321] but also, where it is targeted at combating disadvantage or improving societal outcomes, it may offer, or lead to, more coherent and effective long-term solutions to intractable problems, irrespective of whether the area of policy in question is one of Community or national competence. Potentially the OMC can serve as an instrument for strengthening integration while allowing for a diverse range of localised responses to globalisation.[322]

In seeking to develop the OMC, the challenges for the EU are fourfold. First, the methodology of the OMC, particularly data collection and benchmarking, has to be strengthened and applied more systematically. Secondly, greater emphasis needs to be placed on 'delivering' the qualitative aspects of the SPA. Thirdly, ways and means must be found to address the 'participation deficit' by including 'stakeholders' in the process of defining, implementing and reporting under the OMC in order to enhance its legitimacy. Fourthly, more attention should be given to compliance with recommendations or other forms of guidance and developing a system by which individual Member States and the European Council can be made more accountable for their actions.

---

[318] COM(2001) 428, p 20.

[319] See A5-O291/2000. For further discussion, see Syrpis, n 203 above at 280–81.

[320] For a classic exposition of this argument, see CAR Crosland, *The Future of Socialism*, Revised edn (Jonathan Cape, London, 1964) pp 64–7.

[321] See K Abbott and D Snidal, 'Hard and Soft Law in International Governance' (2000) 54 *International Organization* 421 at 423.

[322] See S Sciarra, 'Global or Re-nationalised? Past and Future of European Labour Law' in F Snyder (ed) *The Europeanisation of Law: The Legal Effects of European Integration* (Hart, Oxford, 2000) 269–91 at 280–83.

Is the maturing EES capable of meeting these challenges? The 2002 'employment package' offers mixed messages.[323] According to data presented to the Barcelona European Council, the employment rate in the EU reached 64 per cent in 2001,[324] within a whisker of the Commission's mid-term projection of 1997. If the present rate of growth continues the target employment rate of 67 per cent by 2005 is attainable, although the attacks on the US on 11 September 2001 will undoubtedly have serious direct and indirect economic and social consequences.[325] The apparent success of the EES in terms of employment growth, which may be largely accounted for by benign economic circumstances and the activities of the markets, belies the fact that the relative performance of the Member States has been extremely variable and only very limited progress has been made in the direction of promoting 'quality in work'.

Underneath the surface, however, the performance of individual Member States is far from satisfactory. The Commission's detailed assessment of the implementation of the 2001 Employment Guidelines reveals that most Member States have failed to set overall or specific national employment targets,[326] an option suggested in Horizontal Objective A of the Employment Guidelines.[327] One group of Member States have already reached, or are very close to reaching, the employment target and have set ambitious national targets.[328] Another group have comparatively low overall employment rates, in some cases below 60 per cent and have failed to set comprehensive national targets.[329] In the 2002 Recommendation on the implementation of Member States' employment policies,[330] the main emphasis is on structural problems that stand in the way of Member States in the second group achieving the target employment rates. While the individual recommendations touch upon quality issues concerning adaptability and equal opportunities, particularly the importance of lifelong learning, the focus is on employability (incentives to work) and entrepreneurship (incentives to create jobs).

Whereas most Member States have made some progress towards meeting the quantitative targets and have sought to respond to the individual

---

[323] Adopted by the Council on 3 Dec 2001. See COM(2002) 89, p 7.

[324] COM(2002) 14, p 8. For detailed statistics, see the draft joint employment report for 2001, COM(2001) 438.

[325] COM(2002) 14, p 5.

[326] SEC(2001) 1398.

[327] Decision 2001/63/EC, OJ 2001, L22/18, Annex.

[328] SEC(2001) 1398, pp 7–8. Member States in this group are: Austria, Denmark, Sweden, Finland, the Netherlands, Portugal, and the UK. Only Denmark, the Netherlands, Sweden, and the UK exceed the 2010 target for overall employment and women's employment. Denmark is the top performer with 76.3% overall and 71.6% among women.

[329] *Ibid*. This group includes: Belgium, France, Greece, Ireland, Italy, Spain, Germany, and Luxembourg. Italy has the lowest participation rates of 53.5% overall and 39.6% among women.

[330] Decision 2002/178/EC, OJ 2002, L60/70.

recommendations, the Commission note that the majority have not engaged with the idea of quality.[331] Where quality is addressed in the NAPs, it tends to be linked to labour supply rather than quality in work.[332] Member States have placed the most emphasis on the employability and entrepreneurship pillars in the NAPs, which is hardly surprising in the light of the bias in the recommendations.[333] Some progress has been made in developing indicators and benchmarks at local level and involving the social partners in the process.[334] At this stage, however, there is little evidence to indicate that the introduction of quality and partnership as horizontal objectives will have a significant impact on the next round of NAPs.

Over time, the introduction of the horizontal objectives may help to redirect the EES towards the quality issues highlighted in the SPA but the signs are not encouraging. The Commission's preparatory report for the Barcelona European Council highlights a 'delivery gap' across the board with specific reference to the mainly quantitative 'best performance' indicators.[335] In response, the Council has proposed a simplification, but not watering down, of the process and, in particular, fewer employment guidelines.[336]

In conclusion, the SPA has at last provided EU social policy with a rationale[337] 30 years on from the Paris declaration that 'economic expansion is not an end in itself'.[338] After Lisbon, economic strength and rising social standards are regarded as indissoluble. It follows that fundamental social rights and values can be asserted both as a justification for autonomous action under the Social Chapter and as a foundation for a reoriented 'European social model'. We can also see that globalisation begets a process of Europeanisation that carries with it opportunities to manage and shape change at the level of the individual, while Member States retain responsibility for preserving and reinforcing the essential values of social solidarity.

Nevertheless, prospects for a fusion of the economic and the social will depend upon an equal 'pull' of compliance. At Barcelona the Member States determined to synchronise the two sets of guidelines,[339] once again exhibiting 'the same resolve to converge'. However, such integrationist rhetoric will lack conviction so long as the employment guidelines remain formally subordinate to the economic guidelines and while the recommendations to individual Member States are not backed up with sanctions. While this imbalance persists, social policy responses will continue to be driven by the

---

[331] SEC(2001) 1398, p 6.
[332] *Ibid* p 9.
[333] *Ibid* p 6.
[334] *Ibid.*
[335] COM(2002) 14, pp 5–9.
[336] Barcelona European Council Presidency Conclusions, Part II, p 14.
[337] See Szyszczak (2001, *Common Market Law Review*) n 7 above at 1126.
[338] Oct 1972. See *Bulletin of the European Communities Supplement* 2/74, p 14.
[339] Barcelona European Council Presidency Conclusions, Part II, p 14.

strict budgetary discipline of the Stability and Growth Pact. Moreover, the dextrous language of 'modernisation', 'employability', 'adaptability', and 'flexibility' remains highly contested. In this climate of uncertainty there is a danger that tensions within the employment guidelines will be exacerbated, leading perhaps to more jobs at the expense of better jobs,[340] flexibility before security, and social exclusion rather than inclusion. Two possible scenarios can be contemplated. One possibility is that targeted hard law within the Community sphere, supplemented by the OMC, co-operation, and 'bottom-up' partnership in the national sphere, can improve the prospects for delivery of 'high quality' social policies. Another possibility is that sophisticated, often technocratic, forms of soft law such as the OMC, although presented as a 'more legitimate' and 'inclusive' alternative to the 'flawed' Community method, may be used as a smokescreen behind which the welfare state can be dismantled.[341] Such is the fluidity of these reflexive, self-regulatory processes[342] that each of these scenarios is perfectly valid. It is precisely for this reason that individuals require a visible EU guarantee of fundamental social rights to cement in place the new consensus on social policy.[343]

[340] See Ball, n 36 above at 367.

[341] For a helpful analysis of the arguments, see Trubek and Mosher, n 6 above at 3.

[342] See I-J Sand, 'Understanding the New Forms of Governance: Mutually Interdependent, Reflexive, Destabilised and Competing Institutions' (1998) 4 *European Law Journal* 271 at 272.

[343] See C Barnard and S Deakin, 'Social Policy in Search of a Role: Integration, Cohesion and Citizenship' in A Caiger and D Floudas (eds) *1996 Onwards: Lowering the Barriers Further* (Wiley, Chichester, 1996) 177–95 at 195.

12

The EU Charter of Fundamental Rights—Towards a European Social Constitution?

I INTRODUCTION

EUROPE'S 'ECONOMIC CONSTITUTION'[1] has been painstakingly constructed over a 50-year period. Economic freedoms and market integration form its predominant rationale. Until recently employment and social policies have been advanced as a function of the economic integration process rather than an independent aspiration. The significance of the Social Policy Agenda[2] lies with the fact that it subverts the liberal economic paradigm by positing employment and social policies based on the 'quality of work' as intrinsic elements of the efficient process of market functioning. Nonetheless, at its core, the EU still lacks a *social constitution*. Indeed, what is often portrayed as Europe's 'social deficit'[3] will persist so long as the notion of EU citizenship is located within the domain of economic freedoms rather than social values such as solidarity and participation. The high level proclamation of the EU Charter of Fundamental Rights[4] marks a symbolic attempt to place indivisible rights—civil,

---

[1] See M Streit and W Mussler, 'The Economic Constitution of the European Community: From "Rome" to "Maastricht"' (1995) 1 *European Law Journal* 5; C Joerges, 'European Economic Law, the Nation-State and the Maastricht Treaty' in R Dehousse (ed) *Europe After Maastricht: An Ever Closer Union?* (Law Books in Europe, Munich, 1994) 29–62; N Walker, 'European Constitutionalism and European Integration' [1996] *Public Law* 266; and M Poiares Maduro, *We the Court: The European Court of Justice and the European Economic Constitution* (Hart, Oxford, 1998).

[2] COM(2000) 379, approved at the Nice European Council, 7/9 Dec 2000, Presidency Conclusions, Annex I. Discussed in ch 11.

[3] See M Poiares Maduro, 'Striking the Elusive Balance Between Economic Freedom and Social Rights in the EU' in P Alston (ed) *The EU and Human Rights* (OUP, Oxford, 1999) 449–72; and P Davies, 'Market Integration and Social Policy in the Court of Justice' (1995) 24 *Industrial Law Journal* 49.

[4] The Charter was issued as a 'solemn proclamation' by the European Parliament, the Council and the Commission on 7 Dec 2000. For the full text, see OJ 2000, C364/1. For essential explanatory documentation, see the Charter website at: <http://europa.eu.int/comm/justice_home/unit/charte/index_en.html>.

political, economic and social—at the centre of the EU's enterprise and, despite its non-binding status, may yet act as a portent for the emergence of a European social constitution based on a foundation of shared social values.

In this final chapter we will explore the potential of the Charter as a tool for constitutionalising fundamental social values within the EU legal order. In the first part the origins of the Charter will be traced before proceeding to consider several inter-related questions in the remaining sections. What is the substance of the fundamental social rights, freedoms and principles that form the Charter's 'common values'?[5] What is its legal scope? Finally, in the light of the 'post-Nice agenda'[6] of constitutional reflection,[7] to what extent does the Charter offer a new framework for the development of justiciable social rights and recognition of basic social entitlements for European citizens?

II THE ORIGINS OF THE CHARTER

The lineage of the social elements of the Charter can be traced back to the Tindemans Report of 1975[8] and an attempt in the 1980s by the Economic and Social Committee to draw up a catalogue of 'inalienable basic social rights' derived from the Treaties and international law. Significantly, the Committee's aim was to remind the Community institutions and the Member States of *existing* social rights and not to draw up a separate 'Social Charter'.[9] Nevertheless, the Commission proceeded with its own proposal for a Community Social Charter that, although adopted only as a non-binding 'solemn declaration' by a majority of Member States,[10] has been a catalyst for legislative and programmatic action at Community and national levels.[11] The Social Charter seeks to persuade Member States to guarantee fundamental social rights for 'workers' but as we discussed in Chapter 4, all references to social citizenship were deleted from the final text. Europe's 'social identity' was—and indeed remains—highly contested[12] and the time

---

[5] First recital of the preamble.

[6] See especially, J Shaw, 'The Treaty of Nice: Legal and Constitutional Implications' (2001) 7 *European Public Law* 195 at 211–13.

[7] See K Lenaerts and E De Smijter, 'A "Bill of Rights" for the European Union' (2001) 38 *Common Market Law Review* 273 at 299.

[8] COM(75) 481.

[9] Doc CES 270/89.

[10] At the Strasbourg European Council, Dec 1989. The text of the Charter is reproduced in *Social Europe* 1/90, pp 46–50.

[11] By early 2001 there were 43 references to the Social Charter in Community legislation. See further, L Betten, 'The EU Charter on Fundamental Rights: a Trojan Horse or a Mouse?' (2001) 17 *International Journal of Comparative Labour Law and Industrial Relations* 151 at 158.

[12] See M Poiares Maduro, 'Europe's Social Self: "The Sickness Unto Death"' in J Shaw (ed) *Social Law and Policy in an Evolving European Union* (Hart, Oxford, 2000) 325–49 at 326.

was not yet ripe for a broad inclusive vision of social citizenship within a European integration project that lacked a human rights foundation. However, in the wake of the post-Maastricht 'legitimacy crisis', issues of citizenship, social solidarity and fundamental rights were swiftly brought to the fore.

The immediate process leading to the Charter stemmed from the March 1996 report of an ad hoc *Comité des Sages*.[13] Significantly, the authors of the report sought to end the tradition schism[14] between civil and political rights, on the one hand, and economic and social rights, on the other, by proposing a 'bill of rights' encompassing *indivisible* civic and social rights to be incorporated into the Amsterdam Treaty. The objective was to render the embryonic concept of EU citizenship meaningful in the eyes of the people of Europe. In the event, the revised EC Treaty left the limited EU citizenship provisions unchanged and contained only a small nod in the direction of social rights. Article 136 [ex 117] EC proclaims that the Community and the Member States shall have in mind *fundamental social rights*, such as those set out in the ESC and the Community Social Charter, when pursuing their social policy objectives. In itself, however, this generalised commitment does not form a basis for establishing justiciable social rights.

In the aftermath of the Amsterdam Treaty the Commission sought to rekindle the flame ignited by the *Comité*. The Social Affairs Directorate appointed a group of legal experts who published a report on affirming fundamental rights in the European Union.[15] The experts called for recognition of both economic and social rights contained in the ECHR, the ESC and ILO conventions, and concluded that all rights should be set out in a single text to be inserted into the Treaties.[16] The timing of the experts' report was propitious. 1998 marked the fiftieth anniversary of the Universal Declaration of Human Rights[17] an event heralded by a range of activities,[18] including a separate Commission report calling for, inter alia, the establishment of a centre for monitoring human rights based on the model of the Racism Monitoring Centre.[19] Moreover, the adoption of the Revised

---

[13] *For a Europe of Civic and Social Rights* (European Communities, Luxembourg, 1996).

[14] See M Gijzen, 'The Charter: A Milestone for Social Protection in Europe?' (2001) 8 *Maastricht Journal* 33 at 35.

[15] *Affirming Fundamental Rights in the European Union Time to Act* (European Commission, Brussels, 1999). Available at: <http://europa.eu.int/comm/justice_home/unit/charte/index_en.html>.

[16] *Ibid* p 17.

[17] GA Res 217A (III) 10 Dec 1948.

[18] See G de Búrca, 'The Drafting of the European Union Charter of Fundamental Rights' (2001) 26 *European Law Review* 126.

[19] *Leading by Example: A Human Rights Agenda for the European Union for the Year 2000* (EUI, Florence, 2000). For an adapted version, see P Alston and J Weiler, 'An 'Ever Closer Union' in Need of a Human Rights Policy: The European Union and Human Rights' in Alston, n 3 above, 3–66.

ESC in 1996,[20] and the launch of the ILO's Declaration on Fundamental Principles and Rights at Work in 1998,[21] increased the visibility of fundamental social rights on the international stage. At Cologne, in June 1999, the European Council finally accepted responsibility to act by declaring that:[22]

Protection of fundamental rights is a founding principle of the Union and an indispensable prerequisite for her legitimacy. The obligation of the Union to respect fundamental rights has been confirmed and defined by the jurisprudence of the European Court of Justice. *There appears to be a need, at the present stage of the Union's development, to establish a Charter of fundamental rights in order to make their overriding importance and relevance more visible to the Union's citizens.*

Once again the Union was deploying the language of rights for the twin purposes of legitimation and integration.[23] The European Council added substance to its rhetoric by referring both to the ECHR and the common constitutional traditions of the Member States, and also to the citizens' 'guarantee' of economic and social rights in Article 136 [ex 117] EC derived from the Community Social Charter and the ESC.[24] This declaration was significant not only because of the expressed desire to deepen the culture of fundamental rights in the EU, but also as a bold attempt to place classic civil liberties and core social rights on an equal footing. However, from the outset, there was an underlying ambiguity behind the whole exercise. The idea of the Charter was seen as an alternative to Community accession to the ECHR[25] or incorporation of the ESC.[26] Moreover, in a barely concealed compromise, the European Council indicated that, when the Charter was eventually adopted, it would be in the form of a non-binding political declaration and it 'will then have be considered whether and, if so, how the

---

[20] The Revised ESC entered into force in July 1999. For discussion, see N Casey, 'The European Social Charter and Revised European Social Charter' in C Costello (ed) *Fundamental Social Rights: Current Legal Protection and the Challenge of the EU Charter of Fundamental Rights* (Irish Centre for European Law, Dublin, 2001) 55–75.

[21] Available at: <www.ilo.org>. For discussion, see J Bellace, 'The ILO Declaration of Fundamental Principles and Rights at Work' (2001) 17 *International Journal of Comparative Labour Law and Industrial Relations* 269.

[22] Presidency Conclusions, 3–4 June 1999, Annex IV, para 1. Emphasis added.

[23] For a prescient analysis, see G de Búrca, 'The Language of Rights and European Integration' in J Shaw and G More, *New Legal Dynamics of European Union* (Clarendon Press, Oxford, 1995) 29–54 at 39–43.

[24] Cologne Presidency Conclusions, para 2.

[25] In *Opinion 2/94* [1996] ECR I–1759, the Court ruled, on the basis of the principle of conferred powers in the first paragraph of Art 5 [ex 3b] EC, that the Community had no competence to accede to the ECHR, as human rights were not included among the Community's objectives in Art 2 EC. For discussion, see *The Human Rights Opinion of the ECJ and its Constitutional Implications* (CELS Occasional Paper No 1, Cambridge, 1996); G Gaja, 'Opinion 2/94, Accession by the Communities to the European Convention for the Protection of Human Rights and Fundamental Freedoms' (1996) 33 *Common Market Law Review* 973; and L Betten and N Grief, *EU Law and Human Rights* (Longman, Harlow, 1998) pp 111–23.

[26] For discussion of this option, see ch 4.

Charter should be integrated into the treaties'.[27] Hence, on the one hand, the European Council wished to keep alive the pretence of a legally binding Charter as a token gesture to the minority of Member States that might support such a move,[28] while, on the other hand, the driving purpose behind the initiative was to offer a visible declaration of the EU's existing commitments directed, as de Búrca observes, not at lawyers or politicians but the ordinary citizen to 'help to secure a degree of popular legitimacy for a political entity which continues to be contested and questioned'.[29]

In order to furnish the Charter with legitimacy, the European Council constituted a novel EU 'body' composed of representatives of the Governments, the Commission, the European Parliament and national parliaments.[30] The body, which renamed itself the 'Convention', was established outside the Treaties and signified a new form of constitution building in Europe.[31] The Convention consulted widely and set up working parties. Representatives of the Court of Justice and the European Court of Human Rights sat as observers and a wide variety of expert groups were invited to submit their opinions. The Convention established a powerful inner core group, the grandiloquently titled 'Praesidium', to work through the detailed text and produce drafts. The idea was to have the widest possible exchange of views and maximum transparency. Indeed the Convention's inclusiveness was intended to mark a fresh approach, running counter to the exclusiveness and opacity of the traditional IGC process, which was running in parallel.[32] As a decision-making body, however, the Convention was criticised for lacking a formal mechanism for the participation of 'civil society' in its work, except through hearings and the involvement of parliamentary representatives.[33] Nevertheless it represented an open, inherently flexible and more inclusive forum for constitutional development in the EU.

While the structure and working methods of the Convention were innovative, its work was hampered by a fundamental difference of perception among the participants that reflected the contradictions and ambiguities of the whole project.[34] According to Lord Goldsmith, the UK Government's

---

[27] Cologne Presidency Conclusions, para 4.

[28] As an indication, in *Opinion 2/94*, the compatibility of accession to the ECHR was broadly supported by eight Member States (Austria, Belgium, Denmark, Finland, Germany, Greece, Italy and Sweden) and opposed by five (France, Ireland, Portugal, Spain and the UK).

[29] See de Búrca (2001, *European Law Review*) n 18 above at 130.

[30] The formal representation was: Member State governments (15); European Commission (1); European Parliament (16); national parliaments (30). Therefore parliamentary representatives were in a clear majority with 46 out of a total of 62 seats. For the details, see the Tampere European Council Presidency Conclusions, 15–16 Oct 1999, Annex.

[31] See de Búrca (2001, *European Law Review*) n 18 above at 126.

[32] *Ibid* at 132.

[33] See T Eicke, 'European Charter of Fundamental Rights—Unique Opportunity or Unwelcome Distraction' [2000] *European Human Rights Law Review* 280 at 281.

[34] See de Búrca (2001, *European Law Review*) n 18 above at 128.

representative, the discussions were 'not about minting new rights but rather an exercise in increasing the visibility of existing rights'.[35] Many NGOs sought to use the Convention as a platform to argue for new rights not yet firmly established at international level and were, not surprisingly, disappointed.[36] Moreover, shortly after the first draft of the Charter was published in July 2000,[37] it became abundantly clear that the final text would be issued in the form of a non-binding political declaration and the question of legal force would be deferred to a later date.[38] In order to breathe fresh life into the process, and unite the disparate members of the Convention around a common objective, the President, Roman Herzog,[39] successfully recommended that the Charter should be drafted 'as if' it had 'mandatory legal force'.[40] The Convention wished to send a clear signal 'to the outside world that the European Union must not be any less bound to its citizens than are the Member States under their own constitutional laws'.[41] This led to a period of intensive negotiations before publication of the final text in October 2000.[42] In a remarkably smooth process the Charter was endorsed at political level at a meeting of Union leaders in Biarritz[43] before its adoption at Nice on 7 December 2000.

The publication of the Charter as a 'solemn proclamation' of the European Parliament, the Council and the Commission was intended to send a message of unity of purpose as a prelude to a decisive act of constitution building at the Nice IGC in preparation for the enlargement of the Union to include the countries of central and eastern Europe, the Baltic region and the eastern Mediterranean.[44] In the event any feelings of optimism associated with the proclamation of the Charter were swiftly dispelled

---

[35] See Lord Goldsmith, 'A Charter of Rights, Freedoms and Principles' (2001) 38 *Common Market Law Review* 1201 at 1207.

[36] *Ibid.*

[37] CHARTE 4422/00, CONVENT 45. An online version can be found at: <http://www.eiro.eurofound.ie/2000/08/Features/eu0008268f.html>.

[38] Both the Commission and the European Parliament advocated the case for the Charter to become legally binding. See COM(2000) 644, para 11, and European Parliament resolutions A5–0064/2000, especially points 7(a) (f) and (g) and B5–767/2000. See also, Economic and Social Committee Resolution 105/2000 and Committee of the Regions Resolution 140/2000.

[39] Formerly President of Germany.

[40] See COM(2000) 559 final, para 3.

[41] Doc CHARTE 4105/00.

[42] CHARTE 4487/00, CONVENT 50. For the text with explanatory notes produced by the Praesidium, see CHARTE 4473/00, CONVENT 49. Regrettably the version in the Official Journal does not include the explanatory note even though it is indispensable. See further, D Curtin and R van Ooik, 'The Sting is Always in the Tail: The Personal Scope of Application of the EU Charter of Fundamental Rights' (2001) 8 *Maastricht Journal* 102 at 103.

[43] 13/14 Oct 2000. This was not a formal European Council meeting. A summary of the proceedings can be found at: <http://www.presidence-europe.fr/pfue/static/acces5.htm>.

[44] Following the decision at the Helsinki European Council of Dec 1999 to pursue negotiations with an additional six countries, making a total of 13 possible entrants between 2005 and 2015 including: Czech Republic, Hungary, Poland, Romania, Bulgaria, Slovakia, Slovenia, Estonia, Latvia, Lithuania, Cyprus and Malta. Negotiations with Turkey are on hold.

by four days of 'bad-tempered squabbling'[45] on the French Riviera. The draft Treaty of Nice[46] that emerged is primarily concerned with adapting the institutional design of the Union.[47] The main changes concern the representation of the Member States in the composition and appointment of the institutions and their operational efficiency in a Europe of 20 or more countries.[48] For the time being, however, the Treaty and the whole process of enlargement is on hold following a negative vote in the Irish referendum of 7 June 2001. In the meantime, attention has been focused on a declaration annexed to the draft Treaty, which calls for a 'deeper and wider debate' on the future of the Union involving wide-ranging discussions with all interested parties including civil society.[49] This process should address, inter alia, the status of the Charter along with other 'post-Nice' issues such as a more precise delimitation of powers between the EU and the Member States, simplification of the Treaties and a review of the role of national parliaments in the 'European architecture'.

Following the launch of a Declaration on the Future of the European Union at the Laeken European Council of December 2001,[50] a Convention on the Future of the European Union has been established closely modelled on the Convention formed to draft the Charter. The new Convention, chaired by the former French President, Valery Giscard d'Estaing, is due to draw up recommendations on a possible 'Constitution of the European Union' in time for a decision to be taken at a further IGC to be held in 2004. In the meantime the Convention's discussions will be in the public domain and organisations representing civil society will receive regular information through a network called the Forum.[51] This means that any decision to incorporate the Charter in a new 'basic treaty', or to accede to the ECHR,[52] will have to be considered as part of a broader constitutional package.[53]

III THE CHARTER'S SOCIAL RIGHTS AND PRINCIPLES—TEXT AND STRUCTURE

The EU Charter of Fundamental Rights is divided up into three discrete parts: a preamble; the main body consisting of 50 enumerated 'rights,

---

[45] See Shaw, n 6 above at 195.

[46] OJ 2000, C80/1. The Treaty was formally adopted on 26 Feb 2001.

[47] See K St C Bradley, 'Institutional Design in the Treaty of Nice' (2001) 38 *Common Market Law Review* 1095.

[48] *Ibid* at 1097.

[49] Declaration No 23 annexed to the Final Act of the Conference.

[50] Issued on 15 Dec 2001. Available at: <http://europe.eu.int/futurum>.

[51] See A Arnull, 'Editorial: From Opinion 2/94 to the Future of Europe' (2002) 27 *European Law Review* 1 at 2.

[52] Laeken Declaration, Part II.

[53] See B de Witte, 'The Legal Status of the Charter: Vital Question or Non-Issue?' (2001) 8 *Maastricht Journal* 81 at 88.

freedoms and principles'[54] set out in six chapters; and a final chapter of 'horizontal' provisions that define its legal scope and the level of protection that it offers.

As with the Social Charter, the preamble serves as a point of reference for the value orientation[55] of the document and the aspirations of its signatories. From the outset the authors sought to legitimate the whole enterprise by proclaiming that the 'peoples of Europe' wish to 'share a peaceful future based on common values'.[56] Moreover, just as fundamental rights are regarded as indispensable for legitimacy,[57] the process of European integration—or 'ever closer union'[58]—is dependent upon the furtherance of these shared values. In other words, should the Charter be integrated into the Treaties, its core values, or what Fitzpatrick describes as the apex of the EU pyramid,[59] would be based, for the first time, on fundamental rights. Next, the central aspirations are presented thus:[60]

Conscious of its spiritual and moral heritage, the Union is founded on the *indivisible, universal* values of human dignity, freedom, equality and solidarity; it is based on the principles of democracy and the rule of law. It places the individual at the heart of its activities, by establishing the citizenship of the Union and by creating an area of freedom, security and justice.

This highly nuanced paragraph contains three interlinked strands, each of which offers a tantalising glimpse of the *potential* of the Charter if not the *actualité*. First, the values espoused in the Charter are declared to be indivisible, an ambition that is underlined by references to both civil and political rights—'human dignity, freedom and equality'—and social rights— 'solidarity'. Within the EU's conception of fundamental rights, the inclusion of solidarity among the Charter's common values has the effect of elevating social rights to the level of human rights[61] and is perhaps the most important achievement of the Charter in its present form as a political declaration. The EU institutions, not least the Courts, will be bound to take note of the central position that social values now occupy when carrying out their obligations. Therefore, the Charter's social values are capable of having a mainstreaming effect[62] for new legislation and programmatic

---

[54] Seventh recital of the preamble.
[55] See M Weiss, 'The Politics of the EU Charter of Fundamental Rights' in B Hepple (ed) *Social and Labour Rights in a Global Context* (CUP, Cambridge, 2002, *forthcoming*).
[56] First recital.
[57] See A von Bogdandy, 'The European Union as a Human Rights Organization? Human Rights and the Core of the European Union' (2000) 37 *Common Market Law Review* 1307 at 1307.
[58] First recital.
[59] See B Fitzpatrick, 'Converse Pyramids and the EU Social Constitution' in Shaw, n 12 above, 303–24.
[60] Second recital. Emphasis added.
[61] See Gijzen, n 14 above at 42.
[62] *Ibid.*

action, and also serve as a basis for judicial interpretation of EU law within the scope of application of the Treaties. Secondly, the Charter's values are presented as universal. Most of the enumerated rights are guaranteed to 'everyone' or 'every worker'.[63] Where this is the case, the logic of the principle of universalism suggests that the reach of the Charter must extend to third-country nationals who are seeking to rely on social rights falling within the scope of EU law.[64] Thirdly, the Charter fills a void, identified previously by O'Leary,[65] by making an explicit link between fundamental rights and EU citizenship. Although the citizenship provisions in the Charter merely restate the *acquis*,[66] the inclusion of solidarity, along with civil and political rights, offers the prospect of an emerging social conception of citizenship which fits more closely with Marshall's classic definition of citizenship as 'full membership of a community'.[67]

The remaining recitals reflect the compromises reached by the Convention in the light of the Cologne mandate and what was likely to be acceptable to the Member States. First, reference is made to respect for the diversity of the cultures and traditions of the peoples of Europe as well as the national identities of the Member States.[68] In the area of social policy, where the Community defers to 'diverse forms of national practices',[69] this statement provides a pretext for imposing conditions on the exercise of rights and the recognition of principles. Hence, several of the provisions concerning employment law and social security rights are conditional upon 'national laws and practices'.[70] Secondly, the delicate balance between 'new' rights and making existing rights more visible is reflected by a recital that refers to the need to strengthen the protection of fundamental rights 'in the light of changes in society, social progress and scientific and technological development'.[71] The Charter is presented as a 'living instrument' that the Courts can interpret teleologically rather than the regressive creation that Weiler feared.[72] Thirdly, the

---

[63] See C Costello, 'The Legal Status and Legal Effect of the Charter of Fundamental Rights of the European Union' in Costello, n 20 above, 127–50 at 144.

[64] See Gijzen, n 14 above at 38; and Lenaerts and De Smijter, n 7 above at 278.

[65] See generally, S O'Leary, 'The Relationship between Community Citizenship and the Protection of Fundamental Rights in Community Law' (1995) 32 *Common Market Law Review* 519.

[66] See N Reich, 'Union Citizenship—Metaphor or Source of Rights?' (2001) 7 *European Law Journal* 4 at 6.

[67] See T Marshall, *Citizenship and Social Class and Other Essays* (CUP, Cambridge, 1950). For further discussion, see Reich, *ibid*.

[68] Third recital.

[69] Art 136 [ex 117] EC.

[70] Art 27 (workers right to information and consultation within the undertaking); Art 28 (right of collective bargaining and action); Art 30 (protection in the event of unjustified dismissal); Art 34 (social security and social assistance); Art 35 (health care); Art 36 (access to services of general economic interest).

[71] Fourth recital.

[72] See J Weiler, 'Editorial: Does the European Union Truly Need a Charter of Rights?' (2000) 6 *European Law Journal* 95 at 96; cf Eicke, n 33 above at 286.

Charter 'reaffirms' rights derived from the common constitutional traditions of the Member States, the Treaties and international law—including the two 'Social Charters'—but preserves the 'powers and tasks of the Community and the Union' in accordance with the principle of subsidiarity.[73] In this way the Charter recognises a wide range of sources of fundamental rights without transferring any competences from the national to the Union level. Fourthly, the enjoyment of the rights in the Charter entails unspecified 'responsibilities and duties' with regard to other persons, the 'human community' and future generations.[74]

Finally, the preamble refers to the 50 'vertical' provisions that follow as 'rights, freedoms and principles'.[75] This phrase suggests a distinction between specific enforceable rights and general unenforceable principles.[76] Goldsmith explains that this formulation was arrived at after a 'long and difficult' debate.[77] As the UK Government representative he argued assiduously, and with some success, for the inclusion of what he describes as a 'new concept' that the economic and social rights in the Charter are mere 'principles' that will only be realised as exercisable rights 'to the extent that they are implemented by national law or, in those areas where there is such competence, by Community law'.[78] In essence, Goldsmith argues that economic and social rights are different and, by implication, inferior to civil and political rights because they are 'usually not justiciable' and are recognised and given effect to in different ways in the Member States who have primary competence in most of these areas.[79] Goldsmith's contention strikes at the heart of the notion of indivisibility of rights. It is based on an assumption that economic and social rights, such as those contained in the ESC,[80] or the UN International Covenant on Economic, Social and Cultural Rights[81] are less important because they are not subject to judicial oversight. In fact, both the Council of Europe[82] and the UN[83] have introduced

---

[73] Fifth recital.

[74] Sixth recital.

[75] Seventh recital.

[76] See A Heringa and L Verhey, 'The EU Charter: Text and Structure' (2001) 8 *Maastricht Journal* 11 at 14.

[77] Goldsmith, n 35 above at 1212.

[78] *Ibid* at 1213.

[79] *Ibid* at 1212.

[80] For a summary of the social rights contained in the ESC and Revised ESC, see ch 4, pp 112–3.

[81] 999 UNTS No 3. See also, the UN International Covenant on Civil and Political Rights, 999 UNTS No 171. Both Covenants were adopted in 1966.

[82] Following the 1991 Amending Protocol of the ESC, a more effective European Committee of Social Rights has replaced the Committee of Independent Experts. See further, Casey, n 20 above; and T Novitz, 'Remedies for Violation of Social Rights within the Council of Europe' in C Kilpatrick, T Novitz and P Skidmore (eds) *The Future of Remedies in Europe* (Hart, Oxford, 2000) 231–51.

[83] The UN Committee on Economic, Social and Cultural Rights. See further, M Craven, 'A View from Elsewhere: Social Rights, the International Covenant and the EU Charter of Fundamental Rights' in Costello, n 20 above, 77–93 at 87.

increasingly sophisticated supervisory committees that have developed an impressive body of legal assessments on the interpretation of these instruments. Further, Member States retain primary competence in many of the areas included among the civil and political rights in the Charter but this does not prevent them from being recognised as fundamental rights. Goldsmith's distinctive conception of 'rights' and 'principles' is not referred to in the explanatory text issued by the Praesidium. Moreover, he was not entirely successful. Eventually, after lengthy negotiations, the Chapter on 'Solidarity' emerged as a mix of clear individual rights, guiding principles that the EU recognises and respects, and pure objectives.[84] As we shall see, this compromise creates particular difficulties of interpretation and leaves a question mark over the status of social rights within the Charter's construct of fundamental rights.

The Charter's substantive rights are set out in six chapters headed: Dignity; Freedoms; Equality; Solidarity; Citizen's Rights and Justice. The rights and principles of most relevance to EU employment and social law are found mainly, but not exclusively, in the chapter on Solidarity. In this section the main provisions will be presented, and briefly developed, before analysis, in the next section, of their legal scope and effectiveness as determined by the horizontal clauses in Articles 51–54.

Included within chapter I on Dignity we can find rights to human dignity,[85] to the integrity of the person,[86] and the prohibition of slavery and forced labour.[87] Article 1 declares that: 'Human dignity is inviolable. It must be respected and protected'. The dignity of the human person occupies the pole position because it is not only a fundamental right in itself but constitutes the real basis of each of the substantive fundamental rights laid down in the Charter.[88] Therefore, consistent with the Court's interpretation of fundamental rights in *P v S*,[89] human dignity is an integral part of the principle of non-discrimination, which is contained in Article 21. Furthermore, Article 31(2) grants workers the right to working conditions that respect their 'health, safety and dignity'. The source of this provision is

---

[84] See B Hepple, 'The EU Charter of Fundamental Rights' (2001) 30 *Industrial Law Journal* 225 at 228.

[85] This is drawn from the preamble of the 1948 Universal Declaration of Fundamental Rights where it is declared that: 'Whereas recognition of the inherent dignity and of the equal and inalienable rights of all members of the human family is the foundation of freedom, justice and peace in the world'. It follows that the Charter must not be used to harm the dignity of another person and that the dignity of the human person is part of the substance of the rights laid down in the Charter (see CHARTE 4473/00, CONVENT 49, p 3).

[86] Art 3.

[87] Art 5.

[88] See the explanatory note, CHARTE 4473/00, CONVENT 49, p 3.

[89] See Case C–13/94, *P v S and Cornwall CC* [1996] ECR I–2143, para 22, where the Court held that: 'To tolerate [discrimination against transsexuals] would be tantamount, as regards such a person, to a failure to respect the dignity and freedom to which he or she is entitled, and which the Court has a duty to safeguard'.

Article 26 of the Revised ESC, which refers to the obligation on the parties to promote awareness, information and prevention of sexual harassment in relation to work and the need to take appropriate measures to protect workers from such conduct.[90] This provides a platform for advancing legislation and programmatic action under Articles 13 and 141(3) [ex 119] EC.[91]

Furthermore, Article 5(2) on the prohibition of forced or compulsory labour, although explicitly derived from Article 4(2) ECHR,[92] owes its origins to the long-established principle that 'labour is not a commodity'.[93] Hence, Article 5(2) reinforces the Court's finding in *Katsikas*[94] that, under the Acquired Rights Directive,[95] an employee cannot be compelled to continue in an employment relationship with an employer because such an obligation 'would jeopardise the fundamental rights of the employee who must be free to choose his employer and cannot be obliged to work for an employer that he has not freely chosen'.[96]

Chapter II on Freedoms contains the following provisions, inter alia, drawn, for the most part, directly from the ECHR:

—right to liberty and security (Article 6);[97]
—respect for private and family life (Article 7);[98]
—protection of personal data (Article 8);[99]
—right to marry and found a family (Article 9);[100]
—freedom of thought, conscience and religion (Article 10);[101]
—freedom of expression and information (Article 11);[102]
—freedom of assembly and association (Article 12);[103]

---

[90] See the explanatory note, CHARTE 4473/00, CONVENT 49, p 29.

[91] Stemming also from Commission Recommendation 92/131/EEC on the protection of the dignity of men and women at work, OJ 1992, L49/1. See now, Art 2(3) of the Race Equality Dir, 2000/43/EC, OJ 2000, L180/22; Art 2(3) of the Framework Employment Dir, 2000/78/EC, OJ 2000, L303/16; and the Commission's revised proposal to amend Dir 76/207/EC on equal treatment between men and women, COM(2001) 321, draft Art 1a. Discussed in ch 9.

[92] See the explanatory note, CHARTE 4473/00, CONVENT 49, p 7.

[93] See further, P O'Higgins, "Labour is not a Commodity'—An Irish Contribution to International Labour Law' (1997) 26 *Industrial Law Journal* 225.

[94] Cases C–132/91 and C–138–139/91, *Katsikas v Konstantinidis* [1992] ECR I–6577.

[95] Dir 77/187/EEC, OJ 1977, L61/26.

[96] Paras 31–2. See B Hepple, 'Social Values and European Law' [1995] *Current Legal Problems* 39 at 52–4.

[97] Conveys the same meaning and scope as Art 5 ECHR.

[98] Corresponds to the rights contained in Art 8 ECHR.

[99] Derived from Art 286 [ex 213b] EC and Dir 95/46/EC on the protection of individuals with regard to the processing of personal data and the free movement of such data, OJ 1995, L281/31. See also, Art 8 ECHR and Council of Europe Convention of 28 Jan 1981 for the Protection of Individuals with regard to the Automatic Processing of Personal Data, ratified by all EU Member States.

[100] This is broader than Art 12 ECHR, which refers only to 'men and women of marriageable age'.

[101] Corresponds to Art 9 ECHR.

[102] Follows Art 10 ECHR.

[103] Based on Art 11 ECHR.

—right to education (Article 14);[104]
—freedom to choose an occupation and engage in work (Article 15);[105]
—freedom to conduct a business (Article 16).[106]

Article 52(3), discussed below, provides that where the rights laid down in the Charter correspond with those in the ECHR 'the meaning and scope of those rights shall be the same'. In respect of the right to freedom of assembly and association in Article 12, for example, this has been interpreted by the Strasbourg Court in the context of Article 11 ECHR, as including both the right to join and not to join a trade union—a 'negative right of association'.[107]

Article 15(3) contains the only express reference to nationals of third-countries 'who are authorised to work in the territories of the Member States and are entitled to working conditions equivalent to those of citizens of the Union'. Viewed in isolation, this provision conveys a broad conception of citizenship as a 'common bond transcending nationality'.[108] However, neither the citizenship provisions in the EC Treaty, which are tied to nationality of a Member State,[109] nor the requirement for unanimity for legislative measures in respect of the working conditions of third-country nationals,[110] are affected, a situation that would remain unchanged even if the Charter were to become legally binding.[111]

Chapter III on Equality enumerates the following rights:

—equality before the law (Article 20);[112]
—non-discrimination (Article 21);[113]
—cultural, religious and linguistic diversity (Article 22);[114]

---

[104] Derived from the common constitutional traditions of the Member States and Art 2 of the Protocol to the ECHR. The right to education also includes vocational and continuing training—Art 10 ESC and point 15 of the Social Charter. Art 14(2) states that this right 'includes the possibility to receive free compulsory education'. According to the explanatory note, CHARTE 4473/00, CONVENT 49, p 16, this does not require all establishments that provide education to be free of charge. Nor does it exclude certain specific forms of education having to be paid for, if the State takes measures to grant financial compensation.

[105] Drawn from Art 1(2) ESC and the case law of the Court of Justice—eg Case 44/79, *Hauer v Land Rheinland-Pfalz* [1979] ECR 3727.

[106] Based on case law: eg Case 4/73, *Nold v Commission* [1974] ECR 491.

[107] *Sigurjonnson v Iceland* [1993] Series A no 264; *Young, James & Webster* [1981] Series A no 44. See also, Art 5 ESC, Art 22 of the International Covenant on Civil and Political Rights; Art 8 of the International Covenant on Economic, Social and Cultural Rights; and ILO Convention Nos 87 and 98.

[108] See AG Jacobs in Case 274/96, *Bickel & Franz* [1998] ECR I–7637, at paras 23–4 of his opinion. See further, Reich, n 66 above at 10–13.

[109] Art 17(1) [ex 8] EC.

[110] Under Art 137(3) EC.

[111] See Reich, n 66 above at 23.

[112] This is a basic tenet of national constitutions. Also recognised by the Court of Justice: eg Case 283/83, *Racke v Hauptzollamt Mainz* [1984] ECR 3791.

[113] Based on Art 12 [ex 6] EC and Art 13 EC. Further sources are Art 14 ECHR and Art 11 of the Convention on Human Rights and Biomedicine.

[114] Derived from Art 6 [ex F] TEU and Art 151 [ex 128] EC, the provisions on culture.

—equality between men and women (Article 23);
—rights of the child (Article 24);[115]
—rights of the elderly (Article 25);[116]
—integration of persons with disabilities (Article 26).[117]

Article 21(1) lays down a general right to non-discrimination as follows:[118]

Any discrimination based on any ground such as sex, race, *colour*, ethnic or *social* origin, *genetic features*, *language*, religion or belief, *political or any other opinion*, *membership of a national minority*, property, *birth*, disability, age or sexual orientation shall be prohibited.

Article 22(2) replicates the prohibition of discrimination on grounds of nationality contained in Article 12 [ex 6] EC. By contrast, the grounds of discrimination emphasised above are in addition to those referred to in the exhaustive list in Article 13 EC,[119] although the words 'racial or ethnic origin' in that provision may imply discrimination based on colour, genetic features and membership of a national minority.[120] There is a danger that the inclusion of additional classifications of discrimination may further accentuate the hierarchical essentialist model of EU equalities law and raise unrealistic expectations of programmatic and legislative action in areas that fall outside the competence of the Community. Conversely, the reference to discrimination on the grounds of social origin, which had been specifically excluded during the drafting stage of Article 13 EC, amounts to a political recognition of disadvantage arising from multiple or cumulative discrimination in society.[121]

Article 23 on equality between men and women states that:[122]

Equality between men and women *must be ensured in all areas*, including employment, work and pay.

The principle of equality shall not prevent the maintenance or adoption of measures providing for specific advantages in favour of the under-represented sex.

---

[115] Based on the New York Convention on the Rights of the Child of 20 Nov 1989, ratified by all EU Member States.

[116] Drawn from Art 23 of the Revised ESC. See also points 24–25 of the Social Charter. This article did not appear in the original draft.

[117] Based on Art 15 ESC and point 26 of the Social Charter.

[118] Emphasis added.

[119] Art 13 EC provides that: 'Without prejudice to the other provisions of this Treaty and within the limits of the powers conferred upon it by the Community, the Council, acting unanimously on a proposal from the Commission and after consulting the European Parliament, may take appropriate action to combat discrimination based on sex, racial or ethnic origin, religion or belief, disability, age or sexual orientation'.

[120] The Race Equality Dir, 2000/43/EC, OJ 2000, L180/22, contains no specific definition of the term 'racial or ethnic origin' although it is made clear in recital 6 that the EU rejects theories that attempt to determine the existence of separate human races and the use of the term 'racial origin' does not imply acceptance of such theories.

[121] See ch 9 for discussion of these concepts.

[122] Emphasis added.

On the face of it the right to equality between the sexes appears to be no more than a concise version of Article 141 [ex 119] EC. Article 23 does, however, shift the emphasis from formal to substantive equality by declaring that equality between men and women 'must be ensured'. In the light of Article 23, there is potential for the Court to reconsider its case law in this area, in particular the need for a comparator in sex discrimination cases,[123] on the basis that the absence of a comparator should not be allowed to undermine the fundamental rights guarantee. The second paragraph of Article 23 contains the essence of Article 141(4) EC but, as part of the Charter, it is indicative of not just a right to equal opportunities but also of meaningful participation in society.[124] Further, by contrast with Article 21, where the prohibition of discrimination is expressed negatively, Article 23 amounts to a positive commitment to the principle of equality and serves to reinforce the Court's approach in recent cases such as *Badeck*,[125] *Gerster*[126] and *Schröder*.[127] Nevertheless, while Article 23 holds the potential for a more positive approach it will, at the same time, have to be reconciled with the clear wording of the equality directives.

Moreover, by stressing the application of the equality principle 'in all areas', Article 23 is consistent both with the general obligation to promote gender equality in Articles 2 and 3(2) EC and the practice of mainstreaming and specific actions targeted at increasing the participation of women. In addition, it provides a platform for advancing the alternative paradigm of imposing positive duties on states, public bodies and employers to promote equality in their respective spheres.[128]

Chapter IV on Solidarity comprises employment rights, social entitlements and other miscellaneous rights to, inter alia, access to a free placement service,[129] health care,[130] and a 'high level' of environmental and consumer protection.[131] Employment rights and social entitlements include:

—information and consultation within the undertaking (Article 27);
—collective bargaining and action (Article 28);
—protection in the event of unjustified dismissal (Article 30);

---

[123] For a recent example, see Case C–218/98, *Abdoulaye v Renault* [1999] ECR I–5723.

[124] See Weiss, n 55 above.

[125] Case C–158/97, *Badeck and others v Hessischer Ministerpräsident* [2000] ECR I–1875.

[126] Case C–1/95, *Gerster v Freistaat Bayern* [1997] ECR I–5253.

[127] Case C–50/96, *Deutsche Telekom AG v Schröder* [2000] ECR I–743. See ch 10 for a full discussion of this case law.

[128] See S Fredman, 'Equality: A New Generation?' (2001) 30 *Industrial Law Journal* 145 at 163–64.

[129] Art 29—based on Art 1(3) ESC and point 13 of the Social Charter. This is no more than a right for job seekers to receive information about employment vacancies and, as such, can also be implied from Art 15(1) on the 'right to engage in work and to pursue a freely chosen or accepted occupation'. See further, Weiss, n 55 above.

[130] Art 35—derived from Art 12 ESC and point 10 of the Social Charter.

[131] Arts 37 and 38.

—fair and just working conditions (Article 31);
—prohibition of child labour and protection of young people at work (Article 32);
—family and professional life (Article 33);
—social security and social assistance (Article 34).

It is immediately apparent that the chapter on Solidarity does not provide a comprehensive catalogue of fundamental social rights. The drafting Convention appears to have taken a rather cursory view of the ESC and the Social Charter despite the explicit reference to the 'visibility' of these instruments in the Cologne mandate. For example, the right to work,[132] the right to a fair remuneration[133] and the right to housing are among provisions in the ESC or Revised ESC that are not included in the negotiated text of the Charter.[134] In his insightful analysis of the workings of the Convention, Goldsmith justifies this vanishing act on the grounds that 'social and economic rights are usually not justiciable in the same way as other rights'.[135] It is undoubtedly the case that certain social rights, such as the right to social assistance or housing, concern positive social entitlements provided by governments but that does not mean that they are inherently non-justiciable.[136] Goldsmith rather lamely suggests that it would be difficult to provide for a right to an adequate level of housing in a legal text[137] but this does not absolve the EU and the Member States from responsibility to formulate policies and programmes in a manner consistent with international guidance.[138]

The distinction between 'rights' and 'principles' in the solidarity provisions is far from clear. For example, Article 27 states that workers or their representatives at the appropriate levels are 'guaranteed' the right to information and consultation within the undertaking in good time 'in the cases and under the conditions provided for by Community law and national laws and practices'.[139] The precise legal effect of these conditions will be considered in the next section, with particular reference to Article 28 on the right of collective bargaining and action,[140] and Article 30 on protection in the event of unjustified dismissal,[141] where the same rider is attached.

[132] Now Art 1 ESC.
[133] Art 4 ESC and point 5 of the Social Charter.
[134] Art 31 of the Revised ESC.
[135] Goldsmith, n 35 above at 1212.
[136] See Craven, n 83 above at 87.
[137] Goldsmith, n 35 above at 1212.
[138] Craven, n 83 above at 89. Craven refers to the General Comment of the UN Committee on Economic, Social and Cultural Rights on the Right to Adequate Housing which encompasses more than simply a 'roof over one's head' and includes matters such as security of tenure, availability of services, affordability, habitability, accessibility, location and cultural adequacy—General Comment No 4 (1991) UN Doc E/1992/23, annex III, paras 7–8.
[139] Art 27 is consistent with Art 21 of the Revised ESC and points 17–18 of the Social Charter. It also incorporates the notion of social dialogue contained in Arts 138 and 139 [ex 118b] EC.
[140] Based on Art 6 ESC and points 12–14 of the Social Charter.
[141] Draws on Art 24 of the Revised ESC.

For now it is important to note that several of the provisions in the Solidarity Chapter are not expressed as freestanding 'rights'.

Directive 2002/14 on establishing a general framework for informing and consulting employees in the European Community[142] can be seen as an attempt to secure this objective through Community law while, as Article 27 indicates, allowing for national diversity. In effect, Article 27 reaffirms the existing obligation on the Community to act in this area but it does not resolve the issue of what level is appropriate and under what conditions the guarantee will operate.[143] Furthermore, the Charter makes no reference to the right of workers, contained in the Revised ESC,[144] to take part in the determination and improvement of the working conditions and working environment. The absence of any reference to workers' participation is a striking indication of the failure of the Charter to fully address the issue of inequality in the employment relationship.[145]

Article 27 is a good example of a 'right' that is derived primarily from Community law. Articles 31, 32[146] and 33(2)[147] also fall into this category. For example, Article 31(1), providing that 'every worker' has the right to working conditions which respect his or her 'health, safety and dignity', is derived mainly from the Framework Directive on Safety and Health at Work.[148] It should be noted, however, that the term 'working conditions', drawn from Article 140 [ex 118] EC, is used rather than the much wider 'working environment' found in Article 137(1) [ex 118a] EC.[149] Article 31(2), which grants 'every worker' the right to limitation of maximum working hours, to daily and weekly rest and an annual period of paid leave, is based on the Working Time Directive.[150] While the exclusion of certain sectors and activities from that Directive is now being addressed,[151] the law, even after the implementation of a series of supplementary sectoral directives,[152] will still not contain an unfettered right to any of the proclaimed rights apart from a minimum of four weeks paid annual leave. The main area of contention is likely to concern Article 18(b)(i) of the Working Time

---

[142] Dir 2002/14/EC, OJ 2002, L80/29.

[143] See Hepple (2001, *Industrial Law Journal*) n 84 above at 228–29.

[144] Art 22 of the Revised ESC.

[145] See the case made by Hepple (1995, *Current Legal Problems*) n 96 above at 52.

[146] Art 32 is based on Dir 94/33/EC on the protection of young people at work, OJ 1994, L216/12. See also, Art 7 ESC and points 20–23 of the Social Charter.

[147] Art 33(2) contains the basic rights set out in the Pregnancy and Maternity Dir, 92/85/EEC, OJ 1992, L348/1; and the Parental Leave Dir, 96/34/EC, OJ 1996, L145/4. See also Art 8 ESC and Art 27 of the Revised ESC. Art 33(1) provides for a more general family right, based on the right in Art 16 ESC to 'legal, economic and social protection'.

[148] Dir 89/391/EEC, OJ 1989, L183/1. Other sources include Art 3 ESC, Art 26 of the Revised ESC and point 19 of the Social Charter.

[149] See further, Case C–84/94, *United Kingdom v Council* [1996] ECR I–5755.

[150] Dir 93/104/EC, OJ 1993, L307/18. See also, Art 2 ESC and point 8 of the Social Charter.

[151] See Dir 2000/34/EC, OJ 2000, L195/41.

[152] Dir 99/63/EC, OJ 1999, L167/33 and Dir 99/95/EC, OJ 2000, L14/29 (both concerning seafarers) and Dir 2000/79/EC, OJ 2000, L302/57 ('mobile' airline staff).

Directive which allows Member States discretion to provide for an individual 'opt-out' from the maximum working week provisions where workers agree to an employer's request to perform such work. In the UK, where this 'opt-out' is available, it has been widely suggested that, in practice, many workers have little option but to agree to such requests. It is difficult to see how this clause can be reconciled with Article 31.

Under Article 34(1) the Union 'recognises and respects' a range of entitlements to social security benefits and social services.[153] Article 34(3) applies the same language to the right to social and housing assistance 'so as to ensure a decent existence for all those who lack sufficient resources' in order to combat social exclusion and poverty.[154] The purpose of this Article is to reaffirm the European model of social protection while also respecting the competence of the Member States in these areas. This is consistent with the principle of subsidiarity and helps us to distinguish between general principles and the pursuit of specific policies.[155] Therefore, although Article 34 may have only a limited practical impact, it provides some political ballast for the preservation of welfare states in Europe based on the notion of social rights as positive entitlements.

Finally, before we turn to the legal scope and effectiveness of these provisions, it is important to note that Chapter VI on Justice includes a number of rights concerned with access to justice including: the right to an effective remedy,[156] a fair trial,[157] the presumption of innocence and the right of defence.[158]

IV THE LEGAL SCOPE OF THE CHARTER

Chapter VII, Articles 51–54, contains general provisions that are intended to define the legal scope of the Charter and the level of protection it offers,

---

[153] Based on Arts 137(3) and 140 [ex 118] EC, Art 12 ESC and point 10 of the Social Charter. Art 34(1) refers to social entitlements 'in cases such as maternity, illness, industrial accidents, dependency or old age, and in the case of loss of employment, in accordance with the rules laid down by Community law and national laws and practices'.

[154] This paragraph draws on Arts 30–31 of the Revised ESC and point 10 of the Social Charter.

[155] On this point, see the explanation by Hepple (1995, *Current Legal Problems*) n 96 above at 50.

[156] Art 47, first paragraph, derived from Art 13 ECHR and buttressed by more extensive protection provided by the Court of Justice guaranteeing an effective remedy: Case 222/84, *Johnston v Chief Constable of the RUC* [1986] ECR 1651; Case 222/86, *UNECTEF v Heylens* [1987] ECR 4097; and Case C–97/91, *Borelli v Commission* [1992] ECR I–6313.

[157] Art 47, second and third paragraphs. Included within this provision is a right to legal aid for those who 'lack sufficient resources in so far as such aid is necessary to ensure effective access to justice'. In *Airey* [1979] Series A vol 32/11, the European Court of Human Rights held that provision should be made for legal aid where the absence of such aid would make it impossible to ensure an effective remedy.

[158] Art 48—corresponding with Art 6(2) and (3) ECHR.

on the assumption that it may become a binding document in due course.[159] Therefore, in order to determine both the effectiveness of the Charter as a soft law instrument and its potential legal scope in the future if it is incorporated into the Treaties, it is necessary to explore these provisions in depth.

Article 51 outlines the scope of the Charter. Under Article 51(1) the provisions in the Charter are addressed to the 'institutions and bodies'[160] of the Union 'with due regard to the principle of subsidiarity' and to the Member States 'only when they are implementing Union law'. In accordance with their respective powers they shall 'respect the rights, observe the principles and promote the application' of the Charter. Therefore, on the one hand, the purpose of the Charter is to enhance the legitimacy of the EU by ensuring that it complies with internationally recognised standards of fundamental rights in all of its activities, without granting the Union a specific competence to accede to the ECHR or ESC. The national government representatives were clearly determined to block the notion of an independent EU human rights policy, as advocated by Alston and Weiler.[161] Hence, the reference to subsidiarity, which is intended to prevent the Charter having a centralising effect.[162]

The Member States, on the other hand, are regarded as individually bound by the obligations in the Charter under international law.[163] In fact this is not strictly the case as many Member States have not signed up to, for example, the Revised ESC, or all relevant ILO Conventions. However, the adoption of the Charter as a high level inter-institutional political declaration, and the unique manner of its drafting, strengthens its legitimacy and creates an expectation of conformity with the individual fundamental rights that it enumerates without creating a strict legal obligation on the Member States.[164] Further, a clear message is being sent to applicant states that the Charter now provides the reference point for the assessment of the fundamental rights criteria required for EU accession.[165]

---

[159] See Costello, n 63 above at 128.

[160] According to the explanatory note, this would include all institutions listed in Art 7 [ex 4] EC and bodies set up by the Treaties or secondary legislation. See CHARTE 4473/00, CONVENT 49, p 46. For discussion, see Curtin and van Ooik, n 42 above at 104–8.

[161] See n 19 above. For a powerful critique, see von Bogdandy, n 57 above.

[162] See von Bogdandy, *ibid* at 1316.

[163] A point that is reinforced by Art 6(1) [ex F(1)] TEU, which refers to Member States' observance of common principles including 'liberty, democracy, respect for human rights and fundamental freedoms, and the rule of law'.

[164] See especially, J Kenner, 'EC Labour Law: the Softly, Softly Approach' (1995) 11 *International Journal of Comparative Labour Law and Industrial Relations* 307; and F Snyder, *Soft Law and Institutional Practice in the European Community*, EUI Working Paper LAW No 93/5 (EUI, Florence, 1993).

[165] In this respect the Charter is to be read in conjunction with Art 7 TEU whereby a Member State found to have been guilty of 'a serious and persistent breach' of fundamental rights and other principles listed in Art 6(1) [ex F(1)] TEU can have certain of their EU rights suspended. Under the draft Treaty of Nice, Art 7 TEU will be strengthened to allow action to

Nevertheless, unlike the Social Charter, the Charter of Fundamental Rights is not directly addressed to the Member States except in so far as when they are 'implementing Union law'. An earlier draft had used the formulation that Member States would be bound by the Charter only when acting 'within the scope of Community law',[166] a statement that is consistent with the case law of the Court.[167] Rather confusingly, the Convention's explanatory note suggests that Member States will be bound 'when they act in the context of Community law'.[168] Viewed in isolation, Article 51(1) would appear to be a restriction on the Court's powers of interpretation and application of fundamental rights.[169] However, Article 53 states that nothing in the Charter shall be interpreted as restricting or adversely affecting human rights 'in their field of application' by Union law. According to the explanatory text this is intended to maintain the level of protection currently afforded.[170] This would appear to leave the Court free to apply the rights in the Charter 'horizontally' in preliminary references involving private parties, consistent with its case law on sex equality[171] and non-discrimination on grounds of nationality,[172] binding employers and entities which regulate employment.[173]

---

be taken against a Member State where there is a 'clear risk of a serious breach' by that State. The Council may address 'appropriate recommendations' to the State in question, acting by a four-fifths majority and after obtaining the assent of the European Parliament, on a reasoned proposal by one-third of Member States, by the European Parliament or by the Commission. The 'purely procedural stipulations' in Art 7 TEU, which include a procedure for the Member State under review to be heard and for an independent report to be submitted to the Council, will be subject to review by the Court under Art 46 [ex L] TEU. These changes are intended to give the EU power to act where there is a potential violation of human rights principles and have been introduced as a direct response to the events in Austria where, following the electoral success of the far-right 'Freedom Party' in Oct 1999, the EU found itself unable to act decisively.

[166] CHARTRE 4360/00.

[167] See Cases C–60 and 61/84, *Cinéthèque v Fédération Nationale des Cinémas Français* [1985] ECR 2605, para 25; Case C–12/86, *Demirel v Stadt Schwaebisch Gmund* [1987] ECR 3719, para 28; and Case C–260/89, *ERT v Pliroforissis & Kouvelas* [1991] ECR I–2925, para 42, where the Court held that 'it has no power to examine the compatibility with the European Convention on Human Rights of national rules which do not fall within the scope of Community law. On the other hand, where such rules do fall within the scope of Community law, and reference is made to the Court for a preliminary ruling, it must provide all the criteria of interpretation needed by the national court to determine whether those rules are compatible with the fundamental rights the observance of which the Court ensures and which derive in particular from the European Convention on Human Rights'.

[168] See CHARTE 4473/00, CONVENT 49, p 46. See further, L Besselink, 'The Member States, the National Constitutions and the Scope of the Charter' (2001) 8 *Maastricht Journal* 68 at 76.

[169] See de Búrca (2001, *European Law Review*) n 18 above at 137.

[170] See CHARTE 4473/00, CONVENT 49, p 50.

[171] See Case 43/75, *Defrenne v Sabena II* [1976] ECR 455.

[172] See Case C–281/98, *Angonese v Cassa di Risparmio di Bolzano SpA* [2000] ECR I–4139.

[173] See Costello, n 63 above at 144.

The Court has ruled that Member States may be held liable for legislative or administrative decisions in 'all situations which fall within the scope *ratione materiae* of Community law'.[174] For example, the Court has ruled that actions of Member States in areas such as education,[175] vocational training,[176] public transport,[177] and health,[178] may fall within the scope of Community law if they are incompatible with, or a restraint upon, the exercise of *market rights*, such as the free movement rules. In this respect it is important to note that the Race Equality Directive will prohibit discrimination on the grounds of 'racial or ethnic origin' in a wide range of fields including, inter alia, social protection, social security, social advantages, education and healthcare.[179] The new Directive will present a fresh challenge for the Court when ruling on the policy choices of Member States in areas of national competence. Moreover, the Charter's emphasis on 'indivisible values of human dignity, freedom, equality and solidarity'[180] adds weight to Poiares Maduro's suggestion that the Court should 'elevate the assessment of reasonableness of public intervention in the market from market integration rules to the realm of classical social and economic fundamental rights'.[181]

The main thrust of Article 51(1) must be understood in the context of Article 6(2) [ex F(2)] TEU which places a duty on the Union to respect fundamental rights derived both from the ECHR and the constitutional traditions common to the Member States. This means that there is a positive obligation on the Commission when proposing legislation, and the European Parliament and Council when performing their legislative roles, to take full account of the Charter. While this obligation does not carry binding force in itself, the Charter adds meaning and legal certainty to the responsibility of the Community and the Member States in Article 136 [ex 117] EC to have in mind fundamental social rights when pursuing their objectives under the Social Chapter. According to the Commission, the Charter 'will produce all its effects, legal and others, whatever its nature'.[182] In performing their judicial roles, the Court of Justice and the Court of First Instance will be obliged to have cognisance of the rights in the Charter. In particular, the Courts will have to re-evaluate their narrow approach to

---

[174] Case C–85/96, *Martinez Sala v Freistaat Bayern* [1998] ECR I–2691, para 63. For discussion, see Poiares Maduro in Alston, n 3 above at 456–7.

[175] For example, see Case 152/82, *Forcheri v Belgian State* [1983] ECR 2323.

[176] See Case 293/83, *Gravier v City of Liège* [1985] ECR 593; and Case 24/86, *Blaizot v University of Liège* [1988] ECR 379.

[177] See Case 32/75, *Christini v SNCF* [1975] ECR 1085.

[178] See Case C–158/96, *Kohll v Union des caisses de maladie* [1998] ECR I–1931; and Case C–120/95, *Decker v Caisse de maladie des employés privés* [1998] ECR I–1831.

[179] Art 3(1) of Dir 2000/43/EC, OJ 2000, L180/22. See ch 9 for discussion.

[180] Second recital of the preamble.

[181] See Poiares Maduro in Alston, n 3 above at 464.

[182] COM(2000) 644, para 10.

the locus standi rules for non-privileged applicants in judicial review proceedings[183] to ensure compliance with the access to justice provisions in the
Charter.[184]

When carrying out their legislative functions, it will be difficult for the
EU institutions to ignore the Charter.[185] For example, the Commission's
draft directive on working conditions for temporary workers,[186] which is
based on Article 137(1) EC, 'is designed to ensure full compliance' with
Article 31 of the Charter that proclaims the right of *every worker* to fair
and just working conditions.[187] Moreover, the proposal also refers to the
Social Charter,[188] emphasising that it has continuing relevance and a quite
distinctive function because, unlike the Charter of Fundamental Rights, it
places particular responsibility on the Member States to guarantee the fundamental social rights that it enumerates.[189] Hence, the recent Directive on
establishing a general framework for informing and consulting employees,[190] which applies to undertakings with more than fifty employees even
if they are based in only one Member State, demonstrates that the Social
Charter still retains potency as a catalyst for social legislation and is not
wholly superseded by the new Charter.[191]

While Article 51(1) opens up possibilities for utilising the Charter, Article
51(2) limits its scope as follows:

This Charter does not establish any new power or task for the Community or the
Union, or modify powers and tasks defined by the Treaties.

The purpose of this clause is to prevent the Charter being used as a 'Trojan
horse' to expand social policy even if it enters into legal force.[192] For
example, although the Charter 'recognises and respects' the entitlement to
social security and social assistance,[193] this right is purely symbolic, or at

---

[183] With the exception of the privileged institutional applicants, Art 230 [ex 173] EC
restricts standing for judicial review proceedings thus: 'Any natural or legal person may, under
the same conditions, institute proceedings against a decision addressed to that person or
against a decision which, although in the form of a regulation or a decision addressed to
another person, is of direct and individual concern to the former'. For analysis of the Court's
approach, see A Arnull, *The European Union and its Court of Justice* (OUP, Oxford, 1999)
pp 40–9.

[184] Arts 47–50.

[185] COM(2000) 644, para 10.

[186] COM(2002) 149.

[187] Draft first recital of the preamble.

[188] Draft second recital of the preamble, which refers to the achievement of harmonisation
of the living and working conditions of temporary workers in accordance with point 7 of the
Social Charter.

[189] Point 27 of the Social Charter.

[190] Dir 2002/14/EC, OJ 2002, L80/29. This Directive is also based on Art 137(1) EC.

[191] But see Hepple (2001, *Industrial Law Journal*) n 84 above at 230.

[192] The fear expressed by the Confederation of British Industry is that the Charter will be
'a "Trojan horse" imposing social policy through the back door'—*The Times*, 1 June 2000.
See Betten, n 11 above at 151.

[193] Art 34(1).

least adds nothing to existing Community rules concerning free movement and non-discrimination. Further, the limitation in Article 51(2) is reinforced by Article 52(2), concerning the scope of guaranteed rights, which declares that rights recognised by the Charter, which are based on the Treaties, 'shall be exercised under the conditions and within the limits defined by the Treaties'. In order to illustrate the effect of these limitations of scope let us consider two possible scenarios.

The first scenario concerns Article 30, which recognises the right of *every worker* to protection against unjustified dismissal, in accordance with Community law and 'national laws and practices'. According to Goldsmith,[194] the UK had to 'fight very hard' to include this formulation in the final draft. From his perspective, economic and social 'rights' are mere 'principles' that will only be realised as exercisable rights 'to the extent that they are implemented by national law or, in those areas where there is such competence, by Community law'.[195] Goldsmith was acutely aware that the UK's national legislation on unfair dismissal, which excludes workers in the first year of their employment contract, was under threat.[196] Article 137(3) EC provides a legal base for Community legislation to provide protection against dismissal but only subject to a requirement of unanimity in the Council. Thus, although Article 51(1) makes it an imperative for the Commission to bring forward a proposal in this area, the effect of Article 30, read in conjunction with Article 51(2), is that, even if the Charter becomes legally binding, it only creates a moral obligation on the Council to act. In turn, the UK would be entitled to veto such a proposal in its entirety or seek to secure an amendment that would exclude the most vulnerable workers from the 'right' to protection against unjustified dismissal.

Article 28, concerning the right of collective bargaining and action provides us with another interesting scenario. Workers and employers, or their respective organisations have, in addition to the right to negotiate and conclude collective agreements at the appropriate level, the right 'in cases of conflicts of interest, to take collective action to defend their interests, including strike action'. As with Article 30, this right applies only in accordance with Community law and national law and practices. Let us suppose that the Commission wishes to propose a directive to harmonise the law on the right to strike.[197] Immediately this would conflict with the exclusion of the right to strike from the scope of Community legislative action under Article 137(6) EC. The effect of Article 52(2) is, according to the explanatory

---

[194] Goldsmith, n 35 above at 1213.
[195] *Ibid.*
[196] See Betten, n 11 above at 163.
[197] For advocacy of action in this area, see P Germanotta and T Novitz, 'Globalisation and the Right to Strike: The Case for European-Level Protection of Secondary Action' (2002) 18 *International Journal of Comparative Labour Law and Industrial Relations* 67.

note,[198] to preserve the status quo because the Charter does not alter the system of rights and conditions conferred by the Treaties and Community legislation. Further, Article 51(2) may inhibit the Community from exercising its powers in this respect, making it difficult to justify legislation based on another ground such as common market approximation under Article 94 [ex 100] EC.[199] This inconsistency undermines both the visibility of the Charter and its effectiveness. Member States, such as the UK, who have domestic legislation that does not comply with ILO Convention No 87 or Article 6(4) ESC, from which the right in Article 28 is derived, are under no compulsion to act. As Weiss[200] observes, the Community is obliged by the Charter to promote a right in an area where it has no power to harmonise laws, which might lead one to suggest that Article 28 is nugatory in effect.

Article 51(1) will also oblige the Court of Justice and the Court of First Instance, within their respective jurisdictions, to take account of the Charter when carrying out their duties of interpretation under Article 220 [ex 164] EC.[201] This opens up a number of possibilities but also carries with it certain dangers. The Court has developed the concept that 'respect for fundamental rights forms an integral part of the general principles of law protected by the Court of Justice'.[202] Fundamental rights have been utilised incrementally to perform an important gap-filling function, enabling the Court to assert the supremacy of Community law 'within the framework and structure of the Treaties'.[203] As de Witte[204] observes, by using unwritten principles 'instead of, or in addition to, rights expressly contained in the constitution, supreme courts enlarge their scope for creative law-making'. For Weiler[205] the ability of the Court to draw from the legal system of each Member State 'as an organic and living laboratory of human rights protection' is one of the Community's truly original features. Indeed in cases

---

[198] CHARTE 4473/00, CONVENT 49, p 48.

[199] On the basis that this would prevent distortions of competition and help to establish the 'common market' in accordance with Art 2 EC. Utilisation of Art 94 EC in this regard would be possible notwithstanding the limited scope of the narrower 'internal market' concept in Art 14 [ex 7a] EC and its distinct legal base for approximation measures in Art 95 [ex 100a] EC. See ch 3 for discussion of this issue in the context of the Court's judgment in Case C–376/98, *Germany v European Parliament and Council (Tobacco Advertising)* [2000] ECR I–8419.

[200] See Weiss, n 55 above.

[201] This is based on the revised text of Art 220 [ex 164] EC in the draft Treaty of Nice. If ratified, the new Treaty will expand the jurisdiction of the Court of First Instance. See OJ 2000, C80/1. See further Shaw, n 6 above, at 203–8.

[202] See Case 11/70, *Internationale Handelsgesellschaft v Einfuhr-und Vorratsstelle Getreide* [1970] ECR 1125, para 4.

[203] *Ibid*. See B de Witte, 'The Past and Future Role of the European Court of Justice in the Protection of Human Rights' in Alston, n 3 above, 859–97 at 863.

[204] *Ibid* at 865.

[205] See Weiler (2000, *European Law Journal*) n 72 above at 96.

such as *Rutili*,[206] *Johnston*,[207] *Wachauf*[208] and *P v S*,[209] the Court has been able to identify Community provisions as specific manifestations of more general principles enshrined in the ECHR and national constitutions[210] and therefore reflective of common values.[211] The Court has resolved that the Community cannot accept measures that are incompatible with the observance of fundamental rights thus recognised and guaranteed,[212] but it has no power to examine the compatibility with fundamental rights of national rules that do not fall within the scope of Community law.[213] Therefore, fundamental rights as developed by the Court have provided a source of inspiration for the interpretation and application of Community law amounting to an 'unwritten charter of rights'.[214]

Weiler fears that the adoption of the Charter 'runs the risk of inducing a more inward looking jurisprudence and chilling the constitutional dialogue'.[215] Where, for example, rights in the Charter are derived from the case law of the Court this may inhibit further innovation and induce a 'freezing effect'.[216] Equally, the explanatory note may unduly influence the Court even though it has 'no legal value' and is simply intended to clarify the provisions of the Charter.[217] For example, in *D and Sweden v Council*,[218] the issue at stake concerned recognition by the Council of a same-sex

[206] Case 36/75, *Rutili v Minister for the Interior* [1975] ECR 1219, para 32. See P Craig and G de Búrca, *EU Law—Text, Cases and Materials*, 2nd edn (OUP, Oxford, 1998) pp 303–5.
[207] Case 222/84, *Johnston v Chief Constable of the RUC* [1986] ECR 1651, para 18.
[208] Case 5/88, *Wachauf v Germany* [1989] ECR 2609, para 19.
[209] Case C–13/94, *P v S & Cornwall CC* [1996] ECR I–2143, para 18.
[210] See Case 44/79, *Hauer v Land Rheinland-Pfalz* [1979] ECR 3727, paras 14–16.
[211] See Craig and de Búrca, n 206 above p 305.
[212] See Case C–260/89, *ERT v Pliroforissis & Kouvelas* [1991] ECR I–2925, para 41. For a more wide ranging statement, see the opinion of AG Jacobs in Case C–168/91, *Konstantinidis v Stadt Altensteig, Standesamt, & Landratsamt Calw, Ordnungsamt* [1993] ECR I–1191. The AG advised that an EU national is entitled to assume that, wherever he goes in the EU 'he will be treated in accordance with a common code of fundamental values, in particular those laid down in the European Convention on Human Rights. In other words, he is entitled to say 'civis europeus sum' and to invoke that status in order to oppose any violation of his fundamental rights' (para 46).
[213] For examples of the application of this rule, see Case C–299/95, *Kremzow v Austria* [1997] ECR I–2629; Case C–309/96, *Annibaldi v Sindaco del Comune di Guidonia & Presidente Regione Lazio* [1997] ECR I–7493; and Case C–249/96, *Grant v South-West Trains* [1998] ECR I–621. Discussed by de Witte, n 203 above at 870–74. For a lively debate, see J Coppel and A O'Neill, 'The European Court of Justice: Taking Rights Seriously?' (1992) 29 *Common Market Law Review* 669; and J Weiler and N Lockhart, '"Taking Rights Seriously" Seriously: The European Court and its Fundamental Rights Jurisprudence' (1995) 32 *Common Market Law Review* 59.
[214] See Craig and de Búrca, n 206 above, p 296.
[215] Weiler (2000, *European Law Journal*) n 72 above at 96.
[216] See de Witte, (2001, *Maastricht Journal*) n 53 above at 85. De Witte gives the example of Art 41 on the right to good administration.
[217] CHARTE 4473/00, CONVENT 49, p 1. On this point, see Costello, n 63 above at 132.
[218] Cases C–122/99P and C–125/99P [2001] ECR I–4139, at para 97 of the opinion. Noted by E Ellis (2002) 39 *Common Market Law Review* 151.

partnership that was legally recognised in Sweden. In his opinion, AG Mischo considered the term 'spouse' in the Community's Staff Regulations in the context of Article 9 of the Charter on the right to marry and found a family. The AG referred directly to the explanatory note, which states that Article 9 'neither prohibits nor imposes the granting of the status of marriage to unions between people of the same sex'.[219] In the light of this advice he recommended that the Court should follow its earlier case law restricting the meaning of 'spouse' to marital relationships between couples of the opposite sex.[220] In its judgment the Court followed this advice without making direct reference to the Charter.

Although *D* might suggest that, to the extent that the Charter is a point of reference for the Court, it will merely 'consecrate the status quo',[221] the case is perhaps best explained as a classic example of judicial restraint in a situation where, as in *Grant*,[222] new Community legislation had been introduced[223] or was imminent in an area of acute national sensitivity.[224]

Article 28 of the Charter, recognising the right of collective bargaining and action may present the Court with an opportunity to interpret and apply the Charter more creatively, but it also reveals new dilemmas. We have discussed the opinion of AG Jacobs and the judgment of the Court in the pre-Charter case of *Albany International*[225] in a range of contexts, but the Charter now casts a fresh light on the tension between collective labour law and competition law. In his extensive opinion, the AG relied primarily on the case law of the European Court of Human Rights based on Article 11 ECHR concerning freedom of association, the essence of which is replicated in Article 12 of the Charter. The AG was satisfied that, on the basis of the case law of the Strasbourg Court, the ECHR did not establish a general right to bargain collectively, and, while he accepted that the right was recognised by Article 6 ESC and other international instruments upon which the Member States had collaborated,[226] he concluded that there was insufficient convergence of national legal orders and international legal instruments on the recognition of a specific fundamental right to bargain

---

[219] CHARTE 4473/00, CONVENT 49, p 12.

[220] See Case 59/85, *Netherlands v Reed* [1986] ECR 1283.

[221] Weiler (2000, *European Law Journal*) n 72 above at 96.

[222] Case C–249/96, *Grant v South-West Trains* [1998] ECR I–621. See pp 435–42.

[223] An amendment to the Staff Regulations had been introduced but was not yet in force at the material time: Council Reg 781/98/EC, OJ 1998, L113/4. See Ellis, n 218 above at 151.

[224] However, recital 22 of the preamble of the Framework Employment Dir, 2000/78/EC, OJ 2000, L303/16, which prohibits sexual orientation discrimination in employment, states that the Directive is 'without prejudice' to national laws on marital status and benefits dependent thereon.

[225] Case C–67/96, *Albany International BV v Stichting Bedrijfspensioenfonds Textielindustrie* [1999] ECR I–5751.

[226] ILO Convention Nos 87 and 98; Art 22 of the International Covenant on Civil and Political Rights; and Art 8 of the International Covenant on Economic, Social and Cultural Rights.

collectively.[227] The Court did not address the international instruments in its judgment although it too ultimately concluded that collective agreements per se fell outside the competition rules in Article 81 [ex 85] EC.

While the AG's approach is comprehensive, his analysis underplays the status and autonomy of the ESC and, most importantly, the authority of the legal experts on the European Committee of Social Rights (ECSR) that oversees its operation.[228] Once again it reveals a bias in favour of 'first generation' civil and political rights over 'second generation' economic and social rights. There is, however, a serious underlying problem. The ECSR is not a court, even if it is quasi-judicial in nature, and therefore, as Fitzpatrick notes,[229] in dealing with the ECHR, the Court of Justice is in a mode of 'judges speaking to judges', whereas it tends to perceive other bodies as non-judicial and discounts their expertise.[230] The ECSR is gradually maturing as an expert body that produces a regular, coherent overview of the ESC and the Revised ESC,[231] whereas the Strasbourg Court is concerned only with the interplay between the ESC/Revised ESC and the ECHR when interpreting and applying the rights protected by the latter.

The emergence of a Charter based on a core concept of indivisible rights would suggest that the Court is now impelled, in cases concerning the interpretation of provisions derived from the ESC/Revised ESC, to consider the legal assessments of the ECSR. This would provide a foundation for the Court to affirm collective bargaining rights, as set out in Article 28, when ruling on a matter within the scope of Community law.[232] However, Article 52(3) may dissuade the Court from acting boldly. Under that provision, where rights correspond with those guaranteed by the ECHR 'the meaning and scope of those rights shall be the same as those laid down by the said convention'. According to the explanatory note this is intended to ensure consistency between the ECHR and the Charter as determined both by the

---

[227] Para 160. The AG concludes, in para 161, that the right to collective bargaining is sufficiently protected by the general principle of freedom of contract.

[228] The ECSR consists of nine experts assisted by an observer from the ILO. Under the Amending Protocol of 1991 its functions are to examine the national reports and make a legal assessment of the states' observance of their legal obligations. For further discussion, see Casey, n 20 above at 56; and Novitz, n 82 above who notes, at 250, attempts by the Parliamentary Assembly of the Council of Europe to establish either a 'parallel European Court of Social Rights' or the absorption of the ESC within the ECHR 'in order to create the basis for strict legal observance': *Recommendation No 1354 on the Future of the European Social Charter* (1998) para 18.

[229] See B Fitzpatrick, 'European Union Law and the Council of Europe Conventions' in Costello, n 20 above, 95–108 at 101.

[230] *Ibid.* For example, in Case C–249/96, *Grant v South-West Trains* [1998] ECR I–621, the Court was not prepared to draw on the interpretation of the International Covenant on Civil and Political Rights by the UN Human Rights Committee, also a quasi-judicial body.

[231] *Ibid* at 101. Until all Member States of the Council of Europe endorse the Revised ESC the two texts will operate in tandem.

[232] See Costello, n 63 above at 137.

text of the ECHR and the case law of the European Court of Human Rights.[233] The Court of Justice is extremely sensitive about its relationship with its colleagues in Strasbourg, and this feeling of sensitivity has been heightened and reciprocated following the negotiation and adoption of the Charter. In a future case the Court may be inclined to follow the European Court of Human Rights' restrictive interpretation of Article 6 ESC in the context of Article 11 ECHR, for the purposes of judicial consistency and coherence, rather than adhering to the autonomous but only quasi-judicial findings of the ECSR. Significantly, there is no mention of the ECSR in Article 52(3), while the only direct reference to the ESC is in the preamble. The final sentence of Article 52(3) allows Union laws to lay down more extensive protection than the ECHR. This would allow the Court leeway to make direct reference to higher standards laid down in the Charter as 'Union law' if the Charter enters into legal force.

Article 52(3) is also likely to lead the Court to follow the jurisprudence of the Strasbourg Court and review its established case law. This possibility was open to the Court in *D*.[234] AG Mischo, basing his interpretation on the Court's judgment in *Grant*, was not prepared to make a like-for-like comparison between the situations of same-sex and opposite-sex couples. The AG reached this conclusion notwithstanding bolder steps taken in Strasbourg, where the European Court of Human Rights has now held that sexual orientation discrimination is a violation of the right to respect for private life guaranteed by Article 8 ECHR.[235] Further, neither the AG nor the Court referred to the right to non-discrimination in Article 21 of the Charter, which prohibits sexual orientation discrimination on the basis of Article 13 EC and also the general non-discrimination clause in Article 14 ECHR which has been broadly interpreted by the European Court of Human Rights.[236] The AG and the Court were undoubtedly influenced by the fact that only three out of 15 Member States recognised same-sex partnerships at the material time. However, by September 2001 that figure had increased to five with legislation pending in several other countries.[237] This may allow the Court to review its case law on the basis of the 'common constitutional traditions of the Member States' without having to concede that its earlier formulation is clearly at odds with Article 52(3).

Article 53 provides a minimum standards guarantee of the 'level of protection' offered by the Charter:

---

[233] CHARTE 4473/00, CONVENT 49, p 48.

[234] Cases C–122/99P and 125/99P [2001] ECR I–4139.

[235] Appl Nos 33985/96 and 33986/96, *Smith and Grady v United Kingdom* [2000] 29 EHRR 493. In *D* the Court found, at para 59, that Art 8 ECHR was not affected by the Staff Regulations because the refusal to grant the allowance did not affect D's civil status.

[236] Appl No 33290/96, *da Silva Mouta v Portugal* [2001] 31 EHRR 47.

[237] See Ellis, n 218 above at 152. For comprehensive analysis, see R Wintemute and M Andenas, *Legal Recognition of Same-Sex Partnerships: A Study of National, European and International Law* (Hart, Oxford, 2001).

Nothing in this Charter shall be interpreted as restricting or adversely affecting human rights and fundamental freedoms as recognised, in their respective fields of application, by Union law and international law and by international agreements to which the Union, the Community or all Member States are party, including the European Convention for the Protection of Human Rights and Fundamental Freedoms, and by Member States' constitutions.

The purpose of Article 53 is to 'maintain the level of protection currently afforded within their respective scope by Union law, national law and international law'.[238] Consistent with the notion of 'non-retrogression' inherent within Article 137(5) [ex 118a(3)] EC, Article 53 is designed to prevent the Charter being interpreted and applied in such a way as to reduce or level down the protection of rights within the EU and national legal orders. Moreover, if the Charter becomes legally binding, it is intended that it will guarantee the minimum standard or 'floor' of fundamental rights protection that it enunciates, but it should not be seen as a ceiling. For example, existing laws may provide a higher standard of protection, or the Charter may act as a spur for the elaboration or expansion of the rights that it contains. Although some concern has been expressed that Article 53 may replace or weaken Member States' provisions concerning fundamental rights,[239] and may even threaten the supremacy of Community law, it is better understood as a political safeguard against the diminution of the enjoyment of rights based on other rules.[240]

Finally, Article 54 contains a prohibition against 'any right to engage in any activity or to perform any act' aimed at the 'destruction' of any of the rights and freedoms or their 'limitation' to a greater extent than is provided for in the Charter. This is intended to be a straightforward transposition of a corresponding provision in the ECHR.[241] In the context of the Charter, however, the broad span of enumerated rights, many of which are 'polycentric', in the sense that they involve competing interests that may have to be evaluated against each other,[242] may cause particular difficulties. For example, to what extent is the exercise of the right to strike under Article 28 an activity aimed at the destruction or greater limitation of an employer's freedom under Article 16 to conduct a business in accordance with Community law and national laws and practices? Article 52(1) is intended to help resolve this conundrum.[243] Under that provision such limitations are subject to the proportionality principle and will only be permitted if they

---

[238] See the explanatory note, CHARTE 4473/00, CONVENT 49, p 50.

[239] See the concern expressed by the European Parliament's representatives at the Convention, CHARTE 4199/00, CONTRIB 80, point 12 and considerations F and R of the preamble. Discussed by J Bering Liisberg, 'Does the EU Charter of Fundamental Rights Threaten the Supremacy of Community Law?' (2001) 38 *Common Market Law Review* 1171 at 1173.

[240] *Ibid* at 1194.

[241] Art 17 ECHR. See the explanatory note, CHARTE 4473/00, CONVENT 49, p 51.

[242] See Craven, n 83 above at 87.

[243] See the explanatory note, CHARTE 4473/00, CONVENT 49, p 19.

are necessary and genuinely meet objectives of general interest recognised by the Union 'or they need to protect the rights and freedoms of others'. However, as Article 28 contains an identical limitation to that contained in Article 16 such arguments are somewhat circular.

Whilst Articles 51–54 have been drafted on the basis that the Charter will eventually enter into legal force, they also help us to determine its effects as a high-level soft law proclamation. According to the Commission, 'the Charter will become *mandatory* through the Court's interpretation of it as belonging to the general principles of law'.[244] Such an interpretation is certainly consistent with Articles 51 and 53. To date, however, the Court has exercised extreme caution when the Charter has been raised in pleadings. Indeed the solitary reference to the Charter in a judgment has been in a competition case concerning the procedural fairness of the Commission's rules for dealing with complaints.[245] When giving judgment the Court of First Instance applied the Charter to affirm the rights of the individual to both good administration[246] and an effective remedy.[247] The Court's AGs have been less reticent, issuing several opinions where the primary role of the Charter as a tool for interpreting and affirming established rights and making them 'visible' has been emphasised.

For example, in *BECTU*[248] the Court was asked to consider the validity of a trade union challenge to a UK law that denied employees the right to accrue paid annual leave until after the first 13 weeks of their employment. Was this rule compatible with the right of 'every worker' to paid leave under Article 7(1) of the Working Time Directive?[249] The trade union argued that many employees in the entertainment sector were unable to exercise their right to paid leave because they were employed for periods of less than 13 weeks at a time. The UK pointed to the fact that Article 7(1) of the Directive operates 'in accordance with the conditions for entitlement to, and granting of, such leave laid down by national legislation and/or practice'. This formulation, which is strikingly similar to the rider added to several of the provisions in the Solidarity Chapter, is not contained in Article 31(2) of the Charter, which simply refers to the right of 'every worker . . . to an annual period of paid leave'. In his opinion AG Tizzano drew on the Charter thus:[250]

Admittedly . . . the Charter . . . has not been recognised as having genuine legislative scope in the strict sense. In other words, formally, it is not in itself binding. However

[244] COM(2000) 644, para 10.
[245] Case T–54/99, *max.mobil Telekommunikation Service GmbH v Commission* [2002] ECR II (nyr) judgment of 30 Jan 2002.
[246] Art 41(1).
[247] Art 47.
[248] Case C–173/99, *R v Secretary of State for Trade and Industry, ex parte BECTU* [2001] ECR I–4881. For the background and facts of the case, see ch 5.
[249] Dir 93/104/EC, OJ 1993, L307/18.
[250] Opinion, paras 27–8. Emphasis added.

... the fact remains that it includes statements which appear in large measure to *reaffirm rights which are enshrined in other instruments* ...

I think therefore that, in proceedings concerned with the nature and scope of a fundamental right, the relevant statements of the Charter cannot be ignored: *in particular we cannot ignore its clear purpose of serving, where its provisions so allow, as a substantive point of reference for those involved*—Member States, institutions, natural and legal persons—in the Community context. Accordingly, I consider that the Charter provides us with the *most reliable and definitive confirmation* of the fact that the right to paid annual leave constitutes a fundamental right.

In the light of the wording in the Charter, and by reference to other international instruments,[251] the AG advised that the right to paid leave is located among workers' fundamental rights. It follows that the right to paid leave in the Directive is 'an automatic and unconditional right granted to every worker'.[252] The reference in the Directive to national laws and practices concerning the conditions for entitlement means that, although Member States have some latitude in defining the arrangements for the enjoyment of paid leave, it does not permit national rules that negate that right[253] or affect its scope.[254] In its judgment the Court agreed with the AG's interpretation of the Directive but did not refer to the Charter. Therefore, although the clear wording in the Charter affirmed the right to paid leave and helped to guide the AG and, by implication, the Court, it was not regarded as an essential point of reference.

While *BECTU* provides a glimpse of the interpretative potential of the Charter, its limitations have been revealed in *Bowden*,[255] where the Court was asked to consider the scope of the Working Time Directive in a case involving 'non-mobile' workers in the transport sector who were excluded from its provisions.[256] Neither the AG nor the Court referred to the Charter even though the legislative exclusion denied the workers in question the right to paid annual leave that had been deemed 'automatic and unconditional' by the same AG in *BECTU*. The explanation for this is twofold. First, the Court was acting in deference to the Community legislature that had recently adopted a Directive that would extend the scope of the Directive to cover 'non-mobile' transport workers.[257] Secondly, notwithstanding the unconditional wording of Article 31(2), the general provision in Article 52(2) effectively precludes the Court from applying the Charter in these circumstances because it can only be 'exercised under the conditions and

---

[251] Para 23. The AG referred to Art 24 of the Universal Declaration of Human Rights; Art 2(3) ESC; and Art 7(d) of the UN Charter on Economic, Social and Cultural Rights.
[252] Paras 29–30.
[253] Paras 34–5.
[254] Paras 39–45.
[255] Case C–133/00, *Bowden and others v Tuffnells Parcels Express Ltd* [2001] ECR I–7031.
[256] Art 1(3) of Dir 93/104.
[257] Dir 2000/34/EC, OJ 2000, L195/41.

within the limits' defined by the Treaties. The same logic would apply even if the Charter were legally binding.

Nevertheless, even in its present form, the Charter will have to be taken into account for, as AG Léger observed in *Hautala*:[258]

... aside from any considerations about its legislative scope, the nature of the rights set down in the Charter of Fundamental Rights precludes it from being regarded as merely a list of purely moral principles without any consequences ... The Charter has undeniably placed the rights which form its subject-matter at the highest levels of values common to the Member States ...

As the solemnity of its form and the procedure which led to its adoption would give one to assume, the Charter was intended to constitute a privileged instrument for identifying fundamental rights. It is a source of guidance as to the true nature of the Community rules of positive law.

Moreover, as AG Mischo noted in his opinion in *Booker Aquaculture*, the Charter:[259]

... constitutes the expression, at the highest level, of a democratically established political consensus on what must today be considered as the catalogue of fundamental rights guaranteed by the Community legal order.

These observations highlight the importance of the Charter and its unique place in the hierarchy of Community soft law. As de Witte[260] observes, the 'natural temptation' of lawyers is to dismiss the Charter as a mere political declaration and give unquestioned preference to a legally binding document. Such a temptation must be firmly resisted for several reasons. First, unlike the Social Charter, the Charter of Fundamental Rights is both an inter-institutional declaration and has the unanimous endorsement of the Member States. In addition, it has the cachet of legitimacy bestowed by a drafting Convention dominated by parliamentarians intended to engage with civil society and, above all, to be taken seriously.[261] Secondly, the Charter serves to affirm and 'crystallise'[262] the content of the catalogue of fundamental rights referred to in, inter alia, Article 6 [ex F] TEU and Article 136 [ex 117] EC. Therefore, it places an interpretative obligation on the Court—that will be strengthened if the Charter enters into legal force—to affirm, within the scope of EU law, the existence of justiciable social rights that may have, hitherto, had an uncertain legal footing. Hence, the Charter forms part of the *acquis*, even though it is not binding in itself,

---

[258] Case C–353/99P, *Council v Hautala* [2001] ECR (nyr) paras 80–3 of the AG's opinion delivered on 10 July 2001.

[259] Cases C–20/00 and 64/00, *Booker Aquaculture Ltd & Hydro Seafood GSP Ltd v The Scottish Ministers* [2002] ECR (nyr) para 126 of the AG's opinion delivered on 20 Sept 2001.

[260] De Witte (2001, *Maastricht Journal*) n 53 above at 83.

[261] See de Búrca (2001, *European Law Review*) n 18 above at 132.

[262] For the application of this concept, see O Kahn-Freund, 'The European Social Charter' in F Jacobs (ed) *European Law and the Individual* (North-Holland, Amsterdam, 1976) 181–211 at 197–98.

because it clarifies and designates those fundamental rights that constitute the essence of the 'common constitutional traditions' of the Member States.[263] Thirdly, it places a responsibility on each of the EU institutions and the Member States, acting within their respective competences, to develop a fundamental rights culture within the Union.[264] Fourthly, it provides a point of reference for individuals who wish to rely on the values proclaimed in the Charter to support the exercise of their existing Community law rights.

V CONCLUSION

From the preceding analysis it is clear that the EU Charter of Fundamental Rights, whatever its ultimate legal status, has many flaws. The Solidarity Chapter offers a highly selective and incomplete list of fundamental social rights that distinguishes between enforceable rights, many of which are conditional, and recognition of vague principles.[265] The 'peoples of Europe' are offered tantalising glimpses of 'rights' that are, at once, visible but unattainable. For the EU institutions, the Charter creates an obligation to promote each of the enumerated rights but denies them the capacity to extend their powers or tasks to secure its objectives. At the level of the individual, the Charter neither directly affects workers' and/or citizens' social rights, nor does it guarantee basic social entitlements. Member States will remain free to pursue independent human rights policies and can pick and choose their international obligations. Fundamental rights hover over the Union's activities but their final resting place in the EU constitutional settlement has yet to be determined.

Despite these limitations, the Charter has the *potential* to add a new dimension to the 'post-Nice' process of 'constitutionalising' the Union. Firstly, although the results to date have been inconclusive, the Charter may yet 'add value' to the protection of fundamental rights by the Court. For the first time at Union level a wide range of economic and social rights have been *defined* as both indivisible and justiciable.[266] The Court's approach to applying fundamental rights has been highly selective.[267] With the exception of the principles of equality and non-discrimination, social rights have, hitherto, been perceived as less 'fundamental'[268] and have assumed a secondary position in the Court's catalogue of judicial protection.[269] Only on

[263] See Lenaerts and De Smijter, n 7 above at 299.

[264] See Shaw, n 6 above at 199.

[265] See 'Editorial Comments: The EU Charter of Fundamental Rights still under discussion' (2001) 38 *Common Market Law Review* 1 at 3.

[266] See Betten, n 11 above at 156.

[267] See G de Búrca, 'The Role of Equality in European Law' in A Dashwood and S O'Leary (eds) *The Principle of Equal Treatment in E.C. Law* (Sweet & Maxwell, London, 1997) 13–34.

[268] See de Búrca in Shaw and More, n 23 above at 51.

[269] See Poiares Maduro in Shaw, n 12 above at 338.

a handful of occasions has the Court made direct reference to the ESC and ILO conventions.[270] The Charter has made social rights more visible and, in the process, has altered the hierarchy of rights recognised by the Union. The challenge for the Court is to adjust its vision to reflect this new reality by extending the reach of its jurisprudence in order to take full account of fundamental social rights derived from the ECHR, the ESC and other sources now recognised by the Charter as part of the 'common values' of the Union and the Member States.[271]

Secondly, by placing fundamental rights at the core of the EU's supranational order,[272] the Charter mainstreams the 'common values' that it expounds throughout its activities. As with the Social Charter, the adoption of the Charter of Fundamental Rights may serve as a catalyst or a 'reflex'[273] for legislative and programmatic action at the EU level where it can be justified on the grounds of subsidiarity. Undoubtedly the proclamation of the Charter helped to add impetus to the parallel process of adopting the Commission's 'anti-discrimination' package.[274] Moreover, despite its deficiencies, the inclusion of a Solidarity Chapter in the Charter, co-existing with an autonomous Social Chapter in the EC Treaty conveys a message that social policy can no longer be marginalised. Just as the Social Policy Agenda has provided the EU with a rationale based on the indissoluble link between economic strength and rising social standards, the Charter offers a transcendent vision of a modern European *ius commune* based on a coherent—if not wholly complete—statement of fundamental social values.[275] In order to make the Charter effective, however, the Convention on the Future of the European Union will have to consider, not only, its placement within a putative 'European constitution', but also, the establishment of supervisory mechanisms such as an independent 'committee of experts' empowered to receive complaints, issue reports and make recommendations.[276]

Thirdly, the recognition of a range of social entitlements in the Charter, although expressed in general terms, represents an important step in the process of constructing a 'European social constitution' that would combine justiciable social rights with a guarantee of decent levels of universal social protection. Nevertheless, the rhetoric of social solidarity can only be given substance if further steps are taken. For some the only viable solution lies

---

[270] See for example, Case 149/77, *Defrenne v Sabena III* [1978] ECR 1365; and Case 24/86, *Blaizot v University of Liège* [1988] ECR 379.
[271] See de Witte (2001, *Maastricht Journal*) n 53 above at 85; and Gijzen, n 14 above at 42.
[272] See von Bogdandy, n 57 above at 1333.
[273] See Kahn-Freund, n 262 above at 184. See generally, R Rogowski and T Wilthagen (eds) *Reflexive Labour Law* (Kluwer, Deventer, 1994).
[274] See ch 9.
[275] See the case made by Hepple (1995, *Current Legal Problems*) n 96 aobve at 60.
[276] See Hepple, *ibid* and Weiss, n 55 above.

with a transfer of competence or a reallocation of functions. Poiares Maduro[277] has presented a powerful case for the idea of 'European social entitlements' arising from a criterion of 'distributive justice'. Such a notion builds on the earlier conception of a European *Sozialstaat*[278] and Habermas'[279] thesis that it is no longer possible for the nation state to guarantee the mechanisms and instruments of social solidarity upon which the welfare state has been founded. However, there is little evidence to suggest that a centralised solution based on the EU exercising 'an independent redistributive function'[280] would be effective, desirable or achievable.[281] Rather, an alternative, more diverse and localised approach must be sought, utilising soft law tools such as the 'open method of co-ordination' and partnerships with local actors and networks, to enable individuals and governmental bodies to accept a positive duty to maintain and adapt a European model of social entitlements by reference to the yardsticks in the Charter.

The proclamation of the Charter of Fundamental Rights marks the latest stage of a process of realignment of market freedoms and social rights within the European integration project. In itself, the Charter may yet prove to be an ephemeron, short-lived and of limited use. As part of a broader canvas, however, the Charter has the potential to reinforce a distinctively European conception of social solidarity, in which European citizenship can be envisioned as not merely a metaphor but a source of rights.[282] Post-Amsterdam, European integration is no longer a simple function of the market but the construction of a 'European social constitution' has only just begun.

[277] See Poiares Maduro in Shaw, n 12 above at 340–49.

[278] See S Leibfried and P Pierson, 'Prospects for Social Europe' (1992) 20 *Politics & Society* 333 at 336.

[279] See J Habermas, *The Postnational Constellation* (Polity Press, London, 2000). Discussed by Poiares Maduro in Shaw, n 12 above at 347.

[280] Poiares Maduro, *ibid* at 343.

[281] See the Declaration on the Future of the European Union, issued at the Laeken European Council of 14/15 Dec 2001, where the European Council warned, in Part II, against any attempts to redefine EU competences leading to a 'creeping expansion of the competence of the Union' or an 'encroachment upon the exclusive competence of the Member States'.

[282] See Reich, n 66 above.

Bibliography

ABBOTT K, 'The European Trade Union Confederation: Its Organisation and Objectives in Transition' (1997) 35 *Journal of Common Market Studies* 465

ABBOTT K and SNIDAL D, 'Hard and Soft Law in International Governance' (2000) 54 *International Organization* 421

ABRAMS K, 'Complex Claimants and Reductive Moral Judgments: New Patterns in the Search for Equality' (1996) *University of Pittsburg Law Review* 337

ADINOLFI A, 'The Implementation of Social Policy Directives Through Collective Agreements' (1988) 25 *Common Market Law Review* 291

ALLOTT P, 'European Governance and the Re-branding of Democracy' (2002) 27 *European Law Review* 60

——, 'The Concept of European Union' (1999) 2 *Cambridge Yearbook of European Legal Studies* 31

——, 'The European Community is Not the True Community' (1991) 100 *Yale Law Journal* 2485

ALSTON P (ed) *The EU and Human Rights* (Oxford: OUP, 1999)

ALSTON P and WEILER J, 'An 'Ever Closer Union' in Need of a Human Rights Policy: The European Union and Human Rights' in Alston (1999) 3–66

AMY ELMAN R, 'The Limits of Citizenship: Migration, Sex Discrimination and Same-Sex Partners in EU Law' (2000) 28 *Journal of Common Market Studies* 729

ARMSTRONG K, 'Civil Society and the White Paper—Bridging or Jumping the Gaps?' in Joerges *et al* (2001) Part 10

——, 'Governance and the Single European Market' in Craig and de Búrca (1999) 745–789

——, 'Tales of the Community: sexual orientation discrimination and EC law' (1998) 20 *Journal of Social Welfare and Family Law* 455

ARNULL A, 'Editorial: From Opinion 2/94 to the Future of Europe' (2002) 27 *European Law Review* 1

——, *The European Union and its Court of Justice* (Oxford: OUP, 1999)

——, 'The European Court and Judicial Objectivity: A Reply to Professor Hartley' (1996) 112 *Law Quarterly Review* 411

——, 'Does the Court of Justice have inherent jurisdiction?' (1990) 27 *Common Market Law Review* 683

——, 'The legal status of recommendations' (1990) 15 *European Law Review* 318

——, 'The Incoming Tide: Responding to Marshall' [1987] *Public Law* 383

——, 'Article 119 and Equal Pay for Work of Equal Value' (1986) 11 *European Law Review* 200

ASHIAGBOR D, 'EMU and the Shift in the European Labour Law Agenda: From 'Social Policy' to 'Employment Policy'' (2001) 7 *European Law Journal* 311

ATKINSON R and DAVOUDI S, 'The Concept of Social Exclusion in the European Union: Context, Development and Possibilities' (2000) 38 *Journal of Common Market Studies* 427

AUST A, 'The Theory and Practice of Informal International Instruments' (1986) 35 *International and Comparative Law Quarterly* 787

BALDWIN R and DAINTITH T, 'The European Framework' in Baldwin R and Daintith T (eds) *Harmonization and Hazard: Regulating Workplace Health and Safety in the European Community* (London: Graham and Trotman, 1992) 1–17

BALL S, 'The European Employment Strategy: The Will but not the Way?' (2001) 30 *Industrial Law Journal* 353

BAMFORTH N, 'Sexual Orientation Discrimination after *Grant v South West Trains*' (2000) 63 *Modern Law Review* 694

BARNARD C, *EC Employment Law*, 2nd edn (Oxford: OUP, 2000)

——, 'Flexibility and Social Policy' in de Búrca and Scott (2000) 197–217

——, 'Social dumping and the race to the bottom: some lessons for the European Union from Delaware?' (2000) 25 *European Law Review* 57

——, 'Article 13: Through the Looking Glass of Union Citizenship' in O'Keeffe and Twomey (1999) 375–394

——, 'EC 'Social' Policy' in Craig and de Búrca (1999) 479–516

——, 'The Principle of Equality in the Community Context: *P, Grant, Kalanke* and *Marschall*: Four Uneasy Bedfellows?' (1998) 57 *Cambridge Law Journal* 352

——, '*P v S*: Kite Flying or a New Constitutional Approach?' in Dashwood and O'Leary (1997) 59–79

——, 'The Economic Objectives of Article 119' in Hervey and O'Keeffe (1996) 321–334

——, 'A European Litigation Strategy: the Case of the Equal Opportunities Commission' in Shaw and More (1995) 253–272

——, 'A Social Policy for Europe: Politicians 1:0 Lawyers' (1992) 8 *International Journal of Comparative Labour Law and Industrial Relations* 15

BARNARD C, DASHWOOD A and HEPPLE B, *The ECJ's Working Time Judgment: The Social Market Vindicated* (Cambridge: CELS Occasional Paper No 2, 1997)

BARNARD C and DEAKIN S, 'In Search of Coherence: Social Policy, the Single Market and Fundamental Rights' (2000) 31 *Industrial Relations Journal* 331

—— and ——, 'Social Policy in Search of a Role: Integration, Cohesion and Citizenship' in Caiger A and Floudas D (eds) *1996 Onwards: Lowering the Barriers Further* (Chichester: Wiley, 1996) 177–195

BARNARD C, DEAKIN S and HOBBS R, 'Capabilities and Rights: An Emerging Agenda for Social Policy?' (2001) 32 *Industrial Relations Journal* 464

BARNARD C and HEPPLE B, 'Substantive Equality' (2000) 59 *Cambridge Law Journal* 562

—— and ——, 'Indirect Discrimination: Interpreting *Seymour-Smith*' (1999) 58 *Cambridge Law Journal* 399

BARNARD C and HERVEY T, 'Softening the approach to quotas: positive action after *Marschall*' (1998) 20 *Journal of Social Welfare and Family Law* 333

—— and ——, 'European Union Employment and Social Policy Survey 1996 and 1997' (1997) 17 *Yearbook of European Law* 435

BAXTER R, 'International Law in 'Her Infinite Variety'' (1980) 29 *International and Comparative Law Quarterly* 549

BELL M, 'Anti-discrimination Law after Amsterdam' in Shaw (2000) 157–170

——, 'Article 13 EC: The European Commission's Anti-discrimination Proposals' (2000) 29 *Industrial Law Journal* 79

——, 'Shifting Conceptions of Sexual Discrimination at the Court of Justice: from *P v S* to *Grant v SWT*' (1999) 5 *European Law Journal* 63

——, 'The New Article 13 EC Treaty: A Sound Basis for European Anti-discrimination Law?' (1999) 6 *Maastricht Journal* 5

BELL M and WADDINGTON L, 'The 1996 Intergovernmental Conference and the Prospects of a Non-Discrimination Treaty Article' (1996) 25 *Industrial Law Journal* 320

BELLACE J, 'The ILO Declaration of Fundamental Principles and Rights at Work' (2001) 17 *International Journal of Comparative Labour Law and Industrial Relations* 269

BERCUSSON B, 'Trade Union Rights in EU Law' in Snyder (2000) 195–209

——, 'European Labour Law in Context: A Review of the Literature' (1999) 5 *European Law Journal* 87

——, 'Democratic Legitimacy and European Labour Law' (1999) 28 *Industrial Law Journal* 153

——, *European Labour Law* (London: Butterworths, 1996)

——, 'The Dynamic of European Labour Law after Maastricht' (1994) 23 *Industrial Law Journal* 1

——, 'Social Policy at the Crossroads: European Labour Law after Maastricht' in Dehousse (1994) 149–186

——, 'Collective Bargaining and the Protection of Social Rights' in Ewing *et al* (1994) 106–126

——, *Working Time in Britain, Towards a European Model*, Part I (London: Institute of Employment Rights, 1993)

——, 'Maastricht: a fundamental change in European labour law' (1992) 23 *Industrial Relations Journal* 177

——, 'Fundamental Social and Economic Rights in the European Community' in Cassesse A, Clapham A and Weiler J (eds) *Human Rights and the European Community: Methods of Protection* (Baden-Baden: Nomos, 1991) 195–291

——, 'The European Community's Charter of the Fundamental Social Rights of Workers' (1990) 53 *Modern Law Review* 624

BERCUSSON B, DEAKIN S *et al*, 'A Manifesto for Social Europe' (1997) 3 *European Law Journal* 189

BERCUSSON B and VAN DIJK J, 'The Implementation of the Protocol and Agreement on Social Policy of the Treaty on European Union' (1995) 11 *International Journal of Comparative Labour Law and Industrial Relations* 3

BERING LIISBERG J, 'Does the EU Charter of Fundamental Rights Threaten the Supremacy of Community Law?' (2001) 38 *Common Market Law Review* 1171

BERMAN G, 'Taking Subsidiarity Seriously' (1994) 94 *Columbia Law Review* 332

BERNARD N, 'Legitimising EU Law: Is the Social Dialogue the Way Forward? Some Reflections Around the UEAPME Case' in Shaw (2000) 279–302

BESSELINK L, 'The Member States, the National Constitutions and the Scope of the Charter' (2001) 8 *Maastricht Journal* 68

BETTEN L, 'The EU Charter on Fundamental Rights: a Trojan Horse or a Mouse?' (2001) 17 *International Journal of Comparative Labour Law and Industrial Relations* 151

——, 'The Democratic Deficit of Participatory Democracy in Community Social Policy' (1998) 23 *European Law Review* 20

BETTEN L, (ed) *The Future of European Social Policy* (Deventer: Kluwer, 1989)

——, 'Prospects for a Social Policy of the European Community and its Impact on the Functioning of the European Social Charter' in Betten (1989) 101–141

BETTEN L and SHRUBSALL V, 'The Concept of Positive Sex Discrimination in Community Law—Before and After the Treaty of Amsterdam' (1998) 14 *International Journal of Comparative Labour Law and Industrial Relations* 65

—— and GRIEF N, *EU Law and Human Rights* (Harlow: Longman, 1998)

BEVERIDGE F and NOTT S, 'A Hard Look at Soft Law' in Craig and Harlow (1998) 285–309

—— and ——, 'Gender Auditing—Making the Community Work for Women' in Hervey and O'Keeffe (1996) 383–398

BEVERIDGE F, NOTT S and STEPHEN K, 'Addressing Gender in National and Community Law and Policy-making' in Shaw (2000) 135–154

BIAGI M, 'The Implementation of the Amsterdam Treaty with Regard to Employment: Co-ordination or Convergence?' (1998) 14 *International Journal of Comparative Labour Law and Industrial Relations* 325

BIEBER R and AMARELLE C, 'Simplification of European Law' in Snyder (2000) 219–241

BIEBER R, JACQUÉ J-P and WEILER J, *An Ever Closer Union: A Critical Analysis of the Draft Treaty Establishing the European Union* (Luxembourg: European Communities, 1985)

BIONDI A, 'The Court of Justice and certain national procedural limitations: not such a tough relationship' (1999) 36 *Common Market Law Review* 1271

BLANPAIN R (ed) *Temporary Work and Labour Law* (Deventer: Kluwer, 1993)

BLOM J, FITZPATRICK B, GREGORY J, KNEGT R and O'HARE U, *The Utilisation of Sex Equality Litigation in the Member States of the European Community*, V/783/96-EN (Brussels: European Commission, 1996)

BOCH C, 'Official: During Pregnancy, Females are Pregnant' (1998) 23 *European Law Review* 488

BOOTH C, 'Gender Mainstreaming in the European Union Toward a New Conception and Practice of Equal Opportunities', *ESCR Seminar Series: The Interface Between Public Policy and Gender Equality* (Centre for Regional Economic and Social Research, Sheffield Hallam University, 1999)

BOURN C, 'Amending the Collective Dismissals Directive: A Case of Rearranging the Deckchairs?' (1993) 9 *International Journal of Comparative Labour Law and Industrial Relations* 227

BRADLEY K ST C, 'Institutional Design in the Treaty of Nice' (2001) 38 *Common Market Law Review* 1095

——, 'The European Parliament and Treaty Reform: Building Blocks and Stumbling Blocks' in O'Keeffe and Twomey (1999) 123–139

BRINKMANN G, 'Lawmaking under the Social Chapter of Maastricht' in Craig and Harlow (1998) 239–261

BRITZ G and SCHMIDT M, 'The Institutionalised Participation of Management and Labour in the Legislative Activities of the European Community: A Challenge to the Principle of Democracy under Community Law' (2000) 6 *European Law Journal* 45

BRUNING G and PLANTENGA J, 'Parental Leave and Equal Opportunities: Experiences in Eight European Countries' (1999) 9 *Journal of European Social Policy* 195

BURNS T, 'Better lawmaking? An evaluation of lawmaking in the European Community' in Craig and Harlow (1998) 435–453

BURROWS N, 'Maternity Rights in Europe—An Embryonic Legal Regime' (1991) 11 *Yearbook of European Law* 273

CANOR I, 'Equality for Lesbians and Gay Men in the European Community Legal Order—'they shall be male and female'?' (2000) 7 *Maastricht Journal* 273

CARACCIOLO DI TORELLA E, 'The 'Family Friendly Workplace': the EC Position' (2001) 17 *International Journal of Comparative Labour Law and Industrial Relations* 325

——, 'Childcare, employment and equality in the European Community: first (false) steps of the Court' (2000) 25 *European Law Review* 310

——, 'Recent Developments in Pregnancy and Maternity Rights' (1999) 28 *Industrial Law Journal* 276

CARACCIOLO DI TORELLA E and MASSELOT A, 'Pregnancy, Maternity and the Organisation of Family Life: An Attempt to Classify the Case Law of the Court of Justice' (2001) 26 *European Law Review* 239

CARACCIOLO DI TORELLA E and REID E, 'The Changing Shape of the "European Family" and Fundamental Rights' (2002) 27 *European Law Review* 80

CARANTA R, 'Government Liability after *Francovich*' (1992) 52 *Cambridge Law Journal* 272

CARTER C and SCOTT A, 'Legitimacy and Governance Beyond the European Nation State: Conceptualising Governance in the European Union' in Bankowski Z and Scott A, *The European Union and its Order: The Legal Theory of European Integration* (Oxford: Blackwell, 2000) 131–147

CASEY N, 'The European Social Charter and Revised European Social Charter' in Costello (2001) 55–75

CASS D, 'The Word that Saves Maastricht? The Principle of Subsidiarity and the Division of Powers within the European Community' (1992) 29 *Common Market Law Review* 1107

CASSELL E, 'The Revised Directive on Equal Treatment for Men and Women in Occupational Social Security Schemes—The Dog that Didn't Bark' (1997) 26 *Industrial Law Journal* 269

CECCHINI P, *The European Challenge 1992: The Benefits of a Single Market* (Aldershot: Wildwood House, 1988)

CHALMERS D, *European Union Law Volume One: Law and EU Government* (Aldershot: Dartmouth, 1998)

CHALMERS D and SZYSZCZAK E, *European Union Law, Volume Two: Towards a European Polity?* (Aldershot: Dartmouth, 1998)

CHARPENTIER L, 'The European Court of Justice and the Rhetoric of Affirmative Action' (1998) 4 *European Law Journal* 167

CLAPHAM A and WEILER J, 'Lesbians and Gay Men in the Community Legal Order' in Waaldijk and Clapham (1993) 11–69

CLARK J and HALL M, 'The Cinderella Directive? Employee Rights to Information about Conditions Applicable to their Contract or Employment Relationship' (1992) 21 *Industrial Law Journal* 106

CLOSA C, 'The Concept of Citizenship in the Treaty on European Union' (1992) 29 *Common Market Law Review* 1137

COHEN W, 'The Conseil d'Etat: continuing convergence with the Court of Justice' (1991) 16 *European Law Review* 144

COLNERIC N, 'Making Equality Law More Effective: Lessons from the German Experience' (1996) 3 *Cardozo Woman's Law Journal* 229

CONLON T, 'Industrial Democracy and EEC Company Law: A Review of the Draft Fifth Directive' (1975) 24 *International and Comparative Law Quarterly* 348

CONVERY J, 'State Liability in the United Kingdom after *Brasserie du Pêcheur*' (1997) 34 *Common Market Law Review* 603

COPPEL J and O'NEILL A, 'The European Court of Justice: Taking Rights Seriously?' (1992) 29 *Common Market Law Review* 669

CORBETT R, *The Treaty of Maastricht* (Harlow: Longman, 1993)

COSTELLO C (ed) *Fundamental Social Rights: Current Legal Protection and the Challenge of the EU Charter of Fundamental Rights* (Dublin: Irish Centre for European Law, 2001)

——, 'The Legal Status and Legal Effect of the Charter of Fundamental Rights of the European Union' in Costello (2001) 127–150

CRAIG P, 'Once more unto the breach: The Community, the State and Damages Liability' (1997) 113 *Law Quarterly Review* 67

——, '*Francovich*, Remedies and the Scope of Damages Liability' (1993) 109 *Law Quarterly Review* 595

CRAIG P and DE BÚRCA G (eds) *The Evolution of EU Law* (Oxford: OUP, 1999)

—— and ——, *EC Law: Text, Cases and Materials*, 2nd ed (Oxford: OUP, 1998)

CRAIG P and HARLOW C (eds) *Lawmaking in the European Union* (London: Kluwer, 1998)

CRAUFURD SMITH R, 'Remedies for Breaches of EC Law in National Courts: Legal Variation and Selection' in Craig and de Búrca (1999) 287–320

CRAVEN M, 'A View from Elsewhere: Social Rights, the International Covenant and the EU Charter of Fundamental Rights' in Costello (2001) 77–93

——, *The International Covenant on Economic, Social and Cultural Rights* (Oxford: Clarendon Press, 1995)

CRENSHAW K, 'Demarginalizing the Intersection of Race and Sex: A Black Feminist Critique of Antidiscrimination Doctrine, Feminist Theory and Antiracist Politics' (1989) *University of Chicago Legal Forum* 139

CROMACK V, 'The EC Pregnancy Directive—Principle or Pragmatism?' (1993) 15 *Journal of Social Welfare and Family Law* 261

CROSBY S, 'The Single Market and the Rule of Law' (1991) 16 *European Law Review* 451

CULLEN H and CAMPBELL E, 'The future of social policy-making in the European Union' in Craig and Harlow (1998) 262–284

CURTIN D, 'The Fundamental Principle of Open Decision-making and EU (Political) Citizenship' in O'Keeffe and Twomey (1999) 71–91

——, 'Betwixt and Between: Democracy and Transparency in the Governance of the European Union' in Winter *et al* (1996) 95–121

——, 'The Constitutional Structure of the Union: A Europe of Bits and Pieces' (1993) 30 *Common Market Law Review* 17

——, 'State Liability under Community Law: a New Remedy for Private Parties' (1992) 21 *Industrial Law Journal* 74

——, 'Scalping the Community Legislator: Occupational Pensions after *Barber*' (1990) 27 *Common Market Law Review* 475

——, 'Effective Sanctions and the Equal Treatment Directive: The *Von Colson* and *Harz* Cases' (1985) 22 *Common Market Law Review* 505

CURTIN D and DEKKER I, 'The EU as a 'Layered' International Organization: Institutional Unity in Disguise' in Craig and de Búrca (1999) 83–136

CURTIN D and VAN OOIK R, 'The Sting is Always in the Tail: The Personal Scope of Application of the EU Charter of Fundamental Rights' (2001) 8 *Maastricht Journal* 102

—— and ——, 'Denmark and the Edinburgh Summit: Maastricht without Tears' in O'Keeffe and Twomey (1994) 349–365

DAALDER H, 'The Consociational Democracy Theme' (1974) 26 *World Politics* 606

DAHRENDORF R, *Der Moderne Soziale Konflikt* (Stuttgart: DVA, 1992)

DANKERT P, 'What Parliament for Europe?' in Heukels *et al* (1998) 131–138

DASHWOOD A, 'The Limits of European Community Powers' (1996) 21 *European Law Review* 113

DASHWOOD A and O'LEARY S (eds) *The Principle of Equal Treatment in EC Law* (London: Sweet and Maxwell, 1997)

DÄUBLER W, 'Instruments in EC Labour Law' in Davies *et al* (1996) 151–167

——, 'The Employee Participation Directive—A Realistic Utopia?' (1977) 14 *Common Market Law Review* 17

DAVIES P, 'Transfers—The UK Will Have to Make Up Its Own Mind' (2001) 30 *Industrial Law Journal* 231

——, 'Posted Workers: Single Market or Protection of National Labour Law Systems?' (1997) 34 *Common Market Law Review* 571

——, 'Taken to the Cleaners? Contracting Out of Services Yet Again' (1997) 26 *Industrial Law Journal* 193

——, 'The European Court of Justice, National Courts and the Member States' in Davies *et al* (1996) 95–138

——, 'Market Integration and Social Policy in the Court of Justice' (1995) 24 *Industrial Law Journal* 49

——, 'The Emergence of European Labour Law' in McCarthy W (ed) *Legal Intervention in Industrial Relations: Gains and Losses* (London: Blackwell, 1993) 313–359

——, 'Acquired Rights, Creditors' Rights, Freedom of Contract, and Industrial Democracy' (1989) 9 *Yearbook of European Law* 21

DAVIES P, LYON-CAEN A, SCIARRA S and SIMITIS S (eds) *European Community Labour Law: Principles and Perspectives* (Oxford: Clarendon Press, 1996)

DAVIES P and WEDDERBURN (Lord), 'The Land of Industrial Democracy' (1977) 6 *Industrial Law Journal* 197

DEAKIN S, 'Labour Law as Market Regulation: the Economic Foundations of European Social Policy' in Davies *et al* (1996) 62–93

DEAKIN S and MORRIS G, *Labour Law* (London: Butterworths, 2nd edn, 1998)

DEAKIN S and REED H, 'The Contested Meaning of Labour Market Flexibility: Economic Theory and the Discourse of European Integration' in Shaw (2000) 71–99

DEAKIN S and WILKINSON F, 'Rights vs Efficiency? The Economic Case for Transnational Labour Standards' (1994) 23 *Industrial Law Journal* 289

DEARDS E, 'Curioser and Curioser? The Development of Member State Liability in the Court of Justice' (1997) 3 *European Public Law* 117

DE BÚRCA G, 'The Drafting of the European Union Charter of Fundamental Rights' (2001) 26 *European Law Review* 126

——, 'Reappraising Subsidiarity's Significance after Amsterdam', *Harvard Jean Monnet Working Paper* 7/99

——, 'The Principle of Subsidiarity and the Court of Justice as an Institutional Actor' (1998) 36 *Journal of Common Market Studies* 217

——, 'The Role of Equality in European Law' in Dashwood and O'Leary (1997) 13–34

——, 'National Procedural Rules and Remedies: The Changing Approach of the Court of Justice' in Lonbay and Biondi (1997) 37–46

——, 'The Quest for Legitimacy in the European Union' (1996) 59 *Modern Law Review* 349

——, 'The Language of Rights and European Integration' in Shaw and More (1995) 29–54

——, 'The Principle of Proportionality and its Application in EC Law' (1993) 13 *Yearbook of European Law* 105

DE BÚRCA G and SCOTT J (eds) *Constitutional Change in the EU: From Uniformity to Flexibility* (Oxford: Hart, 2000)

DE GROOT C, 'The Council Directive on the Safeguarding of Employees' Rights in the Event of Transfers of Undertakings: An Overview of Recent Case Law' (1998) 35 *Common Market Law Review* 707

——, 'The Council Directive on the Safeguarding of Employees' Rights in the Event of Transfers of Undertakings: An Overview of the Case Law' (1993) 30 *Common Market Law Review* 331

DEHOUSSE F, 'The IGC Process and Results' in O'Keeffe and Twomey (1999) 93–108

DEHOUSSE, R, 'European Institutional Architecture After Amsterdam: Parliamentary System or Regulatory Structure?' (1998) 35 *Common Market Law Review* 595

——(ed) *Europe After Maastricht: An Ever Closer Union?* (Munich: Law Books in Europe, 1994)

——, 'From Community to Union' in Dehousse (1994) 5–15

——, *Does Subsidiarity Really Matter?* EUI Working Paper LAW No 92/32 (Florence: EUI, 1993)

——, *Integration v Regulation? Social Regulation in the European Community* (Florence: EUI, 1992)

DE LA PORTE C, POCHET P and ROOM G, 'Social benchmarking, policy making and new governance in the EU' (2001) 11 *Journal of European Social Policy* 291

DEMARET P, 'The Treaty Framework' in O'Keeffe and Twomey (1994) 3–11

DEN BOER M, Guggenbühl A and Vanhoonacker S (eds) *Coping with Flexibility and Legitimacy after Amsterdam* (Maastricht: EIPA, 1998)

DESMOND H, 'Older and Greyer—Third Age Workers and the Labour Market' (2000) 16 *International Journal of Comparative Labour Law and Industrial Relations* 235

DE WITTE B, 'The Legal Status of the Charter: Vital Question or Non-Issue' (2001) 8 *Maastricht Journal* 81

——, 'The Past and Future Role of the European Court of Justice in the Protection of Human Rights' in Alston (1999) 859–897

——, 'The Pillar Structure and the Nature of the European Union: Greek Temple or French Gothic Cathedral?' in Heukels *et al* (1998) 51–68

DOCKSEY C, 'The Principle of Equality Between Women and Men as a Fundamental Right under Community Law' (1991) 20 *Industrial Law Journal* 258

——, 'Employee Information and Consultation Rights in the Member States of the European Communities' (1987) 7 *Comparative Labor Law Journal* 32

——, 'Information and Consultation of Employees: The United Kingdom and the Vredeling Directive' (1986) 49 *Modern Law Review* 282

DOCKSEY C and FITZPATRICK B, 'The Duty of National Courts to Interpret Provisions of National Law in Accordance with Community Law' (1991) 20 *Industrial Law Journal* 113

DONOVAN K, *Sexual Divisions in Law* (London: Wiedenfield and Nicholson, 1985)

DOUGAN M, 'The *Francovich* right to reparation: The contours of Community remedial competence' (2000) 6 *European Public Law* 103

——, 'The Equal Treatment Directive: Retaliation, Remedies and Direct Effect' (1999) 24 *European Law Review* 664

DOUGLAS-SCOTT S, 'Affirmative Action in the US Supreme Court: the *Adarand* case—the Final Chapter' [1997] *Public Law* 43

DUMMETT A, 'The Starting Line: A Proposal for a Draft Council Directive Concerning the Elimination of Racial Discrimination' (1994) 20 *New Community* 530

ECONOMIDES K and WEILER J, 'Accession of the Communities to the European Convention on Human Rights: Commission Memorandum' (1979) 42 *Modern Law Review* 683

EDWARD D, 'Judicial Activism—Myth or Reality?' in Campbell A and Voyati M (eds) *Legal Reasoning and Judicial Interpretation of European Law* (Gosport: Trenton Publishing, 1996) 29–67

EHLERMANN C-D, 'Increased Differentiation or Stronger Uniformity' in Winter *et al* (1996) 27–50

——, 'The Internal Market Following the Single European Act' (1987) 24 *Common Market Law Review* 361

EICKE T, 'European Charter of Fundamental Rights—Unique Opportunity or Unwelcome Distraction' [2000] *European Human Rights Law Review* 280

ELLIS E, 'The Recent Jurisprudence of the Court of Justice in the Field of Sex Equality' (2000) 37 *Common Market Law Review* 1403

——, *European Community Sex Equality Law*, 2nd edn (Oxford: Clarendon Press, 1998)

——, 'Recent Developments in European Community Sex Equality Law' (1998) 35 *Common Market Law Review* 379

——, 'Equal Pay for Work of Equal Value: The United Kingdom's Legislation Viewed in the Light of Community Law' in Hervey and O'Keeffe (1996) 7–19

——, 'The Definition of Discrimination in European Community Sex Equality Law' (1994) 19 *European Law Review* 563

——, 'Protection of Pregnancy and Maternity' (1993) 22 *Industrial Law Journal* 63

——, 'Parents and Employment: An Opportunity for Progress' (1986) 15 *Industrial Law Journal* 97

EMILIOU N, *The Principle of Proportionality in European Law* (London: Kluwer, 1996)

EMILIOU N, 'State Liability under Community Law: Shedding More Light on the *Francovich* Principle?' (1996) 21 *European Law Review* 399

——, 'Subsidiarity: an effective barrier against 'the enterprises of ambition'?' (1992) 17 *European Law Review* 383

EVERLING U, 'Reflections on the Structure of the European Union' (1992) 29 *Common Market Law Review* 1056

EVERSON M, 'The Legacy of the Market Citizen' in Shaw and More (1995) 73–90

EVJU S, 'Collective Agreements and Competition Law The *Albany* Puzzle, and *van der Woude*' (2001) 17 *International Journal of Comparative Labour Law and Industrial Relations* 165

EWING K, GEARTY C and HEPPLE B (eds) *Human Rights and Labour Law: Essays for Paul O'Higgins* (London: Mansell, 1994)

FAIRHURST J, 'SIMAP—Interpreting the Working Time Directive' (2001) 30 *Industrial Law Journal* 236

FALKNER G, 'The Maastricht Protocol on Social Policy: Theory and Practice' (1996) 6 *Journal of European Social Policy* 1

FENWICK H, 'From Formal to Substantive Equality: the Place of Affirmative Action in European Union Sex Equality Law' (1998) 4 *European Public Law* 507

——, 'Special Protections for Women in European Union Law' in Hervey and O'Keeffe (1996) 63–80

FENWICK H and HERVEY T, 'Sex Equality in the Single Market: New Directions for the European Court of Justice' (1995) 32 *Common Market Law Review* 443

FITZPATRICK B, 'European Union Law and the Council of Europe Conventions' in Costello (2001) 95–108

——, 'Converse Pyramids and the EU Social Constitution' in Shaw (2000) 303–324

——, 'Straining the Definition of Health and Safety' (1997) 26 *Industrial Law Journal* 115

——, 'Community Social Law after Maastricht' (1992) 21 *Industrial Law Journal* 199

——, 'The Effectiveness of Equality Law Remedies: A European Community Law Perspective' in Hepple and Szyszczak (1992) 67–85

——, 'Equality in Occupational Pensions—the New Frontiers after *Barber*' (1991) 54 *Modern Law Review* 271

FLANDERS A, *Management and Unions: the Theory and Reform of Industrial Relations* (London: Faber, 1970)

FLYNN J, 'How Well Will Article 100a(4) Work? A Comparison with Article 93' (1987) 24 *Common Market Law Review* 689

FLYNN L, 'Whatever Happened to Emmott? The Perfecting of Community Rules on Time Limits' in Kilpatrick *et al* (2000) 51–67

——, 'The Implications of Article 13 EC—After Amsterdam Will Some Forms of Discrimination be More Equal Than Others?' (1999) 36 *Common Market Law Review* 1127

——, 'Equality between Men and Women in the Court of Justice (1998) 18 *Yearbook of European Law* 259

——, 'The Body Politic(s) of EC Law' in Hervey and O'Keeffe (1996) 301–320

——, 'Gender Equality Laws and Employers' Dress Codes' (1995) 24 *Industrial Law Journal* 255

FRANSSEN E, 'Implementation of European Collective Agreements: Some Troublesome Issues' (1998) 5 *Maastricht Journal* 53

FRANSSEN E and JACOBS A, 'The Question of Representativity in the European Social Dialogue' (1998) 35 *Common Market Law Review* 1295

FREDMAN S, 'Equality: A New Generation?' (2001) 30 *Industrial Law Journal* 145

——, 'Affirmative Action and the European Court of Justice: A Critical Analysis' in Shaw (2000) 171–195

——, 'Social Law in the European Union: The Impact of the Lawmaking Process' in Craig and Harlow (1998) 386–411

——, 'Reversing Discrimination' (1997) 113 *Law Quarterly Review* 575

——, 'Labour Law in Flux: the Changing Composition of the Workforce' (1997) 26 *Industrial Law Journal* 337

——, 'The Poverty of Equality: Pensions and the ECJ' (1996) 25 *Industrial Law Journal* 91

——, 'European Community Discrimination Law: A Critique' (1992) 21 *Industrial Law Journal* 119

FREDMAN S and SZYSZCZAK E, 'The Interaction of Race and Gender' in Hepple and Szyszczak (1992) 214–226

FREEDLAND M, 'Vocational Training in EC Law and Policy—Education, Employment or Welfare?' (1996) 25 *Industrial Law Journal* 110

——, 'Employment Protection: Redundancy Procedures and the EEC' (1976) 5 *Industrial Law Journal* 24

GAJA G, 'Opinion 2/94, Accession by the Communities to the European Convention for the Protection of Human Rights and Fundamental Freedoms' (1996) 33 *Common Market Law Review* 973

GARDNER J, 'On the Ground of Her Sex(uality)' (1998) 18 *Oxford Journal of Legal Studies* 167

GEORGE S, *An Awkward Partner: Britain in the European Community*, 2nd ed (Oxford: OUP, 1994)

GERMANOTTA P and NOVITZ T, 'Globalisation and the Right to Strike: The Case for European-Level Protection of Secondary Action' (2002) 18 *International Journal of Comparative Labour Law and Industrial Relations* 67

GIDDENS A, *The Third Way* (Cambridge: Polity Press, 1998)

——, *Beyond Left and Right: The Future of Radical Politics* (Cambridge: Polity Press, 1994)

GIJZEN M, 'The Charter: A Milestone for Social Protection in Europe?' (2001) 8 *Maastricht Journal* 33

GOETSCHY J, 'The European employment strategy from Amsterdam to Stockholm: Has it reached its cruising speed?' (2001) 32 *Industrial Relations Journal* 401

——, 'The European Employment Strategy: Genesis and Development' (1999) 5 *European Journal of Industrial Relations* 117

GOLD M, CRESSEY P and GILL C, 'Employment, employment, employment: is Europe working?' (2000) 31 *Industrial Relations Journal* 275

GOLD M and HALL M, 'Statutory European Works Councils: The Final Countdown?' (1994) 25 *Industrial Relations Journal* 177

GOLDSMITH (Lord), 'A Charter of Rights, Freedoms and Principles' (2001) 38 *Common Market Law Review* 1201

GORMLEY L, 'Reflections on the Architecture of the European Union after the Treaty of Amsterdam' in O'Keeffe and Twomey (1999) 57–70

GRAHL J and TEAGUE P, *1992—The Big Market: The Future of the European Community* (London: Lawrence and Wishart, 1990)

GRANT C, *Delors: Inside the House that Jacques Built* (London: Nicholas Brealey, 1994)

GRAVELLS N, 'State Liability in Damages for Breach of European Community Law' [1996] *Public Law* 567

GREGORY J, 'Sexual Harassment: the Impact of EU Law in the Member States' in Rossilli (2000) 175–191

GUILD E, 'The EC Directive on Race Discrimination: Surprises, Possibilities and Limitations' (2000) 29 *Industrial Law Journal* 416

HAAS E, *The Uniting of Europe: Political, Social and Economic Forces 1950–1957* (California: Stanford, 1968)

HAKIM C, 'Segregated and Integrated Occupations: A New Approach to Analysing Social Change' (1993) 9 *European Sociological Review* 289

HARLOW C, 'A Common European Law of Remedies' in Kilpatrick *et al* (2000) 69–83
——, 'European Administrative Law and the Global Challenge' in Craig and de Búrca (1999) 261–285
——, '*Francovich* and the Problem of the Disobedient State' (1996) 2 *European Law Journal* 199

HARDY S and PAINTER R, 'The New Acquired Rights Directive and its Implications for European Employee Relations in the Twenty-First Century' (1999) 6 *Maastricht Journal* 366

HARRIS A, 'Race and Essentialism in Feminist Legal Theory' (1990) 42 *Stanford Law Review* 581

HARRIS D, *The European Social Charter*, 8th ed (Charlottesville: University of Virginia Press, 1984)

HARRISON V, 'Using EC Law to Challenge Sexual Orientation Discrimination at Work' in Hervey and O'Keeffe (1996) 267–280

HARTLEY T, 'The European Court, Judicial Objectivity and the Constitution of the European Union' (1996) 112 *Law Quarterly Review* 95

HEATH E, *The Course of My Life* (London: Hodder and Stoughton, 1998)

HENDERSON D, 'The UK Presidency: An Insider's View' (1998) 36 *Journal of Common Market Studies* 563

HEPPLE B, 'The EU Charter of Fundamental Rights' (2001) 30 *Industrial Law Journal* 225
——, 'Equality and Discrimination' in Davies *et al* (1996) 237–259
——, 'Social Values and European Law' [1995] *Current Legal Problems* 39
——, *European Social Dialogue—Alibi or Opportunity* (London: Institute of Employment Rights, 1993)
——, 'Has Twenty-five Years of the Race Relations Acts in Britain Been a Failure' in Hepple and Szyszczak (1992) 19–34
——, 'The Implementation of the Community Charter of Fundamental Social Rights' (1990) 53 *Modern Law Review* 643
——, *Main Shortcomings and Proposals for Revision of Council Directive 77/187* (Brussels: European Commission, 1990)
——, 'Social Rights in the European Economic Community: A British Perspective' (1990) 11 *Comparative Labor Law Journal* 425
——, 'The Crisis in EEC Labour Law' (1987) 16 *Industrial Law Journal* 77
——(ed) *The Making of Labour Law in Europe: A Comparative Study of Nine Countries up to 1945* (London and New York: Mansell, 1987)

——, 'Harmonisation of Labour Law in the European Communities' in Adams J (ed) *Essays for Clive Schmitthoff* (Abingdon: Professional Books, 1983) 14–28

——, 'The Effect of Community Law on Employment Rights' (1975) 1 *Poly Law Review* 50

HEPPLE B and SZYSZCZAK E (eds) *Discrimination: The Limits of the Law* (London: Mansell, 1992)

HERINGA A and VERHEY L, 'The EU Charter: Text and Structure' (2001) 8 *Maastricht Journal* 11

HERVEY T, 'Up in Smoke? Community (anti) tobacco law and policy' (2001) 26 *European Law Review* 101

——, 'Social Solidarity: A Buttress Against Internal Market Law?' in Shaw (2000) 31–47

——, 'Putting Europe's House in Order: Racism, Race Discrimination and Xenophobia after the Treaty of Amsterdam' in O'Keeffe and Twomey (1999) 329–349

——, *European Social Law and Policy* (Harlow: Longman, 1998)

——, 'The Future of Sex Equality Law in the European Union' in Hervey and O'Keeffe (1996) 399–413

——, 'Migrant workers and their families in the European Union: the pervasive market ideology of Community law' in Shaw and More (1995) 91–110

——, 'Legal Issues concerning the *Barber* Protocol' in O'Keeffe and Twomey (1994) 329–337

——, 'Small Business Exclusion in German Dismissal Law' (1994) 23 *Industrial Law Journal* 267

——, *Justifications for Sex Discrimination in Employment* (London: Butterworths, 1993)

——, 'Justification of Indirect Sex Discrimination in Employment: European Community Law and UK Law Compared' (1991) 40 *International and Comparative Law Quarterly* 807

HERVEY T and O'KEEFFE D (eds) *Sex Equality Law in the European Union* (Chichester: Wiley, 1996)

HERVEY T and ROSTANT P, 'After *Francovich*: State Liability and British Employment Law' (1999) 25 *Industrial Law Journal* 259

HERVEY T and SHAW J, 'Women, Work and Care: Women's Dual Role and Double Burden in EC Sex Equality Law' (1998) 8 *Journal of European Social Policy* 43

HEUKELS T, BLOKKER N and BRUS M (eds) *The European Union After Amsterdam: A Legal Analysis* (The Hague: Kluwer, 1998)

HIGGINS T, 'Anti-essentialism, Relativism and Human Rights' (1996) 19 *Harvard Women's Law Journal* 1419

HIMSWORTH C, 'Things Fall Apart: The Harmonisation of Community Judicial Protection Revisited' (1997) 22 *European Law Review* 291

HODSON D and MAHER I, 'The Open Method as a New Mode of Governance: The Case of Soft Economic Policy Co-ordination' (2001) 39 *Journal of Common Market Studies* 719

HOSKINS M, 'Tilting the Balance: Supremacy and National Procedural Rules' (1996) 21 *European Law Review* 365

HOSKYNS C, 'A Study of Four Action Programmes on Equal Opportunities' in Rossilli (2000) 43–59

HUNT J, 'Success at last? The amendment of the Acquired Rights Directive' (1999) 24 *European Law Review* 215

JACOBS F, 'Enforcing Community Rights and Obligations in National Courts: Striking the Right Balance' in Lonbay and Biondi (1997) 25–36

JASPERS T, 'Desirability of European Legislation in Particular Areas of Social Policy' in Betten (1989) 53–81

JEFFERY M, 'Not Really Going to Work? Of the Directive on Part-Time Work, 'Atypical Work' and Attempts to Regulate It' (1998) 27 *Industrial Law Journal* 193

——, 'The Commission Proposals on 'Atypical Work': Back to the Drawing Board ... Again' (1995) 24 *Industrial Law Journal* 296

JOERGES C, 'European Economic Law, the Nation-State and the Maastricht Treaty' in Dehousse (1994) 29–62

JOERGES C, MÉNY Y and WEILER J (eds) *Jean Monnet Working Paper No 6/01: Symposium: Mountain or Molehill? A Critical Appraisal of the Commission White Paper on Governance* (New York: New York University School of Law, 2001)

JONES B, 'Sex Equality in Pension Schemes' in Kenner (1995) 85–144

KAHN-FREUND O, 'Industrial Democracy' (1977) 6 *Industrial Law Journal* 77

——, 'The European Social Charter' in Jacobs F (ed) *European Law and the Individual* (North-Holland: Amsterdam, 1976) 181–211

——, 'On the Uses and Misuses of Comparative Law' (1974) 37 *Modern Law Review* 1

——, 'Labour Law and Social Security' in Stein E and Nicholson T (eds) *American Enterprise in the European Common Market: A Legal Profile, Vol 1* (Ann Arbor: University of Michigan Press, 1960) 297–458

KELLER B and SÖRRIES B, 'The New European Social Dialogue: Old Wine in New Bottles?' (1999) 9 *Journal of European Social Policy* 111

——and ——, 'Sectoral Social Dialogue: New Opportunities or Impasses?' (1999) 30 *Industrial Relations Journal* 330

——and ——, 'The New Social Dialogue: Procedural Structuring, First Results and Perspectives' in Towers and Terry (1998) 77–98

KENNER J, 'Employment and Macroeconomics in the EC Treaty: A Legal and Political Symbiosis' (2000) 7 *Maastricht Journal* 375

——, 'The Paradox of the Social Dimension' in Lynch *et al* (2000) 108–129

——, 'The EC Employment Title and the 'Third Way': Making Soft Law Work?' (1999) 15 *International Journal of Comparative Labour Law and Industrial Relations* 33

——, 'Statement or Contract?—Some Reflections on the EC Employee Information (Contract or Employment Relationship) Directive after *Kampelmann*' (1999) 28 *Industrial Law Journal* 205

——, 'A Distinctive Legal Base for Social Policy?—The Court of Justice Answers a 'Delicate Question' (1997) 22 *European Law Review* 579

——(ed) *Trends in European Social Policy* (Aldershot: Dartmouth, 1995)

——, 'Citizenship and Fundamental Rights: Reshaping the European Social Model' in Kenner (1995) 3–84

——, 'EC Labour Law: the Softly, Softly Approach' (1995) 11 *International Journal of Comparative Labour Law and Industrial Relations* 307

——, 'European Social Policy—New Directions' (1994) 10 *International Journal of Comparative Labour Law and Industrial Relations* 56

——, 'Economic and Social Cohesion—The Rocky Road Ahead' [1994] *Legal Issues of European Integration* 1

KILPATRICK C, 'Gender Equality: A Fundamental Dialogue' in Sciarra S (ed) *Labour Law in the Courts: National Judges and the European Court of Justice* (Oxford: Hart, 2001) 31–130

——, 'Production and Circulation of EC Night Work Jurisprudence' (1996) 25 *Industrial Law Journal* 169

——, 'How long is a piece of string? European regulation of the post-birth period' in Hervey and O'Keeffe (1996) 81–96

KILPATRICK C, NOVITZ T and SKIDMORE P (eds) *The Future of Remedies in Europe* (Oxford: Hart, 2000)

KLABBERS J, 'Informal Instruments before the European Court of Justice' (1994) 31 *Common Market Law Review* 997

KLEINMAN M and PIACHAUD D, 'European Social Policy: Conceptions and Choices' (1993) 3 *Journal of European Social Policy* 1

KOLEHMAINEN E, 'The Directive Concerning the Posting of Workers: Synchronization of the Functions of National Legal Systems' (1998) 20 *Comparative Labor Law and Policy Journal* 71

KOLVENBACH W, 'EEC Company Law Harmonization and Worker Participation' (1990) *University of Pennsylvania Journal of International Business Law* 709

KOOPMANS T, 'The Rôle of Law in the Next Stage of European Integration' (1986) 35 *International and Comparative Law Quarterly* 925

KOUTRAKOS P, 'Community law and equal treatment in the armed forces' (2000) 25 *European Law Review* 433

KRIEGER H, 'Participation of Employees' Representatives in the Protection of the Health and Safety of Workers in Europe' (1990/91) 6 *International Journal of Comparative Labour Law and Industrial Relations* 217

KÜCHHOLD K, '*Badeck*—The Third German Reference on Positive Action' (2001) 30 *Industrial Law Journal* 116

LACEY N, 'From Individual to Group' in Hepple and Szyszczak (1992) 99–124

LANGE P, 'Maastricht and the Social Protocol: Why Did They Do It?' (1993) 21 *Politics and Society* 5

LARSSON A, 'Employment is a Matter of Common Concern', *Employment and Industrial Relations International* (Dublin: EIRI, August 1997) 18–21

LAWRENCE R and SCHULTZ C (eds) *Barriers to European Growth: A Transatlantic View* (Washington DC: Brookings, 1987)

LEBEN C, 'Is there a European Approach to Human Rights?' in Alston (1999) 69–97

LEIBFRIED S and PIERSON P, 'Prospects for Social Europe' (1992) 20 *Politics and Society* 333

LEIGHTON P and DUMVILLE S, 'From Statement to Contract—Some Effects of the Contracts of Employment Act 1972' (1977) 6 *Industrial Law Journal* 133

LENAERTS K and DE SMIJTER E, 'A "Bill of Rights" for the European Union' (2001) 38 *Common Market Law Review* 273

LEWIS C and MOORE S, 'Duties, Directives and Damages in European Community Law' [1993] *Public Law* 151

LINDBERG L, *The Political Dynamics of European Economic Integration* (California: Stanford, 1963)

LISTER R, 'Citizenship, Exclusion and "the Third Way" in Social Security Reform: Reflections on TH Marshall' (2000) 7 *Journal of Social Security Law* 70

Lo Faro A, *Regulating Social Europe: Reality and Myth of Collective Bargaining in the EC Legal Order* (Oxford: Hart, 2000)

Lonbay J and Biondi A (eds) *Remedies for Breach of EC Law* (Chichester: Wiley, 1997)

Lorber P, 'Regulating Fixed-term Work in the UK: A Positive Step towards Workers' Protection?' (1999) 15 *International Journal of Comparative Labour Law and Industrial Relations* 121

Louis J-V, 'A Monetary Union for Tomorrow?' (1989) 26 *Common Market Law Review* 301

Lynch P, Neuwahl N and Rees W (eds) *Reforming the European Union: From Maastricht to Amsterdam* (Harlow: Longman, 2000)

——, —— and ——, 'Conclusions: Maastricht, Amsterdam and beyond' in Lynch et al (2000) 235–250

Lyon-Caen G, 'Subsidiarity' in Davies *et al* (1996) 49–62

MacKinnon C, 'Reflections on Sex Equality under Law' (1991) 100 *Yale Law Journal* 1281

Maher I, 'Legislative Review by the EC Commission: Revision without Radicalism' in Shaw and More (1995) 235–251

——, 'National Courts as European Community Courts' (1994) 14 *Legal Studies* 226

Majone G, 'The European Community Between Social Policy and Social Regulation' (1993) 31 *Journal of Common Market Studies* 153

Mancini G, 'The Making of a Constitution for Europe' (1989) 26 *Common Market Law Review* 595

——, 'Labour Law and Community Law' (1985) 20 *Irish Jurist (ns)* 1

Mancini G and Keeling D, 'Democracy and the European Court of Justice' (1994) 57 *Modern Law Review* 175

Mancini G and O'Leary S, 'The New Frontiers of Sex Equality Law in the European Union' (1999) 24 *European Law Review* 331

Marglin S and Schorr J (eds) *The Golden Age of Capitalism: Reinterpreting the Postwar Experience* (Oxford: Clarendon Press, 1992)

Marshall T, *Social Policy* (London: Hutchinson, 1975)

——, *Citizenship and Social Class and Other Essays* (Cambridge: CUP, 1950)

McColgan A, 'Family Friendly Frolics? The Maternity and Paternity Leave etc Regulations 1999' (2000) 29 *Industrial Law Journal* 125

McCrudden C, 'Merit Principles' (1998) 18 *Oxford Journal of Legal Studies* 543

——, 'The Effectiveness of European Equality Law: National Mechanisms for Enforcing Gender Equality Law in the Light of European Requirements' (1993) 13 *Oxford Journal of Legal Studies* 320

——, 'Rethinking Positive Action' (1986) 15 *Industrial Law Journal* 219

McGlynn C, 'Ideologies of Motherhood in European Community Sex Equality Law' (2000) 6 *European Law Journal* 29

——, 'A Family Law for the European Union?' in Shaw (2000) 223–241

——, 'An Exercise in Futility: The Practical Effects of the Social Policy Opt-out' (1998) 49 *Northern Ireland Legal Quarterly* 60

McInerney S, 'Bases for Action Against Race Discrimination in EU Law' (2002) 27 *European Law Review* 72

Meehan E, 'Sex Equality Policies in the European Community' (1990) 13 *Journal of European Integration* 185

MEGARRY R, 'Administrative Quasi-Legislation' (1944) 60 *Law Quarterly Review* 125

MOEBIUS I and SZYSZCZAK E, 'Of Raising Pigs and Children' (1998) 18 *Yearbook of European Law* 125

MONNET J, 'A Ferment of Change' (1962) 1 *Journal of Common Market Studies* 203

MORAVCSIK A, 'Negotiating the Single European Act: National Interests and Conventional Statecraft in the European Community' (1991) 45 *International Organization* 19

MORE G, 'The Principle of Equal Treatment: From Market Unifier to Fundamental Right?' in Craig and de Búrca (1999) 517–553

——, 'Equality of Treatment in European Community Law: The Limits of Market Equality' in Bottomley A (ed) *Feminist Perspectives on the Foundational Subjects of Law* (London: Cavendish, 1996) 261–278

——, 'The Acquired Rights Directive: Frustrating or Facilitating Labour Market Flexibility?' in Shaw and More (1995) 129–145

——, 'The Concept of 'Undertaking' in the Acquired Rights Directive: The Court of Justice Under Pressure (Again)' (1995) 15 *Yearbook of European Law* 135

——, ' "Equal Treatment" of the Sexes in European Community Law: What Does "Equal" Mean?' (1993) 1 *Feminist Legal Studies* 45

MOSLEY H, 'The social dimension of European integration' (1990) 129 *International Labour Review* 147

MÜCKENBERGER U, 'Non-standard Forms of Work and the Role of Changes in Labour and Social Security Regulation' (1989) 17 *International Journal of the Sociology of Law* 381

MURRAY J, 'The International Regulation of Maternity: Still Waiting for the Reconciliation of Work and Family Life' (2001) 17 *International Journal of Comparative Labour Law and Industrial Relations* 25

——, 'Social Justice for Women? The ILO's Convention on Part-time Work' (1999) 15 *International Journal of Comparative Labour Law and Industrial Relations* 3

——, 'Normalising Temporary Work' (1999) 28 *Industrial Law Journal* 269

NEAL A, 'Regulating Health and Safety at Work: Developing European Union Policy for the Millennium' (1998) 14 *International Journal of Comparative Labour Law and Industrial Relations* 217

——, 'Promoting Occupational Safety and Health in the European Union' in Neal and Foyn (1995) 80–99

——, 'The Industrial Relations in SMEs in the United Kingdom' (1993) 26 *Bulletin of Comparative Labour Relations* 75

——, 'The European Framework Directive on the Health and Safety of Workers: Challenges for the United Kingdom' (1990) 6 *International Journal of Comparative Labour Law and Industrial Relations* 80

NEAL A and FOYN S (eds) *Developing the Social Dimension in an Enlarged European Union* (Oslo: Scandinavian University Press, 1995)

NICKELL S, 'Unemployment and Labour Market Rigidities: Europe versus North America' (1997) 11 *Journal of Economic Perspectives* 55

NEILSON J, 'Equal Opportunities for Women in the European Union: Success or Failure?' (1998) 8 *Journal of European Social Policy* 64

NIELSEN R, *European Labour Law* (Copenhagen: DJØF Publishing, 2000)

NIELSEN R, 'The Contract of Employment in the Member States of the European Communities and in European Community Law' (1990) 33 *German Yearbook of International Law* 258

NIELSEN R and SZYSZCZAK E, *The Social Dimension of the European Community*, 2nd ed (Copenhagen: Handelshøjskolens Forlag, 1993)

NIHOUL P, 'Do workers constitute undertakings for the purpose of the competition rules?' (2000) 25 *European Law Review* 408

NOEL E, 'Reflections on the Community in the Aftermath of the Meeting of the European Council in Milan' (1985) 20 *Government and Opposition* 444

NOVITZ T, 'Remedies for Violation of Social Rights within the Council of Europe' in Kilpatrick *et al* (2000) 231–251

NUMHAUSER-HENNING A, 'Swedish Sex Equality Law before the European Court of Justice' (2001) 30 *Industrial Law Journal* 121

NUSSBAUM M, 'Human Functioning and Social Justice: In Defence of Aristotlean Essentialism' (1992) 20 *Political Theory* 202

OBRADOVIC D, 'Accountability of Interest Groups in the Union Lawmaking Process' in Craig and Harlow (1998) 354–385

——, 'Policy Legitimacy and the European Union' (1996) 34 *Journal of Common Market Studies* 191

O'HARE U, 'Enhancing European Equality Rights: A New Regional Framework' (2001) 8 *Maastricht Journal* 133

——, 'Equality and Affirmative Action in International Human Rights Law and its Relevance for the European Union' (2000) 4 *International Journal of Discrimination and the Law* 3

O'HIGGINS P, "Labour is not a Commodity'—An Irish Contribution to International Labour Law' (1997) 26 *Industrial Law Journal* 225

O'KEEFFE D, 'Union Citizenship' in O'Keeffe and Twomey (1994) 87–107

O'KEEFFE D and TWOMEY P (eds) *Legal Issues of the Amsterdam Treaty* (Oxford: Hart, 1999)

—— and —— (eds) *Legal Issues of the Maastricht Treaty* (London: Wiley Chancery, 1994)

O'LEARY S, 'The Principle of Equal Treatment on Grounds of Nationality in Article 6 EC: A Lucrative Source of Rights for Member State Nationals?' in Dashwood and O'Leary (1997) 105–136

——, 'The Relationship between Community Citizenship and the Protection of Fundamental Rights in Community Law' (1995) 32 *Common Market Law Review* 519

PADDOA-SCHIOPPA T, *The Road to Monetary Union in Europe: the Emperor, the Kings and the Genies*, revised ed (Oxford: OUP, 2000)

PEERS S, 'Towards Equality: Actual and Potential Rights of Third Country Nationals in the EU' (1996) 33 *Common Market Law Review* 7

PESCATORE P, 'Some Critical Remarks on the Single European Act' (1987) 24 *Common Market Law Review* 9

——, 'The Doctrine of 'Direct Effect': An Infant Disease of Community Law' (1983) 8 *European Law Review* 155

PETERS A, 'The Many Meanings of Equality and Positive Action in Favour of Women under European Community Law—A Conceptual Analysis' (1996) 2 *European Law Journal* 177

PLAZA MARTIN C, 'Furthering the Effectiveness of EC Directives and the Judicial

Protection of Individual Rights Thereunder' (1994) 43 *International and Comparative Law Quarterly* 26

POIARES MADURO M, 'Europe's Social Self: 'The Sickness Unto Death' in Shaw (2000) 325–349

——, 'Striking the Elusive Balance Between Economic Freedom and Social Rights in the EU' in Alston (1999) 449–472

——, *We, The Court: The European Court of Justice and the European Economic Constitution* (Oxford: Hart, 1998)

PRECHAL S, SENDEN L and KOOPMAN B, *General Report 1997 of the Legal Experts Group on Equal Treatment of Men and Women* (Brussels: European Commission, 1999)

PREUß U, 'Problems of a Concept of European Citizenship' (1995) 1 *European Law Journal* 267

QUINN G, 'Human Rights of People with Disabilities under EU Law' in Alston (1999) 281–326

RABIN R, 'Fibreboard and the Termination of Bargaining Unit Work: The Search for Standards in Defining the Scope of the Duty to Bargain' (1971) 71 *Columbia Law Review* 803

RAMM T, 'Workers' Participation, the Representation of Labour and Special Labour Courts' in Hepple (1987) 242–276

RASMUSSEN H, 'Between Self-Restraint and Activism: A Judicial Policy for the European Court' (1988) 13 *European Law Review* 28

REICH N, 'Union Citizenship—Metaphor or Source of Rights?' (2001) 7 *European Law Journal* 4

RHODES M, 'Globalization, Labour Markets and Welfare States: A Future of 'Competititve Corporatism'?' in Rhodes M and Mény Y, *The Future of European Welfare: A New Social Contract?* (Basingstoke: Macmillan, 1998) 178–203

——, 'The Social Dimension after Maastricht: Setting a New Agenda for the Labour Market' (1993) 9 *International Journal of Comparative Labour Law and Industrial Relations* 297

——, 'The Future of the 'Social Dimension': Labour Market Regulation in Post-1992 Europe' (1992) 30 *Journal of Common Market Studies* 23

RIDEOUT R, 'The Great Transfer of Employees Rights Hoax' [1982] *Current Legal Problems* 233

RODRÍGUEZ-PIÑERO M and CASAS E, 'In Support of a European Social Constitution' in Davies *et al* (1996) 23–48

ROGOWSKI R and WILTHAGEN T (eds) *Reflexive Labour Law* (Deventer: Kluwer, 1994)

ROSS M, 'Beyond *Francovich*' (1993) 56 *Modern Law Review* 55

ROSSILLI M (ed), *Gender Policies in the European Union* (New York: Peter Lang, 2000)

RUBENSTEIN M, *The Dignity of Women at Work: A Report on the Problem of Sexual Harassment in the Member States of the European Communities* (Luxembourg: European Communities, 1987)

RYAN B, 'The Private Enforcement of European Union Labour Laws' in Kilpatrick *et al* (2000) 141–163

——, 'Pay, Trade Union Rights and European Community Law' (1997) 13 *International Journal of Comparative Labour Law and Industrial Relations* 305

SAND I-J, 'Understanding the New Forms of Governance: Mutually Interdependent, Reflexive, Destabilised and Competing Institutions' (1998) 4 *European Law Journal* 271

SANDHOLTZ W and ZYSMAN J, '1992: Recasting the European Bargain' (1989) 42 *World Politics* 95

SANDLER A, 'Players and Process: The Evolution of Employment Law in the EEC' (1985) 7 *Comparative Labor Law Journal* 1

SCHACHTER O, 'The Twilight Existence of Nonbinding International Agreements' (1977) 71 *American Journal of International Law* 296

SCHIEK D, 'Positive Action before the European Court of Justice—New Conceptions of Equality in Community Law? From *Kalanke* and *Marschall* to *Badeck*' (2000) 16 *International Journal of Comparative Labour Law and Industrial Relations* 251

——, 'Sex Equality Law After Kalanke and Marschall' (1998) 4 *European Law Journal* 148

——, 'Positive Action in Community Law' (1996) 25 *Industrial Law Journal* 239

SCHMIDT M, 'Representativity—A Claim Not Satisfied: The Social Partners' Role in the EC Law-Making Procedure for Social Policy' (1999) 15 *International Journal of Comparative Labour Law and Industrial Relations* 259

——, 'Parental Leave: Contested Procedure, Creditable Results' (1997) 13 *International Journal of Comparative Labour Law and Industrial Relations* 113

SCHWARZE J, 'The Convergence of the Administrative Laws of the EU Member States' in Snyder (2000) 163–182

SCIARRA S, 'Global or Re-nationalised? Past and Future of European Labour Law' in Snyder (2000) 269–291

——, 'The Employment Title in the Amsterdam Treaty: A Multi-language Legal Discourse' in O'Keeffe and Twomey (1999) 157–170

——, 'Dynamic integration of national and Community sources: the case of night-work for women' in Hervey and O'Keeffe (1996) 97–108

——, 'Collective Agreements in the Hierarchy of European Community Sources' in Davies *et al* (1996) 189–212

——, *How 'Global' is Labour Law? The Perspective of Social Rights in the European Union*, EUI Working Paper No 96/6 (Florence: EUI, 1996)

——, 'Social Values and the Multiple Sources of European Social Law' (1995) 1 *European Law Journal* 60

SCOTT J, 'Law, Legitimacy and EC Governance: Prospects for 'Partnership'' (1998) 36 *Journal of Common Market Studies* 175

SENDEN L, 'Positive Action in the EU Put to the Test: A Negative Score?' (1996) 3 *Maastricht Journal* 146

SERVAIS J-M, 'Labour Law in Small and Medium-Sized Enterprises: An Ongoing Challenge' (1994) 10 *International Journal of Comparative Labour Law and Industrial Relations* 119

SHANKS M, 'Introductory Article: The Social Policy of the European Communities' (1977) 14 *Common Market Law Review* 375

SHARPE A, *Transgender Jurisprudence: Dysphoric Bodies of Law* (London: Cavendish Publishing, 2002)

SHAW J, 'Gender and the Court of Justice' in de Búrca G and Weiler J (eds) *The European Court of Justice* (Oxford: OUP, 2001) 87–142

——, 'The Treaty of Nice: Legal and Constitutional Implications' (2001) 7 *European Public Law* 195

——, 'The Treaty of Amsterdam: Challenges of Flexibility and Legitimacy' (1998) 4 *European Law Journal* 63

——(ed) *Social Law and Policy in an Evolving European Union* (Oxford: Hart, 2000)

——, 'From the Margins to the Centre: Education and Training Law and Policy' in Craig and de Búrca (1998) 555–595

——, 'Citizenship of the Union: First Steps in the European Court of Justice' (1998) 4 *European Public Law* 533

——, 'The Many Pasts and Futures of Citizenship of the European Union' (1997) 60 *Modern Law Review* 554

——, 'Law, Gender and the Internal Market' in Hervey and O'Keeffe (1995) 283–299

——, 'Twin-track Social Europe—the Inside Track' in O'Keeffe and Twomey (1994) 295–311

——, 'The Scope and Content of European Community Social Law: A Review of Progress and a Bibliographical Note' (1992) 14 *Journal of Social Welfare and Family Law* 71

——, 'Positive Action for Women in Germany: The Use of Legally Binding Quota Systems' in Hepple and Szyszczak (1992) 386–411

——, 'European Community judicial method: its application to sex discrimination law' (1990) 19 *Industrial Law Journal* 228

SHAW J and MORE G (eds) *New Legal Dynamics of European Union* (Oxford: Clarendon Press, 1995)

SHONFIELD A, *Europe: Journey to an Unknown Destination* (London: Harmondsworth, 1973)

SHRUBSALL V, 'The Additional Protocol to the European Social Charter—Employment Rights' (1989) 18 *Industrial Law Journal* 39

SIEBERT H, 'Labor Rigidities: at the Root of Unemployment in Europe' (1997) 11 *Journal of Economic Perspectives* 43

SIMITIS S, 'Workers' Participation in the Enterprise—Transcending Company Law' (1975) 38 *Modern Law Review* 1

SIMITIS S and LYON-CAEN A, 'Community Labour Law: A Critical Introduction to its History' in Davies *et al* (1996) 1–22

SKIDMORE P, 'EC Framework Directive on Equal Treatment in Employment: Towards a Comprehensive Community Anti-Discrimination Policy?' (2001) 30 *Industrial Law Journal* 126

——, 'Can Transsexuals Suffer Sex Discrimination?' (1997) 19 *Journal of Social Welfare and Family Law* 105

SNYDER F (ed) *The Europeanisation of Law: The Legal Effects of European Integration* (Oxford: Hart, 2000)

——, 'Europeanisation and Globalisation as Friends and Rivals: European Union Law in Global Economic Networks' in Snyder (2000) 293–320

——, 'EMU—Metaphor for European Union? Institutions, Rules and Types of Regulation' in Dehousse (1994) 63–99

——, *Soft Law and Institutional Practice in the European Community*, EUI Working Paper LAW No 93/5 (EUI, Florence 1993)

SNYDER F, 'The Effectiveness of European Community Law: Institutions, Processes, Tools and Techniques' (1993) 56 Modern Law Review 19

SOSKICE D, 'Industrial Relations and Unemployment: The Case for Flexible Corporatism' in Kregel J, Matzner E and Roncaglia A (eds) Barriers to Full Employment (London: Macmillan, 1988)

SQUIRES J, Gender in Political Theory (Cambridge: Polity Press, 1999)

STEINER J, 'From direct effects to Francovich: Shifting Means of Enforcement of Community Law' (1993) 18 European Law Review 3

STORY J, 'Social Europe: Ariadne's Thread' (1990) 13 Journal of European Intergration 151

STREECK W, 'Competitive Solidarity: Rethinking the 'European Social Model'', MPIfG Working Paper 99/8 (Cologne: Max-Planck-Institut für Sozialforschung, 1999)

——, 'Neo-Voluntarism: A New European Social Policy Regime?' (1995) 1 European Law Journal 31

——, 'Skills and the Limits of Neo-Liberalism: The Enterprise of the Future as a Place of Learning' (1989) 3 Work, Employment and Society 1

STREIT M and MUSSLER W, 'The Economic Constitution of the European Community: From 'Rome' to 'Maastricht' (1995) 1 European Law Journal 5

STUBB A, 'Differentiated Integration' (1996) 34 Journal of Common Market Studies 283

SUPIOT A, Beyond Employment: Changes in Work and the Future of Labour Law in Europe (Oxford: OUP, 2001)

——, 'The Dogmatic Foundations of the Market' (2000) 29 Industrial Law Journal 321

——, 'On the Job: Time for Agreement' (1996) 12 International Journal of Comparative Labour Law and Industrial Relations 195

SYMES V, Unemployment and Employment Policies in the EU (London: Kogan Page, 1998)

SYRPIS P, 'Smoke Without Fire: The Social Policy Agenda and the Internal Market' (2001) 30 Industrial Law Journal 271

——, 'The Integrationist Rationale for European Social Policy' in Shaw (2000) 17–30

SZYSZCZAK E, 'The New Paradigm for Social Policy: A Virtuous Circle?' (2001) 28 Common Market Law Review 1125

——, EC Labour Law (Harlow: Longman, 2000)

——, 'The Evolving European Employment Strategy' in Shaw (2000) 197–220

——, 'The Working Environment v Internal Market' (1999) 24 European Law Review 196

——, 'The New Parameters of European Labour Law' in O'Keeffe and Twomey (1999) 141–155

——, 'Making Europe More Relevant to its Citizens: Effective Judicial Process' (1996) 21 European Law Review 351

——, 'Positive Action After Kalanke' (1996) 59 Modern Law Review 876

——, 'Community Law on Pregnancy and Maternity' in Hervey and O'Keeffe (1996) 52–62

——, 'Social Policy: a Happy Ending or a Reworking of the Fairy Tale?' in O'Keeffe and Twomey (1994) 313–327

——, 'Racism: The Limits of Market Equality' in Hepple and Szyszczak (1992) 125–147

——, 'L'Espace Sociale Européenne: Reality, Dreams, or Nightmares?' (1990) 33 *German Yearbook of International Law* 284

TASH A, 'Remedies for European Community Law Claims in Member State Courts: Towards a European Standard' (1993) 31 *Columbia Journal of Transnational Law* 377

TEAGUE P, 'Monetary Union and Social Europe' (1998) 8 *Journal of European Social Policy* 117

—— and GRAHL J, '1992 and the Emergence of a European Industrial Relations Area' (1990) 13 *Journal of European Integration* 167

TEMPLE LANG J, 'The Fifth EEC Directive on the Harmonization of Company Law' (1975) 12 *Common Market Law Review* 155

TERRY S, 'A Bridge Too Far? Non-Discrimination and Homosexuality in European Community Law' (1998) 4 *European Public Law* 487

TESAURO G, 'The Effectiveness of Judicial Protection and Co-operation between the Court of Justice and National Courts' (1993) 13 *Yearbook of European Law* 1

TIMMERMANS C, 'How can one improve the Quality of Community Legislation?' (1997) 34 *Common Market Law Review* 1229

TOTH A, 'The Legal Effects of the Protocols Relating to the United Kingdom, Ireland and Denmark' in Heukels *et al* (1998) 227–252

——, 'The Principle of Subsidiarity in the Maastricht Treaty' (1992) 29 *Common Market Law Review* 1079

——, 'The Legal Status of the Declarations Annexed to the Single European Act' (1986) 23 *Common Market Law Review* 803

TOWERS B and TERRY M (eds) *Industrial Relations Journal European Annual Review 1997* (Oxford: Blackwell, 1998)

TRIDIMAS T, 'Liability for Breach of Community Law: Growing Up and Mellowing Down?' (2001) 38 *Common Market Law Review* 301

TSOULAKIS L, *The New European Economy Revisited*, 3rd ed (Oxford: OUP, 1997)

TRAXLER F, 'Employers and Employer Organisations' in Towers and Terry (1998) 99–111

TREU T, 'European Collective Bargaining Levels and the Competences of the Social Partners' in Davies *et al* (1996) 269–287

TRUBEK D and MOSHER J, 'New Governance, EU Employment Policy, and the European Social Model' in Joerges *et al* (2001) Part 9, 1–25

TUYTSCHAEVER F, *Differentiation in European Union Law* (Oxford: Hart, 1999)

TWOMEY P, 'The European Union: Three Pillars without a Human Rights Foundation' in O'Keeffe and Twomey (1994) 121–132

USHER J, 'Variable Geometry or Concentric Circles: Patterns for the EU' (1997) 46 *International and Comparative Law Quarterly* 243

——, 'European Community Equality Law: Legal Instruments and Judicial Remedies' in McCrudden C (ed) *Women, Employment and European Equality Law* (London: Eclipse Publications, 1987) 161–177

VALTICOS N and VON POTOBSKY G, *International Labour Law*, 2nd revised ed (Deventer: Kluwer, 1995)

VAN DEN BERGH R and CAMESASCA P, 'Irreconcilable Principles? The Court of Justice Exempts Collective Labour Agreements from the Wrath of Antitrust' (2000) 25 *European Law Review* 492

VAN GERVEN W, 'Of rights, remedies and procedures' (2000) 37 *Common Market Law Review* 501

——, 'Bridging the gap between Community and national laws: towards a principle of homogeneity in the field of legal remedies' (1995) 32 *Common Market Law Review* 679

VENEZIANI B, 'The Evolution of the Contract of Employment' in Hepple (1987) 31–72

VENTURINI P, *1992: The European Social Dimension* (Luxembourg: European Communities, 1989)

VOGEL-POLSKY E, 'What Future is There for a Social Europe?' (1990) 19 *Industrial Law Journal* 65

VON BOGDANDY A, 'The European Union as a Human Rights Organization? Human Rights and the Core of the European Union' (2000) 37 *Common Market Law Review* 1307

VON KROSIGK F, 'A Reconsideration of Federalism in the Scope of the Present Discussion on European Integration' (1970) 9 *Journal of Common Market Studies* 197

VOUSDEN S, 'Albany, Market Law and Social Exclusion' (2000) 29 *Industrial Law Journal* 181

WAALDIJK K, 'The Legal Situation in the Member States' in Waaldijk and Clapham (1993) 71–130

WAALDIJK K and CLAPHAM A (eds) *Homosexuality: A European Community Issue* (Dordrecht: Nijhoff, 1993)

WADDINGTON L, 'Testing the Limits of the EC Treaty Article on Non-discrimination' (1999) 28 *Industrial Law Journal* 133

——, 'Reassessing the Employment of People with Disabilities in Europe: From Quotas to Anti-discrimination Laws' (1996) 18 *Comparative Labor Law Journal* 62

——, *Disability, Employment and the European Community* (Antwerp: Maklu, 1995)

WADDINGTON L and BELL M, 'More Equal than Others: Distinguishing European Union Equality Directives' (2001) 38 *Common Market Law Review* 587

WALKER K, 'Workers' Participation in Management: Problems, Practice and Prospects' in 1974 *IILS Bulletin* (Geneva: International Institute of Labour Studies) No 12, 3–35

WALKER N, 'European Constitutionalism and European Integration' [1996] *Public Law* 266

WARD A, 'Effective Sanctions in EC Law: a Moving Boundary in the Division of Competence' (1995) 1 *European Law Journal* 205

WARD I, 'Amsterdam and the Continuing Search for Community' in O'Keeffe and Twomey (1999) 41–55

——, 'Beyond Sex Equality: The Limits of Sex Equality Law in the New Europe' in Hervey and O'Keeffe (1996) 369–382

WARNER H, 'EC Social Policy in Practice: Community Action on Behalf of Women and its Impact in the Member States' (1984) 23 *Journal of Common Market Studies* 141

WATSON P, 'The Role of the European Court of Justice in the Development of Community Labour Law' in Ewing *et al* (1994) 76–105

——, 'Social Policy After Maastricht' (1993) 30 *Common Market Law Review* 481

——, 'The Community Social Charter' (1991) 28 *Common Market Law Review* 37

——, *Social Security Law of the European Communities* (London: Mansell, 1980)

WEATHERILL S, 'Safeguarding the *Acquis Communautaire*' in Heukels *et al* (1998) 153–178

——, *Law and Integration in the European Union* (Oxford: Clarendon Press, 1995)

——, 'Beyond Preemption? Shared Competence and Constitutional Change in the European Community' in O'Keeffe and Twomey (1994) 13–33

WEATHERILL S and BEAUMONT P, *EU Law*, 3rd ed (London: Penguin, 1999)

WEBB B and WEBB S, *Industrial Democracy* (London: Longmans, 1898)

WEDDERBURN (Lord), 'Consultation and Collective Bargaining in Europe: Success or Ideology?' (1997) 26 *Industrial Law Journal* 1

——, 'Inderogability, Collective Agreements and Community Law' (1992) 21 *Industrial Law Journal* 245

——, 'The Social Charter in Britain—Labour Law and Labour Courts?' (1991) 54 *Modern Law Review* 1

——, 'Workers' Rights: Fact or Fake?' (1991) 13 *Dublin University Law Journal* 1

——, 'Industrial Relations and the Courts' (1980) 9 *Industrial Law Journal* 65

WEILER J, 'Editorial: Does the European Union Truly Need a Charter of Rights?' (2000) 6 *European Law Journal* 95

——, 'Prologue: Amsterdam and the Quest for Constitutional Democracy' in O'Keeffe and Twomey (1999) 1–20

——, 'Epilogue: The European Courts of Justice: Beyond "Beyond Doctrine" or the Legitimacy Crisis of European Constitutionalism' in Slaughter A-M, Stone Sweet A and Weiler J (eds) *The European Courts and National Courts: Doctrine and Jurisprudence* (Oxford: Hart, 1998) 365–391

——, 'Quiet Revolution: The European Court of Justice and its Interlocutors' (1994) 26 *Comparative Political Studies* 510

——, 'The Transformation of Europe' (1991) 100 *Yale Law Journal* 2403

WEILER J and FRIES S, 'A Human Rights Policy for the European Community and Union: The Question of Competences' in Alston (1999) 147–165

WEILER J, HALTERN U and MAYER F, 'European Democracy and its Critique' (1995) 18 *Western European Politics* 4

WEILER J and LOCKHART N, ' "Taking Rights Seriously" Seriously: The European Court and its Fundamental Rights Jurisprudence' (1995) 32 *Common Market Law Review* 59

WEISS M, 'The Politics of the EU Charter of Fundamental Rights' in Hepple B (ed) *Social and Labour Rights in a Global Context* (Cambridge: CUP, 2002, *forthcoming*)

——, 'The European Community's Approach to Workers' Participation' in Neal and Foyn (1995) 100–124

——, 'The Significance of Maastricht for European Community Social Policy' (1992) 8 *International Journal of Comparative Labour Law and Industrial Relations* 3

WELCH J, 'The Fifth Draft Directive—A False Dawn' (1983) 8 *European Law Review* 83

WELLENS K and BORCHARDT G, 'Soft Law in European Community Law' (1989) 14 *European Law Review* 267

WELLENSTEIN E, 'Unity, Community, Union—What's in a Name?' (1992) 29 *Common Market Law Review* 205

WHITEFORD E, 'Occupational Pensions and European Law: Clarity at Last?' in Hervey and O'Keeffe (1996) 21–34

——, 'W(h)ither Social Policy?' in Shaw and More (1995) 111–128

——, 'Social Policy After Maastricht' (1993) 18 *European Law Review* 202

WINTEMUTE R, 'When is Pregnancy Discrimination Indirect Sex Discrimination' (1998) 27 *Industrial Law Journal* 23

——, 'Recognising New Kinds of Direct Sex Discrimination: Transsexualism, Sexual Orientation and Dress Codes' (1997) 60 *Modern Law Review* 334

——, *Sexual Orientation and Human Rights: The United States Constitution, the European Convention and the Canadian Charter* (Oxford: OUP, 1995)

WINTEMUTE R and ANDENAS M, *Legal Recognition of Same-Sex Partnerships: A Study of National, European and International Law* (Oxford: Hart, 2001)

WINTER J, CURTIN D, KELLERMANN A and DE WITTE B (eds) *Reforming the Treaty on European Union—The Legal Debate* (The Hague: Kluwer, 1996)

WISE M and GIBB R, *Single Market to Social Europe: The European Community in the 1990s* (Harlow: Longman, 1993)

WYATT D, 'The Direct Effect of Community Social Law—Not Forgetting Directives' (1983) 8 *European Law Review* 241

WYATT D and DASHWOOD A, *European Community Law*, 2nd ed (London: Sweet and Maxwell, 1993)

YOUNG H, *This Blessed Plot: Britain and Europe from Churchill to Blair* (London: Macmillan, 1998)

Index